哲学前沿问题与方法论

吴根友　黄　超　主编

人 民 出 版 社

序　言

何谓哲学前沿问题？人们常说，边界意识或者说“冲击边界”是哲学思考的基本特征，不触及边界的人类思考不是哲学思考。从这个意义上说，哲学问题即前沿问题，哲学思考必须抵达并力图超越人类和时代思想的前沿，同样，一种有效的哲学方法可以提示并激励人们抵达并超越思想的边界。当前，如何提升哲学学科研究生的前沿意识和方法论意识，已经成为各哲学学科研究生培养教育机构普遍关注的问题。武汉大学哲学学院组织编写的这部《哲学前沿问题与方法论》研究生教材，编辑整理了学院在岗教师和部分外籍学者发表的关于哲学前沿问题与方法论的系列论文，希望这样一种就地取材的编辑思路不仅能够为学生提供“零距离”的鲜活文本，而且能够方便学生随时发起与原作者面对面的讨论。

由于哲学的问题与方法不可能一分为二，方法论问题本身也是哲学前沿问题，因此，在编辑体例上，我们虽然区分出哲学前沿问题和哲学方法论两个部分，但是，这种区分只具有相对的意义，或者说只是为了编辑方便。

在哲学前沿问题部分，我们选取了 10 篇文章。第一篇文章是陶德麟在 1981 年的《哲学研究》第 1 期发表的《逻辑证明与真理标准》，在该文中，陶德麟以一个哲学工作者的身份直接参与改革开放初期的“实践是检验真理的唯一标准”的大讨论，作者从理论与实践统一的马克思主义基本原则出发，既敏锐地抓住了改革开放时代的重大哲学前沿问题，又成功运用和充分展示了逻辑证明的雄辩力量，使得该文成为一篇既具有时代价值，又具有典范意义的马克思主义哲学文献。我们还选取了马克思主义哲学学科的另外两篇重要文章，何萍的《马克思主义哲学的内史与外史的书写》一文，作者通过内史与外史的区分与梳理，强调马克思主义哲学的内史是由实践和辩证法的批判精神与多元化的哲学传统和理论形态相互作用创造出来的，对它的叙述应该构成马克思主义哲学史书写的主线。汪信砚的《西学东渐与马克思主义哲学中国化》一文，作者一方面客观描述了西学东渐与马克思主义哲学中国化之间的密切联系，另一方面又从理论本质、社会性质和社会效应等方面深刻揭示了马克思主义哲学中国化本身并不属于西学东渐的范畴。

与自然科学类似，越是基础性的哲学问题往往越具有前沿性。哲学与哲学史的关系问题就是这类问题。黑格尔在《哲学史讲演录》表达了哲学是哲学史或哲学史是哲学的观点，这一论点在武汉大学哲学学院引起热烈讨论，邓晓芒、赵林明确肯定哲学史是哲学这一论题。我们选取了朱志方的驳论文章《哲学不是哲学史》，该文不仅分析了“哲学是哲学史”的几种可能解释的错误或表达不严格，还从语用学上考察，论述“哲学是哲学史”导致哲学研究以史料研究为主，哲学论文被哲学教学论文所取代。最后强调，哲学的特殊性不在于它与历史的特殊关系，而在于它的题材、问题和方法。与之对应，吴根友在《即哲学史讲哲学——关于哲学与哲学史研究方法的再思考》一文中综合了参与争论的西方哲学学者的观点，并结合当代中国哲学创新的例证，对“哲学与哲学史”的关系问题作出了新的论述。吴根友指出，哲学史的学习与研究是哲学研究与理论创新的必要条件，但不是充分条件。从事哲学创新还需要逻辑思维能力、基本的科学素养和艺术素养。依托哲学史提供的哲学智慧，结合现实给哲学提出的理论问题，从事哲学创新，是哲学研究的基本要求。因此，“即哲学史讲哲学”是可能的，也是必须的。

哲学与宗教的关系问题是一个古老又常新的问题。段德智在《哲学的宗教维度与哲学动力学》一文中从哲学的精神意境、理论品格和致思路向视角界定哲学的宗教维度，认为哲学的宗教维度或宗教性不仅属于哲学静力学的范畴，同时亦属于哲学动力学的范畴。从哲学静力学和哲学动力学的高度来审视哲学与宗教的辩证关系是该文追求的精神境界。

长期以来，武汉大学哲学学院十分重视研究生培养教育的国际化拓展，吸纳众多具有重要国际影响力的西方学者来校任教和讲学。本教材也选取了这些学者发表的具有代表性的四篇论文，希望起到他山之石可以攻玉的借鉴作用。Paul Patton 的 Deleuze's Political Philosophy（《德勒兹的政治哲学》）一文详细考察了德勒兹政治哲学的时代背景，尤其是 1968 年法国五月风暴运动。Paul Patton 认为，与其说德勒兹的政治理论是马克思主义的，不如说它是去政治的。尽管受马克思主义影响较深，但德勒兹的政治理论与传统的马克思主义政治理论相去甚远，他主要从微观政治层面去研究个人与集体欲望同社会变革之间的关系。由于对特殊事件的特征评判提供了一套描述性语言，在此意义上德勒兹与瓜塔里理论的一系列概念是符合规范性的。而且他们后期的理论更是向政治规范性靠拢，并为自由民主国家的公共政治文化服务。Paul Patton 的 Foucault on Power and Government（《福柯论权力和政府》）一文旨在揭示当下已经出版的福柯法兰西学院演讲集所呈现的福柯在 1976—1982 年间权力观的转变。福柯提出了 1975—1976 年讲座课程目的中最为首要的问题，即“权力是什么”，次一级问题则为权力的本质及如何使用恰当术语对权力进行分析的问题。就权力的本质问题，福柯给出了四个答案：其一，在纳粹主义和斯大林主义之后，统治西方社会的最终极的权力形式是规训性权力和至高权力的复杂结合；其二，18 世纪末期“生命政治”诞生；其三，权力的新技术是要应用到人口而非个人或者组织方面，以确保安全机制；其四，欧洲基督教传统之下，牧领权力具有独特性，并且是现代国家治理形式的序曲。Eleonore Stump 在 The Sunflower: Guilt，Forgiveness，and Reconciliation（《向日葵：愧疚、宽恕与和解》）一文中探讨人们对于作恶者赎罪行为的直觉。有人认为：宽恕他人罪行的充分必要条件是作恶者的忏悔和对此作出的补偿，一旦这两个条件被满足，作恶者就应该得到宽恕，其罪行也得到充分清除。这一直觉可以被托马斯·阿奎那的相关阐述进行解释。阿奎那认为：宽恕和爱一样，在道德上具有强制力，宽恕他人是为了达到道德上的善。与此冲突的直觉是：在一些罪大恶极的例子中，即使宽恕具有强制性，忏悔和补偿并不足以使作恶者得到宽恕。因为罪恶所造成的实际伤害和潜在伤害是不可挽回的，而且他人的宽恕并不足以使得作恶者的罪恶清除。Bradley Monton 的“Against Maximizing Expected Utility”(《反对最大化预期效用》)通过分析圣彼得堡悖论（St. Petersburg game）和帕斯卡抢劫（Pascal's Mugging）两个例子，讨论预期效用最大化的不足，即在某些情况下，预期效用最大化的主体（很有可能）会不必要地面临贫穷甚至死亡的后果。因此，我们不应该预期效用最大化。相反地，当涉及到决策时，对于仅有很小概率发生的可能性，无论这些可能性能够带来多少效用，我们应该将其发生的概率降至零。

武汉大学哲学学科历来重视哲学方法论的研究与教学，相关学术成果非常丰富，我们大致按照二级学科的区分收录了 13 篇文章。彭富春在《哲学的主题与方法》中探讨哲学主题与方法的关系问题，该文认为，哲学的主题总是相关于它的方法。在西方哲学传统中，主题和方法的关系还表达为本体与方法的关系或者真理与方法的关系；在中国思想传统中，它则被描述为道与技的关系或者道与术的关系。彭富春强调，所谓的方法就是主题的方法，在这样的意义上，术乃道之术，方法乃缘道而行。一方面，主题在根本上规定了方法；另一方面，一种主题只有在一种与它相适应的方法中才能显示出来。有关马克思主义哲学的研究范式和方法论变革，我们选取了 3 篇重要文章。汪信砚的《当代中国马克思主义哲学的研究范式》指出，以马克思主义哲学中国化为范式开展当代中国马克思主义哲学研究，是马克思主义哲学自身的本质要求和当代中国社会发展的客观需要，也是当代中国马克思主义哲学研究健康发展的重要保证。要真正以马克思主义哲学中国化为范式开展当代中国马克思主义哲学研究，我们首先必须坚决反对各种形式的教条主义，纠正对于马克思主义哲学中国化性质的误读，对马克思主义哲学中国化进行正确的学术定位，并明确以马克思主义哲学中国化为范式的马克思主义哲学研究与对马克思主义哲学中国化这一领域的研究之间的重要区别。何萍的《文化哲学视野中的东西方马克思主义哲学》强调，马克思主义哲学作为当代最重要的哲学思潮的地位要求我们把它作为一个整体的对象加以研究。我们首先必须确定20世纪马克思主义哲学概念，进而研究东西方马克思主义哲学论争以及由此而决定的20世纪马克思主义哲学的基本格局和整体风貌，在此基础上，以文化哲学的研究范式审视20世纪马克思主义哲学。李佃来的《马克思主义哲学的三次方法论变革及其意义》指出，从19世纪到20世纪，马克思主义哲学在形成和发展的不同历史时期，经历了三次重大的方法论变革，由此在很大程度上解决了每个时期所面临的主要理论困难，大大推动了马克思主义哲学理论的发展。这三次方法论变革，分别是指由马克思所策动的辩证法对经验主义的变革、由卢卡奇所策动的总体性对实证主义的变革以及由柯亨所策动的分析的方法对人本主义的变革。另外，何萍的《如何写作马克思主义哲学专业的博士学位论文——以马克思的博士论文为范文》，针对当前马克思主义哲学专业的博士学位论文中存在的问题，论述了马克思主义哲学专业的博士学位论文写作的步骤、写作方法和写作规范的问题，重点论述了如何进行论文选题、如何开展资料搜集工作和如何进行正文的写作问题。

中国哲学史学科一直开设有本二级学科的方法论课程，继往开新，形成了深厚的研究与教学传统。郭齐勇在《中国哲学史方法论问题》中，通过评述武汉大学已故萧萐父教授及该校中国哲学学科点在中国哲学史方法论课程的教学方面的经验，强调经典诠释、创造转化的基础仍在于训诂与考据等处理文献的基本功，而在义理上则主张古今中西的兼通。中国哲学史学科的解释学处境是在中外古今之间，向外国哲学传统开放，同时重视自己的解释学传统。内在性的批评与思想的训练一定要以同情的了解为前提，注重理解的历史性与诠释的相应性。20世纪80年代末，萧萐父先生反省20世纪中国哲学史的研究经验时，曾提出了哲学史研究的“纯化”与“泛化”的关系问题。萧先生所说的“纯化”，即是指“使哲学史纯化为哲学认识论史，以便揭示哲学矛盾运动的特殊规律”。他所说的“泛化”，即是指“哲学史研究可以泛化为哲学文化史。以哲学史为核心的文化史或以文化史为铺垫的哲学史，更能充分反映人的智慧创造和不断自我解放的历程。”吴根友在《再谈哲学史研究的“纯化”与“泛化”》一文中，结合其明清哲学思想的研究，讨论了作者对“纯化”与“泛化”这一新哲学史观和方法论的回应与实践。正是由于将“纯化”与“泛化”的方式结合起来，明清哲学思想得以在《戴震、乾嘉学术与中国文化》一书中立体呈现，在坚持侯外庐、萧萐父等人的“明清早期启蒙说”的同时，主要从学术、哲学思考方式转换的角度讨论中国的早期现代性，不再停留于社会政治、文艺思潮的层面讨论中国传统文化的现代转换。吴根友在《即哲学史讲哲学——关于哲学与哲学史研究方法的再思考》中认为，哲学史的研究方法与类型是多元的，哲学创新的途径也是多元的。而“即哲学史讲哲学”是其中最为基本的方法之一。李维武的《“以哲学史为中心的思想史研究”刍议——对19—20世纪中国哲学研究的方法论思考》一文则反思中国哲学研究面临的问题：如何通过方法论上的探讨与创新，进一步拓展这一研究的思维空间，使这一研究具有更为广阔的视域和更为深刻的阐释。李维武提出的“以哲学史为中心的思想史研究”方法论创新，就是试图在哲学史研究与思想史研究之间加以沟通，使哲学史研究更多地吸取思想史研究的内容。经过十多年的精研深思，李维武又发表了《关于“以哲学史为中心的思想史研究”的再思考》，对“以哲学史为中心的思想史研究”这个新的方法论作了进一步的概括性说明，该文强调，“以哲学史为中心的思想史研究”，尽管也重视“史”，也重视历史的思想碎片，但又必须从“史”中探寻出“思”的内在逻辑与展开脉络，从这些思想碎片中揭示出哲学发展的“一以贯之”之“道”。

除了马哲、中哲比较集中的方法论讨论外，我们也选取了其他二级学科的重要方法论文章。郝长墀在《胡塞尔与黑格尔：政治现象学何以可能？》中比较胡塞尔与黑格尔的现象学文献，认为在胡塞尔的单子多样性的共同体或空间中，单子之间没有内在必要的关系，不可能存在政治关系。黑格尔则为我们提供了一种政治现象学思路，“认可”概念是其政治现象学核心概念，政治空间是关于自我意识如何实现的问题。对于黑格尔来说，政治领域或空间不是为了保护个人私有财产或分配正义的问题，而是在一个共同体中，平等人追求认可的活动，是关系到人的自我意识实现的问题。麻天祥的《宗教哲学方法论的理论探索》一文，从疑虑、诠释、比较和体悟四个方面概括了宗教哲学的研究方法。尤为重要的是，麻天祥直指当前宗教哲学研究中的弊端，指出体悟的方法并非神秘而遥不可及，它既是感觉经验长期积淀的结果，又是以逻辑手段为基础。只有在人们紧张、细密的逻辑思维之后，直觉体悟才能充分展示它的魅力。在宗教哲学中，任何夸大“体悟”神秘性的思想、行为，都是不足取的。麻天祥的《中国思想史哲学史研究的理念与方法》一文，从一条原则、两种内容、三项要求概括中国思想史、哲学史研究的理念与方法。所谓一条原则，即历史和逻辑相结合；两种内容则包括精英思想与平民思想；三项要求分别指三学、三义、三难，治中国学术，有文章、义理和考据之三学，三者缺一不可。治学需厘清三义：字面义、文本义和诠释义，三者缺一不可。为学有三难：淹博难、识断难、精审更难。石长平的《批判性融会与创造性建构——刘纲纪先生学术方法论略》一文指出，刘纲纪的实践本体论美学的理论形态属于马克思主义实践观的哲学美学，马克思主义哲学赋予了刘纲纪美学思想特色鲜明的理论品格。刘先生强调，“我写的每一本书、每一篇文章，都离不开马克思主义的指导，离开了马克思主义的哲学基础，我在大量的错综复杂的感性材料面前，就会感到束手无策，就没有办法将它提升到一定的哲学高度加以认识”。

目　录

第一部分

哲学前沿问题

逻辑证明与真理标准

陶德麟

1978年开始的真理标准问题的讨论，对于破除反马克思主义的现代迷信、冲决思想网罗，起了振聋发聩的作用。但是，对“实践是检验真理的唯一标准”这个命题的认识，在学术界和广大群众中并不一致，甚至还有不小的分歧。例如，有的同志认为经实践检验过的正确理论也可以是检验真理的标准；有的同志认为逻辑证明也可以是检验真理的标准；有的同志认为检验真理的标准不是实践而是客观对象。总之，在这些同志看来，“唯一”标准的说法至少是绝对化、简单化了，不能成立。我个人是同意“唯一”论的。限于篇幅，本文只想就“逻辑标准”问题谈一点粗浅的看法。

为了避免“假争论”，需要先明确一下语词的涵义和论题的意义。第一，这里说的“真理（Truth），是指认识与客观对象的符合，“检验真理的标准”（准确地说，是检验认识的真理性的标准）是指判定认识与客观对象是否符合的标准。第二，这里说的“逻辑”是专指传统的和现代的演绎推理，因为归纳推理和类比推理的结论并没有必然性、强制性，辩证逻辑则还没有形成一套严密的推理规则，它们之不能作为检验真理的标准现在并无争议，没有特别讨论的必要。第三，这里不是一般地讨论逻辑在认识过程中的作用问题，而仅仅涉及逻辑的证明作用问题（后者比前者的范围狭窄得多）。一句话，我们要讨论的问题是：逻辑证明是不是判定认识与对象符合的标准？

一

除了非理性主义者，谁也不会公然否认逻辑有证明的作用。在现代逻辑的研究和应用取得了巨大成就的今天，否认逻辑的证明作用更是荒谬的。问题不在于逻辑有没有证明的作用，而在于它证明的是什么，能不能由它的证明作用得出它是检验真理的标准的结论。而这就需要对逻辑证明的实质和功能作一点考察。

逻辑证明是以确定论题的真实性为目的的演绎推理（反驳是证明的特殊情况，不另讨论）。无论多么复杂冗长的证明，总是由论据、推论和论题组成的演绎推理。论题是待证的命题，是推理的结论，这里无需分析。论据是推理的前提，论证是按照逻辑规则（即正确的推理形式）由前提过渡到结论的思维活动，这两者是需要分析的。

先看论据。

论据可以是一个命题，也可以是若干个命题。要使演绎推理成为逻辑证明（逻辑证明是演绎推理，但并非一切演绎推理都是逻辑证明），第一个必要条件就是论据全部真实，即作为论据的每一命题都与它所反映的对象符合。如果论据全部假、部分假或真假不定，即使推理形式正确，结论在事实上是真的，证明也无效，也不成其为证明。那么，论据的真理性能否由逻辑来确定呢？

作为论据的命题不外以下几类：

（一）陈述经验事实的命题，亦称经验命题或知觉命题

这类命题反映的是可感知的事实，其真假取决于命题的陈述与事实是否符合。要判定这一点，逻辑显然无能为力。符合逻辑和符合事实并不是一回事。说“猫是吃老鼠的”固然符合逻辑，说“老鼠是吃猫的”也决不违反逻辑。假如让一个对猫鼠的生活习性毫无认知的人从逻辑上来判定这两个命题的真假，他一定束手无策。因为对他来说，这两个命题无非是“x 是吃 y 的”和“y 是

吃 x 的”而已，怎么知道孰真孰假？这类命题的真假是只有实践（包括观察和调查）才能“裁决”的。

或曰不然。有些经验命题可以从逻辑上判定真假，例如，“这只百灵鸟是鸟”必真，“这个等边三角形是六边形”必假，又当作何解释？其实，前者是分析命题，谓词就包含在主词之中；后者是矛盾命题，谓词与主词互相排斥。前者相当于说“A 集的一个元素属于 A 集”；后者相当于说“A 集的一个元素属于 A 的补集”。这两种命题虽然看来好象也是陈述某种经验事实的，而其实不是经验命题，而是公理。我们判定“这只百灵鸟是鸟”为真而“这个等边三角形是六边形”为假，并不需要具体的经验知识，而只需要相信公理。至于公理的真实性靠什么证明，正是下面要讨论的。

（二）公理

像逻辑和数学这样的纯演绎科学是以公理为原始论据的，这类科学是公理系统。公理的真实性能不能靠逻辑来证明？不能。有人想去证明充足理由律，想去证明毅氏几何第五公设，结果只是徒劳。这是为什么呢？因为任何演绎系统的基本要求就是不自相矛盾，而要不自相矛盾就会有至少一个命题在本系统中得不到证明（也得不到否证）。假如我们在某一演绎系统中用 A0 证明 A1，用 A1 证明 A2，用 A2 证明 A3，……一直到用 An-1 证明 An，那么用什么来证明 A0 呢？用从 A1 到 An 的任何命题来证明，都陷入了循环证明，等于不证明。可见像 A0 这样的命题在本系统中是不可能被证明的，它只能作为不证自明的公理。

那么，在本系统中得不到证明的命题不能在别的系统中得到证明吗？那要看两个系统的关系怎样。（1）如果 A 系统与 B 系统的命题不相干，显然不能证明。（2）如果 A 系统与 B 系统的命题互相矛盾，也不能证明。例如“平行线不相交”在欧氏几何里是真命题，在非欧几何里却是假命题；“全体大于部分”在有穷集合里是真命题，在无穷集合里却是假命题；这样矛盾的系统当然不可能互相证明。（3）如果 A 系统与 B 系统不相矛盾并且有某种关系，那么在A系统中得不到证明的命题在B系统中是可能得到证明的，但B系统又会有命题在本系统中得不到证明，又得求助于别的系统。这样一直推下去，公理的证明问题还是不能在逻辑的范围内解决。

这当然不是说公理是不反映客观实际的人为约定和任意假设，无所谓真实性，而是说它们的真实性不能由逻辑来判定。欧氏几何和非欧几何的公理当然都是一定的现实空间的特性的正确反映，有客观的真实性，是真理。但逻辑是无法证明这一点的，. 只有无数次的实践所提供的经验事实才能表明它们是真理。这也并不是马克思主义者独有的看法。例如现代著名数理哲学家哥德尔（K.Godel）就认为数学公理要成为科学真理要决定于“经验的检验”。

（三）定理

在纯演绎科学中，定理是以公理为原始论据推论出来的，定理的真实性靠公理的真实性来保证。而如上所述；公理的真实性就不能由逻辑证明来检验，定理的真实性当然也不能由逻辑证明来检验。定理是否与客观现实符合，与什么客观现实符合，只有实践才能判定。

至于在经验科学中，定理（或原理），一般说来并不是从公理演绎出来的，而是从经验事实中概括出来的普遍命题。这些经验事实是从实践中得到的（通过观察、实验、调查等等），因而普遍命题是否真实也只有由实践来确定。这是显然的。不错，现代的经验科学有许多部门采用的已经不是早期实验科学所采用的纯粹经验的方法，“而是研究人员受到经验数据的启发而建立起一个思想体系；一般来说，这个思想体系在逻辑上是用少数的基本假定，即所谓公理，建立起来的。”① 例如爱因斯坦的狭义相对论就是从两个被视为公理的命题出发的（在一切相互作匀速直线运动的坐标系中，光在真空中的速度相同；在一切相互作匀速直线运动的坐标系中，自然定律相同）。但是，第一，这些公理之所以能被提出，首先还是由于研究人员“受到经验数据的启发”，并不是

① 爱因斯坦：《狭义与广义相对论浅说》，上海科技出版社1979年版，第102页。

离开经验凭空构想出来的。第二，这些公理的真实性要在实践中受到检验。例如相对论的第一个公理就是在迈克尔逊—莫雷的著名实验中得到证实的。第三，这样建立起的理论体系（它由一系列相互联系的命题组成）究竟是否符合实际，是否真实，逻辑并不能回答，只有实践才能回答。例如广义相对论是得到了水星近日点的运动、光线在引力场中的偏转、光谱线的红向移动的实验证实的。在得到实验证实以前，爱因斯坦本人也并不认为他的理论就一定符合实际。他在1916年还写道："无论如何在未来的几年中将会得出一个确定的结论。如果引力势导致的光谱线红向移动并不存在，那么广义相对论就不能成立。另一方面，如果光谱线的位移确实是引力势引起的，那么对于此种位移的研究将会为我们提供关于天体的质量的重要情报。"①1924年，亚当斯（Adams）通过对天狼星的伴星的观测证实了谱线红移现象，这才使广义相对论的真实性得到了一个实践上的验证。爱因斯坦完全理解："理论有存在的必要的理由乃在于它能把大量的个别观察联系起来，而理论的'真实性'也正在于此。"② 至于在化学、生物学、人类学等等经验自然科学和各门社会科学中的定理和原理的真实性只有实践才能判定，就无需一一说到了。

（四）定义

以定义为论据是常见的。定义有语词定义和实质定义的区别。

语词定义是对语言符号的意义的规定，被定义的东西不是客观对象而是语词。它无非是说明我们用某一语词去指称某一对象，以便使人们了解我们的陈述，相当于给一个对象取名字。这种定义是约定的，无所谓真假，至多不过要求下定义的时候遵守日常用语或科学用语的习惯而已。我们把"圆"定义为与平面上一定点等距离的点的轨迹，就等于给具有如此这般特性的几何图形命名为"圆"，这就无所谓与客观对象是否符合，无所谓真假。如果有人不愿遵守这个约定，偏要把"圆"定义为别的什么，那么，只要他交待清楚，也不能说

① 爱因斯坦：《狭义与广义相对论浅说》，上海科技出版社1979年版，第107页。

② 爱因斯坦：《狭义与广义相对论浅说》，上海科技出版社1979年版，第102页。

他的定义是假的；至于他在此后的议论中是否首尾一贯，不自相矛盾，那是另一个问题，与定义的真假无关。语词定义既然无所谓真假，当然也就无所谓以什么为标准来检验其真假的问题。

实质定义与此不同，被定义的东西是客观对象。实质定义是对事物的本质或本质属性的断定和陈述，是有真假之分的。与事物的本质或本质属性相符合的断定和陈述就是真的，反之就是假的。那么，逻辑能否判定一个实质定义与它所反映的对象是否符合呢？不能，道理同前述的公理或定理的真假不能由逻辑判定一样。“国家是全民利益的代表”和“国家是阶级压迫的机关”这两个定义哪一个符合国家这个客观事物的本质，从逻辑上是不能判定的，两者都符合逻辑；只有阶级社会中的实践才能回答这个问题。

可见，无论哪一类论据的真实性都不能由逻辑证明来确定。逻辑证明的第一个必要条件，它自身就不能保证，它怎么能成为检验真理的标准？

二

再看论证。

逻辑证明的另一个必要条件，是论证的每一个步骤都合乎演绎推理的规则，即遵守正确的推理形式。那么，正确的推理形式能不能成为检验真理的标准呢？回答也是否定的。

第一，推理的形式正确与否靠什么来检验？这本身就是一个大问题。为什么我们恰恰把如此这般的推理形式看作“正确”的，而把另一些推理形式看作“不正确”的呢？推理形式的正确性靠什么来证明呢？如果用逻辑来证明，那么在一动手证明的时候就不可能不运用这些推理形式本身，就等于把待证明的东西当成已证明的东西，这就违反了逻辑。当然，在证明某种特定推理形式时可以设法避免运用它自身，而只用别的推理形式；但这时别的推理形式是否正确还有待证明。就推理形式的总体看，谁要想从逻辑上去证明推理形式，就无法避免由推理形式自己证明自己，而这也就等于什么也没有证明。可见，推理形式的正确性是不可能由逻辑来证明的，它只能被当作“当然如此”的、“无需证明”的规则来采用。这种“当然如此”和“无需证明”，正是因为它已被千百万次的实践证明过了的缘故。例如，为什么我们在推论时都得遵守同一律呢？因为人类千百万次的实践证明了它。原始人在追捕一条野牛的时候，他们将发现这条野牛在整个追捕过程中始终是一条野牛，具有野牛的一切属性；他们只有始终认定它是一条野牛，采取捕野牛的特殊办法追捕它，才可能达到预期的目的。假如他们一方面认定那是一条野牛，另一方面又认定那不是一条野牛，而是一块石头，试问他们将如何行动，他们的狩猎还要不要进行呢？可见，若不遵守“如果 X 是 A，那么 X 是 A”这样的推理形式，人们就无法行动、无法生活。这种推理形式的“正确性”就是这样经过无数次的实践反映到人的头脑中来，被无数次的实践所证明，而不是被推理形式自己证明的。列宁说得很精辟：“人的实践经过千百万次的重复，它在人的意识中以逻辑的格固定下来。这些格正是（而且只是）由于千百万次的重复才有着先入之见的巩固性和公理的性质。”①

第二，即使把正确推理形式本身如何形成、如何证明的问题存而不论，仅就它形成以后的作用来说，它能不能充当检验真理的标准呢？也不行。正确的推理形式无非是指这样的推理形式。它可以被归结为一个蕴涵式，而这个蕴涵式又是一个重言式，即永真式。检查一种推理形式是否正确，就是看它的相当的蕴涵式是不是一个永真式，如果把前提和结论的关系归结为 $A \supset B$ 的命题形式，而 $A \supset B$ 又是永真式，则推理形式是正确的，否则是不正确的。永真式是什么意思呢？它是指这样的命题形式：无论把具有什么具体内容的名词（或命题）代入它的变项，也无论被代入的命题（如果不是名词而是命题的话）是真是假，得到的命题总是真的。例如“如果 P，那么 P”（P=P），“不可能 P 并且非 P”（$\sim[P \wedge \sim P]$），“P 或者非 P”（$P \vee \sim P$）等等，就是常见的永真式。

① 《列宁全集》第 38 卷，人民出版社 1959 年版，第 233 页。

一个揭示了前提和结论的关系的蕴涵式是永真式，这表明了什么呢？表明了前提和结论的必然关系是不以前提和结论的具体内容及其真假为转移的。可见，正确的推理形式的实质和功能正在于、也仅在于撇开了前提和结论的具体的内容，不管前提和结论事实上真不真，而单从思维的形式结构方面揭示命题间的必然关系。换句话说，推理形式所涉及的只是思维本身的形式结构问题，而不是前提或结论与客观对象是否符合即是否真理的问题。如果问：正确的推理形式能证明什么？回答只能是：能证明前提和结论在命题形式方面的关系，再没有别的。至于前提和结论是不是正确地反映了客观实际，是不是真理，它是不去“管”、也“管”不了的。

正确的推理形式所能证明的仅仅是逻辑上的蕴涵，即命题形式上的蕴涵，而不包括事实上的蕴涵。例如客观世界里的对象或事件之间的因果关系、函数关系等等，是不能由推理形式来证明的。在这一点上，休谟说对了。要想从原因中“演绎”出结果来，是做不到的。同样，演绎也证明不了函数关系。例如，假定我们已知 A 物体的质量为 B 物体质量的两倍，又知道加在 AB 两物上的力相等，我们也就可以断定 A 的加速度必为 B 的加速度之一半。这个断定是不是从两个已知条件“演绎”出来的呢？很像是，其实不是。因为这两个已知条件与我们的断定之间在命题形式上并无必然联系，或者说，虽有必然联系，但只是物理的必然而非逻辑的必然。即使我们作出与此不同的断定，也并不违反逻辑。为什么我们认为只有这样的断定才是正确的呢？是因为我们依据了 F=ma 的经典力学公式。这并不是什么逻辑规则，而是力学公式，它反映的是力、质量、加速度这三个物理量之间的事实上的必然关系（函数关系），而不是三个概念之间的逻辑上的必然关系。这种事实上的必然关系的普遍性是不可能由逻辑推理来证明，而只能由千百万次的实践来证明的。

我国 20 世纪 50 年代讨论逻辑问题时，有的同志主张把“正确性”和“真实性”加以区别，我认为这种意见是很对的，对我们当前的讨论仍有意义。卡尔纳普（R. Carnap）把“逻辑上有效”（L-valid）和“物理上有效”（P-valid）

加以区别的说法也不无合理的成分。所谓“正确”或“逻辑上有效”相当于通常说的“合乎逻辑”，是指推理形式正确（前提蕴涵结论）；“真实性”或“物理上有效”则相当于通常说的“合乎实际”，这才是指命题是真理。逻辑只能证明前者而不能证明后者。人们常常在说到逻辑证明的场合叫“证明”(proof)，而在说到实践证明的场合则叫“证实”(verification 或 confirmation)，这并不是无意义的咬文嚼字，而是为了表示两者在性质和功能上的区别。当然，问题不在于用语，“实践证明”并非不可以说，而在于“实践证明”和“逻辑证明”所解决的问题确实是不同的，不应该混为一谈。

或许有的同志会说：如果前提的真实性已被实践证明，不就可以推出结论的真实性吗？在这种情况下结论的真实性不就是由正确的推理形式确定的吗？是的，看来似乎是这样，但实际上并不是这样。在这种情况下，结论的真实性本来就被蕴涵在前提之中，早就同前提一起被实践证明过了。推理的作用不过是把已被实践证明了的真实性揭示出来而已。打一个不完全恰当的比喻吧：罪犯的性质在他的犯罪行为被查实的时候就已经确定了，并不是等到法庭根据材料进行推论、作出“此人的行为已构成犯罪”的结论的时候才确定的。证明此人是罪犯的并不是推论，而是推论之前的调查。

第三，正确的推理形式之不能检验真理，在前提为假的情况下显示得更清楚。从假前提出发，按照同样的正确推理形式，既可以推出假结论，也可以推出真结论（假前提不仅蕴涵假结论，也蕴涵真结论）。试看下面的两个推理：

（甲）所有的鸟都是植物（假）

所有的狗都是鸟（假）

所有的狗都是植物（假）

（乙）所有的鸟都是哺乳动物（假）

所有的狗都是鸟（假）

所有的狗都是哺乳动物（真）

这两个推理的前提都假，在这一点上没有区别；推理形式都正确，而且是同一个推理形式（“所有的 M 是 P”，“所有的 S 是 M”，所以“所有的 S 是 P”），在这一点上也没有区别。可是得出的结论却一个假，一个真，截然相反。如果一个人根本没有生物学的知识，仅以推理形式为标准，能检验得出究竟哪一个结论是假的，哪一个结论是真的呢？显然是不能的。这就表明了正确的推理形式只能揭示前提和结论的逻辑蕴涵关系，而不能据以确定结论的真假。

三

有的同志说，上面这些道理至多不过说明逻辑不是检验真理的最终标准罢了。这一点我们并不反对。可是不管怎么说，如果前提真并且推理形式正确，则结论必真，这总是无可否认的吧，而这就是逻辑证明的威力所在。我们说逻辑证明也是检验真理的一种标准，也无非就是这个意思。这又有什么不对呢？

是的，逻辑证明作为演绎推理，有它的必然性、强制性。否认了这一点就等于否认了逻辑证明的存在权，连这个名词都该取消了。这当然很荒谬。可是问题在于：这种必然性、强制性是不是无条件的呢？并非如此。逻辑证明的有效性是受到条件的限制的，不过通常把这些条件当作不言而喻的东西，没有提到罢了。当问题涉及逻辑证明是不是检验真理的标准时，对这些条件是不能置之不顾的。

这些条件是什么呢？我想至少应该提到如下两点：

第一，要从真前提合乎逻辑地得出真结论，必须使结论所论及的范围不超出前提的实际有效范围。如果超出了，结论就不是必然真。这种“超出”的情形可能发生吗？完全可能。为什么呢？因为一定的具体实践（实践总是历史的、具体的）虽然可以确切地证明某一命题是真的，但却不能绝对确定它在什么范围内是真的，即不能绝对地确定它的实际有效范围。假如我们以这个命题为前提来进行推理，就不能不按照当时的认识水平对这个命题的有效范围作出一个规定。这个规定与这个命题实际有效范围是否一致呢？可能一致，也可能不一致。如果不一致，那就是说我们对前提本身的有效范围的规定就超出了前提的实际有效范围，因而由此推出的结论也就可能超出前提的实际有效范围，结论的真实性就不是必然的了。当然，如果结论所断定的东西事实上并未超出前提的实际有效范围，事实上是真的，那么，即使不考虑这个“范围”问题也不碍事；正如在篮球场上奔跑的运动员如果事实上没有出界，即使“忘记”了球场的界线也无关紧要一样。可是“范围”毕竟是客观地存在着的，并不因为我们“忘记”了它而消失掉。如果不估计到它，我们在闯出了“界线”之外的时候就会大吃一惊，觉得不可理解。比如说，经典力学的公式当然是真命题。在什么范围内真呢？人们长期没有想到这个问题（因为实践还没有提出这个问题），于是按照当时的认识水平对它的有效范围作了一个规定，然后以它为前提进行推理。这种推理也许进行过亿万次，每次的结论都没有超出经典力学公式的实际有效范围，事实上都是真的，因而也就没有发现这里面还有什么问题。可是，实践的进一步发展终于显示了经典力学公式的真理性的界限，表明了人们原先对它的有效范围的规定超出了它的实际有效范围，推出的结论并非在任何范围内都必然是真的。像这种由于推理的结论超出了前提的实际有效范围，终于被新的实践所揭露、所修正的情况，在科学史以至整个认识史上是层出不穷的。这是大好事。可以说，没有这种“超出”和“修正”就没有科学的发展和认识的进步。试想，如果坚持从经典力学公式合乎逻辑地推出来的结论无条件地是真理，相对论和量子力学还有出世的权利吗？

第二，要从真前提合乎逻辑地得出真结论，还要求前提的总和能正确地反映对象的全体。有时，前提是真的，但并未反映对象的全体，只反映了对象的某些侧面；而在结论中却作出了关于对象全体的断定。在这种场合，结论就不是必然真，很可能假。例如，“光是微粒”是真命题，“光是波”也是真命题，但如果仅以前者为前提，或者仅以后者为前提，得出的结论都不必然真，很可能假。事实上也是如此。例如以“光是微粒”为前提，应该得出的结论是：光在通过一个极小的孔时背幕上出现的是一个亮点；通过互相接近的两个小孔时背幕上出现的是两个互相接近的亮点。可是实验的结果却表明：光在通过一个小孔时背幕上出现的是光环和暗环，通过两个小孔时背幕上出现的是光带和暗带，否定了推出的结论。又如抗日战争初期，“中国是弱国”和“日本是强国”都是真命题，但这两个命题合在一起也没有正确地反映中日关系的全体。以这两个真命题为前提，得出的结论就会是“这次战争的结果是中国失败”，实践证明这个结论是假的。在科学实验中、社会调查中、历史考证中、革命或建设的各项工作中，数据或材料并无错误，推理的形式亦无错误，而得出的结论却不合实际的事，是常常发生的。其原因就在于前提虽真，却未能正确地反映所论对象的全体。

仅从以上两点看，前提真且推理形式正确则结论必真这一逻辑规律的有效性是有条件的，它不是威力无边，而是威力有边。“边”在何处，也只有不断发展着的实践才能逐步地、日益精确地作出回答，逻辑本身是回答不了的。如果由真前提合乎逻辑地得出来的结论就可以保证绝对地、无条件地符合实际，那又何必还要由实践来检验它呢？可是，主张逻辑证明可以作为检验真理的标准的同志也并不否认这种检验的必要。

有一种诘难说：数学定理难道不是真理吗？它们不是由推导来证明、并且仅仅由推导来证明的吗？

数学的来源、对象和本质是数学史和哲学史上长期争论的问题，直到今天也还在激烈争论。这些争论在这里不必赘述。这里需要指出的是：在什么意义上我们说数学定理是真理？我们认为，说数学定理是真理（truth），除了指它们与客观世界的量的关系或空间关系相符合以外，没有别的意义。那么，数学定理是不是正确地反映了这种客观的关系呢？这恰恰是推导所不能证明的。为什么？因为数学的原始论据是公理，推导所遵循的是逻辑规则。公理本身是否与客观现实符合，逻辑规则本身是否普遍有效，推导尚且不能证明，它又怎么能证明由公理推导出来的定理是否与客观现实符合呢？爱因斯坦说过：“‘真实’，这一概念与纯几何学的论点是不相符的，因为‘真实’一词我们在习惯上总是指与一个‘实在的’客体相当的意思；然而几何学并不涉及其中所包含的观念与经验客体之间的关系，而只是涉及这些观念本身之间的逻辑联系。”又说：“几何观念大体上对应于自然界中具有正确形状的客体，而这些客体无疑是产生这些观念的唯一渊源。”① 这些话是对的，不仅适用于几何学，而且原则上也适用于其他门类的数学。数学推导所证明的，只是数学概念之间的逻辑联系，公理和定理之间以及定理和定理之间的逻辑联系。至于这些概念、公理、定理与客观世界的客体（或关系）是否符合，即是否真理，数学推导是没有证明、也不能证明的。只有把这些概念、公理、定理应用于各门经验科学，即通过千百万次的实践，才能解决这个问题。

四

这样说来，逻辑证明对检验真理岂不是没有任何作用了吗？

不，并不是这样。我们说逻辑证明本身不能检验真理，并不是说它在检验真理的过程中没有任何作用。相反，它的作用是巨大的，不可缺少的，而且是不可代替的。

第一，结论的真实性虽然已被蕴涵在前提之中，在前提被实践证明的同时就已被实践证明，但前提与结论的蕴涵关系并不是可以一望而知的。当它还没有明晰化的时候，人们并不容易认识到这种关系的存在。即使知道了前提真，也未必就知道结论真。在欧氏几何中“平行线内错角相等”的命题蕴涵着“三角形三内角之和等于两直角之和”，但是如不经过一番推导，即使知道了前一命题的真，也未必知道后一命题的真。同样，即使知道了方程式 $X^2-7X+12=0$ 正确地反映某种客体间的关系，是真的，但是如不经过一番演算，也未必能一

① 爱因斯坦：《狭义与广义相对论浅说》，上海科技出版社 1979 年版，第 3 页。

眼看出 X=3 或 X=4 是真的。像这样极简单的蕴涵关系尚且如此，复杂的蕴涵关系就更不用说了（有的蕴涵关系要经过几十、几百、几千甚至上亿次的推论才能揭示出来）。逻辑能够把前提和结论的蕴涵关系明晰地揭示出来，把虽然已被实践证明、但还不为人们所知的真理确切地陈述出来，这对于达到检验真理的目的来说就绝不是可有可无的。没有它的辅助，已被实践证明了的真理也往往不为人们所知道、所确认。正如一个人的犯罪行为虽已查实，如不经过合乎逻辑的推论就未必能使人确认此人是罪犯一样。

这里顺便说到，有的同志认为逻辑证明不过是同语反复，根本不能提供任何新知识。此说未免失之偏颇，未敢苟同。事实上，一切演绎推理（证明也在内）的结论都只是蕴涵而不是“包含”在前提之中，关于前提的知识并不等于关于结论的知识。演绎推理能把蕴涵在前提中的结论揭示出来，使人们知道前所未知的东西，这也就是提供了新知识。如果不能提供新知识，那就无异乎说只要承认了为数不多的几条公理就等于精通了某门演绎科学，一切演绎科学的著作就都成了废话集了。

第二，在如何组织实践的检验上，逻辑的辅助作用也不可缺少。如果我们要用实践来检验一个命题的真假，`就不能不碰到这样的问题：用什么实践来检验？通过什么途径来检验？是直接检验这个命题还是通过检验别的命题来检验它？这就需要进行一番“设计”，要使“设计”能达到有效地检验命题的目的，除了借助于已有的经验知识以外，还少不了运用逻辑。即使检验的是最简单的经验命题，也必须如此。例如我们要检验“这只梨是甜的”这个命题真不真，是怎样检验的呢？当然，吃一口就是了。但是，我们怎么知道恰恰是用“吃”这种实践去检验这个命题，而不是用别的实践（例如把梨砸碎、把梨扔到水里等等）去检验呢？这是因为我们从以往的实践经验知道了这样一种必然关系的存在：“x 是甜的，当且仅当 x 被人吃并且人产生甜的味觉。”把这个关系式用于这只梨味的检验，就得到：“如果我吃这只梨并且我尝到甜味（前件），那么这只梨是甜的（后件）。”于是我们的任务就变成了去检验“如果我吃这只梨并且我尝到甜味”这个前件是否真。而这个前件又是“我吃这只梨”和“我尝到甜味”的合取；只有这两个命题都真，前件才真。于是我们的任务又变成了分别去检验这两个命题的真假。首先，我们用行动保证“我吃这只梨”是真的。然后，如果我的味觉没有毛病，因而可以确定“我尝到甜味”也是真的，那么“我吃这只梨并且我尝到甜味”就是真的。前件既然真，后件也必真。这样，“这只梨是甜的”的真实性就被证明了。像这样最简单的经验命题的检验是如此，复杂一点的更是如此。如果要用实践来检验一个普遍命题的真假，其“设计”的复杂，需要调动的逻辑手段之多，就更不用说了。很显然，没有逻辑的辅助，一个待检验的命题摆在我们面前，我们也会不知道用什么实践、通过什么途径来检验它。

第三，在如何确定实践结果对检验真理的意义上，逻辑的辅助作用也是显然的。实践的结果总是某种经验事实。这种经验事实说明了什么呢？它是不是确实证明了我们想要证明的命题呢？要确定这一点，一方面要检查我们的检验“设计”是否合乎逻辑，另一方面还要对实践结果进行逻辑上的分析，也就是说，要仔细检查表述实践结果的命题与待检验的命题之间是否确有逻辑联系，以及这种联系的意义如何。常常有这样的情况：我们想用实践来证明命题 P，实践的结果 Q 所实际证明的并不是 P 而是 P’，而我们却认为 P 已经由 Q 得证。这就弄错了。这种错误，有时大科学家也不能免。巴斯德的著名实验本来并没有证明生命在任何条件下都不能由无生命的东西产生，而他却误认为证明了，就是一例。

总之，逻辑证明在检验真理过程中不是不起作用，而是起着不可缺少的重大作用。这种作用应该充分地估计。我们想说明的只有一点：就是不管它的作用多么重大，就其性质来说也还是一种辅助作用，它不是、也不能是检验真理的标准，因为在确定认识与对象是否符合这一点上，实际的“判决”者并不是逻辑，而是实践。

（原载《哲学研究》1981 年第 1 期）

Deleuze's Political Philosophy [*]

Paul Patton

Much of Deleuze's work, especially the books co-authored with Guattari, has been read as political philosophy.① Deleuze clearly viewed their initial collaboration in this light. In a 1990 interview with Antonio Negri, "Control and Becoming," he remarked that "*Anti-Oedipus* was from beginning to end a work of political philosophy" (N 170). Their biographer, François Dosse, goes even further in suggesting that all of Deleuze's work, "from his first works on Hume to his final reflections on the virtual, is inscribed in the space of the political." ② However, not everyone accepts this image of Deleuze as a thoroughly political thinker. Slavoj Žižek argues that "*not a single one* of Deleuze's own texts is in any way directly political; Deleuze 'in himself' is a highly elitist author, indifferent toward politics." ③

Alain Badiou outlines several reasons for doubting whether Deleuze was first and foremost a political thinker and even whether there is such a thing as a Deleuzian

---

* Earlier versions of this chapter were presented as talks at The University of Sydney in April 2011 and at a workshop at the China Foreign Affairs University in June 2011. I am grateful to the participants on both occasions for their comments, questions and criticisms.

① See for example Paul Patton, *Deleuze and the Political* (London and New York: Routledge, 2000); Ian Buchanan and Nicholas Thoburn eds, *Deleuze and Politics* (Edinburgh: Edinburgh University Press 2008); *New Formations*, 68, 2010 (Special Issue entitled *Deleuzian Politics?*).

② François Dosse, *Gilles Deleuze and Félix Guattari: Intersecting Lives*, trans. Deborah Glassman (New York: Columbia University Press, 2010) p.21.

③ Slavoj Žižek, *Organs without Bodies: Deleuze and Consequences* (New York and London: Routledge, 2004). p.20.

politics.① A first difficulty is that Deleuze never identified the political as a specific object or domain of thought, in the same way that, in *What is Philosophy*?, he singled out art, science and philosophy.② A second, more subjective difficulty is that Deleuze was never very interested in politics. In his solo writings, he never claimed that politics determined his philosophical activity. Unlike many of his contemporaries such as Althusser, Derrida, Lyotard or Nancy he never argued that the primary purpose of philosophy was political. On the contrary, he tended towards a more traditional view of philosophy as the creation of concepts and suggested in a 1985 interview that he was interested in "the relations between the arts, science and philosophy" (N 123) .

A third difficulty concerns the content of Deleuze's political writings. Badiou suggests that there are two distinct objects of Deleuzian politics. The first is aligned with the virtual realm of becoming and pure events that is the ultimate source of creativity and the emergence of the new, while the second is aligned with the actual realm of embodied events, forms of society and historical processes of contestation and change. In *Anti-Oedipus* and again in *A Thousand Plateaus* Deleuze and Guattari outline a theory of universal history involving at least three stages. In the short essay, "Postscript on Control Societies," Deleuze outlines another historical series of types of society modelled on Foucault's analysis of the "diagram" of disciplinary society (N 177-182) . However, Badiou points out, none of this is really the work of a historian. On the contrary, Deleuze subscribes to a violent anti-historicism that leads

---

① A. Badiou, "Existe-t-il quelque chose comme un politique deleuzienne?" *Cités*, 40 (*Deleuze Politique*), 2009, pp.15-20 (talk given in English at "Immanent Choreographies: Deleuze and Neo-Aesthetics," Tate Modern Public Programme, London 21-22 September 2001) .

② Philippe Mengue also points out the absence of any place for specifically political thought in the tripartite division of thought described in What is Philosophy? See Mengue, Deleuze et la question de la démocratie (Paris: L' Harmattan, 2003), p.52. See also Nicholas Thoburn, Deleuze, Marx and Politics (London and New York: Routledge, 2003), pp.5-6.

him to insist more and more on the distinction between history and becoming:

> The thing is, I became more and more aware of the possibility of distinguishing between becoming and history. It was Nietzsche who said that nothing important is ever free from a 'nonhistorical cloud.' This isn't to oppose eternal and historical, or contemplation and action: Nietzsche is talking about the way things happen, about events themselves or becoming. What history grasps in an event is the way its actualized in particular historical circumstances; the event's becoming is beyond the scope of history. (N 170) ①

For Deleuze, it is becomings that are the real object of philosophy. Philosophy as it is defined in *What is Philosophy?* creates concepts that express particular kinds of becoming or 'pure events.' In view of the priority that Deleuze assigns to becoming at the expense of history, Badiou argues that his politics remains divided between an ethics of creation and creativity and a mundane governmental politics that is bound up with history and the analysis of capitalism. Peter Hallward pursues this line of argument by outlining a reading of Deleuze as a theophantic thinker of unworldly creation, to the point of suggesting that Deleuze's ethics of creativity offers no basis for any determinate political activity whatsoever.② In common with another critic of Deleuze's politics,

---

① On Deleuze's relation to history, see Jay Lampert, *Deleuze and Guattari's Philosophy of History* (London and New York: Continuum, 2009), Jeffrey Bell and Claire Colebrook eds *Deleuze and History* (Edinburgh: Edinburgh University Press, 2009) and Craig Lundy, *History and Becoming: Deleuze's Philosophy of Creativity* (Edinburgh: Edinburgh University Press, 2012) .

② Peter Hallward, *Out of This World: Deleuze and the Philosophy of Creation* (London and New York: Verso 2006), *pp*.136-139. Hallward's book has been critically reviewed by a number of Deleuze scholars: see *inter alia* Gregory J. Seigworth, "Little Affect: Hallward's Deleuze," *Culture Machine*, Reviews 2007 ; John Protevi, *Notre Dame Philosophical Reviews*, 2007.08.03 ; and Erinn C. Gilson, *Continental Philosophy Review*, 42, 2009, pp.429-434.

Philippe Mengue, Hallward wavers between denying that Deleuze is a political philosopher and asserting that he is the wrong kind of political philosopher. Jeremy Gilbert summarises their respective conclusions in the following terms:

> Deleuze is a mystic, a nostalgist for elitist modes of avant-gardism which have no purchase on the present, at best an implicit conservative whose romanticism leaves no scope for rational calculation or collective action.①

There is some truth to each of Badiou's claims about Deleuze's relation to politics.

It is also true, as Gilbert suggests, that his work encompasses both political and anti-political moments.② However, these must be understood in their context and especially in their relation to one another if we are to appreciate the character of Deleuze's political thought and his distinctive contribution to political philosophy. While he would undoubtedly not be regarded as a political philosopher by many professional philosophers and political scientists, there are no grounds for the suggestion that Deleuze's philosophy has nothing to offer in relation to politics. Before outlining some of the ways in which the content of his work with Guattari may be read as a contribution to specifically political philosophy, I begin with the subjective, biographical problem raised by Badiou. It is important to read Deleuze against the background of the developments in his thought and to take at face-value his claim that it was only after the tumultuous events of May 1968 in France that he undertook his own "move into politics" (N 170).

---

① Jeremy Gilbert, 'Deleuzian Politics? A Survey and Some Suggestions, *New Formations*, 68, 2010, p.10.

② ibid.

In his 1990 interview with Negri, Deleuze admits that in his early years he was more interested in the creation of new social relations than in the manner in which these were represented. As such, he was "more interested in right than in politics" (N 169) .① François Dosse takes Deleuze's interest in empiricists such as Hume and vitalists such as Bergson, in a period when French philosophy was dominated by marxism and phenomenology, to be evidence not only of originality but also of a certain intellectual "dandyism" that took delight in embracing unfashionable and untimely thinkers.② It is true that he repeated this gesture with an essay on Sacher-Masoch in 1961, at the height of intellectual interest in Sade, and with a suggestion in 1993 that his next and last book would be called "The Importance of Marx" (N 51) . In the same interview in 1993, in which he points out that he was never a member of the Communist Party and never underwent psychoanalysis, Deleuze admits that he did not become marxist until he read Marx in the 1960s (N 51) . Latecomer to politics that he may have been, he was nonetheless the only member of the philosophy department and one of the few professors at the University of Lyon in 1968 to publicly declare his support for the student movement and to take part in assemblies and demonstrations.③ Only after this social and political upheaval, and a long period of ill-health and convalescence, did he become actively engaged in particular causes alongside people such as Guattari, Foucault and Elie Sambar (N 170) . From this point onwards, as Badiou admits, Deleuze wrote a great deal about politics and political issues, both alone and in collaboration with Guattari. Moreover,

---

① The English text of *Negotiations* uses "law" here to translate "droit," thereby obscuring a contrast in the original between "loi" and "droit." For this and for other reasons, it is more appropriate to translate "droit" here as "right" : see Paul Patton, "Immanence, Transcendence and the Creation of Rights" in Laurent de Sutter and Kyle McGee eds *Deleuze and Law* (Edinburgh: Edinburgh University Press 2012) .

② Dosse, *Intersecting Lives*, pp.98, 109.

③ Dosse, *Intersecting Lives*, p.177.

their final co-authored text, *What is Philosophy?*, does claim a political vocation for philosophy. Philosophy is a certain kind of criticism of the present that works through the creation of concepts. These express forms of absolute deterritorialization that can only be thought and can only produce effects in relation to existing forms of relative deterritorialization within a given society (WP 88). Deleuze and Guattari call this point of engagement between philosophy and its social milieu "utopia":"In each case it is with utopia that philosophy becomes political and takes the criticism of its own time to its highest point" (WP 99). This conception of philosophy as utopian engagement with the present raises a number of questions about the kind of political activity envisaged and the precise sense in which this is political philosophy.

Marxist politics or anti-politics?

In answer to the first set of questions about the kind of politics envisaged, we can begin by noting that, like many of their compatriots mobilized by the events of 1968, Deleuze and Guattari were heavily influenced by Marxist approaches to politics.① They focused on the conditions of revolutionary social change rather than the conditions of maintaining society as a fair system of cooperation among its members. In contrast to traditional Marxist politics, however, they were less

① There is extensive discussion of Deleuze's relation to Marxism in the secondary literature on his and Guattari's work. See in particular Eugene Holland, *Deleuze and Guattari's Anti-Oedipus: Introduction to Schizoanalysis* (London and New York: Routledge, 1999); Jason Read, *The Micro-Politics of Capital* (Albany N.Y.: State University of New York Press, 2003); Nicholas Thoburn, Deleuze, Marx and Politics (2003); Isabelle Garo, "Deleuze, Marx and Revolution: What It Means to 'Remain Marxist'" in J. Bidet and S. Kouvelakis eds *Critical Companion to Contemporary Marxism*, Leiden and Boston, MA: Brill, 2007, pp.605–624; the essays in *Deleuze Studies*, 3, 2009, *Issue Supplement: Deleuze and Marx*, edited by Jain Dhruv; and 'Becoming Revolutionary: Marx Through Deleuze" in Simon Choat, *Marx Through Postructuralism* (London and New York: Continuum, 2010).

interested in the capture of state power than in the qualitative changes in individual and collective identities that occur alongside or beneath the public political domain. In their view, all politics is simultaneously a *macropolitics* that involves social classes and the institutions of political government and a *micropolitics* that involves subterranean movements of sensibility, affect, and allegiance. However much they borrowed from Marx's analysis of history and capitalism, their own work focused on the individual and collective forms of desire that constitute the micropolitical dimension of social change. This focus on the politics of desire led them to abandon key tenets of Marxist social and political theory such as the concept of the party as a revolutionary vanguard and the philosophy of history that sustained Marxist class politics. They proposed a non-teleological conception of history along with a more nuanced appreciation of the deterritorializing as well as the reterritorializing aspects of capitalism. They insisted that the impetus for social change was provided by movements of deterritorialization and lines of flight rather than by class contradictions. Their rejection of the organizational and tactical forms of traditional Marxist politics is definitively expressed at the end of *Dialogues* when Deleuze and Parnet abandon the goal of revolutionary capture of State power in favor of the *revolutionary-becoming* of people throughout society: "why not think that *a new type of revolution is in the course of becoming possible*, and that all kinds of mutating living machines conduct wars, are combined and trace out a plane of consistence which undermines the plane of organization of the World and the States?" （D 147）. This new concept of revolutionary-becoming sought to encompass the multitude of ways in which individuals and groups deviate from the majoritarian norms that ultimately determine the rights and duties of citizens.

The fact that Deleuze read Marx during the 1960s alongside Nietzsche perhaps explains some of the anti-political themes that occasionally manifest themselves in his work（N 51）. There is no discussion of Nietzsche's views on politics and the state in *Nietzsche and Philosophy*, only comments on his theory of culture and, at the end of the book, on the implications of Nietzsche's theory for practice. However, if Deleuze had elaborated a Nietzschean politics on the basis of applying the theory of power outlined in *Nietzsche and Philosophy* to the social and political field, and supposed a simple axiological priority of the active over the reactive and the affirmative over the negative, the argument might run along the following lines. Power is fundamentally active and relational, appearing in the interaction between different kinds and degrees of force. In the state of nature, individual and collective bodies collide in the pursuit of their activities. However, purely chaotic interaction is not a state of social existence: at best, life under such conditions will be uncertain, at worst it will be brutish and short. Hence, it can be argued, the overriding aim of political government is the establishment and maintenance of relatively stable forms of interaction. Social relations require the stabilisation and fixation of certain forms of interaction, including the institution of forms of government which enable stable and predictable forms of action upon the actions of others. In these terms, government is a form of action upon individual or social forces which seeks to limit or constrain their possibilities for action. From the perspective of the forces governed, the government of individual and collective bodies is essentially reactive. Deleuze and Guattari's account of the State as a process of capture operating upon the primary flows of matter and activity in the social field renders explicit this reactive character of the political apparatus. The State, they argue, captures flows of population, commodities, or money in order to extract from these flows a surplus which then becomes a means to maintain and enhance its own power. It is an institution whose primary mode of operation is one of limitation or constraint, a matter of separating active forces from what they can do. In these terms, the State is by definition always a secondary formation, and the political sphere is always reactive by nature. In this way, the argument sketched above would lead to a fundamentally anti-political orientation.

Elements of such an orientation may be found in *Difference and Repetition*, for example, in the form of Deleuze's defence of the singular against the general, the individual against the herd and a resistance to forms of equality and equalisation. This 'anti-political' theme emerges from the conception of the social field (like every other) as a field of free differences and the rejection of representation: every time there is representation there is always "an unrepresented singularity" who does not recognise himself or herself in the representant. Hence the misfortune of speaking for others (DR 52) . Elsewhere in *Difference and Repetition*, Deleuze points out for every philosophy that begins from a subjective or implicit claim about what everybody is supposed to know there is another which denies this knowledge or fails to recognise what is claimed. Such philosophies rely not upon the common man but on a different persona:"Someone who neither allows himself to be represented nor wishes to represent anything" (DR 130) .①

The theory of capitalist society outlined in *Anti-Oedipus* establishes a fundamental dualism within capitalist society between the deterritorializing tendency of capital and the necessary reterritorialization effected by the State and its agents. Moreover, Deleuze and Guattari suggest, the revolutionary path lies not in the attempt to set limits to market forces and the impetus of deterritorialization, but in the opposite direction, pursuing ever further the movement of decoding

---

① In the "Intellectuals and Power" interview with Foucault, Deleuze suggests that it was Foucault who taught the intellectuals of his generation the indignity of speaking for others:"We laughed at representation, saying it was over, but we didn't follow this 'theoretical' conversion through – namely theory demanded that those involved finally have their say from a practical standpoint" (DI 208) . This interview first appeared in the Deleuze issue of *L'Arc* (Paris, 1971) . Another translation appears in Michel Foucault, M. (1977) . *Language, Counter-Memory, Practice: Selected Essays and Interviews*, ed. Donald F. Bouchard, trans. Donald F. Bouchard and Sherry Simon (Ithaca, N.Y.: Cornell University Press, 1977), pp.205-217.

and deterritorialization（AO [Continum 2004]，260）. Much of the analysis of capitalism in *Anti-Oedipus* supports such a reading. For example，the authors describe the capitalist axiomatic as a system of enslavement in which all are subject to the constraint of its axioms. By contrast with the form of slavery established by the Despotic state，which at least retained an apparatus of anti-production distinct from the sphere of production and a corresponding class of masters，capitalism installs "an unrivalled slavery，an unprecedented subjugation" in which "there are no longer even any masters，but only slaves commanding other slaves"（AO [Continuum edition 2004] 276）. Here，there is only one class and bourgeois and proletarian alike are slaves of the social machine. In contrast，Deleuze and Guattari point to "the revolutionary potential of decoded flows" and suggest that the opposition to this machine which is relevant from the point of view of revolutionary politics is not that between capitalist and worker but that between "the decoded flows that enter into a class axiomatic on the full body of capital，and on the other hand，the decoded flows that free themselves from this axiomatic..."（AO [Continuum 2004] 276）.

Other elements of Deleuze and Guattari's mature political philosophy disallow a simplistic anti-political point of view. The axioms of the capitalist social machine do not simply repress a natural state of free and undirected social existence. They are also constitutive of new social forces and forms of life. Deleuze and Guattari are not romantic anarchists who believe in a realm of social being beyond the subjection to political power. It would be an error，they argue，"to take a disinterested stance toward struggle on the level of the axioms"（ATP 463）. The reason is not simply that the conditions of people's lives are at stake in those axioms，but also because forcing changes at the level of the axiomatic is itself an indispensable mechanism of affecting the possibility of future changes. As we have seen，it is a fundamental feature of the axiomatic that it cannot reterritorialize existing flows without creating conditions that will generate new forms of deterritorialization.

Micropolitics, formal normativity and deterritorialization

Deleuze and Guattari's political philosophy does not conform to the disciplinary norms of Anglophone normative political philosophy or German Critical Theory. For the most part, the concepts developed in *Anti-Oedipus* and *A Thousand Plateaus* do not directly address the macropolitical public domain, much less the normative principles on which this should be based. They consider the different forms of modern government only from the Marxist perspective of their subordination to the axioms of capitalist production. From this point of view, authoritarian, socialist, and liberal democratic states are considered equivalent to one another insofar as they function as models of realization of the global axiomatic of capital. They allow that there are important differences among the various modern forms of state but provide little discussion of these differences. They affirm the importance of changes to regimes of public right that come about through struggles for civil and political rights, for equality of economic condition and opportunity as well as for regional and national autonomy. However, they offer no normative theory of the basis of such rights, or of the kinds and degrees of equality or regional autonomy that should prevail (ATP 470–471). They offer no justification for the establishment of basic civil and political rights, for the kinds of differential rights that might apply to cultural or national minorities, or for particular ways of distributing wealth and other goods produced by social cooperation.

Instead, they focus on the micropolitical sources of political change such as the minoritarian becomings that provide the affective impetus for political movements. On their view, the sources of political creativity must always be traced back to shifts in the formations of individual and group desire that in turn lead to changes in sensibility, allegiance and belief. To the extent that such micropolitical movements bring about changes in the majoritarian standards themselves, along with new forms of right or different status for particular groups, they effectively bring about what Deleuze and Guattari refer to as "new earths and new peoples" (WP 99, 101). At the same time, the significance of such minoritarian becomings for public political right depends on their being translated into new forms of right and different statuses for individuals and groups: "Molecular escapes and movements would be nothing if they did not return to the molar organizations to reshuffle their segments, their binary distributions of sexes, classes and parties" (ATP 216–217). In this manner, even though they offer neither descriptive nor normative accounts of macropolitical institutions and procedures, Deleuze and Guattari do provide a supplement to liberal democratic conceptions of political order. They invent a language in which to describe micropolitical movements and infrapolitical processes that give rise to new forms of constitutional and legal order. They outline a social ontology of assemblages and processes that bears indirectly on the forms of public right. They invent concepts such as becoming-minor, nomadism, smooth space, and lines of flight or deterritorialization that are not meant as substitutes for existing concepts of freedom, equality, or justice but that are intended to assist the emergence of another justice, new kinds of equality and freedom, as well as new kinds of political differentiation and constraint.①

---

① This is by no mean an exhaustive list of Deleuzian concepts which might be supposed relevant to political philosophy. Other concepts that have been taken up in this connection include Deleuze's concepts of "the missing people," the "event," "dramatization" and "nomadology." In relation to these concepts, see Alain Beaulieu, "Gilles Deleuze's Politics: From Marxism to the Missing People" in Constantin V. Boundas ed *Gilles Deleuze: The Intensive Reduction* (London and New York: Continuum, 2009), pp.204–217; Tom Lundborg, *Politics of the Event: Time, Movement, Becoming* (London and New York: Routledge, 2011); Iain Mackenzie and Robert Porter, *Dramatizing the Political: Deleuze and Guattari* (Houndmills, Basingstoke and New York: Palgrave Macmillan, 2011); Eugene Holland, *Nomad Citizenship: Free-Market Communism and the Slow-Motion General Strike* (Minneapolis and London: University of Minnesota Press, 2011).

Although this political ontology does not include normative political concepts of equality, freedom and justice, it does include a kind of formal normativity. Moreover, there is a progression in Deleuze and Guattari's work from a focus on this formal normativity in the earlier work towards increasing engagement with explicitly political normativity in their later work. By "formal normativity" I mean the way in which *Anti-Oedipus* discusses political institutions only from the perspective of a universal theory of society and history. The specifically political organization of society plays no independent role in this theory. Rather, it is treated as continuous with the coordination and control of flows of matter and desire in non-state societies governed by the Territorial machine with its systems of alliance and filiation.① Deleuze and Guattari present the state as a new mechanism of alliance rather than as the embodiment of any ideal treaty or contract on the part of its subjects (AO [Continuum 2004] 213) . They argue that the state form appeared in human history in the guise of the different kinds of Despotic machine, each with its own mechanisms of overcoding the flows of desire, before becoming subordinate to the "civilized machine" that is global capitalism. What they call the Territorial, Despotic, and Civilized social machines are treated only as different regimes of coordination and control of the local desiring machines that constitute individual, familial, and social life. There is no discussion of the norms that regulate modern political life, only the normativity inherent in the typology of desiring machines as embodying either the paranoiac, reactionary, and fascistic pole of desire or the schizoid and revolutionary pole (AO [Continuum 2004] 373) . For this reason, their "schizoanalytic" theory

① "In *Anti-Oedipus* … every society, every form of social production is nothing but a specific organisation and articulation of desiring-production, assigning it specific goals and aims." Jason Read, "Fetish is always actual, Revolution is Always Virtual," *Deleuze Studies*, 3, 2009, *Issue Supplement: Deleuze and Marx*, 98–99.

and practice of desire proposes neither a political program nor a project for a future form of society.

A Thousand Plateaus broadens and generalizes Deleuze and Guattari's social ontology so that it becomes a general theory of assemblages and the manner in which these are expressed throughout human history. The last vestiges of Marxist teleology are removed from their universal history such that social formations are defined by processes or becomings and "all history does is to translate a coexistence of becomings into a succession" (ATP 430). The successive plateaus provide a series of new concepts and associated terminology with which to describe different kinds of assemblages. These include concepts designed to express social, linguistic, and affective assemblages, such as strata, content and expression, territories, lines of flight, or deterritorialization; the terminology employed to outline a micro- as opposed to macro-politics, along with concepts such as body without organs, intensities, molar and molecular segmentarities, and the different kinds of line of which we are composed; the terminology employed to describe capitalism as a nonterritorially based axiomatic of flows of materials, labor, and information as opposed to a territorial system of overcoding; and finally, they include a concept of the state as an apparatus of capture that, in the forms of its present actualization, is increasingly subordinated to the requirements of the capitalist axiomatic, along with a concept of abstract machines of metamorphosis, or nomadic war machines, that are the agents of social and political transformation.

This machinic theory of society is normative in a specific and formal sense, namely that the different kinds of assemblage amount to a world in which systematic priority is accorded to minoritarian becomings over majoritarian being, to planes of consistency over planes of organization, to nomadic machines of metamorphosis over apparatuses of capture, to smooth rather than striated space, and so on. Deleuze and Guattari's political ontology presents certain kinds of movement as primary: becoming-minor as a process of deviation from a majoritarian standard, lines of flight or deterritorialization rather than processes of reterritorialization or capture, and so on. In this sense, their ontology of assemblages is also an ethics or an ethology. This ethics might be characterized in the language of one or other of the plateaus as an ethics of becoming, of flows or lines of flight or as an ethics and a politics of deterritorialization.① It is "political" only in the very broad sense that it enables us to conceptualize and describe transformative forces and movements as well as the forms of "capture" or blockage to which these are subject.

In order to appreciate the complexity of this ontology and the kind of description that it allows, consider Deleuze and Guattari's concepts of *deterritorialization* and *reterritorialization*. In the concluding statement of rules governing some of their most important concepts at the end of *A Thousand Plateaus*, deterritorialization is defined as the movement or process by which something escapes or departs from a given territory, where a territory can be a system of any kind: conceptual, linguistic, social, or affective (ATP 508). By contrast, reterritorialization refers to the ways in which deterritorialized elements recombine and enter into new relations in the constitution of a new assemblage or the modification of the old. Systems of any kind always include "vectors of deterritorialization," while deterritorialization is always "inseparable from correlative reterritorializations" (ATP 509). Deterritorialization can take either a negative or a positive form. It is negative when the deterritorialized element is subjected to reterritorialization that obstructs or limits its line of flight. It is positive when the line of flight prevails over the forms of reterritorialization and manages to connect with other deterritorialized elements in a manner that extends its

① Patton, *Deleuze and the Political*, pp.9, 136.

trajectory or even leads to reterritorialization in an entirely new assemblage. As well as distinguishing negative and positive deterritorialization, Deleuze and Guattari further distinguish between an absolute and a relative form of each of these processes. Absolute deterritorialization refers to the virtual realm of becoming and pure events, while relative deterritorialization concerns only movements within the actual realm of embodied, historical events and processes. In the terms of their ontology of assemblages, it is the virtual order of becoming that governs the fate of any actual assemblage.

Finally, in accordance with their method of specification of concepts by proliferating distinctions, they distinguish between the *connection* and *conjugation* of deterritorialized elements in the construction of a new assemblage. The effective transformation of a given element of social or political life requires the recombination of deterritorialized elements in mutually supportive and productive ways to form assemblages of connection rather than conjugation. Absolute and relative deterritorialization will both be positive when they involve the construction of "*revolutionary connections* in opposition to the *conjugations of the axiomatic*" (ATP 473). Under these conditions, absolute deterritorialization "connects lines of flight, raises them to the power of an abstract vital line or draws a plane of consistency" (ATP 510).

Deleuze and Guattari's concepts are normative in the sense that they provide a descriptive language within which to judge the character of particular events and processes. They enable us to pose question such as: Is this negative or positive reterritorialization? Is this a genuine line of flight? Will it lead to a revolutionary new assemblage in which there is an increase of freedom, or will it lead to a new form of capture or worse? (D 143–144). In this sense, the judgments enabled by Deleuze and Guattari's ontology of assemblages and processes are entirely practical and pragmatic. They enable a form of reflective judgment, although one that is closer to Kant's aesthetic judgment than to his determinative judgments of practical or theoretical reason. Philosophy, Deleuze and Guattari suggest, "is not inspired by truth. Rather, it is categories like Interesting, Remarkable or Important that determine success or failure" (WP 82) .

Deleuze's Turn Toward Political Normativity

Deleuze and Guattari's machinic social and political ontology has a normative dimension in so far as it presents a world of interconnected machinic assemblages, the innermost tendency of which is toward the "deterritorialization" of existing assemblages and their "reterritorialization" in new forms. Nevertheless, their ontology remains formal in relation to actual societies and forms of political organization. Disagreements with Marxism aside, all of their political theoretical innovations were carried out within a broadly Marxist perspective that envisaged the emergence of new and better forms of social and political life. However, at no point did they address the normative principles that inform their critical perspective on the present, much less the question how these might be articulated with those principles that are supposed to govern political life in late capitalist societies. Nowhere did they engage directly with the political norms embedded in liberal democratic political institutions and ways of life, such as the equal moral worth of individuals, freedom of conscience, the rule of law, fairness in the distribution of material goods produced by social cooperation, and so on. The principled differences between liberal democratic, totalitarian, and fascist states were mentioned only in passing in the course of their analysis of capitalism and present-day politics as a process of axiomatization of the social and economic field.

Read in the context of Western Marxism during the 1960s and 1970s, Deleuze and Guattari's failure to engage directly with the political values and normative concepts that are supposed to inform the basic institutions of modern liberal democracies is not surprising. Their political philosophy predates widespread understanding and acceptance of the ways in which Marx's critique of capitalist society is bound up with concepts of distributive justice, as it does the efforts to identify the relevant principles of justice that occurred under the impact of so-called analytic Marxism in the course of the 1980s. Since then, there have been numerous attempts to combine Marxist social theory with the normative principles informing varieties of left-liberal political theory.① While these developments had little impact in France, there was a similar rediscovery of ethical and political normativity in French political thought during this period. This was expressed, for example, in a renewed interest in human rights, subjectivity, justice, equality, and freedom in the work of contemporaries such as Foucault and Derrida. Guattari became involved in electoral politics during the latter part of the 1980s, standing as Green candidate in 1992 regional elections.

Deleuze's writings and comments in interviews from the 1980s mark a significant shift in his thinking about such normative issues. For example, he responds to the renewed interest in human rights during this period by insisting on the importance of jurisprudence as the means to create new rights. While he criticizes the manner in which human rights are represented as "eternal values" and "new forms of transcendence," he makes it clear that he is not opposed to rights

① For an example of one such attempt, see Rodney Peffer, *Marxism, Morality and Social Justice* (Princeton: Princeton University Press, 1990). For more general discussions of so-called "analytic marxism," see G.A. Cohen, *Karl Marx's Theory of History* (Oxford: Oxford University Press, 2000); Will Kymlicka, *Contemporary Political Philosophy* (Oxford: Oxford University Press, 2002), pp.166-207; and Andrew Levine, *A Future for Marxism?* (London: Pluto Pres 2003).

as such but only to the idea that there is a definitive and ahistorical list of supposed universal rights. He argues that rights are not the creation of codes or declarations but of jurisprudence, where this implies working with the "singularities" of a particular situation (N 153). He returns to the question of rights and jurisprudence in his *Abécédaire* interviews with Claire Parnet, recorded in 1988–1989, where he affirms the importance of jurisprudence understood as the invention of new rights, along with his own fascination for the law.① In his 1990 interview with Negri, he reaffirms the importance of jurisprudence as a source of law with reference to the question what rights should be established in relation to new forms of biotechnology (N 169). Deleuze's endorsement of rights and jurisprudence clearly commits him to the existence of a rule of law and the kind of constitutional state that this implies. In the case of societies that seek to govern themselves in this manner, the concept of a right implies that certain kinds of action on the part of all citizens will be protected by law and, conversely, the enforcement of limits to the degree to which citizens can interfere with the actions of others.

Deleuze's political writings from the 1980s onward provide evidence not only of his commitment to the rule of law but also to democracy. His 1979 "Open Letter to Negri's Judges" already adopted the speaking position of a democrat committed to certain principles in relation to due process and the rule of law (TRM [2007 edition] 169). His concern with democracy becomes more pronounced in *What Is Philosophy?* where there are a series of highly critical remarks about actually existing democracies. Far from dismissing the democratic ideal, these comments imply

① *Gilles Deleuze from A to Z*, 3-DVD Set, directed by Pierr-André Boutang, trans. Charles J. Stivale, New York: Semiotext (e), 2011: see *G comme Gauche*. On Deleuze's understanding of the invention of rights, see Patton, "Immanence, Transcendence and the Creation of Rights," in de Sutter and McGee eds *Deleuze and Law*, 2012.

that other actualizations of the concept or "pure event" of democracy are possible. *What Is Philosophy?* offers no more direct account of principles that are supposed to govern modern democratic societies than *A Thousand Plateaus*. In this sense, it offers no theory of public right. Many of the elements of Deleuze and Guattari's prior commitment to Marxism remain in the diagnosis of the present outlined in *What Is Philosophy?* For example, the analysis of the isomorphic but heterogeneous character of all states with regard to the global capitalist axiomatic is reproduced in identical terms. From this perspective, there are political differences between different kinds of state but also complicity with an increasingly global system of exploitation. They suggest that even the most democratic states are compromised by their role in the production of human misery alongside great wealth（WP 107; N 173）. They maintain their commitment to the revolutionary-becoming of people rather than the traditional Marxist concept of revolution, even as they point out that the concept of revolution is itself a philosophical concept par excellence, one that expresses "absolute deterritorialization even to the point where this calls for a new earth, a new people"（WP 101）.

What Is Philosophy? argues for the inherently political vocation of philosophy. Philosophy is defined as the creation of concepts where these serve an overtly utopian function:"*We lack resistance to the present*. The creation of concepts in itself calls for a future form, for a new earth and people that do not yet exist"（WP 108）. In the present, the task of philosophy is aligned with the struggle against capitalism. Deleuze and Guattari suggest that philosophical concepts are critical of the present to the extent that they "connect up with what is real here and now in the struggle against capitalism"（WP 100）. At this point, the outline of a new concept appears in their political philosophy. *What Is Philosophy?* contrasts the actual universality of the market with the virtual universality of a global democratic state and describes philosophy as it is envisaged here as reterritorialized on a new Earth and a people to come quite unlike those found in actually existing democracies. Deleuze and Guattari's neo-Marxist support for becoming-revolutionary as the path toward a new Earth and a people to come is combined with a call for resistance to existing forms of democracy in the name of a "becoming-democratic that is not to be confused with present constitutional states" (WP 113). In contrast to the formal normativity of their earlier work, the political normativity of Deleuze and Guattari's later philosophy is defined by this relation between becoming-revolutionary and becoming-democratic. On this basis, in full recognition of their differences from liberal normative political philosophy, it nevertheless becomes possible to compare their later work with that of a left-liberal political philosopher such as John Rawls.①

Immanent Utopianism and Becoming-Democratic

In *Justice as Fairness: A Restatement*, Rawls identifies four purposes served by his kind of reconstructive liberal normative political philosophy: First, it can help to resolve deeply disputed questions by searching for common philosophical and moral ground between the protagonists. Second, it can serve the task of orientation that seeks to identify reasonable and rational ends, both individual and collective, and to show "how those ends can cohere within a well-articulated conception of a just and reasonable society." ② Third, it can address the task of reconciliation by showing the limits of what can be achieved within a democratic society characterized

① See Patton, 'Utopian Political Philosophy: Deleuze and Rawls,' *Deleuze Studies*, 1:1, 2007, pp.41-59; *Deleuzian Concepts: Philosophy, Colonization, Politics* (Stanford: Stanford University Press, 2010), pp.185-2010.

② John Rawls, *Justice as Fairness: A Restatement* (Cambridge, MA: Harvard University Press, 2001), p.3.

by the existence of "profound and irreconcilable differences in citizen's reasonable comprehensive religious and philosophical conceptions of the world." ① Finally, it serves the "realistically utopian" task of "probing the limits of practicable political possibility." It asks what a just and democratic society would be like, given the "circumstances of justice" that obtain in the actual historical world in which we live, but also what it would be like "under reasonably favourable but still possible historical conditions." ② Rawls notes that the limits of the practicable are not simply given by the actual because we can and do change existing social and political institutions. However, he does not pursue any further the question of what determines the limits of the practicable or how we might ascertain what are these limits.③

Deleuze's conception of philosophy is concerned above all to challenge the limits of our present social world. *What Is Philosophy?* presents a conception of the political vocation of philosophy with far more radical ambitions than those acknowledged in Rawls' realistic utopianism. Of the four functions of political philosophy identified by Rawls, Deleuze's philosophy does not address those of resolution, orientation, or reconciliation. It does address the utopian function, although not by setting out normative principles against which we might evaluate the justice or fairness of social institutions. The sense in which Deleuze and Guattari's political philosophy is utopian must be understood in terms of the connection between the absolute deterritorialization pursued in philosophy and the relative deterritorializations at work in its social milieu: "There is always a way in which absolute deterritorialization takes over from a relative deterritorialization in a given field" (WP 88) . The utopian vocation of philosophy can be achieved only when the concepts that it invents engage

---

① ibid.

② Rawls, *Justice as* Fairness*: A Restatement*, p.4.

③ Rawls, *Justice as* Fairness*: A Restatement*, p.5.

with existing forms of relative deterritorialization. This conception of philosophy therefore implies an immanent utopianism in the sense that it does not simply posit an ideal future but rather aims to connect with processes of relative deterritorialization that are present in but stifled by the present milieu, extending these and taking them to extremes. To the extent that these processes or "lines of flight" encompass resistant political forces *along with the ideals or opinions that motivate them*, this immanent utopianism cannot avoid drawing on elements of present political normativity to suggest ways in which the injustice or intolerability of existing institutional forms of social life might be removed. In this manner, because the concept of democracy ties together a number of the values at the heart of contemporary political thought, elements of that concept may be used to counteractualize certain forms of resistance to the present in public political culture. These elements in turn provide the components of the concept of "becoming-democratic" which serves the utopian task of political philosophy by probing the limits of democratic processes in contemporary society.

Deleuze offers no detailed account of "becoming-democratic." However, it is possible to fill out the concept with elements of his prior work with Guattari as well as occasional comments in interviews. For example, in his interview with Negri, he suggests that new rights in relation to the situations created by modern biology should be proposed by "user-groups" rather than "supposedly well-qualified wise men" (N 170) . In effect, he invokes the principle that decisions ought to be taken in consultation with those most affected by them. This is one of the founding principles of modern democratic governance, and Deleuze is not the only theorist to recommend its extension and application to new contexts. This suggests that the opening-up of decision-making procedures throughout society might constitute a vector of "becoming-democratic."

Minoritarian becomings provide another vector of "becoming-democratic." These are defined as the variety of ways in which individuals and groups fail to conform to the majoritarian standard（ATP 105-106）. They have given rise to a succession of measures to extend the scope of the standard and thereby broaden the subject of democracy: first，in purely quantitative terms by extending the vote to women and other minorities; second，in qualititative terms by changing the nature of political institutions and procedures to enable these newly enfranchised members to participate on equal terms. Efforts to change the nature of public institutions in ways that both acknowledge and accommodate many kinds of difference are ongoing，for example in relation to sexual preference and physical and mental abilities，as well as cultural and religious backgrounds. Deleuze and Guattari's support for minoritarian becomings affirms the importance of efforts to enlarge the character of the majority. By their nature，processes of minoritarian-becoming will always exceed or escape from the confines of any given majority. Nevertheless，they embody the potential to transform the affects，beliefs，and political sensibilities of a population in ways that can lead to the advent of a new people. To the extent that a people is constituted as a political community，the transformations it undergoes will affect its conceptions of what is fair and just. In turn，these will affect the distribution of rights and duties as well as the presence of minority citizens in the public institutions and political functions of the society.

A third vector of "becoming-democratic" involves efforts to achieve a more just distribution of material social goods. Deleuze is often critical of the way that modern democratic states fail to live up to this aspect of their egalitarian promise（WP 106-107; N 172）. However，his suggestion that democratic states are morally and politically compromised by their role in the perpetuation of this form of injustice implicitly raises the normative question: What principles of distribution should apply in a just democratic society? Should we advocate radically egalitarian principles that would treat any undeserved inequality of condition as unjust, or should we be satisfied with Rawls's difference principle according to which social and economic inequalities are allowed but only when they are attached to positions open to all and when they are "to the greatest benefit of the least advantaged members of society" (Rawls 2005, 6)?[①] Should the principles of distributive justice apply globally or only within the borders of particular democratic states? Deleuze does not provide us with the means to answer these normative questions but they are inevitably raised by his criticisms of existing states of affairs.

Conclusion

Deleuzean philosophy as it is presented in *What is Philosophy?* is clearly political in the sense that it has an inherently political vocation. The creation of concepts serves the larger project of bringing about new earths and new peoples. Deleuze and Guattari propose a novel kind of utopian political thought that is neither Marxist nor liberal. They rely upon a political ontology of assemblages rather than individual subjects of interest and right. Their goal is the transformation of existing political norms and institutions rather than the reconstruction of the normative principles implicit in existing liberal democratic institutions into a coherent political theory. Despite the substantive differences that separate their approach from that of liberal normative political philosophy, there is at least a degree of convergence between them. Deleuze and Guattari's collaborative work moves from a formal to a more substantive engagement with the explicitly political concepts and norms

① Rawls, *Political Liberalism: Expanded Edition* (New York: Columbia University Press, 2005), p.6.

that make up the public political culture of liberal democratic states. The concept of a “becoming-democratic” at the heart of their later political philosophy points to the role of elements of existing concepts of democracy in historical struggles to implement or expand democratic government.

References

* Earlier versions of this chapter were presented as talks at The University of Sydney in April 2011 and at a workshop at the China Foreign Affairs University in June 2011. I am grateful to the participants on both occasions for their comments，questions and criticisms.

1.See for example Paul Patton，Deleuze and the Political（London and New York: Routledge，2000）；Ian Buchanan and Nicholas Thoburn eds，Deleuze and Politics（Edinburgh: Edinburgh University Press 2008）；New Formations，68，2010（Special Issue entitled Deleuzian Politics?）.

2.François Dosse，Gilles Deleuze and Félix Guattari: Intersecting Lives，trans. Deborah Glassman（New York: Columbia University Press，2010）p.21.

3.Slavoj Žižek，Organs without Bodies: Deleuze and Consequences（New York and London: Routledge，2004）. p.20.

4.Badiou，“Existe-t-il quelque chose comme un politique deleuzienne?” Cités，40（Deleuze Politique），2009，pp.15-20（talk given in English at “Immanent Choreographies: Deleuze and Neo-Aesthetics，” Tate Modern Public Programme，London 21-22 September 2001）.

5.Philippe Mengue also points out the absence of any place for specifically political thought in the tripartite division of thought described in What is Philosophy? See Mengue，Deleuze et la question de la démocratie（Paris: L’Harmattan，2003）， p.52. See also Nicholas Thoburn, Deleuze, Marx and Politics (London and New York: Routledge, 2003), pp.5-6.

6.On Deleuze's relation to history, see Jay Lampert, Deleuze and Guattari's Philosophy of History (London and New York: Continuum, 2009), Jeffrey Bell and Claire Colebrook eds Deleuze and History (Edinburgh: Edinburgh University Press, 2009) and Craig Lundy, History and Becoming: Deleuze's Philosophy of Creativity (Edinburgh: Edinburgh University Press, 2012).

7.Peter Hallward, Out of This World: Deleuze and the Philosophy of Creation (London and New York: Verso 2006), pp.136-139. Hallward's book has been critically reviewed by a number of Deleuze scholars: see inter alia Gregory J. Seigworth, "Little Affect: Hallward's Deleuze," Culture Machine, Reviews 2007; John Protevi, Notre Dame Philosophical Reviews, 2007.08.03; and Erinn C. Gilson, Continental Philosophy Review, 42, 2009, pp.429-434.

8.Jeremy Gilbert, 'Deleuzian Politics? A Survey and Some Suggestions, New Formations, 68, 2010, p.10.

9.ibid.

10.The English text of Negotiations uses "law" here to translate "droit," thereby obscuring a contrast in the original between "loi" and "droit." For this and for other reasons, it is more appropriate to translate "droit" here as "right" : see Paul Patton, "Immanence, Transcendence and the Creation of Rights" in Laurent de Sutter and Kyle McGee eds Deleuze and Law (Edinburgh: Edinburgh University Press 2012).

11.Dosse, Intersecting Lives, pp.98, 109.

12.Dosse, Intersecting Lives, p.177.

13.There is extensive discussion of Deleuze's relation to Marxism in the secondary literature on his and Guattari's work. See in particular Eugene Holland, Deleuze and Guattari's Anti-Oedipus: Introduction to Schizoanalysis (London and

New York: Routledge，1999）；Jason Read，The Micro-Politics of Capital（Albany N.Y.: State University of New York Press，2003）；Nicholas Thoburn，Deleuze，Marx and Politics（2003）；Isabelle Garo，“Deleuze，Marx and Revolution: What It Means to ‘Remain Marxist’” in J. Bidet and S. Kouvelakis eds Critical Companion to Contemporary Marxism，Leiden and Boston，MA: Brill，2007，pp.605–624; the essays in Deleuze Studies，3，2009，Issue Supplement: Deleuze and Marx，edited by Jain Dhruv; and ‘Becoming Revolutionary: Marx Through Deleuze” in Simon Choat，Marx Through Postructuralism（London and New York: Continuum，2010）.

14.In the “Intellectuals and Power” interview with Foucault，Deleuze suggests that it was Foucault who taught the intellectuals of his generation the indignity of speaking for others:“We laughed at representation，saying it was over，but we didn't follow this ‘theoretical’ conversion through – namely theory demanded that those involved finally have their say from a practical standpoint”（DI 208）. This interview first appeared in the Deleuze issue of l'Arc（Paris，1971）. Another translation appears in Michel Foucault，M.（1977）. Language，Counter-Memory，Practice: Selected Essays and Interviews，ed. Donald F. Bouchard，trans. Donald F. Bouchard and Sherry Simon（Ithaca，N.Y.: Cornell University Press，1977），pp.205-217.

15.This is by no mean an exhaustive list of Deleuzian concepts which might be supposed relevant to political philosophy. Other concepts that have been taken up in this connection include Deleuze's concepts of “the missing people，” the “event，” “dramatization” and “nomadology.” In relation to these concepts，see Alain Beaulieu，“Gilles Deleuze's Politics: From Marxism to the Missing People” in Constantin V. Boundas ed Gilles Deleuze: The Intensive Reduction（London and New York: Continuum，2009），pp.204-217; Tom Lundborg，Politics of the Event: Time，

Movement, Becoming (London and New York: Routledge, 2011) ; Iain Mackenzie and Robert Porter, Dramatizing the Political: Deleuze and Guattari (Houndmills, Basingstoke and New York: Palgrave Macmillan, 2011) ; Eugene Holland, Nomad Citizenship: Free-Market Communism and the Slow-Motion General Strike (Minneapolis and London: University of Minnesota Press, 2011) .

16."In Anti-Oedipus … every society, every form of social production is nothing but a specific organisation and articulation of desiring-production, assigning it specific goals and aims." Jason Read, "Fetish is always actual, Revolution is Always Virtual," Deleuze Studies, 3, 2009, Issue Supplement: Deleuze and Marx, 98-99.

17.Patton, Deleuze and the Political, pp.9, 136.

18.For an example of one such attempt, see Rodney Peffer, Marxism, Morality and Social Justice (Princeton: Princeton University Press, 1990) . For more general discussions of so-called "analytic marxism," see G.A. Cohen, Karl Marx's Theory of History (Oxford: Oxford University Press, 2000) ; Will Kymlicka, Contemporary Political Philosophy (Oxford: Oxford University Press, 2002), pp.166-207; and Andrew Levine, A Future for Marxism? (London: Pluto Pres 2003) .

19.Gilles Deleuze from A to Z, 3-DVD Set, directed by Pierr-André Boutang, trans. Charles J. Stivale, New York: Semiotext (e), 2011: see G comme Gauche. On Deleuze's understanding of the invention of rights, see Patton, "Immanence, Transcendence and the Creation of Rights," in de Sutter and McGee eds Deleuze and Law, 2012.

20.See Patton, 'Utopian Political Philosophy: Deleuze and Rawls,' Deleuze Studies, 1:1, 2007, pp.41-59; Deleuzian Concepts: Philosophy, Colonization, Politics (Stanford: Stanford University Press, 2010), pp.185-2010.

21.John Rawls, Justice as Fairness: A Restatement (Cambridge, MA: Harvard

University Press，2001），p.3.

22.ibid.

23.Rawls，Justice as Fairness: A Restatement，p.4.

24.Rawls，Justice as Fairness: A Restatement，p.5.

25.Rawls，Political Liberalism: Expanded Edition（New York: Columbia University Press，2005），p.6.

Paul Patton，“Deleuze’s Political Philosophy”，pp.198-219 In Daniel W. Smith，Henry Somers-Hall（Eds.），The Cambridge Companion to Deleuze

中文简介

《德勒兹的政治哲学》

德勒兹的许多作品，特别是与瓜塔里（Guattari）合著的书，都被视为政治哲学。德勒兹本人也清楚地从这个角度看待了他们最初的合作。在 1990 年对安东尼奥·内格里（Antonio Negri）的一次采访“控制与成为”（Control and beging）中，他说“《反俄狄浦斯》是一部从头到尾的政治哲学著作”。他们的传记作者弗朗索瓦·多塞（François Dosse）更进一步指出，德勒兹的所有作品，“从他对休谟的第一部作品到他对虚拟世界的最后思考，都铭刻在政治的空间里”。然而，并不是每个人都接受德勒兹作为一个彻底的政治思想家的形象。齐泽克（Slavoj Žižek）认为，“德勒兹自己的文本中没有一个是直接政治性的；德勒兹自己是一个高度精英化的作家，对政治漠不关心。”

阿兰·巴迪欧（Alain Badiou）概述了怀疑德勒兹是否首先是一位政治思想家，甚至怀疑是否存在德勒兹式政治理论的几个理由。第一，德勒兹从未把政治定义为一个特定的思想对象或领域，就像给哲学提供定义一样。他特别提到了艺术、科学和哲学，但是并没有提到政治哲学。第二，更主观的说，德勒兹对政治从来就不是很感兴趣。在他的个人著作中，他从未声称政治决定了他的哲学活动。与他同时代的许多人如阿尔都塞、德里达、利奥塔或南希不同的是，他从不认为哲学的主要目的是政治性的。相反，他倾向于更传统的哲学观，认为哲学是概念的创造，并在1985年的一次采访中表示，他对“艺术、科学和哲学之间的关系”感兴趣。

第三，是德勒兹政治著作的内容。巴迪欧认为德勒兹政治有两个不同的目标。第一种是与成为和纯粹事件的虚拟领域相一致，这是创造和新事物出现的最终来源；第二种是与具体事件的实际领域、社会形式以及竞争和变化的历史进程相一致。在《反俄狄浦斯》和《一千个高原》中，德勒兹和瓜塔里勾勒了一个至少涉及三个阶段的普遍历史理论。在短文《控制社会的后记》中，德勒兹以福柯对惩罚性社会“图”的分析为模型，描绘了另一系列惩罚性社会的历史。然而，巴迪欧指出，这些都不是真正的历史学家的作品。相反，德勒兹赞同一种极端的反历史主义，这使得他越来越坚持历史与“成为”（becoming）的区别：“问题是，我越来越意识到区分成为和历史的可能性。尼采曾说过，没有什么重要的东西能从“非历史的云层”中解脱出来，这并不是为了反对永恒和历史，或是沉思和行动：尼采是在谈论事情发生的方式、事件本身或成为。历史对一个事件的把握，是它在特定历史环境中的实现方式；事件的发生超越了历史的范畴”。

对德勒兹来说，“成为”是哲学的真正研究对象。什么是哲学？创造一些概念来表达某种特定的“成为”或“纯粹的事件”。鉴于德勒兹赋予“成为”以牺牲历史为代价的优先权，巴迪欧认为，他的政治仍然是分裂的，既有创造和创造的伦理道德，也有与历史和资本主义分析相联系的世俗政府政治。彼得·哈尔沃德（Peter Hallward）对德勒兹作为一位超自然创造的神幻思想者的解读，追寻了这一论点，以至于认为德勒兹的创造伦理并没有为任何确定的政治活动提供任何基础。与另一位德勒兹政治评论家菲利普·门格（Philippe Mengue）一样，哈尔沃德在否认德勒兹是政治哲学家和断言他是错误的政治哲学家之间摇摆不定。杰里米·吉尔伯特（Jeremy Gilbert）用以下术语总结了他们各自的结论："德勒兹是一个神秘主义者，一个怀旧的精英模式的前卫主义者，他目前没有市场，充其量是一个含蓄的保守主义者，其浪漫主义没有为理性计算或集体行动留有余地"。

巴迪奥关于德勒兹与政治的关系的每一个说法都有些道理。正如吉尔伯特所说，他的工作包含了政治和反政治两个方面。然而，要理解德勒兹政治思想的特点和他对政治学的独特贡献，就必须从德勒兹政治思想的语境中去理解，尤其是从德勒兹政治思想的相互关系中去理解。

The Sunflower: Guilt, Forgiveness, and Reconciliation

Eleonore Stump

Introduction

It is often thought that the remedy for guilt is forgiveness and that repentance and the making of amends on the part of a wrongdoer are both necessary and sufficient for forgiveness. The making of amends is generally considered to have two parts, namely, reasonable reparation of any damage done by the wrongdoer, and then also something extra, some penance, that compensates for the injustice in the wrongdoing. On this view, a wronged person should not forgive the wrongdoer without his repenting and making amends; but if the wrongdoer has repented and made amends, then the wronged person is unreasonable if she refuses to forgive the wrongdoer. If she does forgive him, then the wrongdoer is relieved of his guilt; and since his guilt is removed, nothing stands in the way of her reconciliation with him and his restoration to his usual place in the human community.

On the other hand, however, consider Simon Wiesenthal's book The Sunflower: On the Possibility and Limits of Forgiveness.[①] In that book, Wiesenthal tells the story of a dying German soldier who was guilty of horrendous evil against Jewish men, women, and children, but who desperately wanted forgiveness from and

---

① Simon Wiesenthal, *The Sunflower: On the Possibility and Limits of Forgiveness* (NY: Schocken Books, 1960).

reconciliation with at least one Jew before his death. Wiesenthal, then a prisoner in Auschwitz, was brought to hear the German soldier's story and his pleas for forgiveness. In the story as Wiesenthal presents it, it seems that the German soldier was completely and genuinely repentant. Because he was dying, there was little he could do to make amends; but his broken-heartedness over his evil and his self-excoriating confession of it to Wiesenthal was as much reparation and penance as was possible for him. In the circumstances, in remarkably admirable ways, Wiesenthal dealt humanely with the dying soldier. But when the soldier's confession was finally complete, Wiesenthal got up and left him without a word. As Wiesenthal understands his own reaction to the German soldier, he did not grant the dying soldier the forgiveness the man longed for.

In The Sunflower, Wiesenthal presents reflections on this story by numerous thinkers, many of them noted scholars or eminent religious authorities in differing traditions. He invites these thinkers to consider whether they would have forgiven that soldier. Their responses are noteworthy for the highly divergent intuitions they express.

A number of respondents claim with conviction that the repentant dying soldier should be forgiven. So, for example, the influential former president of Notre Dame, Theodore Hesburgh, C.S.C, says,

"My whole instinct is to forgive…. Of course, the sin here is monumental. It is still finite and God's mercy is infinite. If asked to forgive, by anyone for anything, I would forgive because God would forgive." ①

But other equally thoughtful respondents report that they share Wiesenthal's reaction. In their view, the soldier's evil was great enough to destroy forever his

① Wiesenthal 1960, p.169.

chance at forgiveness. As they see it, by his monstrous acts, the soldier cut himself off permanently from any reconciliation with others or restoration into ordinary human society. And this evaluation of the soldier would not be altered, in their view, even if he had lived to do some severe penance, even if it were possible for there to be reparation for the unspeakable harm that he had done. For these respondents, the soldier should not be forgiven. On their view, there is no way the soldier's guilt can be removed; there is no way the soldier can be restored to any acceptable place within the human community.

On this view, it is not the case that repentance, reparation, penance are sufficient for forgiveness or that these things together with forgiveness are sufficient to remove guilt. Reconciliation may be denied and guilt may remain even where there is repentance with whatever reparation and penance is possible.

In this paper, I want to consider the account of guilt and forgiveness represented by the conflicting views about forgiveness on the part of the respondents in The Sunflower.

In what follows, I will briefly summarize Thomas Aquinas's account of love and the correlative account of forgiveness, as I understand them.[①] On Aquinas's account of love, love is always morally obligatory, and therefore so is forgiveness. Consequently, the view that repentance and making amends are necessary for forgiveness should be rejected. For these reasons, it seems to me that those respondents in The Sunflower convinced that forgiveness should be denied the dying German soldier are mistaken. Nonetheless, I will also argue in support of their vehement rejection of any kind of reconciliation with the dying German soldier. In my view, that rejection is based on intuitions which must also be taken seriously. I

① *Wandering in Darkness. Narrative and the Problem of Suffering*, (Oxford: Oxford University Press, 2010).

will try to show that, in some cases of grave evil, repentance and making amends are not sufficient for the removal of guilt and that reconciliation may be morally impermissible even if forgiveness is morally obligatory.

Consequently, on the account I will defend in this paper, reparation, and penance are not necessary for forgiveness; and for very serious wrongdoing, repentance, reparation, and penance are not sufficient for the removal of guilt. But if they are not sufficient for the removal of guilt, then they are not sufficient for reconciliation either, not even for reconciliation with a person who is forgiven.

Forgiveness and reconciliation therefore can come apart. One reason for this fact is that, unlike forgiveness, reconciliation and the removal of guilt cannot be unilateral and unconditional. For the removal of guilt and reconciliation with a wrongdoer, something is required from the wrongdoer; and if the wrongdoer cannot give what is needed to remove his guilt, then reconciliation may be morally unavailable. Consequently, at least in cases of very serious wrongdoing, guilt may remain even after forgiveness is granted.

The account I will argue for below, then, helps to explain the divergent reactions of the respondents in The Sunflower. Those who feel strongly that the soldier should be forgiven are right. And yet those opposed to forgiving the soldier are also right, at least insofar as they are conflating forgiveness with reconciliation. What these respondents are in effect rejecting is the idea that the soldier's repentance and penitential confession are sufficient to remove his guilt. That is why they refuse any reconciliation with him. But their view is compatible with the convictions of those in favor of forgiving the soldier, because for very serious evil, even with forgiveness granted, repentance, reparation, and penance can fail to be sufficient for the removal of guilt.

The case of John Newton

It helps in thinking about these issues to have in mind a historical case of serious moral wrongdoing in which there is not only grave evil but also exemplary repentance, reparation, and penance. So consider the case of John Newton. On three different occasions, when Newton was still a young man, he was the captain of a slave ship; and, on those three ships alone, he was responsible for transporting many Africans. The conditions on the ships were unspeakable. A large percentage of the Africans transported died during the voyage. Their suffering was heartbreaking, but the suffering of those who survived was worse. They were sold into harsh slavery, and their descendants were born into it.

A lengthy religious conversion changed Newton's life dramatically. First, he left the life of a seaman; then he got a theological education; and eventually he was ordained as an Anglican priest. Gradually, he took on an increasing role in the cultural and religious life of England. Somewhere in the course of this conversion, Newton became horrified at what he had done in the slave trade; he became stricken at the suffering he had helped to bring about.

In his fervent repentance, Newton worked hard, in formal and informal ways, to help bring about the abolition of the slave trade in England. Among other things, he wrote a pamphlet Thoughts Upon the Slave Trade in which he presented in great detail to public view the horrible suffering he had visited on the Africans on his ships, and he spared himself no humiliation in revealing what he had done. On the contrary, he held himself up to public shock and revulsion for his actions as a slave-trader. Newton's pamphlet was widely read and highly influential, and it made a great difference to the debate in Parliament over the slave trade.

Newton lived long enough to see his efforts victorious. The Slave Trade Act, which abolished the slave trade in England, was passed in 1807; and Newton died shortly after it passed. Newton's efforts at ending the slave trade were his reparation and penance. In his efforts for abolition, and in his public excoriation of himself in his pamphlet, Newton did what he could to make reparation and do penance for the evil of his slave-trading.

What should one say about Newton? Is it morally acceptable to forgive him? Were his repentance, reparation, and penance sufficient for the removal of his guilt? Were they sufficient for his reconciliation with the Africans transported on his ships? Were they sufficient to restore him to a place in the human community from which his morally evil actions would otherwise have excluded him?

In what follows, I will argue that forgiveness is not only morally permissible in such a case; rather, like love, it is morally obligatory. On the other hand, by themselves alone, even repentance, reparation, and penance may not be sufficient for the removal of a wrongdoer's guilt, or for his reconciliation with those harmed by his grave wrongdoing, or for his restoration to human community.

Love and forgiveness

To see the point about forgiveness, it helps to begin with a brief discussion of the nature of love. Although many contemporary philosophers have presented varying accounts of the nature of love, the best account I know is that of Thomas Aquinas.[①]

① I have argued for this comparative claim in "Love, By All Accounts," *Proceedings and Addresses of The American Philosophical Association*, Vol.80, No.2, November 2006, pp.25-43.

For Aquinas, ① love requires two interconnected desires:②

(1) the desire for the good of the beloved, ③and

(2) the desire for union④ with the beloved.⑤

Aquinas recognizes different kinds and degrees of love between persons.⑥ For

---

① Aquinas uses four words for love; in Latin, they are '*amor*', '*dilectio*', '*amicitia*', and '*caritas*'. (Cf. ST I-II q.26 a.3.) The first of these is love in its most generic sense, which is included in all the other kinds; for Aquinas, even a rock falling from a higher to a lower place can be said to have love for the place to which it falls, in this generic sense of 'love'. (Cf. ST I-II q.26 a.1.) The second, '*dilectio*', emphasizes the element of voluntariness in the love of rational persons; and the third, '*amicitia*', picks out the dispositions of love in friendship. But, for Aquinas, the fourth, '*caritas*', is the word for love in its real or complete sense. Since Aquinas privileges *caritas* in this way, I will focus on *caritas* in explaining his account of love, although I understand his views of *caritas* in light of what he says about the more generic *amor*.

② See, e.g., ST II-II q.25, a.3.

③ Cf. ST I-II q.26 a.4, where Aquinas says that to love is to will good to someone. Cf. also ST I-II q.28 a.4, where Aquinas explains the zeal or intensity of love in terms of the strength of a lover's desire for the good of the beloved.

④ By 'union' in this connection, I mean being at one with another, where, clearly, the kind of oneness brought about by two or more human beings is a function of what elements of life and psyche they are sharing. A mother shares some parts of herself and her life with her newborn; musically gifted friends composing an opera together share other parts of themselves with each other. Union comes in degrees at least in part because a human being, and a human life, is a composite; and it is possible to share some parts of this composite without sharing others. That is why it is possible to desire union with humanity as a whole: one can desire that all human beings be at one with each other, so that war, injustice, and all oppressive inequality cease.

⑤ Cf., e.g., ST I-II q.26 a.2 ad 2, and q.28 a.1 s.c., where Aquinas quotes approvingly Dionysius's line that love is the unitive force. Cf. also ST I-II q.66 a.6, where Aquinas explains the superiority of charity to the other virtues by saying that every lover is drawn by desire to union with the beloved, and ST I-II q.70 a.3, where Aquinas explains the connection between joy and love by saying that every lover rejoices at being united to the beloved. For an interesting recent attempt to defend a position that has some resemblance to Aquinas's, see Robert Adams, "Pure Love," *Journal of Religious Ethics*, 8 (1980), pp.83–99. Adams says: "It is a striking fact that while benevolence (the desire for another person's well-being) and *Eros*, as a desire for relationship with another person, seem to be quite distinct desires, we use a single name, 'love' or '*Agape*', for an attitude that includes both of them, at least in typical cases" (p.97).

⑥ There are many other details of Aquinas's account of love that are important but that cannot be explored in passing here. For a fuller treatment, see my *Wandering in Darkness. Narrative and the Problem of Suffering*, (Oxford: Oxford University Press, 2010), Chapter 5.

example, he thinks that it is possible to desire the good for humanity in general and also to desire some sort of union with all humanity — say, in the shared beatific vision of heaven;① and so, on Aquinas's account of love, a person can have an impartial love of all human beings. But Aquinas also supposes that some loves are and ought to be greater than others;② a person ought to love all human beings, but not equally. She should love some people more than others in virtue of having certain relationships with them which ought to make her love for them greater than her love for humanity in general.

Certain things are also worth noting with regard to the desires of love.

To begin with the second desire first, whatever exactly the union is, which is desired in love on Aquinas's account, the desire for it is not equivalent to the desire to be in the company of the beloved.③ Other philosophers have remarked that one can love a person without desiring to be in that person's company, ④ and being in someone's company is obviously not equivalent to being united to her. It is manifestly possible to be in the company of someone when one is alienated from her, rather than united to her. So desiring union with a person might not include a desire to be in that person's company, at least not now, as that person currently is.

With regard to the first desire, the goodness in question is not to be identified

---

① If there is a relationship between persons in which it is not appropriate for one person to desire the good for and union with the other, then the relationship is not a relationship of love. Insofar as it is possible to have a general love of humankind, however, then there is no connection between persons which is not also in effect a relationship for which some species of love is appropriate and therefore also obligatory. For some discussion of the claim that obligations and rights are not correlative, see my "God's Obligations", in *Philosophical Perspectives* 6, James Tomberlin (ed.), (Atascadero, CA: Ridgeview Publishing, 1992) pp.475-492.

② ST II-II q.26 a.6-12.

③ For Aquinas's views on the nature of this union, cf., e.g., ST I-II q.28 a.1, where real union is described as a matter of presence between lover and beloved.

④ David Velleman, "Love as a Moral Emotion," *Ethics 109* (*1999*), *p*.353.

with moral goodness only. It is goodness in the broader sense that encompasses beauty, elegance or efficiency, and metaphysical as well as moral goodness.① Furthermore, because Aquinas holds that there is an objective standard of goodness, the measure of value for the goodness at issue in love is also objective.② Given Aquinas's ethical views, then, the good of the beloved has to be understood as that which truly is in the interest of the beloved and which truly does conduce to the beloved's flourishing.

With this brief summary of Aquinas's account of love, it should be clear that it has implications as regards the nature of forgiveness.③ That is because, whatever exactly is required for forgiveness, ④ it must involve some species of love for the person in need of forgiveness. A person who refuses to forgive someone who has hurt her or been unjust to her is not loving towards the offender, and a person who does forgive someone who has treated her badly also manifests love of one degree or

---

① The two desires of any love are therefore included under the more general heading of the desire for goodness, as Aquinas understands it. For detailed discussion of Aquinas's views of goodness, understood in this broad sense, see my *Aquinas*, (New York: Routledge, 2003), Chapter 2.

② The claim that the good desired for the beloved is an objective good therefore results from Aquinas's analysis of the nature of love together with his meta-ethics. It is not itself implied by Aquinas's analysis of love. I am grateful to Ish Haji for calling my attention to the need to make this point clear.

③ For more detailed discussion of forgiveness in connection with Aquinas's account of love, see Chapter 5 in Stump (2010).

④ There is by now a huge literature on forgiveness, which cannot be dealt with in passing here. A good recent review of the literature can be found in Charles L. Griswold, *Forgiveness. A Philosophical Exploration*, (Cambridge: Cambridge University Press, 2014). The differences between the account I give and Griswold's are sketched here. My account of forgiveness is not incompatible with the standard account of forgiveness as the forswearing of resentment, but it encompasses also forgiveness as including the desire for union with a wrongdoer.

another towards him. So whatever else a person's forgiveness is,[①] it seems to include a kind of love of someone who has harmed her or committed an injustice against her.

Since love emerges from the interaction of two desires, for the good of the beloved and for union with him, the absence of either desire is sufficient to undermine love. To the extent to which love is implicated in forgiveness, the absence of either desire undermines forgiveness, too.

So failure to forgive can find expression not only in resentment or vengefulness but also in a rejection of the desire for union with the wrongdoer. On Aquinas's account of love, Paula forgives Jerome only if she desires the good for Jerome and union with Jerome even in the face of his bad treatment of her. If Paula lacks either desire of love where Jerome is concerned, she does not forgive Jerome.

It is important to see that, on Aquinas's account of love, it is possible for Paula to forgive Jerome unilaterally, without repentance on Jerome's part, because it is up to Paula alone whether she desires the good for Jerome and union with him.

On the other hand, the way in which the desires of love are fulfilled, or whether they are fulfilled at all, will depend crucially on the condition of the wrongdoer being forgiven. When in forgiveness Paula forms the two desires of love for Jerome, the nature of the appropriate fulfillment of those desires has to be a function of Jerome's state. Whether Paula can and should have any continued companionship of any kind with Jerome, and the character and extent of such company, depends on Jerome's

---

① In fact, although on my view love is necessary and sufficient for forgiveness, it is not the case that forgiveness is nothing but love or that forgiveness reduces to love. Analogously, being risible is necessary and sufficient for being human – anything that is risible is human and nothing that is not risible is human – but being human is not reducible to being risible. Risibility picks out human beings by an accident which is had by all and only human beings, but the nature of human beings is not nothing but risibility. It is not part of my purposes here to define forgiveness, and so I leave to one side what else might need to be added to love for a definition of forgiveness. I am grateful to Michael Rea for calling my attention to the need to make this point explicit.

state. If Jerome poses a serious threat to Paula's having what is good for her, then Paula's staying with Jerome or otherwise allowing Jerome to harm her enables Jerome to violate the desires of love for her. But his failure at loving her is not good for Jerome. So Paula is not loving Jerome in letting him harm her or treat her unjustly; rather, she is violating the desires of love with regard to Jerome in being an enabler of his wrongdoing against her.①

For Aquinas, then, a person can forgive unilaterally, as she can love unrequitedly. But the desires of love in forgiveness, like the desires of love generally, are inefficacious by themselves to bring about what they desire. A person who forgives, like a person who loves, has to be responsive to the person who is the object of her desires; and so she cannot have what she wants, in love or forgiveness, just by wanting it. Paula's desire for the good for Jerome cannot be fulfilled if, in self-destructive impulses, Jerome refuses the good offered him. And Paula's desire for union with Jerome cannot result in any kind of union with him as long as his state

---

① It might appear that Aquinas's account of love succumbs to the same problems as those that seem to some people to afflict an ethics of care. If the value of loving others or caring for others is the fundamental ethical value, then it is not easy to explain why it is morally acceptable to withhold care for others in the interests of pursuing one's own projects. And yet if there is no morally acceptable way of doing so, caring, or loving, can become deeply destructive, dreadfully unjust, with regard to the one doing the caring or loving. So, for example, Virginia Woolf describes the "angel in the house" who loved others totally, who cared for them completely, in this way:

she never had a mind or a wish of her own, but preferred to sympathize always with the minds and wishes of others... I did my best to kill her. My excuse, if I were to be had up in a court of law, would be that I acted in self-defence. Had I not killed her she would have killed me." (From "Professions for Women," quoted in Jean Hampton, "Feminist Contractarianism," in *A Mind of One's Own. Feminist Essays on Reason and Objectivity*, ed. Louis Anthony and Charlotte Witt [Boulder, CO: Westview Press, 1993], 231.)

In my view, considerations similar to those showing that Paula is not loving Jerome in enabling him to harm her apply also to the case in which Paula allows herself to be harmed by myriad others. She is not loving others in allowing them to hurt her, even if the harm done to her takes the actions of a whole group to accomplish.

of character and current condition keep her from being close to him.

Finally, as I explained at the outset, on Aquinas's account, love is obligatory, in the sense that, for any person, the absence of love is morally blameworthy, and the presence of love is necessary for moral good or excellence.① Given the connection between love and forgiveness, it follows that forgiveness is also obligatory in the same way and to the same extent. It does not follow that any given wrongdoer Jerome has a right to forgiveness from any person Paula whom he has hurt or against whom he has committed an injustice. On Aquinas's view (as also on many contemporary accounts), rights and obligations are not correlative.② Paula can have an obligation with regard to Jerome even if Jerome does not have a correlative right with regard to Paula. So even though Jerome has no right to Paula's forgiveness, on Aquinas's views Paula would be subject to appropriate moral censure if she refused to forgive Jerome. In refusing to forgive him, Paula would be unloving towards him; and in being unloving, Paula would be worthy of moral disapprobation. On this account of forgiveness, it is a mistake to suppose that repentance and making amends are necessary for forgiveness. Nothing on the part of the wrongdoer is necessary for forgiveness of him.

On this view of love and forgiveness, then, forgiveness even of the German soldier in the story in The Sunflower is obligatory, and it would still be obligatory even if the soldier had not repented. It does not follow, however, that Wiesenthal's

---

① For more discussion of this claim, see my "The Non-Aristotelian Character of Aquinas's Ethics: Aquinas on the Passions," *Faith and Philosophy* 28.1 (2011) :29-43.

② I have argued for this claim at length in "God's Obligations," in *Philosophical Perspectives* 6, ed. James Tomberlin (Atascadero, CA: Ridgeview Publishing, 1992) :475-492. To see the point here, consider, by way of analogy that if Paula were a very rich tourist traveling in a very poor country, she would be obligated to give some of her money away for charitable purposes in that country if she were solicited to do so; if she refused all such solicitations, she would be subject to appropriate moral censure. But it would not be the case that any particular recipient of her donations would have a right to her money.

behavior with respect to the soldier should have been otherwise. As I will argue, in cases of grave evil, forgiveness, even with the wrongdoer's repentance and his making what amends he can, may not be sufficient for the removal of guilt or for the moral permissibility of reconciliation. Silently leaving the soldier may have been all that was morally permissible for Wiesenthal to do, as many of the respondents in The Sunflower so fervently maintain.

The problems of guilt

It helps in this connection to consider the problems that guilt produces for a perpetrator of serious wrongdoing, and Newton's case is helpful here.

When Newton was in his slave-trading years, one problem for him lay in defective states of his psyche. In that period of his life, Newton thought that slave-trading was acceptable, and he wanted to engage in it. So the first problem for a guilty person lies in himself, in his morally wrong states of intellect and will and the corrupt habits from which they stem or to which they contribute.

Furthermore, these defects of intellect and will do not exhaust the problem in Newton, however important they are. There are also other psychic defects, more subtle but not less damaging to Newton.

For example, there is memory. The very memory of having engaged in a great evil that caused cruel suffering to others diminishes something morally good in the wrongdoer's psyche too. By staying in memory, the evil a person such as Newton did remains part of Newton's present. His remembering his slave-trading is not itself an evil act, but there is something morally lamentable about the continued presence of his evil acts in his memory nonetheless. That may be one reason why people who have done monstrous evil find their memories an affliction.

So defects of psyche are the first problem for a person guilty of serious wrongdoing. The second problem lies in the world, in the effects of the wrongs done. The suffering of the human beings Newton kidnapped and enslaved was horrible, and he was responsible for it. Just restoring Newton's intellect and will to the state and condition of a morally good person, through repentance, for example, leaves unaddressed the suffering he caused.

This second problem can itself be subdivided into two further problems. First, there is the actual harm that a wrongdoer did, by his action or his omission, so that in one sense or another the world is worse because of him. And then there is the injustice of his acting as he did. In most cases, of course, harm and injustice go together, as they do in Newton's slave-trading; but it is helpful to see that they can be disassociated, because seeing their separability helps illuminate the fact that, typically, a wrongdoer such as Newton has two different problems as regards the effects of his wrongdoing on the world. There is the harm he has caused, but there is also the injustice of what he has done. Just fixing the harm he has done is generally not enough to fix the injustice. That is why, in addition to reparation, penance is often supposed to be required for forgiveness.

The consequence of both the first and the second problem of guilt have the further effect of altering the wrongdoer's relations with others in his society, or, as in the case of the dying German soldier, with the whole human community. The state of the wrongdoer's psyche and the facts about the damage and injustice he has done can leave others angry at him and alienated from him. The victims of his wrongdoing may resent or reject him, and others who learn of his wrongdoing may share those attitudes even if they were not themselves harmed by his wrongdoing. They might nonetheless hate him or turn away from him as someone with whom they refuse to associate, because of what he is and what he has done.

These, then, are the major problems of guilt.

The role of repentance, reparation, and penance in the removal of guilt

It is clear that repentance alone can remove some of the defects introduced in the wrongdoer by his morally wrong actions. So, for example, after his repentance, Newton lost the morally wrong states of intellect and will he had during his slave-trading years, and he replaced them with the states of intellect and will of a morally decent person as regards slave-trading. Through repentance, then, with respect to slave-trading, Newton's intellect and will became like those of the abolitionists in his society.

At least in cases of grave moral wrongdoing, repentance alone cannot repair the damage the wrongdoer did or restore the wrongdoer to the place in community he had before his wrongdoing; but reparation and penance help in this connection. For ease of reference, I will refer to reparation and penance together as 'making amends' or 'satisfaction'. The word 'satisfaction' comes from the Latin term 'satisfacere', and the etymology of the Latin term comes from 'satis' (enough) plus 'facere' (to do). To make satisfaction by reparation (with regard to the damage one has done) and by penance (with regard to the injustice one has done) is to do what one can and by this means to make amends.

It is important to see, though, that satisfaction cannot undo the harm done in the original wrongdoing. Newton could not take away the sufferings of the Africans who had been transported on his ships and had lived to become slaves; he could not restore to life those who had died. Nonetheless, in giving himself to the cause of the abolition of the slave trade, a repentant Newton did all that he could. By the time

Newton died, he was not only friends with these abolitionists, he was in fact held in honor by them. Newton's satisfaction was successful in making him a different man from the man he had been, even from the man he was when he first repented. His repentance for his slave-trading healed the psychic defects in his intellect and will, and his work of satisfaction tried to undo the damage and the injustice for which he had been responsible. In consequence, it also altered his relationships with others. When Wilberforce was friends with Newton at the time the Slave Trade Act passed, Wilberforce was friends not just with a repentant slave trader; he was friends with a powerful enemy of the slave trade.

*The limits of repentance and satisfaction*①

Consequently, repentance and satisfaction, such as that engaged in by Newton, have a useful purpose insofar as they alter both the wrongdoer and the things in the world damaged by his wrongdoing. Certainly, Newton is highly commendable for the way in which he tried to make amends. But contrary to what the reflections about repentance and satisfaction might lead one to suppose, repentance and the attempts at satisfaction on the part of a person such as Newton are not sufficient to remedy the whole problem of guilt. That is because none of these things is sufficient to change the past, to make it not the case, for example, that Newton did the damage or injustice that he did.

---

① In this section of this paper, I am significantly altering the conclusion I argued for in an earlier paper, "Personal Relations and Moral Residue," in *History of the Human Sciences: Theorizing from the Holocaust: What is to be Learned?*, Paul Roth and Mark S. Peacock (eds.), Vol.17 No 2/3 (August 2004), pp.33-57. I stand by the arguments of that paper, but they now seem to me not sufficient to establish the conclusion. What else is needed, as I indicate in the conclusion of this paper, is a well-worked out theory of atonement.

Consider, to begin with, Newton's relations with others harmed by him or alienated from him in his slave-trading year. Newton's repentance and satisfaction are not sufficient to restore these relationships of Newton's to the condition they had or would have had before his wrongdoing.

Someone might object here that the relationship between a wrongdoer and those wronged by him should be healed even by the wrongdoer's repentance alone. When the wrongdoer repents, then, as far as his past morally wrong action goes, he has the beliefs and desires of a morally decent person. And so, someone might suppose. others should adopt towards the wrongdoer the same attitudes they would have had towards the wrongdoer before the wrongdoer's bad acts, that is, the same attitudes they would take towards any morally decent person.

But this objection rests on the mistaken assumption that a relationship is not affected by the past states of the persons in it, that only their present condition is relevant to the relationship. In fact, however, for Newton and those who were wronged by him or who know his history, Newton's past lives on in memory.

Newton wrote about his slave trading past,

"I hope it will always be a subject of humiliating reflection to me, that I was once an active instrument in a business at which my heart now shudders." ①

No doubt, Newton did well to shudder at what he had done on the sea in the slave ships. But if it is always a subject of shuddering for Newton, then it is hard to see that his repentance and satisfaction are sufficient to undo all the morally lamentable effects on his psyche wrought by his slave trading. Something that would have been wholesome and healthy in Newton is diminished and replaced by shuddering in virtue of this memory of his past acts. Furthermore, it is hard not to

---

① See John Newton, *Thoughts Upon the African Slave Trade*.

share Newton's view that he must never forget these acts. There would be something terrible about his forgetting the evil of his participation in the slave trade. In fact, it is not unreasonable to suppose that there is a duty to remember wrongdoing if the wrongdoing is serious enough.①

So, Newton's repentance and satisfaction may heal his intellect and will, but they cannot erase the past evil from his memory; and the same point holds for his victims and others stricken at the story of his acts in the slave trade.

If Newton's repentance and satisfaction are not enough to remove the problems of guilt for Newton in his psyche and in his relationships with others, are they nonetheless sufficient to remove his guilt as regards the damage and injustice he did? Satisfaction is a matter of doing what one can and so doing enough. And Newton is exemplary in having done all he could, so that on this score it seems that he did enough and more. Consequently, it seems that, in this respect at any rate, his guilt is removed, so that his relationships with others can be restored and he can be reconciled with his victims.

But this optimistic view is not right either, is it? Satisfaction such as Newton's is enough if it is considered relative to Newton, that is, relative to what Newton could do. But there is no reason to think that it is enough relative to the victims. How could anything Newton did be enough for those who had suffered from his slave-trading? How did his work of satisfaction help those who had suffered on his slave ships, or whose children suffered in virtue of having been born into slavery? Nothing in Newton's subsequent efforts to abolish the slave-trade in England altered the terrible suffering of those who died on his ships and the even worse suffering of those who lived to be slaves and to see their children enslaved as well. Nothing in what Newton

---

① See, for example, Jeffrey M. Blustein, *Forgiveness and Remembrance*, (Oxford: Oxford University Press, 2014).

did as satisfaction could make up to them the suffering Newton's evil caused them.

One can think of this insoluble difficulty for a perpetrator of serious evil as an analogue to a problem much discussed with regard to the problem of evil.

On some proposed theodicies or defenses, the benefit supposedly justifying God in allowing the suffering of some particular person goes to humankind as a whole, and not to the sufferer in particular. But, as objectors to such accounts point out, this seems not to solve the problem of evil, but only to move it. How could a good God allow one human being to suffer for some benefit that goes only to the species as a whole? Goodness requires that any putative benefit justifying someone in allowing suffering he could readily prevent should go primarily to the sufferer.

By parity of reasoning, if the satisfaction Newton made constituted a benefit for all those who might have been victimized after 1807, when the slave trade was abolished through his efforts, then the benefit garnered by his satisfaction does not go primarily to those afflicted by him in his slave-trading years. But if all people, or all people of his time and society, are benefited by Newton's satisfaction, then it seems that those Africans who suffered horribly from his slave-trading suffered for the sake of a benefit that went to everyone. In what sense, then, has Newton done anything to amend their suffering in particular? And if there is no acceptable answer to this question, as it seems clear that there is not, then in what sense does Newton's satisfaction remove his guilt with respect to those he enslaved and transported?

Consequently, why should the victims of his wrongdoing, or anyone else horrified at his actions, think his repentance and satisfaction are sufficient to remove Newton's guilt or to restore Newton to the place he would have had in the human community before his slave trading?

Conclusion

Although forgiveness, like love, is always obligatory, even for unrepentant wrongdoers, reconciliation does not follow immediately on forgiveness. For perpetrators of grave evil, even their fervent repentance and self-sacrificial satisfaction may not be enough for reconciliation. So it can be obligatory to forgive and nonetheless not morally permissible to be reconciled with a wrongdoer, even when that wrongdoer has repented and made satisfaction. A relationship is an on-going interaction among persons, and it is dependent on the characteristics of all the persons in the relationship. If, because of his past acts, a perpetrator of evil is not now the person he was, then others affected by him or aware of his past evil cannot treat him as if he now were the person he once was. They cannot unilaterally re-form the relationship they had or might have had with him when he was a different person from the person he now is. Consequently, if a person's moral wrongdoing is a great enough evil, it can obstruct or obviate reconciliation with him even if he is genuinely and whole-heartedly repentant. Repentance and satisfaction can make a wrongdoer a different person from the person he was when he engaged in wrongdoing. But even such exemplary repentance and satisfaction as Newton's cannot remove all the problems of guilt.

The highly divergent views of the respondents in Wiesenthal's the Sunflower can therefore all be justified. Those who argue in favor of the forgiveness of the dying German soldier are surely right. Forgiveness of him is obligatory, just as love is. But those who repudiate with fervor any forgiveness of him are also right, if we suppose that under the heading of 'forgiveness' they understand the removal of guilt, reconciliation, and restoration to human community. Even a lifetime's worth of satisfaction, if the soldier had had another lifetime to complete it, coupled with heartbroken repentance, could not remove his guilt or restore him to his former place in human society. The damage and injustice he did were so great that their past effects on others and their on-going effects on the soldier and others who remember what he did put the soldier at a distance of light-years from ordinary human community.

Anselm's account of the atonement of Christ is based on the idea that although human beings owe a great debt because of the evil they have done, they are unable to pay that debt. On his view, that is why Christ, who is both human and divine, pays this debt for them. Because he is human, he is a member of the species that owes the debt; and because he is God, he has the resources to pay the debt. Consequently, as Anselm sees it, only Christ can make satisfaction for the debt incurred by human wrongdoing.

On Anselm's view, the debt in question is owed to God. Elsewhere I have argued against Anselm's account of the atonement, but what the reflections of this paper show is that at least one part of Anselm's account is surely right. In consequence of grave evil, a human being may incur a debt of recompense so monumental that nothing he could do would ever repay it. Only, contrary to Anselm's account, the reflections of this paper imply that the debt is owed to the victims of human evil. If there is an account of Christ's atonement on which Christ's satisfaction removes the guilt of human beings, whatever else is contained in that account, it will have to portray Christ's work of satisfaction as satisfaction made to the victims of human evil. Only human beings owe the debt to the suffering victims of their evil; but it may be true, as Anselm thought, that only God could pay the debt incurred by human evil–a debt that is owed to other human beings, even if it should also be owed to God, as Anselm argued.

In this connection, I want to conclude by pointing out that, on Newton's own view of the matter, the story of Newton's satisfaction as I have told it here is incomplete. Newton did not suppose that his own efforts at satisfaction were what had removed his guilt or enabled him to be reconciled to others, including even the victims of his slave-trading. As his most famous hymn expresses, Newton believed that it was the amazing grace of God that found and restored him. Newton's work of satisfaction manifests his great gratitude for that grace — and for the satisfaction of Christ, which did what Newton himself could not have done alone to make amends for the evil he had done.

These theological considerations are too complicated to be dealt with briefly in passing. I mention them only to end on a more optimistic note than the preceding reflections might otherwise imply. Aquinas thought that there is no wrongdoing so evil that the wrongdoer cannot afterwards be restored to an even more admirable condition in himself and in human community than he would have had before the wrongdoing. But Aquinas thought so because of the implications of the account of Christ's satisfaction which Aquinas himself accepted. On that Thomistic account of Christ's atonement for human sin, it is right to see Newton as a hero in the history of the slave trade, as many people (me included) do. And, on that Thomistic account, even the dying German soldier can be not only forgiven but in fact restored in reconciliation and in community with all others. But these optimistic conclusions about the removal of guilt even for great evil are grounded in the Thomistic interpretation of the theological doctrine of Christ's atonement. And it implies that what is owed to the victims of human evil and what is needed to heal the psyche of a wrongdoer is provided by the satisfaction of Christ. When Christ's atonement is added to the story of guilt and forgiveness, then it turns out that those who refuse reconciliation with the dying German soldier in Wiesenthal's Sunflower story are after all wrong. Christ can make satisfaction for that soldier in such a way that the soldier's guilt is fully and finally removed.

But whether this optimistic conclusion regarding human evil is right, or whether the more pessimistic attitude of those who refuse reconciliation with the German soldier is right rests in the end, then, on theological considerations.①

References

1.Simon Wiesenthal, *The Sunflower: On the Possibility and Limits of Forgiveness* (NY: Schocken Books, 1960).

2.Wiesenthal 1960, p.169.

3.Wandering in Darkness.Narrative and the Problem of Suffering, (Oxford: Oxford University Press, 2010).

4.I have argued for this comparative claim in "Love, By All Accounts," *Proceedings and Addresses of The American Philosophical Association*, Vol.80, No.2, November 2006, pp.25-43.

5.Aquinas uses four words for love; in Latin, they are '*amor*', '*dilectio*', '*amicitia*', and '*caritas*'. (Cf. ST I-II q.26 a.3.) The first of these is love in its most generic sense, which is included in all the other kinds; for Aquinas, even a rock falling from a higher to a lower place can be said to have love for the place to which it falls, in this generic sense of 'love'.(Cf. ST I-II q.26 a.1.) The second, '*dilectio*', emphasizes the element of voluntariness in the love of rational persons; and the third, '*amicitia*', picks out the dispositions of love in friendship. But, for Aquinas, the fourth, '*caritas*', is the word for love in its real or complete sense. Since Aquinas privileges *caritas* in this way, I will focus on *caritas* in explaining his account of

① A longer version of this paper is published in "Guilt and Forgiveness." in *Forgiveness: Philosophical Essays*. Edited by Michael McKenna. New York: Oxford University Press, 2018.

love, although I understand his views of *caritas* in light of what he says about the more generic *amor.*

6.See, e.g., ST II-II q.25, a.3.

7.Cf. ST I-II q.26 a.4, where Aquinas says that to love is to will good to someone. Cf. also ST I-II q.28 a.4, where Aquinas explains the zeal or intensity of love in terms of the strength of a lover's desire for the good of the beloved.

8.By 'union' in this connection, I mean being at one with another, where, clearly, the kind of oneness brought about by two or more human beings is a function of what elements of life and psyche they are sharing. A mother shares some parts of herself and her life with her newborn; musically gifted friends composing an opera together share other parts of themselves with each other. Union comes in degrees at least in part because a human being, and a human life, is a composite; and it is possible to share some parts of this composite without sharing others. That is why it is possible to desire union with humanity as a whole: one can desire that all human beings be at one with each other, so that war, injustice, and all oppressive inequality cease.

9.Cf., e.g., ST I-II q.26 a.2 ad 2, and q.28 a.1 s.c., where Aquinas quotes approvingly Dionysius's line that love is the unitive force. Cf. also ST I-II q.66 a.6, where Aquinas explains the superiority of charity to the other virtues by saying that every lover is drawn by desire to union with the beloved, and ST I-II q.70 a.3, where Aquinas explains the connection between joy and love by saying that every lover rejoices at being united to the beloved. For an interesting recent attempt to defend a position that has some resemblance to Aquinas's, see Robert Adams, "Pure Love," *Journal of Religious Ethics*, 8 (1980), pp.83–99. Adams says: "It is a striking fact that while benevolence (the desire for another person's well-being) and *Eros*, as a desire for relationship with another person, seem to be quite distinct desires, we use a single name, 'love' or '*Agape*', for an attitude that includes both of them, at least in typical cases" (p.97).

10.There are many other details of Aquinas's account of love that are important but that cannot be explored in passing here. For a fuller treatment, see my *Wandering in Darkness. Narrative and the Problem of Suffering*, (Oxford: Oxford University Press, 2010), Chapter 5.

11.If there is a relationship between persons in which it is not appropriate for one person to desire the good for and union with the other, then the relationship is not a relationship of love. Insofar as it is possible to have a general love of humankind, however, then there is no connection between persons which is not also in effect a relationship for which some species of love is appropriate and therefore also obligatory. For some discussion of the claim that obligations and rights are not correlative, see my "God's Obligations", in *Philosophical Perspectives* 6, James Tomberlin (ed.), (Atascadero, CA: Ridgeview Publishing, 1992) pp.475-492.

12.ST II-II q.26 a.6-12.

13.For Aquinas's views on the nature of this union, cf., e.g., ST I-II q.28 a.1, where real union is described as a matter of presence between lover and beloved.

14.David Velleman, "Love as a Moral Emotion," *Ethics 109* (*1999*), *p*.353.

15.The two desires of any love are therefore included under the more general heading of the desire for goodness, as Aquinas understands it. For detailed discussion of Aquinas's views of goodness, understood in this broad sense, see my *Aquinas*, (New York: Routledge, 2003), Chapter 2.

16.The claim that the good desired for the beloved is an objective good therefore results from Aquinas's analysis of the nature of love together with his meta-ethics. It is not itself implied by Aquinas's analysis of love. I am grateful to Ish Haji for calling my attention to the need to make this point clear.

17.For more detailed discussion of forgiveness in connection with Aquinas's account of love，see Chapter 5 in Stump（2010）.

18.There is by now a huge literature on forgiveness，which cannot be dealt with in passing here. A good recent review of the literature can be found in Charles L. Griswold，*Forgiveness. A Philosophical Exploration*，（Cambridge: Cambridge University Press，2014）. The differences between the account I give and Griswold's are sketched here. My account of forgiveness is not incompatible with the standard account of forgiveness as the forswearing of resentment，but it encompasses also forgiveness as including the desire for union with a wrongdoer.

19.In fact，although on my view love is necessary and sufficient for forgiveness，it is not the case that forgiveness is nothing but love or that forgiveness reduces to love. Analogously，being risible is necessary and sufficient for being human – anything that is risible is human and nothing that is not risible is human – but being human is not reducible to being risible. Risibility picks out human beings by an accident which is had by all and only human beings，but the nature of human beings is not nothing but risibility. It is not part of my purposes here to define forgiveness，and so I leave to one side what else might need to be added to love for a definition of forgiveness. I am grateful to Michael Rea for calling my attention to the need to make this point explicit.

20.It might appear that Aquinas's account of love succumbs to the same problems as those that seem to some people to afflict an ethics of care. If the value of loving others or caring for others is the fundamental ethical value，then it is not easy to explain why it is morally acceptable to withhold care for others in the interests of pursuing one's own projects. And yet if there is no morally acceptable way of doing so，caring，or loving，can become deeply destructive，dreadfully unjust，with regard to the one doing the caring or loving. So，for example，Virginia Woolf describes the "angel in the house" who loved others totally, who cared for them completely, in this way:

"she never had a mind or a wish of her own, but preferred to sympathize always with the minds and wishes of others... I did my best to kill her. My excuse, if I were to be had up in a court of law, would be that I acted in self-defence. Had I not killed her she would have killed me." (From "Professions for Women," quoted in Jean Hampton, "Feminist Contractarianism," in *A Mind of One's Own. Feminist Essays on Reason and Objectivity*, ed. Louis Anthony and Charlotte Witt [Boulder, CO: Westview Press, 1993], 231.)

In my view, considerations similar to those showing that Paula is not loving Jerome in enabling him to harm her apply also to the case in which Paula allows herself to be harmed by myriad others. She is not loving others in allowing them to hurt her, even if the harm done to her takes the actions of a whole group to accomplish.

21.For more discussion of this claim, see my "The Non-Aristotelian Character of Aquinas's Ethics: Aquinas on the Passions," *Faith and Philosophy* 28.1(2011):29-43.

22.I have argued for this claim at length in "God's Obligations," in *Philosophical Perspectives* 6, ed. James Tomberlin (Atascadero, CA: Ridgeview Publishing, 1992) :475-492. To see the point here, consider, by way of analogy that if Paula were a very rich tourist traveling in a very poor country, she would be obligated to give some of her money away for charitable purposes in that country if she were solicited to do so; if she refused all such solicitations, she would be subject to appropriate moral censure. But it would not be the case that any particular recipient of her donations would have a right to her money.

23.In this section of this paper, I am significantly altering the conclusion I argued for in an earlier paper, "Personal Relations and Moral Residue," in *History of the Human Sciences: Theorizing from the Holocaust: What is to be Learned?*, Paul Roth and Mark S. Peacock (eds.), Vol.17 No 2/3 (August 2004), pp.33-57. I stand by the arguments of that paper, but they now seem to me not sufficient to establish the conclusion. What else is needed, as I indicate in the conclusion of this paper, is a well-worked out theory of atonement.

24.See John Newton, *Thoughts Upon the African Slave Trade*.

25.See, for example, Jeffrey M. Blustein, *Forgiveness and Remembrance*, (Oxford: Oxford University Press, 2014).

26.A longer version of this paper is published in "Guilt and Forgiveness." in *Forgiveness: Philosophical Essays*. Edited by Michael McKenna. New York: Oxford University Press, 2018.

中文简介

《向日葵：愧疚、宽恕与和解》

人们常常认为，愧疚的解药是宽恕。而犯错之人的悔改和补偿是宽恕的必要条件和充分条件。一般认为，这种补偿分为两部分，即犯错之人所造成损害的合理补偿，以及犯错之人的悔过，这种悔过作为其造成的不公的额外弥补。按照这种观点，一个受害者不应该在没有悔改和补偿的情况下原谅这个犯错之人。但是如果这个犯错之人已经悔改和补偿了，那么如果受害者拒绝原谅这个犯错之人，我们可能会认为，这个受害者拒绝原谅的做法是不合理的。如果受害者原谅了犯错之人，那么就免除了犯错之人的愧疚；既然他的愧疚消除了，就没有什么能阻止双方的和解，使犯错之人恢复到在自己社区中的正常角色。

不过，西蒙·维森塔尔的书《向日葵：宽恕的可能性和限度》一书给出了不同的看法。在此书中，维森塔尔讲述了一个垂死的德国士兵的故事，他对犹太人男女和儿童犯下了可怕的罪行，但他死前迫切希望从至少一个犹太人那里得到宽恕和和解。当时是曾经在奥斯威辛集中营被关押过的维森塔尔被带去听这位德国士兵的故事和他宽恕的请求。在维森塔尔所讲述的故事中，这位德国士兵似乎完全而真诚地忏悔了。因为他快要死了，他几乎没什么办法去弥补；但是他对自己的罪恶痛心，他对维森塔尔进行忏悔，表达自己愿意尽可能多的补偿和悔过。在这种情况下，维森塔尔以非常令人钦佩的方式仁慈地面对这名将死的士兵。但当士兵的供词终于完成时，维森塔尔站起来，一言不发地离开了这个士兵。按照维森塔尔自己对德国士兵的反应的解读，他没有给予将死的士兵所渴望的宽恕。

在《向日葵》中，维森塔尔列举了很多思想家对这个故事的思考，其中许多是著名学者。他邀请这些思想家回答，他们是否会原谅那个士兵。他们的回应是值得深思的，因为这些人表达了非常不一样的直觉。

一些被调查者坚信，这个悔过自新的将死士兵应该得到宽恕。例如，有影响力的圣母大学前校长西奥多·赫斯伯格认为，“我的治具是原谅…。当然，这里的罪恶是巨大的。它仍然是有限的，上帝的仁慈是无限的。如果有人要求我原谅，我会原谅，因为上帝会原谅的。”

但其他同样深思熟虑的受访者报告说，他们也赞同维森塔尔的反应。在他们看来，这个士兵的邪恶足以永远摧毁他获得宽恕的机会。在他们看来，士兵的可怕行为使自己永远无法与他人和解，也无法恢复在正常的人类社会中的位置。在他们看来，即使他活着的时候，做了一些痛心的忏悔，甚至他所做的难以形容的伤害对受害者来说有可能得到一定的补偿，但是我们对这个士兵的评价也不会改变。对这些受访者来说，士兵不应该被原谅。在他们看来，士兵的愧疚感是不可能消除的；士兵也不可能恢复到在人类社会中任何可以接受的角色。

在这种观点下，悔过、补偿、忏悔不足以获得他人的宽恕。同时，这些东西加上宽恕也不足以消除施害者自身的愧疚感。和解可能会被拒绝，即使在有任何可能的补偿和忏悔悔改的情况下，愧疚感可能仍然存在。

在这篇论文中，我想考虑的是《向日葵》中被调查者对宽恕的相互冲突的观点背后所呈现的关于内疚和宽恕的不同理论。接下来，我将简要地总结托马斯·阿奎那对爱的叙述和我所理解的宽恕的相关叙述。根据阿奎那爱的理论，爱在道德上总是必须的，因此宽恕也是必须的。因此，认为悔改和补偿是宽恕的必要条件的观点不会被阿奎那接受。基于这些原因，在我看来，一方面，《向日葵》中的那些受访者的观点，即应该拒绝宽恕这个垂死的德国士兵，是错误的。但是，另外一方面，我会支持他们强烈反对与垂死的德国士兵达成任何的和解。我认为，这种拒绝是基于直觉的，我们也必须认真对待这种直觉。我将尽力表明，在某些严重的罪恶情况下，悔改和赔罪不足以消除愧疚。而和解在道德上可能是不被允许的。

Foucault on Power and Government

Paul Patton

Introduction

Initial assessments of Foucault's work by English language political theorists were almost entirely negative. In the early 1980s, after the English publications of Discipline and Punish (1977), History of Sexuality Volume 1 (1978) and Herculine Barbin (1980), he was denounced by leading figures in Critical Theory for his failure to provide normative foundations for his critical enterprise, resulting in a form of partisanship and relativism (Frazer 1981; Habermas 1987) . From the perspective of liberal democratic theory, Charles Taylor accused him of being incoherent in his use of the concepts of power and freedom and incapable of articulating a positive political vision (Taylor 1984) . Michael Walzer characterised him as an anarchist and nihilist, and attributed the 'catastrophic weakness of his political theory' to the absence of any consideration of democratic citizenship and the liberal state (Walzer 1983) . Defenders of Foucault have tended to agree that his genealogies of power and subjectivity have little to offer normative political theory.①

① Comments such as the following are representative: 'Foucault criticizes, in effect, the entire enterprise of political theory as conceived by liberal thinkers such as Walzer' (Constable 1991:269) ; 'Foucault's analysis [of liberalism] sets him at odds with the dominant Anglo-American philosophical conversation insofar as he denies the theoretical centrality of the normative problem of liberal justice.' (Hibbard-Swanson 2014:252) .

Much of this received view rests on confusion about the aim of Foucault's genealogies and about the nature of his approach to power. Commentators tend to overlook his repeated insistence that he was not interested in a theory of power as such but rather in an 'analytics' that would be useful for the analysis of historically specific mechanisms of power.① Critics and defenders alike tend to overlook his self-critical analysis of his earlier views in the course of his 1975-1976 lectures, 'Society Must Be Defended, ' along with the shift of focus from micropower to techniques for the exercise of power over populations in his 1977-1978 and 1978-1979 lectures (Foucault 2003, 2007, 2008) . There is some excuse for this in relation to those initial responses in the 1980s, since these lectures were not published and not widely available. In retrospect, however, the most striking feature of those initial responses to Foucault on the part of political theorists is the extent to which they were ignorant of the new developments in his political philosophy in the course of his lectures at the Collège de France from 1975 to 1979. Now that these lectures are published and available in English translation, there is good reason to re-examine what has become the orthodox view of his approach to power.

The lectures on security and governmentality in 1977-1978, Security, Territory, Population, and on liberalism and neoliberalism in 1978-1979, Birth of Biopolitics, are especially interesting for a number of reasons. It is only in the course of his 1977-1978 lectures that Foucault begins to formulate an alternative to the 'war - repression' model of power that he utilized in his work before 1976. The shift from micropower to governmentality eventually led to a new analytics of power as the government of conduct that Foucault summarized in 'The Subject and Power' (1982) . While this did not provide normative criteria for acceptable as

① See for example Foucault 1978:82 and 2000:327.

opposed to unacceptable forms of power, it did provide conceptual resources with which to respond to some of the claims of conceptual confusion advanced by Fraser, Habermas, Taylor and others (Patton 1989, 2013) . Foucault's 1978-1979 lectures, The Birth of Biopolitics, outlined some of the distinguishing features of liberal government as it emerged in Europe around the middle of the eighteenth century before turning to the analysis of German and American neoliberalism. They directly refute Walzer's accusation of neglect of the liberal state, even if they do not approach it from the perspective of normative political theory.①

This aim of this paper is to outline the development of Foucault's conception of power during the 1970s and to show how this is reflected in his essay 'The Subject and Power,' first published as an appendix to Dreyfus and Rabinow in 1982. This essay is the closest thing Foucault ever wrote to a definitive statement of his approach to the study of power. Many commentators, myself included, have tended to treat it as more or less continuous with the approach spelt out in DP, HS1 and a number of interviews during the early to mid 1970s, even though this text employs terminology and concepts that were absent from the earlier work. Until 1976 Foucault relied upon an impersonal language of bodies, forces and struggles, whereas 'The Subject and Power' reverts to a more familiar language of human agency and freedom to describe the conditions under which power is exercised. Even though this essay was first

---

① One reviewer suggests that these lectures represent Foucault's one and only 'diversion into contemporary political philosophy,' so long as we understand that his interest does not involve the juridical tradition of contractarian and natural rights philosophy asssociated with Rawls and Nozick but rather the political economic tradition: 'Think of the tradition that goes from Hobbes, Hume and Adam Smith to Milton Friedman, Friedrich Hayek, David Gauthier, and contemporary evolutionary game theory' (Guala 2006:429.431) . François Ewald expresses a similar view in a discussion with Gary Becker when he comments that Foucault's lectures propose a theory of liberalism but without a single quotation from a philosophical thinker of liberalism: 'The sole thinkers of liberalism, in Foucault's account, are economists' (Ewald 2012) .

published in 1982, it is unclear precisely when it was written. I agree with Arnold Davidson that ‘there is compelling internal evidence that parts of it were written several years earlier’（Davidson 2011，39 fn4）. However, I will attempt to show why it is most likely that the key sections defining power as action upon the actions of others were written after Foucault's discovery of the rich theme of government and governmentality in 1978. Before discussing this essay, it is helpful to explore what the now published lectures tell us about the changes in his understanding of power between 1976 and 1982.

Foucault's re-examination of power 1: the diagnostic question

The opening lecture of his 1975-1976 course ‘Society Must Be Defended’ begins with the statement of an intellectual crisis. Foucault says that he has had enough and would like to bring to a close the series of projects that he has pursued in preceding years. He describes these as mere fragments of research on diverse topics such as the history of penal procedure, the intellectual and institutional history of psychiatry in the nineteenth century, some reflections on sophistry and on Greek coins, the outline of a history of sexuality or of knowledge about sexuality, and so on. All this, he suggests, has become very repetitive, ‘always falling into the same rut, the same themes, the same concepts’（SMD，3）. He connects this intellectual crisis to ‘changes in the conjuncture’ but he also reiterates his conviction that the effectiveness of the various kinds of ‘subjugated knowledges’ that he has spent so much time reactivating has to do precisely with their discontinuous, particular and local character（SMD，6）.

Following these critical reflections on his overall research project and the manner in which it has been pursued up to this point, Foucault specifies the aims of his 1975-1976 course by means of a nested series of questions. At the highest level, his question is: what is power? At the next level below, this general question branches into an historically specific, diagnostic question about the nature of power in the present, and a conceptual question about the most appropriate terms in which to analyze power. The diagnostic question asks, in historically situated terms, what is the form of power that has reigned supreme in the West since the collapse of Nazism and the retreat of Stalinism (SMD, 13). In the course of these lectures, Foucault offers two distinct answers to this question. The first, in the second lecture, argues that Western societies are ruled by a complex combination of disciplinary power and a democratized version of sovereign power:

on the one hand, a legislation, a discourse and an organization of public right articulated around the principle of the sovereignty of the social body and the delegation of individual sovereignty to the State; and we also have a tight grid of disciplinary coercions that actually guarantees the cohesion of that social body. Now that grid cannot in any way be transcribed in right, even though the two necessarily go together. A right of sovereignty and a mechanics of discipline. It is, I think, between these two limits that power is exercised. (SMD, 37).

A second answer to the diagnostic question comes in the final lecture of this course where he argues that a new, non-disciplinary technique of power emerged towards the end of the eighteenth century: "something that is no longer an anatomo-politics of the human body, but what I would call a 'biopolitics' of the human race" (SMD, 243). This new technology of power is addressed to populations rather than individual bodies. It involves efforts to control the fertility and reproduction of the population, to impose forms of public hygiene, and to control the natural and urban environments directly affecting the lives of human beings, as well as measures to deal with old age, accidents and infirmities of various kinds. In contrast to the old sovereign power of taking life, what emerged was a power that sought to sustain and develop the conditions in which human life could persist and flourish. This new modality of power was different from but not incompatible with disciplinary power:

We are, then, in a power that has taken control of both the body and life or that has, if you like, taken control of life in general – with the body as one pole and the population as the other (SMD, 253).

These are not the only answers Foucault gives to the diagnostic question posed above. In his first lecture of the 1977-1978 course, Security, Territory, Population, he outlines a more refined account of the new technology of power exercised over the conditions of life by describing security mechanisms. These are applied to populations rather than to individuals or groups. They deal with probable rather than actual events and seek to respond to these on the basis of calculations of cost and in terms of a norm of acceptable outcomes rather than a binary division between the permitted and prohibited. At this point, he toys with the idea of a further answer to the diagnostic question by asking whether it might be the case that 'the general economy of power in our societies is becoming a domain of security?' (STP, 10-11). ①

After the shift of focus from mechanisms of security to the forms and rationalities of government in the 1978 lectures, Foucault offers further epochal claims about the nature of power. He insists on the unique character of pastoral power as it developed within European Christianity and its difference from political power up until the end of the eighteenth century, but also on its role as a prelude to the modern forms of state government that developed from this point onwards. While he

① At the end of the fourth lecture (1 February 1978) in which he reorients the focus of this course towards a history of governmentality, he suggests that we still live in the era of a governmentality discovered in the eighteenth century: this is a form of government that acts on the population, that relies upon a form of economic knowledge or political economy and that 'would correspond to a society controlled by apparatuses of security' (STP, 110).

does not claim in these lectures that modern power is essentially pastoral, he does come close to this kind of claim in 'The Subject and Power,' where he suggests that the contemporary state can be seen as 'a modern matrix of individualization, or a new form of pastoral power' (EW3, 334).①

Foucault's re-examination of power 2: the conceptual question

Foucault approaches the conceptual question in his 1976 lectures by suggesting that our understanding of power has long been permeated by a form of economism. Both the juridical, contractarian conception of sovereign power and the Marxist conception share a certain 'economism' in their understandings of power, although this takes a quite different form in each case. The juridical conception understands political power as analogous to the commodity form in so far as it is built from rights possessed by individuals that can be transferred to a sovereign. For the Marxist conception, 'political power finds its historical raison d'être in the economy' to the extent that power is considered a means to reproduce class domination and associated relations of production, (SMD, 14). To answer the question whether the analysis of power can be divorced from any reference to the economy, Foucault considers two theses that point towards a non-economic analysis of power: firstly, the idea that power is something that exists only in being exercised, and secondly the idea that power is primarily a relation of force.

These two theses immediately raise further questions to which we find ready-made, widely accepted answers. First, if power is something that exists

① His 1979 Tanner lectures refer to the 'welfare state problem' as one of many ways in which the delicate adjustment between political power wielded over legal subjects and pastoral power wielded over living beings is played out in the contemporary world (EW3, 307).

only in its exercise, in what does that exercise consist? How is power exercised? The first widely accepted answer, which Foucault calls Reich's hypothesis, is that power consists in repression: 'Power is that which represses. Power is that which represses nature, instincts, a class or individuals' (SMD, 15). Second, if power is primarily a relation of force, what is the nature of the relationship between different forces? The widely accepted answer, which Foucault calls Nietzsche's hypothesis, is that power is essentially a matter of struggle or conflict between opposing forces: 'Power is war, the continuation of war by other means' (SMD, 15). ①

Together, these two hypotheses form the principle alternative to the economistic approach to power outlined above: the war-repression schema in opposition to the contract-opppression schema. Foucault admits that in his discussions of power in previous years he sought to apply the war – repression schema. ② Nevertheless, at this point in 1976, he has reached the conclusion that both elements of this schema need to be modified and perhaps ultimately abandoned (SMD, 17). He proposes to devote the following one or two lectures to a critical re-examination of the idea of

---

① Foucault could equally have called this Deleuze's hypothesis in the light of the latter's reconstruction of Nietzsche's theory of the will to power on the basis of his conception of active and reactive force (Deleuze 1983, 49-68). In their 1972 Interview 'Intellectuals and Power,' and again in a 1983 interview, Foucault acknowledged the influence of Deleuze's *Nietzsche and Philosophy* on his own thinking about power: 'underneath the old theme of meaning, signified and signifier etc, at last the question of power, of the inequality of powers and their struggles....' (LCP, 205-217; EW2, 445).

② In his 1973 lecture course *The Punitive Society*, Foucault commented that 'Power, the legality that it serves and the illegalisms that it manages or struggles against must all be understood as a particular way of pursuing civil war' (Cited in Nigro 2011, 144). Earlier in the 1976 course, in answer to the question what was at stake in the genealogical exercise of identifying and resuscitating buried and disqualified knowledges, he relies on the struggle schema in suggesting that 'Both the specialized domain of scholarship and the disqualified knowledge people have contained the memory of combats …. And so we have the outline of what might be called a genealogy, or of multiple genealogical investigations. We have both a meticulous rediscovery of struggles and the raw memory of fights' (SMD, 8).

repression. This promise is not kept, apart from some brief remarks about the sources of the concept of repression at the end of the second lecture and the beginning of the third. The History of Sexuality Volume One, published later the same year, develops a more detailed argument against the repressive hypothesis. The real focus of the 1976 lectures is the hypothesis associated with Nietzsche:

> I would like to try to see the extent to which the binary schema of war and struggle, of the clash between forces, can really be identified as the basis of civil society, as both the principle and motor of the exercise of political power. "Are we really talking about war when we analyze the workings of power? Are the notions of 'tactics,' 'strategy,' and 'relations of force' valid? To what extent are they valid? Is power quite simply a continuation of war by means other than weapons and battles?" (SMD, 18) .

There are both historical and conceptual questions at play here. However, it is Foucault's answer to the historical question that occupies centre stage: "How, when, and why was it noticed that or imagined that what is going on beneath and in power relations is a war?" (SMD, 47) . Daniel Defert rightly insists that the bulk of this course is not about war, the analysis of power or racism. Rather, it is concerned with the emergence of a form of analysis in terms of war and race (Defert 2001, 59) . The bulk of these lectures are devoted to a genealogy of the historico-political discourse that took war to be a permanent feature of social relations, 'the ineradicable basis of all relations and institutions of power' (SMD, 49) . Foucault locates the emergence of this discourse in the writings of Levellers and Diggers during the English Civil War. He points to its reappearance in France at the beginning of the eighteenth, in the writings of French aristocrats such as Henry de Boulainvilliers engaged in a rearguard struggle against the establishment of absolute monarchy. He surveys the reappearance of this form of history once more in the nineteenth century, first in the writings of historians of the revolutionary period, such as Sieyès, Augustin Thierry, Montlosier and Guizot, and then later in the writings of biological racists and eugenicists. Among its distinguishing features, this kind of history relied upon a binary division of the social field as involving struggle between contending groups, races or nations. As such, this 'political historicism provided the discursive framework in which emerged some of the defining themes of politics in the twentieth century, including state racism, class war and the idea of revolution (SMD, 111).

In raising these historical and conceptual questions about the war-repression model, Foucault is doing two things. First, he is undertaking a critical intervention in the political present in which they were written.1975 and 1976 were the years in which the Marxist orthodoxy that had sustained radical political movements in France since the 1960s began to crumble. These were also years in which a significant number of those in the European extreme left began to take up arms. This led to assassinations and kidnappings by groups such as the Italian Red Brigades and the German Red Army Fraction. While the recourse to armed struggle was largely avoided in France, this was not because many were not tempted. Foucault's questions about the model of war and its implications for political activity were directly related to the ideas that informed this temptation. His first lecture on 7 January 1976 pointed out that the inversion of Clausewitz's aphorism concerning the relation between war and politics carried the implication that ultimately, the settlement of political conflict came down to a 'trial by strength in which weapons are the final judges' (SMD, 16). His lecture of 28 January quotes a letter from Marx to Engels in 1882 that identifies the French historians who wrote about race struggle as the source of their ideas of class struggle, in order to suggest that the idea of revolution and the history of revolutionary practice is indissociable from this form of 'counterhistory' that presented the social order as an ongoing war between races or classes: 'Where would the revolutionary project, the revolutionary idea, or revolutionary practice be without the will to rekindle the real war that once went on and which is still going on, even though the function of the silent order of power is to mask and smother it …?' (SMD, 79) . Questions such as these served to reinforce the doubts being raised among former militants about the desirability of revolution or the recourse to arms (Le Blanc and Terrel 2003, 22) .

Second, Foucault is directly challenging his own thinking about power up to this point. The 'micro-physics' of disciplinary power outlined in Discipline and Punish relied extensively on the militaristic language of 'tactics,' 'manoeuvres' and 'strategies.' It presupposed that power relations are grounded in relations of force and that 'one should take as the model for power relations 'a perpetual battle rather than a contract regulating a transaction or the conquest of a territory' (DP, 26) . The History of Sexuality, Volume One, which was not published until after these lectures in December 1976, famously argued that 'power must be understood in the first instance as the multiplicity of force relations immanent in the sphere in which they operate' and that the condition of possibility of all power relations must be sought in 'the moving substrate of force relations which, by virtue of their inequality, constantly engender states of power' (HS1, 92-93) . The same passage offered a more nuanced view of the usefulness of battle as the model for power relations, suggesting that the difference between war and politics was not a difference in kind but a difference of strategy whereby the force relations present in a given society could be played out either in the forms of war or politics.①

It is surprising that The History of Sexuality, Volume One continues to rely on the language of forces and strategies, given that the text was not finalized until after the 1976 lectures in which he explicitly questioned the applicability of concepts such as antagonism, rivalry or confrontation and struggle between contending parties to the analysis of power (Defert 1994, 49) .② Comments in interviews during this period indicate that he was actively questioning this aspect of the war-repression schema. For example, in the 'Truth and Power' interview, which took place in June 1976, he rehearses some of the questions raised by the assimilation of power to war and comments that 'it's astonishing to see how easily and self-evidently people talk of warlike relations of power or of class struggle without ever making it clear whether some form of war is meant, and if so what form' (EW3, 124) . Similarly, in 'The Eye of Power' interview conducted around the same time, he comments on the frequency with which people use the term 'struggle' without questioning what is implied by this term: 'Is the relation of forces in the order of politics a warlike one? I

---

① Foucault's discussion of power in *The History of Sexuality*, *Volume One* draws a distinction that is obscured in the English translation between power in general, as it is exercised in local relations throughout society, and 'the power' understood as the overall system of domination and control: 'power insofar as it is permanent, repetitive, inert and self-reproducing' (HS1, 93) . Foucault's nominalist understanding of the latter relies on the military metaphor: '"the" power is not an institution, and not a structure; neither is it a certain strength with which some are endowed; it is the name that one attributes to a complex strategical situation in a particular society' (HS1, 93 translation modified) . The original reads: 'le pouvoir, ce n'est pas une institution, et ce n'est pas une structure, ce n'est pas une certain puissance dont certains seraient dotés: c'est le nom qu'on prête à une situation stratégique complex dans un société donnée' (FHS1, 123) .

② Arnold Davidson's Introduction to 'Society Must Be Defended' notes Foucault's questioning of the war model of power in interviews, but then curiously disregards this critical dimension of the 1976 lectures by suggesting that 'Foucault's preoccupation with the schema of war was central to this formulation of the strategic model of power, of force-relations, a strategic model that would allow us to reorient our conception of power' (SMD, xviii) . Foucault's preoccupation with the schema of war was rather the beginnings of a shift in his thinking about power away from the strategic model.

don't personally feel prepared to answer this with a definite yes or no' (PK, 164) .

Perhaps one reason that Foucault continued to rely on the language of war in talking about power is that, at this point, he had not settled on any alternative. The 1975-1976 lectures do not provide one. After having raised questions about power at the outset, Foucault is still searching in the third lecture for a more precise specification of the conceptual question: what is the role of concepts related to war and the conduct of war in the analysis of power? He reformulates the question in terms of the search for a theory of domination, or the forms of domination, rather than a theory of sovereignty. He does not at this point question the assumption that relations of power culminate in systems of domination. Rather, he asks how does domination operate, by what techniques and by means of what effects of subjugation are relations of domination established and maintained? In particular, he asks whether the concept of war and war-like relations provide an appropriate framework for the analysis of power relations:

> To what extent can a relationship of domination boil down to or be reduced to the notion of a relationship of force? To what extent can the relationship of force be reduced to a relationship of war? (SMD, 46)

Here too, there are both conceptual and historical questions in play, even though as noted earlier it is the historical question that becomes the real focus of the lectures that follow. The conceptual questions raised by asking whether or not concepts derived from the conduct of warfare such as strategy and tactics provide adequate instruments for the analysis of power relations are not answered in the 1975-1976 lectures (SMD, 47) . However, the conditions of a negative answer are established in the final lecture when he identifies a new kind of power directed at populations rather than individuals or groups and employing different mechanisms that sought to maintain regularity in the conditions that sustain human life. As several commentators have noted, the effects of biopower and the means by which they were achieved are not readily explained by reference to binary relationships of domination or violent struggle between contending forces.①

The breakthrough in Foucault's conceptual analysis of power, and the beginnings of an answer to the conceptual questions raised in 1976, occurs two years later in his 1977-1978 lectures, Security, Territory, Population, when he begins to analyse in more detail the technologies of biopower. Mechanisms of security do not involve direct confrontation between contending forces, but forms of action on a population, where this is supposed to be a natural phenomenon subject to various kinds of regular behaviour: economic, demographic, epidemiological, and so on. As such this kind of power required knowledge of the relevant dimensions of the behaviour of populations. The new sciences of statistics and political economy no longer considered a population as a collection of subjects of right but as 'a set of processes to be managed at the level and on the basis of what is natural in these processes' (STP, 70). Together, these mechanisms of security and the forms of knowledge associated with them represented a shift from a political order characterized by the exercise and maintenance of sovereignty to one characterized by government. Henceforth, it is in terms of government rather than war that Foucault understands the exercise of power.

The lecture of 18 January 1978, devoted to proposals put forward in the middle of the eighteenth century to deal with the problem of grain shortage, shows what is at stake in the analysis of power as government rather than war. Grain shortage was a

① See Fontana and Bertani 2003, 283; Le Blanc and Terrel 2003, 16.

threat to governments since it could lead quickly to revolt on the part of a population deprived of food. Previously, it had been dealt with by regulations intended to prevent such shortages from occurring: price controls, prohibitions on hoarding, limits on the export of grain and control of the extent of land under cultivation. From the end of the seventeenth century politicians and their economic advisors became aware that the free circulation of grain was a better mechanism to ensure food security. Proposals such as those put forward in 1763 by Louis-Paul Abeille recommended the removal of restrictions on hoarding, on the export and import of grain, and on the extent of land devoted to its production (STP, 35-44). These measures are aimed at the security of food for the population at large, but they work through the decisions of individual producers, merchants and consumers by allowing the free circulation of goods. As components of a market mechanism of security, they do not involve the direct confrontation and struggle of contending forces, as suggested by the schema of war. Nor do they involve direct action upon the forces of individuals and groups in the manner of disciplinary techniques. Rather, they ensure food security by establishing conditions under which market incentives would cause individuals to act in ways that address any problem of shortage. Foucault returns to the market mechanism for ensuring food security in the final lecture of the 1978 course, in order to suggest that it pointed towards a new, liberal form of government. Rather than the regulative mechanisms favoured by the eighteenth century science of police, this involved the integration of freedom into the art of government. Certain kinds of freedom had to be respected and failure to do so amounted to 'ignorance of how to govern properly' (STP, 353).

This new form of government becomes the subject matter of his 1978-1979 lectures, The Birth of Biopolitics. Liberal government as it emerged during the eighteenth century sought to adjust the exercise of state power to the realities of the market. As such, it depended on the existence of freedoms such as the freedom to trade, the freedom to exercise property rights, freedoms of discussion and expression, and freedom from monopolies. Such freedoms are not given but must be produced. Liberal government did not simply endorse freedom but established limitations, controls and various forms of coercion to ensure the kinds of freedom needed for the effective operation of markets. In the early twentieth century, state intervention to maintain market economies developed to a point of crisis in liberal governmentality, where the forms of regulation themselves came to be seen as a threat to the very market freedom they were supposed to protect. Foucault's lectures on neoliberalism analyzed the response to this crisis that sought to redefine the role of government by insisting on the importance of competition as the essence of markets and the real objective of government policy. Neoliberalism reinvented the aims as well as the techniques of liberal government and sought to extend the reliance on market mechanisms to areas of civil and social life that were previously exempt: 'a state under the supervision of the market rather than a market supervised by the state' (BB, 116).

Foucault's lectures on liberalism and neoliberalism do not reflect on what he later called the 'conceptual requirements' of studying this kind of power. The closest he came to a definitive statement and response to the conceptual questions posed in his 1976 lectures was in 'The Subject and Power,' published for the first time in English in 1982 (EW3, 326-348). This text reiterates his insistence, in The History of Sexuality, Volume One and elsewhere, that the analysis of power relations and the forms of its exercise requires not so much a theory of power as an 'analytics' that would provide the concepts required for the analysis of particular modalities of power (HS1, 82). The bare object of study, namely power, does not provide a sufficient basis for an adequate conceptualization: 'We have to know the historical conditions that motivate our conceptualization. We need a historical awareness of our present circumstances' (EW3, 327). In these terms, we can read the second part of this text entitled 'How is Power Exercised?' as setting out the conceptual requirements for the study of liberal governmental power.

Foucault begins by distinguishing power relations from relations of communication and from the power exercised over things through the exercise of particular physical, technical or organizational capacities. All of these may be involved in a given social institution or activity, but the specificity of power relations is that these involve action upon the action of others:

In effect, what defines a relationship of power is that it is a mode of action that does not act directly and immediately on others. Instead, it acts upon their actions: an action upon an action, on possible or actual future or present actions (EW3, 340).

This understanding of power relations as action upon the field of actions open to others is significantly different from Foucault's earlier conception of power relations as a matter of conflict or struggle between opposing forces. The most important differences include, firstly, the fact that the parties to relations of power are now conceived as agents endowed with a degree of freedom. The exercise of power presupposes that those on whom it is exercised are subjects capable of action and that they are in fact free to act in a number of ways. The exercise of power can take a variety of forms including inducement or incitation to act in particular ways, but also constraint or prohibition on acting in other ways: "Power is exercised only over free subjects, and only insofar as they are 'free'" (EW3, 342). The scare quotes around 'free' here indicate that this is not a natural freedom but rather specific kinds of freedom such as those produced and maintained for the efficient operation of markets. A second difference relates to the kind of subject that is presupposed. For liberal governmentality, this is a subject of interests and rationality, endowed with a capacity to calculate courses of action that serve its interests. For neoliberal governmentality, homo oeconomicus is not simply a subject seeking to maximize its satisfaction in a market but also an enterprise. It is a subject endowed with interests and rationality but also with capital of various kinds that can be increased in competition with others.

The definition of power as action upon the actions of others confirms Foucault's rupture with economism in the theory of power, with the juridical conception of power and with the war model. Power is not something possessed that can be exchanged or transferred. It does not essentially involve either contracts or violence, which does not mean that the exercise of power cannot in particular cases involve the obtaining of consent or the threat of violence. Nor does it essentially involve struggle between contending forces. Rather, power acts on the 'field of possibilities' that circumscribes the actions of others. It is a way of directing or governing the actions of others:

> Basically, power is less a confrontation between two adversaries or their mutual engagement than a question of 'government' … The relationship proper to power would therefore be sought not on the side of violence or of struggle, nor on that of voluntary contracts (all of which can, at best, only be the instruments of power) but, rather, in the area of that singular mode of action, neither warlike nor juridical, which is government. (EW3, 341).

Power, Strategy and Neoliberal Governmentality

'The Subject and Power' answers many of the conceptual questions about power first raised in Foucault's 1976 lectures. At the same time, this intriguing text raises further questions about his approach to the analysis of power, especially in relation to the neoliberal governmentality discussed in 1979. The final section returns to the question of strategy and its role in relations of power. Building on the centrality of freedom to this concept of power as action on the actions of others, Foucault asserts that there is an intransigence of freedom and a corresponding 'agonism' at the heart of power relations (EW3, 342). He argues that, as a result of the ineliminable freedom presupposed by this kind of power, there is no power relationship without the possibility of escape, flight or resistance on the part of those over whom power is being exercised. This implies that a particular exercise of power will always fall somewhere on a continuum between 'the free play of antagonistic reactions' and the achievement of stable mechanisms that imply the ongoing possibility of governing or directing the conduct of others. The attainment of such mechanisms is both an aim of the exercise of power and the temporary overcoming or suspension of the agonism between power and freedom. It is an internal limit of power relations. Conversely, the free play of antagonistic reactions is another limit of power. Once this point is reached there is no longer government of others but only action and reaction: 'instead of manipulating and inducing actions in a calculated manner, one must be content with reacting to them after the event' (EW3, 347). The result is that antagonistic relations are in constant danger of giving rise to the establishment of more or less stable relations of power, while conversely such relatively stable relations of power are in constant danger of falling back into adversarial or antagonistic relations. Foucault concludes from this perpetual instability that it is always possible to interpret the mechanisms employed in particular relations of power in strategic terms: the same events and the same transformations may be interpreted 'either from inside the history of struggle or from the standpoint of power relationships' (EW3, 347). Moreover, he argues that the disparity between these two ways of reading history makes visible the fundamental phenomenon of domination.①

This points to an important feature of the analysis of power as this is carried out in Foucault's lectures on neoliberal governmentality, namely the perspective from which this form of governmental power is analyzed. This is not the perspective from below that is advocated in Foucault's retrospective account of his approach to power at the beginning of his 1975-1976 course. Nor is it simply the perspective of the state which exercises governmental power in the form of public policy, legislation and institutional design that shapes the field in which individuals act as subjects of interest and enterprise. He notes that the state is by far the most important institution in modern societies, since it sets the parameters of operation for the entire range of basic social institutions. However, as he argued in taking up the study of governmentality in 1978, it is important to study institutions from the perspective of the technologies of power that they embody (STP, 116-120). These technologies of power imply, among other things, a system of differentiations that enable action on the actions of others, particular objectives pursued by those exercising power, modes of exercising power, forms of institutionalization and degrees of rationalization (EW3, 344). Foucault's lectures on neoliberal governmentality focus on the objectives, modes of exercise and forms of rationalization of this kind of power, rather than the strategies by which they were introduced or the struggles they have provoked. They help to understand the objectives and rationality of this kind of power, but they do not pursue the strategy outlined in the first part of 'The Subject and Power' that consists in taking forms of resistance against particular modalities of power as the 'starting

① He defines these in a manner reminiscent of his definition of 'the power' in a given society at a given time in *The History of Sexuality*, *Volume One*: systems of class, caste or group domination are the result, at the level of an entire society, of 'the locking-together of power relations with relations of strategy and the results proceeding from their interaction' (EW3, 348).

point' or the 'catalyst' for their analysis (EW3, 329). They do not address the different political dynamics that allowed what David Harvey calls the construction of consent in favour of neoliberal government policies, much less the kinds and degree of economic restructuring and social differentiation that followed (Harvey 2005). None of this should be surprising when we consider that these lectures were delivered shortly before the election of Margaret Thatcher's government in Britain in May 1979 and over a year before the election of Ronald Reagan as US president in 1980. It is noteworthy, however, that in terms of the strategic and conceptual resources for the analysis of power set out in 'The Subject and Power,' these lectures fall short of a critical analysis of neoliberal governmentality.

References

Comments such as the following are representative: 'Foucault criticizes, in effect, the entire enterprise of political theory as conceived by liberal thinkers such as Walzer' (Constable 1991:269); 'Foucault's analysis [of liberalism] sets him at odds with the dominant Anglo-American philosophical conversation insofar as he denies the theoretical centrality of the normative problem of liberal justice.' (Hibbard-Swanson 2014:252).

See for example Foucault 1978:82 and 2000:327.

One reviewer suggests that these lectures represent Foucault's one and only 'diversion into contemporary political philosophy,' so long as we understand that his interest does not involve the juridical tradition of contractarian and natural rights philosophy asssociated with Rawls and Nozick but rather the political economic tradition: 'Think of the tradition that goes from Hobbes, Hume and Adam Smith to Milton Friedman, Friedrich Hayek, David Gauthier, and contemporary evolutionary game theory'（Guala 2006:429.431）. François Ewald expresses a similar view in a discussion with Gary Becker when he comments that Foucault's lectures propose a theory of liberalism but without a single quotation from a philosophical thinker of liberalism:'The sole thinkers of liberalism，in Foucault's account，are economists'（Ewald 2012）.

At the end of the fourth lecture（1 February 1978）in which he reorients the focus of this course towards a history of governmentality，he suggests that we still live in the era of a governmentality discovered in the eighteenth century: this is a form of government that acts on the population，that relies upon a form of economic knowledge or political economy and that 'would correspond to a society controlled by apparatuses of security'（STP，110）.

His 1979 Tanner lectures refer to the 'welfare state problem' as one of many ways in which the delicate adjustment between political power wielded over legal subjects and pastoral power wielded over living beings is played out in the contemporary world（EW3，307）.

Foucault could equally have called this Deleuze's hypothesis in the light of the latter's reconstruction of Nietzsche's theory of the will to power on the basis of his conception of active and reactive force（Deleuze 1983，49-68）. In their 1972 Interview 'Intellectuals and Power，' and again in a 1983 interview，Foucault acknowledged the influence of Deleuze's Nietzsche and Philosophy on his own thinking about power:'underneath the old theme of meaning，signified and signifier etc，at last the question of power，of the inequality of powers and their struggles...'（LCP，205-217; EW2，445）.

In his 1973 lecture course The Punitive Society，Foucault commented that 'Power，the legality that it serves and the illegalisms that it manages or struggles against must all be understood as a particular way of pursuing civil war'（Cited in Nigro 2011, 144). Earlier in the 1976 course, in answer to the question what was at stake in the genealogical exercise of identifying and resuscitating buried and disqualified knowledges, he relies on the struggle schema in suggesting that 'Both the specialized domain of scholarship and the disqualified knowledge people have contained the memory of combats ... And so we have the outline of what might be called a genealogy, or of multiple genealogical investigations. We have both a meticulous rediscovery of struggles and the raw memory of fights' (SMD, 8).

Foucault's discussion of power in The History of Sexuality, Volume One draws a distinction that is obscured in the English translation between power in general, as it is exercised in local relations throughout society, and 'the power' understood as the overall system of domination and control: 'power insofar as it is permanent, repetitive, inert and self-reproducing' (HS1, 93). Foucault's nominalist understanding of the latter relies on the military metaphor: "'the' power is not an institution, and not a structure; neither is it a certain strength with which some are endowed; it is the name that one attributes to a complex strategical situation in a particular society" (HS1, 93 translation modified). The original reads: 'le pouvoir, ce n'est pas une institution, et ce n'est pas une structure, ce n'est pas une certain puissance dont certains seraient dotés: c'est le nom qu'on prête à une situation stratégique complex dans un société donnée' (FHS1, 123).

Arnold Davidson's Introduction to 'Society Must Be Defended' notes Foucault's questioning of the war model of power in interviews, but then curiously disregards this critical dimension of the 1976 lectures by suggesting that 'Foucault's preoccupation with the schema of war was central to this formulation of the strategic model of power, of force-relations, a strategic model that would allow us to reorient our conception of power' (SMD, xviii). Foucault's preoccupation with the schema of war was rather the beginnings of a shift in his thinking about power away from the strategic model.

See Fontana and Bertani 2003，283; Le Blanc and Terrel 2003，16.

He defines these in a manner reminiscent of his definition of ‘the power’ in a given society at a given time in The History of Sexuality，Volume One: systems of class，caste or group domination are the result，at the level of an entire society，of ‘the locking-together of power relations with relations of strategy and the results proceeding from their interaction’（EW3，348）.

Bibliography

Artières，P. et al eds（2011）Michel Foucault，Paris: Éditions de L’ Herne.

Behrent，Michael C.（2009a）‘Liberalism Without Humanism: Michel Foucault and the Free-Market Creed，1976-1979，’ Modern Intellectual History，6:3，539-568.

———.（2009b）‘A Seventies Thing: On the Limits of Foucault’s Neoliberalism Course for Understanding the Present，’ S. Binkley and J. Capetillo eds A Foucault for the 21st Century: Governmentality，Biopolitics and Discipline in the New Millenium，Newcastle upon Tyne: Cambridge Scholars Publishing，16-29.

Buisson-Fenet，E.（2004）‘La mémoire ébréchée de la deuxième gauche，’ Vacarme: Michel Foucault 1984-2004，29，46-49.

Constable，M（1991）‘Foucault and Walzer: Sovereignty，Strategy and the State，’ Polity，24:2，269-293.

Davidson，A.（2011）‘In Praise of Counter-Conduct，’ History of the Human Sciences，24:4，25-41.

Defert，D.（1994）‘Chronologie’ in FDEI，13-64.

———.（2001）‘Le “dispositif de guerre” comme analyseur des rapports de pouvoir,' J-C Zancarini ed Lectures de Michel Foucault: A propos de "Il faut défendre la société," Lyon: ENS Éditions, 59-65.

Deleuze, G. (1983) Nietzsche and Philosophy, translated by Hugh Tomlinson. Minneapolis: University of Minnesota Press.

———. (1988) Foucault, translated by Seán Hand, foreward by Paul Bové, Minneapolis: University of Minnesota Press.

———. (1995) Negotiations 1972–1990, Martin Joughin, trans. New York: Columbia University Press.

———. (2007) Two Regimes of Madness: Texts and Interviews 1975–1995, translated by Ames Hodges and Mike Taormina. New York: Semiotext (e) [Revised Edition] .

Dreyfus H. and Rabinow, P. (1982) Michel Foucault: Beyond Structuralism and Hermeneutics, Chicago: The University of Chicago Press.

Ewald, F. (2011) 'Entretien avec François Ewald' in Artières et al eds, 47-52.

———. (2012) '"Becker on Ewald on Foucault on Becker," American Neoliberalism and Michel Foucault's 1979 Birth of Biopolitics Lectures: A conversation with Gary Becker, François Ewald, and Bernard Harcourt,' Chicago Institute for Law and Economics Working Paper No.614 (2nd series) ; Public Law and Legal Theory Working Paper No.401.

Fontana, A. and Bertani, M. (2003) 'Situating the Lectures' in C-SMD, 273-293.

Frazer N (1981) 'Foucault on Modern Power: Empirical Insights and Normative Confusions,' Praxis International, 1:3, 272-287. Reprinted in Unruly Practices (Minneapolis: University of Minnesota Press, 1989) .

Guala, F (2006) Critical Notice of Michel Foucault, Naissance de la biopolitique: Cours au Collège de France, 1978-1979 (Seuil/ Gallimard, 2004),

Economics and Philosophy，22，429-439.

Habermas J（1987）The Philosophical Discourse of Modernity，trans. Frederick G. Lawrence，Cambridge，Mass.: MIT Press.

Hibbard-Swanson J（2014）‘Liberalism，’ in L. Lawlor and J. Nales eds The Cambridge Foucault Lexicon，New York and Cambridge: Cambridge University Press，251-253.

Gros，F.（2011）‘De la supériorité des cours’ in Artières et al eds，156-159.

Harvey，D.（2005）A Brief History of Neoliberalism，Oxford: Oxford University Press.

Le Blanc，G. and Terrel，J.（2003）‘Foucault au Collège de France: un itinéraire，’ in Le Blanc，G. and Terrel，J. eds（2003）Foucault au Collège de France: un itinéraire，Bordeaux: Presses Universitaires de Bordeaux，7-26.

Nigro，R.（2011）‘Les enjeux d’une confrontation avec Marx，’ in Artières et al eds，142–146.

Patton，P.（1989）‘Taylor and Foucault on Power and Freedom，’ Political Studies XXXVII，260-276.

———.（2005）‘Foucault，Critique and Rights，’ Critical Horizons，6:1，December，267-287.

———.（2010）‘Foucault and Normative Political Philosophy’ in Timothy O’Leary and Christopher Falzon eds Foucault and Philosophy，Wiley-Blackwell，204-221.

Senellart，M.（2007）‘Course Context’ in C-STP，369-401.

———.（2011）‘Le cachalot et l’ écrivisse. Réflexions sur la rédaction des Cours au Collège de France’ in Artières et al eds，147-155.

Taylor C（1984）‘Foucault on Freedom and Truth，’ Political Theory 12（2）:152-183. Reprinted in Foucault: A Critical Reader，ed. David Couzens Hoy，

Oxford: Basil Blackwell，1986，69-102.

Walzer M（1983）‘The Politics of Michel Foucault,’ Dissent，30:481-90. Reprinted in Foucault: A Critical Reader，ed. David Couzens Hoy，Oxford: Basil Blackwell，1986，51-68.

Paul Patton ‘Deleuze’s Political Philosophy’ pp.198-219 In Daniel W. Smith，Henry Somers-Hall（Eds.），The Cambridge Companion to Deleuze © Cambridge University Press 2012.

中文简介

《福柯论权力和政府》

英语世界的政治理论家们对福柯作品的最初的评价几乎完全是否定的。20世纪80年代初，在英文翻译的《规训与惩罚》（1977）、《性史》第1卷（1978）和《巴班》（1980）出版之后，批评理论界的主要人物谴责福柯未能为自己的批评事业提供规范性基础，导致了一种党派主义和相对主义（弗雷泽1981；哈贝马斯1987）。从自由民主理论的角度来看，查尔斯·泰勒指责福柯在使用权力和自由概念时语无伦次，无法阐明积极的政治愿景（泰勒1984）。沃尔泽（Michael Walzer）将福柯描述为一个无政府主义者和虚无主义者，并将其“政治理论的灾难性弱点”归因于缺乏对民主公民和自由国家的任何考虑（沃尔泽1983）。福柯的捍卫者们倾向于同意，福柯关于权力和主观性的谱系理论确实没有为规范的政治理论做出太多贡献。

这一观点大多建立在对福柯的谱系理论的目的和他对权力的态度的混淆基础之上。批评者往往忽略了他一再坚持的观点，即他对权力理论本身并不感兴趣，而是对一种有助于分析历史上特定权力机制的“分析理论”感兴趣。批评者和捍卫者都倾向于忽视他在1975—1976年的系列演讲“必须捍卫的社会”中对自己早期观点的自我批评分析，以及在1977—1978年和1978—1979

年系列演讲中，将焦点从微观权力转移到对大众行使权力的技术（福柯 2003、2007、2008）。这与 1980 年代的最初反应有关，因为这些讲座没有出版，也没有广泛流传。然而，回顾过去，政治理论家们对福柯的最初的回应，体现了他们对福柯 1975 年至 1979 年在法兰西学院（Collège de France）的演讲中的福柯政治哲学的新发展一无所知。既然这些讲座已经出版并有英文译本，我们就有充分的理由重新审视福柯对权力的正统看法。

1977—1978 年关于安全和治理的讲座，1978—1979 年关于安全、领土、人口，以及 1978—1979 年关于自由主义和新自由主义的讲座，“生物政治学的诞生”，特别有意思。在 1977—1978 年的演讲过程中，福柯才开始提出一种替代 1976 年之前他在作品中使用的“战争—镇压”的权力模式。从微观权力到治理的转变最终导致了一种新的权力分析，即福柯在 1982 年《主体与权力》中总结的政府的治理行为。虽然这并没有为可接受或反对不可接受的权力形式提供规范标准，但它确实提供了概念资源，用以回应弗雷泽、哈贝马斯、泰勒和其他人提出的一些认为福柯自己的概念混乱的主张（帕顿 1989 年、2013 年）。福柯 1978—1979 年的演讲《生物政治学的诞生》概述了在 18 世纪中叶左右出现在欧洲的自由政府的一些显著特征，然后他转向了对德国和美国新自由主义的分析。这些直接驳斥了沃尔泽对于福柯忽视自由国家的指责，即使福柯的这些讨论没有从规范政治理论的角度来看待自由国家。

本文旨在概述福柯权力观在 20 世纪 70 年代的发展历程，并展示其论文“主体与权力”（The Subject and Power）是如何反映这一点的，该论文于 1982 年首次作为《德莱弗斯与拉比诺》的附录出版。这篇文章是福柯写过的最接近于他对权力研究方法的明确陈述的文章。包括我在内的许多评论者，倾向于将其视为或多或少地与在 1970 年代早期到中期的一些访谈中所阐述的方法保持一致，尽管其论文使用的术语和概念是早期工作中没有的。直到 1976 年，福柯一直依赖于一种身体、力量和斗争的客观语言，而“主体和权力”则回归到一种更为熟悉的语言，即人类的能动性和自由，用以描述权力行使的条件。

Against Maximizing Expected Utility

Bradley Monton

1. Introduction

The key concept of this paper is the concept of *expected utility*; I'll start by explaining that concept. According to orthodox decision theory, an agent's opinions and preferences should be modelled by a probability function and a utility function. The probability function captures an agent's subjective degree of belief: for example, if you believe that there is an 80% chance of rain tomorrow, then your opinion is modelled with a probability function that assigns 0.8 to the proposition that it will rain tomorrow. The utility function captures how much an agent values various states of the world. For example, you might not want it to rain tomorrow – your utility function might assign 5 units of utility (called "utiles") to the state of the world where it doesn't rain tomorrow, and -3 utiles to the state of the world where it does rain tomorrow.

Since the utility function captures your preferences, to fulfill your preferences you want to maximize utility. But typically you are uncertain about which states of the world will obtain – in the face of such uncertainity, orthodox decision theory says that one should maximize *expected* utility.① To calculate expected utility, divide the

① For example, to quote Alan Hájek (2014, 555-6): orthodox decision theory "specifies that decision makers should maximize expected utility – period. It says that it is wrong always, everywhere, and for anyone, to do otherwise."

possible states of the world into a mutually exclusive and exhaustive set，multiply the probability times the utility for each state，and then add. For example，consider a coin flip，where the probability of Heads is 1/2，the probability of Tails is 1/2，you will get 4 utiles if the coin lands Heads，and -2 utiles is the coin lands Tails. The expected utility of the coin flip is calculated as follows:

EU（coin flip）= P（Heads）xU（Heads）+ P（Tails）xU（Tails）

=1/2 x 4+1/2 x（-2）

=1

Assuming that nothing happens if one doesn’t do the coin flip，then EU（not doing coin flip）=0. Since the expected utility of doing the coin flip is greater than the expected utility of not doing the coin flip，then if these are one’s only two options，according to orthodox decision theory one should maximize expected utility and do the coin flip.

I reject orthodox decision theory. I will argue maximizing expected utility is sometimes an unreasonable – perhaps even irrational – decision procedure to follow. Moreover，I maintain that this is something that we（collectively）should have known for about 300 years（going back to the St. Petersburg game，which I’ll discuss shortly）. Those who have been aware that maximizing expected utility is a bad rule to follow have made proposals for how to avoid maximizing expected utility. In this paper，I’ll present and defend one particular proposal: when it comes to decision-making，for possibilities that have very small probabilities of occurring，we should discount those probabilities down to zero，regardless of the utilities associated with those possibilities.

I don’t necessarily think that this proposal is the right one – I can be very happy if this paper inspires readers to come up with a better proposal for how to avoid maximizing expected utility. But what is interesting about the proposal I defend in this paper is that it has been proposed multiple times, independently, by various philosophers and probability theorists, starting from around 300 years ago. Despite that, discussions of the proposal in the literature are few and far between. I'll give a far more systematic discussion of the proposal than I have ever seen in the literature, by presenting and critically evaluating six different justifications of the proposal.

I've stated my proposal in one sentence above, but as you can imagine, that sentence leaves open questions about the actual content of the proposal. After talking about the six different justifications of the proposal, I'll give answers to three important open questions about the content of the proposal. As you'll see, my discussion will bring up issues closely related to Pascal's Wager – Pascal's pragmatic argument for believing in God, on the basis that doing so maximizes expected utility. My last main section of the paper will take up Pascal's Wager. And stick around for the conclusion, with a big-picture thought about decision theory.

2. The St. Petersburg Game

In 1713, Nicolaus (I) Bernoulli (who I'll call "Nicolaus" for short) wrote a letter presenting the St Petersburg game; in 1738 his cousin Daniel Bernoulli first published the game.[①] The game is played by flipping a fair coin until it lands heads, and then the game stops. The prize is $\$2n$, where n is the number of flips.[②] The game is treated as paradoxical because the expected value of the game is infinite, but

① Robert Martin (2017) says that Nicolaus and Daniel are brothers, but this is (as far as I can tell) mistaken; Dutka (1988, 18) says that they are cousins, and explains the family relationships carefully. Spieß (1975, 563) also says that they are cousins.

② In Daniel Bernoulli's (1738) version of the game, the price is $2n/2$ ducats, but the formulation I give is the standard contemporary one. Daniel Bernoulli says that he would pay 20 ducats to play the St. Petersburg game; presumably he would pay \$40 to play the standard contemporary version.

intuitively people aren't willing to pay that much to play – in fact, it is intuitively irrational to give the majority of one's wealth to play a game that only has a tiny chance of yielding significant reward.

Some people are tempted to reject that intuition. Harris Nover and Alan Hájek (2004, 309) write:

> in response to the St. Petersburg paradox, there is something to be said for the bullet-biting response: 'the game *should* be valued infinitely, and any intuition to the contrary should be dismissed as an artifact of our finite minds not fully appreciating the true nature of the game; we should learn to live with decision theory's verdict' .

I maintain that this bullet-biting response is mistaken. Let's suppose that our finite minds cannot appreciate the true nature of infinite games. Admitting that doesn't resolve the paradox, because there is a finite version of the St. Petersburg game that is also paradoxical. The paradox arises in the finite case because the expected value of the game is high, while rational people are not willing to pay more than a low amount to play.

Suppose that we truncate the St. Petersburg game at 999 tosses – if one gets tails 999 times in a row, then the game ends and the prize is what one would get if heads landed in the 1000th toss ($21000) . The expected value of this game is $1000. But rational people aren't willing to pay more than about $100 to play the original St. Petersburg game, and this finite version is worth even less, so again there is a disconnect between what rational people are willing to pay and what the strategy of maximizing expected utility recommends.

Daniel Bernoulli's (1738) now-standard (and correct) reply to the original

St. Petersburg game is that money has diminishing marginal utility, so while the expected monetary *value* of the finite game may be $1000, the expected *utility* of the game is much less. But we can just present new versions of the St. Petersburg game, replacing monetary values with utilities.

My favorite version is a days-of-life version, because I do not treat life-days as having diminishing marginal utility. I value two days of living twice as much as I value one day of living, I value 10,000 days of living 10 times as much as I value 1,000 days of living, and so on.[①] Suppose that you discover that, if you do nothing, you will die on The Critical Day, which is currently 1000 days from now. But you are offered a pill that with probability 1/2 will extend your day of death past The Critical Day by exactly 2 days, with probability 1/4 will extend your day of death past The Critical Day by exactly 4 days, and so on. (For a finite version of this game we can cap it at 21000 days.) This pill has a cost though – it brings The Critical Day closer to the present by X number of days. How large would X have to be before you are unwilling to take the pill?

Since I do not treat life-days as having diminishing marginal utility, according to orthodox decision theory my expected utility of taking the pill (ignoring the cost) is an infinite number of life days (for the uncapped version) or 1000 life-days (for the capped version) . But for either version, I am not willing to take the pill if the cost is moving The Critical Day 999 days closer to the present – I wouldn't take the pill if X were more than 50. Why not? If I take the pill when X=999, there's a 7/8 chance that I'll live for less than 10 more days, and that would be sad. If I don't take the pill I'll

① Some interlocutors have objected that as a practical matter I couldn't have such insight into the details of my own utility function. I think that I do, but instead of arguing that point, we can just set me aside: imagine a hypothetical agent who does treat life-days in the way I'm describing, and consider how you would advise such a hypothetical agent who is presented with the days-of-life version of the St. Petersburg game that I will describe.

live for 1000 more days – much better! But orthodox decision theory says that I should take the X=999 pill, because the expected utility of taking the pill is greater than the expected utility of not taking it. I am not willing to maximize expected utility here, and I maintain that maximizing expected utility here is an unreasonable thing to do.①

Now is a good time to make explicit that the scope of my paper is not limited to non-ideal boundedly rational agents like you and me; I intend my reasoning to also apply to imaginary ideally rational agents. My rejection of the orthodox decision-theoretic answer to the finite days-of-life version of the St. Petersburg game has nothing to do with the fact that I am bounded in my rationality – it's not the case that, if only I were more rational or could do some more sophisticated math, I could see that taking the X=999 pill is the right choice. For an agent who shares my utilities about days of life, taking the X=999 pill is so unreasonable that I take giving that answer as a datum in determining what counts as irrational behavior.

Note that there's not an unreasonable amount of idealization in the setup of the finite days-of-life version of the St. Petersburg game. Hájek points out that for the original infinite version of the St. Petersburg game, we are "up to our necks in idealization" (Hájek 2014, 565), and he gives that as a reason to accept the prima facie surprising orthodox-decision-theoretic claim that the game should be valued infinitely. But the finite days-of-life St. Petersburg game isn't overly idealized like that – while we may not currently have the medical resources to make such pills, we are still operating within the general constraints of the actual world (we are not

---

① One might object that there is a disutility associated with the feeling of sadness, and that needs to be taken into account in deciding whether to take the X=999 pill. I agree, but for me at least, the disutility associated with such a feeling of sadness is very small compared to the full amount of utility associated with each day of life, so such feelings do not play a significant role in my expected utility calculation. Those who follow the adage "don't cry over spilt milk" should be on board with not assigning much disutility to these feelings of sadness or regret at the game not going the way one wanted.

dealing with infinite bankrolls or infinite sequences of coin flips, for example) .① So when orthodox decision theory gives an unreasonable prescription for the finite days-of-life version of the St. Petersburg game (the prescription that one should take the X=999 pill), we shouldn't defend orthodox decision theory by saying that the prescription is permissible because we're talking about a highly idealized impossible situation. We're talking about a situation within the realm of future possible development, and orthodox decision theory gives the wrong answer, so orthodox decision theory has to go.

3. Pascal's Mugging

These St. Petersburg-style games are effective in illustrating a problem with orthodox decision theory, but the games are more complicated than they need to be to illustrate the problem. The relevant feature of the St. Petersburg-style games is that there is a very low probability of getting a very high reward. For a simpler game with that feature, consider Pascal's Mugging (Bostrom 2009) .

Pascal's Mugging is a game where an agent named 'Pascal' has an opportunity to pay some money for a very small probability of getting a very large (but finite) amount of utility from a seeming mugger – utility both for Pascal and for lots of sweet little orphans. (In Bostrom's scenario the probability is one in 10 quadrillion.)

① Anti-aging and life-extension technologies are actively under development by reputable scientists, but immunity from accidental death is (alas) not. So to make the game more realistic, we could add utility that compensates for the chance that (via accidental death) one might not live that long. We could do that by, for example, offering to give the person more and more money the longer they live. Some interlocutors have been skeptical of the possibility of a pill accomplishing all that I describe. But the pill is just an artifice for simplicity – a more realistic account involves a game-playing, coin-flipping league of assassins and life-extension scientists.

Since the utility associated with the mugger's offer is high enough, Pascal calculates that the expected utility of giving the money is positive. No matter what non-zero probability Pascal assigns to the hypothesis that he and the orphans will get the large amount of utility, there is a corresponding utility that he and the orphans could be offered such that Pascal deems the expected utility of the game to be positive, and hence gives the mugger the money.

Proponents of consequentialism should be concerned about Pascal's Mugging. Consequentialists hold that "What we ought subjectively to do is the act whose outcome has the greatest *expected* goodness" (Parfit 1985, 25). For example, effective altruists are (typically) consequentialists; they donate with the goal of maximizing expected utility, and they are explicit that it can be more valuable to donate to a cause that has a small chance of having a large impact than a cause that has a large chance of having a small impact. By blindly maximizing expected utility as Bostrom's Pascal does above, effective altruists could spend an unreasonably large amount of money to, for example, slightly reduce the probability of a catastrophic scenario that already has a very small probability of occurring. (More on this in Section 5.6.)

Those who maximize expected utility will most likely end up with undesirable results when presented with the situations above. They will spend a lot of their wealth to play the St. Petersburg game, or give it to the grandiosely-promising mugger, or donate it to address very-small-probability causes – and they can foresee that, based on their own probability judgements, it's very likely that they will have nothing to show for it. Expected utility maximizers, when faced with 1000 more days of life, will take a pill that will cause them to most likely end up with just a few more days of life. In short, in these situations, expected utility maximizers are needlessly (with high probability) poor and on death's door, and I do not want to be one.

In the next section, I'll discuss how to avoid maximizing expected utility. But first, let's consider an objection. Some might admit that in the situations I've presented above, expected utility maximizers would most likely end up poor and on death's door, but point out that it doesn't follow that they are irrational. The objectors might say that the situation is analogous to what the two-boxers face in Newcomb's problem. In Newcomb's problem, a predictor puts $1 million in a box for you to take if and only if the predictor predicts that you will not also take a box with $1000. According to two-boxers like David Lewis (1981), the rational thing to do is to take both boxes, even though you will most likely not get the $1 million as a result: "The reason why we [two-boxers] are not rich is that the riches were reserved for the irrational" (Lewis 1981, 377). Could the expected utility maximizer make a similar move?

My answer is "no"; the situations are importantly disanalogous. In Newcomb's problem, the reason the two-boxers aren't rich is that there is an agent, the predictor, who is rewarding irrationality. As two-boxers Gibbard and Harper (1978, 153) put it, "If someone is very good at predicting behavior and rewards predicted irrationality richly, then irrationality will be richly rewarded."① Even if one replaced the predictor in Newcomb's problem with an inanimate predicting machine, it is still the case that the person playing the game is being analyzed and (from the two-boxer's perspective, at least) the fact that the person has a rational intention-forming mechanism leads to the person being penalized. For people presented with a St. Petersburg-style game or Pascal's Mugging, in contrast, there is no evaluation of their mental state by another agent or a machine. As a result, there is nothing external that penalizes the people for the decisions they make – when expected utility

① The original quote has a semi-colon in place of the comma; I read that as a typo.

maximizers end up poor and on death's door, they've done it to themselves.

4. Discounting Very Small Probabilities

So how can we avoid the fate of the expected utility maximizers? The simplicity of Pascal's Mugging makes clear that there are only two factors that are put in to yield the problematic result: the high-utility possibility and the small probability associated with that possibility. So to avoid the fate of the expected utility maximizers, we need to either limit that high utility number or discount that small probability number.①

The limiting utility move is not viable. A utility cap would be needed, but such a cap is ethically problematic. Here's why a cap would be needed: if one instead endorsed a principle that slowed the growth of utility without imposing a cap, then I could simply present a new version of the St. Petersburg game or Pascal's Mugging that offered utilities high enough to overcome the slowing-growth principle. But a cap is ethically problematic because one can always add more agents into the utility calculation – one can always consider the possibility of more sweet little orphans (either in existence now or in the future) who can benefit from one's decisions. I maintain, and so should you, that the utilities of those added sweet little orphans matter, regardless of how many sweet little orphans are already in existence.②

So limiting the high utility number isn't viable. This leaves the only other option: when it comes to decision-making, one should discount small probabilities, down to

① At least, those are the two options under the assumption that preferences of an agent should be modeled via a utility function and a probability function; I'll say more about that in the conclusion.

② What if there are already an infinite number of sweet little orphans in existence? Even then I maintain that adding more ones matters, as I argue in Monton 2010.

zero.①

Here's why going to zero is needed: if one instead had a principle that lowered the probability numbers without reducing them to zero, I could simply present a new game that offered utilities high enough to compensate for those reduced probabilities. (For a mathematical example of this, see Buchak 2014, 73.)

Here's why the "when it comes to decision-making" qualifier is in there. When it comes to one's doxastic state, and updating one's doxastic state in response to new evidence, one should not discount small probabilities down to zero. The reason is that, in the Bayesian framework at least, a proposition that receives probability zero will always receive probability zero; an agent who assigns zero probability to a hypothesis is insensitive to new evidence regarding that hypothesis. But one should be sensitive to new evidence regarding propositions to which one initially assigns a small but non-zero probability, so when it comes to updating, one should not discount such probabilities down to zero.

My proposal is that for decision-making, small probabilities should be discounted down to zero but I know you're itching to ask: "how small?" My answer for now is "very small". Don't hate me! I'll have much more to say about this below.

This discounting idea is not original with me – in fact, it originated with the person who came up with the St. Petersburg paradox, Nicolaus (I) Bernoulli

---

① There are also mixed options: instead of just limiting the utilities, or just discounting the probabilities, one could combine the moves – one could hold that high-utility possibilities need discounts on their probabilities, and high-probability possibilities need limits on their utilities. I'm not a fan of mixed options; there are situations where they give unreasonable prescriptions. Imagine, for example, that you seem to experience death and then show up in a wonderful afterlife, and hence have you good reason to assign a high probability to the high-utility hypothesis that heaven exists and you are in it. It strikes me as unreasonable to discount the probability of that hypothesis just because that hypothesis has high utility – when all the evidence points to heaven existing and you being in it, it's unreasonable to say "this is too good to be true". (of course, there are many reasons to doubt one's perceptions, but high utility by itself is not a good one.)

himself.[①] In 1714, Nicolaus, in a letter to Pierre Rémond de Montmort, endorses the following solution to his St. Petersburg paradox:"cases that have a very small probability must be neglected and assumed to be zero" [②], and as a result he says that the expected utility assigned to the St. Petersburg game by orthodox reasoning is too high. Nicolaus, unfortunately, doesn't have much more to say about his solution, but he does say: "This is a remark which deserves to be thoroughly studied." [③] That thorough study has not yet happened; this paper is my belated attempt to rectify that.

I'll henceforth neologistically call that discounting-to-zero procedure "Nicolausian discounting". I endorse the doctrine that one should engage in Nicolausian discounting. But why? Why, when it comes to decision-making, should very small probabilities be discounted down to zero? There's a sense in which I've already given an answer: in the games presented in the previous section, we rational agents don't want to maximize expected utility, and capping utilities is a bad option, so discounting probabilities must be the good option. But I recognize that more would need to be said – and indeed, here and there in the literature, some more has been said. Building on those limited discussions in the literature, I'll now present and critically evaluate six reasons for engaging in Nicolausian discounting, in order from my least favorite to my most. (Impatient readers have permission to skim ahead – my discussion of the first two reasons is less suited for those uninterested in decision-theory history.)

---

① Interestingly, none of the people I discuss in this paper who endorse something akin to Nicolaus's discounting move (d'Alembert, Daniel Bernoulli, Buffon, Smith, Schwitzgebel, Buchak, Borel, Jordan, and Condorcet) cites Nicolaus as being the originator of this idea. In fact, the three contemporary philosophers I focus on in the next section (Smith, Schwitzgebel, and Buchak) do not cite anyone as being a precursor; they each introduce the idea *de novo*. (I don't mean this as a critique – it's just interesting.)

② This is my translation; the original is "les cas qui ont une tres petite probabilité doivent être negligés et censés pour nuls". Nicolaus's letter is published in Spieß 1975, 558-9.

③ This is my translation; the original is "C'est une remarque qui merite d'étre bien approfondie."

5. Six Reasons for Discounting

5.1 D'Alembert and "Certainement"

Jean Le Rond d'Alembert (1761) was the first to propose in print discounting very small probabilities down to zero.① D'Alembert endorses the following rule: "when the probability is very small, it must, in the ordinary course of life, be regarded as zero, & treated as such." ② His initial rationale for this looks promising. He considers the standard rule of valuing a game by calculating the expected value (multiplying the probabilities and the utilities, and summing), and he says that the St. Petersburg game shows that this rule is flawed.③ If instead one follows the rule of discounting very small probabilities down to zero and then valuing the St. Petersburg game via its expected value, one gets a more reasonable valuation for the game. (At least, one does if one picks a suitable threshold for what probabilities count as very small – more on this later.) So d'Alembert says that the fact that his discounting rule enables one to assign a reasonable value to the St. Petersburg game is evidence in

① The historian of probability Isaac Todhunter (1865, section 644, page 344) incorrectly writes: "The doctrine that a very small chance is practically zero is due to D'Alembert". But we can give d'Alembert credit for being the first to propose the idea in print.

② D'Alembert 1761, Memoir 10, Section 13, page 11, my translation. The original is: "On peut donc, ce me semble, poser pour régle, que quand la probabilité est fort petite, on doit dans l' usage ordinaire de la vie, la regarder comme zéro, & la traiter comme telle."

③ D'Alembert (1761), Memoir 10, Section 2, page 2. He imagines the St. Petersburg game offered to Pierre, and says the standard way of valuing games has the consequence that Pierre must give an infinite sum for the game to be fair. He then writes: "independent of the fact that an *infinite sum* is a chimera, there is no person who would give it in order to play this game, I say no infinite sum, nor even a rather modest sum. The rule [of valuing a game via its expected value] appears therefore to be flawed". This is my translation; the original is: "indépendamment de ce qu'une *somme infinie* est une chimere, il n'y a personne qui voulût donner pour jouer à ce jeu, je ne dis pas une somme infinie, mais même une somme assez modique. La régle paroît donc être en défaut".

favor of his rule.

So far，I agree. But d'Alembert recognizes that he needs to give more justification for his rule than that it gives a reasonable value to the St. Petersburg game，and it is in this further justification that he makes some problematic moves. D'Alembert considers a simplified version of the St. Petersburg game – essentially a Pascal's Mugging scenario. Pierre has the opportunity to pay 1 écu to play a game where if a coin lands heads for the first time on the hundredth toss，Pierre will get 2100 écus，and otherwise he'll get nothing. By the orthodox way of calculating the value of that game in terms of the expected value，the game is fair，but d'Albembert says that Pierre should not play. Why not?

There's an interesting translation issue here，so let's start with the French:

> Pierre ne doit pas donner cet écu; parce qu'il le perdra *certainement*，& que *croix* arrivera *certainement* avant le centiéme coup，bien qu'il ne doive pas arriver *nécessairement*.（d'Alembert 1761，Memoir 10，Section 10，pages 8-9）

You might think that this should be translated as something like:

> Pierre must not give this écu，because he will *certainly* lose it，& heads will *certainly* arrive before the hundredth toss，even though it will not *necessarily* arrive.

And indeed，this is the sort of way it is standardly translated.[1]

The problem with this translation is that it has the consequence that what

[1] See Todhunter（1865，section 472，page 262），Samuelson（1977,43），and Pulskamp（2009,4）.

d'Alembert is saying doesn't make sense – at least, in this context, I don't see how to understand this distinction between the claim "X will certainly happen" and the claim "X will necessarily happen". We should wonder whether that translation is uncharitable – and indeed, there is another way to translate "certainement" besides as "certainly". It can also mean "most probably" or even "probably". ① On that more charitable interpretation of d'Alembert, we have him saying:

> Pierre must not give this écu, because he will most probably lose it, and heads will most probably arrive before the hundredth toss, even though it will not necessarily arrive.

It's true that most probably, Pierre won't get 100 tails in a row. The problem now is that we lose the motivation for d'Alembert to say that Pierre should not give the écu. It's true that he most probably will lose it, but he might get a huge reward. What's so bad about that?

The *certainement/nécessairement* distinction isn't the only one d'Alembert uses to try to elucidate his point. He also says that getting 100 tails in a row is not "possible *physiquement*", even though it is "*métaphysiquement* possible" (d'Alembert 1761,

---

① For "most probably" see *Collins French Dictionary*, https://www.collinsdictionary.com/dictionary/french-english/certainement, archived on 2017-6-22 at http://www.webcitation.org/6rPE8Vq9m; and http://www.french-linguistics.co.uk/dictionary/certainement.html, archived on 2017-6-22 at http://www.webcitation.org/6rPFZ2Upb. For "probably" see *Cambridge Dictionary*, http://dictionary.cambridge.org/dictionary/french-english/certainement, archived on 2017-6-22 at http://www.webcitation.org/6rPEaLAsm.

D'Alembert's contemporary Buffon also used the term "certainement" to describe a measure of probability that comes in degrees – see Hey, Neugebauer, and Pasca (2010, footnote 2): "we should warn readers at the outset that Buffon uses the word certainty not in the absolute sense that we currently use.… He refers to certainties of different orders and hence uses the word certainty as a synonym for probability or likelihood."

Memoir 10, Section 12, page 10). The distinction between physical possibility and metaphysical possibility makes sense in this context; the problem is that the claim that it's physically impossible to get 100 tails in a row seems false. On the contemporary standard way of understanding physical possibility, at least, getting 100 tails in a row is physically possible – in fact, that string of results has the same probability as any other string of results one gets from flipping a fair coin 100 times.

But let's again be charitable to d'Alembert – he's working with a different understanding of physical possibility. He clarifies this when he considers rolling double-sixes on two dice 100 times in a row, and says that such a sequence of events is physically impossible "because this has never happened, and will never happen."①

This claim is interestingly non-alethic. D'Alembert is not saying that such a sequence of events *could* not happen; he's just saying that it has not happened in the past, and it will not happen in the future. His claim may be correct.② But suppose it turns out that just moments ago, Lily flipped a fair coin and got 100 tails in a row – d'Alembert's reasoning about the St. Petersburg game would no longer go through. This is unreasonable – we shouldn't have to change our philosophical analysis of the St. Petersburg game as a result of what Lily just did with her coin.

Let's sum up. D'Alembert infamously got lots of things wrong when it comes to probability theory (he endorsed the gambler's fallacy, for example). And I'm not particularly impressed by the reasons he gives for this rule of discounting very small probabilities down to zero. But I think he's right to endorse the rule, even if he hasn't hit on the right reasons. Let's see if his contemporary, Georges-Louis Leclerc de

---

① D'Alembert 1761, Memoir 10, Section 12, page 10; the original is "parce que cela n'est jamais arrivé, & n'arrivera jamais."

② I intend this to, in part, be an explanation of d'Alembert's reasoning in response to Paul Samuelson (1977, 43), who disdainfully quotes d'Alembert with parenthetical interrogation marks, as follows: "it is *physically* impossible because it has never [?] happened and never will [??] happen."

Buffon, can do any better.

5.2 Buffon and the Probability of Dying in a Day

Buffon (1777, Section 16) considers the St. Petersburg game, and says that there are two reasons the game should not be valued highly. One reason is the diminishing marginal utility of money; the other is:"the probability must be considered as zero as soon as it is very small, that is, below 1/10,000" .① Setting aside the issue of diminishing marginal utility, Buffon's 1/10,000 threshold would lead one to value the St. Petersburg game with prize \$2*n* at \$13, since the probability of getting heads on the 13th toss is 1/8, 192, while the probability of getting heads on the 14th toss is 1/16, 384. So Buffon's discounting strategy gives a reasonable result to the St. Petersburg game, and that provides some evidence in its favor, but what further reason does Buffon give for his discounting strategy? And why the 1/10,000 threshold?

Buffon's reasoning starts by considering what sorts of possibilities people ignore, and what the associated probabilities are for those possibilities. For an possibility one doesn't care about that much, one might be willing to ignore it even if the probability is not very low. So Buffon considers an important possibility that one cares a lot about: death. But he is not interested in just any person's fear of death – he's interested in the fear of death in someone "when reason has attained its full maturity and the experience all its force", and he considers a 56-year-old man to be such a person (Buffon 1777, Section 8) . Consulting mortality tables, he sees that the probability of a 56-year-old man dying in the course of 24 hours is 1/10,189. But such a man who is doing well "has no fear of death in the 24 hours" . Buffon then says:

from this I conclude that any equal or smaller probability must be regarded as zero, since any fear or any hope below ten thousand must not affect us or even

① All quotations in this subsection on Buffon are from the excellent translation by Hey, Neugebauer, and Pasca (2010) .

occupy for a single moment the heart or the mind. (Buffon 1777, Section 8)

Since such a man is willing to treat his death in a day as a zero-probability possibility, we should treat any probability below 1/10,000 as zero. (Buffon calls the sort of certainty such a man has that he will not die in a day "moral certainty", and distinguishes it from the stronger notion of "physical certainty" .)

Daniel Bernoulli, intriguingly, endorses Buffon's discounting strategy, though Bernoulli takes issue with the choice of threshold. Buffon quotes from a 1762 letter that Bernoulli sent him, where Bernoulli writes:

> I strongly approve, Sir, your way to estimate the limits of moral probabilities; you consult the nature of man by his actions … you conclude that one ten-thousandth of probability should not make any impression in the mind of man, and consequently this one ten-thousandth has to be regarded as an absolute nothing. (quoted in Buffon 1777, Section 8, footnote 3)

Bernoulli then says that some 56-year-old men are ill, and such men would rightly fear dying in the next day. Bernoulli points out that only healthy men would regard the probability of their death in the next day as an absolute nothing. Since the mortality table for 56-year-old men includes both ill men and healthy men, the probability of death of a healthy man is much less than 1/10,000. Bernoulli concludes: "I do not fight your principle, but it seems rather to lead to 1/100,000 rather than to 1/10, 000." (quoted in Buffon 1777, Section 8, footnote 3)

After quoting this letter, Buffon makes a slight concession: "there is maybe a little more than ten thousand to bet against one, that a man, healthy and strong will not die in the twenty-four hours; but it is hardly necessary to increase this probability to one hundred thousand." Buffon then says that "this difference [between a 1/10,000 threshold and a 1/100,000 threshold], although very large, changes nothing of the main implications that I draw from my principle." And indeed, I agree. With the 1/100, 000 threshold, the value the St. Petersburg game with prize \$2*n* would be \$16; so that's also a reasonable result. But what about the reasoning that leads to either of these thresholds?

Well, there is certainly a lot to criticize in the details. First, people other than 56-year-old men have the full maturity of reason and the full force of experience – though perhaps a 21st-century Buffon would argue that, whatever a healthy person's mortality rate is in a day, that determines what that person's probability-discounting threshold is.

Second, many even healthy people do rationally fear dying in the next 24 hours – for many healthy people, there are moments where the fear of immediate death occupies their hearts and their minds. Perhaps Buffon would maintain that that only happens in frightening situations, where the probability of death in a day is greater than 1/10,000. But even in everyday life situations, some rational-seeming people are generally more fearful – such people would sometimes worry about death even if the probability is much below 1/10,000.

Third, why the restriction to a day? Why not two days, or 17 seconds? Buffon doesn't give a reason for that arbitrary time frame.

Fourth, Buffon picks a person's own death because he says that "of all the possible moral probabilities, the one that most affects man in general is the fear of death", but that is arguably false. One could care more about the death of one's family than one's own death. Effective altruists are taking steps to reduce the probability of human civilization ending, and while that has a lower probability than the death of a 56-year-old man in a day, it's a correspondingly more significant event.

But despite my criticisms of the details, there's something to be said for the general idea that we should look to rational-seeming people's behavior to adjudicate between decision theories. There are very-small-probability possibilities that rational-seeming people ignore (for example, no one is worried about death via half of their brain quantum-tunneling out of their body in the next day), and we want our decision theory to capture that. One could object that the *ideally* rational agent should take all such possibilities into account, in the standard-decision-theoretic way – but this would lead to the ideally rational agent giving up many days of life to play the days-of-life version of the St. Petersburg game, and handing over the money in a Pascal's mugging scenario. Those are not reasonable results.

So let's continue to look for reasons to follow the "Nicolausian discounting" rule I'm endorsing: when it comes to decision-making, for possibilities that have very small probabilities of occurring, we should discount those probabilities down to zero, regardless of the utilities associated with those possibilities.

5.3 The Virtues (and Vices) of Tolerance

Nicolausian discounting enables one to assign a reasonable value to the St. Petersburg game. It also enables one to assign a reasonable value to the Pasadena game, a game invented by Nover and Hájek (2004), that is like the St. Petersburg game, but with the distinctive feature that the possible outcomes of the game switch in value between negative and positive, depending on whether the game ends with an odd or even toss.① Nover and Hájek show that the Pasadena game has the

① My claim that Nicolausian discounting allows one to assign a reasonable value to the Pasadena game is controversial. For example, Kenny Easwaran (2008) argues that the correct value of the Pasadena game is $ln 2, and Hájek (2014, page 551, footnote 12) proves that a discounting strategy like mine cannot assign the Pasadena game that irrational value. But I don't know of anyone who believes that the case for valuing the Pasadena game at $ln 2 is conclusive – for example, Easwaran (2008, 634) suggests that his reasoning has more of a "pragmatic" than a "rational" basis. So my rejection of the $ln 2 value is simply a bullet I have to bite.

problematic feature that it has no unique expected utility, because there is no unique value for the sum of the probability times the utility for each of the infinite possible outcomes of the game.

Nicholas J. J. Smith (2014) wants to solve the problems for orthodox decision theory posed by the Pasadena game, and to do so he endorses the following principle:

For any lottery featuring in any decision problem faced by any agent, there is an *e*>0 such that the agent need not consider outcomes of that lottery of probability less than *e* in coming to a fully rational decision. (Smith 2014, 472)

Smith calls this the "Rationally Negligible Probabilities principle" (RNP).

D'Alembert, Buffon, Nicolaus and Daniel Bernoulli, and I all endorse RNP. In fact, we endorse a claim that's stronger than RNP – we endorse the claim that one *should* not consider very-small-probability outcomes in coming to a fully rational decision, while Smith just holds that it is *rationally permissible* not to consider such very-small-probability outcomes.

Why does Smith endorse RNP? One reason is that it can yield a reasonable result for the Pasadena game. But Smith recognizes that more would need to be said – so he gives the following argument based on *tolerance* reasoning. His argument in a nutshell is: decision theory specifies that rational agents should ignore outcomes with zero probability; given that decision-making is a practical activity, infinite precision cannot be required; so instead "there must be some finite tolerance – some positive threshold such that ignoring all outcomes whose probabilities lie below this threshold counts as satisfying the norm" of rationality (Smith 2014, 472).

I have concerns with decision-theoretic reasoning based on tolerance. Obviously I am happy with RNP, but my worry is that if one blindly applies tolerance-based reasoning one will get unacceptable results. Here are two examples of what I have in mind.①

First, suppose that you assign proposition A some probability *k*, and you assign its negation, ~A, probability 1-*k*. In accordance with the probability calculus, you assign proposition A&~A probability 0. But now let's apply tolerance reasoning: decision-making is a practical activity, so infinite precision cannot be required, so there is an *e* >0 such that it's rationally permissible to assign proposition A&~A probability *e*. It follows that P（A）+ P（~A）+ P（A&~A）>1, and hence by tolerance reasoning it's rationally permissible to believe that probabilities can sum to greater than 1. I conclude that this tolerance reasoning is unacceptable.

Here's one more argument for that same conclusion. Suppose you are a scientist who assigns probability *b* to hypothesis B, and probability *c* to hypothesis C. It's taken you much research to arrive at these probability assignments, and you've done so with the goal of answering the important scientific question of whether *c* is higher than *b*. You have discovered that *c* is slightly higher. But by tolerance reasoning: decision-making is a practical activity, and infinite precision cannot be required, so it's rationally permissible to treat *c* as slightly lower than *b*. So you report the results of your research as showing that hypothesis C is less likely than hypothesis B, despite the fact that *c* > *b*.

I maintain this is unreasonable – and Smith would presumably agree. What this shows is that Smith does not endorse tolerance reasoning in general in decision theory – tolerance reasoning can be used to support RNP, but it can also be used to support unreasonable results. Perhaps there is a more limited form of tolerance reasoning that supports RNP but elegantly evades the unreasonable results – I'd be happy to see that reasoning spelled out, and in principle I'd be happy to endorse it. But I don't

① And for many more pages of trenchant criticism of Smith's "tolerance" move, see Hájek（2014, 551-560）– my criticism here is complementary to his.

see that reasoning spelled out by Smith, and I don't have any insights to add. For now, my view is that there are better, non-tolerance-based, reasons to support RNP – I'll present three such reasons in the next three subsections. (But for the first two reasons, I still have some qualms, as you'll see.)

5.4 Loss Aversion

I think that it is sometimes rationally permissible to desire to maximize expected utility. But there are other desires that are rationally permissible too, that conflict with the desire to maximize expected utility. One such desire is the desire to *avoid loss*. Eric Schwitzgebel (2015, 283), for example, has this desire: he says that he will sometimes make a decision that increases the chances of avoiding loss, even if that decision is not the one that maximizes expected utility. He goes on to say:

> I might even reasonably decide that at some level of improbability –1/1030?– no finite positive or negative outcome could lead me to take a substantial almost-certain loss. And if the time and cognitive effort of sweating over decisions of this sort itself counts as a sufficient loss, then I can simply disregard any possibility where my credence is below that threshold. (Schwitzgebel 2015, 283)

By endorsing Nicolausian discounting, in a Pascal's Mugging scenario Schwitzgebel can avoid the almost-certain loss of giving the mugger his money, regardless of what positive finite utility the mugger is offering. And for the St. Petersburg game, the 1/1030 threshold would lead Schwitzgebel to value the game at $99– in the ballpark of reasonableness.[①]

---

① The probability of getting heads for the first time on the 99th toss is 1/299, which is about 1.6x10-30; the probability of getting heads for the first time on the 100th toss is 1/2100, which is about 8x10-31, less than the 10-30 threshold.

Schwitzgebel's rationale that time and cognitive effort themselves count as a loss is an promising but limited one. It is promising in that it offers good pragmatic justification in some contexts for ignoring small-probability options. Our time and cognitive effort in this life is limited, so it's not worth worrying about possibilities that are very unlikely to occur. But Schwitzgebel's rationale is limited because it only apples to non-ideal agents who need to spend time and cognitive resources to think. An ideal agent would be able to think about arbitrarily complex topics infinitely quickly, and so wouldn't face that limitation. But I maintain that even an ideal agent should not spend a lot of utility to play the St. Petersburg game, and should not hand over money to Pascal's mugger.

Let's set aside the idea that time and cognitive effort themselves count as a loss, and look directly at the connection between loss aversion and Nicolausian discounting. While I share Schwitzgebel's desire to avoid loss, and I agree with Schwitzgebel that we should do Nicolausian discounting, I want to raise two worries regarding the connection between that desire and that strategy.

Here is a story to illustrate my first worry. Imagine that Schwitzgebel, tired of spending time and cognitive effort managing his vast wealth, hires Bernie as his money manager. Schwitzgebel, worried that Bernie might invest in a Pascal's Mugging scenario, tells Bernie to disregard any possibility where the probability is below the threshold of 1/1030, regardless of the finite outcome associated with that possibility. Bernie then transfers Schwitzgebel's money from Bank A to Bank B, where the transfer fee is a 1/1031 chance of Bernie getting all of Schwitzgebel's money.

Bernie can truthfully tell Schwitzgebel that things will (most probably) be fine. But Bernie is exposing Schwitzgebel to a potential loss that Schwitzgebel didn't need to be exposed to – Bernie's action is not an action that a loss-averse person would approve.

Here is the lesson I draw from this. Nicolausian discounting is a rational thing to do, and having the desire to avoid loss is a rational desire. For Pascal's Mugging, that strategy and that desire cohere, and both give the result that one should refrain from giving the mugger money. What the money transfer scenario shows is that there are other situations where the relationship between that strategy and that desire is more complicated than Schwitzgebel suggests.

Here is my second worry regarding the connection between avoiding loss and Nicolausian discounting – but unlike with the first worry, I think that this second worry is fully resolvable. The worry is that engaging in Nicolausian discounting makes one a potential money pump, where one faces potential loss with no countervailing gain. This is not the sort of situation a loss-averse agent would want to find herself in. Continuing the story above, imagine that Bernie excitedly does the transfer, only to find that he did not get the money. He then decides to set up an automated system that transfers Schwitzgebel's money back and forth until Bernie hits jackpot with the transfer fee.

The lesson to be learned here is that an agent engaging in Nicolausian discounting will have to evaluate potential gambles collectively – the choices the agent makes may be different than when evaluating gambles individually. But this sort of thing is true for orthodox decision theory too – consider for example the immortal person with the ever-better bottle of wine, where each day she is better off not drinking the wine, but those choices taken together will lead to her never drinking the wine. She will have to evaluate her choices collectively to avoid ending up in the clearly inferior situation where she never drinks the wine.①

5.5 The Unbearable Amorphousness of Very Small Probabilities

Let's turn to another reason to engage in Nicolausian discounting. In the Pascal's Mugging game, there is one salient very-small-probability possibility – that paying the mugger yields a vast increase in utility. But there are other very-small-probability possibilities that aren't made salient but are also prima facie relevant to deciding what one should do. For example, there is the possibility that another mugger is waiting a five-minute walk down the road, and this mugger will offer Pascal vastly more utility for the money Pascal would have given the first mugger. There is the possibility that Pascal is wrong about his moral judgements, and increasing the utility of sweet little orphans is actually a morally horrendous thing to do. The list goes on and on, and we shouldn't expect Pascal to even be aware of the space of all such remote possibilities, let alone have precise probability assignments for each of the possibilities. Pascal should recognize that his probability assignments for such possibilities are very small, but beyond that we should expect his probability assignments to be *amorphous*.

As a practical matter, we aren't cognitively capable of making well-thought-out precise probability assignments for that immense space of remote possibilities. Hence, it would be irrational to focus on one such possibility simply because the mugger has made it salient, when there are other such possibilities that would also

① For many more orthodox-decision-theoretic examples, see Arntzenius, Elga, and Hawthorne 2004. Evaluating gambles collectively allows one to avoid the objection to Smith's RNP (and, by extension, Nicolausian discounting) by John Matthewson, as presented in Hájek 2014, pages 561-562. The objection presents a gamble with an infinite set of possibilities that, taken together, give one probability 1/2 of getting $1, but holds that Smith could unreasonably value that gamble at less than $0.50, because some of the possibilities in the gamble have very low probability. I maintain that a proponent of Nicolausian discounting should evaluate the possibilities collectively, and hence value the gamble correctly at $0.50.

need to be taken into account to make a considered decision. Because we aren't cognitively capable of taking them all into account, and because the probabilities associated with the possibilities are all very small, the rational thing to do is to ignore all such possibilities, by discounting their probabilities to zero.

Let's compare my amorphousness argument to the symmetry argument given by Ord, Hillerbrand, and Sandberg (2010, 203) . Imagine that you find yourself worrying that dropping a pencil will destroy the world. They write: "for events like the dropping of a pencil which have no plausible mechanism for destroying the world, it seems just as likely that the world would be destroyed by not dropping the pencil. The expected losses would thus balance out." A similar argument is given by Schwitzgebel (2015, 283) : he says that his "credences about such extremely remote possibilities appear to be approximately symmetrical and canceling", and hence the remote possibilities should be discounted.

The symmetry argument is different from my amorphousness argument above. I'm not saying that for every remote possibility there is a symmetric countervailing possibility with equal probability. To say that would require too much cognitive sophistication – it would require an unreasonable amount of knowledge of the immense space of remote possibilities, and also an unreasonable level of precision in making probability assignments to this space of possibilities. So I reject the symmetry argument.

I'm a fan of my amorphousness argument, but I recognize that it has limitations. I'll point out two.

One limitation is that my amorphousness argument only applies to rationally limited agents – it does not apply to a rationally perfect being who is aware of the whole space of possibilities, and can assign probabilities and utilities to each of those possibilities. But I maintain that even such ideally rational agents should not give a high value to the St. Petersburg game, and should not give the money to the mugger.

Another limitation of my amorphousness argument is that, even for rationally limited agents like us, it does not apply in all situations. Consider a group of effective altruists who have $10 billion to give away, so they spend years developing the cognitive sophistication to assign precise probabilities to all the remote possibilities they are aware of. And suppose it turns out that, while their credences about these remote possibilities are *approximately* symmetrical and canceling, they are not *exactly* symmetrical and canceling. Should the altruists then simply do the math and spend the $10 billion in whatever way maximizes expected utility, even if it is spent on a possibility associated with a very small probability?

I want to say "no", but I don't think my amorphousness argument provides a strong enough reason to say "no" . We can get a better argument by coupling that amorphousness argument with a judgement-stability line of reasoning: we should prefer to make life-changing decisions that we would not call into question upon making tiny adjustments in our probability assignments. The effective altruists should recognize that there are competing possibilities with respect to how a group of rationally-minded people would make such judgements. If a different cognitively sophisticated group would get a vastly different judgement about the most effective action by making a tiny change in the probability assignments, this should lead the initial group to recognize that their judgements are not very *stable*. Moreover, one should expect such instability, given that one is dealing with very small probabilities.

But even when we add the judgement-stability line of reasoning, my amorphousness argument is limited. The effective altruists could recognize that their judgement is imperfect, and that there are probably still other remote possibilities they haven't even thought about yet. But at some point one has to act. Maybe the $10 billion will disappear if they don't give it away, or maybe they simply recognize that, if they don't give it away, future decision-makers will also feel uncertain in their judgement, and will have the same reason to not give it away. One never reaches a stage where one can say with certainty 'all the judgements have been made; all the information is in'– Neurath's ship keeps sailing. So at some point, even in the face of amorphousness and a lack of judgement stability, one has to act. But nevertheless, I maintain that there are situations where that act should not be the one that maximizes expected utility.

5.6 YOLO

It's time for my favorite reason to engage in Nicolausian discounting. The reason is that it is rational to value how your life actually goes. In the end, looking back on your life, it doesn't matter for your well-being to what extent you maximized expected utility. What matters is the utility you actually achieved – how your life actually went. The orthodox decision theorists' exclusive focus on maximizing expected utility is a mistake, because (to quote Goethe's *Clavigo*) "one lives but once in the world" . Or to quote millenials c.2012: "YOLO" – you only live once.

This gives good reason to avoid situations where one has a high probability of having one's life go badly, regardless of whether or not one achieves maximum expected utility. Both the St. Petersburg game and Pascal's Mugging can be used to present situations where the choice that maximizes expected utility also gives one a high probability of having one's life go badly. So don't maximize expected utility! The prescription to maximize expected utility does not take seriously the importance of how one's life actually goes.

It follows that how rational agents value an action that they have the opportunity to repeat over and over might be different than how they value an action that they only have the opportunity to do once. Pascal's Mugging provides a good example of this. Suppose I think that there is a 10-40 chance that the mugger will give me the prize，but I have the opportunity（and the financial resources）to play the game 1050 times（and each trial is independent，and playing the game 1050 times can happen quickly，and so on）. In this situation I would want to play the game – there is a high probability that I will come out ahead. But if I only have the opportunity to play once，I'd pass – there is a high probability that I will come out behind. Orthodox decision theory specifies that I should play the game regardless of whether it is iterated or not – orthodox decision theory specifies that both the one-off version and the iterated version have positive expected utility. But what orthodox decision theory fails to adequately take into account is my probability of *actually* winning money.

Nicolausian discounting allows one to avoid playing the one-off version of the game because the probability is too low that one will win; that probability should be discounted to zero for the purposes of decision-making. For the iterated version of the game，the probability is high that one will win，so – when the iterations of the game are evaluated collectively，as they should be – Nicolausian discounting does not apply.①

To further motivate my YOLO reasoning, let's think about a one-off Pascal's-Mugging-style scenario from the perspective of effective altruists. If the effective

---

① Jeff Jordan (1994, 215-6) endorses a principle closely related to Nicolausian discounting, and argues for it using YOLO-style reasoning. But his argument ends up being confused. For details, keep reading.

Jordan calls the principle he endorses the "Sure Loss Principle" (SLP) :

> if two acts A and –A are such that the EU [expected utility] of A is greater than the EU of –A, but the probability of the favorable consequence of A occurring is such that the performance of A will probably result in a significant net loss for the agent, then the agent ought either to (i) perform –A, if there is no risk of great loss; or (ii) perform neither A nor –A. (Jordan 1994, 215)

Applied to Pascal's Mugging, where A is paying the mugger a significant amount of money and –A is refraining, SLP has the consequence that the agent should perform –A, because paying the mugger will probably result in significant loss. Note that in this situation SLP dictates that the agent should perform –A regardless of how high the expected utility of A is:"According to the SLP one should decline *any* act in which a resultant net loss is practically certain" (Jordan 1994, 215, my emphasis) .

Jordan gives two arguments for the SLP. The first is unproblematic: he says that "something like the SLP is needed whenever infinite utilities are included" . The second is where the trouble arises. Jordan writes:

> Secondly, a violation of the SLP will lead, almost certainly in the short term and often in the long, to the agent suffering a loss of the stake with little, if any, gain. Even if one has great resources, a net loss is practically certain, given the Law of Large Numbers. (Jordan 1994, 216)

If we look at a one-off version of the Pascal's Mugging game, then indeed a net loss is practically certain, and that's a reason to decline to play – that's YOLO-style reasoning. But Jordan is mistaken to say that the law of large numbers implies that a net loss is practically certain in a sufficiently iterated version of the Pascal's Mugging game. Since the expected utility of the game is positive, then what the law of large numbers implies is that in the long run the person playing the Pascal's Mugging game will come out ahead. (Think about it in a casino context: the house, with its positive expected utility and great enough bankroll, always wins in the long run.)

So what was Jordan thinking? He continues the discussion from the quote above by applying the law of large numbers to a single iteration of the St. Petersburg game. But his discussion of violating the SLP "in the long" term, and his mention of the person being offered the game having great resources, implies that at that point he was thinking of a situation where the game in question is iterated. My interpretation is that Jordan got confused here, but we can set aside the confusion and recognize that there's a YOLO-style insight at the core of his second argument. The insight is that a violation of the SLP can lead to an agent suffering a significant loss with near certainty, and that is a good reason to endorse something like the SLP.

altruists' only desire were to maximize expected utility, then (let's suppose) they would give all their donation money to a very-small-probability cause. But rational effective altruists could have other desires too, such as the desire to *actually do good*. In a situation where they have these multiple reasonable yet conflicting desires, it would be rational for them to reject the option that maximizes expected utility but has a very small probability of doing good, and instead donate in such a way that has lower expected utility but a higher probability of actually doing good.

At this point some interlocutors have objected: the effective altruists who lower the probability of something bad happening count as actually doing good, simply because they have lowered the probability. I maintain that this is mistaken – at least, this is not what I mean by "actually doing good". Here's an intuition-pumping example. Imagine that, 10 years from now, scenario A will occur with high probability, or scenario B will occur with low probability, and the scenarios are mutually exclusive and exhaustive. If scenario B occurs, there is a very high probability that everything will be fine, but there is a very low probability that something catastrophic will happen. Suppose that a group of people spend billions of dollars and years of their lives to reduce the chance of something catastrophic happening in scenario B. Then, scenario A occurs. It's true that those people lowered the probability of something bad happening. But there's an important sense in which their work was in vain – they did not actually accomplish anything. Looking back, we could feel regret that they didn't spend their time and money on actually doing good. And, if the initial probability of catastrophe is low enough, then at the time that they are deciding how to proceed, it is rational for them to spend their time and money in such a way that may have lower expected utility, but a higher probability of actually doing good.

5.7 What About Risk?

We're done with my discussion of the six reasons to engage in Nicolausian discounting. But you might wonder why I didn't talk about *risk*. Lara Buchak (2014) has a beautiful risk-weighted decision theory, which I'm on board with – I would want to incorporate Buchakian risk-weighting into my preferred decision theory. But does such risk-weighting help resolve the St Petersburg paradox or Pascal's Mugging?

Buchak (2014, 73) recognizes that, for a normal risk-weighting function that does not drive probabilities to zero, the answer is 'no'. In either game, the utilities can be increased to compensate for the risk of loss, in such a way that even a risk-averse agent would deem a suitable version of the St. Petersburg game to have infinite risk-weighted expected utility, and a suitable version of the Pascal's mugging game to have positive risk-weighted expected utility.

Intriguingly, Buchak does give a proposal for how we can avoid the judgement that the St. Petersburg game has infinite expected utility: her proposal is that the agent utilize a risk-weighting function that has the mathematical effect of discounting very small probabilities to zero. But Buchak gives only a one-sentence justification for this proposal: "we might think that we ought not consider the chance of a good outcome in our calculations if that good outcome is extremely unlikely to happen" (Buchak 2014, 74). What I've tried to do in this section is give reasons for thinking that.

6. Three Open Questions

A key feature of Nicolausian discounting is the low-probability threshold below which, for the purposes of decision-making, one discounts probabilities to zero. This leads to three unresolved questions. Is this threshold subjective or objective? Does the value of the threshold depend on context, or is it invariant? How should one handle probabilities greater than but close to the threshold? I'll give my own answers to those three questions now – but of course someone could be a fan of Nicolausian discounting and yet give different answers to these questions.

6.1 Is the Threshold Subjective?

People who believe that the threshold is objective face the burden of telling us what the value of the threshold is – and to their credit, Buffon and Daniel Bernoulli are happy to provide numbers. They aren't the only ones: Le Marquis de Condorcet, for example, endorses a threshold of 1/144,768. Condorcet's argument for this threshold is that it is the difference between the probability that a 47-year-old man would die in the course of a day and the probability that a 37-year-old man would, and that is a difference that would keep no man awake at night.①

The fact that this is so amusing in its specificity is an indicator that it can't be objectively right. Contrast that experience with the experience of having some objectively true philosophical insight – such as reading Gettier's (1963) paper and saying "oh yes, now I see, knowledge is not justified true belief". I can't imagine having an experience like that with Condorcet's argument – "oh yes, now I see, the threshold is 1/144,768". I can't think of any argument for an objective threshold that fares better than Condorcet's in that amusingness regard, so I conclude that the threshold is *subjective*.②

At least, it is subjective within reason. If someone set the threshold to, for

---

① Condorcet criticizes Buffon's choice of threshold, and then provides his own; he calls 1/144,768 "the greatest risk that can be regarded as null". This is my translation, the original is "le risque le plus considérable qu'il foit permis de regarder comme nul" (Condorcet 1785, page cxiii).

② My appeal to subjectivity defangs the critique of arbitrariness from Kenneth Arrow (1951, 414): "This principle [of engaging in Nicolausian discounting] seems extremely arbitrary in its specification of a particular critical probability [i.e. the threshold]". I say: a choice of threshold is unproblematically arbitrary because it is based on subjective preference, in the same way that a choice between eating vanilla ice cream or chocolate ice cream is unproblematically arbitrary.

example, 1/2, I'd deem them irrational (and, with their resultant poor decision-making skills, they would probably not be long for this world) . And if someone set the threshold to an astronomically small number, I'd deem them at least unreasonable – they would, for example, be willing to assign too high a value to playing the St. Petersburg game.

So what is your threshold? One way to get insight is to contemplate how much you would pay to play a utility-based version of the St. Petersburg game with no diminishing marginal utility. For me, the finite days-of-life version I presented in Section 2 is such a game, and recall that I wouldn't be willing to give up more than 50 days of life to play the game. So for me, the threshold is somewhere between 1/250 and 1/251. That means that, for the purposes of decision-making, I am treating the probability of getting tails 50 times in a row, and then heads on the 51st toss or later, as a probability 0 event. The number 1/250 is about 9x10-16, while 1/251 is about 4x10-16, so my threshold is about 5x10-16– about 1 in 2 quadrillion. I'm happy with that as my threshold – in the course of decision-making, I'm happy to ignore possibilities with probabilities less than 1 in 2 quadrillion.

6.2 Is the Threshold Context-Dependent?

Suppose you use the above method of introspecting how many days of life you would give up in the finite days-of-life version of the St. Petersburg game to determine your threshold. Now we can ask the question: is this your threshold for all contexts, or just contexts where your life is at stake? Perhaps one's threshold should be larger for less important contexts, like deciding what to have for dinner, and one's threshold should be smaller for more important contexts, like when the fate of the whole world is at stake.

Émile Borel, who is a proponent of Nicolausian discounting, maintains that one's threshold should vary depending on the context. I'll present his position, and then reject it.

In Borel's 1943 book *Le Probabilités et la Vie* (translated into English as Borel 1962), Borel endorses this claim:

Events with a sufficiently small probability never occur; or at least, we must act, in all circumstances, as if they were *impossible*. (Borel 1962, 3)

In this ensuing discussion, it's clear that he's not really acting *in all circumstances* as if they were impossible – he's happy to do math calculations involving very small probabilities where he gives the right answer, which is a non-zero answer. The charitable way to read Borel is that he is talking about *decision-making* circumstances. So I take Borel to be endorsing Nicolausian discounting.①

But what is Borel's threshold? Borel gives four different numerical thresholds, for probabilities which are negligible on the human scale, the terrestrial scale, the cosmic scale, and the supercosmic scale. His corresponding threshold values are 10-6, 10-15, 10-50, and 10-500. The human scale corresponds to possibilities regarding the life of a person; the terrestrial scale corresponds to possibilities regarding human civilization as a whole; the cosmic scale corresponds to possibilities regarding the observable universe, and the supercosmic scale corresponds to possibilities regarding violations of the laws of physics.

---

① But *why* does Borel endorse Nicolausian discounting? It's not clear. Borel says on the first page of his book that the calculus of probabilities permits prediction as a result of "the *single law of chance*", which is "phenomena with very small probabilities do not occur" (Borel 1962, 1). I take Borel to be endorsing Antoine-Augustin Cournot's (1843) claim this single law of chance is what gives empirical meaning to probability theory. While I am skeptical of this foundational claim, discussing it is beyond the scope of this paper. (See Shafer and Vovk (2006, 73) for some discussion.)

① nomenclature note: this foundational claim is sometimes called "Cournot's Principle", but sometimes "Cournot's Principle" is just used to refer to something more like the rule that one should engage in Nicolausian discounting. Let's give credit where credit is due; since Cournot was the first to state the foundational claim, let's call *that* claim "Cournot's Principle".

This initially has an air of reasonableness, that the threshold should vary depending on the types of possibilities under consideration. But I will argue that a reasonable person should have a single threshold that does not vary with context.

To start my argument, let's look at what Borel says about carrying an umbrella. Suppose that you're in France, it's 10 am, the weather is nice, you haven't seen a weather forecast, and you're about to head out the door. Borel guesses that the probability is somewhat larger than 1/1000 that in such a situations, it rains in the afternoon. But unless you're frail, "we will not consider [you] careless" if you go out without an umbrella (Borel 1962, 30). So far I agree. But Borel is using this umbrella example to illustrate the following claim:

much larger probabilities [than the human-scale threshold of 10-6] must also be disregarded in the numerous cases where the event corresponding to such probabilities does not represent for us a grave misfortune, but merely a disagreeable incident. (Borel 1962, 30)

What this shows is that, by Borel's lights, there aren't just four thresholds; there are many, corresponding to the relative graveness of the possible misfortune under consideration. Thus, in Borel's decision theory, an agent's preferences would have to be modeled not only by a probability function and a utility function, but also a complicated threshold function. (Borel doesn't spell it out that way (he doesn't spell it out at all), but I think that's how the account would most reasonably go.)

I reject this proposal of a threshold function. Orthodox decision theory already has the resources to explain the decision not to carry an umbrella in the situation Borel describes. When you're about to leave your house at 10 am, you (at least implicitly) do an *expected utility calculation* to decide whether it's worth it to carry the umbrella. Consider the process of carrying the umbrella – just the act of carrying itself, setting aside the umbrella's usefulness if it rains. This process of carrying the umbrella has some negative utility for you, and the expected utility calculation determines whether carrying the umbrella is all-things-considered worth it, given the small chance of it doing any good for you. We don't need Borel's threshold function to account for umbrella-carrying behavior; orthodox decision theory does just fine.

But that just implies that using Borel's threshold function is unnecessary; I'll now show that it's a mistake. By the lights of orthodox decision theory, if the process of carrying the umbrella had zero utility for you, then you're irrational if you don't carry it, since there's a chance it will do some all-things-considered good. But by Borel's lights, you should apply the threshold to treat the probability of rain in the afternoon as a zero-probability event, and hence you should be indifferent between carrying the umbrella or not. Orthodox decision theory is closer to the truth here – it's irrational (or at least careless) *not* to carry the umbrella, in a situation where the process of carrying it doesn't have any negative utility.

I'm not aware of any proposal to have the threshold vary with context that is better than Borel's proposal, and Borel's proposal fails. So that's a reason to conclude that a reasonable person should have a single threshold that does not vary with context. Here is another consideration in favor of that conclusion – or at least, here is my explanation for why I personally have a single threshold that does not vary with context.

Consider the finite days-of-life version of the St. Petersburg game, and recall that I'm willing to give up 50 days of life to play the game. What if I am making the choice, not for my life, but for the life of a chinchilla? Or what if I am making the choice for all of human civilization, so that civilization as a whole will end in 1000 days unless I play the game to determine when civilization as a whole will actually end? Whether it's for a chinchilla or civilization, I still make the choice to give up 50 days to play the game, and hence my threshold in both these contexts is about 1 in 2 quadrillion. But the death of a chinchilla and the end of civilization are vastly different contexts; this provides evidence that *my* threshold, at least, does not depend on context.

6.3 How Should One Handle Probabilities Close to the Threshold?

Let's suppose that 1/1000 is our threshold. How should we treat probabilities greater than but close to this threshold, like 1/999 and 1/998– should we discount them somewhat? D'Alembert poses this question, asking:

If we do not look at these probabilities as smaller than they actually are, I ask how the probability 1/999 suddenly becomes =0 in the case where it is 1/1000? Can the expression of probability thus shift sharply & without gradation, from a finite expression to a null value?①

D'Alembert does not give answers to these questions – he simply concludes that "the general rule for the calculus of probabilities is defective in certain respects." ② With this I agree, but nevertheless, working within the context of Nicolausian discounting, we can answer his questions.

My answer is: yes, in a decision-making context, the expression of probability does shift sharply and without gradation to zero when one reaches the threshold. At least, this is the answer I give as an agent with limited cognitive resources. While I share d'Alembert's implicit worry that the difference between 1/999 and 0 is large, I do not feel the same about the difference between 1/2000000000000000 and 0 – with my limited cognitive resources, these numbers seem really close. Moreover, if I were

① This is d'Alembert 1761, Memoir 10, Section 13, page 11, my translation. The original is:"S'il ne faut pas regarder ces probabilités comme plus petites qu'elles ne sont en effet, je demande comment la probabilité 1/999 devient tout d'un coup =0 dan le cas où elle est 1/1000? L'expression de la probabilité peut-elle passer ainsi brusquement & sans gradation, d'une expression finie à une valeur nulle?"

② D'Alembert 1761, Memoir 10, Section 14, page 12. This is my translation; the original is "la régle générale du calcul des probabilités est défectueuse à certain égards."

to try to implement some discounting function that discounts probabilities close to the threshold to a lower but non-zero number，that needlessly adds to my already-limited cognitive load. Would an ideal agent implement a discounting function instead of a single threshold? Perhaps; my limited cognitive resources prevent me from giving a more definitive answer.

Nicolaus himself worried both about the issue of what the threshold is，and the issue of how handle probabilities near the threshold. In a 1728 letter to Gabriel Cramer，Nicolaus writes:

it is necessary ⋯ to determine how far the quantity of a probability must diminish，in order for it to be considered as zero; but this is impossible to determine，whatever supposition one may make，one always finds difficulties; the limits of these small probabilities are not precise，but they have a certain latitude which cannot be fixed easily⋯ ①

To put this in contemporary philosophy-speak: there is an element of vagueness with respect to the threshold. Fortunately，philosophers have now solved the problem of vagueness，and that solution can be used in this case as well.

Oh，is that not yet true at the time that you are reading this? Then my resolution of this open question is just a partial one. I'm most happy with the ‘draw a definite line’ move to determine the threshold，even if it seems arbitrary，but I'll defer to the vagueness literature for further discussion.

① This is my translation; the original is “Il faut donc ⋯ determiner jusqu' où la quantité d'une probabilité doit diminuer，afin qu'elle puisse étre censée nulle; mais voilà ce qui est impossible de determiner，quelque supposition que l'on fasse，on rencontre toujours de difficultés; le limites de ces petites probabilités ne sont pas precises，mais elles ont une certaine latitude que l' on ne peut pas fixer aisément⋯”. This letter is published in Spieß 1975，page 562.

7. Objection: Domination (and, Pascal's Wager)

There's no point in worrying about the open questions if Nicolausian discounting itself is a fundamentally flawed decision-theoretic procedure. In this section, I'll consider the one objection I find most pressing.

I endorse Nicolausian discounting with a threshold of 5x10-16. You might think that it follows that, when it comes to decision-making, I treat the following two possibilities indifferently, with respect to their expected utility:

Option A: getting $2 with probability (1-10-50), and losing $1 with probability 10-50

Option B: getting $2 with probability (1-10-50), and losing all one's money with probability 10-50

But the objector would say: surely (surely!) when it comes to decision-making, one should not be indifferent between Option A and Option B, and hence Nicolausian discounting is a flawed decision procedure.

To orthodox decision theorists who present such an objection, I reply: *tu quoque*. As Hájek (2014, 556-7) points out, orthodox decision theory faces the same sort of problem of prescribing indifference between options that shouldn't be considered indifferently. According to orthodox decision theory, these two options both have expected utility of 0:

Option 1: A fair coin is flipped an infinite number of times in a finite amount of time; you go to heaven if the coin lands heads on every toss, and get nothing otherwise.

Option 2: Same as above, except you go to hell if the coin lands heads on every toss.

Surely, we should not be indifferent between those two options.

But "tu quoque" by itself isn't a solution to the problem posed by the objection; it just means that orthodox decision theorists and Nicolausian-discounting decision theorists are in the same boat when it comes to solving the problem.

I (following Hájek) propose to the orthodox decision theorists that they solve the problem by specifying that indeed, when faced with a choice between the zero-probability heaven and hell options, they prescribe that a rational agent choose the dominating heaven option. They need to supplement the ranking of options based on expected utility with dominance reasoning. But the dominance reasoning should only be implemented when it is cost-free. It's not worth spending any time or money to get the heaven option over the hell option, since the two options have the same expected utility.

I propose that Nicolausian-discounting decision theorists make the same move. When faced with the choice between Option A and Option B as specified above, they should choose Option A, but only if it is cost-free. It's not worth spending any time or money to get Option A over Option B, since, post-Nicolausian-discounting, the two options have the same expected utility.

I understand if you feel uncomfortable with this thought of not placing any value on small-probability possibilities in decision-making contexts, especially if such possibilities lead to ruin (losing all one's money, for example) . But I maintain that you, 21st-century intellectual that you are, already make such disregarding judgements in the course of decision-making – and moreover, you are correct to do so.

To see this, let's (finally) take up Pascal's Wager – Blaise Pascal's argument that it is pragmatically rational to believe in God, even if one initially assigns a small probability to the hypothesis that God exists, because of the possibility of obtaining the infinite reward offered in heaven. Let's focus on a hell-based version of Pascal's

Wager – consider the hypothesis that the traditional Christian God exists, and all and only redeemed believers go to heaven; everyone else goes to hell.① 21st-century intellectual that I am, my probability for that hypothesis is very low. But it's not zero – I recognize that there is a tiny chance that that hypothesis is correct. Moreover, when I consider other hypotheses that involve the possibility of ending up in hell (the hypothesis that God sends all and only theists to hell, for example) those hypotheses strike me as less probable than the traditional Christian hypothesis, in part because of the number of believers involved. (It is striking that millions of people believe that I am going to hell, and I assign a very low but non-zero probability that they are correct.) So out of all the hypotheses that involve people going to hell, I consider the traditional Christian one most likely. Specifically, the probability I assign to that hypothesis is 10-50. But now let's apply orthodox-decision-theoretic reasoning: the disutility associated with hell is, if not infinite, at least vastly more than 1050 times larger than the utility I get from my godless earthly life, so orthodox decision theory specifies that the action that maximizes expected utility is to try to become a redeemed believer.

Nicolausian discounting can be utilitized to provide a response to Pascal's Wager. By my lights, any hypothesis that involves people spending eternity in hell has probability below my threshold, and hence, for the purposes of decision-making, I discount the probabilities of such hypotheses to zero. The process of trying to become a redeemed believer has negative utility for me; hence I rationally decide to refrain from trying to become a redeemed believer.

---

① Whether Pascal himself endorsed a hell-based version of Pascal's Wager is controversial – see Section 4 of Hájek 2017. See all of Hájek 2017 for an excellent overview of Pascal's Wager issues – in my brief discussion here, I will of necessity be eliding some of the intricacies and controversies that Hájek takes up.

Perhaps you were uncomfortable with engaging in decision-making while disregarding the small-probability possibility in Option B above, where there was a small chance of losing all your money. Are you, 21st-century intellectual that you are, similarly uncomfortable with engaging in decision-making while disregarding the small-probability possibility that you will spend eternity in hell? I'm guessing – and hoping – that you are in fact comfortable disregarding such silly eschatological hypotheses; it's not healthy to make life decisions with the worry that one might end up in hell. But, from a doxastic standpoint, it's unreasonable to assign all such hypotheses zero probability; there is a chance that such a hypothesis is right, unlike, say, there being a chance that 2+2=5. So I maintain that, when faced with Pascal's Wager, you are already implicitly engaging in Nicolausian discounting. What I have tried to do in this paper is to make such reasoning explicit, and defend its reasonableness.

8. Conclusion

The St. Petersburg game and Pascal's Mugging show that orthodox decision theory is flawed, and I have put forth Nicolausian discounting as a means of avoiding some of the problematic prescriptions of orthodox decision theory. My guess is that open-minded decision theorists are intrigued but unsatiated. Perhaps they want a calculus of decision into which I can input my prior probability and utility functions to get a cardinal ranking of actions that captures all the decision-theoretic preferences I've expressed above. Or maybe they want something analogous to a representation theorem that shows how all my decision-theoretic preferences can be represented as resulting from some utility function and probability function. I admit, I don't have that calculus, and I don't have that theorem. In fact, I'm skeptical of the view that it's correct to express decision-theoretic preferences solely in terms of a utility function and a probability function. (And, as much as I admire Buchak's work, I'm also skeptical of the view that it's correct to express decision-theoretic preferences solely in terms of a utility function, a probability function, and a risk function.) We need to go back to the drawing board; this paper is just providing an impetus to do that.

I admire orthodox decision theory, but orthodox decision theory is predicated on a mistake. A key feature of orthodox decision theory is that maximizing expected utility is the rational thing to do, but (as you've gathered by now) I think that that is problematic. I admire orthodox decision theory because it gets the right answer in a lot of cases, and because it helps people see that often their intuitive judgements about probability are the wrong ones. But it turns out that some of the decisions prescribed by orthodox decision theory are the wrong ones too.

The formal system that orthodox decision theorists have developed is impressive, but the existence of an impressive formal system does not entail that the theory is giving the right prescriptions for decisions. We shouldn't let the existence or non-existence of a formal system blind us to the fact that maximizing expected utility is sometimes an unreasonable – perhaps even irrational – decision procedure to follow.

References

Arntzenius, Frank, Adam Elga, and John Hawthorne (2004), "Bayesianism, Infinite Decisions, and Binding", *Mind* 113:251–83.

Arrow, Kenneth (1951), "Alternative Approaches to the Theory of Choice in Risk-Taking Situations", *Econometrica* 19:404-37.

Borel, Émile (1962), *Probabilities and Life*, New York: Dover Publications.

Bostrom, Nick (2009), "Pascal's Mugging", *Analysis* 69:443-5.

Buchak, Lara (2014), *Risk and Rationality*, Oxford: Oxford University Press.

Bernoulli, Daniel (1738 [English translation 1954]), "Exposition of a New Theory on the Measurement of Risk", *Econometrica* 22:23–36.

Condorcet, Le Marquis de (1785), *Essai sur l'application de l'analyse à la probabilité des décisions rendues à la pluralité des voix*, Paris: L'Imprimerie Royale.

Cournot, Antoine-Augustin (1843), *Exposition de la théorie des chances et des probabilités*, Paris: Hachette.

d'Alembert, Jean le Rond (1761), *Opuscules Mathématiques ou Mémoires sur différens sujets de Géométrie, de Méchanique, d'Optique, d'Astronomie &c., Tome Second*, Paris: David.

Dutka, Jacques (1988), "On the St. Petersburg Paradox", *Archive for History of Exact Sciences* 39:13–39.

Easwaran, Kenny (2008), "Strong and Weak Expectations", *Mind* 117:633-641.

Gettier, Edmund (1963), "Is Justified True Belief Knowledge?", *Analysis* 23:121-3.

Gibbard, Allan and William Harper, "Counterfactuals and Two Kinds of Expected Utility", in C. A. Hooker, J. J. Leach, and E. F. McClennen (eds.), *Foundations and Applications of Decision Theory*, *Volume 1*, Dordrecht, Holland: D. Reidel, pages 125-62.

Hájek, Alan (2014), "Unexpected Expectations", *Mind* 123:533-567.

Hájek, Alan (2017), "Pascal's Wager", *The Stanford Encyclopedia of* Philosophy, Edward N. Zalta (ed.), https://plato.stanford.edu/archives/fall2017/entries/pascal-wager.

Hey, John, Tibor Neugebauer, and Carmen Pasca (2010), "Georges-Louis Leclerc de Buffon's 'Essays on Moral Arithmetic'", Luxembourg School of Finance

Research Working Paper Series, available at: http://www.lsf.lu/eng/Research/Working-Papers/2010.

Jordan, Jeff (1994), "The St. Petersburg Paradox and Pascal's Wager", *Philosophia* 23:207-22.

Lewis, David (1981) 'Why Ain'cha Rich?' *Noûs* 15:377-80.

Martin, Robert (2017), "The St. Petersburg Paradox", *The Stanford Encyclopedia of Philosophy*, Edward N. Zalta (ed.), https://plato.stanford.edu/archives/fall2017/entries/paradox-stpetersburg.

Monton, Bradley (2010), "Against Multiverse Theodicies", *Philo* 13:113-135.

Nover, Harris, and Alan Hájek (2004), "Vexing Expectations", *Mind* 113:305-17.

Ord, Toby, Rafaela Hillerbrand, and Anders Sandberg (2010), "Probing the Improbable: Methodological Challenges for Risks with Low Probabilities and High Stakes", *Journal of Risk Research* 13:191-205.

Parfit, Derek (1985), *Reasons and Persons*, reprinted with corrections, Oxford: Oxford University Press.

Pulskamp, Richard (2009), "Jean Le Rond d'Alembert on Probability and Statistics", available at http://cerebro.xu.edu/math/Sources/Dalembert. Memoir 10 archived on 2017-06-21 at http://www.webcitation.org/6rOw6h63E.

Samuelson, Paul (1977), "St. Petersburg Paradoxes: Defanged, Dissected, and Historically Described", *Journal of Economic Literature* 15:24-55.

Schwitzgebel, Eric (2015), "1% Skepticism", *Noûs* 51:271-290.

Shafer, Glenn and Vladimir Vovk (2006), "The Sources of Kolmogorov's *Grundbegriffe*", *Statistical Science* 21:70-98.

Smith, Nicholas J. J. (2014), "Is Evaluative Compositionality A Requirement of Rationality?”, *Mind* 123:457-502.

Spieß, Von O.（1975），“Zur Vorgeschichte des Petersburger Problems”, in BL van der Waerden（ed.），*Die Werke von Jakob Bernoulli*，*Bd.3: Wahrscheinlichkeitsrechnung*，Basel: Birkhäuser，pp.557-67.

Todhunter，I.（1865），*A History of the Mathematical Theory of Probability From the Time of Pascal to That of Laplace*，Cambridge and London: Macmillan and Co.

中文简介

《反对最大化预期效用》

从具有悖论性质的“圣彼得堡游戏”和“帕斯卡的抢劫”中得到的经验是，在某些情况下，预期效用最大化者将不必要地（以高概率）落入贫穷和终结，因此，我们不应该是预期效用最大化者。相反，当涉及到决策时，对于发生概率非常小的可能性，我们应该将这些可能性视为零，而不管这些可能性的相关效用。

本文的核心概念是预期效用（EU，expected utilities）。我将从解释这个概念开始。根据传统的决策理论，行为主体的意见和偏好应该用概率函数和效用函数来建模。概率函数捕捉了一个行为主体的信念的主观强度：例如，如果你认为明天有 80% 的可能性下雨，那么你的观点就被一个概率函数模拟，这个概率函数为明天下雨的命题指定了 0.8。效用函数捕捉一个行为主体对世界不同状态的所认可的价值。例如，你可能不希望明天下雨，你的效用函数可能会将 5 个效用单位（称为“utiles”）分配给明天不下雨的世界状态，将 3 个效用单位分配给明天下雨的世界状态。

因为效用函数捕捉你的偏好，为了满足你的偏好，你需要最大化效用。但通常情况下，你不确定某种外部世界状态将获得这种最大化效用。而正统的决策理论认为，一个人应该最大化预期效用。要计算预期效用的话，需要将世界上可能的状态划分为一个互斥的并且是穷尽的集合，再乘以每个状态的概率，乘以每个状态的效用，最后相加。例如，假设抛掷一个硬币，其中正面的概率是 1/2，反面的概率是 1/2，如果硬币正面着地，你得到 4 个单位的效用，硬币背面着地，你得到 2 个单位的效用。硬币翻转的预期效用计算如下：

EU（硬币翻转）=P（正面）xU（正面）+P（反面）xU（反面）

=1/2x 4+1/2x（−2）

=1 个

假设如果一个人不掷硬币，什么也不会发生，那么 EU（不掷硬币）=0。由于抛硬币的预期效用大于不抛硬币的预期效用，因此，如果这是一个人仅有的两个选择，根据正统的决策理论，一个人应该最大化预期效用，就是去抛硬币。

我反对传统的决策理论。我认为最大化预期效用有时是一个不合理的，甚至是一个非理性的决策过程。此外，我坚持认为，这是我们（集体）在大约 300 年前就应该知道的结论。那些已经意识到最大化预期效用是一个不好遵循的规则的人已经提出了如何避免最大化预期效用的建议。在这篇文章中，我将提出并捍卫一个特别的建议：当涉及到决策时，对于发生概率很小的可能性，我们应该将这些可能性划归为零，而不管这些可能性涉及到什么效用。

我不一定认为这个建议是正确的，如果这篇文章能激励读者提出一个更好的建议，以避免期望效用最大化，我将非常高兴。但有趣的是，我在这篇论文中提出的这个建议，从大约 300 年前开始，已经被许多哲学家和概率论者独立地多次提出。尽管如此，文献中对这一建议的讨论还是很少。我将通过提出并批判性地评价这项建议的六种不同理由，对这项建议进行一次比我在文献中看到的更为系统的讨论。

在讨论了提案的六个不同理由之后，我将回答关于提案内容的三个重要的公开问题。如你所见，我的讨论将提出与帕斯卡的赌注密切相关的问题——帕斯卡相信上帝的实用主义的论证，其基础是这样做能最大限度地实现预期效用。我的论文的最后一个主要部分将讨论帕斯卡的赌注。我将坚持自己的结论，通过一个关于决策理论的全局性思考来进行论证。

哲学的宗教维度与哲学动力学

段德智

一、“哲学的宗教维度”之两重含义：哲学的宗教性与对宗教的哲学反思

哲学的宗教维度所意指的既非哲学的外在部件或外部印记，也非哲学的内部构成，而是意指哲学的精神意境、理论品格和致思路向，这也就是我们所说的哲学的宗教性。朱熹所谓“敬字功夫，乃圣门第一义”① 所昭示的便是儒学的宗教性。

我们不仅可以对哲学的宗教性作静态的逻辑的分析，而且还可以对之作动态的发生学的考察。这就是说，哲学的宗教性不仅属于哲学静力学的范畴，它同时亦属于哲学动力学的范畴。

哲学的宗教维度还有一重含义，这就是对宗教的哲学反思或哲学考察。在这种情况下，我们所谓哲学的宗教维度也就是一种狭义的宗教哲学。对宗教哲学可以有两种理解：一是将其理解为“宗教性的哲学”（religious philosophy），一是将其理解为“关于宗教的哲学”（philosophy of religion）。前者意指的是宗教化了的哲学而不是非宗教化了的哲学，而后者意指的则是对宗教的哲学反思或哲学考察，它本质上属于哲学而非宗教，前者关涉的是“宗教的哲学维度”，后者关涉的则是“哲学的宗教维度”。

就研究对象论，哲学的宗教性的研究对象为历史的和现实的哲学形态，而

---

① 朱熹：《朱子语类》卷十二第一册，（宋）黎靖德编，王星贤点校，中华书局 1986 年版，第 210 页。

对宗教的哲学反思的研究对象则为宗教及其经典和神学。

从哲学学的角度看，哲学的宗教性关涉的是哲学的理论品格和发展动因问题，而对宗教的哲学反思所关涉的则是哲学的研究范围问题，亦即哲学究竟有无“禁区”的问题。

本文的全部内容即是围绕着哲学的宗教维度的这样两重含义展开的。但是，鉴于无论哲学的宗教性还是对宗教的哲学反思都关涉到哲学与宗教的“关系”问题，故而，我们在对哲学的宗教性和对宗教的哲学反思这两个方面作出说明之前，需要先行地对哲学与宗教的“关系”问题作出初步解释。

二、对“双重真理论”的误读：哲学与宗教的“绝缘”

在我国哲学界，长期存在着一种孤立地研究哲学的倾向。许多研究者刻意避谈宗教神学对哲学的影响，把宗教神学视为与哲学研究毫不相干的东西。这样一种理论倾向不仅极大地妨害了我国哲学研究的理论视野，而且也极大地妨害了我国哲学研究的理论深度。这种倾向，从政治层面看，显然与我国过去很长一段时间推行的把宗教神学视为理论禁区的“左”的政策及其后遗症有关。但从认识层面看，显然与人们对历史上流行过的“双重真理论”的误读相关。

一般认为，“双重真理论”是由阿拉伯哲学家伊本·鲁西德（Ibn Rushd，1136—1198）最早提出来的。神秘主义思想家安萨里（al-Ghazālī，1058—1111）在《哲学家们的矛盾》等著作中曾强调哲学与宗教的矛盾和对立。针对这种观点，伊本·鲁西德写出了《论宗教与哲学的一致》和《矛盾的矛盾》等著作，在反驳安萨里的基础上提出和阐述了他的双重真理论，不仅断言真理有两种：一种是“哲学真理”或“推证真理”，另一种是“神学真理”或“经文真理”，而且还强调了这两种真理之间的一致性。他明确宣布：“哲学并不包含任何反乎伊斯兰教的东西。”① 他从哲学真理的立场论证说：“论证的真理和经文的真理是不可能相冲突的。因为既然这种宗教是真实的，是召唤人们去进行通往真理的知识的研究，则穆斯林社会就当确切地知道：论证的研究决不会导致与经文给予我们的真理相冲突的结论。因为真理不可能反乎真理，而只可能与真理相一致，并为真理作证。”② 伊本·鲁西德承认在哲学真理（论证真理）与宗教真理（经文真理）之间也存在有某种表面上的冲突，这主要是由于人们一味地对经文做字面解释的缘故。如果我们对经文既做字面的解释又做“隐喻式的解释”，则这样的冲突即可以避免。③ 显然，伊本·鲁西德对经文做隐喻式解释的要求，在事实上提出了哲学真理高于神学真理、推证真理高于经文真理的原则。正因为如此，双重真理论后来曾被一些中世纪神学家谴责为异端。

由此看来，从理论源头上看，双重真理的原始义至少有下述几点值得注意。首先，双重真理论旨在捍卫哲学真理而不在于贬低哲学真理。其次，双重真理论旨在强调哲学真理与宗教真理的一致而非强调它们之间的矛盾或对立。第三，双重真理论旨在强调它们之间的相关性和哲学真理的普遍适用性。因为所谓对经文的隐喻式解释强调的即是对经文哲学解释的可能性或哲学真理的普遍适用性。后来，托马斯·阿奎那在《反异教大全》和《神学大全》中明确阐述了我们借哲学和理性也能够对包括上帝存在、上帝本质和上帝属性在内的信仰真理有所认知的观点，他所依据的也正是经他修正过的伊本·鲁西德的双重真理论。④

因此，双重真理论的基本义并不在于强调哲学真理与宗教真理的无关和绝缘。那种把哲学真理与宗教真理、哲学研究与宗教研究绝对对置起来的观点，显然是对双重真理的误读。哲学的根本规定性即在于它以“完全普遍的对象”

---

① Arthur Hyman and James J. Walsh ed., *Philosophy in the Middle Ages*, Indianapolis: Hackett Publishing Company, 1973, p.292.

② Arthur Hyman and James J. Walsh ed., *Philosophy in the Middle Ages*, p.292.

③ Arthur Hyman and James J. Walsh ed., *Philosophy in the Middle Ages*, p.295.

④ Thomae De Aquino, *Summa Contra Gentiles*, I, cap.7, 1; I, cap.8, 1.

作为内容。哲学之同于艺术和宗教而异于各门具体科学，究其深层原因，全在于此。[①] 哲学是门关于“一切皆一”和“一皆一切”的学问。那种企图给哲学研究设置种种“禁区”以获取某种“安全感”的做法显然是以牺牲哲学研究的本质属性为巨大代价的，是与哲学家或哲学工作者的身份完全不相称的。从哲学与宗教的绝缘走向哲学与宗教的联姻，是当代双重真理论者应当作出的理性选择。

三、哲学的宗教性与“哲学动力学”

哲学真理与宗教真理的统一性或兼容性将我们引向了“哲学的宗教性”和“对宗教的哲学反思”这样两个话题。尽管在“哲学的宗教性”这个话题下，我们的考察对象是哲学形态而非宗教形态，而在“对宗教的哲学反思”这个话题下，我们的考察对象是宗教形态而非哲学形态，但无论是“哲学的宗教性”还是“对宗教的哲学反思”，我们着眼的都是哲学形态与宗教形态的关联，都是哲学真理与宗教真理的统一性或兼容性。

哲学真理与宗教真理的统一性和兼容性并不是一个纯粹的理论问题，它首先表现为一个事实问题或历史问题。在西方哲学史上，我们始终可以窥见西方宗教的踪影。我们通常将西方哲学史区分为希腊罗马哲学、中世纪哲学、近代哲学和现代哲学这样几个发展阶段，但有谁能够说西方哲学的这些发展阶段与西方宗教没有任何关联呢？我们谈到希腊哲学时常常非常自然地会想到它的理性性质和它的人文性质，会想到苏格拉底的“认识你自己”、柏拉图的理念论和亚里士多德的“人是理性的动物”，但是有谁能够据此来否认它的宗教气质和神学意蕴呢？希腊哲学家梯利曾说过：“希腊哲学以宗教始，以宗教终。”[②] 另一个著名的西方哲学史家文德尔班径直将希腊哲学的希腊化–罗

---

① 参见黑格尔：《哲学史讲演录》第 1 卷，贺麟、王太庆译，商务印书馆 1981 年版，第 62 页。

② 参见梯利：《希腊哲学》，罗忠恕译，商务印书馆 1944 年版，第 9—10 页。

马时期称作“宗教时期”，强调：“人类学运动最早进入希腊科学时不过是为了转移兴趣，不过是为了改变提问题的方式，但到了希腊化-罗马时期越来越发展成为考虑世界的真正原则了，最后与宗教需要联合起来占领了整个形而上学领域。”① 其实，即使希腊古典时期的苏格拉底的“认识你自己”也是以神谕的形式颁布出来的。无怪乎近代西方理性主义哲学集大成者黑格尔在谈到古希腊罗马宗教时，也断言：早期希腊哲学“局限在希腊的异教信仰范围内”，局限在“民间宗教”或“希腊宗教”范围内，罗马时期的哲学则局限在罗马民族宗教和基督宗教范围内。② 近代西方哲学是在笛卡尔“我思故我在”的旗帜下向前挺进的，几乎没有人怀疑它的理性主义性质，然而有谁能够据此来否认它的宗教背景和神学前提呢？当我们看到笛卡尔将上帝宣布为“绝对实体”而把自我规定为“相对实体”时，我们不是终究发现了笛卡尔理性哲学的终极秘密了吗？黑格尔在谈到西方近代哲学的神学意蕴时，曾发出由衷的感叹：“神在近代哲学中所起的作用，要比古代哲学中大得多。”③ 这位理性主义哲学大师的这样一种判断绝不是空穴来风的。当代存在主义大师萨特曾宣布存在主义是一种人道主义，然而另一位存在主义大师海德格尔却补充说存在主义不仅讲人道，而且还讲“天道”，讲天、地、神、人（作为此在的人）的“四相圆舞”。有谁能说，海德格尔的这样一种补充偏离了存在主义的哲学原则了呢？中国哲学不仅有“天命之谓性，率性之谓道，修道之谓教”的说法，而且还有“朱子道，陆子禅”的说法。有谁能够否认中国哲学的这样一种宗教性或准宗教品格呢？由此看来，中外哲学在其发展的道路上都有宗教这样一个挥之不去的东西。黑格尔把“哲学涉及宗教，宗教也涉及哲学”说成是一个“既成的事实”，④ 即是谓此。因此，当我们思考

① 文德尔班：《哲学史教程》上卷，罗达仁译，商务印书馆 1987 年版，第 351 页。

② 参阅黑格尔：《哲学史讲演录》第 1 卷，贺麟、王太庆译，商务印书馆 1978 年版，第 77—78 页。

③ 黑格尔：《哲学史讲演录》第 4 卷，贺麟、王太庆译，商务印书馆 1978 年版，第 184 页。

④ 参阅黑格尔：《哲学史讲演录》第 1 卷，贺麟、王太庆译，商务印书馆 1978 年版，第 65 页。

哲学或哲学问题时，我们当首先面对的就是这样一个“既成事实”。那种纯而又纯的与宗教或神学思想毫无瓜葛的哲学体系似乎是从来不曾存在过的。哲学真理与宗教真理不仅存在有历史的统一性和兼容性，而且还存在有逻辑的统一性和兼容性。哲学真理与宗教真理在逻辑层面的统一性和兼容性最根本的即是黑格尔所指出的它们都以“完全普遍的对象”为内容。而所谓“完全普遍的对象”也就是我们说过的“一切皆一”中的那个“一”，亦即世界的“终极实存”或“普遍存在”。也正是基于这一点，黑格尔将宗教与哲学一起规定为“绝对精神”的基本形态，并且针对宗教为非世间事物的认识而哲学乃世间事物的智慧这一割裂哲学与宗教的说法，强调指出：“哲学并非世间的智慧，而是对非世间者的认识”，是“对永恒者、作为上帝者以及与其自然相关联者之认识”。“哲学对宗教进行阐释，也就是对自身进行阐释；对自身进行阐释，也就是对宗教进行阐释。……哲学乃是同宗教并无二致的活动。”① 诚然，在黑格尔看来，哲学与宗教之间也有区别，但其区别却不在于“内容”而仅仅在于“形式”，仅仅在于哲学是以“概念”或“思想”的形式表达其内容的，而宗教则主要是以“感情”和“表象”的方式来表达其内容的。② 其实，黑格尔对哲学与宗教关系的这样一种看法，早在古希腊哲学家亚里士多德那里便已经初露端倪。亚里士多德不仅明确宣布“神学”乃“第一哲学”，而且还断言神乃“万物的原因，而且是本原”以及第一哲学乃研究万物的“为什么”即“根本原因”和“不动的实体”的学问。③ 他的这样一种理路与黑格尔并无本质的区别。托马斯·阿奎那虽然不赞成亚里士多德关于神乃“不动实体”的看法，但他却不

---

① 黑格尔：《宗教哲学》（上），魏庆征译，中国社会科学出版社 1999 年版，第 17 页。

② 参阅黑格尔：《哲学史讲演录》第 1 卷，贺麟、王太庆译，商务印书馆 1978 年版，第 78 页；《法哲学原理》，范阳、张企泰译，商务印书馆 1979 年版，第 351 页。黑格尔在其中说道：“宗教和哲学有一共同的内容，只是形式不同罢了。”

③ 参见北京大学哲学系外国哲学史教研室：《西方哲学原著选读》上卷，商务印书馆 1981 年版，第 120 页。

仅明确地将上帝宣布为“一”或“绝对单纯者”,① 而且还明确地宣布上帝乃“存在本身”或“存在活动”。② 他的这样一种非实体主义处置不仅将哲学的最高范畴与宗教信仰的最高对象鲜明地对应起来甚至等同起来，从而为哲学与宗教的统一性和兼容性提供了直接的逻辑根据，而且他将之作为上帝的存在本身理解成一种生生不已的创造活动的做法倒是更接近黑格尔的思想了。

哲学真理与宗教真理的统一性和兼容性不仅有其历史根据和逻辑根据，而且也是哲学发展本身所需要的。如所周知，哲学不仅是追求“多”中之“一”的反思活动，而且还是追求“一切”中之“一”的活动，但哲学研究的主体却总是处于一定的时空之中，总是作为“多”或“一切”中的一分子存在于世的。这就给哲学研究达到其终极目标的努力预设了种种障碍。为了克服这些障碍，哲学研究的主体就需要不断地提升自身的精神境界，逐步实现其自身与“一切皆一”中之“一”的契合，实现思维主体与思维客体的合一。张载所谓“民吾同胞；物吾与也”,③ 即是谓此。然而，若要达到这样一种境界，没有助力是不可能实现的。柏拉图因此而提出了“哲学乃死亡的排练”的著名命题。④ 然而，排练死亡无疑需要一种超越生死的境界，否则这个关隘是断然穿越不了的。而宗教信仰在推动人们臻于超越生死境界、与终极实存（即作为“一”的神）合一方面无疑有其妙用。这也是许多大哲学家即使不具有宗教信仰也总是具有某种宗教情怀或宗教意境的根由。为什么中世纪哲学能够突破希腊哲学实体主义的藩篱而走向非实体主义？为什么中世纪哲学能够突破希腊哲学中“魂学”的局限而达到“全整的人”的概念？为什么中世纪哲学能够突破古希腊哲学“类”意识的局限而提出“个体化原则”？所有这一切显然都与基督宗教信仰的推动

① 参阅托马斯·阿奎那:《论存在者与本质》，段德智译，《世界哲学》2007 年第 4 期。

② Cf. Thomae de Aquino, *Summa Contra Gentiles*, I, cap.22, 7.

③ 张载:《正蒙·乾称篇第十七》,《张载集》，中华书局 1978 年版，第 62 页。

④ 柏拉图:《斐多篇》64A，67E，81A，载《柏拉图全集》第一卷，王晓朝译，人民出版社 2002 年版，第 60、65、85 页。

不无关系。[①] 我们常常说"经院哲学不仅是一种指向性极强的形而上学，而且还是一种指向性极强的生存论",[②] 究其根本原因，也在于此。无论如何，离开了基督宗教及其神学思想的深刻影响，中世纪哲学，特别是经院哲学的成就是根本不可设想的。

宗教不仅在西方哲学发展的历史上扮演过重要的角色，而且在中国哲学发展的历史上也发挥过至关紧要的作用。我们知道，宋明理学是中国儒学发展历史上的一个极其重要的阶段，而它对先秦儒学的超越最根本的就在于它之具有更为鲜明的形而上学色彩。先秦儒学采取"就事论理"的进路，强调的是形而上与形而下的关联性与浑然一体性。而宋明儒学采取的则是"就理论理"的进路，开始强调形而上与形而下的区分，自觉地将自己的哲学思考定格在形而上的层面上。朱熹不仅将"无形的理"规定为自己哲学的最高范畴，而且把这一点说得很明白:"形而上者，无形无影是此理。形而下者，有情有状是此器。"[③] 尽管朱熹强调"性即理"，而陆九渊和王阳明强调"心即理"，但他们之强调"无形的理"或"形上的理"则是一致的。然而，促成宋明儒学迈出这一步的一个重要动因便是中国宗教。朱熹坦然承认道家道教对宋明理学的影响。他曾经说过:"至妙之理，有生生之意焉，程子所取老氏之说也。"[④] 陆九渊虽然声明他的心学"因读孟子而自得之",[⑤] 但是他的心学却还是被朱熹说成是"昭昭灵灵"的禅学。[⑥] 明末清初的潘平格（1610—1677）讲"朱子道，陆子禅"，

---

① 参见段德智:《试论经院哲学的学院性质及其学术地位》，载徐志伟主编:《基督教思想评论》，上海三联书店 2008 年版，第 11—13 页。

② 段德智:《经院哲学与宗教文化研究丛书·总序》，翟志宏:《阿奎那自然神学思想研究》，人民出版社 2008 年版，第 7 页。

③ 朱熹:《朱子语类》卷九十五第六册，(宋) 黎靖德编，王星贤点校，中华书局 1986 年版，第 2421 页。

④ 朱熹:《朱子语类》卷一百二十五第八册，(宋) 黎靖德编，王星贤点校，中华书局 1986 年版，第 2995 页。

⑤ 陆九渊:《陆九渊集》卷三十五，中华书局 1980 年版，第 471 页。

⑥ 朱熹:《朱子语类》卷一百二十四第八册，(宋) 黎靖德编，王星贤点校，中华书局 1986 年版，第 2978 页。

看来此言不诬也。由此看来，离开了中国道教和中国佛教的影响，宋明理学的学术成就是很难设想的。①

诚然，按照马克思的唯物史观，哲学的发展归根到底是由经济决定的。但是，这似乎并不排除宗教及其神学对哲学发展的影响。这是因为唯物史观虽然强调经济对哲学意识形态及其发展的决定性影响，但却并未因此而认为经济直接决定哲学的历史形态及其发展过程，而是认为经济对哲学历史形态及其发展过程的影响是间接的，是要经过包括宗教在内的许多中间环节的，从而宗教对哲学的影响不仅是存在的，而且还是直接的而非间接的。关于这个问题，恩格斯下面一段话是发人深思的。恩格斯说道："政治、法、哲学、宗教、文学、艺术等等的发展是以经济发展为基础的。但是，它们又都相互作用并对经济基础发生作用。并非只有经济状况才是原因，才是积极的，其余一切都不过是消极的结果。"② 就我们当前的话题论，我们可以从恩格斯的这段话中得出如下两个结论：首先，宗教对哲学的"作用"是存在的，正如哲学对宗教的"作用"是存在的一样。其次，宗教对哲学的"作用"不是"普通"的，而是"因果性"的，有可能是"积极"的，而并非只是"消极"的。诚然，推动哲学发展的还有经济、政治、法律、文学和艺术等，但无论如何，宗教及其神学也是哲学发展的一项重要动力。而且，如果我们考虑到宗教不只是一种社会意识形态，而且还是一种具有重大影响的社会组织、社会群体和社会存在，则在对哲学影响的力度和广度方面，宗教对哲学的影响之远远超出政治观念、法律观念、道德和文学艺术等社会意识形态就是一件完全可能的事情了。恩格斯在谈到基督宗教及其神学在西方中世纪意识形态体系中"万流归宗"的地位时，曾经说道："中世纪把意识形态的其他一切形式——哲学、政治、法学，都合并到神学中，使它们成为神学中的科目"，"中世纪的历史只知道一种形式的意识形态，即宗

① 参阅段德智：《宗教学》，人民出版社 2010 年版，第 321 页。

② 《马克思恩格斯选集》第 4 卷，人民出版社 1995 年版，第 732 页。

教和神学”。① 至少对于西方中世纪的哲学来说，基督宗教及其神学对于哲学的影响是其他社会意识形态所远远不及的。

从哲学动力学的高度来审视宗教与哲学的关系乃本文的一项重要目标。

四、对宗教的哲学反思与哲学无“禁区”

本文的另一项主题是对宗教的哲学反思。如前所述，对宗教的哲学反思与对哲学的宗教反思不同，后者属于宗教及其神学，关涉的是“宗教的哲学维度”，前者则属于哲学，关涉的则是“哲学的宗教维度”，更具体地说，关涉的是哲学的“研究范围”问题或哲学究竟有无“禁区”的问题。

因此，当我们在考察对宗教的反思时，可能遇到的首要的和基本的问题便在于我们的哲学研究应不应、要不要以及如何对宗教作出哲学思考的问题。既然我们在前面已经指出，哲学的发展事实上总同宗教掺和在一起的，既然哲学的内容与宗教的内容并无二致，既然在哲学的发展历史上，宗教常常扮演积极的助推的角色，则我们似乎也就从中获得了将宗教作为我们哲学研究对象的应然性或必要性的某些理据，从而在这里我们也就无需赘述了。下面，我们就把话题转到我们的哲学研究究竟要不要以及如何对宗教作出哲学思考这样两个问题上。

要不要对宗教进行哲学反思这个问题虽然与应不应对宗教进行哲学思考有逻辑上的关联，但它首先涉及的却是哲学研究的范围问题。诚然，对哲学研究的范围问题，人们也有不同的理解。哲学这个词据说最早是由毕达哥拉斯提出来的。他当时用的是 philosophia 这个希腊词，其基本意思是爱好智慧，也就是爱好追求真理，爱好探求万物的本原。1847 年，日本启蒙家西周在《百一新论》中用“哲学”汉译英文单词 philosophy，其后于 1896 年前后康有为等将

① 《马克思恩格斯选集》第 4 卷，人民出版社 1995 年版，第 255、235 页。

西周的这个译法引进到我们中国。西周的这个译法虽然有其创新之处，但与我国传统哲学对哲学的理解颇为契合。因为我国传统哲学中的“哲”虽然也有“哲人”的含义，但毕竟也内蕴有“哲学”的意涵。那么，究竟什么才算爱好智慧呢？在哲学史上，爱好智慧所意指的无非是人们探究隐藏在自然现象、社会现象和人类思维现象背后的东西，也就是黑格尔所说的“完全普遍”的、被视为终极实存的东西。这种“完全普遍”的、被视为终极实存的东西本身为“一”，但它却能产生、支配宇宙万物，亦即它能产生、支配“一切”。这种“一”在古希腊哲学中，先是被称作“始基”、“存在”、“数”、“火”和“原子”等，后来又被称作“理念”和“实体”等。而在古代中国，则被称作“天”、“道”和“理”等。这就是说，哲学研究的既是“一切皆一”的“一”，也是“一皆一切”的“一”，从而宽泛地讲，没有什么东西应该逃逸出哲学视野之外。换言之，在哲学面前是没有任何禁区可言的。对哲学设定禁区，也就意味着哲学不再以“完全普遍”的东西为自己的研究对象和内容，从而也就因此而丧失了哲学的本性不复是哲学了。更何况从宗教诞生之日起，宗教就一直是最为重要的社会现象和精神现象之一，并对人类社会的发展和人类文化的进步产生了无可替代的影响。因此，倘若将宗教设定为哲学研究的禁区，则哲学之为哲学也就成了一个非常值得怀疑的事情了。把哲学视野转向宗教不仅为面向世界、面向现实的哲学家或哲学工作者所必须，而且也为哲学家或哲学工作者之为哲学家或哲学工作者所必须。我们这样说不是说每个哲学家或哲学工作者都应该成为潜心研究宗教的专门学者，而是说任何一个哲学家或哲学工作者都不应当将宗教完全置放到自己的理论视野之外并且对于宗教研究持完全排拒的态度和立场。

如何对宗教进行哲学反思似乎是一个更为复杂的问题。一些学者简单地用理性与信仰的关系来框照和界定哲学与宗教神学的关系使得我们对这样一个问题的讨论越来越步履维艰。因此，在这里我们首先需要指出的便是这样一个公式的简单化和荒谬性。宗教神学固然要讲信仰，但它却并不因此而完全排拒理性。神学这个词在希腊文和拉丁文中为 theologia，源自 theos（神）和 lógos（理性，对……的研究，对……的理性思考，关于……的学问)，因此，其基本意思是“对神的研究”、“对神的理性思考”或“关于神的学问”。而“研究”和“学问”就不是单纯的信仰，而同样具有“理性思考”的意味。我们中文中的“神学”这个字眼也同样有两个方面的意涵：“神学”一方面是“神”的学，另一方面又是神的“学”，既关涉到宗教信仰对象，也关涉到对宗教信仰对象的理性思考。因此，信仰和理性就像马德堡半球那样结合在神学之中，离开了宗教信仰或宗教信仰对象固然无神学可言，但是，倘若离开了理性思考和理性推证，同样也没有任何形式的神学。神学即是对宗教信条所做的种种理性推证。德尔图良（145—220）在《论基督的肉身》中曾说过“惟其不可能，我才相信”。而路德则甚至骂过“理性娼妓!”这样的咒语。① 乍一看他们两个人似乎都蛮不讲理，但是深究起来他们之不讲理其实也就是在讲理，在作理性推证。

其次，是神学与宗教性哲学的关联与区别问题。神学与宗教性哲学虽然都讲理性推证，但理性推证的前提却有所区别。一般来说，神学的理性推证往往是以宗教经典和宗教传统为其理论前提和基本理据的，而宗教性哲学则是以哲学原理为其理论前提或基本理据的。中世纪著名思想家托马斯·阿奎那有两部重要的著作，其中一部为《反异教大全》，另一部为《神学大全》。《反异教大全》虽然旨在站在基督宗教立场上反对其他宗教对基督宗教的攻击从而捍卫基督宗教神学，但托马斯却认为《圣经》和《圣传》对于基督宗教及其神学虽然重要，但却不被其他宗教所承认，因此倘若以它们为理论前提和理论依据来反对和驳斥其他宗教便势必毫无效果，故而他在《反异教大全》中基本上不引用《圣经》作为理据，而是注重以哲学原理作为理据。在《反异教大全》中，托马斯把这一点讲得很明白。他写道：“异教徒是既不接受《旧约》也不接受《新约》的。所以，我们必须诉诸于自然理性（naturalem rationem)，因为对自然理性，

① 参阅巴雷特：《非理性的人》，段德智译，上海译文出版社 2007 年版，第 99—100、28 页。在其中，作者曾称赞德尔图良为“非凡的有识之士和有影响的作家”。

所有的人都是不能不认同的”。[①] 也正因为如此,《反异教大全》也被称作《哲学大全》。与《反异教大全》不同,《神学大全》不仅以哲学原理(自然理性)为理据,而且还以《圣经》和《圣传》为理据,故而它从总体上看属于神学著作。[②] 诚然,无论是神学还是宗教性哲学都具有为宗教教义做理性推证的宗旨和性质,但它们理性推证的前提却有明显的区别。在《神学大全》中,阿奎那不仅明确地称自然神学为“哲学之一部分”(pars philosophiae),而且还明确地将其作为“哲学之一部分”而与“作为神圣学问的神学”对置起来,宣称“作为神圣学问的神学同作为哲学之一部分的神学分属不同种类(differt secundum genus)的学问”。[③] 托马斯的这样一种努力可以说是与我们殊途同归。

第三,我们之作为对宗教哲学反思的宗教哲学是既有别于神学也有别于宗教性哲学的。如上所述,神学以宗教始以宗教终,宗教性哲学以哲学始以宗教终,而我们所谓宗教哲学则以哲学始以哲学终。这就是说,我们之作为对宗教哲学反思的宗教哲学之所以不同于神学,乃是因为它不仅以哲学始而非以宗教始,而且还以哲学终而非以宗教终。而我们之作为对宗教哲学反思的宗教哲学之所以不同于宗教性哲学,则是因为它虽然也以哲学始但它却以哲学终而非以宗教终。神学和宗教性哲学虽然都内蕴有理性推证,但却都是以论证宗教教义为宗旨和归宿的,从而也都在所难免地具有护教学的色彩。我们之作为对宗教哲学反思的宗教哲学虽然与宗教性哲学一样也都以哲学始,但其理性推证的目标却在于普遍的理性结论或哲学结论,从而完全祛除了护教学色彩而具有鲜明的思辨品格和形上意蕴。例如,安瑟尔谟(1033—1109)关于上帝存在的本体论证明虽然是以柏拉图的理念论为其理论前提或理论依据的,但他的这一理性证明的根本目标却在于维护基督宗教关于上帝存在的教义和信仰。托马斯的关

① Thomae de Aquino, *Summa Contra Gentiles*, I, cap.2, 4.

② 《神学大全》各集的情况也有所不同。例如,其中第 1 集明显地具有宗教性哲学的意味,而第 3 集则典型地具有神学意味。

③ Thomae de Aquino, *Summa Theologiae*, Ia, Q.1, a.1.

于上帝存在的宇宙论证明也是如此。它虽然以亚里士多德的形而上学和认识论为其理论前提或理论依据，但他的这一理性证明的根本目标也是在于维护基督宗教关于上帝存在的教义和信仰。而我们之作为对宗教哲学反思的宗教哲学则不是这样，它作为对宗教的哲学反思，虽然也是以哲学原理为其理论前提或理论依据，但其目标却不在于维护某个宗教的教义和信仰，而是在于从中得出关于宗教普遍本质和一般发展规律的哲理性的结论。例如，当我们用唯物史观对世界诸宗教及其神学作出考察后得出“宗教神学归根到底是一种人学”这样一个结论时，其目标便不在于为某一宗教教义和宗教信仰作出辩护，而是在于昭示世界诸宗教的人学本质。再如，当我们用辩证唯物史观考察宗教的功能时，我们立足于从宗教功能“二律背反”这样一个角度和立场，不仅旨在阐述宗教的正功能，而且对其负功能也有所涉猎，这就表明我们之考察宗教功能不仅根本没有为某一宗教的教义和信仰辩护这样一种企图，甚至也根本没有为世界诸宗教及其教义和信仰进行辩护的企图，而只是在于对世界诸宗教的功能作出哲学的说明。最后，当我们考察《圣经》中的“立约之道”时，我们的目标也不在于对“西奈山缔盟”和“登山宝训”事件的宗教气氛作出刻意的渲染，而是在于挖掘潜存于其中的“契约精神”和“法治意识”及其现时代意义，故而与护教学大相径庭。

写作本文的一个隐秘的意图在于充当“牛虻”的角色，呼唤我国哲学界同仁更多地关注哲学的宗教维度，更多地注重对宗教及其经典进行深入的哲学思考，以期我国的哲学臻于新的高度，出现新的局面。因此本文的根本目标是哲学学的或者说是哲学动力学的。从哲学学和哲学动力学的高度来审视哲学与宗教的辩证关系乃本文追求的精神境界。

（原载《外国哲学》第 26 辑）

马克思主义哲学的内史与外史的书写

何 萍

一、本题研究之必要性

自黑格尔创立哲学史这门学科以来，哲学的内史和外史就成为哲学史书写中必须讨论的问题。所有的哲学家，凡是撰写哲学史的著作，都会在其导论或绪论中专门讨论这一问题。

哲学家们之所以要讨论这一问题，是由哲学史的研究对象的特殊性决定的。哲学史的研究对象是哲学的一般。这里所说的哲学的一般，不是单个的哲学理论，不是讲的哲学和现实关系的问题，而是讲的哲学的本质和个别哲学派别和哲学形态之间的关系。哲学的本质是一，是逻辑的东西；个别哲学派别和哲学形态是多，是历史的东西。个别哲学派别和哲学形态的历史又有两种：一种是无数个别的哲学派别和哲学形态之间的联系和发展。这种历史构成了哲学自身发展的历史，即哲学的内史；一种是无数个别哲学派别和哲学形态产生的历史条件，主要指一定时代和民族的文化，与哲学发生联系的各种文化形式，即宗教、神话、科学、艺术、文学、语言等等。这些都是哲学发展的外在因素，构成了哲学的外史。由于哲学史的研究对象具有这双重的历史，所以，哲学家在叙述哲学史之前，必须研究哲学史中的历史的东西，区分哲学的内史和外史，以便确定哲学史应该叙述什么样的历史，以及如何叙述这一历史。由此可见，区分哲学的内史和外史，是哲学家对于哲学史书写的一种方法论的反思，体现了哲学史研究的自觉意识。

但是，哲学史本身又是一门发展的学科。哲学史这门学科的发展是与哲学的发展相联系的：哲学的变革是哲学史观变革的内在根据，而哲学史观的变革是哲学变革的完成。也就是说，一种哲学，只有当它能够进入哲学史的叙述，能够证明它与前此哲学之间的联系和区别，能够比前此哲学更深刻地展示哲学的一般的时候，它变革哲学的意义才能得到肯定。直到这时，它的变革才算完成。这种通过哲学史来研究哲学、检验哲学变革的意义、证明某种哲学的合理性的思路，是黑格尔在建立哲学史这门学科时提出来的，也是黑格尔创立哲学史这门学科的目的。自黑格尔之后，这种哲学研究的思路得到了普遍的认同，从而成为了哲学的研究方式和哲学自我证明的方式。正是这样，每一时代的哲学家，为了证明他们的哲学的合理性，都要去研究哲学史，以新近发展起来的哲学去改写以往叙述出来的哲学史。哲学史这门学科就在哲学变革的推动下发展起来。这一点，在文德尔班批评黑格尔的哲学史观中得到了鲜明的体现。文德尔班是新康德主义的哲学家，也是著名的文化哲学的哲学家。文化哲学不同于近代理性主义哲学的一个根本特点，就是它把哲学的对象看作是历史，而不是科学；强调哲学的根据是历史科学，而不是自然科学。从这一观点出发，文化哲学在哲学理论上建立了历史的形而上学，以对抗近代理性主义哲学的科学的形而上学；在哲学史的叙述上以历史科学的个别化方法取代自然科学的普遍性方法，揭示哲学发展的文化必然性。在文化哲学的这两个方面的创造中，文德尔班在哲学史研究方面的贡献更大，文化哲学对于哲学变革的意义、它的理论的合理性，就是在他的哲学史书写中得到证明，并最终得到普遍认可的。他在《哲学史教程》的绪论中，首先对包括黑格尔在内的前此哲学家的哲学观念进行了批判。他指出，从古希腊以来的哲学虽然有种种不同的观点，但是，在把科学作为洞见人生观和价值观的基础，在把哲学“置于有更普遍意义的‘科学’概念之下”[①] 这一点上则是共同的。这种哲学观念的根本缺陷在于，只看

---

① 文德尔班：《哲学史教程》（上卷），罗达仁译，商务印书馆 1987 年版，第 12 页。

到了哲学中的逻辑的东西，而没有看到哲学中的历史的东西。进而，他指出了黑格尔哲学史观的荒谬之处。他指出，黑格尔把哲学史定义为理性范畴不断获得明确意识并进而达到概念形式的过程，强调哲学史的研究就是要揭示理性范畴的内在联系，这是对哲学史本质的说明；只有通过这一说明，哲学史才第一次成为科学。这是黑格尔对于哲学史这门学科建立所作的贡献。但是，这并不意味着黑格尔的哲学史观是完全正确的。在如何叙述理性范畴的演化过程上，黑格尔由于受哲学是普遍科学概念的指导，只强调逻辑的东西，而删除了历史的东西。在他那里，哲学的内史只是抽象的理性概念结构，个别哲学家的历史创造活动是没有意义的，是根本不能进入哲学内史的；哲学的外史虽然对哲学的发展产生影响，但是，它们对于哲学史的叙述来说，却是一些无关的东西，是需要被排除的东西。由于删除了历史的东西，黑格尔就只能借助于一种想像的必然性来说明一种范畴向另一种范畴的过渡。他这样叙述哲学史，的确保证了哲学史的哲学性质，保证了哲学史的内在逻辑的清晰性，但却使哲学史失去了历史的内容，从而"经常违背历史事实"①。从这一方面看，黑格尔有关哲学内史和外史的观点，又是需要修正的。文德尔班从对黑格尔哲学史观的这一批评出发，对哲学的内史和外史作了新的阐发。他提出，哲学史固然"只能通过思想内在的必然性和'事物的逻辑'去理解"②，但是，哲学史中的思想的内在必然和"事物的逻辑"不应该是黑格尔所理解的科学的逻辑，而应该是历史的逻辑，不应该是理性的必然性，而应该是文化的必然性。历史的逻辑、文化的必然性包含着黑格尔所要求的理性的东西、逻辑的东西，同时，又要求结合哲学家个人的哲学创造活动，在无数哲学家个人的思维中去揭示哲学的理性的和逻辑的东西。由此决定，哲学的内史是由思维的普遍性和哲学家个人的哲学创造活动结合而成的结构，其中，思维的普遍性是逻辑的东西，是哲学一般的方面，哲学家个人的哲学创造活动是历史的东西，是决定哲学一般的性质的

① 文德尔班：《哲学史教程》（上卷），罗达仁译，商务印书馆1987年版，第20页。

② 文德尔班：《哲学史教程》（上卷），罗达仁译，商务印书馆1987年版，第21页。

方面；正是由于后者，思维的普遍性才具有了文化必然性的特性，而不致于变成抽象的、片面的、想像的理性。除此之外，哲学的外史，对于哲学史的叙述来说，也不是无关紧要的，因为，哲学家个人的创造活动总是与他们的生活环境相联系的，与他们时代的各种文化因素相联系的，因此，哲学史只有通过考察哲学家的生活环境、考察一定时代的哲学思想与其他文化的关系，才能揭示哲学的一般，才能使哲学史变成"批判—哲学的科学"[①]。在这里，文德尔班通过重新定义哲学的内史和外史，建立了文化哲学的哲学史观。根据这一哲学史观，哲学史是"欧洲人用科学的概念具体表现了他们对宇宙的观点和对人生的判断"[②]的过程，是"种种不同的单个的思维活动的产物"[③]，由此决定，哲学的历史进程必然是形形色色和多种多样的。这样一来，文德尔班就描绘了一幅完全不同于黑格尔的哲学史的图景。

我认为，考察文德尔班对黑格尔哲学史观的批判和对哲学内史与外史的界定，对于我们思考中国马克思主义哲学史的研究现状，有着十分重要的方法论意义。因为，它给了我们一种研究马克思主义哲学史的规范。这一规范包括两个方面的内容：其一，马克思主义哲学史，不论具有什么样的特殊性，只要想成为一门科学，就必须首先符合哲学史这门学科的一般规定，而要获得哲学史学科的一般规定，就必须反思它的内史和外史，建立起马克思主义哲学史学科的自觉意识；其二，马克思主义哲学史的研究必须扎根于一个半多世纪的全部哲学思想发展的历史之中，尤其是要扎根于20世纪的马克思主义哲学发展的历史之中。因为马克思主义哲学内部诸多传统的形成和多种形态的演变，只到20世纪才得到充分的发展和显现，所以，我们只有研究20世纪的马克思主义哲学，才能看清马克思主义哲学发展的内在逻辑，也才能把握马克思主义哲学的一般，而只有深刻地把握了马克思主义哲学的一般，马克思主义哲学史的

---

① 文德尔班：《哲学史教程》（上卷），罗达仁译，商务印书馆1987年版，第25页。

② 文德尔班：《哲学史教程》（上卷），罗达仁译，商务印书馆1987年版，第18页。

③ 文德尔班：《哲学史教程》（上卷），罗达仁译，商务印书馆1987年版，第20页。

叙述才能够称得上是哲学的，马克思主义哲学史也才能由此而成为一门相对独立的科学。我国的马克思主义史研究最欠缺的恰恰就是这两个方面。就第一个方面而言，我国的马克思主义哲学史研究因为没有经过方法论的讨论而缺乏哲学史的自觉意识，所以，在马克思主义哲学史的叙述中，大量叙说的是历史的东西，而非逻辑的东西；历史的东西成了主题，逻辑的东西只是作为历史东西的一种点缀而出现。按照这种方式叙述出来的哲学史，或许符合了逻辑与历史相一致的原则，却也难以称得上是真正的哲学史，因为哲学史作为一门独立的学科的首要条件，是它所叙述的逻辑的东西必须是哲学的一般，凡是不具有哲学一般的性质，凡是没有揭示出哲学一般的“哲学史”，都不能成为真正意义上的哲学史。可见，对于哲学史这门学科来说，发现哲学史的内在要求，是比强调逻辑与历史相一致的原则更为重要的方面。就第二个方面而言，我国的马克思主义哲学史研究所遵循的辩证唯物主义和历史唯物主义理论不是从马克思主义哲学的全部历史发展中抽象出来的，而是从马克思主义哲学的教科书中搬过来的。马克思主义哲学教科书中的哲学理论只是诸多马克思主义哲学形态中的一种，绝不是马克思主义哲学理论的全部；它是马克思主义哲学的特殊，而不是马克思主义哲学的一般。用这种特殊的理论去叙述全部的马克思主义哲学史，必然会出现许多违背事实的东西。我国马克思主义哲学史研究中出现的种种问题，比如，把西方马克思主义哲学排除于马克思主义哲学史的系统之外，对第二国际马克思主义哲学的贬斥，等等，都是由此而引起的。鉴于此，本文立足于一个半多世纪以来的马克思主义哲学发展的历史，以20世纪马克思主义哲学的发展为历史的和理论的视角，讨论马克思主义哲学的内史和外史，以此说明马克思主义哲学史的书写问题。

二、马克思主义哲学的内史及其书写

我国的马克思主义哲学史叙述中出现的内容庞杂、逻辑线索不清的种种问题，都是因为没有理清和确定马克思主义哲学的内史造成的。因此，从方法论的高度探讨马克思主义哲学的内史及其书写的问题，应该成为本文研究的重点。

按照哲学史这门学科的规范，哲学的内史必须是哲学自身发展的历史，因而也必定是哲学史书写的主线。遵循这一规范，马克思主义哲学的内史，必须是马克思主义哲学自身发展的历史。那么，马克思主义哲学自身发展的历史是什么？它的本质和核心理论是什么？是以辩证唯物主义和历史唯物主义理论为核心展开的历史，还是以实践和辩证法为核心展开的历史？对于这个问题，我国学者在马克思主义哲学的理论研究领域，已经作了许多的研究，却很少从马克思主义哲学史观的角度加以研究。从哲学研究的思路来说，从理论的角度研究问题和从哲学史观的角度研究问题是不同的。从理论的角度研究问题，讲的是理论本身，或者说，是具体的理论问题，而从哲学史观的角度研究问题，讲的是理论的深层结构，或者说，是理论的构造机制。前者是对理论的静态的说明，后者是对理论的动态的、历史发展的说明。由于两者之间存在着这种差别，所以，理论的研究不能代替哲学史观的研究，理论研究的成果可以为哲学史观的研究所用，但不能是简单的搬用，而应该把它纳入到哲学史研究的系统中作重新阐释。这一点也适合于我国的马克思主义哲学的理论研究和哲学史观研究的关系。在理论研究中，我国学者通过对马克思和恩格斯哲学的关系、马克思哲学和马克思主义哲学关系、西方马克思主义哲学和马克思主义哲学的关系等多方面的讨论，提出，马克思主义哲学的本质不是原有的马克思主义哲学教科书中的辩证唯物主义和历史唯物主义的基本原理，而是马克思的实践和辩证法。这一研究成果应该成为马克思主义哲学史观研究的理论基础，但是，马克思主义哲学史观的研究不能简单地把这一成果运用于叙述马克思主义哲学的发展史，如果这样的话，那么，它只是用一种理论标准代替另一种理论标准，用一种马克思主义哲学排挤另一种马克思主义哲学。这样叙述出来的马克思主义哲学史与以往的马克思主义哲学史著作叙述出来的马克思主义哲学史并无实质性的差别。然而，如果从马克思主义哲学史观研究的视角来反思这一成果，情况就不同了。在这里，马克思的实践和辩证法不是理论的研究对象，而是哲学史的研究对象。作为哲学史的研究对象，研究马克思的实践和辩证法所要解答的问题是：马克思的实践和辩证法的内在结构如何？它是如何成为马克思主义哲学的本质的？又是如何构造出一部哲学史的？解答这些问题，就是解答何为马克思主义哲学的内史的问题。这也就是我在这里所要论述的问题。

实践和辩证法成为马克思主义哲学的本质，严格地说，是几代马克思主义哲学家创造的结果，因而，是一种历史的产物。不可否认，把实践和辩证法作为新唯物主义学说的本质是马克思首先提出来的，但是，马克思在提出这一观点时，并不是用它来定义整个的马克思主义哲学，而是讲的他自己的哲学品格。这种哲学如果不经几代马克思主义哲学家的创造性发展，如果不发生形态上的变化，那么，它就会如同康德的批判哲学和黑格尔的辩证法那样，永远都只能和马克思个人的名字连在一起，永远都只是马克思个人的哲学，而绝不能发展为一种哲学传统、一种哲学思潮。然而，当马克思以后的马克思主义哲学家把马克思的实践和辩证法定义为马克思主义哲学的本质并在学理上发展这一哲学时，马克思哲学的命运就不同了，它不再是马克思个人的哲学，而是世界各民族进步力量共同创造的思想财富。这一事实，要求我们联系一个半多世纪马克思主义哲学的发展，尤其是20世纪马克思主义哲学的发展，来思考马克思主义哲学本身的历史。这就是马克思主义哲学史研究的历史主义原则。

历史地看，马克思主义哲学家对马克思的实践和辩证法的阐释主要是从两个层面上展开的：第一个层面，是把实践和辩证法当作一种精神、一种哲学理念，来阐释它们对于马克思主义哲学革新的方法论意义；第二个层面，是结合时代的变革和本民族的哲学传统，赋予实践和辩证法不同的含义，创造不同形态、不同传统的马克思主义哲学理论。前者建立起不同时代、不同地域的马克思主义哲学之间的深刻的联系，后者则创造了马克思主义哲学在不同时代、不同地域的差别，从而展示了马克思主义哲学的变革。马克思主义哲学正是在这两个看似矛盾的层面中创造了自己的传统，从而获得了不同于其他哲学的本质。因此，我们要把握马克思主义哲学的本质，对马克思主义哲学的内史作出界定，就必须历史地考察这两个层面的内容以及它们之间的关系。

实践和辩证法作为一种精神、一种哲学理念，是马克思最早阐发出来的。博士论文是马克思从事哲学创造的第一部哲学著作。马克思在写作这部著作时，他的唯物史观的理论还远远没有形成，但是，他的唯物史观理论中所包含的新的哲学精神却已经在这部著作中先阐发出来了。在这部著作中，马克思以偶然性为核心范畴，通过对原子偏斜意义的说明，阐发了个体自由的精神及其在现实世界中的实现问题。在阐发这一问题中，他提出了著名的“世界的哲学化同时也就是哲学的世界化”的论断。这一论断揭示了哲学与现实之间的相互否定关系，强调了哲学的批判精神。① 在《关于费尔巴哈的提纲》中，马克思进一步把哲学的批判精神概括为：“环境的改变和人的活动或自我改变的一致”和“改变世界”的哲学 ②。当他把这一精神贯穿于对政治的、意识形态的和资本主义经济的批判之中，贯穿于对工业的批判性研究之中时，他就超越了青年黑格尔派的哲学，超越了他同时代其他的哲学，而创立了历史唯物主义的理论。这一过程表明，马克思的实践和辩证法绝不只是一些能够说明人类历史规律的理论，它还包含了哲学不断趋向现实，并通过理论的反思和批判而又超越现实的诉求，包括了彻底批判的辩证法精神。马克思之后的马克思主义哲学家把马克思哲学中的这种现实的批判精神概括为一种历史的辩证方法，一种哲学创造的原则。罗莎·卢森堡在批评那些教条式地对待马克思思想的观点时，反复强调：“只是在经济领域内才谈得上马克思创立了一个或多或少完整的理论体系。相反，他的理论中最有价值的唯物主义的辩证的历史观却只表现为一种研究方法、一些天才的指导思想，它们使人有可能展望一个崭新的世界，开辟独

---

① 对马克思博士论文中的这一思想的详细论述，见拙文《马克思博士论文中的本体论问题》，《学术月刊》2002 年第 9 期。

② 参见《马克思恩格斯选集》第 1 卷，人民出版社 1995 年版，第 55、57 页。

立活动的无限远景，激励我们的思想大胆地飞进尚未研究的领域。”① 在这里，罗莎·卢森堡把马克思的哲学当作一种思想解放的力量，一种反对教条主义的武器。正因为有了这个武器，她才能够突破了旧的理论框架，立足于19世纪末西欧资本主义的发展和世界历史的新变化，分析帝国主义现象，修改马克思的资本积累公式，创造帝国主义理论。所以，从理论内容上看，她的资本积累理论与马克思的资本积累理论有着巨大的差异，而从方法论上看，她却是把马克思的辩证法原则到底了，从而体现了她的哲学与马克思的哲学之间深刻的一致性。罗莎·卢森堡的这一马克思主义哲学的创造方式也体现在列宁的哲学创造活动之中，体现在西方马克思主义哲学家的哲学创造活动之中，同样地，也体现在毛泽东的哲学创造活动之中。马克思主义哲学的本质就是在这些马克思主义哲学家的连续不断地批判和创造活动中形成的。正是这种连续不断地批判和创造活动，把不同时代、不同民族的马克思主义哲学家的思想和观点联结下来，使他们之间具有了共同性，而这种共同性就是马克思主义哲学的本质。这一历史事实表明，马克思主义哲学的本质是它充满活力的创造精神，是辩证的批判方法，而不是某种既成马克思主义哲学理论，因此，它是开放的，而不是封闭的。那种把马克思主义的某一哲学理论当作马克思主义哲学的本质，以此衡论其他的马克思主义哲学形态的观点，其实就是我们通常所说的一种教条主义的马克思主义哲学观，是一种需要批判和摒弃的马克思主义哲学史观。

实践和辩证法作为一种哲学理论，就是被马克思称之为“实践的唯物主义”的学说。这一学说本身也是历史发展的。早在马克思和恩格斯那里，“实践的唯物主义”就已经包含了哲学各个领域的内容，本体论的、认识论的、辩证法的、意识形态的、语言学的、自然观的、历史观的、伦理学的，等等，但是，马克思和恩格斯从来就没有建立起关于这一学说的完整体系，其中的有些部分，比如本体论、认识论、意识形态、语言学、伦理学等，还根本没有充分

① 《卢森堡文选》上卷，人民出版社1984年版，第472页。

发展起来，有些部分，比如唯物主义的历史观、辩证法等，虽然有了较为完整的论述，但在理论的结构上、在研究的向度上，都打上了自由资本主义时代的印记，属于他们所处时代的理论。这些都为以后的马克思主义哲学理论创造留下了广阔的空间。从 19 世纪末开始，世界各国的马克思主义哲学家结合资本主义的新变化，结合资本主义在本民族发展的状况，对马克思和恩格斯创造的“实践的唯物主义”学说的各个部分都进行了结构性的改造，创造出不同的马克思主义哲学传统和不同的哲学形态。不同的马克思主义哲学传统，是马克思主义哲学与不同国家、民族哲学传统文化相结合的产物，体现了马克思主义哲学在空间上的拓展。这种空间上的拓展，在世界性范围内，形成了马克思主义哲学的东方传统和西方传统之别；而在这两种马克思主义哲学的内部，又有不同的哲学传统。在东方，有苏联马克思主义哲学传统与中国马克思主义哲学传统之别；在西方，有批判的马克思主义哲学传统与科学的马克思主义哲学传统之别，等等。不同的马克思主义哲学形态，是时代变革的产物，体现了马克思主义哲学在时间上的发展。从 19 世纪末到今天，马克思主义哲学曾经历了三次大的变革：第一次是 19 世纪末至 20 世纪初，面对西欧资本主义内部的变化、帝国主义现象的出现以及所引发的无产阶级革命，第二国际的马克思主义哲学家从资本主义存在的历史环境的角度研究资本主义崩溃的问题，创立了帝国主义理论，从而改变了唯物史观研究的向度；第二次是 20 世纪 20 年代至 60 年代，包括苏联和西方马克思主义哲学在内的马克思主义哲学家，围绕着无产阶级革命实践的问题，开展了马克思主义哲学的研究，从本体论上更新了马克思主义哲学，西方马克思主义哲学家还相继创造了文化的意识形态理论、日常生活批判理论等；第三次是 20 世纪 60 年代末至今，面对全球问题的出现，东西方马克思主义哲学家以全球化和现代性批判为主题，重新思考了马克思主义哲学的自然观和历史观，创造了生态学马克思主义哲学和分析的马克思主义哲学等等。马克思和恩格斯创立的“实践的唯物主义”学说正是在哲学传统的分流和哲学形态的变革中形成了多元发展的格局。这种多元发展的格局表明，马克思主义哲学的发展不是一个范畴的演进过程，而是哲学传统的分流和哲学形态的变革过程，因此，它的发展不可能是一元的、直线式的，而是多元的、立体式的。正是有了这种多元的、立体式的发展，实践和辩证法的本体论、认识论、意识形态、语言学和伦理学等理论才能被建构起来，马克思主义哲学也才能由此而成为20世纪主要哲学思潮之一。在这个意义上，可以说，如果没有几代马克思主义哲学家的创造，马克思和恩格斯创立的“实践的唯物主义”学说的全部哲学意义，尤其是它的现代意义，是根本不能呈现出来的，也谈不上有马克思主义哲学史。

从逻辑的角度分析，实践和辩证法的批判精神和多元化的哲学传统和理论形态共同构造了马克思主义哲学发展的内在机制。其中，批判精神体现了实践和辩证法的内在要求。这种内在要求有两种：一种是方法论意义上的；一种是理论创造意义上的。方法论意义上的内在要求，针对的是哲学的批判精神，是每一时代、每一民族的马克思主义哲学家在创造新的马克思主义哲学理论时，都必须坚持的东西，因而也是把每一时代、每一民族的马克思主义哲学联结起来的共同点。理论创造意义上的内在要求，针对的是具体的理论革新，它要求每一理论必须有时代的、民族的内容，有哲学家富有个性的创造。这种要求一旦满足，哲学的理论必然是多元化的，而不是一元化的。也就是说，理论创造意义上的内在要求构造的是马克思主义哲学发展的差异性。多元化的哲学传统和理论形态就是实践和辩证法的批判精神创造的成果，当然也是这双重要求的实现。从马克思主义哲学发展的历史形成看，多元化的哲学传统和理论形态又是后来的马克思主义哲学创造的历史起点。正是有了这个起点，后来的马克思主义哲学家的创造活动才有了新的内容，马克思主义哲学才有了阶段性的变化。在这个意义上可以说，多元化的哲学传统和理论形态构造了马克思主义哲学发展的不同阶段，不同环节。马克思主义哲学的历史就是在实践和辩证法的批判精神和多元化的哲学传统和理论形态的相互作用中创造出来的。

根据上述历史的叙述和逻辑的分析，实践和辩证法的批判精神和多元化的哲学传统和理论形态的相互作用及其所创造的历史，就是马克思主义哲学的内史，也是马克思主义哲学史叙述的主线。为要清晰地展现这一主线，马克思主义哲学史的叙述要遵循三个原则：第一，准确地描述各个哲学家的创造活动。实践和辩证法的批判精神是决定马克思主义哲学本性的方面，但这一精神不是预成的，而是通过个体的哲学家创造出来的，因此，要叙述马克思主义哲学的精神及其发展，就必须研究哲学家个体的富有个性的思想创造。这是从整体上叙述马克思主义哲学史的基础。第二，以问题为中心，研究不同时代马克思主义哲学发展的特点和独特的形态，通过哲学形态的变革揭示哲学发展的质变，从而建立起马克思主义哲学史叙述的时间向度。第三，以民族文化为背景，研究不同国家、民族的马克思主义哲学传统的形成及其历史演变，特别是比较东西方马克思主义哲学的传统，通过这些不同的哲学传统比较，叙述马克思主义哲学发展的世界化和多元化，从而建立起马克思主义哲学史叙述的空间向度。

三、马克思主义哲学的外史及其书写

一部马克思主义哲学史的著作，读起来，让人感到内容庞杂、逻辑线索不清，这是内史书写的问题，但是，如果读起来，让人感到全是历史背景的叙说、全是政治性的评论，则属于外史书写的问题了。通常，这两个部分的缺陷是分不开的，一部哲学史著作叙述得不成功首先是内史的书写出了问题，但是，对内史书写的检讨并不能代替对外史书写的反思，因为，即使内史的书写方式弄清了、明确了，还有一个是否需要书写外史和如何书写外史的问题。何况，书写外史，对于马克思主义哲学史来说，比之其他任何哲学史都显得更为重要和迫切。这是由马克思主义哲学的性质决定的。因为，马克思主义哲学在把“改变世界”作为自己的目的，强调外部世界是哲学的一个须臾不可分离的部分时，就已经注定了外史的书写要成为马克思主义哲学史叙述中的不可或缺的部分。所以，在检讨了马克思主义哲学内史的书写之后，马克思主义哲学外史书写的问题就凸显出来了。

哲学外史的书写一般说来包括三个方面的内容：第一个方面是哲学与时代的关系；第二个方面是哲学与其他学科之间的关系；第三个方面是一个民族哲学与其他民族哲学之间的关系。这三个方面的内容又可分为两类：一类是由第一个方面的内容所表现出来的哲学与现实之间的关系；一类是由第二和第三两个方面表现出来的学术联系。马克思主义哲学外史的书写，也应该包含这两类的关系。不过，由马克思主义哲学的性质所决定，马克思主义哲学史的叙述有自己独特的内容和书写方式。

就第一类的关系而言，马克思主义哲学外史的书写应该紧紧扣住以机器生产为标志的工业革命和资本主义生产方式及其变化。哲学与时代的关系，也就是哲学与现实生活的联系，但是，现实生活是复杂的、多方面的，并不是每一个方面都会对哲学起作用，而只有那些决定时代性质的方面才会对哲学起作用，哲学史的叙述就是要选取其中对哲学起主要作用的方面。这是从客观的方面而言的。从主观的方面看，有一个哲学家对现实生活中的某些方面感兴趣的问题，这种兴趣是与他们判断现实生活中的哪些因素对人们的精神生活、对该时代的哲学更有意义这一问题相关的。每一时代的哲学家，在创造自己的哲学时，都会指出该时代的现实生活中那些决定社会生活、历史发展和人类的精神生活一般性质的因素，然后用这些因素去说明现实生活的其他方面，以此建立起该时代的哲学。此外，同一时代的哲学家对现实生活的理解总有不同，对现实生活中起支配作用的思想的判断也不相同，这就决定了他们创造出来的哲学必然不同。哲学史上的科学主义和人文主义思潮的兴起与发展，就源于哲学家对现实生活中支配人们精神生活因素的判断不同：科学主义的哲学家把自然科学的思想作为支配人们精神生活的东西，于是，把哲学置于自然科学思维的基础之上，并且借助自然科学的思维方式建构起科学理性的形而上学；人文主义的哲学家把文学、历史学、伦理学、语言学等人文科学看作是人们精神生活的主要方面，于是，把这些学科的思维方式当作哲学思维的基础，建立道德伦理学说、政治哲学、历史哲学，直到建立起历史的形而上学。哲学与现实关系的这些不同反映到哲学史的研究上，就是，不同的哲学家对现实生活叙述有着不同的要求。在西方哲学家那里，对每一时代的哲学起支配作用的现实生活的叙述，大都集中于政治、自然科学和人们道德生活的变化等因素上，所以，他们主要通过这些因素的分析来叙述哲学与时代的关系。马克思主义哲学家也肯定政治、自然科学和人们道德生活的变化是现实生活中对哲学起支配作用的因素，但是，在马克思主义哲学家看来，在现代社会，政治、自然科学和人们道德生活的变化归根到底是从工业革命和资本主义生产方式及其变化中产生出来的，它们的性质、对哲学起作用的方式，也是由工业革命和资本主义生产方式的发展状况所决定的，因此，工业革命和资本主义生产方式及其变化是社会生活中更为根本的方面，也是对哲学起主导作用的因素，政治、自然科学和人们道德生活的变化对哲学的作用，都只能通过工业革命和资本主义生产方式及其变革这一中介来实现。这样，马克思主义哲学家就在工业革命和资本主义生产方式及其变化中找到了哲学与时代的本质联系，并根据工业的发展和资本主义生产方式的变化，创造不同时代的马克思主义哲学。在马克思和恩格斯那里，实践概念明显地包含着工业和资本主义批判的内容，马克思对实践唯物主义的所有原理的论述、对费尔巴哈哲学的批判，也都是从工业对于人的本质、对人类历史发展所带来的革命性影响这一角度展开的。自马克思、恩格斯之后，马克思主义哲学从第二国际到第三国际的发展，从东方到西方的拓展，无不是在研究工业革命和资本主义生产方式的变化中发展起来的。由此决定，马克思主义哲学史要叙述哲学与时代的关系，就应该抓住工业革命和资本主义生产方式的变化这条主线，而把政治、自然科学和人们道德生活的变化作为这条主线上的不同方面来论述。除此之外，马克思主义哲学史在论述工业革命和资本主义生产方式的变化时，要着重那些与哲学发生本质联系的东西，而不是罗列工业革命和资本主义生产方式变化的细节，具体地说，是以实践和辩证法的批判精神来审视工业革命和资本主义生产方式变化对马克思主义哲学的产生和发展所起的作用，说明每一时代的工业发展状况和资本主义生产方式变化的特点与该时代马克思主义哲学的关系。

就第二类的关系而言，马克思主义哲学外史的书写应该重点叙述马克思主义哲学与各民族文化传统之间的关系问题。西方哲学家在论述哲学的外史时，已经肯定了哲学的民族性特征，强调，哲学总是一定民族的思想、民族的精神，因而，哲学是民族的，但是，他们并不认为所有民族的思想都能称得上是哲学，而只有具有充分发展的理性思维形式的西方思想、西方文化，才能成为哲学，由此得出的结论是：西方哲学具有哲学的一般性质，是世界哲学。这是典型的西方中心论的思想。与西方哲学不同，马克思主义哲学产生于西欧的文化土壤，但它绝不是西方民族的，而是世界性的。这里所说的世界性，不是指的马克思主义哲学的世界性传播，而是指它具有世界文明的共同性和普遍性的内容。这种共同性和普遍性的内容主要有两点：一是指它具有建立在资本主义创造的世界性的生产方式之上的思维内容和形式；二是指它的共同性和普遍性的获得是在世界历史的形成中，通过改造各民族的文化传统而实现的。这样一来，各民族的文化传统既是马克思主义哲学获得共同性和普遍性的经验基础，也是马克思主义哲学共同性和普遍性的内容之一；马克思主义哲学要走进各民族的无产阶级革命实践，首先要走进各民族的文化传统，要在与各民族文化传统的融合中，创造出一种新的思维方式，被该民族所接受。由此决定，我们在叙述马克思主义哲学的世界性发展时，不能仅仅讲马克思主义哲学与各国无产阶级革命实践的关系，而必须讲马克思主义哲学与各民族文化传统之间的关系，叙述它在不同民族所形成的思维方式的特点，揭示它与各民族文化传统之间的学术联系。只有通过这一叙述，马克思主义哲学的学术思想内容才能充分地展示出来。相反，如果只讲马克思主义哲学与无产阶级革命实践的关系，而不理马克思主义哲学与民族文化传统之间的学术联系，就会把马克思主义哲学封闭在一个狭隘的圈子里，变成一种仅仅服务于政治的工具。这显然是降低了马克思主义哲学世界性发展的意义，也根本不符合马克思主义哲学发展的历史和逻辑，最重要的是，它不能展示马克思主义哲学作为思想史的内容。事实上，通过不同民族的哲学思维的相互交流、相互碰撞来考察一定民族的思维方式，是马克思研究哲学史的一个重要方法。早在《神圣家族》中，马克思就通过考察 18 世纪法国唯物主义者接受英国唯物主义的方式，说明、考察一个民族怎样吸收和改造其他民族的哲学思想，就能发现该民族的时代内容和哲学的思维传统。① 我以为，马克思提出的哲学史叙述的这一方法也适用于我们对马克思主义哲学外史的学术关系的书写。长期以来，我国学术界把马克思主义哲学与政治画等号，没有揭示出马克思主义哲学在中国传播和发展的学术价值，没有说明它对于改造中国传统文化，推动中国传统文化实现现代转型的意义，就是因为没有考察中国的马克思主义哲学与中国近代其他哲学传统的关系。自 20 世纪 90 年代开展起来的马克思主义哲学中国化研究给予了我们书写马克思主义哲学史一个重要的方法论启示，这就是，要求我们重视马克思主义哲学与各民族哲学传统之间的关系，通过考察马克思主义哲学与其他哲学传统的相互碰撞、相互吸收的过程，揭示马克思主义哲学内部传统的形成和哲学形态的变化。这一哲学史的研究方法，不仅为书写马克思主义哲学中国化的历史进程所必须，而且也为书写西方马克思主义哲学和北美的马克思主义哲学所必须。

以上对马克思主义哲学内史和外史的书写问题的探讨，其实是我以文化哲学的范式对马克思主义哲学史所作的一种解读。这种解读的历史基础就是 20 世纪的马克思主义哲学。我认为，20 世纪的马克思主义哲学，无论在理论的内容上，还是在思维的形式上，都是沿着文化哲学的路向发展的，通过这种发展，马克思主义文化哲学的传统不仅被开发出来，而且还表明，马克思主义哲学的发展，并不是像先前人们所以为的那样是受单纯的技术理性支配的，而是受文化的必然性支配的，是由内部诸多哲学传统和哲学形态构成的有机整体。这一点一旦被揭示出来，变革马克思主义哲学史观的任务也就提出来了，而这

① 对这一观点的详细论证，见拙著:《马克思主义哲学史教程》上卷，人民出版社 2009 年版，第 106—108 页。

种变革的方向，就是破除先前看待马克思主义哲学史的那种片面的、单一的理性主义的范式，采用文化哲学的范式来解读马克思主义哲学的历史，说明它内部的诸多哲学传统和哲学形态产生的历史必然性和合理性，展示它的完整风貌。如果说，先前的那种片面的、单一的理性主义研究范式使我们的马克思主义哲学史研究陷入了种种困境，那么，文化哲学的研究范式则给予了我们走出这种种困境的可能。

哲学不是哲学史

朱志方

黑格尔表达了哲学是哲学史或哲学史是哲学这样一个观点，这是由他的哲学体系引出的许多论断中的一个。在《哲学史讲演录》的结论中，黑格尔说："到了现在，世界精神到达了。那最后的哲学是一切较早的哲学的成果；没有任何东西失掉，一切原则都是保存着的。……精神的概念自身配合着自己整个具体的发展……。发展自己并且由自身中前进。它永远向前迈进，因为只有精神是前进的。……精神的这种认识自我，寻求自我的活动，就是精神自身，就是精神生活。它的成果就是它认识到自我的概念；哲学的历史就是蕴涵在历史中的精神。"而邓晓芒、赵林则明确表达了哲学史是哲学这一论题。"当我们全身心地投入研究一个又一个哲学家的思想之后，我们也就相继超越了一个又一个哲学家；我们不断地变换自己的立场，训练着对一个哲学观点的快速领悟力和把控力。长此以往，我们就逐渐拥有了一种能力，能够面对一种陌生的观点或思潮迅速洞察其要点，并作出自己的评价的能力，这就叫作'哲学素养'。正是在这种意义上，学习哲学史就是学习哲学，或者如黑格尔所说，哲学史就是哲学。"①（P6）本文是对"哲学是哲学史"的几种可能解释及其后果的讨论。由此得出的结论是，虽然哲学与哲学史有密切的关系，但哲学不是哲学史。

---

① 参见 Alex Rosenberg：Lessons from biology for philosophy of the Human Sciences，Philosophy of Social Sciences，2005（1）。作者的本意是要论证，生物科学和人文社会科学一样是历史学科。即使作者的论证不充分，但它所预设的前提，即人文社会科学是历史学科，却是多数哲学家都接受的。

一、“哲学是哲学史”的几种可能解释

“是”作为联系词，不论是在汉语里还是在英语里，都是多义的，它可以表达等值关系、子集关系、元素关系（Membership）、实体—属性关系、因果关系和手段—目的关系（如“你是我心中永远的痛”、“团结就是力量”、“坚持就是胜利”）、相似关系（隐喻，如“长征是播种机、是宣传队”，“儿童是祖国的花朵”）。假定“哲学史”与“哲学”的定义是已知的，说“哲学是哲学史”，这其中“是”表达的是什么关系呢？在黑格尔那里，它表达等值关系；但这个黑格尔主义的论题后来经历了逐步退却或弱化，往往解释作“哲学史是哲学的一部分（子集）”、“学习哲学史是学习哲学的途径”（手段—目的）。下面对这几种解释做一一考察。

（一）哲学等于哲学史

“哲学是哲学史”这个论题，如果理解为哲学等于哲学史，只有在黑格尔哲学的框架内才是成立的。黑格尔把整个世界看作绝对精神，把世界的历史看作绝对精神展开、发展并最终达到自我认识的历史。哲学的历史就是绝对精神自我认识的历史。在这个意义上，哲学是哲学史。但是，只要我们抛弃黑格尔的本体论，我们就必须抛弃“哲学是哲学史”这一论题。

首先，我们没有任何证据证明世界历史发展的过程就是绝对精神或绝对概念自我展开、自我发展和自我认识的过程。现代自然科学能够有说服力地说明宇宙和生命的起源和发展，现代社会科学也能够有说服力地说明人类社会的起源和发展，在此基础上再加上一个绝对精神或绝对概念，完全是多余的。其次，绝对精神完全是一个大而空的概念。与之相联系的概念有“时代精神”、“人类精神”、“世界精神”等。什么是时代精神？时代精神是否是时代的主流精神或一个时代多数人的精神？它与一个时代各色人等的信念、思想、欲望、追求、价值等是什么关系？如果它与这些东西无关，它又如何成为时代精神？

如果它与这些东西有关，一些人的卑劣的欲望、迷信、狂妄、对人类的仇恨、称霸全球的野心等等是否也是时代精神的一部分？如果不是，用什么标准来区分？谁能制定这个标准？黑格尔宣称，世界精神在他的哲学体系里达到了。现在人类历史又过去了一百多年，现代科学、现代数学和逻辑、现代社会科学的进步是否已经包含在他的世界精神中了？可见，时代精神和世界精神之类的概念并不能用来说明任何事情，反倒是需要说明的概念。

（二）哲学史是哲学的一部分

邓晓芒、赵林主张“哲学史就是哲学”，这显然不能理解为“哲学史等于哲学”。如果这样，“哲学史”与“哲学”就是在一切外延语境中都是可交换的。但是，“罗尔斯的政治哲学”显然不等于“罗尔斯的政治哲学史”。当然，有人可能不接受形式逻辑，或者把形式逻辑看作低等逻辑，把辩证逻辑看作高等逻辑。但是，不论辩证逻辑如何高等，它都不能是对形式逻辑的否定，而必须以遵守形式逻辑为前提。如果在辩论中我们连基本的逻辑规则都不要，就不成其为辩论，就无法进行辩论。如果把“哲学史是哲学”解释为“哲学史是哲学的一部分”，这个命题是可以接受的，但这个命题是没有价值的。在某种意义上，每个学科的历史都是该学科的一部分。因此，说哲学史是哲学的一部分，做了一个正确而没有价值的陈述，而不是一个深刻的陈述。

显然，断定“哲学是哲学史”的学者是要做一个有价值的、深刻的陈述。而且，断言哲学史就是哲学，就算是对的，也是一种错误的表达方式。如果把它的意义解释为“哲学史是哲学的一部分”，那么哲学史与哲学是部分与整体的关系，而部分与整体的关系是不能用“是”来表达的。我们可以说，“湖北是中国的一部分”，但不能说“湖北是中国”，更不能反过来说“中国是湖北”。

（三）学习哲学史就是学习哲学

这个论题的一般解释为，我们要通过学习哲学史来学习哲学。如何才能学习哲学并学好哲学？要学好哲学，需要一些条件。学习哲学史是必要条件还是充分条件？还是必要且充分的条件？显然，它不是充分条件。这就是说，要学好哲学，仅仅学习哲学史是不够的。要学好哲学，还必须学习逻辑学和数学、自然科学和人文社会科学。虽然不一定对这些领域都很精深，但必须有足够的了解。而且，在个别情况下，它甚至不是一个必要条件。一些哲学家并不了解哲学史。老子、泰勒斯学过哲学史吗？我们也没有证据表明，维特根斯坦学过哲学史。但一般来说，学习哲学史是学习哲学的必要条件，大多数哲学家都熟悉和了解哲学史，至少了解哲学史的某些重要部分。但是把A是B的必要条件表达为“A是B”，至少是一个错误的表达。因此，不论一位学者对“学习哲学史是学习哲学的必要条件”这一论题的论证是多么有力，也不能得出“哲学史是哲学”的结论。

当我们学习哲学史的时候，我们看到的是，有多少个哲学家就有多少种哲学史。每个历史上的杰出的哲学家对待哲学史的态度，恰恰是不利于论证“哲学是哲学史”这一论题的。每一个哲学家，必须先有了自己的哲学，才有他自己的哲学史。康德认为，只有超越哲学史才有自己的哲学。综观历史上的哲学研究，尤其是大哲学家们往往把过去的哲学或哲学的历史用作他们进行哲学研究或哲学构造的材料，而他们总是重构哲学史。如果说把哲学史用作哲学研究的材料就使我们有理由断定哲学是哲学史，那么，我们也可以说木头就是椅子，这显然是荒谬的。我们是否可以说一个哲学家所写的哲学史就是他的哲学？也许可以说，这是他表达自己哲学思想的一种方式，却不一定是主要的方式，我们了解黑格尔的哲学，主要是读他的《逻辑学》《精神哲学》《历史哲学》之类，而主要不是他的《哲学史讲演录》。当然，多数人最好先学习一些哲学史然后才进行哲学研究。但这并不足以确立哲学是哲学史这一论题。每一个做哲学研究的首先必须吃饭，但我们不能说，哲学就是吃饭。

断定学习哲学史就是学习哲学，忽略了一个重要的方面。当我们说到哲学的时候，我们不仅指学习哲学，而且指研究哲学以及由哲学研究得出的理论见解。学习哲学史与做哲学研究相差甚远。说学习哲学史就是学习哲学，因此哲学史就是哲学，我们就是把哲学同哲学教育混为一谈了。

邓晓芒和赵林认为，“通过学习哲学史，我们就逐渐拥有了一种能力，能够面对一种陌生的观点或思潮迅速洞察其要点，并作出自己的评价”。这样就拥有了“哲学素养”。这样说来，学会哲学就太轻松了。学习哲学史，我们只是拥有了一些哲学思想史的素材，离哲学的思考还有相当的距离。学习哲学，不仅要学习哲学史，而且还要学习如何做哲学研究。这就是要在老师的指导下去从事哲学研究。哲学研究不是单凭老师教就能学会的。一个哲学学者如何构想出一种新的而能够得到充分辩护的哲学观点，没有逻辑和方法论的辅助是行不通的。如对有关问题的研究情况的了解、推理和论证能力，科学和社会知识等。要研究问题，首先要寻找、选择问题。问题可能来自于哲学史，也可能来自于哲学史之外，来自于社会实践、自然科学和社会科学的最新发展成果。在这个意义上，学习哲学史也不是学习哲学的充分条件。的确，学习哲学史是一个重要条件，但还有一些同等重要的条件，如对逻辑、科学和科学史、社会和社会科学史的深入了解。如果承认问题选择的重要性，我们还必须承认，一些重要的哲学问题可能来自哲学史之外。对哲学史的解释可以有新意，但创新的可能性是受有限的。另一方面，邓、赵二位教授只讲到对于历史上的哲学“作出自己的评价”，但是，他们没有讲这是否就算学会了哲学。评价主要是对某种哲学理论作对与错、好与不好的判断。一些文章，全文就是“某某说，某某认为”，最后说几句这个人哪些地方说对了，哪些地方说错了。某某观点有什么现实意义、理论意义。这同当前的公文格式差不多。我以为，哲学论文（且不谈专著）必须做到以下三点：第一，对于一个已有的论题作出新的论证；第二，对于一个已有的论题做出新的反驳；第三，提出一个新论题并进行严密的论证。没有这三点，就不是论文，就只具有教学的意义，只不过是把课堂讲授的内容搬到了打印纸上。提出新论题而没有论证，是毫无意义的。仿照“我思故我在”的格式，我们一眨眼就可以提出一大堆新观点来：我吃故我在，我睡故我在、我说故我在、我吹故我在、我消费故我在、我忧愁故我在……以及把这些命题都倒过来说。

目前哲学界有两种偏向：一种是把讲哲学史当作讲哲学，黑格尔怎么说，伽达默尔怎么说，再加上他们说的某某话特别重要这样的价值判断（这就叫评价）；一种是讲一大堆的大话和空话而不作论证，这种风格在哲学史上也有渊源，如绝对精神、时代精神、人类精神、科学之科学、真善美的统一、引领时代之类。

现在，哲学家大多数不再说大话了，很难找到构建无所不包的哲学体系而又能说服人的人了。分析哲学、大陆哲学这样的区分，本身是成问题的。我们只有哲学和哲学问题。不论是分析哲学还是大陆哲学，都只是我们进行哲学研究和思考的材料，而不是哲学本身。哲学不是哲学史，哲学史也不是哲学。

二、对于"哲学是哲学史"的几种辩护

（一）哲学是历史学科，① 因此，哲学是哲学史

哲学是历史学科，这一点是正确的。说哲学是历史学科，不是说哲学是关于历史的学科，而说哲学这门学科是历史性的。哲学的界线、哲学问题、哲学研究，都有离不开它的历史。哲学的问题在一定的历史过程或历史处境中产生，哲学的活动受到历史条件的制约，哲学的答案有其历史的渊源。另一方面，哲学陈述即使有效，也是在一定的历史条件下有效，在一定的文化背景下有效。与自然科学相比，哲学似乎显示出两个突出的特点。第一，自然科学的陈述如果是有效的，那就是在所有的时间和地点都是有效的。而我们很难说哲学的陈述在所有的时间和地点都有效，依此而言，可以说哲学无定论。第二，与自然科学相比，读经典原著对哲学具有更重要的作用。但是，说哲学是历史

① 参见 Alex Rosenberg：Lessons from biology for philosophy of the Human Sciences，Philosophy of Social Sciences，2005（1）。

学科，不能推导出哲学是哲学史。有一些学者认为，生物学也是历史学科，[①]但由此不能推出生物学是生物学史。由学科 X 是历史学科，不能推导出“X 就是它的历史”。

每一门学科都同它的历史有密切的联系。从这个意义上来说，自然科学也是历史学科。“范式”、“科学传统”这些具有历史含义的概念在当代科学哲学中也是众所周知的。在 20 世纪 90 年代，科学哲学据称也发生了“解释的转向”[②]，一些科学哲学家主张自然科学也融入了理解、解释和历史。因此，在一定的程度上，可以说所有的学科，包括人文社会科学和自然科学都是历史性的。但是，我们显然不能说物理学史是物理学，社会学史是社会学。因此，我们同样不能因为哲学同哲学史有密切联系、哲学是历史学科，就断定哲学是哲学史。

（二）历史是一切发生的事情，因此哲学是哲学史

按照这种论证，现在发生的事情也是一个历史事件，如果是一个重要的历史事件，它将被写进历史。我们不反对对历史可以有不同的定义，这样的历史定义也是可以考虑的。但是，如果这样来定义历史，我们就必须说，物理学是物理学史，天文学是天文学史。因为物理学、天文学的当前研究活动，都是历史事件，或者将成为历史事件。我们在使用“××史”时，不能采取双重定义。当说到哲学史时，指的是过去、现在和将来发生的一切事件，而说到物理学史时，指的是过去发生的事件。只要上过中学，就是物理学家、生物学家、天文学家、数学家、逻辑学家，因为它们毕竟都知道历史上的一些科学，如阿基米德静力学。更重要的是，这一解释使用了一个未经证明的前提：所有的学科都是它的历史。然而，正好是“所有的学科都是它的历史”

---

① 参见 Alex Rosenberg：Lessons from biology for philosophy of the Human Sciences，Philosophy of Social Sciences，2005（1）。

② 参见 The *Interpretive Turn*，eds. by David R. Heily，James F.Bohman and Richard Shusterman，Cornell University Press，1991。集 T.Kuhn，H.L.Dreyfus，J.Rouse，C.Taylor 等人的论文，讨论自然科学的解释特性。

这一全称命题使“哲学是哲学史”这一单称命题变得毫无价值，就如说“某某人将会死去”一样。

三、“哲学是哲学史”的语用学意义

就如“词的意义就是它的用法”一样，每个命题的意义都要从它的语境和它导致的结果去理解。

（一）“哲学是哲学史”产生于极左的学术政治

在极“左”的思想路线的支配下，人们一度认为，一种哲学的价值就在于它对于马克思主义哲学的产生是否起了积极的作用。德国古典哲学是马克思主义哲学的来源，因此，黑格尔“哲学是哲学史”一说受到极度的重视，几乎成为哲学史学者的公理。于是哲学的主要教育就是学习“三史”：马克思主义哲学（史）、中国哲学史、西方哲学史。现代西方哲学就是“资产阶级哲学批判”，其他的学科不用学，因为哲学是一切科学的精华和总结，学了哲学就什么都懂，或者说，学了哲学史就等于什么都懂。

（二）“哲学是哲学史”带来的现实的和可能的后果

哲学是哲学史，学习哲学史就是学习哲学，而世界上有各种各样的哲学史著作。它的典型格式是“某某说，某某认为，某某又说，简评”。于是，学习者成为“学者”之后写作“论文”的通常格式就是“某某说，某某认为，某某又说，简评”。近二十年来，学习哲学史造就的大量的学者写的就是这样的论文，其实只能说是文章，只有教学参考的意义，算不上论文。由于它只是重复哲学史，因此连文章也说不上。我们培养的不是哲学家，而是大量的有生命的哲学思想的复印机。正是这个论题，导致了“天下文章一大抄”。

说“哲学就是哲学史”，导致严重反科学主义。由于使人误解为“学好哲学史就学好了哲学”，而哲学史上的哲学夹杂着许多迷信和宗教神话，一些哲学理论自封为“科学之科学”，指斥科学是有限的、追求偶然真理的，而吹嘘哲学是无限的、追求绝对真理的。于是，一些学习者不学习现代科学，而对反科学的东西津津乐道。把反对科学当作思想深刻。把科学和逻辑当作道德邪恶的替罪羊。不说某某人为了私利去污染环境，而说科学技术导致环境污染。甚至把科学技术指斥为“工具理性”，把逻辑看作它的同谋。

说哲学就是哲学史，导致复古主义和学术停滞。一个词的意义就是它的用法。“哲学史”是什么意思，就看我们用这个词来表达什么。一般我们用它来表示距我们时间比较遥远的哲学的历史。我们写哲学史，一般写到 20 世纪初。也许一百年后写到 21 世纪初。近期发生的事情，我们不叫它历史。这样，这个论题的含义就是叫人学习哲学史，学到黑格尔就差不多了。最好是主要学习古希腊或先秦，因为越早越历史。一些沉浸在历史中的哲学家总是对我们说，古人多么智慧，多么崇高，你们忘了历史，是不要祖先，同禽兽没有分别。而对于当代国际学术，他们所知甚少，而且会轻蔑地说：那不重要。没有一个物理学家只懂得阿基米德就是国际一流。而一个哲学家只要多读亚里士多德或孔子，就可以训斥全世界。这是“哲学是哲学史”的悲哀。

四、哲学学科的特殊性

我接受以下命题：(1) 哲学是爱智慧的；(2) 哲学同它的历史有密切联系；(3) 哲学的问题研究必须在一定程度上追溯它的历史；(4) 哲学是无定论的。

这些命题都是真的。但是，对以上命题，有两点必须说明：第一，从上述 4 个命题，不论是它们的析取还是它们的合取，都不能推导出哲学史是哲学或哲学是哲学史。第二，以上几个命题中的谓词不仅适合于哲学，而且适合于其他一切学科。也就是说，所有的学科都是爱智慧的，每一学科都同它的历史有密切的联系，每一学科的问题研究都必须在一定程度上追溯该问题研究的历史，每门学科都是无定论的。这里就第一个和第四个命题多说几句。

哲学一词来自于希腊，它的直接意义是爱智慧。但是，从古希腊到近代，这个词的意义就是理论科学或理论学科。所以，说哲学是爱智慧的意思是科学是爱智慧的，即人文社会科学和自然科学是爱智慧的，所有的科学都是爱智慧。现在所说的哲学，有很大一部分是古希腊时候的第一哲学。用近代德国哲学的话说，哲学是科学之科学。但哲学是否具有如此之高的地位，在今天是一个大有争议的问题。那么，哲学与其他学科的不同之处，是否在一个爱字上？其他科学是智慧，哲学是爱智慧。其他科学得到的是智慧，哲学得到的是爱。如果作为一种诗意的说法，我们没有更多的话可说。如果是一个可以讨论的命题，那么就必须说清楚，哲学所追求、研究的"爱"是什么。

再看哲学无定论这一命题。从肯定的角度说，这是出自16—18世纪哲学的破产。那时，哲学家大多追求知识的确实性，个别哲学家，如休谟，否定我们有确实的经验知识，因此，被指斥为怀疑论者。但是，了解现代科学和现代认识论的人都知道，科学也是没有确实性的。在这个意义上，这是一个正确的论题，即科学和哲学都不拥有绝对真理。如果所有的科学都没有确实性，那么，说哲学无定论并没有把哲学与科学区分出来。但是，这里还有否定的方面，即在某种意义上，它是一种相对主义。虽然除了逻辑和数学之外（这也是有争议的），一切学科皆无定论，但这并不意味着我们无法对两个题材相同的论题进行比较和评价。我们总是可能说它们之间有一个得到更多的证据支持。因此，我们同休谟一样，既不是怀疑论者，也不是相对主义者。拿亚里士多德的物理学和哲学来说，他的物理学仅仅具有历史素材的意义。但是，他的哲学似乎还在活动：现在还有很多亚里士多德主义者。这不是说，所有的哲学，至少所有的在历史上曾经伟大过的哲学，都是同样好或同样不好。这是哲学研究的特点决定的。过去的哲学问题都是大问题。小问题比较容易回答或其回答比较容易论证或反驳。如某一物体的体积、重量。对大问题的回答要进行论证和反驳都非常困难。在理论科学中，我们时常见到一些古代观念的复活。我们致力于研究和辩论，表明我们认定，尽管哲学命题可能是错的，但有些命题比另一些命题有更充分的理由。

哲学学科的特殊性，并不在于我们在上面说到的几个命题，而在于它的题材、它所研究的问题、它回答问题的方式。这一点需要专门论述。本文的主题是，哲学不是哲学史。

即哲学史讲哲学

——关于哲学与哲学史研究方法的再思考

吴根友

哲学与哲学史的关系，经过黑格尔的阐述以后，长期以来成哲学界与哲学史领域里的重要问题之一，20 世纪中国哲学界对此问题尤其关注。武汉大学哲学学院西方哲学界的同仁于 2006 年 6 月 17—19 日，曾对此问题举办过一场认真、细致的讨论。仔细阅读争论双方的观点，发现他们对于“哲学史”这一概念的理解，虽然也有一些“重叠共识”，如认为哲学史就是历史上已经出现的哲学家们的思想。但由于他们关于“哲学”的认识不同，对哲学史与哲学研究的正相关性的理解发生了很大的分歧。概括地讲，以研究德国哲学为主的一批学者，他们比较倾向于维护黑格尔的“哲学”与“哲学史”观，将哲学与哲学史均理解为一个动态发展过程，研究哲学史绝不仅仅意味着对历史上某些过去了的哲学家及其思想面貌的认识与还原重构，而是将这些个别的哲学家的思想看作是哲学思想发展链条上的一个有机环节，进而考察哲学在具体的历史时空里不断展开的历史过程。以研究分析哲学与逻辑学的一批学者为主，他们反对黑格尔的“哲学”与“哲学史”观，主要将哲学理解为一种“理智探索活动”，其基本任务是“凭借恰当的语言来研究思想和世界”①。或者将哲学看作是一种“智力活动”，主要方法是“通过清晰的概念和合理的论证来形成正确

① 张志林：《如何做哲学——兼论哲学与哲学史》，载邓晓芒主编：《哲学名家对谈录——英美分析哲学 PK 欧洲大陆哲学》，湖南教育出版社 2007 年版，第 305 页。（下面所引该书，只注页码）

的理论”[1]。或者哲学就是指一些“哲学问题”[2]。他们不承认哲学是一个有机的发展过程。而“哲学史”无非就是历史上已经出现的哲学家的思想。哲学史的研究，无非是对“历史上曾经出现的哲学问题，给出的是别人曾经所做的概念分析、逻辑论证和反思平衡”。相对于哲学研究的“理性重构”而言，哲学史的研究无非是“历史重构”。[3] 由于争论双方在“哲学”观方面有巨大的差异，他们有关“哲学史”及其研究的价值的认识自然产生了巨大的分歧。笔者在他们讨论的基础上，综合两家的观点，并结合当代中国哲学创新的几个例证，试图对“哲学与哲学史”的关系问题再做一点新的论述，希望能够深化对此问题的讨论。

一、分析哲学研究者的主要观点及其评价

试图通过“哲学不是哲学史”，或“哲学史不是哲学”命题的证明，进一步强调哲学研究与哲学史之间没有什么必然的关系，进而否定“通过哲学史研究哲学”途径的重要性，是一些专门从事分析哲学与逻辑学研究者的主要观点。而在他们呈现出的主要观点背后，实际上隐藏着一种未加言明的哲学史观，即哲学史无非是历史上已经出现的一些哲学家的思想。这些哲学思想是历史性的东西，与哲学的创新性思维没有什么直接的关系。他们既不承认黑格尔整体的哲学观与哲学史观，也反对“时代精神”等的类似说法，[4] 就他们对哲学与哲学史关系的论述而言，大体上可以分为三种表达类型：

---

① 程炼：《哲学史作为哲学的真子部分》（提纲），载邓晓芒主编：《哲学名家对谈录——英美分析哲学 PK 欧洲大陆哲学》，第 307 页。

② 徐明：《哲学不是离开哲学问题的哲学史》，载邓晓芒主编：《哲学名家对谈录——英美分析哲学 PK 欧洲大陆哲学》，第 310 页。

③ 张志林：《如何做哲学——兼论哲学与哲学史》，载邓晓芒主编：《哲学名家对谈录——英美分析哲学 PK 欧洲大陆哲学》，第 306 页。

④ 参见朱志方《哲学不是哲学史》，载邓晓芒主编：《哲学名家对谈录——英美分析哲学 PK 欧洲大陆哲学》，第 296—297 页。

其一，强调哲学对于哲学史的绝对优先性，进而割裂哲学史与哲学的关系。其典型、激进的代表命题是："没有哲学，哲学史是不可能的；没有哲学史，哲学是可能的。"① 其温和性的命题有：(1) 哲学不可能仅仅是哲学史，如果从来都没有新的哲学思想，那也不可能有什么哲学史。② (2) 其引申性的表达式："每一个哲学家，必须先有了哲学，才有他自己的哲学史。"③"不做哲学研究，写不好哲学史"④ (3)"哲学不能离开当前的哲学问题，而哲学史也不应离开历史上的哲学问题。""所以，在西方哲学的研究和教学中，应以哲学问题为主，以哲学史为辅。"⑤

其二，把哲学史与哲学之间复杂、深刻的内在关系化约为一个现代分析哲学的命题——"哲学是哲学史"或"哲学史是哲学"，然后分析这一命题的三种意思，对这一命题的辩护进行想象性的分析与反驳（因为作者没有举出一个实例，故称是想象性的），再从语用学的角度指出这一命题的历史根源及其危害性，进而给出反命题："哲学不是哲学史"。这一类型的论证过程中，提出了一些有启发性的观点，但其中的一些论证用语在逻辑上是不严格的，也缺乏哲学史的史实，有些地方不符合哲学史研究的实际情况。其表面的用语与实际上想表达的意图之间有很大的差异。

其三，反对"哲学就是哲学史"的命题，但有限地承认"哲学史对于哲学研究的必要性"。此处的"必要性"并能等同于形式逻辑上的"必要条件"，至

① 张志林：《如何做哲学——兼论哲学与哲学史》，载邓晓芒主编：《哲学名家对谈录——英美分析哲学 PK 欧洲大陆哲学》，第 305 页。

② 叶峰：《从"先天综合判断"问题看哲学史与哲学研究的关系》，载邓晓芒主编：《哲学名家对谈录——英美分析哲学 PK 欧洲大陆哲学》，第 277 页。

③ 朱志方：《哲学不是哲学史》，载邓晓芒主编：《哲学名家对谈录——英美分析哲学 PK 欧洲大陆哲学》，第 297 页。

④ 程炼：《哲学史作为哲学的真子部分》（提纲），载邓晓芒主编：《哲学名家对谈录——英美分析哲学 PK 欧洲大陆哲学》，第 307 页。程炼的这一命题巧妙地回避了哲学史对于哲学的作用。如果我们追问："没有哲学史的基本常识，能做哲学研究吗？"

⑤ 徐明：《哲学不是离开哲学问题的哲学史》，载邓晓芒主编：《哲学名家对谈录——英美分析哲学 PK 欧洲大陆哲学》，第 310 页。

多是“哲学史研究在哲学活动中有不可替代的作用”。[①] 但这种富有弹性的“不可替代”一词的意思，是（1）“孩子的成长过程中，母亲的作用是不可替代的”这一句式中的“不可替代”，还是（2）“人体健康，蛋白质的作用是不可替代的”这一句子中的“不可替代”？作者未及深论。如果是（1）句式中的“不可替代”，只是强调了其重要程度，并没有形式逻辑中“必要条件”非它不可的意思。因为在父亲作为单亲的家庭中，孩子没有母亲也能够长大，并不一定就会死亡。只是这样的单亲家庭里长大的孩子可能有各种各样的心理疾病或情感上的问题。而（2）句子中的“不可替代”，就是形式逻辑中的“必要条件”的意思，如果完全没有蛋白质提供营养，人会死亡的。至于人是从哪些食物中摄取的蛋白质，那是次要的。

上述三点的归纳还没有完全穷尽上述分析哲学研究者关于“哲学与哲学史”关系的具体讨论。如有论者说：“在个别条件下，它（指哲学史，引者注）甚至不是一个必要条件。”一些哲学家，如“老子、泰勒斯学过哲学吗？我们也没有充分证据表明，维特根斯坦学过哲学史。”[②]

“学习哲学史，我们只是拥有了一些哲学思想史的素材，离哲学的思考还有相当的距离。”[③]

（哲学上的问题），“可能来自于哲学史，也可能来自于哲学史之外……在这个意义上，学习哲学史也不是学习哲学的充分条件。的确，学习哲学史是一个重要条件，但还有一些同等重要的条件，如对逻辑、科学和科学史、社会和社会科学史的相当了解。”[④]“说哲学就是哲学史，导致复古主义和学术

① 程炼：《哲学史作为哲学的真子部分》（提纲），载邓晓芒主编：《哲学名家对谈录——英美分析哲学 PK 欧洲大陆哲学》，第 307 页。

② 朱志方：《哲学不是哲学史》，载邓晓芒主编：《哲学名家对谈录——英美分析哲学 PK 欧洲大陆哲学》，第 297 页。

③ 参见朱志方《哲学不是哲学史》、程炼《哲学史作为哲学的真子部分》（提纲），载邓晓芒主编：《哲学名家对谈录——英美分析哲学 PK 欧洲大陆哲学》，第 297、307—309 页。

④ 朱志方：《哲学不是哲学史》，载邓晓芒主编：《哲学名家对谈录——英美分析哲学 PK 欧洲大陆哲学》，第 298 页。

停滞"①。

以上列出的这些具体的论述与观点，有些论述与观点已经滑向了否定哲学史学习之于哲学研究的重要性了，将哲学研究仅仅看作是对纯粹的哲学问题的研究。

非常遗憾的是，由于从事分析哲学研究的一些论者忽视对哲学史本身的研究，所以他们举出的例证，如维特根斯坦不熟悉哲学史，实际情况并不像他们想象的那样。维特根斯坦的哲学，无论是其前期的逻辑哲学创作时期，还是其后期的语言哲学时期，与哲学史都有深刻而内在的关系。前期的维特根斯坦如果不是师从大哲学家罗素，就根本不可能有逻辑哲学的相关思想的产生。而后期维特根斯坦如果不是从逻辑学家弗雷格、牛津日常语言学派摩尔以及德国语言学家毛特纳等那里获得哲学思想的灵感，还有从圣·奥古斯丁、叔本华、克尔凯郭尔、陀斯妥耶夫斯基、托尔斯泰、帕斯卡等人那里获得哲学思想的启迪，也根本上就不能成为现代西方哲学界首屈一指的大哲学家。②对于维特根斯坦，我们可以说他没有系统地研究过西方哲学史，甚至不像黑格尔那样，在他的时代允许的条件下系统地研究了世界哲学史，但并不能以他为例，说他的哲学研究与哲学史上的思想无关，或者基本上没有关系。如果对"哲学"不作分析哲学式的理解，而将它看作是人类的精神现象学，即广义的哲学思想，追求智慧的学问，那么，一些宗教、文学、语言学、逻辑学的著作中本来就包含着哲学思想在其中。至于老子、泰勒斯等人，他们所处的时代虽然没有我们今天意义上的哲学史著作可以学习，但他们的哲学思想也不是凭空产生的，王弼本的《老子》中，多处有"建言有之"的说法。而所谓的"建言"，一般的注释均释为古之格言。因此，以老子、维特根斯坦等人与哲学史的关系为例证，

① 朱志方：《哲学不是哲学史》，载邓晓芒主编：《哲学名家对谈录——英美分析哲学 PK 欧洲大陆哲学》，第 301—302 页。

② 参见叶秀山、王树人总主编《西方哲学史》（学术版）第八卷（上），《现代英美分析哲学》（上），载江怡主编，凤凰出版社，江苏人民出版社 2005 年版，第 150—151 页。

并不证明哲学可以与哲学史基本上不发生关系。

不过，仔细分析一些从事分析哲学研究者关于“哲学史与哲学关系”的主要观点，可以发现他们的主要思想倾向是，想通过否定或弱化哲学史与哲学研究的关系，来实现哲学研究的创新。从他们的理论目标来看，笔者认为是可以接受的。但有些论者主要从他们所理解的“哲学史研究”现象出发，如把哲学史研究看作是记诵古人的哲学思想，或者是引经据典，把前人的哲学观点当作现成的结论，进而否定哲学史的研究对于哲学研究及哲学创新的价值和意义(参见朱志方的文章)。如果是否定这一特定的“哲学史研究”类型，则与黑格尔在《哲学史讲演录》中所否定的某一类哲学史写作的观点是一致的，那我们也是会接受并赞同的。而且，我们也反对只有引经据典，而没有哲学理性分析的经学式的哲学史研究方法。所不同的地方在于：

一是哲学观上的不同。我们不把哲学仅仅看作是一种“理智活动”或“智力活动”，或表现为一些“哲学问题”，它是一种观念体系和行为方式。这套观念体系与行为方式涉及人对世界、自我的认知与价值评价。仅就认知的方面来说，哲学是关于人如何从无知到知，从知之甚少到知之甚多，直到智慧境界的思想发展过程。对于作为个体的人类而言是如此，对于整体的人类而言也是如此。所有哲学性的认知都处在一个动态的链条过程之中，无论哲学家本人承认还是不承认这一点。我们可以抛弃黑格尔以“绝对精神”为核心的关于哲学发展的封闭思想体系，但需要继承他关于哲学发展是一个过程的合理性的思想。

二是我们认为，好的哲学史研究就是在研究哲学，而不是重复或记诵古代哲人的话语。而且通过哲学史的研究，寻找并发现哲学思想发展的阶段性特征，以及前人哲学思考的局限，对于一些历久而弥新的哲学问题，如人生的意义问题，死亡之于人的意义，有限性与无限性问题等，在前人理论终止的地方继续向前推进。这可以说是“接着讲”。按照笔者的观点看，这就是“即哲学史讲哲学”。

三是哲学史和纯哲学问题研究，对于哲学的创新各有胜场，并不相互排斥。逻辑思维与语言分析有助于哲学思维的训练，但仅靠逻辑思维与语言分析，也不能有什么哲学创新。逻辑思维一般只能整理已有的思想观念，让其合乎思维的理性路径展开；而语言分析只是澄清一些问题，并不能直接达到哲学观念的创新，它可能有助于澄清我们思想表达时一些似是而非的想法。而哲学史的研究与学习，与逻辑思维训练与语言分析能力的培养，对于哲学创新而言，可以并行不悖。

四是哲学既具有与自然科学相似的逻辑思维方法，同时还具有人文理想的内容，一些哲学洞见及其表达，还可以是诗的形象思维方式。从哲学教育的角度看，哲学研究者的科学思维能力与素质的训练非常重要，人文理想的教育与想象思维的训练同样重要。不应该以科学思维的训练排斥人文理想的教育与想象思维训练的重要性。就哲学教育而言，科学思维、人文理想、想象思维，都具有历史的继承性特征。哲学史的学习与研究过程中，通过真诚地讨论与争论，避免古人的思维过失，吸收历史上合理的思维方式与人文理想，然后推陈出新。

笔者的基本观点是：

第一，哲学是一套观念体系与行为方式，它虽然不是黑格尔意义上的“绝对精神”的自我运动的封闭体系，但人类的哲学思想在国别史的时代表现为一个个相对独立的思想体系，整体上具有前后相续的关系，并处在发展的过程中。

第二，哲学史之于哲学研究而言，是必要条件，但不是充分条件。它与哲学概念的逻辑展开，以及分析哲学所提倡的哲学研究方法，其重要性是同等的，不应遭到轻视，更不能遭到排斥与否定。他们二者之间的关系是相互补充的，而不是相互排斥的。正如植物的生长，水是必要条件，适宜的温度与光合作用，也是必要条件。

第三，无论从思维方式，还是学科类型或曰学问类型、知识类型来看，“哲学”不是自足的。没有一种先验的、纯而又纯的“哲学”思维，也没有一个先验的、纯而又纯的“哲学”学科（或学问类型、知识类型）。哲学思维是从原始混沌的宗教、神学、历史、政治、艺术诸思维中慢慢分化、独立出来的；哲学学科也是如此。因此，把“哲学”看作是哲学史的先决条件这一观点，并不能成立。

第四，所有门类的知识都具有历史性特征，了解一个学科和一门学问的前提条件，或曰必要条件是了解他的基本问题史与研究方法史。哲学学科也不例外。因此，哲学史的学习与研究构成了我们的哲学研究与创造的必要条件，而不是什么辅助条件；也不是分析哲学研究者所说的语义模糊的“必要性”（见上文分析）。即使哲学发展到了今天，离开了哲学史提供的一系列哲学问题，离开了哲学史提供的思维方式、分析工具，今天的哲学研究是不可能展开的。今天分析哲学家们津津乐道的一些理性思维与分析工具，也是以往哲学家提供的，不是他们与生俱来的。形象地说，哲学史是通达哲学研究过程中“过河的桥”或上屋顶的梯子，当然也可说是到达某一哲学问题研究平台的直升机。具体哲学研究工作者的哲学史修养可厚可薄，但不能没有基本的哲学史训练。

第五，从学术史的角度看，为了澄清此一问题的真相，我们有必要重新回到黑格尔《哲学史讲演录（一）》之中，把握黑格尔对“哲学史与哲学关系”的真正意思，进而帮助我们重新思考哲学史与哲学的关系。

二、黑格尔《哲学史讲演录（一）》对“哲学史与哲学”关系的论述

通过对当代部分分析哲学研究者有关“哲学史与哲学”关系论述的研究与分析，笔者觉得有必要重新回到黑格尔在《哲学史讲演录（一）》的具体论述之中。就黑格尔原书中所说的话而言，黑格尔只是强调哲学史的研究要有哲学，哲学史的研究不是陈述过去的哲学家的意见，并没有说“哲学史就是哲

学”，或者说“哲学就是哲学史”[①]。至于有些中国哲学史研究者可能表达了上述两个命题的意思，但并不是黑格尔本人的思想或观念。

就黑格尔本人的观点看来，“哲学是关于真理的客观科学，是对于真理之必然性的科学，是概念式的认识；它不是意见，也不是意见的产物。”[②] 正因为“哲学的目的即在于用思维和概念去把握真理”，因此，“在哲学史里我们所研究的就是哲学本身。”[③] 在这句话里，黑格尔强调的是哲学史研究的任务不是个别哲学家的个人意见，而是在哲学家的著作中研究那种属于哲学，即是真理的内容。这一有关哲学史研究的任务与目标的观点，他还有另外的表达式：“哲学是理性的知识，它的发展史本身应当是合理的，哲学史本身就应当是哲学的。”[④] 就“哲学史本身应当是哲学的”的这句话来看，如果哲学史本身不是哲学的，那哲学史本身也不成为哲学史了。可见，黑格尔并没有用“哲学史”来规定“哲学”，相反，是用“哲学”来规定“哲学史”的。但这种规定并不是分析哲学研究者所认为的那样，是逻辑上的先后关系，而是就哲学史研究的任务与目标而言。我们可以不同意黑格尔的“哲学”观，但不能把他有关哲学史与哲学的关系化为“哲学是哲学史”，或“哲学史是哲学”这样形式化的哲学命题。

黑格尔不仅将哲学看作是关于真理的科学，而且还将哲学比拟为一种生命的现象，认为“哲学是在发展中的系统”[⑤]。揭示哲学理念的发展可以有两种方式，一种是逻辑的形式，“即揭示出理念各种形态的推演和各种范畴在思想中的、被认识了的必然性，这就是哲学自身的课题和任务。”另一种是理念在经

---

① 参见何卫平《对黑格尔的哲学与哲学史的关系学说的再认识——参照西方现代解释学的立场和观点》，载邓晓芒主编：《哲学名家对谈录——英美分析哲学 PK 欧洲大陆哲学》，第 333—334 页。

② 黑格尔著，贺麟、王太庆译：《历史哲学讲演录》第一卷，商务印书馆 1959 年版（以下只注页码），第 17—18 页。

③ 黑格尔著，贺麟、王太庆译：《历史哲学讲演录》第一卷，第 24 页。

④ 黑格尔著，贺麟、王太庆译：《历史哲学讲演录》第一卷，第 12—13 页。

⑤ 黑格尔著，贺麟、王太庆译：《历史哲学讲演录》第一卷，第 33 页。

验时间里所展现出的各种哲学理论体系，用黑格尔的原话说："亦即理念的不同阶段和不同发展环节之出现在时间中，在变化的形态中，在某些特殊的地域中，在这个或那个民族里，在某些政治环境里，或在由政治环境而引起的错综复杂的关系里，——简言之，出现在经验的形式内——这就是哲学史所要揭示给我们的一幕一幕的戏剧。"① 而正是从哲学在经验时间发展的角度看，"哲学史的研究就是哲学本身的研究，不会是别的。"② 而且，"哲学史也是在发展中的系统"。③ 这即是说，在一个非常严格的限定性条件下，当且仅当（1）哲学是发展的系统；（2）作为该发展系统的哲学在经验的时间里展开的条件下："哲学史的研究就是哲学本身的研究，不会是别的。"在此双重限制性条件下，哲学史的研究也只能是哲学，而不是哲学家的意见或其他的内容。由此也不能推断出："哲学史是哲学"，或者"哲学是哲学史"这样两个命题。因此，"哲学是哲学史"，以及它的反命题："哲学不是哲学史"，只是今天某些研究者对于黑格尔有关哲学史与哲学关系认识的歪曲的、甚至是错误的简化式表达，并不是黑格尔有关哲学史与哲学关系的本来陈述。

通过以上简要的辨析，我们似乎可以把黑格尔关于"哲学史与哲学关系"的论述予以重新表述：

第一，哲学的性质规定了哲学史研究的任务。哲学是关于真理的科学。因此哲学史就不能以客观的描述方式铺陈历史上具体哲学家们的意见。"在哲学史里我们所研究的就是哲学本身。"引申一点说，哲学史是研究具体历史过程中的"真理"或曰真理性的认识，以之作为人类进一步认识的台阶或阶梯。

第二，与上述表达平行的另一表达式："哲学是理性的知识，它的发展史本身应当是合理的，哲学史本身就应当是哲学的。"

这一表达式，按照笔者的理解，实际上是关于理想状态下的"哲学"本身

① 黑格尔著，贺麟、王太庆译：《历史哲学讲演录》第一卷，第 34 页。

② 黑格尔著，贺麟、王太庆译：《历史哲学讲演录》第一卷，第 34 页。

③ 黑格尔著，贺麟、王太庆译：《历史哲学讲演录》第一卷，第 33 页。

的认识，而不是说历史上各个哲学家的具体哲学思想或观念都是“理性的知识”。理想状态的哲学史研究恰恰是要剔除一些个人性的哲学意见，从一大堆纷繁复杂的意见中寻找到或提炼出一些带有真理性的“理性知识”。

第三，作为（1）和（2）的递进式表达，“哲学是发展的系统”。而“发展”有两种形式，一是概念的逻辑展开，二是哲学在经验的时间与地域里展开的历史发展。前者是思想的纯粹逻辑展开，具体的哲学家在这一维度里主要运用逻辑思维展开哲学的研究与思考，与具体的哲学史可以不发生关系。后者则是一般意义上的哲学历史的研究。而这一维度的哲学研究，正是分析哲学研究者要加以削弱、抑制，甚至是加以贬低的维度。但是，就黑格尔本人而言，即使是哲学在经验时间里的发展这一层意义上来说，他也将哲学史的任务规定为是对哲学的研究，而不是对个别哲学家意见的记诵，或对这些历史上哲学思想原貌的重构或还原。他说：“哲学史的研究就是哲学本身的研究，不会是别的。”这样，实际上并不存在分析哲学研究者化约式的说法：“哲学史是哲学”，或“哲学是哲学史”。

要而言之，上述三条黑格尔关于哲学史与哲学关系的表述，并没有“哲学史是哲学”或“哲学是哲学史”的句式意思，而只是从他自己所理解的“哲学”性质的角度来阐述哲学史研究的任务与性质，并将哲学史研究的任务与性质规定为是哲学研究本身，而不是其他。换句话说，如果哲学史的研究不是在从事哲学本身的研究，那他就不配享有哲学史研究或哲学史家的称号。实际上，从黑格尔对当时流行的一些哲学史研究方式的蔑视与颇有点刻薄的批评观点中，也可以佐证上面的说法。他说：“我们并不缺乏卷帙繁多、甚至学问广博的哲学史，在这些哲学史里，他们所费力寻求的关于哲学实质的知识反而没有。这样的哲学史家有点像某些动物，它们听见了音乐中一切的音调，但这些音调的一致性与和谐性，却没有透进它们的头脑。”① 当然，我们完全可以有理由不认

① 黑格尔著，贺麟、王太庆译：《历史哲学讲演录》第一卷，第5页。

同，甚至批评黑格尔关于哲学史研究任务与目标的规定，因为，“哲学史”作为历史学的一个分支，它的另一个任务是还原历史上的哲学家思想的面貌。这一类型的研究对于哲学创造而言也许没有多少必要性，但对于思想史追求历史真相而言则是必需的（不管这一真相是否能真的完全达到）。黑格尔虽然强调了哲学史研究的科学性，但在他庞大的客观唯心主义的思辨哲学体系里，“科学性”一词似乎还缺乏历史唯物主义思想体系里所包含的对经验历史真相的把握这一思想内涵。

为了更完整地、更深入地理解黑格尔本人对于“哲学史与哲学”关系的认识，有必要对于他提出的哲学史研究的四条原则进行简明扼要地再叙述。

第一条原则：“全部哲学史是一有必然性的、有次序的进程。这进程本身是合理性的，为理念所规定的。偶然性必须于进入哲学领域时立即排除掉。概念的发展在哲学里是必然的，同样概念发展的历史也是必然的。这种发展的主导力量是各种多样性的形态之内在的辩证法则。”①

第二条原则：“每一哲学曾经是、而且仍然是必然的，因此没有任何哲学曾经消灭了，而所有各派哲学作为全体的诸环节都肯定地保存在哲学里……那被推翻了的并不是这个哲学的原则，而只不过是这个原则的绝对性、究竟至上性。”②

第三条原则：“我们特别限制于对原则的讨论。每一原则在一定时间内都曾经是主导原则。当整个世界观皆据此唯一原则来解释时，——这就叫做哲学系统。”在讨论到这些更具体的哲学系统时，“我们又必须注意到这些原则的主要发展和应用。那些从低级原则出发的哲学每每是不联贯的；它们虽不无深刻的识见，但这些深刻的识见每每超出所据以出发的原则之外。”③

第四条原则：哲学史虽然也是历史，“但它所研究的却并不是业已过去的

① 黑格尔著，贺麟、王太庆译：《历史哲学讲演录》第一卷，第 40 页。
② 黑格尔著，贺麟、王太庆译：《历史哲学讲演录》第一卷，第 40—41 页。
③ 黑格尔著，贺麟、王太庆译：《历史哲学讲演录》第一卷，第 41—42 页。

东西。哲学史的内容是理性的科学成果。而科学的成果是不能消灭的东西。在哲学领域内劳作所得的成就乃是真理，而真理是永恒的，它不是这时存在，他时就不复存在的东西。”①

在以上四条原则中，黑格尔特别对第四条原则做了富有诗意的阐发，他认为，如果一个哲学家在从事真正的哲学史研究工作，则他的工作任务在于：“把潜伏在精神深处的理性，（这理性最初只是潜伏在那里的内在本质或内心本性）揭示出来，提到意识前面，成为知识——哲学的工作实在是一种连续不断的觉醒。”② 因此，哲学史的研究就不是在“记忆的庙宇里”寻找“过去年代的古董”，因为真正哲学著作中的“原则”不是以帆布、大理石、纸张、图像和纪念碑等可以变灭的东西作为媒介而得以保存，历史上真正哲学著作中的“原则”乃是用“思想（概念），精神中不变灭的本质，作为媒介，这媒介是虫所不能蛀蚀的，贼所不能偷窃的。思维所创获的成果，就其为思想而言，构成了精神自身的存在。这种哲学的知识因此也并不是博闻强记——一种对于已死去了的、埋葬在地下的、腐朽了的事物的知识。哲学史所研究的是不老的、现在活生生的东西。”③

由上述四条原则出发，黑格尔对哲学的发展历史也有如下三点结论：第一个结论是：“最初期的哲学是最贫乏最抽象的哲学。在这些哲学里面，理念得着最少的规定，它们只停滞在一般的看法上，没有充实起来。”④ 而由此结论似乎可以推导出更进一步的规定：“最晚出的、最年轻的、最新近的哲学就是最发展、最丰富、最深刻的哲学。”⑤ 对于第一条结论，黑格尔还进一步严肃认真地告诫我们，“必须认清这点，才可不至于在古代哲学里面去寻找较多于应找

① 黑格尔著，贺麟、王太庆译：《历史哲学讲演录》第一卷，第42页。
② 黑格尔著，贺麟、王太庆译：《历史哲学讲演录》第一卷，第42页。
③ 黑格尔著，贺麟、王太庆译：《历史哲学讲演录》第一卷，第42—43页。
④ 黑格尔著，贺麟、王太庆译：《历史哲学讲演录》第一卷，第44页。
⑤ 黑格尔著，贺麟、王太庆译：《历史哲学讲演录》第一卷，第45页。

得到的东西。”[①] 这就是说，在从事哲学史研究的时候，不要把后来人，或者今人的一些观念放到古人的思想当中。

第二条结论涉及对古代哲学的研究方法问题。“我们不要动辄去责备过去的一些哲学家，假如我们在他们的哲学里面找不着在他们的文化水平里尚没有出现的思想。同时复可以使我们妄加一些结论和论断给过去的哲学家，这些结论和论断他们从没有做过，也从没有想到过，虽说我们可以正确地从他们的哲学思想里推演出来。”[②] 黑格尔的这一结论似乎可以从两个方面去解读，第一，哲学史的研究要实事求是，不要让古人“穿”今人的“衣服”。第二，从价值评价的角度看，不要因为古人没有提供我们今人所需要的观念，就指责古人。由此得出结论，黑格尔进一步规定了哲学史研究工作的任务：“哲学史所研究的只是这些思想之发展和发挥出来的次序。某些范畴是很正确地自某一原则推出的，但是这些范畴是否已经很明白地发挥出来，乃完全是另一问题。”[③]

第三条结论的内容较长，但仍然需要较完整地加以引用。“一如在思想的逻辑系统里，每一思想的形态有它的独自有效准的地位，并且通过进一步向前的发展而被贬降为附从的环节，同样每一个哲学在全部过程里是一特殊的发展阶段，有它一定的地位，在这地位上有它的真实意义和价值。必须依照这样的规定去认识它的特殊性格，必须承认它的地位，对于它才有正确合理的处理。也就因为这样，我们对于它的成就，不可要求并希望得过多。我们不要在它里面去寻求须于较高发展的知识里才可提供的满足。我们不必相信，我们思想上的问题，或现代世界感兴趣的问题，可以在古代哲学家那里去找到答案。”[④]

为了比较充分地说明这一点，黑格尔列举了两个典型的例证，一是在柏拉图那里找不到“关于自由的性质、罪恶的起源、神的意旨”等问题的答案，二

① 黑格尔著，贺麟、王太庆译：《历史哲学讲演录》第一卷，第44页。
② 黑格尔著，贺麟、王太庆译：《历史哲学讲演录》第一卷，第46页。
③ 黑格尔著，贺麟、王太庆译：《历史哲学讲演录》第一卷，第47页。
④ 黑格尔著，贺麟、王太庆译：《历史哲学讲演录》第一卷，第48页。

是找不到“自我本身的独立性或自为性”的观念。① 特别是有关现代人所需要的“自由”的观念，黑格尔作了比较详细的说明，他说：

“至于说到一个人本身就是自由的，依照他的本质，作为一个人生来就是自由的，——这点柏拉图不知道，亚里士多德也不知道，西塞罗不知道，罗马的立法者也不知道，虽说惟有自由意志这一概念才是法律的泉源。只有在基督教的教义里，个人的人格和精神才第一次被认作有无限的绝对的价值。一切的人都能得救是上帝的旨意。基督教里有这样的教义：在上帝面前所有的人都是自由的，所有的人都是平等的，耶稣基督解救了世人，使他们得到基督教的自由。这些原则使人的自由不依赖于出身、地位和文化程度。这的确已经跨越了一大步，但仍然没有达到认识自由构成人之所以为人的概念的看法。多少世纪，多少千年以来，这种自由之感曾经是一个推动的力量，产生了最伟大的革命运动。但是关于人本性上是自由的这个概念或知识，乃是人对于他自身的知识，这却并不古老。”②

上述黑格尔的第三个结论及其延伸性的解读，有很多值得玩味之处。就其结论而言，黑格尔要求我们不要做思想上的懒汉，我们自己时代的问题要通过自己的理性思维去加以解决，不要指望古人那里有现成的答案。就其延伸性的解读，如对“自由”观念发展史的解读而言，的确为哲学史的研究提供了很好的范例。一些哲学概念出现比较早，但其概念的具体内涵是不一样的。现代人所拥有的自由观念，尤其是将自由作为人之所以为人的根基意义的自由观念，在传统的哲学里是找不到的。黑格尔以自由思想史纲的形式勾勒“自由”观念在西方哲学史的演进历史进程，高度肯定了基督教教义对“自由”观念深化的意义，但仍然没有拔高基督教教义对现代“自由”观念的作用。这些延伸性说明，对于我们今日的观念史、范畴史的研究，均提供了颇有借鉴意义的方法。不过，在哲学史的研究过程中，我们也不能忽视古人的哲学智慧对于我们的启

① 黑格尔著，贺麟、王太庆译：《历史哲学讲演录》第一卷，第 51 页。

② 黑格尔著，贺麟、王太庆译：《历史哲学讲演录》第一卷，第 51—52 页。

示。那些未能充分发展而又包含着深刻洞见的思想观念，经过时代的问题意识的激发，恰恰可以成为新的时代里有价值的思想酵母。如中国传统哲学中仁的概念与观念，道家的“自然”概念等。因此，对于古代思想观念的价值，我们并不完全同意黑格尔的观点。

上述黑格尔关于哲学与哲学史关系的四条原则与三点结论，我们并没有必要全盘接受，甚至可以对其展开讨论与批判，对于哲学与哲学史的关系做出新的论述。但从上述相对完整、扼要的梳理中可以看出，一些从事分析哲学研究的学者对于黑格尔有关哲学与哲学史的认识，运用形式化的语言简单表述为“哲学史就是哲学”，或“哲学就是哲学史”，进而否认哲学史对于哲学家研究的重要性，甚至直接否定哲学史与哲学的关系，实际上与黑格尔本人对于哲学史与哲学关系的认识并没有很直接的关系。特别是那种将“哲学”看作是一自足的概念，而没有历史发展过程的观点，由此特定的“哲学观”出发，将“哲学”与“哲学史”对立起来的极端性的观点，更不足取。不过，上述这些简化的，甚至漫画式的哲学史与哲学关系的表达式，倒也重新提醒人们重新回到黑格尔的哲学文本之中，让人们对于此问题通俗化、简单化的表述有一个更加正确的认识。

三、“即哲学史讲哲学”的可能性与现实性

在阐述此一观点之前，我们有必要重申一下关于哲学史的两种认识，一种是黑格尔式的哲学史观，将哲学史看作是哲学的展开，因而历史上出现的各种哲学观点，都是哲学自身发展的一个逻辑环节。这是一种系统的哲学史观。另一种哲学史观则将历史上的哲学思想看作是过去发生的一些思想现象，而哲学史研究即是对这些已有的哲学家思想进行一种“历史重构”，或者说是一种历史还原，其目的是将历史上出现的哲学思想的真实意思与面貌揭示出来。而这些前后出现的哲学思想之间未必如黑格尔所设想的那样，有一种逻辑上的次第

关系。这种哲学史观大体上是分析哲学研究者有关哲学史研究工作性质的认识。在我们看来，哲学史的历史展开过程，虽然未必像黑格尔所设想的那样，是“绝对精神”的自我展开，但历史上出现的一些重要的哲学思想观念，大体上还是有前后之间的逻辑联系。相同的哲学概念，后出现的总比它先前出现的概念内涵要丰富、饱满。而后出现的哲学体系也往往包含了先前哲学体系的一些主要哲学原则。哲学史研究过程中的“历史重构”工作虽然不是从时间与逻辑展开的角度来研究观念的发展史，但如果真能将历史上一个个哲学家的思想原貌揭示出来，也非常有助于后来者更准确地认识哲学的历史与逻辑的发展进程，尽管分析哲学研究者并不喜欢这样的看问题方式。就笔者的观点来看，哲学观念的“历史重构”工作与哲学发展的历史与逻辑进程研究之间并不一定是矛盾的，而是可以兼容的。我们提倡即“即哲学史讲哲学”，按照冯友兰先生的观点来看，就是接着前贤的哲学问题与观念往下讲。而我们不用“接着讲”的说法，主要是强调依托整个哲学史提供的思想经验来从事哲学创造的工作，并且强调经验时间上的直接对接或链接关系。而“即哲学史”之“即”字，有依托、顺着哲学史展开的意思。按照黑格尔的观点，哲学理论既可以按照逻辑的次第展开，也可以在经验的时间里依照前后的次序加以发展。后来者的哲学在吸收了前人哲学思想的基础上，可以将前贤的哲学思想的主要原则降低为自己哲学理论体系的一个有机环节，让哲学理论朝着更加丰满、更加丰富的方向发展。

笔者提出的“即哲学史讲哲学”的命题，并不只是局限于哲学史的文本诠释来从事哲学的创新工作。其更为具体、深入的表述应当是，通过对哲学史上重要范畴、问题的梳理与解释，结合当前社会实践提出的一系列重大的社会、政治问题，从哲学的角度给出新的解释或提供新的思想方案。对于这样一种哲学研究与创作的方法，笔者将其称之为“即哲学史讲哲学”的方法。这一方法与以往中国哲学界提出的“照着讲”与“接着讲”的两种方法相比，更接近于“接着讲”的方法。与当前中国哲学界有些人提出的“讲自己”的方法也不矛盾，当然与分析哲学研究者提出的理性分析方式也不矛盾。不过，与“接着讲”的具体说法不尽相同的是，我们不一定仅仅依托中国哲学史的问题或中国社会提出的问题，而是放眼世界哲学问题，当前主要是放眼西方哲学传统，特别是现当代西方哲学传统提出的哲学问题，来展开当代中国哲学的研究与创作。

当代中国仍然处在古今中西之争的交汇点之上，中国的现代哲学家们已经从不同的角度对此问题给出了自己的历史回答。当代中国哲学家中，也有一些哲学家接着现代哲学家提出的问题给出了新的回答，如冯契对金岳霖的哲学问题——“以得之经验之道还治经验”的知识何以可能的哲学问题，从马克思唯物主义的实践论角度给出了新的回答，指出“知识”不仅是可能的，还进一步提出了“由知识到智慧”的“转识成智”问题，将金岳霖的狭义的认识论发展成“广义的认识论”。而陈来则以“仁学本体论”回应了冯友兰的理本论、李泽厚的“情本体论”的问题。还有像张世英、杨国荣等人，分别以“横向超越”、“具体形而上学”的新哲学理论，回应西方哲学几千年来的形而上学问题，尤其是针对西方后现代主义取消形而上学的哲学主张，在综合中国传统哲学思想资源，吸收马克思主义唯物论哲学基础上，重建了哲学的形而上学。还有张立文在中国传统“贵和”，重视“天人合一”的思想传统基础之上，尝试创立了当代的“和合学”这一中国化的哲学理论体系。笔者认为，上述这些哲学新理论均体现了“即哲学史讲哲学”的现实形态。从哲学理论体系的内在自洽性的角度来说，这些哲学理论是否包含真理的内容，能否经得起时间的检验，那是另外一回事。哲学理论的创立与人类其他的科学研究活动一样，既可能是成功的，也可能是失败的。检验的标准当然是长期的社会实践对这些理论的接受程度。但是，即使是一些并不成功的哲学理论，作为一种哲学研究与创作的方法，也具有思想的启迪意义，有时可以作为反面的思维的陷阱，让我们避免一些思想的过失。“即哲学史讲哲学”，其主要意思是依托更加宽广的世界哲学史的知识视野与思想视野，来建构当代中国的哲学理论形态。

就笔者本人目前的哲学研究与创作而言，还不敢奢谈自己的哲学。但在具体的哲学史研究过程中，也尝试讲出哲学史中的真正“哲学”，而不再是个别思想家的思想重构。具体而言，在明清哲学研究的过程中，参照现代西方哲学的实证主义与语言哲学的思路，将清代哲学的方法论提升到一种“人文实证主义”方法论的高度，试图从哲学方法论的高度来考察清代经学考据学与历史考据学中蕴涵的历史还原主义方法，并从哲学的统合角度将其提升为一种实证主义的方法论。由于清代的考据学主要是人文学的，而非自然科学的，故将其视为人文学的实证主义方法，简称为“人文实证主义”方法。另外，本人曾依托中国传统哲学“通”的概念与观念，结合当代世界互联网的现实状态，尝试建立以“通”为形上学的哲学形上学，以此来推进传统哲学以道为形上学的理论建构。目前，此项工作还在尝试的过程之中，发表过一篇论文。整体上还没有比较成熟的想法。

举出上述几个例子旨在说明，哲学史的研究可以不采取“历史重构”的方式展开，亦不需要重复前人讲过的话，而是可以通过对哲学史上诸问题的澄清或批评，以激发研究者的思考，从而推进哲学研究与哲学创作。

笔者的基本结论是：

第一，虽然多元的哲学史研究不等于哲学研究，但也没有必要把哲学研究与哲学史研究对立起来。

第二，哲学史是研究哲学的必要条件，但不是充分条件。由于哲学学科涉及的问题具有广泛性，有些哲学问题是由其他科学，如数学、逻辑等引发的；在现代社会主要由物理学、生物学所引起的；还有些哲学问题主要是由巨大的政治运动、宗教运动引起的。

第三，依托哲学史研究而展开哲学研究和哲学创作，是一条可行的道路或方法，但不是唯一的方法。它不排斥哲学研究和哲学创作的其他方法，如依据哲学概念的逻辑展开的方式。

第四，作为人类精神经验现象之一的哲学思想及其发展历史，简洁地说，即哲学与哲学史的关系，合理的说法是相互定义的。如果从纯粹的逻辑角度看，认为先有哲学，然后才有哲学的历史的说法，类似于先有鸡，还是有鸡蛋的问题一样。哲学思想作为人类的精神现象之一，是从非哲学的思想类型中逐渐产生的。早期的哲学思想与原始宗教、政治等门类的思想是结合在一起的。哲学作为一门相对独立的学问是非常后起的事情。没有一个先验的、绝对的“哲学”存在于人类的精神发展史的过程之中。对此，黑格尔十分正确地说道：“哲学作为一个时代的精神的思维和认识，无论是怎样先验的东西，本质上却也是一种产物。”而“一个民族的精神文明必须达到某种阶段，一般地才会有哲学。”①

第五，笔者认为，黑格尔关于哲学史与哲学关系的论述，全面而完整的理解应当是：哲学这门知识或学问类型是由哲学史这门学科建构起来的。这可以从两个方面去理解，其一，是通过哲学史的研究，让哲学概念得以真正的建立起来。如黑格尔说：“哲学有这样一种特性，即它的概念只在表面上形成它的开端，只有对于这门科学的整个研究才是它的概念的证明，我们甚至可以说，才是它的概念的发现，而这概念本质上乃是哲学研究的整个过程的结果。”② 而哲学史恰恰是对哲学这门科学的整个过程研究的学问。它不仅面向历史，也面向未来。其二，是哲学史这门学科通过将“哲学”知识类型实体化，进而因为实体化而获得主体化的资格，使得自己的学科得以与自然史、科学史、艺术史等学科分别开来。从这一角度说，作为知识类型之一的“哲学”赋予了哲学史以实体和主体的双重特性。

我们希望所有的哲学史著作都能体现写作者自己的哲学，但哲学的研究与创作既可以沿着人类哲学史的大道向前迈进，也可以结合时代要求从事纯粹的哲学思考，以逻辑的力量来展开哲学的论证。但从事哲学思考的理性思维能力与逻辑分析能力，仍然是由哲学史所提供的。因此，我们强调哲学史的学习与

① 黑格尔著，贺麟、王太庆译：《历史哲学讲演录》第一卷，第 53 页。

② 黑格尔著，贺麟、王太庆译：《历史哲学讲演录》第一卷，第 6 页。

研究是我们从事哲学研究的必要条件，但不是充分条件。每位哲学家都需要必要的哲学史训练，但不必成为哲学史专家。哲学家除了要有基本的必备的哲学史训练之外，还需要有更多的科学与文学艺术的素养，但要想成为哲学家，哲学史的基本训练是必需的。我们不否定从事“历史重构”式的哲学史研究的价值与意义，因为这种哲学史研究可以拓展我们关于哲学“知识视野”与“思想视野”。但哲学研究如果追求一种理论的创新，我们更倾向于从哲学发展的动态过程来考察哲学观念的发展史，对前贤的思想得失进行辨证与批评，并结合时代需要创造新的哲学理论。因此，笔者主张，“即哲学史讲哲学”，即通过对历史上诸哲学家和哲学体系的研究、学习，分析其理论的得失，提升我们的哲学理论思维水平，结合时代的需要，并根据哲学思想自身的逻辑要求，创造新的哲学体系。

西学东渐与马克思主义哲学中国化

汪信砚

在近年来的马克思主义哲学中国化研究中，人们开始将探索的目光投向马克思主义哲学中国化的一个重要的历史和理论背景，即一百多年来的西学东渐史，并对西学东渐与马克思主义哲学中国化的关系作了一些探讨。其中，有学者论说过西学东渐对于马克思主义哲学在中国传播的推动作用，有学者考察过西学东渐过程中马克思主义哲学与各种“西学”的思想交锋，还有学者辨析过马克思主义哲学与“西学”之间的归属关系。[①] 应该说，这类探讨大大拓展了马克思主义哲学中国化研究的视野，能够深化我们对马克思主义哲学中国化的理解。但是，到目前为止，这类探讨还不够深入，人们在这类探讨中提出的某些看法和得出的某些结论也是大可商榷的。鉴于此，本文拟对西学东渐与马克思主义哲学中国化的关系问题作一专门的考察和论析。

一

学界通常所说的“西学东渐”，主要是指 1840 年鸦片战争以后近现代西方人文社会科学理论和学说特别是近现代西方政治法律思想和哲学理论在中国的传播。这种意义上的西学东渐，客观上为马克思主义哲学在中国的传播创造了有利条件，并由此构成了马克思主义哲学中国化的一个重要历史前提。

---

① 参见张金荣：《近代西学东渐对马克思主义在中国传播的推动作用》，《湖南师范大学社会科学学报》2010 年第 4 期；刘放桐：《西学传入与“五四”前后中西文化和哲学的碰撞——西方哲学百年反思之一》，《东南学术》2001 年第 2 期。

首先，在西学东渐的过程中，马克思主义被介绍到了中国，从而使马克思主义哲学在中国的传播有了可能。

鸦片战争以后西学东渐的主体，最初是来华的西方人，特别是传教士，后来则主要是清政府出使西方和日本的外交人员、赴欧美和日本学习的留学生、主张改革的知识分子以及中国早期资产阶级代表人物和无政府主义者。虽然这些人背景不同、目的各异，并不认同甚至也未真正理解马克思主义，但他们在向中国传播西方文化和学术思想的过程中，附带地、零星地介绍了马克思主义。

从19世纪70年代开始，清政府的外交人员和主张改革的知识分子如崇厚、张德彝、王韬、高从望、黎庶昌、李凤苞、汪凤藻等人就曾在他们的记述、报道和著作中以不同的方式提到了社会主义。例如，1871年初，清政府派兵部左侍郎崇厚出使法国，兵部候补员外郎张德彝以英文翻译人员的身份随行。他们到达法国后，恰逢巴黎公社革命爆发。崇厚将其所目睹的情况写入日记中，而张德彝则根据其所见所闻撰写了《三述奇·随使法国记》一书。王韬也翻译和撰写了许多关于巴黎公社的报道，并汇编成《普法战记》，于1873年由中华印务总局刊印发行。此外，高从望撰写的《随轺笔记》、黎庶昌撰写的《西洋杂志》、李凤苞撰写的《使德日记》、汪凤藻翻译的《富国策》等著作，也都从不同侧面介绍了社会主义。①

1899年4月，西方基督教会在上海设立的出版机构——广学会主办的《万国公报》连载了由英国传教士李提摩太节译、蔡尔康笔述的《大同学》一文。该文系英国哲学家本杰明·颉德（Benjamin Kidd）所著的《社会进化》（*Social Revolution*）一书的前四章，文中首次提到了马克思的名字和《共产党宣言》中的一段文字："近代学派，有讲求安民新学之一家，如德国之马客偲，主于

① 参见张金荣：《近代西学东渐对马克思主义在中国传播的推动作用》，《湖南师范大学社会科学学报》2010年第4期。

资本者也。”[①] 这里所谓的“安民新学”即社会主义学说，而所谓“主于资本者”即马克思对于资本的研究。

1900 年至 1901 年，中国留日学生主办的《译书汇编》连载了日本著名法学家有贺长雄著、坂崎斌译的《近世政治史》，这是一部关于欧洲 19 世纪政治斗争史的著作。该书共七章，其中，第三章第一节第一部分“万国工人总会及德意志支部”介绍了马克思流亡伦敦、召集各国工人之首领创立万国工人总会（第一国际）的情况，简述了第一国际的宗旨、规约、组织机构、斗争纲领及其在伦敦、日内瓦、洛桑、伯尔尼、巴塞尔等地召开会议的决议，还述及了德国社会民主党领导人黎白克内脱（李卜克内西）和败败而（倍倍尔）在万国工人总会领导下进行革命活动的情况。据考证，这是在中国人创办的报刊上第一次出现“社会主义”一词，并首次把马克思的名字与社会主义学说联系起来。[②]

19 世纪末 20 世纪初，资产阶级改良派代表康有为、梁启超也对社会主义和马克思主义作了一些介绍。康有为 1884 开始编写《人类公理》，1901 至 1902 年避居印度时最后完稿并定名为《大同书》，他在该书中构建其大同理想时介绍并吸收了社会主义学说的某些思想，梁启超甚至称康有为的哲学是一种“社会主义派哲学”[③]。他在《大同书》中说：“夫人事之争，不平则鸣。乃势之自然也。故近年工人联党之争，挟制业主，腾跃于欧美，今不过萌蘖耳。又工党之结联，后此必愈甚，恐或酿铁血之祸，其争不在强弱之国，而在贫富之群矣。从此百年，全地注目者，必在于此。故近者人群之说益昌，均产之说益盛，乃为后此第一大论题也。”[④] 这里所谓的“人群之说”就是指社会主义学说，而“均产之说”则是指共产主义学说。从 1902 年 10 月起，梁启超在《新民丛报》

---

① 李提摩太译、蔡芝绂撰文：《大同学第三章　相争相进之理》，《万国公报》第 123 卷，1899 年 4 月。

② 参见林代昭、潘国华：《马克思主义在中国从介绍到传播》，《世界政治资料》1983 年第 1 期。

③ 梁启超：《康有为传》，参见楼宇烈整理：《康南海自编年谱》（外二种），中华书局 1992 年版，第 253 页。

④ 康有为：《大同书》，中华书局 1935 年版，第 356 页。

上连续发表了《进化论革命者颉德之学说》《二十世纪之巨灵托辣斯》《中国之社会主义》等文，简述了马克思的思想。在《进化论革命者颉德之学说》一文中，梁启超称马克思是“日尔曼人，社会主义之泰斗也”，并引用本杰明·颉德的话说：“今之德国有最占势力之二大思想，一曰麦喀士（即马克思——引者注）之社会主义，二曰尼志埃（即尼采——引者注）之个人主义。”“麦喀士谓今日社会之弊在多数之弱者为少数之强者所压伏。”① 据说，这是中国人在自己的著作中提到马克思的最早记载。在《二十世纪之巨灵托辣斯》一文中，梁启超又称马克思是“社会主义之鼻祖，德国人，著书甚多”。他写道：“观夫近今社会党之生计学者，其论托辣斯也，不惟无贬词，且以其有合于麦喀士之学理，实为变私财以作公财之一阶梯而颂扬之。故知天下事有相反而相成、并行而不悖者，此类是已。”② 而在《中国之社会主义》一文中，梁启超指出：“社会主义者，近百年来世界之特产物也，概括其最要之义，不过曰：土地归公，资本归公，专以劳力为百物价值之原泉。麦喀士曰：现今之经济社会，实少数人掠夺多数人之土地而组成之者也。”③ 虽然这些介绍并不完全准确，但它们在帮助人们了解马克思主义方面起到了积极的作用。

与此同时，资产阶级革命派代表孙中山、马君武、宋教仁、朱执信、胡汉民、戴季陶、叶夏声、廖仲恺等人也在各自的著述中以不同的方式介绍了马克思主义。1903 年 2 月，马君武在日本东京中国留学生主办的杂志《译书汇编》上发表了《社会主义与进化论比较——附社会党巨子所著书记》一文，在论述社会主义学说发展史时介绍了马克思及其思想，并称“马克司者，以唯物史解历史学之人也。马氏尝谓：阶级竞争为历史之钥。”④ 该文所附《社会党巨子所著书记》列举了 26 部研究社会主义的著作，其中包括《英国工人阶级状况》《哲

① 梁启超：《进化论革命者颉德之学说》，《新民丛报》第 18 号，1902 年 10 月 16 日。

② 梁启超：《二十世纪之巨灵托辣斯》，《新民丛报》第 42、43 号合本，1903 年 12 月 2 日。

③ 梁启超：《中国之社会主义》，《新民丛报》第 46、47、48 号合本，1904 年 2 月 14 日。

④ 莫世祥编：《马君武集（1900—1919）》，华中师范大学出版社 1991 年版，第 84 页。

学的贫困》《共产党宣言》《政治经济学批判》《资本论》5部马克思、恩格斯的重要著作。这是最早在中文书刊中出现的对于马克思主义经典著作书目的介绍。1905年8月，孙中山在东京成立中国同盟会。在孙中山的影响下，同盟会成员积极介绍西欧的社会主义思想，其中包括马克思的科学社会主义理论。1906年，同盟会机关刊物《民报》第2、3号连载了朱执信撰写的《德意志社会革命家小传》(署名势伸)，第一次比较详细地介绍了马克思和恩格斯的生平活动，并简述了《共产党宣言》和《资本论》的主要内容。

1907年以后，中国的无政府主义团体及其刊物也开始介绍马克思主义。1908年1月，中国最早宣传无政府主义的刊物《天义》第15卷刊载了恩格斯1888年为《共产党宣言》英文版撰写的序言，这是在中国发表的第一篇比较完整的恩格斯著作中译文。这一卷的《天义》还对其后将发表民鸣翻译的《共产党宣言》全文作了预告。后来,《天义》虽然并未发表《共产党宣言》全译文，但刊载了其前两章内容，并在16—19卷合刊上发表了刘师培为《共产党宣言》写的译序。该合刊还摘译了恩格斯的《家庭、私有制和国家的起源》中的一些段落。另一本无政府主义的刊物《新世界》也曾先后载文介绍《共产党宣言》和《资本论》，并于1912年连载了由施仁荣翻译的恩格斯的《社会主义从空想到科学的发展》(原译名为《理想社会主义与实行社会主义》)，这是中国人对该书的最早翻译。

所有这些对马克思主义的介绍，虽然不够系统也不完全准确，更没有明确区分马克思主义理论的不同组成部分和专门申述马克思主义哲学的内容，但它们毕竟使中国人初识了马克思主义，为马克思主义哲学在中国的传播作了铺垫和准备。

其次，西学东渐使各种西方学说在中国社会受到了鉴别和检验，并使近代中国先进的知识分子自觉地选择了马克思主义哲学。

西学东渐把西方各种人文社会科学理论介绍到中国，使中国思想界成为西方各种社会政治思想和哲学理论的竞技场，也使各种西方学说在中国社会受到了鉴别和实践检验。在这一过程中，近代中国先进的知识分子逐渐认识到各种西方学说都不能适应中国社会的需要，最后自觉地选择了马克思主义哲学。关于这一过程，毛泽东曾作过非常精辟的分析和论述。他指出："自从1840年鸦片战争失败那时起，先进的中国人，经过千辛万苦，向西方国家寻找真理。洪秀全、康有为、严复和孙中山，代表了在中国共产党出世以前向西方寻找真理的一派人物。那时，求进步的中国人，只要是西方的新道理，什么书也看。向日本、英国、美国、法国、德国派遣留学生之多，达到了惊人的程度。国内废科举，兴学校，好像雨后春笋，努力学习西方。……学了这些新学的人们，在很长的时期内产生了一种信心，认为这些很可以救中国，除了旧学派，新学派自己表示怀疑的很少。要救国，只有维新，要维新，只有学外国。那时的外国只有西方资本主义国家是进步的，它们成功地建设了资产阶级的现代国家。日本人向西方学习有成效，中国人也想向日本人学。在那时的中国人看来，俄国是落后的，很少人想学俄国。这就是十九世纪四十年代至二十世纪初期中国人学习外国的情形。"① 那么，近代中国人学习各种西学的结果如何呢？毛泽东说："帝国主义的侵略打破了中国人学西方的迷梦。很奇怪，为什么先生老是侵略学生呢？中国人向西方学得很不少，但是行不通，理想总是不能实现。多次奋斗，包括辛亥革命那样全国规模的运动，都失败了。国家的情况一天一天坏，环境迫使人们活不下去。怀疑产生了，增长了，发展了。"② 最后，"十月革命一声炮响，给我们送来了马克思列宁主义。十月革命帮助了全世界的也帮助了中国的先进分子，用无产阶级的宇宙观作为观察国家命运的工具，重新考虑自己的问题。"③ 毛泽东在这里所说的"无产阶级的宇宙观"，指的就是马克思主义哲学。可见，近代中国先进的知识分子是在对各种西方学说进行鉴别、使其在中国社会受到实践检验并发现它们并不能解决中国的问题后才转而自觉

---

① 《毛泽东选集》第四卷，人民出版社1991年版，第1469—1470页。

② 《毛泽东选集》第四卷，人民出版社1991年版，第1470页。

③ 《毛泽东选集》第四卷，人民出版社1991年版，第1471页。

地选择了马克思主义哲学的。

值得特别注意的是，近代中国先进的知识分子首先都是一些爱国主义者，他们因其爱国情怀和救国救民的抱负而努力向西方国家寻找真理，并由此都曾这样那样地成为西方文化的笃信者。且不说洪秀全、康有为、严复和孙中山这些“代表了在中国共产党出世以前向西方寻找真理的一派人物”是如此，就是陈独秀、李大钊、李达等中国共产党的创始人也不例外。所不同的是，洪秀全、康有为、严复和孙中山等人要么终生都未能走出对于西方文化的迷信，要么始而倡导西方文化、终则退回到文化保守主义的立场，甚至沦为封建帝制的卫道士和守灵人；而陈独秀、李大钊、李达等人则经过艰难的探索最终摆脱了早先痴迷西方文化的梦魇，自觉选择了马克思主义及其哲学。

陈独秀在五四运动以前是中国思想界“全盘西化”论的代表人物之一。他曾说：“欲建设西洋式之新国家，组织西洋式之新社会，以求适今世之生存，则根本问题，不可不首先输入西洋式社会国家之基础，所谓平等人权之新信仰”①。正是基于这种认识，他把“介绍西方学说，改造社会”视为他所主编的《新青年》杂志的“唯一之宗旨”②。从哲学上看，与康有为、梁启超、严复、孙中山等人一样，陈独秀、李大钊也都曾是近代西方进化论思想的信奉者；反映在政治上，他们最初都曾是资产阶级民主主义者，对西方近现代资产阶级的民主思想和民主制度推崇备至，其中，陈独秀还曾经历了从康梁改良主义的追随者到资产阶级激进民主主义者的转变，而李大钊则曾经是一个带有改良主义色彩的资产阶级民主主义者。然而，第一次世界大战结束后巴黎和会上美、英、法等西方列强的无耻分赃活动及其对中国主权和利益的出卖，警醒了他们崇拜西方文化的迷梦，使他们认清了西方资产阶级民主思想和民主制度的局限性和虚伪性；而辛亥革命后民主共和的名存实亡和民国社会的混乱局面，则使他们逐渐认识到西方资产阶级的民主思想和民主制度并不适用于中国，并迫使

① 《陈独秀文章选编》上册，三联书店 1984 年版，第 148 页。

② 《陈独秀文章选编》上册，三联书店 1984 年版，第 165 页。

他们对中国的前途和未来重新进行思考。正当他们悲观、苦闷之际，俄国爆发了推翻沙皇专制政权的二月革命，引起了他们的高度关注并使他们深受鼓舞。而在俄国十月革命的感召下，李大钊毅然放弃了资产阶级民主理想，公开宣称自己信奉马克思主义理论。随着对十月革命的了解日益全面和深入，同时也因受李大钊对马克思主义的积极宣传的影响，陈独秀亦很快告别了旧的资产阶级民主理想，转而认同和信仰马克思主义及其哲学。

至于李达对马克思主义理论的接受和认同，则经过了一种形式不同而实质无异的心路历程。1913 年和 1917 年，具有强烈爱国热情的李达抱着实业救国的理想两次东渡日本，并考入日本第一高等学校，学习探矿冶金。然而，就在李达两次东渡日本期间，日本军国主义者趁西方列强忙于第一次世界大战而无暇东顾之机加强了对中国的侵略扩张，并向中国政府提出了旨在把整个中国都置于日本控制之下的“二十一条”无理要求；而在国内，“各派新旧军阀都勾结一个帝国主义作后台，发动内战。全国人民在蔓延的战火中，受着军阀们的剥削和压迫，都感到活不下去。”① 严酷的现实，使抱有实业救国理想的李达在思想上陷入了极度的迷茫，感到自己“就像在漫漫长夜里摸索道路的行人一样，眼前是黑暗的，内心是极端苦闷的”②。李达彷徨苦闷之际，俄国十月革命爆发并取得了胜利，给了他极大的振奋和鼓舞，使他在黑暗中看到了救国救民的希望，并使他“初步树立了对马克思主义的信心和对苏俄的向往”③。1818 年 5 月，段祺瑞政府与日本秘密签订了反苏卖国、引狼入室的“中日共同防敌军事协定”。留日中国学生闻讯后义愤填膺、忍无可忍，并于 5 月 7 日在东京集会抗议，被军警拘捕多人。在这种情况下，留日中国学生决定全体罢学抗议，并组织“留日学生救国团”归国请愿。李达率救国团先遣队于 5 月中旬抵达北平，并与许德珩等人一起组织和发动了于 5 月 21 日举行的北平学生向总统府

① 《李达文集》第 4 卷，人民出版社 1988 年版，第 732 页。

② 《李达文集》第 4 卷，人民出版社 1988 年版，第 732 页。

③ 《李达文集》第 4 卷，人民出版社 1988 年版，第 733 页。

和段祺瑞政府示威请愿的活动。这次示威请愿活动有北平各院校的两千多学生参加，是中国历史上较早的一次大规模的学生爱国运动，其影响遍及上海、天津、南京等地，并成为次年五四运动的预演和先导。虽然这次示威请愿活动并没有达到预期的目的，但它对于李达最终告别本质上属于资产阶级的意识形态并带有某种改良主义色彩的实业救国理想、自觉接受和认同马克思主义理论却具有决定性的意义。后来他自己回忆说："这次挫折，使我们深切地觉悟到：要想救国，单靠游行请愿是没有用的；在反动统治下'实业救国'的道路也是一种行不通的幻想。只有由人民起来推翻反动政府，像俄国那样走革命的道路。而要走这条道路，就要加紧学习马克思列宁主义的理论，学习俄国人的革命经验。"① 于是，李达当年再次东渡日本，并毅然放弃了理科的学习，转而全力钻研马克思主义及其哲学。

再次，西学东渐所激起的新文化运动使中国一批先进的知识分子完全转变成为马克思主义者，并促成了马克思主义哲学在中国的广泛传播。

从思想文化发展的角度看，新文化运动是由西学东渐所激起的西学与中学或东西文化之间的矛盾和冲突的一次总爆发。这是因为，新文化运动所大力倡导的科学和民主精神是近现代西方文化的基本内核，它们与中国几千年的封建专制和封建迷信是恰相对峙的。新文化运动前期(1915 年 9 月至 1919 年 5 月)，陈独秀、李大钊、鲁迅、胡适等新文化运动的主将以《新青年》杂志为阵地，高举"民主"和"科学"两面旗帜，对以往几千年的封建思想和封建文化进行了猛烈的抨击。尽管这一时期的新文化运动还属于旧民主主义的文化运动，但作为中国历史上前所未有的伟大的思想启蒙运动，它为马克思主义及其哲学在中国的传播扫清了思想障碍。1919 年的五四运动以后，陈独秀、李大钊、瞿秋白、李达等人迅速转变成为马克思主义者，他们不仅反对封建主义，而且反对各种资产阶级思潮，而他们所运用的重要理论武器就是马克思主义，特别是

---

① 《李达文集》第 4 卷，人民出版社 1988 年版，第 733—734 页。

唯物史观。因此，五四运动以后的新文化运动已成为宣传马克思主义及其哲学和以马克思主义及其哲学为指导的新民主主义的文化运动。正是在五四新文化运动的促动下，全国各地传播马克思主义及其哲学的刊物和社团如雨后春笋般出现。据统计，五四运动以前，倡导新文化的刊物只有《新青年》《每周评论》和《新潮》等少数几种；而五四运动后的一年里，全国新出版的进步刊物猛增到 400 多种，新成立的进步社团达三、四百个。这些刊物和社团不仅发表了大量研究和宣传马克思主义及其哲学的文章，而且积极致力于马克思主义经典著作的翻译和出版。在它们的推动下，马克思主义及其哲学在中国的传播呈现出迅速燎原之势。

当然，西学东渐背景下的马克思主义及其哲学在中国的广泛传播不可能是一帆风顺的，马克思主义及其哲学必然面临着并实际经历了与各种西学、各种反马克思主义思潮的思想交锋和论战，如关于中西文化的论战、关于“问题”与“主义”的论战、关于科学与玄学的论战。在五四运动以后的中西文化论战中，李大钊、陈独秀、瞿秋白运用唯物史观对文化复古主义进行了深刻的批判；在“问题”与“主义”的论战中，李大钊用马克思主义哲学反击了胡适的实用主义；科玄论战虽然是现代西方哲学中的科学主义和人本主义两大思潮在中国思想界的论争，但其中也有中国马克思主义者的声音，陈独秀、瞿秋白、邓中夏等人就曾运用马克思主义哲学对二者的片面性作了批判。从 1919 年到 1923 年，中国马克思主义者还经历了与以张东荪和梁启超为代表的资产阶级改良主义、以黄凌霜和区声白为代表的无政府主义等各种反马克思主义思潮的论战。通过这些思想交锋和论战，在中国思想界抢滩登陆的各种西方学说和“主义”要么很快偃旗息鼓，要么完全销声匿迹，而马克思主义及其哲学则逐渐成为中国思想文化发展的不可遏制的主潮流。

正因为西学东渐在客观上促成了马克思主义哲学在中国的广泛传播，所以它构成了马克思主义哲学中国化的一个重要历史前提。人们通常把中国马克思主义哲学发展史划分为马克思主义哲学在中国的传播和马克思主义哲学中国化两个阶段，认为马克思主义哲学在中国的传播并不归属于马克思主义哲学中国化过程。这种把马克思主义哲学在中国的传播与马克思主义哲学中国化截然二分的观点是完全没有根据的。事实上，马克思主义哲学中国化进程恰恰肇始于马克思主义哲学在中国的广泛传播。如果说五四运动之前马克思主义哲学在中国还只是由不同背景和立场的人并非自觉地作了一些零星的介绍，那么，五四运动以后马克思主义哲学在中国广泛传播的过程，一开始就是中国的马克思主义者自觉把马克思主义哲学"作为观察国家命运的工具"、运用马克思主义哲学回答"中国向何去处"这一时代大问题的过程。换句话说，早期中国马克思主义者一开始就是自觉地结合中国的具体实际即通过运用马克思主义哲学考察中国社会的问题来传播马克思主义哲学的。李大钊、陈独秀、瞿秋白、李达等人对马克思主义哲学的传播清楚地表明了这一点。例如，1920 年至 1921 年，李达连续发表了《张东荪现原形》《社会革命的商榷》《马克思还原》《讨论社会主义并质梁任公》《无政府主义之解剖》《马克思派社会主义》等文章，运用马克思主义理论、特别是唯物史观的基本原理，尖锐地批评了当时中国思想界以张东荪和梁启超为代表的研究系、以黄凌霜和区声白为代表的无政府主义等反马克思主义思潮，明确地回答了中国要不要走社会主义道路、能不能走资本主义道路的问题。而在 1923 年的《马克思学说与中国》一文中，他认为"马克思学说之在中国，已是由介绍的时期而进入实行的时期了"，并具体讨论了目前的中国是否可以应用马克思学说改造社会、中国无产阶级应该怎样准备和实行应用马克思学说改造社会、中国无产阶级掌握政权后应该采用何种政策等三个问题。① 实际上，在五四运动以后中国思想界的一系列论战中，马克思主义哲学也正是因为能够帮助人们正确回答"中国向何处去"的时代大问题才战胜了当时中国思想界的各种反马克思主义思潮。因此，尽管马克思主义中国化命题是由毛泽东在 1938 年正式提出的，但马克思主义哲学在中国的广泛传播

---

① 参见《李达文集》第 1 卷，人民出版社 1980 年版，第 202—203 页。

实际上就已开启了马克思主义哲学中国化的进程。由是观之，西学东渐客观上促成了马克思主义哲学在中国的广泛传播，实质上也就揭开了马克思主义哲学中国化的序幕。

二

西学东渐不仅仅是马克思主义哲学中国化的一个历史前提，即不仅仅只是客观上促成了马克思主义哲学在中国的广泛传播，它也构成了马克思主义哲学中国化理论目标的实现和理论功能的发挥的一个必要条件。西学东渐引发了中国哲学历史发展过程中的重大变革，它促成了中国哲学的古代传统向近代传统的转变，从而为马克思主义哲学中国化在中国现代哲学的建构中发挥积极的主导作用提供了可能。

马克思主义哲学中国化的理论目标是建构中国马克思主义哲学。那么，什么是中国马克思主义哲学呢？金岳霖曾在为冯友兰的《中国哲学史》一书所写的《审查报告》中指出，“中国哲学”这个名称存在一个困难问题。他说：“所谓中国哲学史是中国哲学的史呢？还是在中国的哲学史呢？”① 对于“中国马克思主义哲学”这一概念来说，也存在一个类似的问题，即中国马克思主义哲学到底是一种已成为中国哲学或中国现代哲学的有机组成部分的马克思主义哲学，还是一种“在中国”的马克思主义哲学。这也就是人们通常所说的中国马克思主义哲学作为中国哲学或中国现代哲学的合法性问题。

中国马克思主义哲学作为中国哲学或中国现代哲学的合法性问题原本是一个早已解决了的问题。中国马克思主义哲学是通过马克思主义哲学中国化建构的，而所谓马克思主义哲学中国化，就是把马克思主义哲学与中国的具体实际相结合。在这里，“中国的具体实际”是指特定时代中国的历史、现实和未来

---

① 冯友兰：《中国哲学史》下册，中华书局1961年版，附录第5页。

发展趋势的总和，它包括两个方面的内容：一是中国的文化传统，特别是中国历史上绵延数千年的哲学传统，它曾深刻地影响并必将继续不断地影响着中国人的精神世界；二是中国的现实，包括特定时代中国社会的政治、经济、文化等各个方面的发展状况及其各种复杂的影响因素，它既延传和积淀着中国的历史文化传统，也包孕着中国社会未来发展的种种可能和趋势，既以当前世界作为自己存在和发展的外部环境又是当前世界的一个不可分割的组成部分。与此相应，马克思主义哲学中国化也包括两大方面的内容：一是把马克思主义哲学与中国的文化传统相结合，即运用马克思主义哲学来审视、反思和改铸中国的文化传统，推动和促进中国先进文化的形成和发展，包括实现中国传统哲学的现代化，同时又努力吸取中国传统文化、特别是中国传统哲学的精粹，用以丰富马克思主义哲学的内容和创造中国马克思主义哲学的民族化形式；二是把马克思主义哲学与中国的当前现实相结合，即运用马克思主义哲学考察和分析中国的当前现实，从中提升出具有时代性和普遍性的哲学问题，并通过对这些问题的创造性的回答，指导中国的当前实践，推进马克思主义哲学的发展。上述两个方面，内在地包含着毛泽东曾经强调过的马克思主义中国化的两个维度：既"使马克思主义在中国具体化"，即"把马克思列宁主义的理论应用于中国的具体的环境"①，又使中国"丰富的实际马克思主义化"②。而作为上述两个方面之统一，马克思主义哲学中国化必然使马克思主义哲学从内容到形式完全变成中国的东西，必然使马克思哲学具有"为中国老百姓所喜闻乐见的中国作风和中国气派"③，由此所创造的中国马克思主义哲学必然以中国的形式和内容体现着马克思主义哲学的精神实质，从而必然既是中国的又是马克思主义的，即既是中国哲学又是马克思主义哲学。例如，作为马克思主义哲学中国化的第一个标志性成果，毛泽东哲学就是这样一种中国马克思主义哲学。1945 年 4 月，

---

① 参见《毛泽东选集》第二卷，人民出版社 1991 年版，第 534 页。

② 《毛泽东文集》第二卷，人民出版社 1993 年版，第 374 页。

③ 《毛泽东选集》第二卷，人民出版社 1991 年版，第 534 页。

刘少奇在党的七大上所作的关于修改党章的报告中说："毛泽东思想，就是马克思列宁主义的理论与中国革命的实践之统一的思想，就是中国的共产主义，中国的马克思主义"，它"完全是马克思主义的，又完全是中国的。"① 整个毛泽东思想是这样，毛泽东哲学亦复如此。

中国马克思主义哲学还不只是一般意义上的中国哲学，它事实上早已成为中国现代哲学的主潮流，是 20 世纪以来中国哲学现代形态的最重要的创造者。五四新文化运动以后，中国马克思主义哲学的形成和发展构成了现代中国哲学发展的主脉。特别是新中国成立以后，马克思主义哲学的真理性和主导地位更是得到了中国哲学界的普遍认同。1953 年，李达先生在恢复和重建武汉大学哲学系时，曾明确主张马克思主义哲学应该成为一切科学中的首席科学，并提出了"一体两翼"的建系方针，即认为哲学系的建设必须坚持以马克思主义哲学为"体"、以中国传统哲学和西方哲学为两"翼"②。这一建系方针生动而深刻地体现了中国哲学建设必须坚持马克思主义哲学的指导地位的思想，它在当时的中国哲学界是极有代表性和示范性的。那时，许多过去长期专治中国传统哲学和西方哲学而不了解马克思主义的著名学者，如冯友兰、金岳霖、贺麟等，也都满腔热情地自觉学习马克思主义，努力用马克思主义哲学指导自己的学术研究。20 世纪 90 年代以来，虽然挑战马克思主义哲学的指导地位的鼓噪声一直不绝于耳，但它们并没有消解掉马克思主义哲学在中国哲学建设中的主导作用，马克思主义哲学的指导地位也是其他任何一种哲学所不可能取代的。

然而，在今日中国哲学界，仍然有人置上述基本的历史事实而不顾，这样那样地质疑和否定中国马克思主义哲学作为中国哲学或中国现代哲学的合法性。其中，以某些文化保守主义者的看法最为典型。在他们看来，近百年来的中国马克思主义哲学史不过是一种"马克思主义哲学在中国"的历史，而"马

---

① 《刘少奇选集》上卷，人民出版社 1981 年版，第 333、335 页。

② 参见陶德麟：《缅怀李达老校长——在纪念李达同志重建武汉大学哲学系 50 周年大会上的讲话》，《武汉大学学报》（人文科学版）2007 年第 2 期。

克思主义哲学在中国”一如“进化主义在中国”、“唯意志论哲学在中国”和“实用主义在中国”，它们全都是“在中国”的哲学而并不真正属于中国哲学或中国现代哲学，或者说，它们都只是中国哲学或中国现代哲学这个家族中的“客人”而非“主人”或“成员”。按照他们中一些人的描述，作为19世纪中叶以后伴随着西方列强的入侵而出现的西方文化潮水般地涌入中国的一种表现，马克思主义哲学约一百年前传播到了中国，然后就指导中国革命取得了胜利并成为中国社会的主流意识形态，使中国社会历史发生了深刻的变化，其自身也经历了相当曲折的进程。① 在这幅题为“马克思主义哲学在中国”的漫画式图景中，马克思主义哲学中国化和中国马克思主义哲学都纯属子虚乌有的事情，马克思主义哲学甚至成了中国哲学或中国现代哲学“恕不接待”的“客人”。除文化保守主义者外，也还有学者以其他的方式质疑和否定中国马克思主义哲学作为中国哲学或中国现代哲学的合法性。例如，近年来中国哲学界流行的“中、西、马对话”的话语方式，就其把中国哲学、西方哲学和马克思主义哲学视为互为他者的三种不同哲学而言，实际上也是否定中国马克思主义哲学作为中国哲学或中国现代哲学的合法性的。

人们质疑和否定中国马克思主义哲学作为中国哲学或中国现代哲学的合法性的一个重要理由是，认为马克思主义哲学与中国哲学有着很不相同的传统，即西方哲学传统和中国哲学传统，而在鸦片战争之前这两大哲学传统之间并没有真正的交流和实质性的影响，因此，马克思主义哲学是无法接上中国哲学的传统而成为中国哲学或中国现代哲学的②。

这种对中国马克思主义哲学作为中国哲学或中国现代哲学的合法性的质疑，问题恰恰出在对中国哲学传统的理解上，即把中国哲学传统理解为一成不变的东西。其实，虽然传统具有极强的稳定性，但任何传统都不可能是永恒不

① 参见王守常等:《马克思主义哲学在中国》，首都师范大学出版社2002年版，第1页。

② 参见李维武:《20世纪中国哲学视域中的马克思主义哲学中国化研究》，《哲学分析》2010年第4期。

变的。美国学者 E. 希尔斯曾专门考察过传统的变迁问题。他认为，传统的变迁，可能源于某种“内部因素”的影响，也可能因某种“外部因素”的影响而发生。“当传统的拥护者被带到或来到其他传统的面前时，传统便发生了变化。外来传统支持者的经济、政治和军事力量，外来传统明显的方便性和有效性，以及在既有传统的假设之内的知识上令人信服的优越性——所有这些都促使既有传统发生变迁。”① 虽然 E. 希尔斯所考察的是一般传统的变迁，但他的分析对我们理解中国哲学传统及其变化也是很有启发意义的。

众所周知，中国古代哲学曾经经历了从殷周之际到明清时代的长期演变。大致产生于殷周之际的中国哲学，至春秋战国时代，出现了百家争鸣的繁荣局面。孔子创立的儒家思想在汉代取得了主导地位，成为自此以后中国古代哲学发展的主流，并因此构成了中国哲学的古代传统。直到 1840 年的鸦片战争前，中国哲学的古代传统的确未曾受到过西方哲学传统的实质性影响，但这并不意味着中西方不同的哲学传统永远也不会发生碰撞和交融。事情的根本变化恰恰是从鸦片战争开始的。鸦片战争以后的西学东渐，使西方文化潮水般地涌入中国，导致了中西文化大碰撞，激起了中国思想界异常激烈的“古今中西”之争，包括关于中、西哲学的论争，并最终引发了中国哲学传统的重大变革。借用 E. 希尔斯的话来说，西学东渐正是促成中国哲学传统发生变迁的关键“外部因素”。

对于 1840 年鸦片战争以后中国哲学传统的重大变革，一些中国哲学史的研究专家早有明确的认知和精辟的论述。冯契先生就曾分析过包括中国哲学传统在内的整个中国文化传统在近代的革命性转变。他说：“现在人们一谈到传统，往往专指古代传统。我们有五千年民族文化传统，这是足以自豪和需要批判地加以继承的，但是，构成当代人直接精神背景的，却不是原封不动的古代传统。古代文化中那些在当代仍然有生命力的东西，大多是经过近代历史的筛

---

① E. 希尔斯：《论传统》，上海人民出版社 1991 年版，第 321 页。

选，并发生了不同程度变形的东西。所以，批判继承民族文化传统的问题，首先应该注意的是自1840年以来一百余年间（主要是20世纪）形成的近代传统。在这期间，与中国经历了巨大的社会变革相联系，也发生了一场重大的哲学变革。'变革'，那就是说，哲学思想、哲学范畴在这期间发生了质的变化。"[①]在他看来，伴随着整个文化传统的转变，中国哲学传统也经历了由古代传统向近代传统的转变。他指出："中国近代哲学既是古代哲学的延续，又发生了革命性的变革，形成了新的近代传统。"[②]对于中国哲学的这种"新的近代传统"，冯契先生着重就中国近代哲学家们所关注的不同于中国古代哲学的中心问题作了分析："在中国近代，时代的中心问题就是'中国向何处去'的问题。灾难深重的中华民族，如何才能获得解放，才能不受帝国主义的压迫、欺凌、奴役？一百年来的志士仁人就是为了解决这个问题而前仆后继。这个时代的中心问题在政治思想领域表现为'古今、中西'之争，其内容就是如何向西方学习，并且对自己的传统进行反省，来寻求救国救民的真理，以便引导我们这个民族走上自由解放的道路。这一政治思想领域中的关于'古今、中西'的论争，是中国人民反帝反封建的现实斗争的反映。"[③]"在中国近代史上，很多有成就的思想家并不是专搞哲学的，他们研究哲学主要是为了回答'中国向何处去'的问题。"[④]"研究中国近代哲学，首先要看到这一特点：中国近代史上很多思想家是爱国者，是革命家，他们代表了中华民族的希望，代表了中华民族的优秀传统。他们的热情、意志、思想都集中在解决'中国向何处去'的问题。而'中国向何处去'的问题，就表现为政治思想领域的'古今、中西'之争制约着哲学的发展。为什么在中国近代，有的哲学问题显得突出了，有的哲学问题没有被注意，最主要的原因就在于此。"[⑤]显然，按照冯契先生的理解，既然"古今

---

① 冯契：《智慧的探索》，华东师范大学出版社1994年版，第557页。

② 《冯契文集》第9卷，华东师范大学出版社1998年版，第513页。

③ 冯契：《古今、中西之争与中国近代哲学革命》，《上海社会科学院学术委刊》1985年第1期。

④ 冯契：《古今、中西之争与中国近代哲学革命》，《上海社会科学院学术委刊》1985年第1期。

⑤ 冯契：《古今、中西之争与中国近代哲学革命》，《上海社会科学院学术委刊》1985年第1期。

中西”之争是“中国向何处去”这一时代中心问题在政治思想领域的表现并制约着中国近代哲学的发展，构成了中国近代哲学传统的特点，而“古今中西”之争又是由近代以来的西学东渐激起的，那么，中国近代哲学革命即由中国哲学的古代传统向近代传统的革命性转变就是由西学东渐促成的。

近代以来西方哲学东渐的过程，是从严复等人开始的。严复引入西方近代经验主义传统和现代经验证实原则，在经验论的基础上解析了中国古代哲学的话语方式和范畴体系，以牛顿力学、特别是达尔文的进化论为框架建构了中国哲学史上第一个完全近代意义上的哲学体系，并由此成为促使中国哲学的古代传统向近代传统转变的枢机人物。正如冯契先生所说：严复“坚决主张向西方学习，用西学来代替中学，用新学来代替旧学。他用科学的进化论作为思想武器，拿西方近代资产阶级的先进的世界观与中国封建社会腐朽落后的统治思想作比较，来鼓励人们向西方学习，树立中华民族自主、自强的信心，激发人们的爱国热情。这在当时起到了一定的革命作用。可以说，这是标志着中国近代哲学发展第一阶段革命的开始。”① 冯契先生强调指出：“过去中西哲学（以及其他民族的哲学）各自独立地发展，它们各是世界哲学的一部分，没有统一的世界哲学史”，而“由于中国近代的哲学革命，中西哲学、中西文化在中国的土地上开始汇合了”，因此，“对于中国近代哲学论争，我们还是应该把中国传统哲学与西方近现代哲学联系起来加以考察。中国近代哲学是从中国传统哲学演变而来的；同时，它又在一定意义上重复了西方近代哲学发展史。”② 这也就是说，由严复开启的中国哲学的近代传统同时融汇了中国哲学的古代传统和西方哲学传统。

正是因为由西学东渐促成的中国近代哲学传统同时融汇了中国哲学的古代传统和西方哲学传统，它使得最初在西方哲学传统中产生的马克思主义哲学可

---

① 冯契等：《古今中西之争与哲学革命——兼论中国近代哲学的特点和规律》，《哲学研究》1982 年第 8 期。

② 冯契：《古今、中西之争与中国近代哲学革命》，《上海社会科学院学术季刊》1985 年第 1 期。

以通过中国化而对接上中国哲学传统并转化成中国哲学，马克思主义哲学中国化才能够在中国现代哲学的建构中发挥积极的主导作用。1938 年，毛泽东在正式提出马克思主义中国化命题时曾经指出，"从孔夫子到孙中山，我们应当给以总结，承继这一份珍贵的遗产。"[①] 有学者认为，毛泽东在这里实际上强调了这样一点，即要实现马克思主义哲学中国化，就应该注重总结和继承中国哲学的古代哲学传统和中国哲学的近代传统，因为孔夫子可以说是中国文化和中国哲学的古代传统的代表，而孙中山则可以视为中国文化和中国哲学的近代传统的象征[②]。事实也是如此。近百年来，中国的马克思主义者努力把马克思主义哲学与包括中国哲学传统在内的中国的具体现实相结合，通过探索和回答"中国向何处去"这一时代大问题，不断推进马克思主义哲学中国化。尽管这一过程颇为曲折，很是艰难，但它使马克思主义哲学早已成为中国现代哲学的主潮流则是一个不争的事实。

三

正因为西学东渐是马克思主义哲学中国化的一个重要历史前提，并构成了马克思主义哲学中国化理论目标的实现和理论功能的发挥的一个必要条件，所以从一定意义上说，没有西学东渐就不可能出现马克思主义哲学中国化，不深入研究西学东渐及其与马克思主义哲学中国化的关系就不可能真正理解马克思主义哲学中国化。从这个角度看，对西学东渐的漠视确是以往马克思主义哲学中国化研究的一个重大缺陷。在近年来的马克思主义哲学中国化研究中，有些学者也已经意识到了这一问题，并试图考察和分析西学东渐与马克思主义哲学中国化之间的关系，但他们并没有正确地理解和把握这一关系，竟然认为马克

---

① 《毛泽东选集》第二卷，人民出版社 1991 年版，第 534 页。

② 参见李维武：《20 世纪中国哲学视域中的马克思主义哲学中国化研究》，《哲学分析》2010 年第 4 期。

思主义哲学中国化本身就属于西学东渐的范畴。在笔者看来，这是对马克思主义哲学中国化的严重误读，它甚至会造成比以往马克思主义哲学中国化研究对西学东渐的漠视更为严重的后果。实际上，虽然马克思主义哲学中国化与近代以来的西学东渐有着密切的联系，但它并不是西学东渐史的一个组成部分。

首先，马克思主义哲学与人们通常所说的各种西学具有不同的理论本质。

人们通常所说的“西学”是一个与“中学”相对应的概念，它有广义和狭义之分。广义的西学概念是西方文化的总称，其中也包括西方近代以来迅速发展起来的自然科学。显然，这种意义上的西学概念是很不严密的，今天人们一般也不再在这种意义上使用西学概念，因为自然科学是没有中、西之分的。狭义的西学概念则是指西方近现代的资产阶级思潮，特别是政治法律思想和哲学理论，它们是西方近现代资产阶级价值诉求的理论表达。毛泽东曾把这种意义上的“西学”称为“新学”。按照他的说法，“西方资产阶级民主主义的文化，即所谓新学”，它“和中国封建主义的文化即所谓旧学是对立的”①。对于这种意义上的“西学”，我们不能望文生义地加以理解和解释，尤其是不能将其简单地视同为“西方人之学”或西方人创立的思想和理论，因为西方人创立的思想和理论并不一定就是西方近现代资产阶级价值诉求的理论表达，它完全可能超越西方近现代资产阶级的狭隘视界，马克思主义哲学就是如此。虽然马克思、恩格斯都是西方人，但他们所创立的理论表明他们是生长在西方的“世界公民”；虽然马克思主义哲学产生于西方国家，但它是全部人类思想积极成果的结晶，它所表达的是无产阶级和全人类的价值诉求，它的理论旨归是整个人类的解放和每个人的自由全面发展，因而它是一种从根本上超越了地域的、民族的和阶级的片面性和局限性的“世界的文学”②。因此，无视马克思主义哲学与各种西方近现代资产阶级思潮之间的本质区别，把它们都笼而统之、等而视之地称之为西学，并因此认为马克思主义哲学中国化是近代以来西学东渐的一

---

① 《毛泽东选集》第四卷，人民出版社 1991 年版，第 1470 页。

② 参见《马克思恩格斯选集》第 1 卷，人民出版社 1995 年版，第 276 页。

个组成部分，这种观点在理论上是极其错误的，它丝毫无助于我们对于马克思主义哲学中国化及其深远意义的理解，只会带来诸多的理论混乱。

值得进一步指出的是，长期以来，国内外学界有些学者不仅把原初形态的马克思主义哲学即由马克思、恩格斯创立和阐述的马克思主义哲学划归西学的范畴，甚至断言整个马克思主义哲学都属于西方哲学①。这是一种比上述把原初形态的马克思主义哲学与各种“西学”混为一谈更加错谬的观点，因为它不仅抹平和掩盖了马克思主义哲学与各种西学的本质区别，而且还歪曲了马克思主义哲学发展的历史事实。这些学者断言整个马克思主义哲学都属于西方哲学，无非还是因为马克思主义哲学最初产生于西方，是由马克思、恩格斯这两个西方人创立并以马克思的名字命名的。但是，如果说有人认为原初形态的马克思主义哲学属于西方哲学虽并不正确却还事出有因的话，那么，断言整个马克思主义哲学都属于西方哲学则表现出对于马克思主义哲学发展的历史事实的极端漠视。稍有一点常识的人都知道，马克思主义哲学诞生160多年来经历了一个世界化与民族化相统一的发展过程。虽然马克思主义哲学最初产生于西方国家即德国，但由于集中地反映了时代的本质特点，适应了时代发展的需要，它很快就超越了其创立时期的狭隘地域和民族界限，在世界范围内得到了广泛的传播，产生了普遍而深刻的影响，并在20世纪以来的社会主义实践中发挥了巨大的指导作用。在马克思主义哲学的这一世界化进程中，特别是20世纪以来，各国的马克思主义者和共产党人纷纷地把马克思主义哲学与本民族、本国家的具体实际相结合，从而使马克思主义哲学又不断地民族化，出现了苏俄的马克思主义哲学、中国的马克思主义哲学、越南的马克思主义哲学、朝鲜的马克思主义哲学、古巴的马克思主义哲学、当代西方的马克思主义哲学等各种不同的马克思主义哲学民族化形式。虽然它们所经历的发展道路各不相同，在

---

①　赵敦华教授曾概括了学界对于马克思主义哲学与西方哲学之关系的两种完全相反的理解，其中之一就是认为“马克思主义哲学属于西方哲学”，“把马克思主义哲学当作西方哲学的一个部分”。参见赵敦华：《研究马克思哲学与西方哲学的“正本清源”方案》，《学术研究》2006年第3期。

理论视角、所关注的问题及研究问题的思路和方法等许多方面都有很大的差异，甚至在一些问题上还存在着相当大的分歧，但这些差异和分歧只是马克思主义哲学内部的差异和分歧。作为马克思主义哲学的民族化形式，它们不仅具有一些最基本的共同点，而且在马克思主义哲学的研究上都取得了独特的理论成就，都从不同的维度为马克思主义哲学的丰富和发展作出了重要贡献，因而都属于整个马克思主义哲学的有机组成部分。显然，这样一种内在地包含着各种不同的民族化形式的马克思主义哲学，无论如何都是不能被归入西方哲学的范畴的。

其次，马克思主义哲学中国化与西学东渐具有不同的目的和社会性质。

西学东渐并不是一种单纯的文化传播现象，它受到不同目的的制导并因而具有极其复杂的社会性质。一方面，西学东渐是西方国家文化殖民的一种表现，它原本是为西方殖民主义服务的。这从西学东渐早期来华西方人、特别是传教士所起的作用以及西学东渐是由西方资本主义国家的坚船利炮开道的等方面就可以看得很清楚。人们通常认为，西学东渐大体上经历了两个重要时期。一是明末清初时期。这一时期西学东渐的主体是来华西方人、特别是耶稣会传教士，他们在传播基督教教义的同时，也译著了大量西学书籍，对西方的科技和学术思想作了介绍。1605 年意大利耶稣会传教士利玛窦撰著的《乾坤体义》，被《四库全书》编纂者称为“西学传入中国之始”。从总体上看，这一时期传入的西学对中国思想界的影响并不大，人们所着重注意的主要是西学的技术层面，如天文历法、测量以及所谓的“西洋奇器”等等。二是鸦片战争以后。从鸦片战争开始，西方殖民主义者用坚船利炮撞开了中国以往长期闭锁的国门，也按照殖民主义的惯常逻辑开始了对中国的大规模文化入侵，从而使西学东渐迅速成燎原之势，并造就了近代中国半殖民地社会的文化特征。毛泽东在论述帝国主义列强如何使近代中国变成半殖民地时曾说：它们除了对中国进行军事侵略、政治压迫和经济剥削以外，“对于麻醉中国人民的精神的一个方面，也不放松，这就是它们的文化侵略政策。传教，办医院，办学校，办报纸和吸引留学生等，就是这个侵略政策的实施。其目的，在于造就服从它们的知识干部和愚弄广大的中国人民"①。即使是在今天，西学东渐也仍然带有这种文化殖民的性质，因为西方国家的文化侵略政策从来都没有改变。在当代，西学东渐已成为西方国家全球化策略的一个重要组成部分，是西方国家借以传播其价值观念的重要途径，它是为西方资本的全球扩张服务的。虽然西学东渐客观上促进了西方科学知识的传播和东西方之间的文化交流，但我们在任何时候都不应忘记、更不能否定其所带有的文化殖民的性质。另一方面，西学东渐又是中华民族救亡图存和奋发图强的一种表现，是中国先进的知识分子为了拯救危亡中的中华民族和推进中华民族的伟大复兴而奋起向西方学习的结果。西方国家文化殖民的需要只是西学东渐的外因，如果没有某种内因起作用，西学东渐是很难在短时间内大规模地展开的，这也是明末清初时期西学既已开始传入但并没有对中国思想界产生重要影响的原因。真正给西学东渐以有力推动的内因是在鸦片战争以后形成的，这就是中华民族救亡图存的需要。鸦片战争使晚清政府的一些人士认识到必须"师夷长技以制夷"，但最初人们重视的仍然是西方文化的器物方面，这突出地表现在 19 世纪 60 年代出现的洋务运动上。当时的洋务派人士对待西学的基本态度是"中学为体、西学为用"，其所关注的主要是西方先进的武器、器械及相关技能。甲午战争以后，中华民族的危机进一步加重。为了救亡图存，梁启超、康有为、谭嗣同等一大批知识分子开始全面地向西方学习，他们不仅致力于西方的自然科学理论和政治、法律思想的引入，更是积极主张和要求政治上的变革。直到这时，西方文化和学术思想才真正开始大规模地传入中国，各种西学才开始对中国思想界产生深刻的影响，并引发了中国思想界关于东西文化的持续不断的大论战，出现了东西文化大激荡的局面。当代以来，特别是改革开放以后，为了促进中国社会经济和思想文化的发展，中国知识界又以饱满的热情译介、传播和研究各种西学，努力学习、借鉴

① 《毛泽东选集》第二卷，人民出版社 1991 年版，第 629—630 页。

和吸收西方国家的优秀思想文化成果，把西学东渐推向了一个新的高潮。由此可见，西学东渐是西方列强的殖民主义运动与中华民族的救亡图存和自我振兴运动共同作用的结果，它带有西方国家文化入侵和中华民族救亡图存和奋发图强的双重性质。

与西学东渐不同，马克思主义哲学中国化的根本目的是要用马克思主义哲学改造中国、回答“中国向何处去”这一时代大问题。它是中国的马克思主义者自觉把马克思主义哲学与中国的具体实际相结合，谋求国家独立、民族解放和人民生活幸福的过程中所发生的历史事件。从原则上讲，西学东渐的主体可以是任何背景和立场的人，除非他是那种极端的文化保守主义者。就西学东渐的历史看，实际情况也是如此。且不说那些来华西方人和传教士与中国人对西学看法上的差异，就是近代以来曾以不同方式传播和倡导西学的中国人对西学的基本态度也是不尽相同的，其中，有的主张“中体西用”，有的主张“全盘西化”，还有的主张“中西互补”，但这些人对待西学的不同看法和态度，并不妨碍他们都为西学东渐作出了自己的积极努力。与此形成鲜明对照的是，马克思主义哲学中国化的主体只能是中国的马克思主义者。因为人们只有真正认同和信仰马克思主义哲学，才有可能把马克思主义哲学与中国的具体实际相结合、自觉运用马克思主义哲学改造中国和探索“中国向何处去”这一时代大问题。关于这一点，我们仅从马克思主义哲学在中国的早期传播就可看得非常清楚。虽然新文化运动之前某些来华的西方传教士也曾偶尔提到马克思的名字和学说，但他们中没有一个人真正专门介绍过马克思主义及其哲学。蔡元培先生曾称赞严复是在中国介绍西洋哲学的第一人，[1] 但作为资产阶级启蒙思想家，严复始终避而不提马克思主义哲学。虽然梁启超等资产阶级改良派介绍过马克思的学说，但他们并不认同马克思主义及其哲学，他们传播马克思主义及其哲学的目的仅限于胁迫清政府实现君主立宪。梁启超本人就曾直言不讳地说：中

① 参见《蔡元培全集》第4卷，中华书局1984年版，第351页。

国当时“民族主义尚不暇及，何论于社会主义大同理想哉？曰：吾明知不能骤致大同，而实欲立大同之基也。立大同之基何？曰：在迫朝廷改专制政体而为立宪政体。”① 孙中山等资产阶级革命派也曾为传播马克思主义及其哲学作过贡献，但他们同样并不信仰马克思主义及其哲学，其传播马克思主义理论的目的仅仅是想借此而预防未来中国社会出现马克思所激烈批判过的那些资本主义的弊病。孙中山本人曾经坦言：“我国提倡社会主义，人皆斥为无病之呻吟，此未知社会主义之作用也。处今日中国而言社会主义，即预防大资本家之发生可矣。此非无病之呻吟，正未病之防卫也。”② 与上述这些人截然不同，李大钊、陈独秀、瞿秋白、李达等人在新文化运动中已转变成为马克思主义者，他们受俄国十月革命胜利的鼓舞而立志用马克思主义哲学改造中国、回答“中国向何处去”这一时代大问题，并且开始紧密地结合中国的具体实际来传播马克思主义哲学，致力于“建立普遍与特殊之统一的理论”（李达语），由此不仅推动了马克思主义哲学在中国真正大规模的广泛传播，而且开启了马克思主义哲学中国化的历史进程。可见，即使仅就马克思主义哲学在中国的早期传播来看，它与具有双重性质的西学东渐也是完全不同的。

再次，马克思主义哲学中国化与西学东渐具有不同的结果和社会效应。

正如前述，马克思主义哲学中国化即把马克思主义哲学与中国的具体实际相结合，它的理论目标在于建构中国的马克思主义哲学，而它的根本目的则是要以马克思主义哲学改造中国、回答“中国向何处去”这一时代大问题。近百年来的马克思主义哲学中国化历程，实际上也就是这样一种理论目标和根本目的不断实现的过程。当然，这一过程是相当曲折的。虽然早期的中国马克思主义者已开始紧密结合中国的具体实际传播马克思主义哲学、从而开启了马克思主义哲学中国化的进程，但他们对马克思主义哲学和中国的具体实际的理解还不深刻和全面，特别是他们中的一些人曾把马克思主义哲学与中国传统文化和

① 梁启超：《秘密结社之机关报纸》，《新民丛报》第38、39号合本，1903年10月4日。

② 孟庆鹏编：《孙中山文集》，团结出版社1997年版，第339页。

传统哲学完全对立起来，对中国传统文化和传统哲学进行了激烈批判和根本否定，因而还不可能真正实现马克思主义哲学中国化的理论目标。1938 年 10 月，毛泽东在中共中央六届六中全会上作了《论新阶段》的政治报告，深刻地认识到了早期中国马克思主义者的上述缺陷，明确提出了“从孔夫子到孙中山，我们应当给以总结，承继这一份珍贵的遗产”的问题，并较系统地阐述了马克思主义中国化思想[①]。直到这时，中国的马克思主义者才真正达致马克思主义哲学中国化的理论自觉，并开始了中国马克思主义哲学的伟大创造，逐渐形成了毛泽东哲学思想，为马克思主义中国化的第一个标志性成果即毛泽东思想奠定了理论基础。在毛泽东思想的指导下，中国马克思主义者和共产党人不仅实现了中国传统文化的创造性转换，建构了现代中国的革命文化，重塑了中国人的精神世界，而且成功地找到了一条中国特色的民主革命道路，完成了国家独立和民族解放的伟业，实现了中国历史上最广泛最深刻的社会变革，开启了中华民族发展进步的新的历史纪元。新中国成立后，特别是近三十多年来，中国的马克思主义者在总结历史上正反两方面的经验教训的基础上不断推进马克思主义哲学中国化，使中国马克思主义哲学不断发展，为马克思主义中国化的又一个标志性成果即中国特色社会主义理论体系奠定了重要理论基础。在中国特色社会主义理论体系的指导下，中国共产党带领全国人民进行了改革开放的新的伟大革命，开创、坚持和发展了中国特色社会主义，推动中国社会主义现代化建设在政治、经济、文化等各个方面都取得了举世瞩目的伟大成就。可见，马克思主义哲学中国化对于作为中国现代哲学主潮流的中国马克思主义哲学的建构，同时也就是对中国现代社会主流思想文化的理论基础和哲学内核的建构，它从根本上改变了中国社会发展的历史进程，成为中华民族走向繁荣富强和伟大复兴的根本理论法宝。

与马克思主义哲学中国化相比较，西学东渐的结果和社会效应则呈现出另

① 参见汪信砚：《马克思主义中国化的思想源流》，《武汉大学学报》（人文科学版），2008 年第 6 期。

一番景象。虽然西学东渐也曾使各种西学在中国思想界和中国社会激起了这样那样的涟漪，但由于各种西学本质上是西方近现代资产阶级价值诉求的理论表达，现代中国社会缺少其赖以扎根的历史条件和现实土壤，因而它们始终没有真正进入中国人的精神世界，更没有对中国社会的发展产生实质性的影响。近代以来，在中国思想界和中国社会盘桓时间最久、产生影响最大的西学当数自由主义思潮，但西学东渐史终究也不过是自由主义的一曲哀歌。应当承认，近代中国知识分子是抱着向西方寻求救国救民真理的目的而把西方自由主义介绍到中国来的，而西方自由主义传入中国后也确曾在反对封建文化的斗争中起过积极作用。例如，严复对西方古典自由主义思想的系统介绍，为近代中国的维新变法运动提供了思想武器；胡适是杜威功利自由主义的追随者并被称为中国“第一代自由主义知识分子代表”①，他在五四新文化运动中倡导文学革命，对旧文学和封建文化进行了无情的批判。不过，在严复时代，自由主义并没有在中国大规模传播开来；胡适倒是一度使自由主义在中国知识分子中获得了不小的市场，但他的自由主义思想在“问题”与“主义”的论战中受到了马克思主义者的严厉批判，而他主张通过改良而实现中国社会进步的自由主义政治理想也在中国革命的洪流面前彻底幻灭了。抗日战争结束后，自由主义思潮在中国思想界重新泛起，储安平等中国自由主义知识分子提出了所谓“中间路线”的政治主张，即认为中国既不能是半殖民地半封建社会，也不能是无产阶级领导的人民共和国，而应该建立一个资产阶级共和国，自由地发展资本主义。然而，随着国民党独裁野心的暴露和全面内战的爆发，这种“中间路线”的自由主义政治主张也迅速破产。新中国成立以后，自由主义在中国一次又一次地卷土重来，但其向马克思主义和中国社会主义制度发起的一次又一次的进攻均被击退。最近十多年来，西方新自由主义思潮又在中国思想界蔓延，中国的新自由主义者甚至在政治、经济、思想文化等各个方面都提出了一整套纲领，企图

① 参见梅荣政：《用马克思主义引领社会思潮》，武汉大学出版社 2008 年版，第 97—98 页。

使新自由主义成为中国社会的主流意识形态，严重地干扰了中国的改革开放和社会主义现代化建设事业，因而受到了中国马克思主义者的严厉批判。可以预料，自由主义与马克思主义之间的较量在中国思想界和中国社会还将继续下去，但自由主义或新自由主义企望把中国变成资本主义国家的政治图谋是注定不可能得逞的。

单从哲学方面看，除了前述客观上促成了马克思主义哲学在中国的广泛传播及中国哲学的古代传统向近代传统的转变以外，西学东渐在中国哲学界激起的最强烈的回应，莫过于20世纪上半叶那些力图融汇古今中西哲学资源的现代哲学体系的建构。应该承认，没有西学东渐，就不会有新文化运动，也很难设想会有20世纪上半叶中国哲学界的“古今中西”之争和在融汇古今中西哲学资源基础上的哲学创造。李维武曾指出：“经过新文化运动，中国哲学的现代转型进入了全面的发展时期，不仅通过科学与玄学论战，提出并探讨了科学与哲学、知识论与本体论诸关系问题，而且出现了一批分属不同思潮的中国哲学家，融汇中西古今哲学资源，创造了具有个性特征的现代形态哲学体系。”① 这些融汇古今中西哲学资源的现代哲学体系的最典型代表，就是熊十力的“新唯识论”、冯友兰的“新理学”、贺麟的“新心学”和金岳霖的“道论”，它们可谓是中国传统哲学之树在历经西学近百年的浸染后结出的最实在的果实。然而，即便是这些融汇古今中西哲学资源的哲学创造，客观上并没有对中国现代思想文化和中国人的精神世界产生实质性的影响，更没有在中国社会发展的历史进程中真正发挥解决中国现实问题的作用。不仅如此，冯友兰、金岳霖、贺麟在新中国成立后还都放弃了他们自己原来的哲学思想，转而接受和认同马克思主义哲学。

马克思主义哲学中国化和西学东渐所历经的两种完全不同的历史命运绝不是偶然的。实际上，前述的马克思主义哲学与各种西学在理论本质上的区

---

① 李维武：《马克思主义哲学中国化与中国哲学的两种传统》，《江汉论坛》2008年第11期。

别，一开始就决定了马克思主义哲学可以中国化而各种西学从总体上看却只能“在中国”。而这样一种结果，大概是近代像严复那样一些为了救亡图存而在中国倡导各种西学却唯独对马克思主义哲学讳莫如深的知识分子根本未曾料想到的。

（原载《中国社会科学》2012 年第 7 期）

第二部分

哲学方法论

哲学的主题与方法

彭富春

当代哲学面临许多问题：理论的和实践的、历史的和现实的、民族的和国际的，如此等等。但当代哲学面临的最大的问题是自身越来越成为了问题。对此，任一种主张具有时代意识的哲学思考都不可能简单地回避。

所谓的问题首先是哲学的死亡。它意味着哲学已经终结、完成，对于当代思想不再具有规定性。但它是何种哲学的死亡？哲学作为一个学科、哲学系作为一个建制，在全球范围内的大学不仅存在，而且还兴旺发达。显然这种死亡的哲学具有一个独特的名字，即西方的形而上学。形而上学不仅是西方哲学的一个学科，其作为第一哲学不同于其他哲学，而且也是西方哲学的基本本性。形而上学的本性是追问存在者整体：上帝、世界和灵魂，同时追问其存在的根据。这些根据就是真善美，是人的认识、意愿和情感的对象。形而上学的死亡既不是由于"他杀"，也不是由于"自杀"，而是它自身的"寿终正寝"。这也就是说它自身已经完成了其思想使命，达到完满，聚集于其最大的可能性之中。（参见海德格尔，1988 年，第 61—63 页）

其次是哲学和非哲学的界限消失。我们姑且不论作为西方形而上学的哲学的死亡，而将哲学看成一个依然富有生机的思想现象，但也不得不承认这个哲学自身的同一性已经瓦解了。传统的哲学具有自己独特的领地，不同于科学和文化。不仅如此，它还是科学之王，为各种科学提供原则，就是如现在所说的世界观和方法论。但当代的哲学与科学、文化的关系变得模糊。一方面哲学的独有领地被非哲学的学科所占有：自然哲学让位给自然科学，如数学、物理学和化学，甚至让位给现代技术，如原子（核）技术、生物技术和计算机技术。

道德哲学的一些问题也被人类学、社会学、文化学、政治学和法学所代替。另一方面，不是哲学给其他学科制定原则，而是其他学科为哲学给出原则。现代语言学对于哲学以及相关学科的关系是最典型的例证。无论是语言哲学还是结构主义和后结构主义，都从语言学那里获得思想资源，由此语言学似乎成为了先导学科。鉴于上述情况，哲学和非哲学的边界是不确定的。一个文本，既可以是哲学的，也可以是文学的、文化的，还可以是语言的。

第三是哲学的多元化，并表现为其学科分类的复杂化。哲学的一些传统学科依然存在，甚至还是主导性的，如认识论、伦理学和美学等。但是每一个学科自身都在分离出一些新的学科。如认识论和心理学、认知科学的嫁接，形成新的认识论；伦理学出现了生命伦理学、生态伦理学；美学诞生了身体美学和环境美学等。此外，哲学内部其他的一些学科也在不断生长。政治哲学、经济哲学（博弈论）等正成为哲学领域中的热点。这些不同的哲学学科之间存在着巨大的差异，以至人们可以说，哲学自身不同学科之间的差异大于它们各自与其相关的非哲学学科的差异。

当然，当代哲学的问题还有许多。但仅仅这里所说的哲学的死亡、哲学边界的消失和哲学学科的多元化，就会使人们提出一个问题：什么是这个哲学？这一提问本身就是一个哲学式的提问。所谓“什么是”就是追问事物的本质和本性，“什么是这个哲学”就是追问哲学的本质和本性。但是这样一个哲学有其本质和本性吗？也许当代哲学的本质和本性刚好是反本质和反本性，正因如此，它才成为了当代哲学。如果事情是这样的话，那么我们既不能如同先秦那样把哲学思考描述为“爱道”的事情，也不能像古希腊那样将它规定为“爱智慧”，不管是“智慧之爱”还是“爱的智慧”，也不能和近代一样，将哲学等同于科学的世界观和方法论。如果哲学不是如同它历史上所曾是的那样，那么它自身还能是什么？在此我们不再试图对哲学的本性作一个规定，而是探讨它可能的主题和方法。

一

哲学的主题一般被理解为它的内容、对象、事情和问题等，但所有这些都和思想相关。哲学作为思想，其所思想的就是其主题。不过，中西哲学对此主题在其历史上都有不同的理解。虽然中国传统哲学包括了许多深刻和丰富的问题，但其主题也许就是道。道家阐释了自然之道，儒家解释了社会之道，禅宗说明了心灵之道。与此相似，西方也在其不同的时代讨论了世界、上帝和理性之类的问题，现代和后现代甚至将主题变得更加多元化。

尽管如此，无论对于何种哲学来说，存在问题始终是其基本问题。但什么是存在自身的意义，却是无确定性的。因此存在问题又一直是晦暗不明和争论不休的。首先，存在问题是否具有普遍性？显然它只是一个西方形而上学的问题，而不是中国传统思想的问题。当然我们可以将中国所说的“道”与西方所说的存在进行比较，认为道具有与存在相似的意义，但惟有西方思想将存在形成了主题。其次，存在的意义在历史上是否是同一的？柏拉图的存在等同于亚里士多德的存在吗？古希腊思想的存在等同于德意志唯心主义的存在吗？最后，令当代存在问题的追问者着迷的是：存在的哲学上的语义是否就是其语言学上的语义？这就是说，存在只是系词“是”的不定式，还是这之外的其他什么？对于第一个和第二个问题的回答已经给出：存在问题既不是普遍的，也不是同一的。因此我们的重心将集中在对于第三个问题的探讨，即它的哲学与语言学的语义的不同及其多重性。

在我们讨论存在时，最凸显的存在是与虚无相对的存在。虚无在此不意味着虚空和虚幻，而是意味着不存在。这样，存在是指一切不是虚无的东西，凡不是虚无的东西就是存在。在此意义上，不仅自然万物，而且人类社会，还有思想、语言、文字等等都属于存在。虚无不存在，因此是不可思考和不可言说的，存在存在，而且是可思考和可言说的。存在和虚无在此看起来是相对的，却又具有某种隐秘的关联。虽然虚无不存在，但只要虚无是虚无的话，那么虚无也作为虚无存在。这样存在问题甚至越过了自身的边界，它不仅包括了自身，而且还包括了自身的对立面，亦即虚无。对于存在问题，形而上学将它作为自身的基础问题提出：为什么只是存在者存在而不反倒是虚无存在？根据海德格尔的观点，这不是一随意的问题，而是所有问题中的第一问题。在这种意义上，它是最宽广、最深入和最本源的问题，因为它切中了存在者的存在。首先，此问题是宽广的。它包括了所有的存在者，达到了存在者最远的和不可逾越的边界，由此边界而表明了存在者的整体，此整体还包容了虚无。其次，此宽广的问题也是最深入的，因为它追问存在者的根据。追问根据不仅相关于存在和非存在的区分，而且相关于对于存在和非存在的决定，即什么是必须存在的和什么是必须不存在的。最后，此问题是最本源的，它自身说明根据和建立根据，于是它作为形而上学的问题是一切问题中最本源的问题。（参见海德格尔，1987 年，第 2—5 页）

存在除了被理解为与虚无相对之外，还与思想相对。思想泛指一切意识、心灵和精神的东西，它或者表现为主观的形态，或者表现为客观的形态。与思想相对的存在就是思想之外的万物，是被思考的，并因此是被思考之物。在这样的意义上，存在就不再包括思想，而只包括自然和人类。如此的存在甚至被理解为物质和物质性的。因为存在等同于物质，所以存在和思想的关系就变成了物质和思想的关系。在物质和思想之间的优先性上，凡是认为物质是第一性的，就是唯物主义，凡是认为思想是第一性的，就是唯心主义。当然就唯物主义自身而论，如果从自然物质出发，那么就形成所谓的自然本体论，一些旧唯物主义就是如此；如果从人类物质出发，并且强调人与自然的差异，那么就形成人类（学）本体论，其中，如果将人类物质理解为人类物质生产，那么就形成了马克思主义的历史唯物主义的基本原则。就唯心主义而论，把主观精神作为出发点的，就是主观唯心主义；将客观精神作为出发点的，就是客观唯心主义。不管何种唯物主义，也不管何种唯心主义，它们都追求存在和思想的合一。这就是存在和思维的同一性问题，也就是真理问题。思想和存在的符合就是真理，否则就是谬误。由此而来，真理是“是”，谬误是“非”。也正因如此，真理是存在的，且必须是存在的，而谬误是不存在的，且必须是不存在的。但真理如何可能？也就是存在和思想的同一如何可能？这根本上在于首先存在自身是真的，显明真相，然后思想归属于存在，而成为真知。

比较了存在和虚无、存在和思想之后，还要进一步描述存在与变化、存在与现象的关系。变化不仅是从一物到另一物的转变，而且是从无到有的生成和从有到无的消失。但存在不同于变化。如果说存在就是变化的话，那么它一方面可能是：存在产生于存在。但如果存在产生于存在，那么就是存在产生于自身，它与自身是同一的，而这是没有意义的。另一方面则可能是：存在是从无到有，和从有到无。但从无到有意味着存在曾尚未存在，从有到无则意味着存在将不再存在。这两者都是和存在的本意相矛盾的，因为存在不可能同时存在又不存在，或者不存在又存在。存在作为存在是一个不动的静止的整体。它不可能产生于虚无，并归于虚无。存在不仅不同于变化，而且也不同于现象。现象当然是存在的显现，但它却不是存在自身。现象具有几种不同的形态。现象一般被理解为假象，它似是而非，看起来如此却并非如此，或者看起来并非如此却是如此。于是作为假象的现象遮盖了存在自身。现象也被理解为表象，它如同疾病的某种症候，显示出某种自身不显现的东西，这样现象就成为了某物的现象，亦即存在的现象。这两种形态的现象都与存在自身是具有差异性的。只有第三种现象，即现象学意义上的现象才与存在是同一的。这种现象被理解为显现，它是作为显现自身的显现者。（参见海德格尔，1993 年，第 34—39 页）而它正是存在自身。在此存在和现象的矛盾得以克服。

存在问题又始终关联于真善美的问题。真善美不仅是人类永远追求的目标，也是哲学永恒的主题，由此形成了认识论、伦理学和美学等。尽管哲学上对于真善美没有统一的规定，甚至对于真善美和假恶丑的界限缺少明确的划定，但人类历史的每个阶段对真善美都有约定并形成惯例。不过，对于哲学来说，真善美是作为理性的对象。真是认识的对象，善是意志的对象，美是情感的对象。于是真的领域是自然，善的领域是自由，美的领域是艺术。（参见康德，1993年a，第36页）在此意义上，真善美不仅各属自身的领域而且和存在没有直接的关联。但现代思想在完成从理性哲学到存在哲学的转变的同时，也建立了存在和真善美的直接关系。这就是说，真善美是存在的真善美，是存在显现的不同维度。据此，真首先是存在问题，然后才是认识问题；善既不只是一个内在的道德问题，也不只是一个外在的伦理问题，而是一个人类的存在问题，即人如何生存在这个世界上的问题；美不再是存在的幻相或假象，也不再只是一个情感的对象或一个艺术问题，而是存在自身生成的完满显现。

最后，存在问题集中于人的存在特别是个人的存在问题。在存在者的领域内，有不同的存在者：自然、人类和神灵等，人只是其中之一。人的存在显然不能等同于存在自身，甚至也不是存在的中心，如同人类中心主义所构想的那样。但人的存在是一特别的存在，中国传统认为人是万物之灵，西方认为人是理性的动物。但马克思强调人是劳动的动物，是有意识的生命存在。对于海德格尔和许多现代思想家来说，人的独特存在则在于他是语言性的存在。语言不仅显示了人自身的存在，而且打开了人通往世界其他存在者存在的通道。因此存在和人的存在的真实关系表明为：人的存在开启了存在自身，同时存在自身规定了人的存在。但在人的存在自身，个体的存在显然又不同于一般的人类的存在。对于个体存在特性的标划是由所谓的死亡哲学和身体哲学所给予的。死亡哲学认为，人是走向死亡的存在者，因而是一个要死者。不仅自然是永恒的、神灵是长存的，而且人类也是绵延不绝的。惟有个体是要死亡的。由于死亡的根本规定，个体的存在凸显出来了。但死亡是个体存在的边界，是生存的另一面。正是在此边界处，显示了个人存在的不可替代和不可重复，因而表明了其唯一性。身体哲学则思考了人的活生生的肉身。肉身的活动是人的个体的最直接的存在。每一个身体所展现的时空都是有限的，同时每一个身体都是不同的和他样的。身体的差异性不仅体现在性别，即所谓男女的性的区别，而且体现在超出性别的其他方面，甚至人的身体自身也是不断具有差异性的。正是我与他者的差异，才使我获得了我的规定，同时也正是我与自身的差异，才使我始终自我更新。

上述关于存在的哲学语义的不同层面的探讨只是理解存在问题的一个方面。另一方面，我们不能不面临对于存在的语言学语义探讨的挑战。

对于语言学的探讨来说，存在问题只是一个西方的问题。这是因为“存在”一词只是来源于印欧语系的系词“是”的不定式，它从古希腊文经拉丁文到现代德文和英文都是如此。“存在”一词不相关于古代汉语和现代汉语的“是”，因为汉语没有“是”的不定式及其变化。因此，如果将作为西方哲学历史上的基本主题的存在只是狭义地等同于系词“是”的不定式的扩大化使用，那么这不仅否认了存在问题的普遍性，而且也使存在本身的意义变得没有了。对此，现代的分析哲学的工作已经充分地予以了揭示：“存在”如同“虚无”一样都是语言的误用，是形而上学的虚构。于是通过语言分析的工作可以消除存在问题，并克服形而上学。

存在（广义的存在）与“是”的不定式（狭义的存在）的关系的探讨其实古已有之。古希腊前苏格拉底时期的哲学家们所讨论的主题并非作为“是”的不定式的狭义的存在，而是广义的存在。海德格尔在《形而上学导论》中分析了这一时期谈论的三个主题：逻各斯、自然和无蔽。逻各斯不仅是言谈，而且是聚集；自然不是指自然物，而是指发生、生成和涌现；无蔽则意味着真理、真相和存在自身。当然巴门尼德也在狭义上说了“存在者存在，非存在者不存在”，但使存在形成主题的是亚里士多德。在《形而上学》中他指出，哲学这一门科学的任务是探讨存在者之所以为存在者以及存在者作为存在者所具有的各种属性。（参见亚里士多德，1005a，87）这里所说的“存在者之所以为存在者”，指的正是包含着一切存在者的存在或一切存在者所以为存在者的理由——终极原因。他区分了存在，并分析了存在的十种方式。在他那里，存在的意义主要依据于“是”的不定式形态。

在近代，特别是德意志唯心主义哲学虽然思考理性，但也关注作为“是”的不定式的存在问题。康德在《纯粹理性批判》中指出，存在不是一个真实的谓词，而是一种设定，或者说是事情自身的规定。从逻辑上看，存在只是一个系词。譬如上帝是全能的，这包括了两个对象：上帝和全能。其中“是”只是一个系词，并没有给主词添加任何东西。但在表达式“这是上帝”和“上帝是”中，“是”已经构成了一种意义的变化。这个“是”不再是系词而是成为了实义动词，一个不及物动词。但“上帝是”这句话是没有意义的，“上帝是上帝”这句话也是同语反复。只有当我们说“上帝是全能的”时，这个包括了“是”的句子才是有意义的。与康德不同，黑格尔在《逻辑学》中指出，存在就是事情自身无差别的同一性。正是在此意义上，存在即虚无，只要它们是无中介性和无规定性的。至此，西方哲学中存在问题的危险已经浮出，即将存在变成一个实体性和对象性的东西。

现代哲学当然将存在问题凸显了出来，并给予存在许多规定，如尼采的“创造力意志”和马克思的“物质生产”等，但惟有海德格尔将存在问题作为问题进行了追问。首先，海德格尔反对将存在实体化和对象化。他区分了存在和存在者，认为存在不是存在者，甚至也不是存在者的存在，而是存在自身。作为如此的存在就是虚无。为了避免对于这种意义的存在作实体化和对象化的误解，他还特意给“存在”这个语词打叉。其次，海德格尔反对将广义的存在等同于作为系词“是”的狭义的存在。他阐释了许多作为系词“是”的不定式的存在之外的意义，如存在作为让、存在作为给予、存在作为生成等。同时存在的这些语义又包括了自身的悖论：让在场是让离去，给予是反离，生成是剥夺等。（参见彭富春，2000 年，第 45—50 页）最后，海德格尔也试图将存在问题转换成语言问题。如果作为存在的存在不是实体化和对象化的，同时存在的语义不是系词“是”的不定式，从而不是关于某物的判断，那么它的本源之地就是语言性的。正是作为“道”的语言才是让、给予和生成。

但存在问题的真正消解只是实现于后现代思想那里。德里达通过“替补”

否认了作为在场的存在本源性。“替补”有两重含义：一方面是增补，即增加于已有的东西。存在是有缺陷的，甚至自身就是一个虚空；另一方面是替代，即以某物代替另一物，这样就没有永远的在场和不变的中心。在《系动词的替补：语言学之前的哲学》中，德里达深入分析了存在问题。第一，存在的本源不是实义动词，而是系动词“是”的不定式。但“是”只有语法功能，而没有述谓的意义，没有明确的所指。第二，“是”由动词转向了名词，完成了由无意义的系词向主语的转化。主语指涉一个超验的存在，由此一个虚幻的东西成为了真实。第三，如果将作为名词的“是”回到作为系词的“是”，那么“是”就要联系主词和谓词，始终是“什么是什么”。但主词和谓词不可能是同一的，同时谓词也不可能是唯一的，而是不断置换的，因而是一个未知数。于是主词的意义只能在无穷差异中呈现，而且不具有终极的意义。第四，系动词“是”之后的未知数就是增补。增补始终是对于存在空白的增补。这里原物隐而不现，甚至根本就没有原物，没有绝对。于是西方哲学上的存在问题就彻底终结了。

二

与存在一样，思想也是哲学的基本主题之一。特别是当人们谈论“存在和思维”的同一性的时候，思想的主题地位达到了非凡的高度。不管是存在规定思想，还是思想规定存在，思想都是一个不可轻视的问题。除去作为哲学的主题不谈，思想也是哲学自身。哲学就是思想，而且是关于思想的思想。正是在思想之中，哲学从事着自己的工作。然而什么是这个思想？

从事实来说，思想是人的身体中的大脑的一种行为。人的身体当然是存在者之一，甚至是一特别的物质。但身体不能只是理解为肉体，而是要把握为活生生的生命。它是有意识的生命活动。这样身体本身包含了意识或者思想。但人的大脑的思维活动既不能等同于人的手脚的活动，也不能等同于眼耳等五官的感觉。因此它既不是身体的一部分，也不是身体性的。虽然“我在思考”和“我思考某物”是一个显而易见的事实，但思想却不如物质那样是实体性和对象性的，而是像幽灵一般，很难获得其规定性。于是身体和思想所形成的身心关系不能理解为一种单一的关系。身体和思想不是如二元论所设想的那样是分离的：前者是广延性的，后者是思维性的。但也不能简单地统一到物质或者精神那里去，如同传统的唯物主义和唯心主义所做的那样。思想和身体关系的复杂性表现为：对身体来说，思想不是身体自身，但思想是既内在又超越的。思想是内在于身体的，这是因为思维是人的大脑的机能。一块石头不思维，一棵树不思维，一个动物在理性的意义上说也不能思维，惟有人能思维。因此人是思维的动物和理性的动物。但思想也是超越于身体的，这是因为身体的界限并不是思想的界限。思想不仅思考身体及其相关物，而且思考身外之物，甚至思考天下万物。

但思想作为人体的大脑活动，非常容易等同于心理或者被心理主义所误解。心理受制于人的自然的生物和生理条件，它相关于时空和因果关系等。因此心理事实是人类的，同时也是经验的。由此它也会导致相对主义和怀疑主义，只要从心理主义出发来理解思想或者意识自身的规定性的话。哲学所关注的思想在根本上不能等同于一个关于思想的经验性的心理事实。因此作为哲学主题的思想既不相关于某一个别的作为心理主体的思想者，也不相关于某一具体的心理（包括思想）过程，甚至不相关于在某种时空条件下的心理物，而是相关于在所思当中所表明的思想自身的本性和形式，它一般被命名为纯粹思想或者是纯粹意识。在这样的意义上，思想有自身独特的规律、逻辑和道路。它超出了现实主义和经验主义的局限，同时它也能摆脱相对主义和怀疑主义的阴影，而提供真理性的知识。

当然，这个与身体和心理不同的思想包括了多种要素，主要是三种：感性、知性和理性。作为思想的感性既不是对象的感性，也不是人的活动的感性，而是感性认识，是人的感官及其感觉，因此是感性直观。对于康德而言，感知接受了时空中的事物。但这在于感性具有先验地知觉时间和空间的能力。由此心灵不仅能够知觉时空中的事物，而且还能知觉时空自身。感性提供了思想的材料，但它必须被知性所思考。与感性的直观活动不同，知性主要是运用概念和判断的思想过程。概念是关于事物自身的把握，判断则通过概念之间关系的建立而规定事物的本质。康德分析了知性的十二个判断，并由此揭示了量、质、关系和模态四种范畴。所谓知性就是凭借这些范畴的判断活动，从而获得了知识。在思想的结构中，理性无疑占据最高的地位。理性是思想自身关于原则的能力。在这样的意义上，它建立根据和说明根据。如果说感性主要是依靠直觉、知性依赖于概念的话，那么理性则凭借于观念，由此它将知性的规律置于更高的原则之下，而统一知性的判断。根据康德的批判学说，理性在理性心理学中把一切心理活动置于"灵魂"的观念之下，在理性宇宙论中把一切物理事件置于"自然"的观念之下，在理性神学中将一切现象置于"上帝"的观念之下。但上帝观念是最高的观念。

因为理性在思想结构中具有如此特殊的地位，所以它是思想的本质，并往往等同于思想。于是思想自身在历史上就是在理性意义上的思想。如此，思想自身就不是经验的而是先验的，是人的认识的可能性，因此关于思想的思想一般都是先验主义的。不仅柏拉图的理式哲学是如此，而且康德的先验哲学和胡塞尔的先验现象学更是如此。但理性作为原则的能力，它并不相关于提供或者不提供某种知识，如同感性直观和知性判断所作的那样，而是只相关于自身，并且就是它自身，于是理性在本性上是纯粹理性。按照康德的说法，"纯粹理性在事实上只是从事于自身，而且不可能有其他的事业。"（康德，1993 年 b，B708、633）但因为理性有不同的领域，所以它自身也有一些区分。传统上人们区分了理论理性、实践理性和诗意（创造）理性，它们分属于认识、意志和审美等范围。现代人针对技术社会提出了价值理性和工具理性，针对中国传统思想的特点还提出了实用理性等。但这些已经远离了纯粹理性自身的意义，它们不再是理性自身，而是理性之外的某种东西。

事实上，理性意义的这种变化已经显示出了理性的毁灭的某种征候。但对于理性的怀疑和反抗主要来源于对思想的重新规定。思想自身是理性的还是非理性的？对于现代思想来说，思想在根本上不能理解为理性，而是要理解为经验。当然这种经验不同于近代哲学中和唯理主义相对立的经验主义的所谓经验。经验主义强调经验为知识的源泉或准则，因此没有必然的真理，只有或然的知识。这里所谓的经验就是人的感官对于时空中物的感觉。作为经验的思想也不同于现代思想中具有特征性的体验。体验始终关联于人的生命，因为它是对于人的生命的经历。在它的种种样式中如激动、欢乐和痛苦等情绪中，人与世界相遇，万物向人敞开。但人的感觉和体验都不能描述现代意义的经验。这种经验强调的不是思想和人（感觉和体验）的关系，而是思想和存在的本源性的关系。这就是说思想是存在的思想，由此思想来源于存在并且归属于存在。在这样一种关系中，思想也不是通过判断、推理、计算和设立等来表达自身，而是被存在所规定，成为存在或者事物自身的显示。

但什么是一般思想的现象？思想一般可以被描述为“我在思考”，但“我在思考”不是在思考思想自身，就是在思考思想之外的事物，因此根据胡塞尔的现象学对于意识的分析，“我在思考”的完整表达就是“我思考事情”。这一表达实际上揭示了一般思想活动的结构，即我、思考和事情三个要素。思想的事情当然不能等同于一个自然之物，后者只是自在的；但也不能等同于一个心理之物，后者是随意的。思想的事情在思想中显示自身并且构成自身。作为思考事情的思想自身在此形成了和事情的关联。它一方面是否定性的，即要排除和事情无关的各种意识，而保持思想的纯粹性，以至达到如同中国思想所说的“虚无”和“宁静”。排除的意识包括自然意识和历史意识，同时还包括理论的和日常的观点。它另一方面是肯定性的，即揭示事物的本性并在此过程之中让事物形成自身。思想之所以可能，并不只是因为自我是能思维的，而且是因为自我和事物共同存在于世界之中，同时还因为自我相关于他者，即他者始终会打破自我的限度，使自我越过自身的边界，而无限地思考。

思想虽然展现为“我思考事情”这一结构，但它却最后表现为被思考的和已思考的。因此思想就是已被思考的。这个已被思考的是思想的完成，并因此是思想的整体。如柏拉图的思想、马克思的思想等就是如此。但一个思想的整体有什么意义？它们内部存在什么样的关系？对于思想的整体，海德格尔命名为“思想的事情的规定”。（参见彭富春，1999 年）海德格尔这一表达式实际上源于胡塞尔的现象学。现象学要求思想走向事情本身，事情本身成为了对于思想的规定。海德格尔从此出发确定了“思想的事情的规定”的表达式，但是其中主要的只有两端：事情和思想。这个事情就是存在，它在根本上限定了思想。不过，除了事情和思想之外，规定时常处于一不确定的状态，它有时指事情对于思想的规定，有时指作为与事情和思想不同的第三端，亦即事情和思想所共同可能从属的。海德格尔认为，他的整个思想道路就是运行于“思想的事情的规定”的道路上。博德尔接受了海德格尔的这一遗言，但是他将其朦胧之处变得明晰。他将这一表达式分成三端，并消除了其每一语词的海德格尔的特定含义，如事情不能理解为存在，而应理解为论题；他最关注的是这三端可能构成的各种关系，正是这种种不同关系形成了种种不同的思想形态。于是作为任何一个可能的思想结构的“思想的事情的规定”成为了博德尔理解所有思想的钥匙，并使他自身的思想成为“关系构成的思想”。

不过，思想作为“思想的事情的规定”这一整体事实上是一个尚未封闭而面向开放的整体。这是因为思想在它已思考的其中包含了未思考的，而那正是要思考的。思想的有限性以及应该克服的，不是它自身的不足和弱点，而是它自身不断生成亦即“思想出来”的特性。在这样的意义上，思想从来是一条看不见的且不可预见的道路。

三

也许在历史上哲学的主题只集中于存在和思想的问题而不是语言问题，但任何一个接受过后现代思想洗礼的人，都必须承认语言是当代最重要的哲学主题之一。那么语言如何成为了当代的主题?

显然，无论是在中国还是在西方的历史上，人们对语言并没有一种简单的观念。根据文化人类学的考察，巫术虽然承认语言与现实的差异，但却相信语言和现实的一致。在祈祷和诅咒中，人们试图让语言变成现实。与此不同，在文明社会里，语言和现实的非同一性是一个简明的道理。当然语言有不同的种类。神言是神明的言说，它是神圣的。圣言虽然是人言，但它是圣人之言，是关于天地之道和人类之道的言说，也是不可亵渎的。最后是一般的人言，它只是关于人及其世界的表达。在这种种的语言形态中，有一点是共同的：语言被理解为工具。人们认为，首先是事情，然后是关于事情的思想，最后是作为思想表达的语言。这形成了一个从古到今的模式：存在—思想—语言。在此结构中，语言是被规定的，因此也可能是无关紧要的。

但这并不意味着人们没有思考语言。中国的儒家和道家都关注过“名”的问题，只不过将它限于“仁义”和“道德”的范围内。名家等甚至将关于“名”的思考形成了主题，遗憾的是它被人嘲笑为不是道而是术。当然中国有漫长而丰富的训诂学历史，它所从事的唯一工作就是对于语词作历史的解释。但它没有对于“解释”自身进行解释，从而达到语言的自觉，如同西方的解释学那样。

西方古代哲学对于语言的思考是在一个特别的意义上，即它思考的不是一般的语言，而是作为概念的语言。概念是理性对于存在本质的把握，其意义在于它所表达的思想。凭借概念，理性进行判断，展开了自身的逻辑推理的进程。因此概念不仅是理性的产物，而且也是理性的工具。于是语言在根本上是被理性所规定的。与古代思想不同，现代思想当然注重了语言。人不只是理性的动物，而且是语言性的存在。同时语言自身也是存在性的，因为所谓的存在只有显示为语言，所谓的思想只有表达为语言，它们才是可理解的。伽达默尔的解释学经验关于语言的基本教条就是“能被理解的存在是语言”(伽达默尔，第450页)。作为现代哲学所思考的语言不再是作为理性工具的概念，而是开启存在经验的语词。因此任何一个有意义的语词都能成为现代哲学思考的问题。但语词在此仍然依赖于对于语词之外的存在的经验。因此在现代思想那里，语言是被存在所规定的。

只是后现代思想才将语言真正形成了主题。作为哲学主题的语言不是被规定的，不再依附于作为存在的社会历史根源和作为思维的心灵法则，而是自身规定性的，如索绪尔所说的语言的意义在于符号能指之间的差异性（差异原则），同时能指与所指之间的关系是任意的（任意原则），或者是自身没有任何规定的，如德里达所谓的延异。对于这种情况，我们可以提出一个问题：为什么语言在后现代成为了哲学的主题？其回答当然也只能是语言性的。一方面，我们的后现代生活在一个前所未有的语言的世界里，这个时代被描述为信息时代。不仅报纸、广播和电视等在日益发展，使人们更多地接受语言，而且固定和移动通讯也在突飞猛进，使人们更多地交流语言，至于互联网则敞开了一个语言的虚拟世界，使人们更多地构造语言。这种由现代技术所支配的语言是当代人生存的一个最凸显的事实。另一方面，哲学在思考了存在和思想之后必须揭示语言的尚未思考的意义。因此语言成为哲学的主题实际上是哲学自身发展的结果，是思想内在更新的使命。但语言一旦成为哲学的主题，那么存在和思想的主题就会逐渐消失。同时语言也要不断从存在和思想的规定中剥离，将自身显示出来。

对于语言，后现代思想的首要问题是：谁在说话？谁都知道是人在说话。但这一提问显然是对于这一回答的预先置疑。如果说人在说话，那么就是认为人是语言的主人，拥有它并可以抛弃它。然而也许要反过来，语言是人的主人，语言使人成为人，使人区别于动物并创造了世界。那么是否可以说语言在说话呢？作为对于“人在说话”的置换，“语言在说话”看起来是无意义的同义反复，并且也是“语言”的一种拟人化，但它意在回到语言自身。那么它是什么样的语言？在这样的提问中，“谁在说话”就转换成“说了什么”。这是因为语言显示在它所言说的话语之中。如果问题是如此的话，那么它要求语言的划界，亦即分类。

第一种语言是欲望的语言。欲望作为潜意识借助符号、隐喻和形象等起作用。在此意义上，它就像一种语言。拉康认为，潜意识惟有获得语言之后才开始真正的存在。人不仅有欲望，人甚至就是欲望。欲望表现为需要、匮乏、意愿和愿望等。人的欲望从自身出发，但又指向自身之外。因此欲望是意向性的和对象性的，并始终呈现为对某个东西的欲望。人的欲望原初是身体的欲望，即本能。所谓的基本本能无非是食欲和性欲，前者指向特别的物，后者指向作为异性的人。身体性的欲望逐渐发展成心理的、社会的。最后欲望甚至成为对于欲望的欲望，这种无边的欲望就是人们所说的欲壑难填。

第二种语言是工具的语言。工具是手段，它服务于某个目的。语言的工具性一向为人所知，它是思想的外壳。仅仅把语言理解为工具是片面的，而仅仅将工具理解为外壳更是片面的。语言的工具性表现在许多方面。其一是显示。没有语言，思想是空洞的，存在也是黑暗的。正是语言将思维和存在的本性显示出来。其二是构造。语言在显示存在和思想时，并不是如同镜子般的被动的反映，而是对于思想和存在的积极的建构。因此所谓的存在和思想实际上都是由语言所理解和阐释的存在和思想。只是当语言的建构被忽略不计的时候，人们才能想象在语言之前的那种非语言的存在和思想。但这种想象其实也是语言的建构。其三是传达。语言的传达不是单面的，而是多面的，即它是信息的发出、接受和反馈的系统。这一系统不仅存在于人与人之间的对话中，而且也存在于人与物之间的对话中。

在对话过程中，计算或算计具有决定性的意义。人们会思考：如果我使用这种手段，目的会如何；如果我使用其他手段，目的又会如何。这种对话表现出了语言工具的控制特性。

第三种语言是指引的语言。它是我们所说的道、真理和智慧等等。它既表现为系统的文本形式，也呈现为格言、箴言。这些话语不仅是陈述性的，而且也是虚拟式的、命令式的。智慧是一种知识，特别是关于人的规定的知识。所谓知识就是知道什么是存在的，什么是不存在的。这就形成了哲学上的存在与虚无、是与非、真理和谬误等的对立。关于人的规定的知识的获得不仅依靠于人与动物的区分，而且建基于人与自身的区分。通过这种区分，人成为了具有人性的人。智慧的话语就是这种关于人的规定的言说。它是道，并因此作为道路，成为人可以行走的。

概而言之，欲望的语言是黑暗的，因为它基于人的本能和无意识；工具的语言是镜似的，凭借于它反映或者表达；真理的语言是光明的，这在于它是纯粹的，并穿透那些不纯粹的。

这三种语言在语言整体中形成了复杂的交叉关系。欲望性的语言是原初已经给予的自然事实，它会首先言说。但欲望性的语言必须借助工具性的语言而实现自身，同时它也必须在智慧或者真理性的语言的指引下获得一个属人的历史性的尺度。在此工具性的语言的本性是确定的，即保证欲望性的语言和智慧性的语言实现。不管是欲望性的语言还是智慧性的语言，都有赖于工具的运用。虽然真理的语言达到自身纯粹性，是通过与欲望的语言和工具的语言的区分而实现的，但是真理语言的指引性刚好又在于对欲望语言和工具语言的划界。一方面它给欲望划界，区分可吃的东西和不可吃的东西，可成为性的对象的和不可成为性的对象的。另一方面它给满足欲望的工具划界，区分在吃的过程中可采用的方式和不可采用的方式，在性的过程中可使用的手段和不可使用的手段。在此，真理的语言就是在可能和不可能之间划定一条边界，但这个边界不是固定不变的，而是不断地游移和新生。因此真理的语言形成了一个世界，同时又构成了一个历史。这个历史就是人性的生成。在欲望方面，吃饭不再只是充饥，而是成为美食和礼乐，性交不再只是生殖，而是升华为欢乐和爱情。同时在工具方面，手段不异化为目的，而是保存为手段；它不只是为了欲望，而也是为了真理。

欲望性的话语、工具性的话语和智慧性的话语的关系在语言整体中表现为游戏，因此语言就是欲、技和道的游戏的言说。这才是真正的语言游戏。语言游戏始终发生在人之中，并且将人拉入与语言游戏的关联。人与语言的关系是一种对话关系。人是一言说者，因此人是一语言的存在。人的语言性存在表现为：人言说并倾听语言，由此人与他人打交道并与万物沟通。人在语言之网中，区分、选择、决定并开辟自己的道路。

语言与人的这种关系也说出了语言与世界的可能关系。语言当然不是世界。在语言可能设想的各种世界中，语言只是其中的一种。但是语言相关于这些世界，它包括自然世界、人类世界和精神世界。语言和这些世界只有唯一的关系，即言说。言说除了言说之外便没有其他什么。但它能让存在。言说是人的行为，并且能够变成人的身体的行为，作为手和脚的活动。由此借助于工具，语言便走出了自身，进入了精神世界、人类世界和自然世界。实际上，语言不仅能解释世界，而且能改变世界，更能创造世界。例如，西方历史的世界是基督教的世界，中国历史的世界是儒家的世界，现代世界是关于民主与科学的思想所构建的世界，马克思主义也同样创造了一个社会主义和共产主义的世界。

四

哲学的主题总是相关于它的方法。在西方哲学传统中，主题和方法的关系还表达为本体与方法的关系或者真理与方法的关系；在中国思想传统中，它则被描述为道与技的关系或者道与术的关系。

对于哲学主题和方法的关系，人们似乎有两种极端的看法。对方法持肯定性的观点认为，方法具有非常重要的意义，它本身就是哲学的主题。于是哲学就是方法论和方法研究。与此相反，持否定性的观点认为，没有方法，只有主题。因此哲学所关注的只是主题，不是方法。这两种说法也许都陷入了极端。所谓的方法就是主题的方法，在这样的意义上，术乃道之术，方法乃缘道而行。一方面，主题在根本上规定了方法，另一方面，一种主题只有在一种与它相适应的方法中才能显示出来。

就西方的传统而言，其哲学的方法主要是演绎的方法和归纳的方法。它们都是从作为根据的前提推论出结论。演绎从一般性的命题推论出个别性的命题。与此相反，归纳从个别性的命题推论出一般性的命题。但这两种哲学的方法都有其限度。演绎虽然保证了结论的必然真实，但其作为思想根据、原则和公理的前提的自明性有待于揭示，即它们自身需要建立根据和说明根据。归纳的前提固然是真实的，但这不能保证结论的必然真实，这样它就不可能提供确定性的真理。除了上述有限性之外，演绎的方法和归纳的方法还有一个共同性的问题，即它们都不是从所思考的事情自身出发，而是从事情之外出发来论及事物。这个事情之外的东西或者是事情背后的某种不证自明的原则，如上帝、自我和理性等，或者是事情周边的其他同类事情已揭示的特性。在此，思想的事情自身已经被遗忘和遮蔽了。

中国传统思想也遵循了一般的演绎方法和归纳方法，但特别发展了归纳方法中的类比方法。它从一事物和另一事物的类似性出发，由一事物的某种特性推论出另一事物的某种相似特性。在中国儒道思想中，有两个最大的事物，即天和人。当人们研究天人之际的时候，就设定了天人的类似，并由此将自然的特性赋予人类。如阳和阴是天与地的特性，但也是男与女的特性。然而这种中国式的思维的合理性是值得怀疑的。一方面作为推论基础的天（自然）是自明的，没有追问的。另一方面，人与天是各有差异的，与天相比，人甚至是特殊的。因此天与人的关系不具有一种必然的推论关系。

正是在与传统哲学的演绎的方法和归纳的方法相分离的意义上，胡塞尔所倡导的现象学的方法是革命性的。现象学是关于事物显现的科学。事物在此就是意识，而且是意识活动和意识对象的同一。因此事物的显现就是意识的显现。显现是事物自身揭示自身本质的过程，它通过现象学的还原和现象学的直观得以完成。现象学在方法论上的贡献在于它的口号所说的“走向事情本身”。它既不是从思想的事情后面的某种原则出发，也不是从事情之外的其他同类事情的特性出发，而是从事情自身出发，即从现象也就是意识的显现出发，从而揭示事情的本质。同时，现象学所运用的主要方法不是传统哲学的演绎的方法和归纳的方法的推理，而是对于事情自身本质的直观和描述。不过，“事情自身”既是现象学的开端之处，也是现象学的终结之处。这是因为事情自身也许不是意识，而是语言。一个没有语言的意识仍然是黑暗的、遮蔽的和没有显现的，意识只有显示为语言的时候才是真正的意识和真正的意识的显现。如果事情是这样的话，那么现象学就必然走向终结了。与此同时，现代和后现代思想提出了关于语言问题的多元方法，如解释学对于文本理解和解释的方法，分析哲学对于语言的语义、语法和语用的辨析的方法，结构主义对于从语言结构到社会结构和心理结构描述的方法，解构主义对于文本自身的悖论的揭示的方法，等等。

那么什么是我们所运用的哲学方法？对于我们而言，也许只有“无原则的批判”的思想方法。这听起来容易导致误解，它似乎是一种无可无不可的模糊的不明确的思想态度。但无原则的批判强调的是：思想不从任何既定的原则出发。这里所谓“既定的原则”包括一切已有的立场、观点以及由此形成的各种先见、偏见和成见等，从而不仅包括思想者的立场，而且包括思想的论题所依据的各种原则。因此它不仅仅是无立场的，而且也是无原则的。无原则的批判只是从已给予的思想的论题本身出发，对论题进行批判。对于思想批判而言，已给予的论题首先就是语言现象，或者是已说出的话语，然后是语言所揭示的思想和存在的问题。无原则的批判强化了哲学的批判本性。批判不能简单地等同于否定，似乎只具有一种消极的意义，而是区分和划分边界。边界是一个事物的起点和终点。正是在边界上，一物与它物相区分而成为其自身，获得自身的规定。同时通过边界的变更和游移，一物与自身相区分，而获得自身新的规定。作为划分边界的批判，它就是区分存在与虚无、真实与虚幻、显现与遮蔽等。这使批判自身具有两重特性，一方面是否定性的，是解构，另一方面是肯定性的，是建构。由于思想的否定和肯定的同时进行，批判在根本意义上是生成性的，因此是思想的发生。

一种作为批判的哲学具有普遍性适用的主张，它除了对自身进行批判之外，还对自身之外进行批判，因此对于一切都进行批判。这样批判哲学的范围包括了三个方面：语言批判、思想批判和现实批判。哲学的所在之处是语言的领域，无论是批判自身还是批判对象都是语言的战争。因此批判哲学首先的任务就是给语言划界，指明它到底说出了什么，即语言是否是有意义的，以及有何种意义。在语言基础上，哲学要进行思想批判。思想的现实表现为已思想的，它是各种学说、体系和主义等，同时它也呈现为日常的各种想法和说法。对于思想的批判在于揭示其建筑学结构，检查其基础是否牢靠，其结构是否矛盾。通过语言和思想的批判，哲学最后必须进入现实批判。哲学的现实批判才是哲学自身的真正完成和实现。现实作为人的生活世界、作为社会的存在整体是经济、政治和文化等不同方面的发展。哲学的现实批判的根本任务就是指出现实的真相，分析其问题，并提出可能的道路。

对于中国当代思想来说，值得思考的问题许许多多。但究其根本，大致有三：其一，虚无主义，它否认了存在的基础和目的；其二，技术主义，它将人和万物技术化；其三，享乐主义，它使欲望变得没有规定和没有边界。面对虚无主义、技术主义和享乐主义，哲学能有何作为？哲学只是思想，它除了批判之外无所作为。但批判并不是简单地否认虚无主义、技术主义和享乐主义，而是要为它们区分边界。因此在我们的批判哲学看来，一方面要抛弃存在之外的任何根据，另一方面要给存在自身建立根据；同时，一方面要让技术改变和改善我们生存的手段，另一方面要让自然自在自得，如其所是；最后，一方面要使欲望不断解放自己，另一方面不要让它成为了贪欲。

当代哲学只是批判，此外无他。因此从事哲学就是行走于边界并逾越此边界，这个边界是语言的、思想的和存在的。

中国哲学史方法论问题

郭齐勇

本文有三个方面的内容：一是我们的老前辈萧萐父先生的思考、贡献与启示；二是中西互动中的中国经典诠释的方法学及其展开；三是关于中国哲学研究的多重取径、前景与限制问题。

一、萧萐父先生的思考、贡献与启示

（一）萧先生对方法论问题思考的背景、过程与重点

改革开放以来，武汉大学哲学系由陈修斋老师、杨祖陶老师挂帅的外国哲学史教研室和萧萐父老师、李德永老师、唐明邦老师主持的中国哲学史教研室一起开了一门课，中、西哲学的研究生一起来听，一起来切磋，一起来讨论，这门课就是哲学史方法论。这当然也源自于院系调整后的北京大学。“哲学史方法论”这门课是陈修斋、萧萐父与杨祖陶先生为中外哲学史的研究生共同开设的特色课程。我们在 80 年代初，在陈老师、萧老师、杨老师的带领下受学。当时还有王荫庭老师讲普列汉诺夫，徐瑞康老师也讲了课，也请了校外的老师授课，确实使我们受益匪浅。① 那时硕士生的课主要是讨论课，我们读了大量的马克思主义的经典著作，比如马克思的《〈黑格尔法哲学批判〉导言》《政治经济学批判导言》《1844 年经济学哲学手稿》，还有马克思晚年的人类学笔记

① 当时的部分讲义后来编入陈修斋、萧萐父主编：《哲学史方法论研究》，武汉大学出版社 1984 年版。此外，在萧萐父老师指导与安排下，1989 年以武大哲学系名义出了打字油印本《哲学史方法论新探》，由校印刷厂印出，用于研究生的哲学史方法论课程。

数种，恩格斯的《卡尔・马克思〈政治经济学批判〉》《德国农民战争》《家庭、私有制与国家的起源》《费尔巴哈与德国古典哲学的终结》《自然辩证法》，马恩合著的《神圣家族》《德意志意识形态》及他们的通信，列宁的《哲学笔记》等，对涉及黑格尔哲学史观的《哲学史讲演录》导言部分更是反复地研读，还有康德《判断力批判》导言等。萧先生又很重视引导我们对《庄子・天下》《荀子・非十二子》《韩非子・显学》《淮南子・要略》、司马谈《论六家要旨》诸篇反映的古代学术史论与刘知几、王夫之、章学诚的历史哲学的研读，以为从中吸取我们民族哲学思想的方法学。

萧萐父老师的《吹沙集》现已出了新版，四川的巴蜀书社出了《吹沙集》三卷，武汉大学出版社也出版了萧老师的论著集及萧师与师母的诗书画集等。这些著作里面有关于“方法刍议”的七篇论文及其他栏目的若干论文，这些文章我们都曾学习和讨论过，有的我也曾参与了整理。现在，温故而知新，每读一遍都有很深的感情。改革开放以来，全国的哲学界、哲学史界是如何艰难地跨越了这一步，来真正了解人类文明史上最辉煌的西洋哲学与中国哲学的核心问题，及如何探讨方法学问题的，我们是见证人。

我们可以说是在陈修斋老师、萧萐父老师、杨祖陶老师等前辈指导并与我们一起讨论的过程中，打下了方法论的基础的。老师们是结合自己的专长与研究心得来讲方法论的，萧先生结合明清哲学的研究，陈先生结合西方唯理论、经验论与莱布尼兹的研究，杨先生结合德国古典哲学，主要是康德与黑格尔哲学的研究，王荫庭先生结合普列汉诺夫五项论的研究。陈修斋老师的有关论著，请参见段德智教授编的《陈修斋哲学与哲学史论文集》等，杨祖陶老师的论著有《德国古典哲学逻辑进程》《康德黑格尔哲学研究》等，以上几种精专传世之作都是武汉大学出版社出版的，陈先生的书新版为《陈修斋论哲学与哲学史》，由人民出版社出版。当时我们还修了江天骥先生的科学哲学的课，亦很受库恩的科学革命的结构的启发。江先生关于西方科学哲学的书，我们也是人手一册。以上诸先生的影响，从我 1983 年所写的一篇方法论的文章中可以看到。①

60 年来，一个甲子的中国哲学和西洋哲学关于方法学的讨论，的确是非常有深意的。改革开放刚开始，1978 至 1979 年中外哲学史界著名的芜湖会议、太原会议，1981 年杭州宋明理学讨论会等，都是很重要的会议。通过我们中外哲学史两个学科长期在一起讨论，对教条化、庸俗化、贫乏化的苏联日丹诺夫式的哲学史方法论给予了检讨。关于哲学史研究的对象、范围、重点、方法问题一直是萧老师等前辈们思考的重点。我们知道，这一思考的道路不是平坦的。有人发表批评萧老师和李锦全老师主编的《中国哲学史》教材的文章。我不是说我的老师就不能批评，而是说批评一定要知人论世，一定要同情地理解。我们老一辈先生编的《中国哲学史》虽然在我们现在看来有一些不尽如人意的地方，但在当时来说那其实是非常了不起的贡献。而且这套书出版了十几万册，被许多本科阶段的大学生们捧读，的确是非常了不起的。因为它在方法学上有一个自觉，这个自觉表现在对我们中国哲学史研究的重点、范围、对象问题是加以思考与简择了的。萧先生主要是根据马克思主义方法学的理论和原理来思考和构建中国哲学史的，当时对哲学史的定义就曾参考学习了列宁的《哲学笔记》。萧先生讲关于自然、社会和思维的一般认识的历史，以此来定义哲学史，以区别于哲学与非哲学的界限。大家都知道，当时哲学界有一个认识论的转向，这个认识论的转向使得萧先生的认识史观特重梳理、筛选在宗教、艺术、道德、社会、政治、法律资料中涉及的规律、本质的哲学问题。至于这些学科中的具体问题，则由这些学科自行解决。如若把哲学史作为一门学科加以定义、研究，则一定关涉上述各学科里面的本质、规律等哲学问题。萧先生以黑格尔—马克思的“逻辑与历史相统一”的哲学史观与列宁《哲学笔记》的有关论断为方法论主调，且受到前面所说的哲学界“认识论”转向的影响。

武汉大学、中山大学等九校合编的，萧先生与李先生主编的中哲史教材就

① 参见郭齐勇：《哲学史方法论学习札记》，《武汉大学学报》（社科版）1984 年第 4 期。

是用“螺旋结构”、“历史圆圈”、“范畴研究”、“哲学史是认识史”等路数来重新架构或解读中国哲学的，力图从此前的泛政治化走向学术化。同时，作者非常有深度地研讨了中国哲学的范畴问题。我们知道，要了解中国哲学的范畴问题，首先应对此加以提炼与辨析。我们须探讨中国哲学的天、人、道、气、性、命、心、理、德、知等范畴，宇宙论、本体论、心性论、认识论学说及如何与西方哲学相比照并加以调适上遂的发展的问题。且为了使这些哲学资料更加适合于我们的学子讨论和阅读，就须在教材中梳理出这些主要思想之逻辑发展的规则、轨迹。作者从中提炼出一些非常具有价值的范畴和范畴体系来加以建构。当然，在建构过程中也不免出现削足适履的情况，这是难以避免的，但是中国哲学的哲学性就开始得到了特别的重视。这就是在 70 年代末、80 年代初，也就是在我们读本科生和硕士研究生的时候，整个学界特别是中外哲学史界的一个主要的走向。冯契先生的《中国古代哲学的逻辑发展》及“智慧说”三部曲与萧萐父、李锦全先生主编的《中国哲学史》及萧先生的论著——《吹沙集》三卷，算是一种路数的代表。这是承接着逻辑与历史统一、哲学史就是认识史的路数展开的。另一方面，李泽厚先生的中国古代、近代、现代思想史论之三部曲及 80 年代的文化讨论、文化热，产生了汤一介、庞朴先生的一些论著影响极大。大家知道，我们曾经都是李泽厚先生的粉丝。可以说，当时全国的人文学的研究生，其案头上几乎没有不摆放李泽厚的书的。这就是 80 年代初期中国思想界的一种状况。但我们比较偏重于冯契先生和萧先生这样一个脉络。这个脉络非常重视中西马的融通。对西方哲学的研讨，上至古希腊哲学，下至康德、黑格尔等的德国观念论，一直到马克思主义的经典导读，实与中国哲学相发明。可以说中西马的互动促成了当时这样一种哲学史观与方法学的讨论。

当然，今天我们检讨和回顾一个甲子的中国哲学史的研究及其方法论问题，不能不更往前推。我们这个学科的建设、它的自觉化有将近一个世纪的历程。我们知道，最早是胡适先生的《中国哲学史大纲》卷上。还有冯友兰先生

30年代出版的《中国哲学史》（上下卷）两卷本。这个两卷本《中国哲学史》由卜德翻译成英文。这个英译本结合了西南联大时期冯先生《新原道》中的思想，在英文世界流行甚广，至今仍在起作用。这个英译本因为吸收了《新原道》中的思想，且采用了冯先生一边讲述、译者一边翻译的形式，因此比中文本更好，更能体现冯先生自觉地对于中国哲学史的解读。

我们看金岳霖先生给冯友兰先生的《中国哲学史》所作的审查报告，就特别强调了胡适先生的半部中国哲学史中所带有的那样一种强势的西方人特别是美国商人的眼光。后来经冯先生建议，金先生把“商”字去掉了。这种眼光难免造成诸多成见。按梁任公先生的评价，胡适先生的哲学史大纲，对知识论、逻辑学有石破天惊的创发，但是中国人最得心应手、最有创造性智慧的社会哲学、政治哲学、伦理学、人生哲学却暗而不彰。当然，我们也知道，当时胡适之很困难，他能够从西方的实验主义、逻辑学出发来解读一部分中国哲学史的材料就很了不起了。当时对胡适先生这半部哲学史的推崇，是以蔡元培先生的评价为标准的，那评价是非常高的，认为是创造性的开天辟地之作。当然胡著是一个斩头的哲学史，它把前面很长一段哲学史都斩掉了。我们每一个人都有一定的限制，每一个学者也是这样，不可能不在时代的氛围内做自己的学术研究，因为他（她）必须有学术前史作为基础。所以，胡适、冯友兰，特别是胡先生还是非常了不起的具有开拓性的人物。

萧老师他们反省中国哲学（史）以及方法学的建构时，特别重视的还有他们的前驱，像郭沫若、侯外庐的这样一种研究范式。可以说，1949年以前，有两种范式占主导地位。前面一种范式是用美国或说西方的哲学解释框架或者某一种路数来解读传统中国哲学。比如，冯先生是新实在论的路数，用共相的观念来谈问题，而用共相来谈的“理”就可能成了一个空套子。但不管怎样，他有自己的优长。而冯先生晚年则特重人生哲学、社会哲学等。

郭沫若、侯外庐先生的方式是以唯物史观作为中国哲学讨论的最主要的一个理论指导。在这种框架之下，侯外庐、杜国庠、赵纪彬、邱汉生等的《中国思想通史》于解放前出版了几卷，且解放后继续出版，这成为六十年来中国哲学史和中国思想史最重要的参照，非常了不起。当年，侯外庐专门谈《资本论》、谈亚细亚生产方式，都是我们今天还在讨论的问题。但是我们要看到，当时的讨论的确是以唯物史观作指导来研究中国哲学、中国思想的，这也是具开创性意义的，有很多值得我们肯定的思想财富。此外，张岱年先生新中国成立前写的《中国哲学大纲》，之前出版了一个小本子，但却湮没无闻，一直到 80 年代初期才由中国社会科学出版社正式出版，这时才有了一些影响。但张先生是以范畴论的方式来写这部大纲的。任继愈先生挂帅主编的几个版本的《中国哲学史》也是一个重要的参照。特别是四卷本的那套，“文化大革命”前已出版，1979 年又重新修订出版，成为我们好几代学生重要的教材和参考书。这些都是萧先生那一代人思考中国哲学及其方法论的重要前史。特别值得参考的是，他们用唯物史观的理论与方法来指导中国哲学的研究，重视哲学思想产生的社会历史背景及其对哲学观念的影响，重视发掘被正统史家所湮没的民间下层的思想代表等，都很了不起萧先生会通中西印哲学，非常重视中西印各哲学传统的发展。金克木先生、汤用彤先生都是他的老师，彼此之间特有慧心。萧先生以批评的精神和创造性智慧，转化、发展儒释道、诸子百家思想资源。为总结历史经验教训，他从哲学史方法论的问题意识切入，尽力突破“左”的教条主义的束缚，引入螺旋结构代替对子结构。对子结构也就是唯物主义与唯心主义、辩证法与形而上学对立的这样一种结构。萧先生重视逻辑与历史的一致，强调普遍、特殊、个别的辩证联结，认真探究中国哲学范畴史的逻辑发展与哲学观念史发展的历史圆圈。萧先生由哲学史方法论问题的咀嚼，提出了哲学史的纯化与泛化的有张力的统一观（纯化是把哲学问题提炼出来，泛化是还原到思想史、学术史、文化史或某个部类中去），努力改变五四以降中国哲学依傍、移植、临摹西方哲学或以西方哲学的某家某派理论与方法对中国哲学的史料任意地简单比附、“削足适履”的状况。这可以说是萧先生方法学思考的理论贡献。

（二）萧先生关于经典与史料的研读

萧先生也特别强调经典与史料的研读。萧先生特重章学诚先生的史慧。在文史哲分科之前，我国只有经、史、子、集四部的图书分类方法，还有就是清代的义理、考据、辞章三种学问路向，但这些都不是今天西方社会科学的分科。分科当然非常好，但分科也会带来一些盲点。比如说，经学是中国文化最重要的根源，但经学通过这种分科反而得不到很好的研究。今天我们适度地提倡国学，国学这一学科不可以替代文史哲的分科，但是它可以补救现行文史哲分科后出现的问题。例如，经学中的《诗经》放在了文学科，但放在文学中够吗？《诗经》讨论的只是今天文学范畴内的问题吗？当然不是。《易经》《书经》《春秋》、三《礼》等呢？

萧先生在重视经典和史料研读的过程中，非常重视方法论之前的方法或解释学之前的解释。有的人认为训诂、考据或者文献学的研讨，包括文字、音韵、训诂，一直到校勘、辨伪与辑佚等，不能算作解释学的内容，但它们肯定是解释学之前即我们研读中国哲学文本之前必须要做的基础工作。

我们读书的时候，萧老师给我们开了史料学的课程，专门读梁启超先生的《清代学术概论》等书籍。梁任公论朴学，主张“凡立一义，必凭证据；无证据而以臆度者，在所必摈。”①且强调“孤证不为定说。其无反证者姑存之，得有续证则渐信之，遇有力之反证则弃之。”②还有，作为一名学者为了证明自己的看法或观点，“隐匿证据或曲解证据，皆认为不德。”“最喜罗列事项之同类者，为比较的研究，而求得其公则。”“所见不合，则相辩诘，虽弟子驳难本师，亦所不避，受之者从不以为忤。”“文体贵朴实简絜，最忌‘言有枝叶’。”③即语言不要太枝蔓，要集中到你的论证上来。此外，萧先生还让我们讨论陈垣先生的《元典章校补释例》之《校法四例》，即对校法、他校法、本校法、综

---

① 梁启超：《清代学术概论》，上海古籍出版社 1998 年版，第 47 页。

② 梁启超：《清代学术概论》，上海古籍出版社 1998 年版，第 47 页。

③ 梁启超：《清代学术概论》，上海古籍出版社 1998 年版，第 47 页。

合考证法。这都是我们切实研读文献时须讨论的。关于考据，清儒考据功夫很深，但萧先生启发我们对此也不要迷信。

不要迷信已有考据的成果，清儒考据也有自身的限制。例如关于《大学》，清儒毛奇龄认为《大学》的单行本出现很早，以为《论语》《孟子》《大学》《中庸》《孝经》乃小经，在汉唐时早已单篇独行，不始于宋儒。全祖望《萧山毛检讨别传》就指陈其谬，而且举出的例子有很多实证的方面。比如说，关于毛奇龄对于《新唐书》所载材料的误读就是一例。《新唐书》说修小经、中经、大经，指的是学年时间的概念，并不是说有所谓小经、中经、大经的一个内容上的区别。《新唐书》卷四十四载，《孝经》《论语》一年修，《尚书》《公羊传》《谷梁传》一年半修，《周易》《诗经》《周礼》《仪礼》两年修，《礼记》《左传》三年修。不能因《新唐书》的这条材料，我们就把小经当作单篇别出。清儒朱彝尊这一了不起的学者，也指出单篇别出的《大学》《中庸》出现非常早，不始于宋代，尤其不始于南宋。朱彝尊甚至说司马光所注的《大学广义》是单行的开始，好像铁证如山。但实际上，《礼记》有十多篇在宋代以前已有专篇注解了，并不能因此断言单篇独行。司马光所注《大学》，仍是作为《礼记》的一篇。如按《经义考》，《礼记》有四分之一强的篇章早已单行。我们今天来了解《大学》《中庸》形成的历史，就知道这些问题都较容易解决。《大学》《中庸》单篇别出不是如毛奇龄、朱彝尊所理解的那样的。①

我们还注意到《资治通鉴》几位撰写者的分工问题。胡三省在《新注资治通鉴序》中说："修书分属，汉则刘攽，三国讫于南北朝则刘恕，唐则范祖禹，各因其所长属之，皆天下选也。"但清人全祖望在《通鉴分修诸子考》中提出一条材料，是司马光写给范祖禹的信，信中说：你要看到魏晋南北朝的材料就给刘攽，五代的材料就给刘恕。全祖望据此说胡三省注里讲的分工不对。抗战期间，陈垣先生带研究生，就叫研究生自己写文章来讨论全祖望的说法是否可

① 详见岑溢成：《大学义理疏解》，（台北）鹅湖出版社 2000 年版，第 4—8 页。

靠。陈垣先生的意见是，司马光的这封信的确是信史，确有其事。但那只是他初步的想法，是收集资料做长编时候的考虑，后来并没有这样做。解放后翦伯赞先生写过一篇文章，里面关于《通鉴》的分工，还是按胡三省的说法。马上就有人写文反驳，批评翦伯赞，并举全祖望之说云云。翦伯赞先生回应说，全祖望的说法不对，你还须考证。① 从这些材料的甄别可以看出，中国哲学的难度也在其史料、资料的辨析上。

在我校 2009 年举办的明清学术会议上，一位域外学者引用了邓豁渠《南询录》的材料。他用的是发表在《中国哲学》辑刊第 19 辑上的材料。我就告诉他，那个材料不可用。《南询录》的材料日本人很重视，收藏在他们的东洋文库即内阁文库中，而在中国却失传了。日本有几位大学者如岛田虔次先生、荒木见悟先生等都写了关于《南询录》的论文。有的先生做事疏忽或训诂方面的修养不够，整理中的问题很多。点校是要功夫的。比如说，该书前面引的白沙子的话，其实只有短短一句话，整理者却把一长段话都打上引号，当作陈白沙的话。其实白沙子的书都已整理出版，可以查对。有关《南询录》，应看邓红的整理本。②

又如，有人讲庄子的"判天地之美，析万物之理"如何了不起，值得大力提倡云云，这是对《庄子・天下篇》的误解。其实这本来是庄子学派所批评的一曲之见。《天下篇》作者认为把握道体之"全"，才能"原天地之美，达万物之理"。

我举以上几个例子是想说明，萧先生在训练我们的时候特别重视资料、文献的鉴别、爬梳与点校。这是非常难又很重要的一种训练。萧先生的史料学课程的讲义，通过我们前几届研究生听课并不断整理，老师反复加以修订而成。③ 这是作为我校研究生院的教材，由武汉大学出版社出版的，理应成为我

---

① 详见柴德赓：《资治通鉴介绍》，求实出版社 1981 年版，第 13—14 页。

② （明）邓豁渠著，邓红校注：《南询录校注》，武汉理工大学出版社 2008 年版。

③ 参见萧萐父：《中国哲学史史料源流举要》，武汉大学出版社 1998 年版。

们专业博、硕士生的案头书，这本书不仅讲史料，也讲方法。其中第二讲《古史祛疑》，就是对疑古思潮的反思，属于方法论问题，第三讲《朴学简介》，就是讲文献识别与把握的门径与方法，第四讲则讲地下考古资料与传世文献的互证等，也是方法，即二重证据法。

（三）萧先生强调对已有成果的把握

萧先生不仅非常重视第一手原始资料与文献，而且非常重视对于海内外已有成果的研读，即学术前史的通晓。他训练我们的硕士生、博士生时，强调一定要能够做一个非常好的文献综述。做文献综述中也要贯穿着问题意识。任何思想史上的人物都是接着讲的。当你做硕士论文或博士论文时，一定要切实梳理你的研究方向、论题的现有成果。从对已有成果的反思中发现问题，然后抓住问题深入研究，超越已有成果。我们做的是有思想的学术和有学术的思想。思想离开了学术是空疏的，学术离开了思想是盲目的。“竭泽而渔”是陈垣先生倡导的治学方法。那时萧老师就让我们读《励耘书屋问学记》，让我们反复体会大学问家的治学精神。傅斯年先生讲“上穷碧落下黄泉，动手动脚找东西”。傅斯年先生成立史语所的时候，其宣言尽管用的是唯科学主义的方法，存在问题。但我们知道，现代学术的规范就是要充分理解你所研究的对象，并尽量掌握已有的成果。因此，要全面理解中国的、外国的包括汉学家的、中国学家的、日本的、欧美的已有成果来做学术前史的梳理。所以，假如我们没有对于已有成果的研读和学术前史的梳理，每做一篇文章都有可能失败，因为别人已经说过了，只是你不知道而已。有的人自说自话，孤芳自赏，根本不了解海内外有关人物、课题、著作研究的进展与前沿，那当然不能称之为真正的学术研究。我们现在指导研究生时发现，有些同学比较偷巧，在网上查资料，但找的都是一些地方师专学报等刊物上的文章。而对于研究对象所涉及的一些最重要的文献却并没有去找，特别是思想的演进过程却没有。我们认为，学术方法与学术态度是连在一起的。做学问就要老老实实。“知之为知之，不知为不知，是知也。”在一定意义上，老老实实既是态度，也是方法。诚实的做学问既是态度，又是方法。这是我们的老先生一再强调的。因此，萧老师、陈修斋老师、杨祖陶老师、李德永老师、唐明邦老师都非常重视做人与做学问的一致。对此，萧先生提出二十字方针：“德业双修，学思并重，史论结合，中西对比，古今贯通”。这是一种开放的，以做人为前提的学问之道。我以为这里面包含的内容非常深广。以汤用彤先生、金克木先生为榜样的萧先生有一副对联，也是他一生的努力过程：“多维互动，漫汗通观儒释道；积杂成纯，从容涵化印中西。”萧先生和师母的骨灰现安葬在他们的家乡成都，墓碑上的碑文就是这副对联。这是我们武汉大学以及哲学学院最重要的一个学术传统，也是最重要的一个方法学。我们不应把方法与方法学太过于拘束化了。总之，一定要有广博的知识背景与扎实的学问工夫，精读经典，打好基础。

二、中西互动：中国经典诠释方法学的展开

前面谈了第一个问题，即萧先生的致思趋向、方法学思考与治学方法。这里讲第二个问题，讨论的是中国经典诠释方法学的展开。

（一）诠释学与创造的诠释学

这就要提到美国天普大学教授傅伟勋先生。他和萧先生、刘纲纪先生都是非常好的朋友。傅伟勋先生一共来武大两次，萧先生邀请并让我接待、陪同。傅伟勋先生的创造的诠释学是80年代中后期首次在武汉大学讲的，后来又有所修改。关于诠释学，他很敏感。那时大家还没有像今天这样重视伽达默尔的诠释学。那时傅先生用五层辩证的关系来讨论中国经典诠释。首先是“实谓”，即这个文本实际上说了什么？这一层实际涵盖了我前面所说的点校、训诂、考据、辨伪、辑轶等。要想弄清文本实际上说了什么，就离不开文字训诂等一系列小学功夫与文献学的功夫。假如对前面的思想史遗产完全不了解，就没有办法做个案的研究。第二层是“意谓”，即作者想要表达什么？或他所说的意思到底是什么？这一点傅先生认为非常重要。后来有人讨论说，这才是开始了

真正的诠释学。第三层是“蕴谓”，即作者可能要说什么？或他所说的可能蕴涵着什么？第四层是“当谓”，即原思想家本来应当说出什么？或创造的诠释学者应当为原思想家说出什么？最后一层是“必谓”（后来傅先生修改为“创谓”），即原思想家现在必须说出什么？或为了解决原思想家未能完成的思想课题，创造的诠释学者现在必须践行什么？① 有人批评说，必谓（或创谓）也应放在诠释学之外。也就是说，属于诠释学之内的只有意谓、蕴谓和当谓。实谓是进入诠释学的一个功夫与前提，是前面的准备工作。意谓、蕴谓和当谓才是诠释的过程。必谓（或创谓）则是今人的解读，应排除在诠释过程之外。香港中文大学刘昌元先生对傅伟勋先生创造的诠释学也有所批评。他认为，假如存在这五层创造的诠释的话，就有过渡诠释的嫌疑。他强调孟子所说的读《诗》时“以意逆志”的方法。要分析“说话的主体”与“实际的主体”，以期做到不“以文害辞”，不“以辞害意”。人的意识总是处在一定的处境、制度与风俗之中②。还有，诠释者总是使用一定的语言，这也是伽达默尔所强调的一种诠释对话的理论。我们要勇于突破权威的、独断的说法给我们的限制。这就必须有开放的心态。关于“成见”，伽达默尔也有他自己的解读，大家想必也很熟悉了。此外，刘昌元先生提出了“历史的具体化原则”、“融合原则”和“丰富性原则”。比如，他说方东美先生用道体、道用、道相、道徵四方面来解读“道”，就把《老子》的“道”解释为在形上学上有一超本体论的层次。③ 这些都是刘昌元先生在解释学层面对傅伟勋先生的批评。刘先生还提出有所谓“尊敬的解释学”与“怀疑的解释学”等相对应的观点。关于伽达默尔的诠释学，我们有很多很好的学者来做这方面的研究。伽达默尔所反省的是西方启蒙主义的两大精神：一个是强调理性，一个是否定传统。

---

① 参见傅伟勋：《从西方哲学到禅佛教》，北京三联书店 1992 年版，第 51—52 页。

② 参见刘昌元：《研究中国哲学所需遵循的解释学原则》，载沈清松主编：《跨世紀的中国哲学》，（台北）五南出版公司 2001 年版，第 77—98 页。

③ 参见刘昌元：《研究中国哲学所需遵循的解释学原则》，载沈清松主编：《跨世紀的中国哲学》，（台北）五南出版公司 2001 年版，第 77—98 页。

（二）从黑格尔转向后黑格尔

我接手哲学史方法论这门课程到2009年约有15个年头。我们这门课原来是中西哲学史的老师一起上，后因工作量的问题，就分开了。分开后，我和田文军教授一起来负责。原来这门课是两个学期即一个学年的课，田文军老师与我各带一学期课，后来压缩为一个学期了，我们各带半学期课。我主持这门课时曾请邓晓芒教授、彭富春教授、何卫平教授等到我们这个班给中国哲学专业的研究生来讲西方哲学中最重要的哲学家的方法学。我们一直强调中西互通。我接手之后对这门课程的转型，就是从黑格尔转向后黑格尔。一方面，我们继续研读黑格尔《哲学史讲演录》的导言，对其进行细致的讨论；另一方面，我们更重要的是学习并检讨马克斯·韦伯，学习并反思西方著名汉学家的新成果，学习并讨论伽达默尔的诠释学在中国哲学诠释中的意义。伽达默尔认为，如果否定传统就丧失了我们所理解的视域，而令纯理性的作用几乎成为不可能。现代并不与传统相对立，而是以崭新的方式来形成新的传统。真正达到理解时，社会对现代与传统的理解就实现了“视域融合”。洪汉鼎、沈清松、陈荣华、何卫平等教授在这一方面都有很多贡献，我们主要读洪汉鼎译《真理与方法》及洪先生书数种，沈清松先生著《现代哲学论衡》有专章论哲学诠释学，陈荣华先生著有《葛达玛诠释学与中国哲学的诠释》。沈清松据伽达默尔思想指出，每个人都必须意识到自己隶属于一个传统；同时，我们必须知道我们的历史传统只是各种传统中的一个传统而已。因此，我们必须保持开放性，向印度、西方等不同传统开放。另外，我们最须珍视的是语言的传统。而语言的传统则存在于我们的经典、典章文物、圣贤人格、圣人言论、经史子集、民间民俗文化中。

解释学有它的“游戏”观念，而游戏中又有规则。这一规则与自然科学中的规则不同。自然科学的规则是主客对立。西方社会科学也受到了自然科学这一规则的限制。主客二分作为所谓的普遍规则理论，用到对具体事物的把握上，就造成了像我们今天生态环境遭受严重破坏等后果，这就是科技文化所产生的弊端。所以，须理解老子所谓“道法自然”。我们要费很多口舌来向我们的听众表明“道法自然”这一“自然”不是西方观念下的那个对象化的“自然”。“道法自然”就是道向自己的那个样子而已。有一次一位院士问我，“道法自然”怎么解释，我费了很多口舌来向这位自然科学家解释。伽达默尔诠释学讲到了诠释活动的预设，认为客观的诠释是不可能的，我们的理解总是在先设结构（所有、观念、概念等）的框架内才能实现。比如说，我们解读孟子的“尽其心者，知其性也。知其性，则知天矣。存其心，养其性，所以事天也。”(《孟子·尽心上》）尽心、知性、知天，存心、养性、事天只有从《孟子》全书的脉络中才能得到理解。不仅如此，我们甚至只有从先秦儒学发展的脉络中才能理解这句话。这就是一种先设所有。所以任何一种创造性的理解都离不开我们的传统。我们现在认为理性与传统之间是可以各自分离、彼此独立的。然而解释学告诉我们，在我们彼此之间，在问题与答案之间，通过诠释经验中的对话性，双方可以达到一种互动。这就是一种人文主义的方法学。

（三）中国经典诠释的方法论启示

中国哲学史界近年来的方法学讨论，我觉得最值得重视的是：成中英先生的本体诠释学，汤一介先生的中国解释学，黄俊杰先生以孟子诠释为中心的经典诠释学与东亚经典的诠释学，李明辉先生的康德与儒学的互释，刘笑敢先生的“反向格义”说，还有借现象学解释的路子，如张祥龙教授与陈少明教授等所做的工作。成中英先生认为，西方古典的形而上学是寻找本体的诠释，而他所探讨的中国诠释学是基于本体的诠释。他要重新建构中国诠释学视域下的本体论。黄俊杰先生把两千年来《孟子》的诠释历史加以分析与提炼，总结中国诠释的方法学及时代所附加在《孟子》诠释上的一些内容，使经典与文本得以新的敞开。此外，日本、朝鲜半岛、越南学者对于四书、儒学也有自己不同的诠释，并在此方面做出了积极的贡献。汤一介先生总结了中国古代经典诠释的三种路向：一是“历史事件的解释”；二是“整体性的哲学解释”；三是“社会政治运作型的解释”。这些都是值得我们讨论的一些问题，都可以丰富我们的哲学史研究。伽达默尔一百零一岁时告诫中国学者，不应忽视自己本民族及文化传统中丰富的具有特色的解释学思想的分析与提炼，它也可以给西方提供某种借鉴与启示。① 我们有自己的解释学传统，我们的经学、子学、佛学、理学中都有自身的解释学传统。对此我们应倍加珍惜，我们相信伽达默尔的这番话具有重大的意义。

前些年还有所谓中国哲学“合法性”问题的讨论。对于中国有没有哲学，不能因为一个洋大人来中国走了一遭，说中国没有哲学，只有思想，我们就亦步亦趋。其实，没有必要去争论中国有没有哲学，因为哲学的定义本来就非常繁复。但有人又提出，这么多年以来我们中国哲学的解释完全是“汉话胡说”。那么，我们是不是不要用外国人的思想作为参照不要“胡说”了呢？还有人提出，我们不要“哲学”这一词汇，就用古代的“道术”替代算了。此外，我们该如何应对“以西释中”，是不是可以开出一条“以中释中”的路子呢？有的先生主张“自己讲”和“讲自己”。我们今天已经到了一个中西不可分割的对话的时代，个人以为，已经不可能自说自话了。既然我们处在一个中西互动的时代，那么前面所面临的疑问自然就好回答了。看来，固步自封是不行的。“中国哲学”学科的完善与发展，仍然离不开中外哲学的多方面的更加广泛深入的交流、对话与沟通。今天，我们的解释学处境是在中外古今之间，故针对“以西释中”回到所谓“以中释中”，是不妥当的，其实“中”、“西”都是流动的、变化着的。通过对近十几年来中国经典诠释的方法学及专家们所提出的各种问题进行讨论、解读，可以引发我们对于中国哲学方法学的新思考。

三、21 世纪中国哲学研究的多重取径、前景与限制

下面，我讲第三大问题，本世纪中国哲学研究的多重取径、前景与限制。

---

① 参见余敦康、黄俊杰、洪汉鼎、李明辉：《中国诠释学是一座桥》，《光明日报》2002 年 9 月 26 日。

近十几年来，我在为研究生讲授哲学史方法论课程的教学计划中，有关教学目的，我一直写着这样一句话："重点理解和讨论中国哲学史的特殊的方法论，即不以西方范型为框架的中国人文的方法论，破除将西方社会科学与哲学方法作为普遍方法的迷信，理解中国哲学范畴、价值、意境的特殊性及其普式化。"在我布置的思考题中，有一个题目是："治中国哲学史的一个难题，就是人们的视域、思考方式、方法学训练，主要是依从西方的。试问，您认为如何从心态、方法（包括思想方法和范畴诠释方式）上更好地解释传统？"我开的长长的书单中有张岱年先生的《中国哲学史方法论发凡》和韦政通先生编的《中国思想史方法论文选集》等。近些年，我也发表了好几篇关于哲学史方法论的文章，[①] 以下综合这些论文，简略地谈几个问题。

（一）"中国哲学"学科的主体性与中西哲学的对话性

中国哲学与西方哲学是两种不同的哲学形态，我们不能把西方哲学定于一尊。当年金岳霖先生预设的"普遍哲学"仍然只是以欧洲哲学为蓝本的，是西方一部分哲学的抽象。他以所谓的"普遍哲学"作为唯一尺度，衡量、评估非西方的丰富多彩的哲学。这种观点是应予以检讨的。但凡思考宇宙、人生诸大问题，追求大智慧的，都属于哲学的范畴。关于人在宇宙中的地位、人的尊严与价值、人的安身立命之道等等，都是哲学的题中应有之义。中国哲学在这些方面有自己的智慧。中国哲学与西方哲学当然可以通约，可以比较。不同文化背景下产生的哲学具有某种一致性、互通性，因此相互翻译、诠释、比较的哲学研究工作不仅有可能，而且有意义与价值。所谓内在与超越的关系，学界讨论有没有"内在超越"，或者说超越就一定是外在的吗？关于这个问题，完全可以在中国的天人之学中加以探讨。

---

① 郭齐勇：《中国哲学：保持世界性与本土化之间的必要的张力》，《天津社会科学》2004 年第 1 期；郭齐勇：《"中国哲学"及其自主性》，《文史哲》2005 年第 3 期；郭齐勇：《中国哲学的自主性与哲学对话》，《中国哲学年鉴》（2006），哲学研究杂志社 2006 年；郭齐勇：《建构中国哲学的方法论反思》，《学术月刊》2007 年第 3 期；郭齐勇：《内在式批判与继承性创新》，《河北学刊》2009 年第 2 期。

我们强调“中国哲学”学科成立的正当性，强调“中国哲学”学科自身的特色，并不是把“中国哲学”做静态的处理，其本身即是一个动态的过程。中国哲学（儒、释、道诸家等）有自己的特性。一般说来，中国哲学的实践性很强，不停留于“概念王国”，没有西方哲学中的上帝与尘世、超越与内在、本体与现象、主观与客观、身体与心灵、事实与价值等绝对二分的框架。以天、天命、天道为背景，中国哲人有神圣、高远且强烈的终极关切、理想境界、形上追求、精神信念，同时又有现实关怀，力图把理想在社会大群生活和现世人生中实现出来，其内圣与外王是打通的。有人说“中国人没有信仰”，我看中国人、外国人中都有没有信仰的人，也都有有信仰的人。不能笼统地讲。我是中国人，我就有信仰，当然不能由此推论所有中国人都如此。中国人的信仰在今天的民间仍保留着。我们的老师萧先生、陈先生、杨先生等都有着很深沉的信仰。我们在他们身边能强烈地感受到这种信仰支撑的学术人生。他们的所言、所思、所行无不让我们感觉到，这是有信仰的人。

（二）理解的历史性与诠释的相应性

一旦涉及中国哲学史的方法论问题，当然离不开“理解”与“批判”、“继承”与“原创”、“传统”与“现实”等关系问题。所谓“批判”，是在全面深入理解基础上所作的内在性的批评，而不是不相干的外在批评；所谓“原创”“创新”，不是无源之水、无本之木，不是玄想，不是标新立异，不是剑走偏锋，而是真正在全面继承基础上所作的开拓，是扬弃（既保留又克服）；弘扬传统并不意味着脱离现实，而是调动并创造性转化传统文化资源，以其中的某些因素介入、参与、批判、提升现实，促使传统与现代的互动。

如何历史地、相应地诠释中国哲学，值得我们思考。余英时先生是历史学家，他在解读中国思想史时有很多重要的创获。他所强调的“内在理路说”有一定意义。关于清儒与宋儒的关系问题，就值得深思。因此，我们如果强调问题意识和方法学自觉的话，就要对这些前辈学人的重要的思想成果加以认真研读。海外一些汉学家的成果，我们相当重视。例如葛瑞汉、列文森、史华慈、狄百瑞、杜维明、安乐哲教授等，还有一些日本学者。安乐哲先生曾来我校授课、讲学，他有很多重要的创获，当然也有限制。我们做中国哲学研究的学者、学生有着更加麻烦的工作，就是必须对西方哲学，对海内外的现有成果都给予足够的重视，并加以细致的研读，否则根本谈不上创新。

五四运动以来，片面的、平面的西化思潮及教育体制，使得我们这一代甚至前后几代人逐渐丧失了解读前现代文明（或文献）的能力。故现在我们带领同学们读经，就是拿十三经原本来读，连注疏一起读，从识字、断句开始，慢慢培养我们解读原典的能力。我们请同学们不要看白话解释，所有的白话翻译都是有弊病的。我们要看就直接看古文献。对于自己民族的文化及其经典，应有起码的尊重，起码的虚心的态度，不要信口雌黄，不要相信有所谓名家的中国文化如何如何，西方文化如何如何，那都靠不住。有所谓“新批判主义者”，比“老批判主义者”更荒唐，更靠不住，他们对中国传统哲学的批评，绝大多数是站不住的，因为他断章取义，而且是暴力强加式的，武断宰割的，先入为主的。没有相应的理解，不可能有相应的批评，这是非常重要的方法论问题。

（三）“中国哲学”的特殊性与丰富性

关于有没有所谓“普遍哲学”，刚才我们讨论金岳霖先生的论点时已有所涉及。其实，把西方哲学作为一种普遍性的哲学，把中国哲学作为一种特殊性的哲学，这本身就是有问题的。我们中国哲学不能用狭隘的西方哲学的观念来加以范围。用纯西方哲学的观念来研究中国哲学，收获会让人觉得非常遗憾和有限。我们相信，方法多元与成果多样肯定是未来这个时代的哲学方法学和哲学解释状况的前景。但是任何方法与方法学都有它的限制。

劳思光先生用“基源问题研究法”对中国哲学进行解读，很有创意，很有收获。他认为中国哲学有三种基本的形态。一种是心性论的形态，一种是宇宙论的形态，还有一种是形上学的形态。他的这一特定内涵，分别指向三种建构道德价值之门径。他认为，主体性之自觉活动内在于心性主体之中，从而确定善的价值方向。在劳先生看来，孔、孟哲学就是这种心性论哲学的典范。他认为，以宇宙论为中心的哲学太注重于外在的“天”，这个“天”是以汉儒董仲舒为代表的宇宙论的趋向。形上学的形态则是将价值建基于超经验之“实有”（Reality）上。他认为，北宋的二程哲学是形上学最纯粹的表现。如果要加以定位，他认为宇宙论的哲学是最低的一种形态。形上学的哲学是中间的形态。心性论的哲学则是最高的形态。由此，他对于宋明理学的解读展开了所谓一系三向或三系的说法，这与牟宗三先生的三系说不一样。他在这里就把二程放在中间的层次，把周敦颐、张载隶属于宇宙论的形态，即最低的一个层次。而到陆象山、王阳明则越发凸显心性论这一形态，属于最高的一个层次。他的这种判教的确有新见，当然也有一些限制。因此，大家在检讨劳思光先生四卷本的《中国哲学史》及这种“基源问题研究法”时，提出了一些问题与批评。比如，他的这种架构本身就难免对中国哲学造成伤害。考虑到中国哲学的特殊性，这种方法是否适用于中国哲学的研究值得我们进一步讨论。

哪怕是研究中国的名学、逻辑学、正名学说，如若以西方的纯逻辑的观点或方法来加以解读的话，也不可能得到一个恰当的理解。有时候我们的确需要抽象、分析及理论推演，但我们中国人更重视的是当下的体验，更重视一种特殊的、具体的情势。这种体验方式，当然有它自身的局限性。但我们仍要虚怀地去了解这种生命的、生活的体验方式之重要性。西方人对哲学的分类方法也不适用于中国哲学。我们的天道、人性学说，假若用西方的宇宙论、伦理学来加以解读，就会完全不相干。我们对于中国传统哲学自身的特性及治中国哲学史的方法学，仍在摸索之中。我们应有自觉自识，发掘中华民族原创性的智慧与古已有之的治学方法，予以创造性转化。中国有自己的语言学与语言哲学的传统。中国先民仰观天象，俯察地理，近取诸身，远取诸物，以“六书”为特点的汉字，生命体验，经子之学，有自身诠释文献的方法与智慧。中国人强调经验直观与理性直观地把握、领会对象之全体或底蕴的思维方式，有赖于以身“体”之，即身心交感地“体悟”。这种“知”、“感”、“悟”是体验之知，感同身受，与形身融在一起。我们要超越西方一般知识论或认识论的框架、结构、范畴的束缚，发掘反归约主义、扬弃线性推理的“中国理性”、“中国认识论”的特色。

（四）内在性的批评与思想的训练

我们批评、超越传统，我们从来不拒绝批评。所谓“批评”，是在全面深入理解的基础上所作的内在性的批评，而不是不相干的外在批评。但内在性的批评与思想的训练一定要以同情的了解为前提。因为，必须有深刻的同情的了解才能做好哲学思想史研究，而同情的了解要靠相应的才具。刘述先先生讲：“要了解一家哲学，我们必须要了解这一家哲学产生的时代和文化的背景是什么，所感受到的问题是什么，所提出的解决问题的方向是什么，独特的哲学心灵尤其需要独特的处理，庸俗的眼光未必能够了解崇高的哲学的境界。”“缺乏同情的了解是研究传统中国哲学的一大限制，而时代气氛不同，尤其使我们难于领略过去时代的问题。……故此研究思想史贵在作深入的内在的探讨，外在的论议是其余事。从这一个观点看，胡适与冯友兰的哲学史都不能够算是深刻，因为它们不能作足够的内在的深刻的讨论的缘故。大抵在中国哲学史上，以佛学与理学最不容易处理，以其牵涉到内在的体验的缘故。如果缺乏体验，根本就看不出这些东西的意义。入乎其内，而后才能出乎其外，这是研究一家哲学的不二法门。要了解一个哲学所要解决的问题是什么，着手的方法是什么，所根据的经验基础是什么，这样才能看出这一哲学的优点与缺点所在。”①刘先生认为，由此我们才能理解古人的陈述与陈述背后的洞识，显发古人思想中所潜在的逻辑性，使其具备与内容相适应的理论结构。

我所主张的方法是一种“谦虚”的方法。所谓“谦虚”，或“同情的”、“客观的”理解，或“以继承为前提的创新”、“弱势或软性的诠释”等，不仅是态度，而且是方法。文化立场、心态作为一种做学问的态度或方法对诠释的效果也会产生很大的影响。但它本身也有局限。我们不是不要批评、反思，而是要

① 刘述先：《研究中国史学与哲学的方法与态度》，载韦政通编：《中国思想史方法论文选集》，（台北）水牛出版社 1987 年版，第 221—223、224—225 页。

做难度更大的内在性的、相干性的批评与反思。反思是辩证的扬弃，既保留又克服。反思不是全盘否定或恣意的无根据的乱说。王元化先生曾经说过："黑格尔学说具体的普遍性不同于抽象的普遍性，前者可以将特殊性和个体性统摄于自身之内。我认为这只是存在于黑格尔的逻辑学中，而并不存在于现实中。实际上，普遍性愈大，它所能概括的特殊性和个体性则愈小。设想有一种不同于抽象普遍性的具体普遍性，使这种概括可以放之四海而皆准，那只是美好的空想。"① 因此，我们在拥护这种具体普遍性时，也应看到它自身的局限。主张弘大传统文化精神并不意味着没有现实感、不关注现实或脱离现实，而恰好包含着批判现实，批判现代性的负面与偏弊，批判时俗流弊，批判五四以来相沿成习的某些误解。我们努力对传统儒释道与宋明理学等思想传统作创造性转化，主要是通过生活化的渠道浸润到民间，在现代生活中起作用。

此外，还要注重思想训练与思想力的培养。徐复观先生说："某人的思想固然要通过考证（包括训诂、校勘等）而始能确定；但考证中的判断，也常要凭思想的把握而始能确定。……前后相关的文句，是有思想的脉络在里面的。这即说明考证与义理在研究历程中的不可分割性。就研究的人来讲，作考证工作，搜集材料，要靠思想去导引；检别材料，解释材料，组织材料，都是工作者的思想在操作。而'思想力'的培养，必须通过了解古人的、他人的思想，而始能得到锻炼、拓展、提升的机会。所以思想力的培养，是教学与治学上的基本要求。岂有不求了解古人的、他人的思想而能培养自己的思想力？岂有没有思想力的人能做考据工作？"② 他主张通过了解古人的、他人的思想来锻炼、提升、培养"思想力"，尤其要学会把握古人思想的内在脉络，这才是批判的基础。因此，我们要时时理解中国哲学（每家每派）的边界与限制。当然，首先是自己要老老实实地读书，不要说大话，要有自知之明，自虚其心，自空其

---

① 王元化：《谈谈我的反思》，《文汇报》1995 年 10 月 22 日。

② 徐复观：《治古代思想史方法》，载韦政通编：《中国思想史方法论文选集》，（台北）水牛出版社 1987 年版，第 170 页。

说。这并不妨碍问题意识的产生，而是尽可能避免剑走偏锋。

（五）回顾与瞻望

回顾近三十年中国哲学之研究，中外哲学（及汉学、中国学）与各宗教间的对话逐渐加强，古今会通也受到重视。研读第一手资料的功夫更加扎实，也重视海内外已有的研究成果即研究前史，在此基础上提出创新性见解并给予详实地分析、论证。研究领域进一步扩大，各个时段的思潮、流派、人物、著作与哲学问题的研究都有许多成就。传统哲学与当代的关系、经与经学、佛教、道家与道教、宋明理学、现当代新儒学、出土简帛中的哲学思想研究、从政治哲学的视域研究中国哲学等，已成为热门或显学。当然，这其中也有不尽如人意的地方。如何做到小中见大仍是我们面临的难题。我们研究的对象越小，背景越大，才能越有深度。此外，把东亚（中国、越南、朝鲜半岛与日本）的哲学思想史作为一个整体来研究，把整个东亚作为一个思想背景和解释学处境加以对待，也是富有创新性的思路，这种研究业已展开。

当前的中国哲学研究也存在不少的问题或缺失：第一，学科间交叉、对话不够；第二，学术品质与水平及对古典的研读能力的下降；第三，现实向度不够；第四，面向世界的能力尚待加强；第五，问题意识和理论深度还有待提升；第六，关于少数民族的哲学与古代科学中的哲学问题的研究还比较薄弱；第七，中国哲学史研究在少数重要人物(如孔、孟、老、庄、程、朱、陆、王)及其著作上扎堆的现象急需改变，有许多在历史的某时段某地域颇有影响的人物、学术共同体、著作等都没有得到很好的发掘、整理与细致的研究。中哲史上有很多二、三流的人物，其实也非常了不起，在某时某地很有影响，都亟待我们结合东亚史、地域文化思想史去开拓，首先要下功夫把第一、二手资料给予整理、出版。

中国哲学或中国哲学史当然不同于中国学术史、中国思想史，其研究范围、对象与方法自有不同。一方面，中国哲学更重视哲学形上学与哲学问题的讨论；另一方面，中国哲学研究者并不排斥，相反更重视哲学思想、理念对社会民俗、政治与各种社会制度的作用与影响。这种关怀与对哲学理念的关怀相辅相成。我们的任务是彰明中国哲学之为中国哲学的自身的哲学问题、精神、方法、范畴、特点、风格与传统，深度建构、阐发中华民族几千年来的哲学思维发展史，体现中国人的哲学智慧，特别是在天人之间即超越境界、自然天地与俗世生活之间的体验，社会治理的经验，身心性命的修炼与人生意境，言说论辩方式的特色及其与欧洲、印度、阿拉伯等哲学智慧的同异及世界上几大哲学传统在中华文化区的碰撞与交融。

瞻望未来，我们预计中国哲学界将会在中国哲学学科主体性的确立，中国经典诠释的多样性，中国哲学范畴、命题与精神、智慧的准确把握，西方哲学的中国化与中国哲学的世界化，中国哲学的创造性转化，中国哲学智慧对现代化的参与及对人类社会的贡献等方面继续取得重要进展①。

① 参见郭齐勇、廖晓炜：《60 年来中国哲学思想史研究的思考》，《文史知识》2009 年第 9 期。

中国思想史哲学史研究的理念与方法

麻天祥

关于思想史、哲学史研究，在理念上尤其是方法上大多是相通的。概括为一条原则、两种内容、三项要求。后者主要是从方法和方法论上讲的。简述如下：

一、原则：历史和逻辑相结合

思想史研究，关注的是思想发生发展的历史，其中既包含了对思想内容的探索与诠释，同时也强调对不同时期思想演变的规律的把握，故一般总是把“历史与逻辑相结合”作为思想史研究的原则。司马迁说的“究天人之际，穷古今之变”，其实也是这个意思：穷古今之变的史实；究天人之际的内在逻辑。

存在决定意识，生存方式决定人的思想。这无疑是正确的。但是人类的思想也不是完全被动的被决定的东西。思想不仅能够改变生存状态和生存方式，而且能够昭示人类社会沿着特定的方向前进和发展。

有人界定“人”是社会化的动物，实在不尽准确。因为这只是一个类概念，而没有反映出种差。事实上，人不仅具有社会行为，更拥有思想和情感的世界。人不仅有可见的社会活动，而且还有一个“在而无形”并具有主宰作用的精神世界。因此可以说“人是有思想的动物”。就人类的本质而言，听命的不是外部的环境，而是它自身的观念；唯一要服从的是它的内在的原则和价值取向。从这个意义上讲，思想才是人类真正的上帝！

因此可以说，人是有思想的，人类的历史，就是思想生生不息的历史，它是蒙昧时代的火炬，是古代社会的灯烛，也是现代文明的向导。

有人说：

> You must be careful of your thoughts, because your thoughts will become your words.
>
> You must be careful of your words, because your words will become your deeds.
>
> You must be careful of your deeds, because your deeds will become your habits.
>
> You must be careful of your habits, because your habits will become your characters.
>
> You must be careful of your characters, because your characters will become your destiny。
>
> （你必须留意你的思想，因为你的思想会成为你的语言。
>
> 你必须留意你的语言，因为你的语言会付诸你的行为。
>
> 你必须留意你的行为，因为你的行为会铸就你的习惯。
>
> 你必须关注你的习惯，因为你的习惯会形成你的性格。
>
> 你必须关注你的性格，因为你的性格必将决定你的命运。）

这里说的就是：思想决定语言，语言付诸行为，行为铸就习惯，习惯形成性格，而性格最终决定命运。直接地讲就是思想决定命运。这虽然是就个人而言，但就整个社会立论亦当如是。无论中西古今，人类都把自身和自身以外的存在，作为认识的对象，并给以思考和价值的判断。由此而形成的任何一种思想或者理论，都向人们提供一种价值观念以及思维方法，并以此推动历史的前进。思想和历史的关系如是而已。

当然，思想或者观念不是个人的孤独发明，而是具有群体性。它是一个地域，一个民族，一个国家，由于共同生活的需要，凝结而成的特定的思维方式和价值取向。它既是现实的，是时代精神的反映；又是超前的，甚至是超现实的超前觉悟和终极依托。正是这样强有力的内在呼唤，把不计其数的人凝聚在一起，形成了超越血缘和地理环境的文化的共同体。

黑格尔在《哲学史讲演录》中说过许多非常精辟的话，恩格斯称赞他是第一个想证明历史中有一种发展、有一种内在联系的人。他曾经明确地指出，一定的哲学形态与它基以出现的民族形态同时存在，与受这一特定原则支配的旧国家的没落和新国家的兴起同时存在。也就是说，当一个国家或民族的阶级地位发生变化特别是整个民族濒临没落的时候，民族文化的心理结构也将由于内心的要求与外在的现实裂痕而发生改变，其结果是现实的生活方式、共同的伦理风俗和传统信仰因之动摇。一个思想上的破坏期出现之后，便是新思想的酝酿和兴起，精神在空旷的领域中，开始营建新的理想王国，以反抗现实世界，一个新的思想由此而诞生。因此，任何最终的绝对的思想体系都是和辩证法不相容的，因为思想或者说观念，只是用思维和概念去把握真理，而不等于真理，任何一种能称之为体系的哲学，都有凝固或僵化的倾向而和思想发展的历史进程不相容。思想史就是要以辩证的观念，认识、把握，或者说诠释时代精神，开拓历史前进的方向。据此可以说，思想既是历史和时代决定的时代精神，又是对时代精神的反思和超前觉悟。

换个角度讲，任何一种思潮，其发展首先取决于它自身的内在素质，可以摆脱外在的偶然性，而呈现逻辑的必然性。但如果作为社会思潮或主流文化决不可能离开时代而独立存在。它既是整个客观环境的超前觉悟，又是正在进行反思的时代精神，它与时代是不可分的。因此，它的兴衰必定有特定的社会环境和文化背景。这就是侯外庐先生坚持的结合社会史研究思想史，即重视“社会思潮”研究的方式。

简单地说，思想史研究，不仅要注重思想生成、存在、发展变化的社会背景、历史条件、生存方式等外在环境，尤其要注重思想的内在特征和逻辑必然性，即其与社会符契、反映时代精神的内涵，体现思维深度的逻辑框架，以及昭示未来并与时俱进的厚度和张力。我是这样理解、应用或者说实践“历史和逻辑相结合”的原则的。

二、内容：精英思想与平民思想

中国思想早在两千多年以前已经形成，并在不同的历史阶段而有新思。其特质在于，既重视规范和秩序的建设，又重视个人的自在与超越追求；自强不息，兼包并容；内圣外王，博施济众；究天人之际，穷古今之变；为天地立心，为生民立命；既有对有限的现实关怀，又有对无限的期盼和不懈追求。毫无疑问，中国思想是世界思想文化之宝库。它以儒家思想为主体，兼取佛道，内容宏博，收放自如，于己、于人、于社会、于国家、于世界，都有其现实和深远的意义。然而遗憾的是，过去的思想史作，已有固定范式，难以有所突破，而且大多囿于正史和精英社会，往往忽略了在民间的流布和影响的平民思想。所以今后的思想史研究尤宜注视同日常行事密切相关的平民思想，而搜求于市井草莽之间，予以抉择综合，推陈出新。

思想史研究以精英社会为主干，以正史为依据，无疑能准确反映社会思潮，而穷古今之变。但是，平民文化和平民思想同样是社会思潮的组成部分，哪怕是细流或涓滴。稗官野史中的杂抄，庶民百姓的口口相传，市井里巷、书札尺牍、小说杂记，甚至地摊文化，民俗民情，均有助于反映庶民思想的蛛丝马迹，甚或更真实、犀利、更为鲜活。比如，普遍存在于中国社会的家庭、婚姻、爱情、生死等诸多观念，乃至民间信仰，往往在思想史的“正史”中，普遍地被淡忘，而悄无声息地“被消失”。所有这些观念，对思想史研究自然大有裨益，与精英、正史的追寻应当说是相得益彰。基于这样的思考，我也在最近新作《存在与理性》中，初步尝试而有所改变。

单纯说理是枯燥的，仅举例如下：

> 《芝田录》载：史思明送其子（朝义）樱桃，并附诗云："樱桃一篮子，半青一半黄，一半与怀王，一半与周贽。"部属建议：圣上诗作妙笔生花，若将"一半与周贽"句放在第三句上面，则入韵，亦更为妥帖。史氏怒而斥之："岂可将周贽置于我儿之上！"①

悍将叛乱、称帝，而又附庸风雅若此，令人喷饭。章太炎引此说有韵为诗，无韵非诗，若要说无韵是诗的话，史思明便是无韵诗的祖宗。从中既可见当时社会的另一个侧面，亦可见章太炎博识强记之幽默，乃至其中隐寓的批判意识。又如《古今谭概》：

> 明嘉靖间昆山有人为子聘妇，因儿子患病，经久不愈，且民间有冲喜之说，故即遣媒婆至女方家，商议婚娶大事。女家父母怕耽误女儿终身，拒不应聘，男方坚持婚娶。女方父母无奈，便将幼子男扮女装冒充新娘，搪塞男方。始料不及的是，男方父母以儿子患病不宜同房，遣小女与"新娘"做"姑嫂"同床，无意中竟让他们二人成为夫妻。数月后，女方怕偷梁换柱之事败露，要求假女回门，以为如此便可以神不知鬼不觉地搪塞过去。然而，男方小女却有孕在身，导致亲家变成仇家，对簿公堂。历时数年，难以结案。继有叶御史断案，将男方小女与女方幼子结缡成就两对年轻夫妻，两家亦皆大欢喜。其判词曰：嫁女得媳，娶妇得婿，颠之倒之，左右一义。②

这就是后来流传甚广的"三世三言"中的《乔太守乱点鸳鸯谱》的故事，其社会意义不言而喻。还有：

---

① 冯梦龙：《古今谭概》第六部《无术部·史思明诗》。

② 冯梦龙：《古今谭概》第三十六部《杂志部·嫁娶奇合》。

> 唐贞元年间，王师于青海破吐蕃，杀吐蕃大将。吐蕃军收尸百余人，仪仗庄严，哭声凄惨。有人立于尸侧，为尸替身代语。人问：疮病可疼？替身代答：疼，即有人将膏药涂于伤处。问：欲进食乎？代答：好，便有人喂食。问：穿衣么？答：穿，便以锦衣上身。再问：要回家吗？答：要的。立即备车马运尸回吐蕃。①

这样奇特的仪式，正是吐蕃英雄崇拜的习俗。

《清稗类钞》记：

> 《红楼梦》一书，风行久矣，士大夫有习之者，称为《红学》。而嘉、道两朝，则以讲求经学为风尚。朱子美尝讪笑之，谓其穿凿傅会，曲阿世学也。独嗜说部书，曾寓目者几九百种，尤熟精《红楼梦》，与朋友闲话，辄及之。一日，有友过访，语之曰："君何不治经？"朱曰："予亦攻经学，第与世人所指之经不同耳。"友大诧。朱曰："予之经学，所少于人者，一画三曲也。"友瞠目。朱曰："红学耳。"朱名昌鼎，华亭人。②

可见，乾嘉时期虽然以经学为时代主流，但在知识界和民间亦崇尚说部，《红学》已开始在学术界悄然兴起。

> 京伶小百岁者，丑角也。一日，演《法门寺》，去小监，科白时，谓扮赵廉之生曰："做官亦识字么？吾道你只识洋文，不识国文呢。"又尝于《五花洞》中，自唱"做官不论大小，懂得洋文就好。"其言若有意，若无意。又都中妇女往往喜衔烟卷，一若表其时髦者，而不知泰西唯妓女吸之也。即十三四女郎，亦复如是。伶即假《法门寺》中之科白，谓宋玉姣曰：

① 冯梦龙：《古今谭概》第三十五部《非族部·吐蕃》。

② 徐珂编撰：《清稗类钞》第四册，中华书局1984年版，第1792页。

"千岁赐你锭银，不可将去买烟卷，中含尼古丁质，吸之有毒也。"①

插科打诨，乃丑角之长，如此切中时弊的明嘲暗讽，亦别有一番情致。又：

> 河南祥符、中牟间，有水月庵高衲淡如者，俗姓平，年八十五而示寂。先一日，嘱其徒曰："吾死，当归骨于庵，俟三岁后而发之，如体已败，焚之可矣，否则必有为吾更衣者至，汝识之。"……如期发龛，则淡如端坐于内，衣化尘飞，抚其体，坚过铁石，扣之，铿锵有声。远近观者云集。中牟令韩某亦至，愕然曰："师昨日入吾梦，乞吾银五两有奇，为一衲，其将欲饰金以示不坏之身乎？"遂召匠来，问其所需，果符梦中所乞之数。后进像即奉于龛，士女焚礼不绝。有一营卒心疑其伪，潜以刃刺其臂，血缕缕涌出。营卒大惧，投地忏服，急以金涂所刺处，刃口终不可合。庵僧因加扃键，遇心意虔诚者，始为之启观。②

上引，亦可见当时佛教舍利崇拜在民间的渗透。

至如《水浒》故事，原本就在坊间辗转流传，后又整理加工而成小说，不仅揭露了社会的腐朽阴暗，更多地表现了不拘成法的叛逆精神，以及挑战社会，崇尚暴力的游民倾向，与思想史的主流大不相侔。研究思想史，以此为补充，对于还原历史本来面目，显然会更真实，也更全面。当然，以大众文化形式表现出来的平民思想，其中或许夹杂糟粕，或者说是那时代的垃圾，但对于我们而言，毕竟不能因噎废食，关键在于去粗取精，而有精审之识断。

---

① 徐珂编撰：《清稗类钞》第四册，中华书局 1984 年版，第 1616 页。

② 徐珂编撰：《清稗类钞》第十册，中华书局 1984 年版，第 4856 页。

三、三学、三义、三难

治中国学术，有文章、义理和考据之三学，三者不可缺一。治学需厘清三义：字面义、文本义和诠释义，三者不可缺一。为学有三难：淹博难、识断难、精审更难。

“三学”之说，即文章、义理与训诂（或称考据）。所谓考据以通辞，文章以达意，义理以闻道，三者不可偏废。训诂必不可少，义理必然有得。王先谦在《续古文辞类纂序》中特别指出：“义理为干，而后文有所附，考据有所归”。显然是以义理为归附之所在，对于思想史研究尤其显得重要了。章学诚在《文史通义》的内篇二《原学下》中也说：“义理入于虚无，考证徒为糟粕，文章只为玩物。惟自通人论之则不然，考证即以实此义理，而文章乃所以达之之具。”显而易见，“三学”对于中国思想史研究同样缺一不可。冯天瑜先生也曾详细说明：“义理和考据，是属于文章内容方面的问题。在我们说来，讲究义理就是要求观点正确，论据充分；讲究考据就是要求材料准确。辞章是属于文章形式方面的问题。讲究辞章，在我们说来，就是要求适合于内容的完美的形式。”“走向学术的前沿离不开义理、考据、词章三者的互济，有了敏锐的哲理思辨才能发现问题，以占有和辨析的材料才能生发出带有创造性的结论，有较好的文字表述才能使研究成果张扬开来，这就是我们走向学术前沿必备的条件。”

“三难”是对段玉裁治学方法的转借，是对治学者的高层次要求。段玉裁在《经韵楼集·与胡孝廉世琦书》中说：“定本子之是非，存乎淹博；定作书者之是非，则存乎识断、审定。”所谓定本子之是非，就是对资料真伪的判识，淹博是至关重要的：不仅要求作者知识的渊博，而且要对史料广搜精求，甚至宁滥勿缺。定作者之是非，指的主要是“立说”，其实也就是“义理”：不仅要平情立言、有鲜明的论点，而且要有明晰的辩说、持之有故的论据，以及正确的，或者准确地说是令人信服的结论。这就是淹博、识断与精审。

与上述相比，厘清“三义”首当其冲。这里重点谈谈。

学术研究，核心是“研究”，性质是概念分析，是字的命题、言的命题。而文字有三义，一曰字面义，二曰文本义，三曰诠释义。思想史研究也不外与此。

一般说，上述三义理应完全吻合，但事实上由于作为符号的文字同指称事物的关系只是相关、或然，而非必然，所以字和义并非简单的对应。然而，字和言毕竟是客观的，被结构化的现实，故治学首先必须关注上述三义，尤其在具有数千年传统的汉语语境中的中国学术研究。

三义之别，一则因一词多义，指称不同。如道、理、心、性、法之类。道有道路之道、规律之道、道理之道，乃至宇宙大本大原之道，甚至行政区划之道；既可谓之治理，亦可谓之言说，不一而足。其他亦如是，法有存在之义，亦为规则、仿效、法律种种。诸如此类，不胜枚举。二则意义衍伸，由此及彼，尤其见诸成语、俗谚、典故。如三马同槽，马衍伸为司马氏，指司马懿父子三人，槽乃朝之谐音，意为司马父子擅权朝廷。又如“经纶”原初意为整理丝缕，引申义则为才学、能力，所谓满腹经纶。其他如泰山喻人之崇高，还有作岳父的敬语；贪墨之墨亦非墨汁之墨，而指不义之财。衍伸在哲学领域更为普遍，儒指儒家，道是道家、道教；佛本觉悟，又指释迦，也用来指称一切诸佛。禅更是如此，原本嬗代之禅，和作为礼仪的封禅，一变而为佛教哲学的特殊概念——超二元对立的意境和实现这一意境的方法。其三由于言意、名实关系不相对应性，所谓不可道、不可说、不可名者，故有得意忘言之说。

正因为如此，治学必须留意此三者。首先正确理解字面义，否则不知所云，也就无从对文本义进行探讨。比如“心”、“性”，是哲学上的重要范畴，尤其是中国哲学。心原为象形字，《说文解字》曰“土藏在身之中”，指人体的心脏，即人体解剖学和生理学之心。除此之外另有四义：一曰思维之心，所谓“心之官则思”；二曰道德伦理之心，即善恶之心，通常说的“良心”即此，如孟子说的“四心”（恻隐、羞恶、辞让、是非之心）；三曰意志，如孔子说的“从心所欲而不逾矩”，孟子说的养“浩然之气”的尽心，也包含这一层意思；四专指本心、本性，即生成一切的本体之心，哲学上所谓净心、不染心、率性之心、赤子之心、平常心之心，以及无心、心斋种种，皆属此类。意义悬殊若此，不能把握文本中的字面义，所作诠释势必谬之千里，甚至南辕北辙。郢书燕说“是不必然，亦不必不然”，“故未为无益”（纪昀《阅微草堂笔记》），虽然着眼的是诠释的必要，无疑也是对错解字面义的绝妙讽刺。常有人把本体之心翻译作 mind，显然是对心字的误译，实在应译作 nature 或 second nature。

强调重视原典，就是要重视历史文化背景和整个语境中的文本义的探讨。文本中亦有反其意而用之者，辨析本意，尤其应当谨慎。《诗经》伐檀中“彼君子兮，不素飧兮”；宋人《枫窗小牍》“王介甫（安石）不言所利”，采用的就是反语。老子突出“反者道之动”，故其所用概念多与众不同，所谓“绝圣弃智”、“绝仁弃义”、“绝巧弃利”，以及“生也柔弱”、“死也坚强”，不胜枚举，都应当在老子和道家学派的语境中诠释它的内涵。从意义上讲，文本义有突出重点的不同，意义也就有所差别。《老子》开篇讲：“无，名天地之始；有，名万物之母”，也有断句为“无名”、“有名”，以及后面的“无”和“无欲”、“有”和“有欲”，显然指称不同，内涵也就不尽相同了。这也是《老子》一书文本争论的公案。还有更多的是文本义往往超出字面义的外延，而和字面义不同，甚至背离。禅宗哲学以心性为本体，强调“识得本心便能成佛”、“心净则佛土净”，而有“平常心”的范畴见诸禅门经典。何谓“平常心”，应当不难理解，然而人说人殊，甚至大相径庭。从字面上看，平常心乃日常、寻常，与怪异相反之心，也就是人通常对事物的态度、观念，或者说价值取向，比如情欲、爱恨、荣辱、金钱利禄、以至生死，一般说人们都是喜得患失的，所以认为平常心就是“想做什么就做什么”。这显然不是禅宗思想的文本义。从禅学上讲，平常心就是超越二元对立的意境，不仅不是“想做什么就做什么”，而且是“一定不能做什么”，所谓不一不异、不常不断、不来不去、不生不灭，突出的正是如此。马祖道一对此有精确的文本界定："何谓平常心？无造作，无取舍，无断常，无凡无圣。"可见平常心实在与平常理解有大不同。儒家讲"率性之谓道"，与"平常心是道"说的是同样的意思，字面与文本之间的差别也大体相类。"率性"从字面上既可解释为任凭个人的习性，也可理解为随顺天命的"本然之性"，也就是没有造作、没有分别的平常心。可见文本义同字面义还是有极大差异的，所以对文本义的认真推敲显然是治学的关捩。

就学术研究而言，知上述二义是基本，但对文本的诠释尤为重要，也可以说是治学的显著特点。中国传统讲"义理"，西方哲学重概念分析，以至有诠释学风靡世界。其实，对文本义的探讨实际上已经包含了部分的诠释，但是还远远不够。诠释就是要对文本进行历史的、现实的，逻辑的、形式的，内容的、方法的全面多维的透析和剖判，而且常常带有诠释者个人的观念、情感，尽管这样的主观因素是要尽量摒除的。可以毫不夸张地说，治学之妙，或者说学术研究之妙就在于诠释——不止在证实"是什么"，更重要的在于"为什么"、"如何"、"如之何"。

就拿《老子》在学界耳熟能详的"天地不仁，以万物为刍狗；圣人不仁，以百姓为刍狗"这句话为例，通常诠释为：不仁，是不偏私的意思，故解释为天地、圣人均大公无私，而视万物、百姓为草扎成的狗，而不予珍惜，所谓一视同仁的意思。这样的诠释实在是牵强附会，很难使人信服，但数千年来竟成共议，明显是对老子的误读。其实，"不仁"是动词，是不以……为仁的意思，换句话说就是：天地不会把万物视作无用的刍狗，圣人不会把百姓视作无用的刍狗，并以此为"仁"的，或者说为"荣"的。所以这句话应当是"天地，不仁以万物为刍狗；圣人，不仁以百姓为刍狗。"姑不论孰是孰非，诠释的重要性跃然纸上了。

众所周知，佛家哲学谈空说有，"空"之一字体现了佛教哲学全部内容，但空并非什么都没有，这也是任人皆知的道理，但对"空"的诠释则众说纷纭。在佛门便有我空法不空、我法俱空、相空识不空、般若性空、涅槃实相、实相非相、空名无实之说。在学术研究中，亘古及今，或以空解空，或以有解空，或以儒解空，更有以庄老解空者，在佛门更有以假、中说空的，实际上都是借助不同的工具和方法对“空”的诠释。应当说，佛家的空以缘生理论为立论依据，而视万物为一种超越有、无的存在，既非有，也非无。还是僧肇说得好：“欲言其有，有非真生。欲言其无，事象既形。象形不即无，故曰非无。非真非实有，故曰非有。”对“空”的诠释可以说出神入化。另外，法相宗虽然号称“有宗”，其实是以有解空的，也是对“空”的一种诠释，其入手处是“有”，其着眼点是“空”。诚如章太炎对法相唯识无境的评论——以分析名相始，以排遣、破斥名相终。诠释之法，对“空”这样的概念早已是百花齐放、争奇斗艳了。

还有《论语》中的老生常谈，“未知生，焉知死”，很多人解释为孔子的有意回避生死，或者直接说是不愿论及那些不可知、不可言说的事物。不过现在有更多的学者从语义上分析，应当说是对生死问题的更深刻理解，意思应当是“对生尚且不了解，又怎么能认识死亡呢?”如此诠释，似乎更符合文本的意思，也更符合孔子的学问。再比如，“己所不欲，勿施于人”，“己欲达而达人”，一直被认为是孔子推己及人的忠恕之道，但从现实的层面上论，前者无害于人，故无不可，而后者虽然出于良好的动机，但难免有强加于人之意，自然也就不可取了。又如王门四句教，“无善无恶心之体，有善有恶意之动，知善知恶是良知，为善去恶是格物”，明显是对儒、释性本体论、道德论、方法论、体用关系的诠释和高度概括。王畿、钱德洪对四句教的不同理解，尤其是王阳明对二人的回答，更清楚地可见诠释义在治学中的客观性和重要性。

显而易见，学术研究必须厘清三义。字面义是前提，文本义是关捩，诠释义则是治学的显著特征。于此三义，或同时并举，或循序渐进，非如此不能有所创获，非如此则南辕北辙、郢书燕说，也可能是三纸无驴，而贻笑大方。下面二则小品，或许能从反面给治学者些许启迪。

《付法藏因缘传》卷二记载：阿难游行，至一竹林，闻有比丘颂法句偈：“若人生百岁，不解水老鹤，不如生一日，而得睹见之。”阿难告比丘曰：此非佛语，更非佛意，应当是“不解生灭法”。比丘反而说，阿难老朽，言多错谬。此比丘既不识字面义，更不解文本义，当然也就谈不上诠释了。

《清稗类钞》诙谐类，以禾音读毛诗：有人读《诗经》，听起来是：“王八骑马，亲家骑驴，就是骑你。”闻者发噱，甚不雅训。其实是《豳风·东山》中句：“皇驳其马，亲结其缡，九十其仪。”这也可以说是不解文义，而荒谬得让人喷饭了。

最后还要说一点决定研究成败的关键问题——要有责任，敢于承担，所谓为往圣继绝学，为万世开太平。古人有“君子谋道不谋食”之说，也就是说，学者要有承担社会责任精神，学术研究是神圣的事业，而不只是谋食的职业。是学者就应当承担学者的责任，任何时候，任何情况下，都要保持学者的良心和知识分子的距离。既不要脱离现实，谋虚逐妄，做高蹈无用之空谈；更不能趋炎附势、哗众取宠，为违心或媚俗之说。唯有如此，才能做到既不诬古人，也不误今人，而开拓将来。

要做到这一点，在学术研究中还需要有“同情理解”的治学态度——不偏不党，更不要有门户之见；既要凭史迹之搜讨，尤其要有心性之体会。如此探赜索隐，方能钩深致远。因为，尽管任何一种思想或者哲学都不可能终极真理，但是，凡是能够载诸竹帛，并传之广远的思想一定有其历史的价值甚至现实的意义。不加拣择的全盘接受固然是错误的，但以“同情理解”之心，广搜精求，见微知著，慎思明辨，取其精华，显然是正确的方法——既是继往圣之学的学术自觉，也是开启将来的必由之路。

“以哲学史为中心的思想史研究”刍议

——对19—20世纪中国哲学研究的方法论思考

李维武

自中国进入改革开放新时期以来，19—20世纪中国哲学的研究工作逐渐得到深入的开展，至今天已成为中国哲学史研究的一个富有生气与成果的领域。现在所面临的问题是：如何通过方法论上的探讨与创新，进一步拓展这一研究的思维空间，使这一研究具有更为广阔的视域和更为深刻的阐释。“以哲学史为中心的思想史研究”，就是试图在哲学史研究与思想史研究之间加以沟通，使哲学史研究更多地吸取思想史研究的内容，从而从方法论上作这样一种探讨和创新。

一、哲学史研究与思想史研究的疏离与沟通

在现代中国学术界，哲学史研究与思想史研究，实际上是分属哲学与历史学两大学科的。哲学史研究属于哲学研究，而思想史研究则属于历史学研究。直到今天，这种状况依然没有改变。

但不可否认，在过去的很长时期里，哲学史研究与思想史研究从内涵与外延上看，似乎缺乏明确的区分，两者实在是很接近很相似。二十多年前，《哲学研究》曾就中国哲学史与中国思想史的关系问题展开讨论，编者按即言：“中国哲学史与思想史的关系问题，长期以来没有得到解决。这与中国古代文、史、哲不分，以及哲学与伦理、哲学与政治密切联系等传统有关。哲学史研究

的基本内容是什么？思想史是不是一门独立的学科？哲学史与思想史有些什么联系与区别？如何正确解决这些问题，关系到哲学史与思想史研究的深入和发展。”这些话确实反映了当时中国哲学史研究和中国思想史研究的实际。如侯外庐等著五卷本《中国思想通史》，虽然称为思想史，但实际上是以哲学史为其主要内容。这种思想史的写法，被后来的一些思想史研究者戏称为“大号哲学史”。

但自20世纪80年代以来，哲学史研究与思想史研究，在距离上明显地被拉开了，变得不相似了。这种学术现象的发生，可以说是哲学史研究者与思想史研究者双方努力的结果。一方面，哲学史家为了摆脱“唯物主义—唯心主义”两军对战的僵硬研究框架，发掘出中国哲学史与西方哲学史不同的内涵及特点，强调从认识史的视域研究哲学史，提出重视哲学范畴的研究，主张从历史上的哲学范畴的形成与演变入手来书写哲学史。这就使哲学史研究更重视在抽象的概念范畴之间开展，而与文化历史出现了明显的疏离。尽管以后哲学史研究中对哲学问题的重视取代了对哲学范畴的重视，但这种哲学问题的探讨仍局限在本体论、认识论、历史观等这些哲学自身的提问及展开上。另一方面，历史学家开始探寻与哲学史不相同的思想史的写法，从主张“思想史就是理论化的人类社会思想意识的发展史”，到主张思想史是“一般知识、思想与信仰世界的历史”，逐渐使思想史研究获得了自己独特的视野和内涵，不再以哲学史为自己的主要书写内容了。如葛兆光著两卷本《中国思想史》，就是不再以哲学史的叙述为其主要内容，而纳入了更多的具体的文化历史的内容，使思想史的写法与哲学史的写法大不相同。

这样一来，就使得哲学史研究与思想史研究出现了疏离，并由之开始出现了真正意义上的分野。哲学史研究主要探讨哲学自身的范畴与问题在历史上的开展，着重于形上的“思”的内容；而思想史研究则走向了对社会生活中的思潮、意识、观念的研究，着重于非形上的“史”的内容。这种疏离与分野，从哲学史研究与思想史研究的发展看，都有其积极的意义：对于哲学史研究而言，思想史研究成为了真正意义上的"他者"；而对于思想史研究来说，哲学史研究也同样如此；哲学史研究与思想史研究既互为"他者"，那么在两者间作认真的审视和相互的吸取也就成为可能。近年来，笔者就19—20世纪中国哲学研究提出开展"以哲学史为中心的思想史研究"，主张在哲学史研究与思想史研究之间加以沟通，使哲学史研究更多地吸取思想史研究的内容，实以此为其背景。

开展"以哲学史为中心的思想史研究"，其哲学史方法论意义何在呢？从根本上说，由于近二十多年的哲学史研究与思想史研究的疏离，使哲学史研究往往更注重哲学自身的逻辑展开，而对于哲学与文化历史之间的联系则被忽略了，往往只知在纯哲学的思辨中打圈子，而看不到还有许多这圈子之外的来自文化历史的丰富而深刻的思想内容。特别是19—20世纪中国哲学，更是与这一时代的文化历史大变迁密切相关联，不论是问题的提出、思潮的展开，还是学派的形成、体系的建构，往往都深深打上了这一时代的文化历史大变迁的印记。如果只探讨"思"而不看到"史"，忽略了哲学与文化历史的联系，19—20世纪中国哲学研究是难以深入开展的。因此，更多地吸取思想史研究的内容，使"思"的探讨与"史"的研究结合起来，使这一研究更有历史感与现实感，就势在必行了。

当然，"以哲学史为中心的思想史研究"，及其所主张的"思"与"史"的结合，对于19—20世纪中国哲学研究来说，是有其具体的内涵的。下面，即立足于这一研究，来对"以哲学史为中心的思想史研究"的方法论内涵，作进一步的具体说明。

二、扩大19—20世纪中国哲学研究的问题域

开展"以哲学史为中心的思想史研究"，首先在于扩大19—20世纪中国哲学研究的问题域，即扩大观察和把握19—20世纪中国哲学问题的视野。

自20世纪90年代以来，哲学史研究开始由对哲学范畴的关注转向对哲学问题的关注。哲学史研究，包括19—20世纪中国哲学研究，要以问题为中心来展开，现在已为越来越多的研究者所认同。但这一转变之中也存在着明显的不足：这就是问题域还不够大，研究工作往往局限于本体论、认识论、历史观这些哲学自身的提问及其展开，而不太关注那些处于哲学史与思想史之间的问题，不太关注那些直接来自文化历史的哲学问题，而这些问题对19—20世纪中国哲学来说确实是非常重要的。

要扩大19—20世纪中国哲学研究的问题域，就首先需要对哲学史上的哲学问题有一个深入的了解。在哲学史研究中，对哲学问题的重视，与对哲学范畴演变的重视，其指向、其意义是不相同的。对哲学范畴演变的重视，所凸显的是哲学观念之间的联系；而对哲学问题的重视，所凸显的是哲学观念与文化历史之间的联系。哲学观念与文化历史之间的联系在于：文化历史确定了哲学观念的特殊性及其在哲学史上的位置。正是这样，哲学观念被分离为一般与特殊两种类型。哲学观念的一般类型，是哲学自身的提问方式和自身的问题，如本体论、认识论等等。这些内容构成了哲学发展的内在的逻辑环节和逻辑进程。哲学观念的特殊类型，是不同时代、不同民族的提问方式及其问题。在这里，不仅有基于时代和传统的不同对哲学自身的提问方式和问题的不同理解，而且还有直接来自具体时代、具体民族的文化历史的特殊提问方式和特殊问题。这些特殊提问方式和特殊问题，往往不属于哲学自身的提问方式和自身的问题，并不是其他民族哲学发展中都会出现的；也往往与哲学自身的提问方式和自身的问题相比，而处于一种哲学史与思想史交叉的边缘性位置，其哲学理论不那么具有思辨性，其哲学意味也不那么浓烈。但正是这些哲学观念的特殊类型，使得哲学发展呈现出不同的时代特征和各异的民族风格。

在19—20世纪中国哲学的发展中，也明显地存在着这样两种提问方式。一个方面，19—20世纪中国哲学的发展，对于哲学自身的提问方式作出了具有时代特色的转换，在本体论、认识论、历史观等问题上多有创获；另一个方面，19—20世纪中国哲学的发展，则对于那些直接来自中国文化历史大变迁的特殊提问方式和特殊问题作出了思考，对近现代中国所面临的时代大问题予以了回答。如全球性现代化运动在近现代中国所引发的中西古今文化关系问题、中国现代化道路问题、全球化问题、现代性问题，特别是由此而引发的“中国向何处去”这一时代的大问题，就是这种直接来自中国文化历史大变迁的特殊提问方式和特殊问题。这些问题，并不是其他民族哲学发展中都会出现的，其思辨性、其哲学味都不那么强烈，可以说处于哲学史与思想史交叉的边缘性位置，但这些问题的提出、思考与探讨，不仅显示了19—20世纪中国哲学独特的内涵与风貌，而且又反过来影响着近现代中国的文化历史运动。

然而，在哲学观念的两种类型之间，在哲学的两种提问方式之间，长期以来哲学史家们往往更为关注前者，而不大关注后者，甚至认为后者的一些内容根本就不是哲学史的研究对象。特别是一些以西方哲学为各民族哲学发展唯一尺度的研究者，总是千方百计地以西方哲学的尺度去裁量19—20世纪中国哲学的发展，以为这些直接来自近现代中国文化历史大变迁的特殊提问方式和特殊问题，不是什么哲学问题，最多只能是思想问题。这就使得对19—20世纪中国哲学研究总是停留在纯粹的哲学范围里，沉浸在形上世界的思辨之中，演绎于抽象的概念范畴之间，而不甚关注这些直接来自文化历史的提问及其思考，缺乏由形上世界走向生活世界的兴趣。这些直接来自近现代中国文化历史进程的哲学提问，往往为哲学史家们所忽视，甚至被摒弃于他们的视域之外。其实，这些哲学问题同样是值得重视、值得研究的，同样是可以而且应当成为19—20世纪中国哲学研究的一个有机组成部分的。甚至可以说，正是由于有了这些问题进入到19—20世纪中国哲学研究中，这一研究才能保持同中国人的文化历史、同中国人的生活世界的更为密切更为鲜活的联系，才能保持鲜明的时代气息和民族根性，也才能不断丰富自己的研究内容、拓展自己的思维空间。因此，尽管这些问题没有在中国古代哲学史上出现过，更不曾在西方哲学史上出现过，也不是那种纯概念纯逻辑的东西，但却有自己的理论价值和实践价值，有自己激动人心的地方，有自己值得哲学史家认真研究、反复发掘的思想底蕴。这正如冯契在反思中国近代哲学史时所说：“中国近代经历了一次哲学革命，这次革命就在回答一个时代的中心问题：‘中国向何处去’？从鸦片战争到1949年，我国第一流的思想家，都在考虑这个问题：灾难深重的中华民族，如何才能获得自由解放，摆脱帝国主义的压迫、欺凌和奴役？一百多年来的志士仁人前仆后继，浴血奋战，就是为了解决这个‘中国向何处去’的问题。”一个关注中国历史命运和未来发展的19—20世纪中国哲学研究者，尤其应当关注19—20世纪中国哲学中这些直接来自文化历史进程的哲学问题，关注这些与“中国向何处去”这一时代的大问题密切相关的哲学问题。

因此，开展“以哲学史为中心的思想史研究”，首先在于扩大19—20世纪中国哲学研究的问题域，把这些处于哲学史与思想史之间的问题凸显出来，使之成为哲学史研究的重要问题。

三、关注19—20世纪中国哲学与中国思想世界的联系

开展“以哲学史为中心的思想史研究”，还意味着要把19—20世纪中国哲学研究的视野，扩大到整个的19—20世纪中国思想世界，关注19—20世纪中国哲学与19—20世纪中国思想世界的联系。换言之，即从19—20世纪中国哲学与中国思想世界的联系上，来深入研究19—20世纪中国哲学的开展。

对于19—20世纪中国思想世界的内涵，近二十年来思想史研究者们作了多方面的发掘与拓展，揭示出了其间的多层面的结构。从层面结构上看，19—20世纪中国思想世界的内涵，主要包含三个层面的思想形态：一是属于精英文化的观念形态的思想内容，二是观念形态与实际运动相结合的社会思潮，三是属于下层民间文化的群体意识与观念。关注19—20世纪中国哲学与近现代中国思想世界的联系，也就要求关注19—20世纪中国哲学与这些不同层面上的思想形态的联系。

首先，19—20世纪中国思想世界中的作为观念形态的思想内容，包含了哲学思想、经学思想、政治思想、宗教思想、史学思想、文艺思想、教育思想等多方面的内容。这些思想内容，都是由思想家们经过反复的思考、学理的探究、理论的论证、文字的表达而形成的思想成果，且多以体系性或理论性的方式阐发出来，具有精英人物个性化思想创造的特点。其中，除了哲学思想以探讨哲学问题为中心外，一些非哲学的观念形态也与哲学问题有着联系：或以哲学问题为框架，来建构自己的思想体系；或以哲学问题为核心，来展开自己的理论说明；或通过文学的、史学的、政治学的、教育学的等等不同的文本书写或体系建构，来表达某种哲学的理念。因此，这些思想内容，虽不属于纯粹哲学的范畴，但却仍然包含着哲学的思考，蕴含有哲学的意味，实是以一种特殊的形式展开了哲学的创作，值得哲学史研究者的关注与探讨。如19—20世纪中国史学发展，就与19世纪以来历史观的演变联系十分密切。魏源的《海国图志》、王韬的《法国志略》、黄遵宪的《日本国志》、郭沫若的《中国古代社会研究》、钱穆的《国史大纲》，在历史叙述中实表达了各自的历史观念；而梁启超的《中国历史研究法》、李大钊的《史学思想史》、翦伯赞的《历史哲学教程》，则更直接地阐发了他们的历史观念。从这些史学著述中，确能直接感触到中国历史观在19—20世纪的空前大变化。这种历史观的空前大变化，正反映了19—20世纪中国哲学的新发展。

其次，19—20世纪中国思想世界中还有一些内容，并不是以纯粹的观念形态的思想内容出现，而是以观念形态的思想内容与实际的社会运动结合在一起而展开的，表现为一种社会思潮。这些社会思潮都是针对并为解决某一重大社会问题而出现的。与作为观念形态的思想内容相比，这些社会思潮与实际生活、社会实践、下层民众有着更为密切的联系，成为19—20世纪中国思想世界中最为活跃的力量。这些社会思潮有着广大的民众的响应与参与，但其新的思想的提出、群众运动的发动、实践活动的开展，则往往是出自思想家的自觉思考与理论探索。因此，这些社会思潮虽然具有强烈的实践性质，但仍然是以思想家的思想创造为其主体的，其间也包含着哲学的框架或哲学的内核，仍然值得19—20世纪中国哲学研究者予以重视和研究。如19—20世纪中国思想世界中女性主义思潮的崛起、近世伦理观念的变化、反基督教运动的发生、乡村建设运动的开展等，都可以说属于这类社会思潮。19世纪末的维新思潮、20世纪初的革命思潮以及1915—1924年的新文化运动，也可以说是这类社会思潮。至于马克思主义哲学中国化进程，更有一个由理论而实践、由少数先进知识分子所掌握的哲学理念转化为有千百万群众投身其间的社会运动的问题。还有一些与某种社会实践相结合的思想运动，虽然规模与范围相对较小，但是持续较长、影响很大，如中国科学社对科学的提倡、宣传与切实的推进，就属于这类社会思潮。对于深入开展19—20世纪中国哲学研究来说，这些社会思潮中的哲学内容当然值得关注和研究，这些社会思潮与实际生活、社会实践、下层民众的联系其实也值得关注和研究。一种哲学理念，由书斋的学问而走向生活世界，而为广大群众所掌握，转化为广大群众的实际运动，往往是通过某种社会思潮来实现的。离开了社会思潮，仅从学理上，有时是难以衡论这种哲学理念的真正价值的。这里正可以用得上王夫之在《读四书大全说》中所说的那句名言："在势之必然处见理"。

再次，19—20世纪中国思想世界，除了观念形态的内容外，还有以非观念形态出现的属于下层民间文化的群体意识与观念。这种群体意识与观念，并非出自思想家的自觉思考与理论探索，而主要表现为广大民众的普遍意识与心理认同。由于缺乏自觉思考与理论探索，这种思想意识往往不是那么明晰、那么条理、那么具有学理性，有的时候还是只言片语，甚至还不见诸文字的记录。但在实际的历史运动中，这种群体意识与观念的影响与作用实是不可忽视的。这种群体意识与观念，尽管远离哲学家的哲学创作，但与哲学运动却有着实际的联系，只是这种联系有时候表现得比较模糊。但只要对19—20世纪中国思想世界作出认真而仔细的考察，就不难发现这种联系的实际存在。具体来看，这种联系大体从两个方面体现出来：一个方面，作为观念形态的哲学思想，通过各种媒介向下层民间文化大量而有力地渗透，使社会下层广大民众也得其时代精神，也感受到并认同于观念形态的变迁；另一个方面，属于下层民间文化的群体意识与观念，也会以不同的形式把自己的要求与意愿反映出来，影响着哲学家、思想家的思考，从而通过哲学家、思想家的思考在观念形态中得到理论的升华和表达。这种中国思想世界中的上下层面的联系与影响，精英哲学创作与民间意识观念的互动，在以往的19—20世纪中国哲学研究中没有引起重视，倒是一些中国思想史研究者作了有价值的探讨。如台湾学者李孝悌近年所著《清末的下层社会启蒙运动：1901—1911》一书，专门探讨20世纪第一个十年中，作为观念形态的新思想，是如何通过当时的白话报刊、阅报社、讲报、演说、戏曲等媒介手段，向广大下层民众渗透，使之也逐渐开化而认同新思想的。

上述三个层面，可以说是19—20世纪中国哲学与中国思想世界相联系的主要层面，也是19—20世纪中国哲学研究需要了解、学习、吸纳中国思想史研究成果的主要层面。

四、凸显19—20世纪中国哲学与文化历史环境的联系

开展“以哲学史为中心的思想史研究”，还在于凸显19—20世纪中国哲学与19—20世纪中国文化历史环境的联系。换言之，即从19—20世纪中国哲学与文化历史环境的联系上，来深入研究19—20世纪中国哲学的开展。

19—20世纪中国哲学与文化历史环境的联系，集中表现为近现代中国文化历史大变迁，给予了中国哲学发展以深刻的影响。自鸦片战争开始，中国被卷入全球性现代化运动，开始进入现代化的历史进程，这就使得中国文化历史原来自成一系的格局被打破了，中西古今文化发生了大碰撞、大交流、大融会，新的生产方式、新的社会力量、新的社会生活出现了，中华民族反抗外来侵略者的斗争与中国人民反对本国反动统治者的斗争交织为时代的主旋律，促

成了中国由封建社会向半殖民地半封建社会再向社会主义社会的发展。

这种文化历史大变迁对中国哲学的最直接的影响，在于促成了中国哲学的转型。19—20世纪中国哲学之不同于以往时代的中国哲学，当然首先在于哲学形态发生了历史性的转换，由古代形态而近代形态而现代形态。在中国哲学的古代形态中，已于明清之际开始孕育近代哲学的因素，形成了影响一时的早期启蒙思潮，但直到鸦片战争前这种新因素仍未能发展出独立的近代形态哲学。正如侯外庐所指出的，这种新因素长期处于一种“难产”状态。正是由于自鸦片战争以来中国哲学的文化历史环境发生了前所未有的大变化，才推动着中国哲学实现了由古代形态而近代形态而现代形态的历史性变化。因此，19—20世纪中国哲学的开展是与中国哲学的文化历史环境密不可分的。

19—20世纪中国，要解决中华民族与帝国主义、人民大众与封建主义两大基本矛盾，最主要的方式只能是政治。因此，这一时代的文化历史大变迁，是以政治为中心而展开的，其中当然有许多重大的政治变动与政治斗争，包括了变法、革命与战争，这些都对19—20世纪中国哲学的开展产生了重要的影响。正是这样，在这一段哲学史上，不少有贡献的哲学家并不是专业哲学家，不少哲学创作并不是在平静的书斋里完成的，即使是专业哲学家也往往亲身经历过时代的风雨洗礼。艾思奇的《大众哲学》和李达的《社会学大纲》，是在同国民党反动派的思想斗争中产生的。毛泽东的《实践论》与《矛盾论》，更是在中国的山沟里写出的。冯友兰的《新理学》和金岳霖的《论道》，也是在抗战之初的南下流亡途中完成的。晚年冯友兰曾深情地谈到时代的大变局对于他与金岳霖哲学创作的深刻影响。他说：“1937年中日战争开始。我同金先生随着清华到湖南加入长沙临时大学。文学院设在南岳，在那里住了几个月。那几个月的学术空气最浓，我们白天除了吃饭上课以外，就各自展开了自己的写作摊子，金先生的《论道》和我的《新理学》都是在那里形成的。从表面上看，我们好象是不顾困难，躲入了‘象牙之塔’。其实我们都是怀着满腔悲愤无处发泄。那个悲愤是我们那样做的动力”。而金岳霖、冯友兰的学生冯契，于20

世纪 80 年代建构起“智慧说”这一个性化和中国化的马克思主义哲学体系，也是与他早年投身革命、接受马克思主义哲学分不开的。

除了这种大的文化历史变迁外，19—20 世纪中国文化历史中的一些具体的新因素新内容，特别是文化教育领域的新因素新内容，对中国思想世界及哲学发展发生了更直接更具体的影响。如近现代出版业的出现与发展，近现代报刊的出现与发展，现代大学及其哲学系的出现与发展，就是如此。19—20 世纪中国思想世界的变动，19—20 世纪中国哲学运动的开展，可以说是与这些文化历史中的新因素新内容分不开的。

中国的近现代出版业，在鸦片战争后，首先在刚刚开埠的上海出现。1843 年，英国传教士麦都思即来上海，建立了上海的第一个近代出版机构——墨海书馆，开始出版西学著作，除了出版有关宣传基督教方面的书籍外，还出版了一批近代自然科学著作。以后，一大批近代出版机构，如在 19 世纪下半叶产生很大影响的江南制造局翻译馆和广学会，在 20 世纪产生很大影响的商务印书馆和中华书局，相继在上海创办，使得上海成为了近代中国的出版中心。近现代出版业的兴起和发达，有力地促进了新知识、新思想、新哲学的传播。反动统治阶级的思想控制和话语霸权，也由于近现代出版业的兴起而被冲破了。邹容撰写的《革命军》，于 1903 年在上海由大同书局出版，在中国内地高举起反清革命的思想旗帜，对革命思想深入人心起了重要的推动作用。陈望道翻译的《共产党宣言》，于 1920 年在上海由社会主义研究社出版，对一大批新青年了解马克思主义、转向马克思主义起了重要的引导作用。中国共产党成立后，先后在上海建立了新青年社、人民出版社、上海书店、华兴书局等出版机构，出版了一批马克思主义著作。一些 19—20 世纪中国哲学家也曾在出版机构中工作或主持出版事业，如王韬曾在墨海书馆任编辑工作，洪仁玕曾在墨海书馆学习西学，陈独秀曾主持新青年社，李达曾主持人民出版社。抗日战争时期，商务印书馆在流亡中艰难支撑，出版了冯友兰的《新理学》、金岳霖的《论道》、熊十力的《新唯识论》等重要哲学著作，这些著作标志着 20 世纪中国哲学发展中几个最有影响力的本体论体系的建立，也使得抗日战争时期成为19—20世纪中国哲学的一个大收获时期。因此，近现代出版业的出现与发展，对19—20世纪中国哲学运动起了直接的推动作用。

报刊，这个中国古代所未有过的新事物，也在鸦片战争后伴随着近现代出版业的兴起而出现了。近现代报刊的出现和发展，使人们之间的信息的传播和思想的交流变得方便快捷了，为新知识、新思想、新哲学传播提供了重要的工具。而这些刊物由于主编者或主笔者的原因，多具有鲜明的思想倾向性，代表着某种观念形态，影响着某种社会思潮的走向。近现代中国的政治变革和思想变革，往往是与近现代报刊相联系的。王韬主编的《循环日报》，使中国人更直接地了解西方世界。梁启超任主笔的《时务报》，对于宣传维新思想起了积极作用。章士钊任主笔的《苏报》，成为宣传反清革命思想的一面旗帜。陈独秀主持的《新青年》杂志，宣告了新文化运动的到来。李达主编的《共产党》杂志，让中国第一次听到了中国共产党的声音。任鸿隽主编的《科学》杂志，对传播科学思想起了重要的作用。吴宓主编的《学衡》杂志，成为了文化保守主义的阵地。储安平主编的《观察》周刊，则集中体现了近代中国自由主义的呼声。一些重要思想论战，往往是通过刊物来开展，如新文化运动时期的东西文化问题论战，首先就是在《新青年》与《东方杂志》之间展开的。一些重要的哲学著作，也是先在刊物上以文章形式发表再结集为书的，如艾思奇的《大众哲学》，最初就是以《哲学讲话》在《读书生活》半月刊上分篇发表的。许多哲学家、思想家都有自己办报刊的经历，这种经历对其学问其思想产生了重要的影响，如徐复观由国民党要员转变成现代新儒学大师，最初的第一步就是从创办学术刊物《学原》而开始的。20世纪50年代，西化派自由主义思潮与现代新儒学思潮在台湾香港地区的新开展及相互间的思想论争，也是依托于《自由中国》与《民主评论》两个刊物。可以说，如果没有这么多的报刊，19—20世纪中国哲学决不会如此丰富多彩。

现代大学及其哲学系在20世纪中国的出现，使得哲学脱离了传统的经学和传统的书院，成为一门专门性的人文学科。进入这门学科的学习者，需要接受较严格的专业性训练，这是中国传统人文教育所不具有的。在这方面，北京大学的哲学专门教育无疑是开展得最早而且是最具代表性的。北京大学中国哲学门在 1912 年设立，标志着中国现代哲学教育的诞生，对于以后中国哲学的发展产生了深远的影响。冯友兰就毕业于北京大学中国哲学门，算得上是中国哲学史上最早一位由中国现代大学哲学系培养、接受过现代哲学专业训练的著名哲学家。清华大学哲学系的建立，则与北京大学哲学系形成了不同哲学风格之间的对比与互动。而在长江流域，武昌中华大学中国哲学门亦于 1915 年设立。后来成为马克思主义思想家的恽代英，是中华大学中国哲学门第一届学生，接受过专业性的哲学训练，学习期间就开始在《新青年》《东方杂志》《光华学报》上发表《新无神论》《怀疑论》《物质实在论》《论信仰》等哲学论文。进入 20 世纪 20 年代后，东南大学、武汉大学也都设立了哲学系。在这些现代大学哲学系中，聚集了一批哲学家，从事专业性的哲学教学和研究，使这些哲学系成为哲学教学和研究的中心，对于现代中国哲学的开展功莫大焉。以 20 世纪上半叶论，在北京大学哲学系，曾聚集过胡适、梁漱溟、熊十力、汤用彤、贺麟等著名哲学家；在清华大学哲学系，曾聚集过金岳霖、冯友兰、张岱年等著名哲学家；在东南大学哲学系，曾聚集过汤用彤、方东美、宗白华等著名哲学家；在武汉大学哲学系，曾聚集过范寿康、张颐、洪谦、金克木等著名哲学家。在这些现代大学哲学系所培养的学生中，出现了一大批有影响的中国哲学家。如在西南联合大学时期金岳霖指导的研究生中，就出了冯契、殷海光、王浩等著名哲学家。此外，一些师范学校也有比较好的哲学教育。如毛泽东在长沙湖南省立第一师范学校就读时，就由杨昌济讲授伦理学，使他开始爱好哲学。还有一些特殊的学校，如 20 世纪 20 年代国共两党合作主办的上海大学、毛泽东亲自创办的湖南自修大学，也很重视哲学教育。瞿秋白曾在上海大学任社会学系主任，讲授唯物辩证法；李达曾在湖南自修大学任学长，讲授唯物史观；这些对于推动马克思主义哲学在中国的传播起过很大的作用。抗日战争爆发后，北京大学、清华大学、南开大学奉命南迁，组建成长沙临时大学—西南联合大学，更集中了一大批优秀的专业哲学家，形成了全国最好的大学哲学系。金岳霖的“道论”、冯友兰的“新理学”、贺麟的“新心学”，这几个著名的融会中西古今思想而成的哲学本体论体系，都是在长沙临时大学—西南联合大学时期建构的。

地域文化的差异，在古代社会生活中，由于交通与信息的不发达、经济的自给自足、政治上的不统一，往往表现得很鲜明。在19—20世纪中国，这种差异并没有因现代化进程而消失。由于传统的地域文化差异的影响，更由于中国现代化进程的不平衡性，使得在地域文化上仍然存在着明显的不同，这对19—20世纪中国哲学开展发生了很大的影响。由于珠江三角洲地区开风气最早，所以在19—20世纪出现了一大批向西方寻求真理的先进思想人物，洪秀全、洪仁玕、郑观应、康有为、梁启超、孙中山、朱执信都是广东籍人士。上海自1843年开埠到19世纪末，迅速成为中国现代化程度最高的大城市，因而成为新思想新哲学最活跃的地区，梁启超主笔的《时务报》、章士钊主笔的《苏报》、陈独秀主编的《新青年》、李达主编的《共产党》、储安平主编的《观察》，这些在19—20世纪中国思想世界影响一时的著名报刊，都是在上海主办和出版的。湖北东部地区，一方面因邻近武汉，能够直接感受到现代化进程的气息，另一方面直到20世纪前期仍然停留在传统农业社会生活中，长期保留着中国文化传统，因此从这里走出的熊十力、徐复观、闻一多、殷海光等思想人物，一方面接受和倡导新思想，另一方面又对传统文化有着程度不同的依恋。而湖南自19世纪起，则成为近代中国政治风雷激荡之地，湘军的崛起、维新的呼唤、自立军的起义、华兴会的斗争、大革命中的农民运动、中国共产党领导的土地革命战争，使得湖南在百年之间出现了一大批政治哲学家，以他们的思想与实践深刻地影响了中国历史进程，曾国藩、郭嵩焘、谭嗣同、唐才常、陈天华、毛泽东、蔡和森、刘少奇等，都属这类人物。因此，地域文化对于19—20世纪中国哲学的影响，以及两者之间的互动，是值得深入研究的。

从上述论析中可以清楚看出，19—20世纪中国哲学的开展，不仅是中国哲学家的个性化的自我创作，而且同时又是与文化历史环境直接相联系的。“思”与“史”、哲学创作与文化历史的密切联系，在这些方面最为鲜活地表现出来。哲学史研究的生命活力与理论深刻性，在很大的程度上，是要从这里吸取的。

（原载《哲学研究》2007年第1期；又载李维武著《中国哲学的现代转型》，中华书局2008年版。《哲学研究》编者把本文题名改为《蕴含思想史维度的哲学史研究——对19—20世纪中国哲学研究的方法论思考》，并对文中有关提法作了相应改动。收入《中国哲学的现代转型》一书时，恢复了原稿的题名及被改动的内容。这里据《中国哲学的现代转型》一书所载文字收录）

关于“以哲学史为中心的思想史研究”的再思考

李维武

开展“以哲学史为中心的思想史研究”，是笔者在十多年前结合自己所从事的19—20世纪中国哲学研究而提出的，希望以此作为拓展和深化19—20世纪中国哲学研究的一种新的方法论。这些年来，笔者在19—20世纪中国哲学研究中，对这个新的方法论作了进一步的思考、探讨与运用。在这里，把自己的所思所得，以“再思考”的形式作一概括性说明，以求教于方家同道。

一、哲学史与思想史的区分

“哲学史”与“思想史”，这两个概念在中国学术史上出现并为学术界广泛使用，已有近百年的时间。新文化运动中，胡适在北京大学主讲“中国哲学史”课程并著《中国哲学史大纲（卷上）》，李大钊在北京大学开设“史学思想史”课程并撰《史学思想史》讲义，就是这两个概念在当时已经广泛使用的证明。此后近百年间，中国学者撰写了许多部题名为“哲学史”或“思想史”的著作。

但长期以来，这些被称为“哲学史”或“思想史”的著作，往往并没有作哲学史与思想史的明确区分，或者把“哲学史”和“思想史”看作是大同小异的概念，或者认为思想史包含了哲学史、哲学史被包含在思想史中。特别是一些标明为“思想史”的著作，主要论述的其实还是哲学史的内容。如吕振羽著《中国政治思想史》、侯外庐著《中国近世思想学说史》以及侯外庐主编的五卷本《中国思想通史》，实际上都是以哲学史为主要内容的思想史著作。这种思想史的书写方式，在今天的一些思想史学者看来，只是一种“大号哲学史”。

中国学术界以自觉的学科划分意识，对哲学史与思想史的各自内涵及其两者关系进行深刻反思，并真正地把哲学史与思想史明确区分开来，则是20世纪80年代的事情。1983—1984年，中国学术界曾就哲学史与思想史的关系问题展开讨论。《哲学研究》发表了一批相关文章，并在“编者按”中指出了所要解决的主要问题：“中国哲学史与思想史的关系问题，长期以来没有得到解决。这与中国古代文、史、哲不分，以及哲学与伦理、哲学与政治密切联系等传统有关。哲学史研究的基本内容是什么？思想史是不是一门独立的学科？哲学史与思想史有些什么联系与区别？如何正确解决这些问题，关系到哲学史与思想史研究的深入和发展。”这场讨论是完全学术性的，规模并不算大，参与者也不很多，但对哲学史研究和思想史研究都产生了很大的影响。

这次讨论的一个重要理论成果，在于厘清了哲学史与思想史的各自内涵，从而使哲学史与思想史开始明确区分开来。通过讨论，人们不仅认识到哲学史与思想史是两种不同的学问，而且认识到哲学史与思想史分属于两个不同的学科：哲学史属于哲学学科，思想史则属于历史学学科。作为哲学学科的分支，哲学史所研究的是哲学发生发展的历史，主要探讨哲学自身的范畴与问题在历史上的逻辑开展；作为历史学学科的分支，思想史所探讨的则是人的精神生活发生发展的历史，走向了对社会生活中的思潮、意识、观念、群体性心理的具体研究。简言之，哲学史着重于探讨形而上的“思”，思想史则着重于探讨非形而上的“史”。“思”是指哲学思维的抽象性、逻辑性，“史”则是指历史运动的现实性、经验性。由此可见，探讨“思”的哲学史与探讨“史”的思想史具有相对的独立性，两者并不是大同小异的，也不是前者包含在后者之中的。

基于对哲学史与思想史关系的新认识，哲学史学者与思想史学者分别作出了努力，凸显了哲学史的“思”的特征和思想史的“史”的特征。在哲学史方面，提出了中国哲学史的“泛化”与“纯化”问题。周继旨的《关于中国哲学史研究对象、范围的“纯化”与“泛化”问题》一文，就集中反映了当时哲学史学者对这一问题的看法，认为“一部内容过于‘泛化’了的哲学史，就混同于一般的思想史，失去了自己应有的特点”，因此需要“对中国哲学史的研究对象来一番‘纯化’，把不属于哲学范畴的内容‘排除’出去”。20世纪80年代在中国哲学史研究中盛行的哲学范畴研究，旨在把抽象性、逻辑性的“思”与现实性、经验性的“史”分离开来，体现了哲学史学者在“纯化”方面所下的功夫。在思想史方面，葛兆光著两卷本《中国思想史》的问世，鲜明地体现了思想史学者把思想史区分于哲学史的自觉。尽管人们对葛著有不同的意见，但有一点看法当是一致的，这就是它已不再是那种以哲学史为主要内容的思想史著作了，改变了那种“大号哲学史”的思想史书写方式。需要说明的是，这里所说的思想史着重于非形而上的“史”，并没有任何贬抑的含意。形而上与非形而上，在这里只是就研究对象的性质和特点言，形而上意味着“思”的抽象性、逻辑性，非形而上则意味着“史”的现实性、经验性，不是说后者不如前者重要。一些对思想史有自觉认识的学者，也是这样看待思想史的。如孙歌著《思想史中的日本与中国》一书，自序的题目即《在形而下层面结构原理》，强调了思想史研究的性质和特点在于立足“形而下层面”。

考察自20世纪80年代以来的哲学史研究与思想史研究，就会发现由于研究者们开始自觉地意识和把握哲学史与思想史不同的性质和特点，使得哲学史研究与思想史研究获得了各自独立的发展空间，从而有力地推进了两者的开展。

二、哲学史与思想史联系的重构

哲学史与思想史被明确区分开来以后，给中国哲学史研究所带来的影响是双重的，既有积极的一面，也有局限的一面。积极的一面在于：在中国哲学史研究中凸显了对形而上的“思”的重视，更重视哲学史内容的抽象性、逻辑性，从而凸显了哲学史的内在逻辑开展，使中国哲学史研究更具有哲学意味，深化了中国哲学史研究。从20世纪80年代开展的中国哲学范畴研究，到20世纪

90年代转而进行的中国哲学问题探讨，可以看到哲学史学者从“思”的方面逐渐深化哲学史研究的轨迹。局限的一面在于：这种对形而上的“思”的重视，又不免疏离了非形而上的“史”，使中国哲学史研究由于过分强调抽象的逻辑开展，而忽视了来自历史文化的现实性、经验性。这样一来，中国哲学史研究往往只知在纯哲学的思辨中打圈子，而看不到还有许多这圈子之外的来自历史文化的丰富而深刻的思想内容。对于哲学史的探讨，当然少不了对哲学演进的内在逻辑的揭示，但又不能使这种逻辑缺乏现实性和历史感，成为了一种纯粹在思辨中开展的抽象的东西。

针对由此所导致的哲学史研究中“思”与“史”的疏离，中国哲学界的有识之士又提出把“思”与“史”重新结合起来、重构哲学史与思想史联系的要求。在这方面，笔者的老师萧萐父先生在1989年写过一篇题为《哲学史研究中的纯化和泛化》短文，表达了他对中国哲学史的“泛化”与“纯化”问题的新思考：“鉴于哲学史研究曾羼入许多非哲学的思想资料，往往与一般思想史、学说史浑杂难分，我们曾强调应当净化哲学概念，厘清哲学史研究的特定对象和范围，把一些伦理、道德、宗教、政法等等非哲学思想资料筛选出去，使哲学史纯化为哲学认识史，以便揭示哲学矛盾运动的特殊规律。但进一步考虑哲学与文化的关系，文化是哲学赖以生长的土壤，哲学是文化的活的灵魂，哲学所追求的是人的价值理想在真、善、美创造活动中的统一实现；哲学，可以广义地界定为‘人学’，文化，本质地说就是‘人化’。因而这些年我们又强调哲学史研究可以泛化为哲学文化史。以哲学史为核心的文化史或以文化史为铺垫的哲学史，更能充分反映人的智慧创造和不断自我解放的历程。”萧老师在这里所说的哲学与文化的关系以及哲学史研究的“泛化”方法，所依据的是马克思的“哲学正变成文化的活的灵魂”的思想，体现了对马克思主义哲学史观的坚持。从主张哲学史研究的“纯化”，到重提哲学史研究的“泛化”，实则提出了哲学史与思想史联系的重构问题，要求在哲学史研究中把“思”与“史”有机地结合起来。萧老师的这篇短文只有几百字，对于这一问题没有作更多的论述，但却是十分富有启发性的。

类似的思考在冯契那里也提出了。进入20世纪90年代后，冯契主编了“中国近代社会思潮研究丛书”，带领一批中青年哲学史学者，把近代中国哲学史研究拓展为以社会思潮史为主体的思想史研究。他在丛书总序中写道：“收入本丛书的著作，它们所研究的，可以主要是哲学思想，或者政治思潮，或者文化及宗教思潮，即每一部著作的侧重面可能颇不相同，但作为丛书整体，强调的是社会思潮。换句话说，不管这些思潮的侧重面在哪里，它们都是对整个社会发生广泛影响的思潮，而不是只在狭窄的专业圈之内发生影响的理论。所以，收入本丛书的著作与一般的近代哲学史或思想史的著作将有很大的不同，它常常需要跨越政治、哲学、宗教、文学艺术、教育乃至俗文化、社会生活方式等诸多领域，从而反映出社会思潮自身的广度与深度。在方法上，本丛书注重研究在中国近代特定的社会历史条件下，西方思想如何传入并影响中国，而中国古代传统又如何被发掘、继承及转化，从而使形成的一系列社会思潮既具有时代特征，又富于民族特点。由于其中相当一部分社会思潮是在西方同类思潮的传播下发展起来的，所以为了把握它们的近代民族特点，又需要通过中西比较的途径。”这清楚表明，19—20世纪中国哲学研究需要有一个更为广大的视域，这不仅是一个研究范围的扩大问题，更是一个研究范式的转换问题；这一思维范式转换的根本点在于，由哲学史所强调的“思”而转向思想史所强调的“史”。萧老师曾同笔者谈到冯契与他的关系，称这一关系为“师友之间”。据笔者的研究和体会，两位先生之间确有许多相似相通之处。在重构哲学史与思想史联系的问题上，两人也有相似相通的地方，这就是重视哲学史研究的现实性和历史感。

正是在这一大背景下，特别是受到萧老师这篇短文的启发，笔者结合自己所从事的19—20世纪中国哲学研究，提出了“以哲学史为中心的思想史研究”的方法论，以求在哲学史研究中把形而上的“思”与非形而上的“史”结合起来，改变那种只注重哲学史自身的逻辑展开而忽视哲学史与历史文化之间联系的状况。具体到19—20世纪中国哲学，笔者认为关注这一时代的中国哲学与历史文化的关联，要着重从三个方面加以把握：一是由历史文化扩大19—20世纪中国哲学研究的问题域；二是建立19—20世纪中国哲学与中国思想世界的联系；三是凸显19—20世纪中国哲学与历史文化环境的联系。下面，就分别从这三个方面，具体说明如何开展“以哲学史为中心的思想史研究”。

三、从思想史发现19—20世纪中国哲学的问题

哲学史要重视问题的研究，这本来是哲学史研究的题中应有之义。20世纪90年代，由于哲学史与思想史的明确区分，以及由此而来的哲学史研究对哲学范畴的重视，中国哲学史研究中的问题意识曾一度被遮蔽、被淡化。进入20世纪90年代后，随着哲学史研究由对哲学范畴的重视转向对哲学问题的重视，问题意识之于中国哲学史的重要性逐渐成为哲学史学者的共识。笔者在1990年完成的博士学位论文《20世纪中国哲学本体论问题》，就从一个方面体现了中国哲学史研究重心由哲学范畴向哲学问题的转移。

但是，中国哲学史的问题有哪些？这些哲学问题从何而来？在这些问题上，哲学史学者却存在着相当大的分歧。在许多人看来，哲学史中的哲学问题当然是历史上的哲学家所提出来的，并为以后的哲学家们反复探讨而逐渐深化，但很难说哪个哲学家能够成为这些哲学问题的终结者。张东荪就说过：“一部哲学史不是问题的解决，乃是问题的翻新。”这些哲学问题，是哲学自身的提问方式和自身的问题。哲学史的核心问题，如本体论与认识论问题，就是这样的问题。还有的问题虽然不能算是哲学史的核心问题，如历史观与文化观问题，但在一定意义上也是这样的问题。哲学家们围绕这些古已有之的问题所展开的反复思考与不断探讨，就构成了哲学史开展的内在的逻辑环节和逻辑进程。冯契在《中国古代哲学的逻辑发展》一书中指出哲学史上提出的广义认识论问题主要有四个：一是感觉能否给予客观实在。二是理论思维能否达到科学

真理。三是逻辑思维能否把握具体真理（首先是世界统一原理、宇宙发展法则）。四是人能否获得自由。这些问题都属于哲学自身的提问方式和自身的问题，因而了解和把握中国古代哲学的逻辑发展必须从这些问题入手。当然，他又指出，西方哲学家和中国哲学家由于各自的历史文化环境的不同，因而对这四个问题的理解各有特点：西方哲学家更注重对前两个问题的思考与探讨，中国哲学家更注重对后两个问题的思考与探讨，由此形成了西方哲学史与中国哲学史各自的特色与精义。但这四个问题都是哲学自身的提问方式和自身的问题，则是没有疑义的。

在中国哲学史上，除了哲学自身的提问方式和自身的问题外，还有一些特殊的提问方式和特殊的问题。这些特殊的提问方式和特殊的问题，来自历史文化、来自社会生活、来自时代，总之是来自马克思所说的“现实世界”；特别是在那些历史文化发生巨变、社会生活充满矛盾、国家民族前途面临选择的时代，就会从现实世界中提出一些需要反复思考与不断探讨的重大问题，受到忧国忧民的哲学家的关注与求索。这些来自现实世界的特殊的提问方式和特殊的问题，不是哲学史上古已有之的，也不是各个民族、各个国家的哲学发展中都会出现的，因而与哲学自身的提问方式和自身的问题相比，不具有那么强的思辨性和那么浓的哲学味，往往处于哲学史与思想史交叉的边缘性位置，以至被人们看成是思想史的问题而不是哲学史的问题。但这些问题由于关乎国家民族的命运与前途，且需要经过哲学家的反复思考与不断探索，因而也同样是十分重要的哲学问题，特别是对于显示一个民族、一个国家哲学史的特殊性具有十分重要的意义。19—20 世纪中国，正是这样一个经历巨变、充满矛盾、选择道路的时代；这个时代的中国哲学家，不仅要面对来自哲学自身的提问方式和自身的问题，而且要面对来自现实世界的特殊的提问方式和特殊的问题。正是这样，冯契在衡论 19—20 世纪中国哲学时，根据自己青年时代投入革命洪流的亲身感受，特别凸显哲学问题的时代性和现实性，特别强调“哲学要把握时代脉搏”、“哲学要回答时代的问题”。可以说，这种哲学与现实世界的密切关联，这种哲学对时代之问的回答，正是19—20世纪中国哲学的显著特点。因此，19—20世纪中国哲学研究，应当关注这些来自现实世界的特殊的提问方式和特殊的问题，把这些内容纳入到哲学史研究中来。

鸦片战争后中国哲学家反复探讨的“中国向何处去”问题，就是这样一个时代大问题。毫无疑问，这个问题是19—20世纪中国哲学的特殊的提问方式和特殊的问题。在西方哲学的开展中，在中国古代哲学的开展中，都不会提出这个问题；只有当中国在鸦片战争后被卷入全球性现代化运动、需要在世界历史整体发展中作出选择时，这个问题才会尖锐地提到中国人面前，成为了19—20世纪中国哲学的重大问题。冯契在《中国近代哲学的革命进程》一书中就指出，近代中国的时代中心问题是“中国向何处去”，“许多有成就的思想家并不是专门研究哲学的，他们研究哲学主要是为了回答‘中国向何处去’的问题”。因此，他强调：“研究中国近代哲学，首先要看到这一特点：中国近代史上很多思想家是爱国者，是革命家，他们代表了中华民族的希望，代表了中华民族的优秀传统。他们的热情、意志、思想都集中在解决‘中国向何处去’的问题。”然而，由于“中国向何处去”这个问题的特殊性，在许多人看来，这个问题只是思想史问题而不是哲学史问题，因而容易为哲学史学者所忽视。

这类容易被忽视的来自现实世界的哲学问题，在19—20世纪中国哲学中还有很多。例如，环绕“中国向何处去”这一时代大问题，一百多年来中国哲学家又探讨了一系列相关的重大问题，诸如封闭与开放、守旧与维新、改良与革命、立宪与共和、启蒙与救亡、旧民主主义与新民主主义、资本主义与社会主义等等。这些看似不属于哲学史而只属于思想史的问题，却构成了19—20世纪中国政治哲学开展的主要内容。政治哲学在21世纪的今天已经受到中国哲学界的广泛重视，但是研究者们或者只重视罗尔斯的著述，或者只重视古代儒家的思想，希望从这些地方发掘出建构21世纪中国政治哲学的资源，而很少关注19—20世纪中国哲学家环绕上述问题所进行的艰苦探索，以此作为21世纪中国政治哲学的直接源头。其所以如此，一个重要的原因，就是感到这些问题以及由此引发的思考和探索，时代性、现实性很强而思辨性、抽象性较弱，既不曾在西方哲学史上出现过，又不曾在中国古代哲学史上出现过，只是属于思想史的内容而不是属于哲学史的内容。

与“中国向何处去”这一时代大问题相联系，还有19—20世纪中国哲学中的历史观与文化观的一些问题。历史观与文化观的一些内容，也可以说是哲学自身的提问方式和自身的问题，如历史的进化问题、规律问题、动力问题，文化的华夷之辨、文质之辨、古今之辨，都是古已有之的；但对于19—20世纪中国哲学来说，历史观与文化观的更主要内容却是今才有之的，是与近现代中国的历史走向和中国文化的重新选择直接联系在一起的。比如：如何看待鸦片战争后中国社会历史所发生的天翻地覆大变局？如何看待由此而来的中西古今文化的碰撞、交流、融合？如何看待中国传统文化在全球性现代化运动中的价值和作用？如何面对西方文化的强烈影响来选择中国文化发展的道路？这些来自现实世界的问题，引起了19—20世纪中国哲学家的普遍关注和反复探讨，直到21世纪的今天这种关注和探讨也还在继续之中。这种关注和探讨所形成的思想成果，不是思辨的历史哲学或文化哲学，而是对中国历史走向和中西古今文化关系的具体阐发，因而往往被看作是思想史的内容而不是哲学史的内容。

笔者提出“以哲学史为中心的思想史研究”，就是希望从思想史视域对19—20世纪中国哲学的问题域加以拓展，把这些处于哲学史与思想史交叉的边缘性位置的问题，把这些看似不属于哲学史而只属于思想史的问题，都纳入到19—20世纪中国哲学研究中来，作为19—20世纪中国哲学的重要问题。因此，笔者主张在看待19—20世纪中国哲学问题时，既重视来自哲学自身的提问方式和自身的问题，又重视来自现实世界的特殊的提问方式和特殊的问题，将这两类提问方式和问题有机结合起来，作一综合性考察和总体性理解。这就形成了19—20世纪中国哲学基本问题的层次性和结构性。从逻辑上看，即从哲学问题由一般到特殊、由抽象到具体看，这些哲学问题集中在三个层面上：

在最抽象的层面上，是本体论与认识论问题；在居中的层面上，是历史观与文化观问题；在最具体的层面上，是政治哲学问题。这样一来，就使19—20世纪中国哲学研究拥有了更为宽阔的问题域，获得了鲜明的时代性和强烈的历史感，能够更完整地展现这一时代中国哲学的丰富内容，更系统地反映这一时代中国哲学家的思想贡献。

四、从思想史拓展19—20世纪中国哲学的研究空间

拓展哲学史的研究空间，对于推进哲学史研究来说，是一项重要的工作。从方法论上看，这一拓展工作大体上包括两个方面的工作：一是哲学史内部的拓展，另一是哲学史外部的拓展。哲学史内部的拓展，主要是对哲学史的内在逻辑进程进行重新梳理以及对进程诸环节研究的深入与细化；哲学史外部的拓展，主要是建构和拓展哲学史与思想史的联系，把更多的与哲学史有关联的思想史内容纳入到哲学史研究中来。这种哲学史外部的拓展，也就是从思想史拓展哲学史的研究空间，构成了"以哲学史为中心的思想史研究"的重要内容。

在19—20世纪中国哲学研究中，如何从思想史拓展哲学史的研究空间，把更多的与哲学史有关联的思想史内容纳入到哲学史研究中来呢？关键一点，在于进入19—20世纪中国思想世界，从中发掘出、梳理出那些具有哲学史意义的思想史内容，由此来重构哲学史与思想史的联系。在这里，笔者感到有三个方面的思想史内容尤其值得发掘和梳理。

一是哲学与其他相邻学科的联系。进入20世纪后，现代学科体系取代传统经学体系在中国得以确立，成为现代学术、教育和知识发展的基本框架。由此而来，不仅有了专门的哲学学科，而且有了哲学与其他相邻学科的联系。这种联系从实质上看是一种思想史的联系：哲学为其他学科提供了思维框架，其他学科则为哲学开展提供了更大空间。不论是哲学与自然科学诸学科的联系，还是哲学与人文科学、社会科学诸学科的联系，都具有这种思想史的意义。因

此，从思想史拓展19—20世纪中国哲学的研究空间，可以从哲学与相邻学科的这种思想史联系入手，从中发掘出哲学对这些学科的影响，梳理出这些学科中所蕴含的哲学因素，将这些内容纳入到哲学史研究中。在这方面，前辈学者已经做了富有启发性的开拓工作。前述李大钊撰写的《史学思想史》讲义，其着力点就在于阐发史学思想史中的历史观开展，指出："历史观本身亦有其历史，其历史亦有一定的倾向。大体言之，由神权的历史观进而为人生的历史观，由精神的历史观进而为物质的历史观，由个人的历史观进而为社会的历史观，由退落的或循环的历史观进而为进步的历史观。神权的、精神的、个人的历史观，多带退落的或循环的历史观的倾向；而人生的、物质的、社会的历史观，则多带进步的历史观的倾向。神权的、精神的、个人的、退落的或循环的历史观可称为旧史观，而人生的、物质的、社会的、进步的历史观则可称为新史观。"他所说的"新史观"，就是唯物史观；而他所说的"旧史观"，则是唯心史观。正是从这些历史观中，他敏锐地发现了史学思想史中所蕴含的哲学思想，发现了哲学与历史学的思想史联系，由此开展了唯物史观史的研究，从唯物史观史来阐发马克思主义哲学。这成为了李大钊在中国传播马克思主义哲学的一大特点。因此，《史学思想史》作为一部思想史著述，对于从哲学与相邻学科的思想史联系入手，发掘和梳理出其中所蕴含的哲学思想，将这些思想史内容纳入到哲学史研究中来，具有示范的意义。

二是观念史研究。观念史研究在进入21世纪后受到了中国学术界的关注。尽管今天人们还很难就何谓观念史达成一致的看法，但大概都会认为观念史是思想史的一种形态或一个分支。作为思想史的观念史，当然重视"史"，包含了许多历史的内容，并非一种抽象的观念演绎。但一般的思想史所重视的"史"，有许多不是以观念形式所表达的思想碎片，甚至表现为群体性的心理动向和精神诉求；而观念史对"史"的重视，集中在思想史中的重要观念的生成与演变，这些重要观念都是由哲学家、思想家所创造和阐释的，也是由以后的哲学家、思想家所承继和发挥的，是思想史中用文字表达、有脉络可寻的内容。这些重要观念具有凝聚人心的作用，集中体现了一个民族、一个国家在一个时代的精神生活；而这些重要观念的变化，则反映了一个民族、一个国家的时代精神和民族精神的变化。由此可见，观念史与哲学史之间存在着交叉、贯通之处。从思想史来拓展19—20世纪中国哲学的研究空间，可以从观念史与哲学史的联系入手。19—20世纪是中国人的精神生活发生大变化的时代，许多新观念为中国哲学家、思想家所引入、所阐发、所高扬，用以建构中国人的新的时代精神和民族精神。“自强”“进化”“维新”“革命”“科学”“民主”“平等”“社会主义”等等，就是这些新观念中的特别重要者，集中体现了中国人精神生活的新变化，高度凝练了中国人复兴民族的理想追求，对塑造现代中国发生了深刻影响。19—20世纪中国的时代主旋律和思想世界的总体走向，正是通过这些重要观念的提出、演变及其影响体现出来。这些重要观念之所以具有如此巨大的影响力，就在于它们不仅反映了时代的要求，而且具有着理论的品格，或者就是哲学观念，或者具有哲学内核，或者多少带有哲学意味。正是这样，这些重要观念的提出、演变及其影响，应当成为19—20世纪中国哲学研究的重要内容。

三是社会思潮史研究。社会思潮史同观念史一样，也是思想史的一种形态或一个分支。所谓社会思潮，都是针对并为解决某种重大社会问题而出现的，与实际生活、社会实践、下层民众有着更为密切的联系，吸引了广大民众的认同、响应与参与，甚至演变为声势浩大的群众运动。正是这样，社会思潮史又与观念史不同，不是凸显历史中观念的发生与演变，而是凸显历史中群体性的思想运动，这就必然涉及更为广泛的“史”的内容。19—20世纪中国，社会生活的巨大变迁和各种社会矛盾的发生发展及其彼此消长、相互影响，激起了不同形态的社会思潮起伏纵横于中国思想世界，并在不同程度上转化为变革中国社会的实际运动。诚如冯契所论：“在短短百年间，特别是在19世纪末至20世纪前半叶的数十年间，如此多的思潮纷呈涌动，在数千年的中华文明史上可以说是没有前例的，它集中地表现了中华民族在近代历史条件下，思想的空前活跃，争鸣的空前激烈，精神的迅速高扬。”社会思潮虽具有广泛的民众性，但并非就与哲学无关。一个能够产生持久有力影响的社会思潮往往具有哲学内核，这个哲学内核在社会思潮的开展中有着自己生成、辐射与更新的过程。因此，就这些社会思潮最核心的内容言，仍然是以哲学家、思想家的思想创造为其主体的，而非仅为群体性的心理认同和心理表达。特别是一些持续时间长、社会影响大、具有鲜明奋斗目标的社会思潮，其间都存在着经过哲学家、思想家的自觉创造而形成的哲学内核。这是因为，一个社会思潮只有具有了自己的哲学内核，才能形成自己思想的原创性的活水源头，才能在较长久的时间中有力地保持自己思想的活力与激情，才能在理论上说服人、在思想上吸引人，从而形成自己掌握群众、动员群众、激励群众的理论力量。在 19—20 世纪中国思想世界中，那些曾在长时间中产生过很大影响的社会思潮，往往都形成了各自不同的哲学内核。改良主义、三民主义、自由主义、科学主义、文化保守主义等，作为社会思潮是如此；一个世纪来深刻影响了中国历史进程的马克思主义，作为社会思潮更是如此。正是这样，对这些社会思潮进行研究，阐发其中的哲学内核，不仅是 19—20 世纪中国思想史研究的重要内容，而且也值得纳入到 19—20 世纪中国哲学研究中来。

这三个方面的思想史内容清楚表明，进入 19—20 世纪中国思想世界，了解和把握其中的思想史与哲学史的具体联系，就能够把更多的与哲学史有关联的思想史内容发掘、梳理出来，纳入到哲学史研究中来。由此观之，从思想史视域出发，确能为 19—20 世纪中国哲学研究拓展出一个相当大的空间。

五、从思想史考察 19—20 世纪中国哲学的历史文化环境

开展“以哲学史为中心的思想史研究”，还在于从思想史考察 19—20 世纪中国哲学的历史文化环境。历史文化环境无疑是影响哲学史的重要因素。但在以往的哲学史研究中，存在着把历史文化环境简单化的问题，基本上只注意到

经济和政治的影响，而没有看到影响哲学史的还有更为复杂的历史文化因素。特别是一些鸦片战争后才出现的新的历史文化因素，如近现代报刊的出现、现代大学哲学系的设立、现代思想文化运动的兴起，就对19—20世纪中国哲学开展产生了十分重要的影响。对这些新的历史文化因素进行专门性研究，现在主要是思想史学者的工作，哲学史学者则很少问津。但是，若要从历史文化环境入手，拓展和深化19—20世纪中国哲学研究，就需要认真看待思想史的相关研究，从中吸取有启发性的内容。

自19世纪中叶起，近现代报刊在中国的出现和发展，为中国人提供了一种中国古代社会从未有过的纸质新媒体，不仅使人们之间的信息传播和思想交流方便、快捷、及时，而且深刻影响了19—20世纪中国哲学发展，推动了中国哲学的现代转型和传统更新。从19世纪与20世纪之交开始，一些中国哲学家自觉地与报刊建立起密切的联系，不仅积极在报刊上发表文章，而且还亲自参与创办、主持报刊。20世纪中国的许多重要哲学家，如严复、章太炎、王国维、陈独秀、李大钊、胡适、张东荪、张君劢、李达、瞿秋白、毛泽东等，都曾有过主办报刊或主笔报刊的经历。近现代报刊与20世纪中国哲学相关密切者主要有三种类型：一是时政—思想性报刊，二是学术性报刊，三是哲学刊物。时政—思想性报刊在报道时政要闻的同时，往往兼有思想性内容，其中也包含哲学的内容。这些哲学的内容虽然有限，但却因与时政评论、时代思潮结合在一起，能够于一时之间对中国思想世界投下很大影响。学术性报刊主要以大学学报和学人刊物为主，也包括一些报纸上的学术副刊。这类报刊以发表学术论文为主，能够容纳更多的哲学内容，特别是能够发表一些专业性强的哲学论文，使之在学术圈和哲学界内传播并产生影响。专业性的哲学期刊在20世纪20年代初开始在中国出现。由尚志学会和中国哲学会先后主持的《哲学评论》，是20世纪上半叶办刊时间最长、学术影响最大的哲学期刊，著名哲学家冯友兰、金岳霖、贺麟都先后参与编辑部工作。这使得《哲学评论》与当时中国哲学开展建立起十分密切的联系。20世纪三四十年代，正是中国哲学家建构现代形态中国哲学体系的时期，有熊十力的“新唯识论”、冯友兰的“新理学”、贺麟的“新心学”、金岳霖的“道论”和“知识论”相继建构，这些体系成为中国哲学的现代转型和传统更新的标志性成果。《哲学评论》发表了这些哲学家的许多专业性论文，有力支持了他们的这一工作，以至晚年金岳霖在回忆录中将这一时期称之为“《哲学评论》时代”。《哲学评论》还发表哲学青年的作品。冯契在师从金岳霖读研究生期间撰写了长篇论文《智慧》，就发表在这个刊物上。在文章的开篇，冯契提出本文的主旨在于探讨“元学怎么可能”这一哲学根本问题；以后他一直沿着这一方向探索，终于在 20 世纪 80 年代建立起“智慧说”这一中国化和个性化的马克思主义哲学新体系。

辛亥革命终结了封建国家对经学教育体制的长期支撑，现代大学哲学系由此在中国开始设立，为中国哲学发展提供了一个新的历史文化环境。现代大学哲学系建构起现代哲学教育制度，按照大学哲学教育的目标，设置现代课程体系，对哲学系学生进行专业培养和专门训练，使之初步具有从事哲学研究的知识结构与能力结构。1912 年，北京大学中国哲学门创建，成为中国最早建立的哲学系；冯友兰是北大哲学门的第二届学生，成为中国哲学史上由现代大学哲学系培养的第一个著名哲学家。1915 年，武昌中华大学中国哲学门设立，是中国南方最早建立的哲学系；恽代英是中华大学哲学门的第一届学生，以后成为中国共产党早期著名革命家兼思想家。现代大学哲学系作为一种教学组织，将不同学术主张的哲学家集合在一起共事，使他们之间有了更密切的联系和更多的交流，从而促进了 20 世纪中国哲学的开展。上述四位建构现代形态中国哲学体系的哲学家，都任教于著名大学哲学系。随着现代大学哲学系的发展，不同大学的哲学系之间逐渐形成了各自的风格和传统。如在 20 世纪 30 年代的北平，北京大学哲学系与清华大学哲学系成为当时国内最为著名的哲学系，分别聚集了一批著名哲学家在其中任教，北大哲学系有胡适、熊十力、汤用彤、张颐、贺麟诸子，清华哲学系有金岳霖、冯友兰、沈有鼎、张申府、张岱年诸子，由此形成了两种不同风格和传统的哲学共同体：北大哲学系更具有传统哲学色彩，偏重于哲学史的研究；清华哲学系则更带西洋哲学色彩，对哲学理论的创造更有兴趣。晚年张岱年根据自己的亲身体会对此作过说明：“在30年代，北京大学哲学系与清华大学哲学系，学风有所不同。北大哲学系在胡适的影响之下，重视考据，重视历史的研究。清华哲学系在金岳霖、冯友兰的领导之下，赞赏英国穆尔（G.E.Moore）、罗素（B.Russell）的逻辑分析方法，致力于建立自己的理论体系。”抗日战争时期，由于长沙临时大学—西南联合大学的组建，这两个大学哲学系融合为一体，不仅形成了一个空前壮观的专业哲学家阵容，而且汇聚了两个哲学系的不同治学风格，使之互为补充，相得益彰。新中国成立后，中国马克思主义哲学家开始创办马克思主义哲学指导下的大学哲学系。20世纪50年代中期，李达主持重建武汉大学哲学系，从筹办之始就确定了明确的目的，要把武大哲学系办成“马克思主义的哲学系”。时任李达学术助手的陶德麟老师后来回忆说：“这种重建不是简单地恢复，而是创办一个有自己特色的新的哲学系。这个哲学系应当以马克思主义哲学为主体，同时在马克思主义指导下建设其他学科。”萧萐父老师也曾对笔者说过，李达当年同他谈话时就明确提出，重建后的武大哲学系，不是办成以讲康德、黑格尔为主的哲学系，也不是办成以讲程、朱、陆、王为主的哲学系，而是办成马克思主义的哲学系。萧老师成为中国马克思主义早期启蒙说的承续者和发扬者，实与李达指导下的武大哲学系这一具体环境相关联。

进入20世纪第二个十年后，中国近现代文化在中西古今文化的碰撞、交流、融合中有了更大的发展，现代思想文化运动开始在中国兴起。1915—1924年的新文化运动，20世纪30年代的左翼文化运动，就是典型的现代思想文化运动。现代思想文化运动虽不是严格意义上的哲学运动，但却对20世纪中国哲学开展产生了深刻影响。新文化运动作为鸦片战争后最为深刻的思想文化革新运动，对中国旧文化、旧思想所展开的猛烈批判，特别是对孔子的批评、对孔教的抨击、对儒家纲常的否定，为中国新文化、新思想的发展开辟了道路，促成了各种新哲学思想的传播和发展，特别是促成了马克思主义哲学作为一大思潮崛起于中国思想世界。新文化运动后，中国哲学家进一步反思这一运动的哲学提问，开始建构现代形态中国哲学体系，形成中国哲学现代传统。因此，新文化运动成为中国哲学古今之变的一大枢纽。左翼文化运动是在中国共产党直接领导下所兴起的现代思想文化运动，是中国马克思主义者在新形势下对新文化运动精神的承继和发扬。这一运动中的唯物辩证法运动，有力地推进了马克思主义哲学中国化，形成了具有中国特点的马克思主义哲学形态。艾思奇的《大众哲学》，李达的《社会学大纲》，毛泽东的《实践论》、《矛盾论》，都是其重要成果。因此，这些现代思想文化运动，不仅发展出延续至今的革命文化和社会主义先进文化，而且对中国哲学的现代形态和现代传统起了重要的塑造作用；至于中国马克思主义哲学的发端与发展，更是与这些现代思想文化运动密切地联系在一起的。

总之，近现代报刊的出现、现代大学哲学系的设立、现代思想文化运动的兴起，这些鸦片战争后新的历史文化因素，对 19—20 世纪中国哲学开展产生了十分重要的影响。从思想史考察 19—20 世纪中国哲学的历史文化环境，这些内容都是必须予以关注、加以研究的重要因素。

六、完整理解“以哲学史为中心的思想史研究”

“以哲学史为中心的思想史研究”，作为 19—20 世纪哲学研究的方法论，需要有一个完整的理解。

这个方法论的提出，其具体背景是哲学史与思想史的明确区分以及由此所带来的“思”与“史”的疏离，而其学理根据实在于马克思所说的哲学与现实世界的联系。马克思在创立自己的哲学时，强调“哲学不是在世界之外”，强调哲学“同自己时代的现实世界接触并相互作用”。“以哲学史为中心的思想史研究”，就是要在 19—20 世纪中国哲学研究中体现马克思哲学的这一精神。

因此，“以哲学史为中心的思想史研究”固然重视哲学史与思想史的联系，但并不是要把属于哲学的哲学史变成属于历史学的思想史。提出和运用这个方法论，旨在改变哲学史研究中忽视哲学史与历史文化之间联系的状况，并不意味着在哲学史研究中可以忽视或遮蔽哲学史自身的逻辑开展。哲学史之为哲学史，就在于从历史上纷纭复杂的精神现象和思想碎片中揭示出哲学开展的内在逻辑进程。这也就要求在重构哲学史与思想史的联系时，对这种新的联系的把握仍然要以哲学史为中心。也就是说，哲学史研究在重申“史”的意义时，不能离开“思”来讲“史”，不能只有“史”而无“思”，而在于把“思”与“史”有机结合起来。

这样一来，可以看出“以哲学史为中心的思想史研究”与历史学的思想史研究在方法论上的区别：历史学的思想史所涉及的“史”，往往是以历史上的思想碎片的形态呈现出来，有的思想史学者通过对这些思想碎片的多方拼接来复原思想史的大致面貌，有的思想史学者即以这些思想碎片作为思想史的本真原貌；而“以哲学史为中心的思想史研究”，尽管也重视“史”，也重视历史的思想碎片，但又必须从“史”中探寻出“思”的内在逻辑与展开脉络，从这些思想碎片中揭示出哲学发展的“一以贯之”之“道”。

这些都表明，“以哲学史为中心的思想史研究”，并不是一般意义的思想史研究，而归根到底仍然是一种哲学史研究。

（原载《中国高校社会科学》2018 年第 6 期）

再谈哲学史研究的“纯化”与“泛化”

吴根友

最近六年来，笔者在明清哲学、现代诸子学研究的过程中，一方面接着萧先生的明清早期启蒙思想与中国现代化的内在根芽的问题意识往下讲，发表了一系列的文章与论著，另一方面也写过几篇研究萧先生的“明清早期启蒙思想”、诸子学思想、比较哲学思想等文章。今年，配合拙著《戴震、乾嘉学术与中国文化》一书的出版，应《哲学分析》杂志之约，回应该书的三篇评论性文章，专门针对萧先生的哲学方法论作了进一步的阐述。在此处将此文的主要观点提出来，向诸位同门学兄及其他几位业内同道请教。

20 世纪 80 年代末，中国著名哲学史家萧萐父先生反省 20 世纪中国哲学史的研究经验时，曾提出了哲学史研究的“纯化”与“泛化”的关系问题。这一有关哲学史方法论的思考收入他 1991 年出版的《吹沙集》。萧先生所说的“纯化”，即是指“使哲学史纯化为哲学认识论史，以便揭示哲学矛盾运动的特殊规律”。他所说的“泛化”，即是指“哲学史研究可以泛化为哲学文化史。以哲学史为核心的文化史或以文化史为铺垫的哲学史，更能充分反映人的智慧创造和不断自我解放的历程。”因为哲学本身可以广义地界定为“人学”，文化，本质地说就是“人化”。① 他的这一说法，与同时代的冯契先生提出的“广义认识论”的说法，有着某种的呼应关系。也是在这样新哲学史观的指引下，笔者对于明清哲学思想的研究，基本上遵循了以哲学史为核心，在学术史与思想史相互动的格局下研究明清时期的思想特征。这是对萧先生“泛化”哲学史观的

---

① 萧萐父：《吹沙集》，巴蜀书社 1991 年版，第 410 页。

一种回应与实践。

比较而言，20世纪的明清学术研究中，梁启超、钱穆、余英时等人主要是学术史的进路，胡适、侯外庐、萧萐父等人主要是思想史、哲学史的进路。现代新儒家群体中的情况比较复杂，有偏重于学术史的，如熊十力、徐复观、刘述先等，有偏重于哲学史与思想史的，如唐君毅、牟宗三等。这些研究进路的差异，使得明清哲学思想的研究呈现出不同的面貌。笔者在《戴震、乾嘉学术与中国文化》一书中采取的方式，就是将“纯化”与“泛化”的方式结合起来，努力展示明清哲学思想的立体面貌。在坚持侯外庐、萧萐父等人的“明清早期启蒙说”的同时，主要从学术、哲学思考方式转换的角度讨论中国的早期现代性，不再停留于社会政治、文艺思潮的层面讨论中国传统文化的现代转换。

一、“道论”与清代哲学史研究的“纯化”

为了揭示明清之际，特别是清代哲学区别于其他历史阶段，如宋明理学的面貌，笔者将这一时期的哲学形上学称之为“道论”或“道本论”，其典型人物可以戴震与章学诚为代表。一般的学术史与哲学史都特别重视戴震的“分理说”，尤其重视其反理学的政治化口号：“以理杀人”的说法。这些关注不能说是错的，但从哲学形上学的角度看，没有抓住戴震思想的实质。20世纪戴震哲学、思想与学术的研究，其主流倾向将他塑造成一个反对理学的哲学家形象，因为这一哲学形象，他既获得了额外的赞誉，也招致了现代新儒家很多不恰当的批评、攻击，甚至是谩骂。更为严重的是，在“反理学”的思维模式下，戴震哲学的自我特征被淹没了，而他的气论与道本论思想与广义宋明理学——张载以降的气本体论思想的内在联系，反而被遮蔽了。

作为哲学家的戴震，他不只是一般意义上的反对宋明理学，他要解构宋明理学中“理本体论”，将“理”下降为具体的“在物之理”，必需要重新建构一个新的哲学本体论，这个新哲学本体论并不是戴震的首创，恰恰是张载以来的

“气化即道”的道本论。戴震提出了“道，恒赅理气”的命题，表明他在哲学的本体论上是有明确的思考，即将宋明理学的理本论与气本论综合起来，以古老的哲学概念“道”来统合理、气本体论。而且，戴震还从传统哲学的名学思想中吸取了思想资源，将中国哲学之名即概念从整体上分成两类：一类是“实体实事”之名，一类是“纯粹中正”之名。用现代的哲学语言来说，实体实事之名是表述客观实在的一类概念，纯粹中正之名是表示价值观念的一类概念，而“道”这一根本概念，从其内容看，是表示实体实事之名，从其为一切价值之根源的角度看，又是表述纯粹中正之名。因此，在戴震的思想中，事实与价值，是与应当的关系，在源头上是统一的。这一点颇不同于休谟要将此二者分开处理的思路。由此可知，仅仅讲戴震的“分理”思想，而不理解戴震的“道论”思想，其实是无法理解作为哲学家的戴震的思想。20 世纪的戴震思想研究基本上忽视了戴震的“道论”思想。

更进一步，相对于中国传统的“道论”思想而言，戴震“道论”思想的新颖之处在于何处呢？这是我们哲学史研究比较忽视的地方，笔者在《戴震、乾嘉学术与中国文化》一书中也未清晰地加以论述。此处可以做一点补充。戴震“道论”思想超越前人的地方，我想有两点：一是从宋明理学的传统看，他以道论统一了气本论与理本论，在哲学理论上是一种综合。二是从实际存在与价值表述二分的角度，将“道”分析为表述“实体实事”与“纯粹中正”的两层意思，以前所未有的、清晰的哲学语言把传统社会“天人合一”的思想阐述清楚了。特别值得肯定的是，他将“人道”的“人伦日用”的客观性与天道的自然自在的客观性做了一个合乎类比思维逻辑的推理，以证明人的一切感性需求的客观性，从而在哲学的层面上为人的欲望的客观性及其满足的合理性做了比较有力的理论辩护。因此，戴震在“理欲之辩”的问题上肯定欲望的合理性论证，相较于王夫之、陈确等人在此问题上的论证而言，更富有哲学的说服力。而这一切，都要依赖对其“道论”思想的整体把握。就笔者目前的阅读视野来看，在此点上，20 世纪的戴震哲学与思想研究，还很少有人如此清楚、明晰地阐述其“道论”与其“理欲之辩”命题之间内在深刻的关系。

章学诚的哲学思想一般而言被低估了，历史学与清代学术史的研究多关注其“六经皆史”与“言性命必究于史”的两个著名命题，很少有人讨论其作为哲学思想的“道论”思想，尤其是很少有人讨论其道论与其“六经皆器”、“六经皆史”两个命题的内在思想关系。就笔者的阅读所见，还很少有人从哲学思想方法论的角度讨论其“言性命必究于史”的命题所体现出的人文实证的哲学思维方法。

作为哲学家的章学诚，其“道论”思想学界长期以来未能给予足够的关注。章氏的“道论”在哲学思想的形式上主要是继承宋明理学中理本论的思想影响，将“道”看作是不可见的抽象实体。但是在“道”的具体属性上，他似乎又吸收了气化论的思想因素，将“道体”看作是变动不居的，尤其是在人道的问题上，他认为圣人所把握的也只是“道”变化、运动的轨迹，而不是“道体”本身，故尔“六经”相对于“道体”而言，也只能是器，而不是道。诚然，“六经皆史”的观念不是章学诚的首创，但从“六经皆器”到“六经皆史”的思想过渡，以往学术界未能给予足够的关注，而这一点恰恰是章学诚重述“六经皆史”命题的新意之所在。由于相对于变动不居的道体而言，“六经”只能是道运动、变化过程中的陈迹，是器，故每个时代的史学家都应该根据变动不居的道，同时参酌“六经”的精神撰写属于自己时代的史著，从而去探究变动不居的大道。在这样的历史哲学的高度，章学诚提出史学家应该研究自己时代的历史，的确是一个具有思想突破意义的史学观念，而不能简单地看作是对现实时王的歌颂。相对于这一深邃的历史哲学而言，其具体的人道历史观——“三人居室而成道”的人道论，突出社会分工对于人道形成的意义，虽然有一定的新意，但若与孟子从社会分工的角度讨论君子与小人的关系相比较，其新意就非常有限了。而且，他的“三人居室而成道”的人道形成论思想，其实并不是基于历史事实的考察，反而是一种历史的想像与推测，对于人类认识自己的历史形成过程来说并无多少实质性的意义。

以上对戴震与章学诚"道论"思想的分析，可以说是本书从哲学史研究的"纯化"方面试图对明清哲学，特别是清代哲学的整体特征所作出的新的阐述，能否成立，期待学界贤达赐教。

二、"古典人文知识的增长"与哲学史研究的"泛化"

从哲学史研究的"泛化"角度看，如何将清代经学、史学的考据研究与哲学思想研究联系起来，这是清代哲学研究中的一个大问题。对于此点，余英时已经有明确的思考，他提出的"儒家智识主义"概念就是试图来回答这一问题。而且，他的这一概念还与现代哲学追求知识的独立性的价值取向有关。余先生称自己的清代思想研究着重从"内在理路"出发。但是，他的"儒家智识主义"的说法，其实还是从隐性的现代性的宏大叙事立场出发，揭示清代考据学的现代思想意义。因此，我认为，余先生在实际上并未完全做到从"内在理路"出发研究清代学术与思想，还是有"外在理路"的痕迹，即借助于科学与知识在现代社会与学术中的独立性来发掘清代"儒家智识主义"的价值与意义。相较于余先生的"儒家智识主义"的说法，笔者用"古典人文知识的增长"这一概念来揭示乾嘉时代经学考据与史学考据的思想意义，既有同于余先生之处，亦有不同的地方。相同之处在于，我们从不同的角度揭示了清代儒者对于知识的兴趣及其实际成就。不同之处在于，我未将这一客观化的学术活动所导致的古典人文知识增长的事实拔高为一自觉的正面理论追求——儒家智识主义。经学考据的实际结果，一方面使经学的附庸——训诂学逐渐成为一种显学，并初步形成了科学的形态。另一方面，经学的语文学（philology）研究的实际成绩，发掘了很多词汇、尤其是一些重要观念的多面意义，向清代的士人阶层展示了古代经典丰富的意义世界。其典型的代表作品有王念孙的《读书杂志》与王引之的《经义述闻》两部著作。史学考据的实际成就，既纠正了官方正统史学著作的一些错误，也发掘了一些新史实，从而也扩大并更新了当时士人对古典古代世界的认识，其典型的代表作品有钱大昕的《二十一史考异》、赵翼的《廿二史札记》与王鸣盛的《十七史商榷》三部著作。

与"古典人文知识增长"的客观社会现象相联系，乾嘉时代的知识分类学的讨论亦颇具有象征意义。官方的《四库全书总目》沿袭古代的图书分类法，将经与经学置于四部分类之首，简化为经史子集四部，体现了"以治道为中心"的知识分类的哲学思想。但作为民间学者的知识分类观颇不同于官方的以图书性质从事知识分类的思路，而是就知识的性质来进行分类，提出了义理、考据、辞章的三分法，或义理、考据、辞章、经济（经世致用之意）的四分法。这一新的知识分类法，有利于学人摆脱经学思想的束缚，迈向新的学术研究途径。这一知识分类思想虽然并没有被官方接受，也未产生相应的社会效果，但作为一种知识分类思想，却能较好地反映中国传统学术发展的内在逻辑，并预示着一种摆脱经学、追求新知的思想发展方向。

以往学术界研究乾嘉考据学兴起与繁荣的原因时，多从清代政治高压的外缘条件入手加以说明。这不能说是错的，但不够充分。余英时从"内在理路"的角度加以揭示，开辟了新的研究视角，值得肯定。但他的具体结论却有待进一步的商榷。清代学问不只是"道问学"而不"尊德性"，即使是主流形态亦不能这样说。更准确地说，清儒的尊德性有两条道路，一条是在道问学的过程中尊德性，如戴震在《答郑丈用牧书》说："立身守二字曰不苟，待人守二字曰无憾"，在学术研究活动中，"不以人蔽己，不以己自蔽。不为一时之名，亦不期后世之名"，剔除"鄙陋之心"而"志存闻道"。① 一条是把尊德性与道问学分开，像惠栋所说的"六经尊服郑，百行法程朱"。惠氏所言，并不是个别学人的人生行为，而是那个时代学人的人生行动准则。其实，乾嘉考据学的兴盛还有更加内在的价值追求，即该时代的学人将求得"真知"看作是一种精神的快乐。上述所引戴震的一段话，已经初步地表达了乾嘉学人"为学术而学术"

① 《戴震全书》（六），黄山书社 1995 年版，第 373—374 页。

的精神，这种精神在章学诚的“道公而学私”的具体论述中亦可找到同调，如章氏说：“道之所在，学以趋之”，①“立言之士”只要传之其人，其道相同，就不必斤斤计较文章的命名权问题。这是一种非常高的精神境界。但更为直接地反映该时代学人以求得“真知”为人生价值归宿的是段玉裁说的一段话，他认为，如果求得真知，考核精当，求得一字一句之安妥，也有“天地位，万物育”的气象，“近以自娱、娱亲，远以娱人”，甚至上可以神交古人，下可以神交后人。② 像段玉裁这样的乾嘉学者将追求“真知”看作是人生的精神寄托，恰恰是乾嘉学术近百年而不衰的内在精神动力之所在。

因此，在本书中，哲学史研究的“泛化”范围已经延伸到人类的心灵史领域，将知识的追求与人生的信仰结合起来，不再局限于哲学认识的历史。在这一点上，笔者接着萧先生的哲学是“人学”的泛化的哲学史观的。

三、现代性的宏大叙事与明清哲学的现代性问题再思考

当代国际学术界，后现代思潮十分强劲，在学术史领域，福柯、利奥塔等人极力反对现代性的宏大叙事，反对将人类的思想史进程描述成一个朝着我们走来的化约式的进化与进步的历程。他们的观点有合理之处。但是，现代性又是一个客观的社会历史事实，欧洲与中国等少数几个主要的民族，在成熟的农业文明基础上又的确开启了形式不同、性质相似的现代性的历史进程。以进化论、进步观等其他简化的形式来描述的现代性可能失之于简约，但现代性所蕴含的人类文明“进步”的观念，在原则上是成立的。这无论就人的存在方式、技术的精密化、人的解放等不同角度来考察，人类文明从整体上表现为进步，或者文明化，是一个无法否认的事实。儒家思想特别强调人禽之别，文野之分，实质上也是持一种文明进步的观念，只是儒家没有发明朝向未来的、单线

① 章学诚著，仓修良编注：《文史通义新编新注》，浙江古籍出版社 2005 版，第 206 页。

② 参见《娱亲雅言序》，《经韵楼集》卷八，《续修四库全书》第 1434 册，第 75 页。

的历史进化观而已。在社会思潮领域，包括文艺领域，明清之际的现代性，梁启超、胡适、侯外庐、萧萐父及其弟子许苏民等人已经做了相当充分的阐述，特别是侯—萧一系的中国的马克思主义学者，发掘了大量的经济史与思想史的资料，有力地论证了明清之际的早期现代性及其特征。从人的解放角度，萧先生用“反对伦理异化”的命题来概括之际的早期现代化的思想性质与具体的历史内容，以别于近现代西方“反对宗教异化”的历史内容，揭示了中西现代性内容的“异中之同”与“同中之异”。我在本书中没有重新复述这些思想，而是着重从学术与思维方式变化的角度，即人文学中所体现的实证精神的角度，考察明清学术、思想中的现代性内容。

以往的学术史与思想史，对于明清的考据学，特别是清代的考据学，往往从“汉宋之争”的思维模式出发，来评判其得失。由于评判者或站在汉学立场，或站在宋学立场上来评价考据学，其争论的结果颇类似于庄子在《齐物论》中所批评的那样，既然同于甲或同于乙，或者异于甲异于乙，就已经失去了评判甲、乙的资格。梁启超、胡适虽然在比较哲学与比较文化的视野里肯定了考据学具有实证、科学的特征，但考据学与处理自然事物的自然科学、处理社会问题的社会科学毕竟不一样，他们面对的历史文献或古代的书面语言及其词汇，其科学性究竟有什么自身的特点，梁、胡二位先贤并未来得及深入思考。本书着重分析了明清学术、思想中的历史事实还原、文本真相还原、词汇意义还原等学术研究特征，进一步揭示这一“还原”的学术研究目标所包含的“求真”精神，进而揭示了明清学术，特别是乾嘉学术活动中所包含的科学精神。在比较哲学的视野里，本书尝试运用“人文实证主义”的方法来概括明清学术，特别是乾嘉学术研究活动中的科学精神。明清时期的学者，特别是乾嘉时代的学者，绝大多数是人文学者，即使像方以智、戴震这样少数的懂得数学史、古代技术史的学者，也不是科学家，而只是科学史家，他们的主要研究领域还是经学。他们的实证方法与手段，与宋明时期学者相比，更具有科学性，但与近现代自然科学通过实验手段而获得证据的实证方法还是有很大区别的。不过，他们在史料研究、语文学资料的使用过程中，的确又采用了科学的归纳方法，语音的历史性与区域性等客观性材料，不再是纯粹的思辨，更不是根据经学的原则来做结论或解释。因此，他们在历史学、历史语言学、语义学等领域里，取得了一些带有一定普遍性与正确性的研究结论，为后人的进一步研究提供了相对可靠的历史前提或出发点。为了区别于现代西方哲学的“实证主义”哲学及其方法，同时又照顾到明清学术中的科学特征，本书尝试运用了“人文实证主义方法”这一概念，并将其作为一个时代的哲学思想方法，以彰显该时代思维方式的突出特点。

余　论

在本书的小型讨论会上，有学者指出，乾嘉学术对于现代中国学人的影响，应该写黄侃而不应该写王力。写余嘉锡而不应该写顾颉刚。这一说法有一定道理，但也不尽然。其实，乾嘉学术对于中国现代学术的影响是全方位的，很难面面俱到。本书着眼于学术的现代性这一特定视角，故选择了一些既对古代学术有创发性的研究，同时又有现代学术精神风貌的一些学者。当然，即使如此，也还有一些应选择而没有选择的学者与思想家。另外，本书虽然在戴震部分触及“人文实证主义”方法与“大其心”方法之间的张力，但如果将“人文实证主义”方法作为该时代哲学的主要方法，还要处理其他学者如焦循、章学诚等人提倡“性灵”的主观性、主体性方法之间的张力，这是可以进一步拓展的研究领域与学术问题。

不过，在写作本书的过程中，笔者深感重要的是另一个问题，即如何运用现代汉语创造一些有思想活力的现代学术概念与哲学概念，改变现代汉语与现代哲学新概念过于依赖对西方哲学翻译与学术著作翻译的现象。当代中国有些学者曾抱怨现代汉语在哲学研究中缺乏词汇的生成能力，不像英语那样从一些旧的词根生成出新的哲学或学术术语。这种抱怨在一定的程度上有它的合理性。毕竟，现代汉语与古代汉语之间有一定的隔阂。但如果巧妙地利用汉语构词的灵活性，如两个名词可以叠加，亦可构造出新汉语哲学词汇，而不必一味地要从古代汉语造出现代汉语哲学的新词，如萧先生构造的“伦理异化”，刘笑敢在研究老子思想时构造的“人文自然”，本书所构造的“人文实证主义”等，似乎可以为现代汉语哲学词汇与学术语汇的创造提供一点借鉴意义。实际上，现代汉语通过两个名词叠加而构造新词的方式，在原理上并不违背古代汉语的两个名词叠加而构造概念的方法，如古代汉语中的道德、心术、道术、方术、技术等，都是如此构成的。不仅如此，有些旧概念如“天下”，亦可像赵汀阳那样，通过新的哲学思考，赋予它新的时代意义。因此，当代中国的人文学术，如何能够在出入中西古今的宏大视野里，以解决问题为中心，广泛吸取现代西方哲学、马克思主义哲学，包括自己的现代哲学精神，运用现代汉语重塑中国学术、中国思想、中国哲学的新话语体系，不只是依赖翻译来增加新词，这不仅是可能的，而且是现实的。

另外，由现代西方学术分类而来的哲学史、思想史、观念史、文化史、社会史等研究范式所带来的中国人文学术分类的变化，也制造出了很多的疆域与壁垒。若借用萧先生哲学史的“纯化”与“泛化”的观念来处理这些问题，我想哲学史、观念史更是哲学史的“纯化”研究，而思想史、文化史、社会史研究，更接近哲学史的“泛化”研究。

马克思主义哲学的三次方法论变革及其意义

李佃来

从19世纪到20世纪，马克思主义哲学在形成和发展的不同历史时期，经历了三次重大的方法论变革，由此在很大程度上解决了每个时期所面临的主要理论困难，大大推动了马克思主义哲学理论的发展。这三次方法论变革，分别是指由马克思所策动的辩证法对经验主义的变革、由卢卡奇所策动的总体性对实证主义的变革以及由柯亨所策动的分析的方法对人本主义的变革。

一、马克思：辩证法对经验主义的变革

众所周知，近代之后、德国古典哲学之前，在西方哲学的理论发展中起主导作用的是经验主义。经验主义既是一种理论形式，也是一种研究方法。根据经验主义，人们只能从对外部事物的感知或心灵的经验中获得知识，从其他途径得来的知识都是不可靠的和值得怀疑的。经验主义顺应现代科学的发展而勃然兴起，既为现代科学的发展扫除了许多思想上的障碍，也为哲学研究提供了许多科学的、实证的材料，由此在很大程度上克服了古代形而上学因为缺乏实证知识而形成的独断论倾向。不过，经验主义所具有的进步意义，并不能掩盖其固有的思维缺陷。黑格尔在《小逻辑》中，从两个方面指认了经验主义的思维缺陷，一是它虽然能够帮助人们获得关于当前事物的直观认识，但却不能把握自由、精神及上帝等超验性的对象；二是它的落点虽在于建立普遍性原理，但却不能达到必然性的反思和满足必然性的认知形

式。[①]当然，在德国古典哲学家中，黑格尔并非对经验主义提出挑战的第一人，毋宁说康德才是第一人。康德对人的认识能力的批判性审查，以及由此而提出的“物自体”概念，打破了经验主义试图根据对可感事物的认知来获得最终真理的梦想，因为以康德之见，人们在经验范围内认识到的只是现象而非真理，在理论理性界限内，人们凭借先验的知性概念是无法把握物自体及与之对应的真理的。康德将物自体与现象界分开来，并强调人们只能认识后者，虽然导致了常被后人所诟病的不可知论，但这却是对经验知识的有效性所进行的一种严格限定，在事实上构成了对经验主义这种思维方法的深刻检视与批判。黑格尔对康德的观点予以了高度评价，不仅认为后者在现象层面来指认基于经验的知性知识及其有限性，乃是其哲学的一个重大思想成果，[②]而且认为他对于知性范畴所必然引起的理性世界之矛盾的审视，以及由此而带动的辩证思维的发展，构成了近代哲学界最重要和最深刻的理论进步[③]。不过，康德虽然在知性和理性、现象和物自体的边界发现了辩证法的存在，但怀有“理性恨”情结的他却是在消极的意义上看待辩证法的，这也是他始终将现象与物自体界分开来的原因之一。黑格尔并不认同康德的这一做法，于是在批判性地考察后者观点的基础上，将现象与物自体缝合了起来，从而在积极意义上、通过逻辑学方式发展了辩证法。根据黑格尔的界划，辩证逻辑包括三个环节，即一是抽象的或知性（理智）的环节，二是辩证或否定理性的环节，三是思辨或肯定理性的环节。[④]这三个环节构成了思维的全过程，缺少任何一个环节，对于事物的认识都将是不完整的。而经验主义之所以存在不能把握超验性事物和不能达及必然性反思的思维缺陷，乃是因为它只停留在辩证逻辑的第一个环节，故而只能形成对外界事物的直观认识和平面把握，而没有能力看到比这更多的东西。

---

① 参见黑格尔：《小逻辑》，贺麟译，商务印书馆 1980 年版，第 46—48 页。

② 参见黑格尔：《小逻辑》，贺麟译，商务印书馆 1980 年版，第 127 页。

③ 参见黑格尔：《小逻辑》，贺麟译，商务印书馆 1980 年版，第 132、133 页。

④ 参见黑格尔：《小逻辑》，贺麟译，商务印书馆 1980 年版，第 172 页。

经过康德和黑格尔对经验主义的反复批判，近代以来的哲学研究方法得到了实质性的提升，这不仅促成了德国古典哲学在理论上的重大突破与发展，而且也为马克思的方法论变革奠定了重要基础。

恩格斯曾经说道："应该用什么方法对待科学？一方面是黑格尔的辩证法，它具有完全抽象的'思辨的'形式，黑格尔就是以这种形式把它留下来的；另一方面是平庸的、现在重新时兴的、实质上是沃尔弗式的形而上学的方法，这也是资产阶级经济学家写他们那些缺乏内在联系的大部头著作时采用的方法。后一种方法，曾被康德特别是黑格尔在理论上摧毁，只是由于惰性和缺乏一种别的简单方法，才使它能够在实际上继续存在。"[①] 显而易见，恩格斯在这段话中指认了两种研究方法，一是黑格尔的辩证法，一是形而上学的方法。后一种方法，实际就是指经验主义方法，因为经验主义虽然不同于古代旧形而上学，但它根据经验和实证的事物来求得普遍原理的思维路数，却又导向了一种新的形而上学。根据恩格斯的审理，这种曾经支配近代哲学的经验主义方法虽然已经被康德特别是黑格尔所摧毁，但却由于惰性和缺乏一种别的简单方法而在黑格尔之后重新复苏，在现代的哲学和科学研究中起着"风向标"的作用。可是，在恩格斯看来，经验主义方法固然能够帮助人们在哲学及科学研究中获得丰富翔实的实证性知识材料，但这一方法固有的思维特点，决定了它没有能力将不同的知识材料连接和综合起来、从而发现相互之间的内在关系。要克服经验主义的此一思维缺陷，就需要接入到从康德到黑格尔的思维传统，使用辩证法这一思维工具来开展哲学和科学研究，"因为只有辩证法才为自然界中出现的发展过程，为各种普遍的联系，为一个研究领域向另一个研究领域过渡提供类比，从而提供说明方法。"[②]

如果说恩格斯的以上论述表明，黑格尔之后的哲学家依然面对一个如何用辩证法来解决经验主义所造成的理论困难的艰巨任务，那么，马克思则比他所

① 《马克思恩格斯文集》第2卷，人民出版社2009年版，第601页。
② 《马克思恩格斯文集》第9卷，人民出版社2009年版，第436页。

有同时代人都更好地完成了这一任务。我们都知道，马克思在写作《资本论》及其手稿时期，是十分注重对政治经济学的研究方法进行前提性的反思和界定的。在《1857—1858 年经济学手稿》中，马克思特别指认和描述了两种政治经济学的研究方法，即一是从具体到抽象的方法，一是从抽象到具体的方法。所谓从具体到抽象的方法，实质就是经验主义方法，因为经验主义始终不变的思维套路，就是从对当前具体事物的认识中抽象出普遍的原理，从而实现对事物的所谓“终极”把握。与之相反，所谓从抽象到具体的方法，也就是辩证的方法，因为根据马克思的界定，“具体”是指许多规定的综合和多样性的统一，故而从抽象过渡到具体，意味着人们的思维所经历的恰恰是一个呈现事物之内在联系的辩证认识过程。作为一种经验主义方法，从具体到抽象由于使“完整的表象蒸发为抽象的规定”①，所以它并不是一种正确的政治经济学研究方法。而相形之下，作为一种辩证的方法，从抽象到具体会引导人们在思维行程中再现出事物的丰富多样性规定和原本样貌，所以它才是一种正确的政治经济学研究方法。

如果说在政治经济学的研究中，马克思主要遵从的是从抽象到具体这一辩证的研究方法，那么亚当·斯密以来的英国古典经济学家们，则主要遵从的是从具体到抽象这一经验主义的方法。早在《1844 年经济学哲学手稿》中，马克思就敏锐地发现了英国古典经济学因为方法论而造成的理论困难，由此这样指出：英国古典经济学“从私有财产的事实出发。它没有给我们说明这个事实。它把私有财产在现实中所经历的物质过程，放进一般的、抽象的公式，然后把这些公式当做规律。它不理解这些规律，就是说，它没有指明这些规律是怎样从私有财产的本质中产生出来的。”② 如果正像马克思在这里所指示的，凭借从具体到抽象的研究方法，英国古典经济学家们虽然提出了关于私有财产的一般规律和理论，但却不能揭示私有财产的本质，那么凭借从抽象到具体的研究方

① 《马克思恩格斯文集》第 8 卷，人民出版社 2009 年版，第 25 页。

② 《马克思恩格斯文集》第 1 卷，人民出版社 2009 年版，第 155 页。

法，马克思则不仅深刻揭示出了私有财产的本质，而且也由此看到了资本主义经济关系的结构性存在和复杂性在场。正是因为洞见到马克思的方法论变革为其政治经济学研究所带来的这一卓尔不凡的成就，列宁才在评价《资本论》时这样说道："这部书（指《资本论》）使读者看到整个资本主义社会形态是个活生生的形态：有它的日常生活的各个方面，有它的生产关系所固有的阶级对抗的实际社会表现，有维护资本家阶级统治的资产阶级政治上层建筑，有资产阶级的自由平等之类的思想，有资产阶级的家庭关系。……《资本论》不是别的，正是'把堆积如山的实际材料总结为几点概括性的、彼此紧相联系的思想'。"①

需要说明的是，马克思是在康德以来德国古典哲学思维传统尤其是黑格尔辩证法的影响下，来厘定其政治经济学的研究方法的，其所讲的从抽象到具体的辩证方法，与黑格尔所讲的从知性到理性的辩证逻辑至少具有形式上的一致性。然而，我们却不能由此而完全退回到黑格尔的水平来理解马克思的方法论变革，因为这样一来，我们就没有理由认为马克思在方法论领域策动了一场重大的变革。换言之，马克思之所以能够策动一场方法论变革，原因之一就在于，他是以根本不同于黑格尔的方式来发展黑格尔的辩证法的。在黑格尔那里，一则是由于辩证法是以逻辑概念的形式展现出来的，二则是由于逻辑概念具有规定事物之存在的本体论地位，所以归根结底，辩证法就是一种并非来自于现实事物、反而创造出现实事物的神秘莫测的东西。从这一点来看，虽然正像马克思所说的那样，"辩证法不崇拜任何东西，按其本质来说，它是批判的和革命的"②，但黑格尔却并未凭借辩证法而发展出一种针对现实矛盾的批判性理论，这是因为从逻辑上来说，辩证法并不可能对自己所创造的东西提出实质性批判，而只会在思维与存在的同质性结构中来呈现它所创造的东西。马克思充分认识到黑格尔辩证法的这一神秘性和非批判性，由此郑重强调："我的辩证方法，从根本上来说，不仅和黑格尔的辩证方法不同，而且和它截然相反。

① 《列宁专题文集　论辩证唯物主义和历史唯物主义》，人民出版社 2009 年版，第 162 页。

② 《马克思恩格斯文集》第 5 卷，人民出版社 2009 年版，第 22 页。

在黑格尔看来，思维过程，即甚至被他在观念这一名称下转化为独立主体的思维过程，是现实事物的创造主，而现实事物只是思维过程的外部表现。我的看法则相反，观念的东西不外是移入人的头脑并在人的头脑中改造过的物质的东西而已。……辩证法在黑格尔手中神秘化了，……在他那里，辩证法是倒立着的。必须把它倒过来，以便发现神秘外壳中的合理内核。"① 如果说马克思把在黑格尔那里倒立着的辩证法重新倒了过来，那么这一对辩证法的改造绝不仅仅具有形式上的意义，而是具有实质性的意义。这不仅意味着马克思不再像黑格尔那样将辩证法论定为某种神秘的东西，而且还使辩证法的空间始终向现实生活世界敞开，从而能够始终保持对现实矛盾的批判能力。实际也正是因为这一点，马克思才真正在思维和方法论层面根本性地超越了英国古典经济学家，形成了对资本主义经济和社会关系鞭辟入里的批判。

二、卢卡奇：总体性对实证主义的变革

受法国哲学家孔德的影响，19 世纪末和 20 世纪初的哲学社会科学领域普遍采用实证主义的方法开展研究。这个情况也波及马克思主义阵营当中，其主要表现，是考茨基、普列汉诺夫等第二国际理论家借助于自然规律来解释社会经济问题以及由此而图绘马克思的研究路径的确立。比如说，考茨基为自己确立的研究路径就是："我是从达尔文出发的。我所研究的首先是达尔文，后来才是马克思；首先是有机体的发展，后来才是经济的发展，首先是物种的生存斗争，后来才是阶级斗争。"② 我们很容易发现，考茨基的这一研究路径，就是严格遵照孔德的实证主义方法确立起来的，因为以孔德之见，社会与自然这两个领域存在高度的相似性和同质性，所以完全可以根据认识自然的方式来认识社会。

① 《马克思恩格斯文集》第 5 卷，人民出版社 2009 年版，第 22 页。

② 考茨基：《唯物主义历史观》第一分册，上海人民出版社 1964 年版，第 17 页。

马克思和恩格斯在《德意志意识形态》中曾经说过："在思辨终止的地方，在现实生活面前，正是描述人们实践活动和实际发展过程的真正的实证科学开始的地方。"[①] 单从马克思和恩格斯的这句话来看，第二国际的实证主义方法似乎是一种符合马克思主义哲学理论特质的研究方法，因为马克思和恩格斯在这里明确使用了"实证科学"这个术语。然而，马克思和恩格斯在此使用"实证科学"这个术语，是为了指代他们正在创立的从生活到意识的历史唯物主义，以便与从意识到生活的德国唯心主义区别开来。所以，我们不能因为马克思和恩格斯使用过"实证科学"的术语，而认为他们也采用了孔德式的实证主义研究方法。实际情况恰恰相反，作为一种实证科学的历史唯物主义不仅不是依靠实证主义方法确立起来的，而且它在本质上是反实证主义的，因为如果说马克思为自己的哲学所制定的目标是"改变世界"而非"解释世界"，那么历史唯物主义就不仅仅是一种关于历史发展规律的理论，而更是一种具有批判性精神品格的理论。从这一点来看，第二国际无疑是马克思主义哲学在发展的过程中所经历的一段"黑暗"时期，因为马克思为哲学所赋予的那种批判和改造世界的精神性品格，必然会随着实证主义方法的盛行而发生衰微。换言之，当第二国际理论家相继用实证方法来注解马克思主义哲学时，"改变世界"无论从理论层面来看还是从现实层面来看，都将是不可能的。

卢卡奇是较早洞察到上述问题的马克思主义理论家，所以，如何将马克思主义哲学从实证主义方法的"包围"中解救出来，由此激活其改变世界的批判性精神，赋予其新的生命力和思想活力，便成为了他着重思考和回答的重大问题。

在《历史与阶级意识》中，卢卡奇郑重指出："正统马克思主义并不意味着无批判地接受马克思研究的结果。它不是对这个或那个论点的'信仰'，也不是对某本'圣'书的注解。恰恰相反，马克思主义问题中的正统仅仅是指方

---

① 《马克思恩格斯文集》第1卷，人民出版社2009年版，第526页。

法。"[①] 由此可见，卢卡奇不仅充分认识到方法对于马克思主义哲学研究的基础性意义，而且还直截了当地将马克思主义哲学的正统论定为方法。不过以他之见，这种作为马克思主义哲学之正统的方法，在本质上绝非是实证和科学方法，而是总体性辩证法，即"总体范畴，整体对各个部分的全面的、决定性的统治地位（Herrschaft），是马克思取自黑格尔并独创性地改造成为一门全新科学的基础的方法的本质。"[②] 在1967年为《历史与阶级意识》所写的"新版序言"中，卢卡奇依然直言不讳地强调这个观点的正确性："毫无疑义，《历史与阶级意识》的重大成就之一，在于使那曾被社会民主党机会主义的'科学性'打入冷宫的总体（Totalität）范畴，重新恢复了它在马克思全部著作中一向占有的方法论的核心地位。"[③]

如果说以总体性取代实证主义，卢卡奇的确如其所愿，重新激活了马克思主义哲学的批判性精神，赋予了其新的生命力和思想活力，那么，这都是因为他借助于总体性方法来重建被第二国际所遮蔽的"理论维度"而实现的。对此，应当如何理解？

众所周知，"理论"是一个与"实践"紧密联系在一起的术语，当人们谈到"理论"时，往往会立即想到它的对应词"实践"。不过，人们通常遵照亚里士多德及康德传统，将理论与实践指定为两种互不相同的活动类型，并由此在哲学形态学的意义上界划和区分出"理论哲学"与"实践哲学"。比如，将寻求知识的认识论哲学界划为理论哲学，将探求公正理想的政治制度的政治哲学界划为实践哲学。由于马克思明确地将哲学的任务指示为改变世界而非解释世界，所以，人们也往往由此而将其所创立的哲学命定为实践哲学，似乎从理论的角度来认定其哲学一定是非法的。但实际上，理论与实践的关系并非是一种非此即彼的关系，而是密不可分的一体之两面：一方面，理论从来就不应是

---

① 卢卡奇：《历史与阶级意识》，杜章智、任立、燕宏远译，商务印书馆1999年版，第49页。

② 卢卡奇：《历史与阶级意识》，杜章智、任立、燕宏远译，商务印书馆1999年版，第79页。

③ 卢卡奇：《历史与阶级意识》，杜章智、任立、燕宏远译，商务印书馆1999年版，第15页。

抽象空洞的东西，而是建立在现实实践的基础上的；另一方面，实践也不应是流离于理论之外的经验行动，而应是在理论的深度参与下所构建起来的历史活动。从这一点来看，马克思哲学作为一种实践哲学，实际也是一种具有理论性的哲学，如果马克思没有从理论的制高点来对资本主义制度及其矛盾予以透彻审视与批判，他也不会提出“改变世界”这一划时代的哲学口号，并由此赋予其哲学以强烈的实践性品格。在这个问题上，海德格尔的如下认识是尤为深刻的：“在马克思那里谈到的是哪样一种改变世界呢？是生产关系中的改变。生产在哪里具有其地位呢？在实践中。实践是通过什么被规定的呢？通过某种理论，这种理论将生产的概念塑造为对人的（通过他自身的）生产。因此马克思具有一个关于人的理论想法，一个相当确切的想法，这个想法作为基础包含在黑格尔哲学之中。”① 海德格尔这一认识的深刻性就在于，他不仅看到了马克思立足于“实践”的哲学也是一种理论，而且还看到了这种理论不是一种具有描述性的经验和实证知识，而是一种对实践起塑造作用、因而彰显着批判性精神品格的规范性话语。

如果以上论述表明，具有实践指向的马克思哲学不仅存在一个不可或缺的“理论维度”，而且其批判性精神在一定意义上，恰恰也就是通过这个理论维度的建立而确立起来的，那么第二国际在遵照实证主义思维方法解读马克思时，正是因为将这个不可或缺的理论维度深深遮蔽了起来，所以才使马克思主义哲学批判和改造世界的精神性品格逐渐衰微，使其在一段时间内变异为一种教条的知识和缺乏思想解释力的原理说教。问题的关键在于：对于卢卡奇而言，他何以能够借助于总体性辩证法来重建被第二国际所遮蔽的“理论维度”？在直接的意义上，总体性辩证法的一个基本思想就是强调理论与实践的统一，而对于这种统一，卢卡奇在《历史与阶级意识》中作了如下限定性说明：“只有当意识的产生成为历史过程为达到自己的目的（这个目的来自人的意志，但不取

---

① 《晚期海德格尔的三天讨论班纪要》，F. 费迪耶等 / 辑录，丁耘 / 摘译，《哲学译丛》2001年第3期。

决于人的任意妄为，也不是人的精神发明的）所必须采取的决定性步骤时；只有当理论的历史作用在于使这一步骤成为实际可能时；只有当出现一个阶级要维持自己的权利就必须正确认识社会这样的历史局面时；只有当这个阶级认识自身就意味着认识整个社会时；只有因此这个阶级既是认识的主体，又是认识的客体，而且按这种方式，理论直接而充分地影响到社会的变革过程时，理论的革命作用的前提条件——理论和实践的统一——才能成为可能。”① 卢卡奇的这段限定性说明告诉我们，他是在强调理论对于实践所具有的先导性意义的前提下来强调这两者的统一的，即在他的心目中，理论并非总是滞后于实践的东西，而是对于实践发挥着批判和引导的功能、因而在一定意义上超前于实践的东西，所以实践性的一定是高度理论性的，而理论性的，才是真正实践性的，理论只有在对于实践的批判与创制作用下，才可能达到与实践的高度统一。如果说卢卡奇的这一认识，也就是其总体性辩证法所要阐释的一个最为重要的思想观点，那么他在方法论层面的重大自觉，必然意味着被马克思为其哲学所建立的理论维度在被第二国际的实证主义所遮蔽之后又获得了历史性的重建，进而也必然意味着马克思主义哲学之“改变世界”的思想诉求又获得了新的历史性奠基。

扩而论之，卢卡奇所策动的总体性对实证主义变革的方法论意义不仅具有特殊性，也具有普遍性。换言之，这一变革不仅构成了卢卡奇解读马克思和发展马克思主义哲学的方法论前提，而且也为之后西方马克思主义的哲学探索提供了一个方法论的范本。受卢卡奇的影响，20 世纪 30 年代至 60 年代末的西方马克思主义哲学家，大都吸收了总体性辩证法的思想精髓，由此特别强调和突出了理论维度在马克思主义哲学中的基础性地位，抵御了实证主义方法对马克思主义哲学的不断侵蚀，维护了马克思主义哲学所特有的批判性精神。在这方面，法兰克福学派是一个尤为典型的例证。众所周知，法兰克福学派将其创

① 卢卡奇:《历史与阶级意识》，杜章智、任立、燕宏远译，商务印书馆 1999 年版，第 50 页。

造的理论指示和命名为"批判理论"。而所谓批判理论，并非指具体针对这个或那个对象进行批判的一种理论，而是指与近代以来经验和实证的理论相异质、能够穿越事物现象从而达及事物本质、具有批判能力的一种特定的理论形式。法兰克福学派理论家认识到，要使这种特定形式的理论具有批判能力并与实证性理论形成分殊，唯一有效的工作，就是以理论的方式或在理论的制高点上来审视现存秩序，因为在以霍克海默为代表的法兰克福学派理论家看来，"如果脱离开理论去思考理论对象，我们就会歪曲理论对象，就会陷入无为主义或顺世哲学。"① 法兰克福学派的这个认识无疑表明，其批判理论，实际就是在卢卡奇所策动的方法论变革的启示下、明确遵照总体性辩证法、通过开显马克思主义哲学的理论维度而构建起来的。对于法兰克福学派与卢卡奇在方法论上的这种师承关系，美国哲学家理查德·沃林作了如下精彩的评述："按照霍克海默的观点，哲学和社会科学这两门学科是必然地相辅相成的。没有一般观念指导的经验研究将是一堆零乱的无意义的材料堆砌，仅仅是材料本身而已。它仅仅呈现了个别的专门学科之日益不相关联的各种结果，而不是对于主流社会趋势的一致而系统的思考；像以前一样，这是一种把社会片断的当前状况提升为某个二次方程式的实践。而且，由于被提高到方法论绝对的姿态，带着对于"事实"的无批判尊重，经验主义表现了对于当下给定的社会秩序的全盘肯定。由于它禁欲主义地看待评价问题或规范问题，由于它完全忽视了社会发展的重大趋势和动力，它以像晚期黑格尔（纵然出于不同理由）把现实性和合理性同一起来那样而告终。因此，为了同实证主义社会科学之自我抵消的唯名论作斗争，霍克海默不得不求助于卢卡奇的一个范畴：总体性。追随于黑格尔和马克思之后，卢卡奇千方百计地把那个范畴重新引入 20 世纪的社会哲学话语之中。因为按照霍克海默的观点，由于忽视了这个范畴，受制于某种严格的知识复制理论的正统社会科学仍被指责为只是反映了当代社会生活的片断及其危

① 霍克海默：《批判理论》，李小兵等译，重庆出版社 1989 年版，第 217 页。

机四伏的性质。只有通过统一于某个理论计划，只有首先牢记作为一个性质全体的社会秩序的观点，经验研究的成果才免于堕入琐碎的和无意义的命运之中。”① 沃林这段评述的精彩之处，其实不仅在于从一般思想史的意义上指认了法兰克福学派与卢卡奇的师承关系，而且也在于从这种指认中，把握到了总体性与实证主义这两种研究方法在 20 世纪马克思主义哲学的发展中所形成的对决及由之而造成的马克思主义哲学理论的重大变迁。这也由此告诉我们，卢卡奇所策动的方法论变革的意义，实际已经远远超出了继承谁与影响谁的一般思想史层面，而关涉到了几乎整个 20 世纪马克思主义哲学的理论发展及其思想实质的重大问题。

三、柯亨：分析的方法对人本主义的变革

进一步讲，马克思固然是在理论维度中实现理论与实践之统一的，但与此同时，他又是以直面资本主义现实、科学研究和批判资本主义经济关系来建立其理论维度的。从这一点来看，马克思所讲的理论并非是空中楼阁，而是对现实矛盾的一种深度和科学把握，离开了科学性，其理论就会退化为与之格格不入的东西。然而，卢卡奇之后的西方马克思主义根据总体性辩证法来开显和重建理论维度，虽然在很大程度上克服了实证主义给马克思主义哲学的发展造成的困难，激发了马克思主义哲学的批判性精神，但由于没有领会到马克思所讲的理论的科学性特质，所以严重疏离了对资本主义经济关系的科学分析和批判，进而一味强调理论对于现实的超越性关系。在哲学形态上，西方马克思主义的这个缺陷的基本表征，便是人本主义的泛滥成灾，具体一点说，就是西方马克思主义哲学家们凭借飘荡无根的理论想象，构建关于人、人的自由、人的异化、人的解放等的话语和叙事结构。对于解读马克思和发展马克思主义哲学

① 理查德·沃林：《文化批评的观念》，张国清译，商务印书馆 2000 年版，第 92—93 页。

理论而言，人本主义作为一种哲学形态，固然为人们提供了一个第二国际和前苏联马克思主义哲学家所不能提供的支点，但却也容易将人们引向纯粹主观主义和唯意志主义这一经验主义的思维老路，对马克思主义哲学的重大基础理论问题作出任意解释，从而与马克思所开创的科学性理论道路渐行渐远。这个情况表明，卢卡奇以来的西方马克思主义在经历了总体性对实证主义这次重大的方法论变革之后，实际又面临着一个如何克服人本主义、回归马克思主义哲学的科学性的重大理论任务。而要完成这个理论任务，显然又需要方法论上的再一次变革。

最早明确意识到上述理论任务的马克思主义哲学家，是阿尔都塞。众所周知，在《保卫马克思》一书中，阿尔都塞区分了科学和意识形态，认为1845年之前的青年马克思处在意识形态的阶段，而1845年之后、特别是《资本论》创作时期的马克思处在构建理论的科学阶段。在阿尔都塞看来，人本主义归根结底就是一种反科学的意识形态，它虽然能够获得青年马克思文本的支持，但却与科学创作时期的马克思的思想背道而驰，所以只有在理论上祛除包括人本主义在内的任何意识形态，并切实回到1845年之后的马克思理论结构中，才能够根本揭示马克思理论的科学性本质。需要特别注意的是，阿尔都塞主要是在理论层面来克服人本主义的，并没有涉及方法论层面的问题。他虽然提出了理解《资本论》的所谓“症候阅读法”，但这种方法只有文本解读的个别意义，而没有方法论变革的全局和普遍意义。但实际上，在西方马克思主义中盛行的人本主义缺少的是一种学理上的坚实性，所以要克服人本主义的任意性和泛滥成灾，一项几乎是必不可少的基础性工作，就是厘清马克思主义哲学理论的基本命题，并全面把握各命题之间的内在联系，由此使马克思主义哲学成为一种具有概念的明晰性和逻辑的严密性的科学理论。由于这项工作已经根本涉及到方法论层面的问题，所以阿尔都塞并没有对此有所推进，这使他在马克思主义哲学的一些基础理论问题甚至是重大基础理论问题上，仍然缺乏严谨和科学的界定与说明，虽然追求科学性是其始终不变的目标。比如说，当他在科学与意识形态之间作硬性划界，并将一切人本主义（或称人道主义）作为意识形态从对马克思理论本质的认知中加以剔除时，他就无法对马克思主义哲学中最基础、最重要的范畴之间的关系，如理论与实践、理想与现实以及事实与规范（价值）、科学与哲学之间的关系作出科学性的界定与说明。阿尔都塞本人也意识到了这个问题，所以在他进行自我反思和自我批评时这样指出："尽管我凸显了理论对于革命实践的极端重要性，尽管我因此揭示了各种形式的经验主义的错误，但是，我并没有探讨'理论和实践相结合'的问题，而这一问题在马克思列宁主义传统中具有举足轻重的地位。……同样，尽管我坚持马克思发现在理论上的革命特征，尽管我指出马克思建立了一个新的科学和一个新的哲学，我却没有明确地说明那把科学与哲学区分开来的极其重要的差别。我没有表明不同于科学而构成了哲学本身的东西：整个哲学（它是理论的原则）在其各种存在形式及各种理论要求之中的和政治的有机联系。我没有指出这种联系的性质。对于马克思主义哲学来说，它和实际的联系没有任何关系。因此，我没有清楚地指明把马克思主义哲学和先前的哲学区分开来的东西。"① 平心而论，只要不能对诸如理论与实践、哲学与科学等的关系作出实至名归的界定和说明，就无法有效地克服人本主义模式在解释马克思及其哲学思想的随意性与非科学性，因而也不能完全揭示马克思主义哲学的科学性本质。要解决这个问题，方法论层面的再一次重大调整与变革是必不可少的。

在这方面作出实质性推进的，是当代分析的马克思主义哲学家G.A.柯亨。在《卡尔·马克思的历史理论：一个辩护》一书的"序言"中，柯亨这样说道："阿尔都塞的《保卫马克思》使我相信，永久重要的马克思是在《资本论》及其准备材料中被发现的。这种确信促使我写这本书，因此我要感谢他。但是当我进而读到阿尔都塞和其他一些人的论文集——《阅读〈资本论〉》时，我却大失所望。我从阿尔都塞那里所得甚少，不管法语是多么的优雅和含混。我喜欢别

---

① 阿尔都塞：《保卫马克思》，顾良译，商务印书馆2010年版，第254页。

的更好一点的东西，特别是巴利巴尔（Balibar）的贡献。但是我不认为它的价值在于它显示了阿尔都塞的影响。首先，我发现《阅读〈资本论〉》极其不明确。逻辑实证主义连同它关于理智活动精确性的坚定主张，在巴黎从未受到欢迎，这或许是一件遗憾的事。英美哲学已经超越逻辑实证主义很久了，但好在它一直同它打交道。阿尔都塞的含混会给英国的马克思主义带来不幸，在那里明晰性是一种严格的传统。”① 从柯亨的这段论述来看，如果说阿尔都塞的《保卫马克思》在很大程度上扭转了卢卡奇以来的西方马克思主义一味倚重马克思早期著作来解释其思想的人本主义传统，并确立起了到《资本论》及其准备材料中来解读马克思的科学主义传统，那么柯亨作为一位分析马克思主义的哲学家，实际是在阿尔都塞所确立的科学主义传统中来理解马克思的。不过，以柯亨之见，由于阿尔都塞在对马克思《资本论》基本概念和命题的界定上存在含混不清和晦暗不明的重大缺陷，所以这一点又对英国马克思主义产生了消极的影响，而只有接受逻辑实证主义之精确性和明晰性的传统，才能够真正有效地克服人本主义，将马克思主义哲学的理论活动实质性地引向科学的道路。我们知道，在 20 世纪的哲学发展中，由逻辑实证主义所催生的理论方法就是分析的方法，而由于柯亨是在方法论层面来认同和接受逻辑实证主义的，所以，分析的方法顺理成章地成为了他开展马克思主义哲学研究的基本方法。由此我们认为，如果说柯亨在马克思主义哲学发展史上同样策动了一场方法论变革，那么这就是分析的方法对人本主义的变革。

进而论之，由于分析的方法的一个基本要求就是追求理智活动的精确性和坚实性，所以从思维进程来看，它属于黑格尔所界划的辩证逻辑的第一个环节，即抽象的或知性（理智）的环节。在科学研究中，虽然仅仅停留在这个环节，并不能认识和呈现研究对象的本真状貌，但如果越过这个环节而直接动用处在更高思维阶段的辩证理性和思辨理性，也不能实现对于研究对象的完整把

---

① 柯亨：《卡尔·马克思的历史理论：一个辩护》，岳长龄译，重庆出版社 1989 年版，序言第 2 页。

握，其所缺少的就是关于研究对象的规定性和思维的坚实性。对于这个问题，黑格尔在《小逻辑》中作了明确说明："思维无疑地首先是知性的思维。……无论如何，我们必须首先承认理智思维的权利和优点，大概讲来，无论在理论的或实践的范围内，没有理智，便不会有坚定性和规定性。"① 黑格尔的这个说明告诉人们，相比知性，他虽然更加推崇辩证法和思辨，但没有知性作基础，辩证法和思辨都只是无源之水、无本之木的东西，在此意义上，知性所具有的坚定性和规定性，乃是达到辩证法和思辨阶段的基石。卢卡奇以来的各种人本主义哲学流派，几乎都没有理解知性与辩证法的这一关系，所以在一味强调辩证法的意义和理论对于实践的规制作用时，也都不约而同地忽视了对于知性思维的运用。

对于马克思而言，他自然如上所示，借助于辩证法而根本超越了以知性为启端和终端的经验主义，进而形成了对资本逻辑的科学认知和批判，但毋庸置疑，他的科学认知和批判活动，又恰恰是从知性开始的，具体一点说，就是从对资本主义活生生的经济关系的分析开始的，离开了这个起点，马克思反倒不可能建立起超越经验主义的辩证思维，由此从方法论层面及理论层面颠覆亚当·斯密以来的英国经济学传统，形成对资本主义社会的透彻批判。同理，我们固然需要从辩证思维的界面和高度来领略、把握马克思哲学的思想命意，但正如黑格尔所指出的，"在哲学里，最紧要的，就是对每一思想都必须充分准确地把握住，而决不容许有空泛和不确定之处"②，所以，在将马克思哲学作为一个对象来予以科学性理解和诠释时，知性也是一个不可空缺的环节。从这一点来看，与知性相对应的分析的方法，不仅不会必然将我们的思维触角引向马克思所反对的经验主义及卢卡奇所反对的实证主义，相反，这一方法是我们理解马克思的一个基础性方法，其重大意义之一，就在于帮助我们辨明马克思哲学文本和理论范畴的原初意义，从而避免对马克思的思想作出空洞抽象的、任

① 黑格尔：《小逻辑》，贺麟译，商务印书馆 1980 年版，第 173—174 页。

② 黑格尔：《小逻辑》，贺麟译，商务印书馆 1980 年版，第 176 页。

意性的解释。就此而言，分析的方法在克服缺乏知性思维的人本主义上，比阿尔都塞通过界划科学与意识形态而作出的努力，无疑是更为有效的。

放大开来，柯亨通过引入分析的方法而策动的方法论变革，其意义并不仅仅在于有效克服人本主义思潮的非科学性倾向，同时还在于为马克思主义哲学的各分支领域建立理论基础和学科前提。这里的问题在于：马克思在19世纪创造其哲学理论时，并未从学科或近似学科的意义上界划和区分出不同的学术领域。但20世纪后期以来直到今天，马克思主义哲学研究的一个重大变化，就是出现和形成了学术化和专门化的趋势，其重要表征之一，便是从作为一个整体的马克思主义哲学理论中，分化出和确立起不同的分支性学术领域和学科方向，如历史哲学、文化哲学、经济哲学、政治哲学、法哲学、价值哲学、人学等领域和方向。实际上，当人们在开辟和确立这些学术领域和学科方向时，就在自觉或不自觉地运用着分析的方法，虽然人们未必意识到这一点。因为众所周知，分析的方法及与之相对应的知性的一个重要特点，就是根据“同一律”来对研究对象予以界定和规定，[①] 而人们只有按照“同一律”来对马克思主义哲学的各理论要素和各学术命题加以区分，才能够确定诸如历史哲学、文化哲学、经济哲学、政治哲学等的边界，从而使它们成为具有自成一系的研究内容和理论规范的学术领域和学科方向。对于柯亨而言，众所周知，其在20世纪90年代之后的学术实践中，从对历史唯物主义的界定与阐释，明确转向了以构建社会主义平等理论为核心旨趣的政治哲学研究，由此在马克思主义学术史上开辟出了规范性政治哲学这个研究领域。实际上，柯亨的这个重大学术转向，与其所使用的分析的方法就有着密切关系：一方面，柯亨正是借助于分析

① 黑格尔在《小逻辑》中，对这个问题作出过如下说明：“知性的定律是同一律，单纯的自身联系。也就是通过这种同一律，认识的过程首先才能够由一个范畴推进到另一个范畴。譬如，在数学里，量就是排除了它的别的特性而加以突出的范畴。所以，在几何学里，我们把一个图形与另一个图形加以比较，借以突出其同一性。同样，在别的认识范围里，例如在法学里，也是主要依据同一律而进行研究。在法学里，我们由一条特殊的法理推到另一条特殊的法理，这种推论，也是依据同一律而进行的。”（黑格尔：《小逻辑》，贺麟译，商务印书馆1980年版，第174页。）

的方法，厘清了马克思主义哲学中事实性命题与规范性命题的内容及相互之间的关系，才得以根据规范性命题界划出了政治哲学的理论问题与学科边界；另一方面，柯亨也正是借助于分析的方法，透彻检视和指证了罗尔斯及诺齐克等的理论缺陷，才形成了与自由主义话语有着异质性学术前提和思想诉求的马克思主义政治哲学话语。由此可见，在马克思主义哲学发展史上，柯亨所具有的卓尔不凡的学术成就和无法取代的理论地位，与其在方法论层面所策动的重大变革是密不可分的。

本文以上论述表明，方法论层面的问题，绝非马克思主义哲学中无关紧要的小问题，而是关系到马克思主义哲学的理论实质与乃至理论命运的大问题。如果说从马克思主义哲学发展的历史来看，方法论上的每一次重大变革都直接引发了理论上的重大突破、推进和跃升，那么方法论上的重大自觉，无疑也构成了当代中国马克思主义哲学理论创新的一个重要前提。

（原载《社会科学战线》2017 年第 1 期）

文化哲学视野中的东西方马克思主义哲学

何 萍

《20世纪马克思主义哲学：东方与西方》[①]，是我对20世纪马克思主义哲学的一种解读。这一解读包括三个方面的内容：第一，20世纪马克思主义哲学是一个有着特定意义的概念，是需要专门提出来加以研究的对象；第二，20世纪马克思主义哲学是由东西方马克思主义哲学共同构成的，因此，要研究20世纪马克思主义哲学，就必须从东西方马克思主义哲学的论争中把握20世纪马克思主义哲学发展的基本格局和整体风貌；第三，运用文化哲学的研究范式审视20世纪马克思主义哲学，提出20世纪马克思主义哲学研究的论题。事实上，从20世纪80年代开始，我就一直在研究这一课题，发表了多篇论文。但是，当我把其中的主要论文集结成书时，我又觉得需要有一个概论的形式，把我所思考的问题和基本观点叙述出来，以便于读者把握全书的结构和内容。本文就是这一概论形式。

一、"20世纪马克思主义哲学"概念解析

我认为，要开展20世纪马克思主义哲学的研究，首先要有"20世纪马克思主义哲学"这一概念。因为只有有了"20世纪马克思主义哲学"这一概念，人们才会把20世纪的马克思主义哲学与19世纪的马克思主义哲学区别开来，才会把20世纪马克思主义哲学作为一个有机整体加以研究，才会发现它在马

① 何萍：《20世纪马克思主义哲学：东方与西方》，人民出版社2012年版。

克思主义哲学发展史上的特殊地位，也才会了解研究它的全部意义。我把本书定名为“20 世纪马克思主义哲学”，就是为了明确“20 世纪马克思主义哲学”这一概念。所以，解析“20 世纪马克思主义哲学”概念就成为本文首先要解决的问题。

对于一个断代哲学的研究，人们可以用时间概念来叙述，也可以用哲学概念来表达。但是，用时间概念叙述出来的东西和用哲学概念表达出来的东西是根本不同的。时间概念是与经验、常识相联系的，由此决定，用时间概念叙述出来的东西，必然是一个断代哲学产生的背景、一定时期哲学产生的经验基础，或者叙述这一时期的哲学与前此哲学之间的联系，说明哲学发展的连续性。这种叙述的目的只在于，把现阶段的哲学归属于前此的哲学，看作是前此哲学理论的延续。这实际上是否定了现阶段哲学存在的价值，是在叙述常识的东西，而绝非哲学的东西。与此不同，哲学概念本质上是批判的，是对一个时代的哲学总观念的表达，因此，运用哲学概念所揭示的，是一个时代哲学的理性结构以及它的理念，总之，是该时代的哲学与前此哲学之间的否定关系。当然，哲学概念的表达也关心现阶段的哲学与前此哲学之间的联系，但它绝不像时间概念叙述的那样，把现阶段的哲学归属于前此哲学，而是要把那些被遮蔽在前此哲学中本质的东西揭示出来，说明这些本质的东西是如何构造成新的哲学传统和哲学形态的，又是如何决定现阶段哲学的性质和风貌的。这一区别表明，时间概念的叙述和哲学概念的表达体现了断代哲学研究的两个相互反对的方向。至于哪一个方向更适合研究的对象，需要研究者根据研究对象的性质和特点作出判断和选择。这种研究方向的判断和选择，对于 20 世纪马克思主义哲学的研究，尤为重要。

长期以来，我国学术界都是以时间概念来叙述 20 世纪马克思主义哲学，认为，20 世纪马克思主义哲学与 19 世纪马克思主义哲学在哲学的观念上、在坚持马克思主义哲学的原理上，没有本质的区别，它们之间的区别只在产生的时代背景不同，因而研究的内容不同：19 世纪马克思主义哲学产生于自由资本主义时代、工人运动刚刚兴起的时代，因此，研究生产力对生产关系的决定作用，研究资本主义发展的规律、研究科学社会主义的理论，是这一时代马克思主义哲学研究的主要内容；20世纪的马克思主义哲学产生于自由资本主义走向垄断资本主义的时代、科学社会主义由理论走向实践时代，因此，研究上层建筑的能动性、批判垄断资本主义的极权统治、探讨社会主义的实践问题，构成了这一时代马克思主义哲学研究的主要内容。而在我看来，时代的不同决定20世纪马克思主义哲学与19世纪马克思主义哲学在研究内容上的区别，这一点是不容置疑的，但是，20世纪马克思主义哲学与19世纪马克思主义哲学的区别还不止于此，它们之间最根本的区别还在形式上，即哲学总观念的区别。可以说，正是由于有了哲学总观念上的区别，才有了20世纪的马克思主义哲学运动，也才会有20世纪马克思主义哲学。因此，单单从内容上来区分20世纪马克思主义哲学与19世纪马克思主义哲学，只能在经验的层面上描述20世纪马克思主义哲学，而不能从理论上说明20世纪马克思主义哲学的特点。我国学术界正是因为没有看到这一点，所以，虽然在哲学研究创新的驱使下，不断地追踪研究20世纪东西方各国马克思主义哲学的派别和代表人物的思想，却始终没有提出“20世纪马克思主义哲学”这一概念，更没有把“20世纪马克思主义哲学”作为一个独特的对象加以研究。我在这里明确地提出“20世纪马克思主义哲学”这一概念，就是要把“20世纪马克思主义哲学”当作一个哲学概念来表达，揭示它与19世纪马克思主义哲学在研究的形式上、在哲学总观念上的区别，以此说明把“20世纪马克思主义哲学”作为一个独特的对象加以研究的意义和必要性。

那么，20世纪马克思主义哲学的总观念是什么？它与19世纪马克思主义哲学的观念有什么实质性的区别？对于这个问题，我们是很难以马克思主义哲学中的某个领域的理论来概括的，而必须在20世纪马克思主义的哲学批判运动中找到说明。事实上，是以马克思主义哲学中的某个领域的理论来定义马克思主义哲学，还是以哲学的总观念来定义马克思主义哲学，恰恰是19世纪马克思主义哲学与20世纪马克思主义哲学在哲学总观念上的区别。

我在这里所说的19世纪马克思主义哲学，当然包括马克思和恩格斯的哲学，但更主要的是指19世纪后半叶的马克思主义哲学，尤其是第二国际的马克思主义者的哲学。马克思和恩格斯是马克思主义哲学的创始人，他们在创造自己的学说的时候，并没有刻意地区分他们学说中的哲学、政治经济学和科学社会主义学说，也没有把其中的某一个部分确定为自己学说的本质。把其中的某一个部分确定为马克思主义学说的本质是马克思、恩格斯之后的马克思主义者所做的工作。这一工作始于19世纪下半叶。19世纪下半叶，正是欧洲工人运动蓬勃兴起的年代，工人运动的健康发展需要科学社会主义理论，于是，传播和发展科学社会主义理论就成为这一时期马克思主义者的主要任务。在这种情况下，西欧的马克思主义者，尤其是第二国际的马克思主义者，明确地把马克思主义学说定义为科学社会主义学说，而马克思主义哲学只是科学社会主义理论的方法。在这一观念主导下，这一时期的马克思主义哲学研究主要有两个特点：其一，把马克思主义哲学等同于历史唯物主义。当时的马克思主义者把马克思主义哲学理解为历史唯物主义，这固然与马克思、恩格斯著作的出版和传播相关①，但更主要的原因还是工人运动和社会主义运动发展的需要，是因为工人运动和社会主义运动急需从历史唯物主义理论中找到对人类历史规律的说明，以此证明工人运动的历史合理性和社会主义学说的科学性。这就使得历史唯物主义成为工人运动和社会主义运动的直接的理论根据；其二，历史方法的研究胜于历史理论的研究。由于研究帝国主义和社会主义运动的需要，这一时期的马克思主义者把历史唯物主义分为理论和方法两个部分，以方法解理论，论证修改和发展马克思、恩格斯的历史唯物主义学说的合理性和合法性，

① 19世纪下半叶在工人运动广泛传播的马克思、恩格斯的著作主要是《共产党宣言》《法兰西内战》《反杜林论》《资本论》《家庭、私有制和国家的起源》等，马克思的早期著作只有梅林、罗莎·卢森堡等马克思主义理论家从马克思哲学的思想起源上、从马克思的辩证法思想形成的角度作过研究。

从而使马克思、恩格斯的哲学能够面对和解答当时实践提出的新问题。有的马克思主义者甚至把马克思、恩格斯的历史唯物主义定义为方法论，从理论上阐发历史唯物主义的方法论内容和内在逻辑。这就使得马克思主义哲学方法论的研究水平超过了理论的研究水平。19 世纪的马克思主义者对马克思主义哲学的这一理解和研究，极大地推动了历史唯物主义学说的发展。在这一时期，历史唯物主义的研究取得了三个大的成就：一是把文化哲学引入了历史唯物主义的研究，开发出对家庭、伦理和道德的起源和历史演变等方面的研究，从而对人类的经济、政治和文化作了起源学的说明，深化了马克思、恩格斯的历史唯物主义理论；二是以资本主义的崩溃为研究视角，分析帝国主义现象，创立了帝国主义理论，同时，也发展了马克思的资本主义危机理论；三是发展了马克思主义的历史主义方法。然而，历史唯物主义研究中的这些成就并没有使马克思主义学说赢得哲学的荣誉，反而使它陷入了危机。这种危机，在理论根源上，首先来自于把马克思主义学说定义为科学社会主义这一总观念。因为，把马克思主义学说定义为科学社会主义，这本身就已经把马克思主义学说归属于社会思潮，而否定了它是一种哲学思潮。由于这一否定，不论是在马克思主义阵营内部，还是在马克思主义阵营外部，人们都自觉或不自觉地将马克思主义学说排除于哲学之外；其次是来自于把马克思主义哲学等同于历史唯物主义这一哲学观念。我们知道，哲学之能成为哲学，之能够把自己与科学、常识和宗教等其他学说区别开来，就在于它有本体论。本体论是哲学的根基处。任何哲学要想改变以往的哲学，要把自己与同时代其他的哲学区别开来，都必须建立自己的本体论。马克思主义哲学也不例外，也需要有自己的本体论。这一点恰恰被 19 世纪下半叶的大多数学者所忽视了。因为忽视了这一点，他们把仅仅是马克思主义哲学的一个方面、一个理论的历史唯物主义当作了马克思主义哲学的总体，并且更强调它的方法论意义，这就阻止了对马克思主义哲学开展总体性的、全面的研究，尤其是阻止了对马克思主义哲学开展本体论的研究，而没有本体论，马克思主义哲学就失去了形上的根基，就不能显示它与其他哲学的区别。当时的哲学家就是抓住了马克思主义的这一理论缺陷而否定马克思主义有自己的哲学。这就是马克思主义哲学的危机。柯尔施重提“马克思主义哲学”时，概括了这一危机状况：“在那个时期，无论马克思主义理论和资产阶级理论在所有其他方面有着多大的矛盾，这两个极端在这一点上却有着明显的一致之处。资产阶级的哲学教授们一再互相担保，马克思主义没有任何它自己的哲学内容，并认为他们说的是很重要的不利于马克思主义的东西。正统的马克思主义者们也一再互相担保，他们的马克思主义从其本性上来讲与哲学没有任何关系，并认为他们说的是很重要的有利于马克思主义的东西。但还有从同样的基本观点出发的第三种倾向；在这整个这个时期内，这是唯一多少更彻底地关心社会主义的哲学方面的倾向。它由各种‘研究哲学的社会主义者’所组成，他们声称他们的任务是用来自文化哲学（Kulturphilosophie）的观念或者用康德、狄慈根、马赫的哲学概念或别的哲学来‘补充’马克思主义。然而，正是因为他们认为马克思主义体系需要哲学的补充，他们也就使人们明白了，在他们的眼里，马克思主义本身是缺乏哲学内容的。”① 事实上，在第二国际的阵营里，也有马克思主义者意识到了马克思主义哲学的这一危机，并力图挽救这一危机。比如，普列汉诺夫就是这样一个马克思主义者。他在《马克思主义哲学的基本问题》中分析了马克思主义陷入哲学危机的理论根源，指出，人们对马克思主义学说性质的种种歪曲和误解，比如，把马克思主义哲学或与康德哲学结合一起，或与马赫哲学结合一起，等等，都是因为仅仅把马克思主义哲学归于唯物主义的历史观，而没有从哲学世界观的高度理解马克思主义哲学。然而，马克思主义哲学从本质上来说，“是一个完整的世界观”，是“现代唯物主义”②。在这里，普列汉诺夫是把唯物主义、哲学的世界观看作高于历史唯物主义的东西，是比之历史唯物主义更具有一般性、更能体现哲学原则的东西，而历史唯物主义只是唯物主义、哲学的世界观下的一个分支理论。普列汉诺夫

① 柯尔施：《马克思主义和哲学》，重庆出版社 1989 年版，第 4 页。

② 参见《普列汉诺夫哲学著作选集》第 3 卷，三联书店 1962 年版，第 134 页。

的这一观点在指出19世纪马克思主义哲学的巨大缺陷上，实际是完全正确的。但是，要使马克思主义走出哲学危机，仅仅把马克思主义哲学理解为一般唯物主义、理解为哲学的世界观是不够的，还必须把哲学看作是马克思主义学说的本质，看作是比科学社会主义更重要的东西。也就是说，要把对马克思主义的本质定义为哲学，而不是科学社会主义。普列汉诺夫没有提出这一任务，所以，尽管他在研究马克思主义哲学的一般性上做了许多的工作，但终究没有摆脱第二国际的马克思主义哲学研究框架。这一任务是由20世纪的马克思主义者明确提出来，并最终完成的。

为了挽救马克思主义哲学的危机，20世纪的马克思主义者做了两个方面的工作：第一，把马克思主义定义为哲学，实现马克思主义哲学观念的变革；第二，重建马克思主义哲学的本体论，阐发马克思主义哲学的现代意义。这两个方面的工作都是针对第二国际的马克思主义哲学观念的。就第一个方面而言，20世纪的马克思主义者认为，第二国际的马克思主义者走向改良主义、走向庸俗的马克思主义，其理论根源就在于，他们把马克思主义仅仅理解为科学社会主义，而没有看到支持科学社会主义的革命理论——马克思的哲学，即革命的辩证法学说，没有看到科学社会主义本质上是从属于马克思主义哲学的。所以，要避免把马克思主义哲学片面化、庸俗化，要使马克思主义哲学走出危机，就必须把马克思看作是一个哲学家，把马克思主义定义为哲学。强调这一点，是比什么都重要的。因为只有这样才能把马克思和马克思主义哲学纳入到西方哲学的传统中加以研究，说明它的理论起源、与先前哲学之间的继承和变革关系，才能看到马克思主义哲学变革的全部意义，从而使马克思主义从它的哲学危机中摆脱出来。柯尔施在《马克思主义和哲学》中提出，要重新思考马克思主义和哲学的关系，就是要改变第二国际的马克思主义观念，建立新的马克思主义观念。这个新观念就是，马克思主义是哲学，是革命的辩证法，而不是科学社会主义。其实，提出变革19世纪马克思主义观念的，绝不止柯尔施一人，而是20世纪马克思主义者的共同观念。在布洛赫那里，在葛兰西、卢卡奇那里，在霍克海默那里，甚至在中国的瞿秋白那里，我们都可以看到他们是如何以不同的形式提出这一变革要求的。科拉科夫斯基在他的《马克思主义的主流》一书的“绪论”中阐明了这一变革的实质。他指出：“虽然现在我们很清楚，马克思是个哲学家，半世纪以前情况可不大一样。在第二国际时期，大多数马克思主义者倒认为他是某个经济、社会理论的创造者。”① 可见，把马克思看作是一位哲学家、把马克思主义定义为哲学，是马克思主义观的一次重大变革，而且是20世纪的马克思主义者所进行的一次自觉的、有意识的马克思主义观的批判和变革活动。正是因为有了这一批判和变革活动，我们才有了马克思主义哲学的观念，才会对马克思主义哲学展开多层面、多视角的研究；就第二个方面而言，20世纪的马克思主义者强调，第二国际的马克思主义者对于马克思主义哲学的理解也是根本错误的，因为他们或者从传统唯物主义，或者从康德主义、马赫主义等唯心主义的哲学来理解马克思主义哲学，不了解马克思主义哲学本质上是现代哲学。从这一观点出发，20世纪的马克思主义者对马克思主义哲学作了方法论和理论的改造。在方法论上，20世纪的马克思主义者探讨了现代哲学与传统哲学在思维方式上的差别，批判了传统哲学的逻辑结构，阐明了现代哲学的逻辑结构，并以现代哲学的逻辑结构重建马克思主义的批判理论。法兰克福学派的批判的社会理论就是在批判传统哲学的思维方式、阐发现代哲学的思维方式的基础上建立起来的②；在理论上，20世纪的马克思主义者以实践和辩证法为核心概念，重建马克思主义哲学的本体论，并结合西方哲学传统的流变，阐发了马克思主义哲学的传统。葛兰西在把马克思主义哲学定义为“实践哲学”时反复强调：“实践哲学是现代文化的一个‘要素’”③，而他的实践哲学就是在批判现代文化的基础上建立的马克思主

---

① 科拉科夫斯基：《马克思主义的主流》（一），远流出版事业股份有限公司1992年版，第11页。

② 详见拙著：《马克思主义哲学史教程》下卷，人民出版社2009年版，第686—692页。

③ 葛兰西：《狱中札记》，中国社会科学出版社2000年版，第300页。

义的实践本体论。自葛兰西之后，在西方资本主义国家，每一次马克思主义哲学的变革都是通过重建马克思主义哲学的本体论而实现的。20 世纪 50 年代，法国存在主义的马克思主义哲学是在阐发实践的生存论意义而建立起来的，而阿尔都塞的科学的马克思主义哲学也是在返回到哲学的本体论，通过对哲学性质的重新规定而建立起来的。[①] 不仅如此，生态学马克思主义也正在经历由经济学到哲学，从历史唯物主义进到具有生态意义的自然本体论的转变[②]；在东方国家，苏联马克思主义者建立了自然本体论的马克思主义哲学。这一哲学曾经对中国的马克思主义哲学产生过强烈的影响。中国马克思主义哲学在 20 世纪 30 年代建构了具有认识论特征的"实践的唯物论"、"实践论"，在 20 世纪 80 年代，走向了"实践本体论"的建构。[③] 正是通过 20 世纪的马克思主义者的这种连续不断的哲学创造活动，马克思主义哲学才展示出自己的独特风貌，从而成为 20 世纪的哲学思潮之一。

20 世纪东西方马克思主义者所做的上述两个方面的工作汇集成了马克思主义的哲学运动，从而表明，20 世纪马克思主义哲学是在"马克思主义本质上是哲学"这一总观念下展开的，而结合 20 世纪的文化开展马克思主义哲学的本体论和认识论等多层面的理论创造构成了 20 世纪马克思主义哲学的深刻而丰富的内容。由此，我们可以得出这样的结论：20 世纪是马克思主义哲学空前创造的时代，也是马克思哲学的理论意义和现代价值得到充分展示的时代。因此，我们要研究马克思的哲学，要了解马克思主义哲学发展的历史，就必须研究 20 世纪马克思主义哲学。也就是说，我们只有把 20 世纪马克思主义哲学当作一个独特的研究对象，进行深入的探讨，才能整体把握马克思主义哲学及其发展的历史。这就是我提出"20 世纪马克思主义哲学"概念的根据。

---

① 详见拙著：《马克思主义哲学史教程》下卷，人民出版社 2009 年版，第 633—634 页。

② 详见拙文：《生态学马克思主义的理论困境与出路》，《国外社会科学》2010 年第 1 期。

③ 详见拙著：《马克思主义哲学史教程》下卷，人民出版社 2009 年版，第 813—824 页。

二、20世纪东西方马克思主义哲学的有机构成

从19世纪末开始，马克思主义哲学开始超出它的发源地西欧，传播到世界各国，并在世界各国发展开来。在这一过程中，马克思主义阵营的内部虽然存在着不同的派别，产生了许多的争论，但是，对于马克思主义哲学的发展最有意义的、决定20世纪马克思主义哲学格局的，还是东西方马克思主义者之间的论争。历史地看，20世纪的马克思主义哲学是在东西方马克思主义哲学的论争中展开的，其中有两场论争对20世纪马克思主义哲学格局的形成起了决定性的作用：第一场论争发生于19世纪末至20世纪初。这场论争是在列宁、布哈林与第二国际的马克思主义者之间展开的，其中最著名的、对于20世纪马克思主义哲学格局的形成产生重要影响的，是罗莎·卢森堡和列宁之间就资本积累、民族自治和社会主义民主等问题展开的论争；第二场论争发生于20世纪20—30年代。这场论争是在以葛兰西、卢卡奇和柯尔施为代表的西方马克思主义者和以斯大林为代表的苏联马克思主义者之间就东西方无产阶级革命的性质和特点以及所采取的革命策略问题所展开的。这两场论争构造了20世纪马克思主义哲学由一元而多元、从普遍性到特殊性的发展格局。因此，我们要走进20世纪的马克思主义哲学，要确立“20世纪马克思主义哲学”的概念，就应该分析这两场论争的性质和特点，说明它们对20世纪马克思主义哲学格局形成产生了哪些影响。

先看发生于19世纪末至20世纪初的第一场论争。

19世纪末至20世纪初，是世界历史形成的时代，第一次世界大战的爆发和十月革命的胜利，把东方世界和西方世界连结成一个整体。在这个整体中，一方面是西欧资本主义国家对东方民族的资本扩张，在东西方国家之间建立起资本的联系，另一方面是西欧资本主义国家为了瓜分殖民地在世界范围内发动的帝国主义战争和被压迫民族为反抗帝国主义战争而进行的无产阶级革命，在

东西方国家之间建立起战争和革命的联系。这两个方面的联系对于东西方国家发展的意义是不同的：在资本的联系中，西欧资本主义以高于东方前资本主义的文明形式而成为主动的、能动的一方，东方国家则是被动的、从属的一方；在战争和革命的联系中，西欧国家和东方国家之间的主动和被动关系就变得十分不确定了。东方国家虽然在资本的联系中处在被动的、从属的一方，但是，它有可能通过战争与革命来改变自己的命运、改变世界的格局，而成为主动的、能动的一方。东西方国家之间的这两个方面的联系，为人们考察世界历史提供了两个不同的视角：一个视角是根据资本的联系，从资本的世界形成和崩溃的角度思考东西方国家之间的关系；另一个视角是根据战争和革命的联系，从无产阶级革命和社会主义胜利的角度思考东方社会对世界历史的作用。罗莎·卢森堡和列宁之间发生激烈的论争就是由于他们分别选取的视角不同而引起的。

罗莎·卢森堡是第二国际的左派思想家，她和列宁一样，赞成无产阶级革命，坚持批判修正主义，并在实际的斗争中与列宁有过融洽的合作，但是，罗莎·卢森堡毕竟主要战斗在德国，又是德国马克思主义者当中批判伯恩施坦的主将，所以，在看待世界历史发展的观点上、在思考理论问题的向度上，都要受到她所批判对象的影响。当时，伯恩施坦的修正主义的哲学观点集中在两点上：一是否定马克思有关社会发展的客观必然性的思想；二是否定马克思的资本主义危机理论，主张从生产关系的适应性上来探讨生产力的发展问题。为了从理论上战胜伯恩施坦的修正主义，罗莎·卢森堡从资本主义生存的价值向度、从资本主义生存的历史环境日益缩小的向度，考察帝国主义现象，发展马克思的资本积累理论和危机理论，以此论证社会发展的客观必然性、无产阶级革命和资本主义制度崩溃的历史必然性。这就形成了她从资本联系方面、从资本的世界形成和崩溃的角度，以历史必然性的观点，分析帝国主义时代的东西方国家的关系，说明帝国主义的本质及其历史趋势和无产阶级革命等问题。与罗莎·卢森堡不同，列宁身处具有东方社会特点的俄国，看到的是帝国主义战争造成的世界历史发展的不平衡性，并从世界历史发展的不平衡性中看到了东方民族崛起的机遇，他希望东方社会能够抓住这一机遇，通过世界范围内的民族解放运动，获得自身的独立，改变自身在世界历史体系中的被动地位，成为世界历史体系中的能动因素。从这一观点出发，列宁从战争和革命的联系方面，考察帝国主义现象，揭示帝国主义发展的不平衡规律，并从意识形态的能动性和历史发展的偶然性的向度，思考帝国主义环境下东方无产阶级革命的出路，分析社会主义首先在东方社会取得胜利的客观条件和可能性。这就形成了他从战争和革命的联系方面，从世界无产阶级革命的角度，以历史偶然性的观点，分析帝国主义时代的东西方国家的关系，说明东方无产阶级革命和社会主义在一国胜利的可能性，以及由此而给世界历史变革带来的积极影响。

由于研究的视角不同，罗莎·卢森堡和列宁在帝国主义的前景、帝国主义时代的战争和革命、社会主义民主制度的建设等各个方面，都持不同的观点，并进行过激烈的论战。罗莎·卢森堡从资本的联系出发看待帝国主义的前景，认为，帝国主义意味着资本主义进入了它的世界体系形成的阶段；在这个阶段，东方非资本主义国家是作为西方资本主义存在的历史环境而进入世界资本主义体系，因而是资本主义世界体系的一个限度；在这个限度内，资本主义世界体系有充分的发展空间，如果超出了这个限度，即东方非资本主义国家完全资本主义化了，帝国主义崩溃的历史条件也就成熟了，到那时，无产阶级革命才能在世界范围内取得生产方式的胜利，从而实现总体的社会主义。这就是她的总体资本主义和总体社会主义的观点。从这一观点出发，她反对在帝国主义时代提民族战争和民族自治的口号，认为，在帝国主义时代，由于资本国际化了，无产阶级革命也必然是国际性的，因此，在这个时代，只有国际资本主义和国际无产阶级的对立、资产阶级国家和人民自治的对立，根本不存在民族独立和民族战争的问题，如果谁要在这个时代谈民族的对立、民族的战争，那他是在谈论一些过时的观点，是一些缺乏国际性的世界历史观点。罗莎·卢森堡的这一观点落实在社会主义的民主制度上，就是反对以战争的、宏观革命的方式来对待社会主义的民主制度。她强调，战争的、宏观革命的方式只能解决社会形态的变革问题，而社会形态的变革只是社会主义民主制度建立的前提，并不是社会主义民主制度建设的全部内容，更不能代替社会主义民主制度的建设，因为，社会主义民主制度的建设是一个法律的问题，必须通过长期的日常斗争，通过人民群众的自我教育和不断地参与社会管理的方式来解决。她正是基于这一观点而对布尔什维克以取消杜马的方式来解决社会主义民主制度建设问题的做法持批评态度，即使在十月革命胜利后承认自己的观点有偏激之处时，她仍然坚持认为，在正常的情况下，社会主义民主制度的建设应该像她所设想的那样做。与罗莎·卢森堡不同，列宁从战争和革命的联系出发看待帝国主义的前景，认为，帝国主义的出现意味着资本主义的危机和濒于崩溃，意味着无产阶级革命的客观条件的成熟，所以，在帝国主义时代，东方国家可以利用帝国主义发展的不平衡规律发动无产阶级革命和在世界范围内开展民族解放运动，在一国或多国首先取得无产阶级革命的胜利，并利用无产阶级政权的力量建立社会主义的国家、建设社会主义的民主制度。从这一观点出发，列宁特别强调革命、无产阶级政党和无产阶级的阶级意识对于建立社会主义国家和社会主义民主制度的意义。所以，他强调意识形态的能动性，强调无产阶级革命理论的能动作用，反对把社会主义民主制度建立在人民群众的自发斗争的基础上。正是基于这一观点，列宁激烈地反对罗莎·卢森堡，认为，她在资本积累的理论上、在对待布尔什维克与孟什维克联合的态度上、在有关帝国主义战争和民族自治的观点上、在对俄国革命和布尔什维克做法的批评上，都犯有错误。

尽管罗莎·卢森堡和列宁因研究的视角不同而在帝国主义现象的认识和社会主义制度的建立等一系列问题上发生尖锐的对立，但是，他们都是立足于世界历史发展的高度来看待这些问题，并且把自己的理论看作是一种普遍性的、具有国际性意义的理论。正是这样，他们之间的论争对 20 世纪马克思主义哲学格局的变化和理论发展产生了深远的影响。20 世纪初，随着十月革命的胜利和苏联社会主义国家的建立，列宁哲学被认为是正确的马克思主义哲学而获得了列宁主义的定义，苏联的马克思主义哲学也由此而取代了西欧马克思主义哲学原有的主导地位，成为世界马克思主义哲学的中心，被看作是正统马克思主义哲学，是裁决其他国家的马克思主义哲学是否正确、能否列入马克思主义哲学阵营的标准。这就构造了20世纪马克思主义哲学发展的一元化格局。在这一格局中，人们只有马克思主义哲学是普遍真理的观念，而没有特殊性和民族化的观念。当然，这只是就列宁与罗莎·卢森堡论争所带来的20世纪马克思主义哲学发展格局的形成而言的。除此之外，他们的论争还对20世纪东西方马克思主义者思考世界历史的变化及20世纪东西方国家的关系等问题产生了深刻而持久的影响。尤其是20世纪80年代到90年代以来，由于东欧剧变和苏联的解体、西方资本主义国家凭借互联网重建世界资本主义体系，人们又开始反思罗莎·卢森堡的资本积累理论和她有关社会主义民主制度建设的思想。这时，人们看到，罗莎·卢森堡和列宁论争的问题，依然是我们这个时代面临的问题，而探讨罗莎·卢森堡和列宁的论争又成为联结东西方马克思主义者，形成东西方马克思主义哲学对话的一个契机。

再看发生于20世纪20—30年代的第二场论争。

罗莎·卢森堡与列宁论争所创造的20世纪马克思主义哲学的一元化格局并没有持续很久。20世纪20年代，在十月革命胜利的推动下发动的西欧各国无产阶级夺取政权的革命运动的相继失败，动摇了人们对于苏联马克思主义哲学的普遍性的信念。以葛兰西、卢卡奇和柯尔施为代表的西方马克思主义者在反思西欧各国无产阶级革命失败的经验教训中，针对苏联社会主义革命和建设的经验和苏联马克思主义哲学普遍化的观点，展开了批判。葛兰西分析了西欧社会和俄国社会结构的差别，指出："在俄国，国家就是一切，市民社会处于原始状态，尚未开化；在西方，国家和市民社会关系得当，国家一旦动摇，稳定的市民社会结构立即就会显露。国家不过是外在的壕沟，其背后是强大的堡垒和工事：不用说，各个国家的数量有别——但是这恰好说明每个国家都需要进行准确的侦察。”[①] 通过这一分析，他强调，苏联社会主义革命和建设的经验是特殊，而不是普遍，因此，西方无产阶级革命既不能照搬俄国十月革命的经验，也不能照抄苏联马克思主义的哲学理论，而应该研究西欧市民社会的性质和结构，建立市民社会的理论，在此基础上，制定无产阶级革命的策略。葛兰西并不满足于这种经验的分析，他还进一步把这种经验的差别上升到理论，创造了马克思主义的实践哲学。这是完全不同于苏联马克思主义哲学的另一种哲学传统。柯尔施是明确提出“西方马克思主义”概念的第一人。他提出“西方马克思主义”概念，首先是针对那种把苏联的马克思主义普遍化的观点，要求建立马克思主义特殊化的观点。他在《我为什么是马克思主义者》中明确指出：“今天的马克思主义的苏维埃国家的公民有一种忘记马克思主义的特殊性的倾向，他们强调马克思主义基本原理的普遍有效性，为的是把包含在他们国家当前宪法中的教义神圣化。”[②] 其次是反对把马克思主义哲学实证化和科学化。在他看来，马克思主义哲学本质上是批判的、革命的，它是具体的、特殊的、历史的，而不是抽象的公式、不是科学的公理。他所说的把马克思主义哲学实证化和科学化，指的是苏联的马克思主义哲学，他所说的马克思主义哲学的批判性和革命性，指的是西方马克思主义的哲学，他所说的具体性、特殊性和历史性，指的是西方马克思主义哲学的原则，即强调每一个马克思主义哲学的基本理论都有与其相应的历史条件和人们的实践活动。这也就是他提出的理论和实践的总体性的含义。在这里，柯尔施从对苏联马克思主义普遍化的经验批判进到了对苏联马克思主义哲学传统的批判，他的“西方马克思主义”就是与苏联马克思主义哲学相对立的新的马克思主义哲学传统。

从葛兰西和柯尔施对苏联马克思主义的批判中，我们可以看到不同于罗莎·卢森堡和列宁论争的特点：罗莎·卢森堡和列宁之间的论争是围绕世界历

---

① 葛兰西：《狱中札记》，中国社会科学出版社 2000 年版，第 194 页。

② 柯尔施：《我为什么是马克思主义者》，载：《马列主义研究资料》1983 年第 3 期，人民出版社 1983 年版，第 247 页。

史的发展和无产阶级革命的前景问题展开的，论争的双方都力图证明自己观点的正确性和对方观点的错误性，所以，他们的论争是在普遍性观念主导下展开的，论争的双方都力图用一种普遍性反对另一种普遍性。然而，葛兰西和柯尔施对苏联马克思主义的批判却不是这样。他们并不反对苏联的马克思主义，而是反对把苏联的马克思主义普遍化。在他们看来，那种把苏联的马克思主义普遍化的观点是教条主义的观点，这种观点实际上是违背了马克思主义的本质，因为，马克思主义的任何哲学原理都是具体的、特殊的。这样，他们就把对苏联马克思主义普遍化的批判上升到对马克思主义普遍性观念的批判，力图以马克思主义的特殊性观念对抗马克思主义的普遍性观念。也就是说，葛兰西、柯尔施与苏联马克思主义者之间的论争是围绕着马克思主义哲学的本质是普遍还是特殊这一问题展开的。这场论争的结果是打破了苏联马克思主义哲学一统天下的格局。

然而，葛兰西、柯尔施对苏联马克思主义哲学的批判，只是整个20世纪马克思主义哲学批判苏联马克思主义哲学的开始。他们的主要贡献在于，通过对苏联马克思主义普遍化的批判，建立了马克思主义哲学的特殊性和民族化的观念。这一观念在他们提出之时，曾经受到了苏联马克思主义者的猛烈批评，他们的哲学也被视为马克思主义哲学的异端而受到排斥。但是，随着马克思主义哲学日益广泛地进入东西方各国的政治的和经济的生活，越来越多国家的马克思主义者接受了马克思主义哲学特殊性和民族化这一观念，并把它运用于马克思主义哲学的再创造过程中，而批判苏联马克思主义哲学的普遍化观念则成为东西方各国马克思主义者进行本国的马克思主义哲学创造的契机。在西方资本主义国家，法国新马克思主义、法兰克福学派等，都是以批判苏联马克思主义哲学的普遍化而创造出批判的马克思主义哲学和批判的社会理论的；在东方国家、在社会主义阵营中，东欧新马克思主义是从批判苏联马克思主义哲学的普遍化中走出来的。中国的马克思主义者虽然不是以西方马克思主义哲学为其哲学起点，也没有与苏联马克思主义者进行直接的论战，但在本国的马克思主义哲学发展的内部，也经历了反对把苏联马克思主义的实践和理论教条化，强调必须使马克思主义哲学具体化、特殊化、民族化的论战。毛泽东提出的要使马克思主义具体化、中国化，就是这场论战的重大理论成果。由于东西方各国的马克思主义者的这些创造活动，自20世纪二三十年代开始，马克思主义哲学朝着多元化的方向发展开来。这一历史过程表明，马克思主义哲学的多元化是与马克思主义哲学的特殊性和民族化的观念相一致的，是马克思主义哲学的特殊性和民族化观念的历史表现。

20世纪马克思主义哲学由普遍而特殊，从一元到多元的发展，从表现上看，是一个由合而分的过程，而在实质上，是一个由分而合的过程。因为在马克思主义哲学普遍性观念主导下的创造和论争，是以理论的对错为标准的；唯要坚持正确的东西，唯要使自己的理论成为普遍，当然要排斥和否定错误的东西，于是，一方的存在必然要以排斥和否定另一方为前提。这就是人们总要在罗莎·卢森堡和列宁的论争中两者择一的原因，也是苏联马克思主义者始终坚持批判和否定罗莎·卢森堡的马克思主义思想的原因。与之不同，在马克思主义哲学特殊性观念主导下的创造和论争，是以理论与实践的统一为标准。这一标准本身就为理论的运用规定了一定的范围。根据这一标准，一种理论的正确性，并不意味着反对它的理论就必然是错误的，因此，一方的存在也不必然要排斥和否定另一方。西方马克思主义者就是以这一态度来对待苏联马克思主义哲学的，所以，他们对苏联马克思主义哲学的批判是有保留的，他们只是要消除苏联马克思主义哲学的普遍化，并不是要完全否定或取代苏联马克思主义哲学。相反，苏联马克思主义者因为遵循马克思主义哲学的普遍性观念，而斥西方马克思主义哲学为马克思主义哲学的异端，或非马克思主义哲学思潮。同样地，毛泽东在反对把苏联马克思主义的经验和理论教条化的时候，也没有否定苏联马克思主义哲学的正确性，他只是强调苏联马克思主义的经验和理论的运用是有限度的，反对不顾中国的实际，照搬照抄苏联马克思主义的经验和理论。正是这样，批判苏联马克思主义哲学的普遍化就成为了东西方各国确立马克思主义哲学特殊性和民族化观念，走向一种开放的马克思主义哲学创造的环节，而东西方各国的马克思主义哲学传统的创造又是马克思主义哲学特殊性和民族化观念的一个又一个的实现，因而必然是马克思主义哲学整体中不可缺少的一部分。从这个角度看，马克思主义哲学的特殊性和民族化观念的合理性只能在东西方各国的马克思主义哲学的共存和相互论争中得到体现和证明，20世纪马克思主义哲学就是由东西方各国的马克思主义哲学传统构成的有机整体。我们研究20世纪的马克思主义哲学，就是要从整体上勾画出它的整体风貌，而不是以理论的正确和错误为标准把东西方马克思主义哲学割裂开来，把20世纪的马克思主义哲学裁切成一些碎片。

三、文化哲学范式中的20世纪马克思主义哲学研究的论题

在确定了“20世纪马克思主义哲学”的概念、考察了19世纪末至20世纪30年代发生的东西方马克思主义哲学的论争以及由此而形成的20世纪马克思主义哲学发展的基本格局和整体风貌后，还有一个如何研究20世纪马克思主义哲学的问题。我认为，解决这个问题，首先有一个哲学研究范式的选择问题。长期以来，我国学术界不能把20世纪马克思主义哲学作为一个总体的对象来研究，而总是在东西方马克思主义哲学中两者择一，究其根源，是我们的哲学研究范式出了问题。这个问题主要出现在两点上：其一，没有把哲学研究范式中的哲学研究意义与哲学史的研究意义区分开来；其二，选择了理性主义的研究范式，而没有选择文化哲学的研究范式。鉴于此，在这里，我力图从哲学研究范式的分析入手，清理和提出20世纪马克思主义哲学研究的论题。

在迄今为止的哲学研究中，哲学的研究范式不外两种：一种是理性主义的研究范式，一种是文化哲学的研究范式。理性主义的研究范式以自然科学的方法为思维工具，寻求建立起具有普遍性的逻辑理性形式，文化哲学的研究范式

以人文科学的方法为思维工具，寻求建立具有特殊性的历史理论形式。① 在维科创立“新科学”之前，这两种研究范式就已经客观地存在于从古代到现代的形而上学的构造之中，德谟克利特的原子论和伊壁鸠鲁的原子论的差别、亚里士多德的物理学和柏拉图的形而上学的差别、笛卡尔哲学与培根哲学的差别，都体现了这两种哲学研究范式的对立。维科的贡献，就是把哲学史上已经存在的哲学研究范式的对立揭示出来，指出，哲学史上的理性主义和经验主义的对立、科学的形而上学和历史的形而上学的对立，本质上是由不同的哲学研究范式决定的，而他的“新科学”，就是从柏拉图和培根的哲学传统中发展起来的文化哲学的研究范式，这种哲学研究范式与笛卡尔的理性主义的哲学研究范式是不相容的。自维科之后，区分这两种不同的哲学研究范式，并在其中两者择一，就成为哲学家们从事哲学创造的自觉意识。不仅如此，哲学家们还把这两种不同的哲学研究范式运用于哲学史的研究，形成了哲学史观的对立。黑格尔的理性主义的哲学史观和文德尔班的文化哲学史观的对立，就是这两种哲学史对立的典型形式。由于黑格尔和文德尔班的工作，理性主义的研究范式和文化哲学的研究范式都获得了双重的意义：一重是就哲学家的哲学理论的创造活动而言的，一重是就反思一定时代、一定民族的哲学史的观点和方法而言的。区分这两重意义是哲学史的研究的前提性工作。因为，任何哲学家在进行哲学史的研究时，都要把自己的哲学史观和哲学史上出现过的哲学区分开来。把哲学史上出现过的哲学作为自己的研究对象。对于自己所要研究的对象，研究的主体不仅允许不同哲学研究范式的并存和相互论争，而且还要尽可能多地纳入哲学史上的不同哲学派别和哲学观点，以便能够对它们进行比较，发现哲学史上的不同哲学传统和内在逻辑，描述哲学发展的全貌；对于自己所要表达的哲学史观，研究的主体为了保持自己研究的一致性和严谨性，绝不允许把多种研究范式和不同观点混杂在一起，而只能在理性主义的哲学史观和文化哲学的哲学

① 详尽的论证见拙著：《马克思主义哲学与文化哲学》第四章第四节“文化哲学的方法论问题”，武汉大学出版社 2002 年版。

史观中两者择一。这就是哲学史研究中的“多”和“一”的关系。“多”是对哲学史的研究对外的要求，即是对研究的客体的要求；“一”是对哲学史观的要求，即是对研究的主体的要求。

弄清哲学研究范式的这种“多”和“一”的关系，对于研究20世纪马克思主义哲学来说，尤为必须。因为，与西方哲学史和中国哲学史的研究相比，马克思主义哲学史的研究中以一种哲学排斥另一种哲学，甚至把另一种哲学删除于哲学史之外的情况更为常见。比如，长期以来，我国的马克思主义哲学史研究以“正确”的马克思主义哲学理论为标准，把不符合这一标准的西方马克思主义哲学家的思想拒斥于马克思主义哲学史的系统之外。这实际上是混淆了哲学理论的研究和哲学史的研究方式：在研究的对象上，没有把20世纪马克思主义哲学当作研究史的研究对象来看待，而在研究的范式上，又缺乏文化哲学的研究视野，不能从理论和实践的统一上去客体地评价西方马克思主义哲学。这不能不影响到我们对20世纪马克思主义哲学，乃至整个马克思主义哲学史的研究。但是，如果我们弄清了哲学研究范式的不同意义，弄清了“多”和“一”的关系，我们就会看到，20世纪马克思主义哲学是由东西方马克思主义哲学共同构成的，西方马克思主义哲学是20世纪马克思主义哲学中一个不可缺少的方面，没有这一方面，就根本谈不上有20世纪马克思主义哲学。因此，要想研究20世纪马克思主义哲学，我们必须厘清哲学研究范式的双重意义，并明确哲学史的研究任务：把20世纪不同马克思主义哲学家的哲学理论创造活动作为研究的对象，在这个意义上，要允许不同的马克思主义哲学传统、不同哲学研究范式的存在，也就是说，要把西方马克思主义哲学看作是与苏联马克思主义哲学、中国马克思主义哲学有同样价值的研究对象纳入20世纪的马克思主义哲学研究之中；在哲学史观的意义上，要选择文化哲学的研究范式，以特殊性和民族化的观念为主导，清理20世纪的马克思主义哲学传统及其派别，确立20世纪马克思主义哲学研究的论题。这是符合20世纪马克思主义哲学由普遍而特殊，从一元到多元发展的历史事实的。

以文化哲学的研究范式审视20世纪马克思主义哲学，我认为，20世纪马克思主义哲学的研究可以在三个论题下展开：

第一，以哲学传统和哲学形态为核心范畴，对20世纪马克思主义哲学作总体性的研究。20世纪出现马克思主义的哲学运动，在客观上是由马克思主义哲学的危机造成的，而在主观上则是由马克思主义哲学创造的主体决定的。20世纪从事马克思主义哲学创造的主体，并不是单纯的马克思主义的实践家，而是具有很高的哲学素养的知识分子，他们中的大部分都是高等院校的教授，比如法兰克福学派的代表人物、法国的阿尔都塞、美国实用主义马克思主义哲学家、英国分析马克思主义的创造者柯亨、中国的李大钊等等。由于具有很高的哲学素养，所以，他们在进行马克思主义哲学的研究和再创造时，自觉地把哲学史作为马克思主义哲学创造的根基，力图从哲学史中找到马克思主义哲学传统的起源，从近代哲学到现代哲学的变革中说明马克思主义哲学的性质及其变革的意义、吸取现代哲学的资源，从本民族的文化传统和当代社会的发展中发现马克思主义哲学与本民族文化传统的接合点，创造既具有时代特征，又具有民族文化特征的新的马克思主义哲学传统。葛兰西、柯尔施、卢卡奇还把自己的哲学与第二国际的马克思主义哲学传统联结起来，强调西方马克思主义哲学是西欧马克思主义哲学传统的继承，以此把西方马克思主义哲学传统与苏联马克思主义哲学传统对立起来，而苏联马克思主义者在进行哲学创造时，不仅研究西方哲学史、俄国哲学史，而且还开创了马克思主义哲学史的研究。这种结合哲学史的研究创造马克思主义哲学的传统和新的理论形态，是20世纪马克思主义哲学创造最重要的特点，它使20世纪马克思主义哲学一开始就在不同哲学传统的创造中、在哲学形态的更替中有序地展开。这些表明，20世纪马克思主义哲学的发展不是辩证唯物主义和历史唯物主义理论的量的积累过程，而是通过哲学传统的更新、哲学形态的变革而形成的质变过程。既然如此，我们就不能以辩证唯物主义和历史唯物主义的概念和理论为主线来考察20世纪马克思主义哲学的形成和发展，而应该深入到20世纪马克思主义哲学家的创造活动之中，以哲学传统和哲学形态为核心范畴，研究20世纪马克思主义哲学在空间上的拓展和在时间上的变革。

第二，开展东西方马克思主义哲学的比较研究。20世纪马克思主义哲学虽然具有多种哲学传统，但是，对20世纪马克思主义哲学格局的形成产生决定性影响、决定20世纪马克思主义哲学的世界性特征的，还是东西方马克思主义哲学之间的论争。20世纪马克思主义哲学的世界发展问题，说到底，就是东西方马克思主义哲学的关系问题。正是这样，自19世纪末开始，无论是西方的马克思主义者，还是东方的马克思主义者，在他们的研究中，都不可能只看西方马克思主义哲学而不理东方马克思主义哲学，或者相反，只看东方马克思主义哲学而不理西方马克思主义哲学。自东西方马克思主义哲学家之间展开第二场论争后，东西方马克思主义哲学家们各自返回到本民族文化的土壤之中，创造具有民族特色的马克思主义哲学传统，但是，这并不意味着，东西方马克思主义哲学的创造就丧失了世界性质，彼此之间就不再发生联系了，不再有世界性的对话了。事实是，自20世纪30年代开始，西方资本主义国家的马克思主义者对列宁哲学的研究、对斯大林哲学、苏联马克思主义哲学的批判就没有间断过，一些西方马克思学的学者还通过对列宁哲学、对毛泽东哲学的研究，说明东西方马克思主义哲学的差别，揭示马克思主义哲学内部的批判哲学和科学主义哲学传统的形成和发展；自20世纪90年代开始，随着中国市场经济建设的全面展开，全球化、现代化成为世界各国的共同话题，西方的马克思主义者也越来越关心中国马克思主义哲学的发展，在西方国家出现了一批研究毛泽东哲学、邓小平哲学等中国马克思主义哲学的著作，中西方马克思主义者的学术交流和对话也日益频繁。而在中国，自20世纪80年代开始，西方资本主义国家的马克思主义哲学理论大量传入中国，成为中国的西方哲学和马克思主义哲学研究中的一个重要领域；进入新世纪，西方马克思主义哲学的许多理论更是被转化为一种方法，为中国马克思主义哲学的研究广泛借鉴和运用。东西方马克思主义哲学之间的这些复杂联系，要求我们破除以往在理性主义哲学研究范式中构造的东西方马克思主义哲学之间非此即彼的关系模式，而在文化哲学的研究范式中开展东西方马克思主义哲学的比较研究。我在这里所说的东西方马克思主义哲学的比较研究，不是要以西方马克思主义哲学批判和否定东方马克思主义哲学，也不是要以东方马克思主义哲学来菲薄西方马克思主义哲学，而是要在世界马克思主义哲学发展的宏大背景下探讨东西方马克思主义哲学之间的互补关系，说明它们之间的差别，它们各自创造的哲学传统产生的历史必然性、合理性和不足之处，以及由此而对于 20 世纪马克思主义哲学发展作出的贡献，等等，总之，要从世界历史的整体性上考察东西方马克思主义哲学，建立总体性的马克思主义哲学史观。结合 20 世纪东西方马克思主义哲学的论争和对话，我认为，开展 20 世纪马克思主义哲学的比较研究，可以分别从方法论和理论两个层面展开。方法论层面的比较研究主要是建立马克思主义哲学研究的世界视野，就是说，不论是研究西方资本主义国家的马克思主义哲学，还是研究东方国家的马克思主义哲学，都要有一个世界视野，都要把它们置于世界马克思主义哲学发展的整体中进行研究和评价，只有这样，才能揭示马克思主义哲学的本质，深入地了解马克思主义哲学的不同传统和形态的内涵。理论层面的比较研究主要是研究 20 世纪马克思主义哲学家之间的论争和对话，研究东西方马克思主义哲学在同一问题上的不同观点、不同的研究路向，从中发现东西方马克思主义哲学的理论交汇点。这两个方面的研究构成了 20 世纪马克思主义哲学研究的多个领域、多重视野。

第三，开展 20 世纪马克思主义文化哲学的理论研究。20 世纪，马克思主义哲学经历了全面、彻底而深刻的文化哲学研究的转向。这种转向是从西方马克思主义哲学的创造开始的，这种转向的全面性和深刻性也是相对于第二国际马克思主义的文化哲学研究而言的。19 世纪下半叶，受文化哲学和文化人类学、历史哲学、地理学等学科发展的影响，第二国际的一些马克思主义者也开展了文化哲学的研究，但是，他们的研究只是片断的，在根本上是从属于历史唯物主义研究。比如，拉法格、拉布里奥拉。他们都很重视文化哲学和文化人类学的成果，并运用文化哲学和文化人类学的成果阐发马克思主义的历史主义方法、研究人类的家庭和伦理思想史、区分人为环境和自然环境、把人为环境当作人的文化存在方式加以叙述。他们开展这些研究，是为了批判当时流行的机械论和因素论的观点，提出历史唯物主义的有机整体观，从而能够把人类历史的发展描述为一个经济系统的演进过程，所以，他们虽然研究了文化哲学，但是，文化哲学并不是他们研究的主流，不是他们理论的全部，而只是方法，只是理论的片断，不仅如此，这些方法和理论的片断都是围绕着论证经济基础决定上层建筑的原理展开的，是作为一种补充形式进入历史唯物主义研究的。与这种片断的、非主流的研究相比，20 世纪西方马克思主义的文化哲学创造是全面的、彻底的和深刻的。因为 20 世纪西方马克思主义的文化哲学创造是从本体论的变革着手的。在葛兰西、卢卡奇那里，在法兰克福学派的批判的社会理论的创立者那里，在法国存在主义的马克思主义者那里，文化哲学的确立都经过了本体论的深刻改造。在这些马克思主义哲学家看来，马克思主义的本体论，不应该是知识论的，而应该是实践的和文化批判的；这种本体论的内在结构是由自觉的、有意识的文化批判活动与自发的、无意识的大众文化构成的，而联结两者的中介就是作为文化的、有内容的语言。从这一本体论的规定出发，他们对马克思主义哲学的内容和理论形式都进行了改造：在内容上，他们改变了马克思主义哲学研究的论题，把马克思主义哲学研究的重心由对经济基础的说明转变成了对文化的政治和意识形态的探讨，从对历史规律的研究转变成了对大众文化的批判；在理论的形式上，他们区分了马克思主义哲学的一般理论与政治哲学和大众文化批判理论，改变了以往的马克思主义哲学的单一化的理论结构，从而使马克思主义哲学理论在批判当代资本主义的文化工业中能够容纳更多的现实内容，同时，在与现代哲学和其他理论的融合中也具有更大的张力。经过这种内容和理论形式的改造，马克思主义哲学的问题、提问方式和思维方式、范畴体系都发生了根本性的变化。对于这种已经变化了的哲学，我们不可能再采用唯物主义和唯心主义对立的模式加以研究，而应该进行文化哲学的研究。当然，20 世纪的马克思主义哲学并不全部是文化哲学。我在这里所说的马克思主义的文化哲学研究，主要是针对 20 世纪马克思主义哲学中属文化哲学传统的那些哲学。由于这些哲学派别构成了 20 世纪西方资本主义国家的马克思主义哲学发展的主线，并对非文化哲学的哲学派别的哲学、对中国的马克思主义哲学，也都有极强的渗透力，所以，研究这些派别的文化哲学理论理应成为 20 世纪马克思主义哲学研究的主要论题。

人类历史已经进入了 21 世纪的第十个年头。对于生活在 21 世纪的人们来说，20 世纪的社会生活已经渐行渐远，再提那个世纪的革命和战争，已经是过时的话题。但是，20 世纪批判的马克思主义哲学家们所创造文化哲学却建立了 20 世纪与 21 世纪的人们在思想上的联系。从 20 世纪 90 年代开始，无论在西方资本主义国家，还是在中国这样的社会主义国家，葛兰西的文化霸权理论、法国存在主义的马克思主义哲学和阿尔都塞的哲学、法兰克福学派的批判的社会理论，都成为哲学家们思考建立 21 世纪的民主制度、反对消费主义、发展和谐的生态经济和和谐的政治环境的重要思想资源。哲学家们之所以重视这些思想，是因为他们认识到，人类所创造的文化，尤其是工业社会发展起来的文化，是束缚人的精神创造、压抑人的个体解放的根源，因此，文化与人的精神、人的解放的关系，依然是当代人们所面临的、必须解决的问题，而生态学马克思主义哲学从 20 世纪末到 21 世纪的发展本身就构筑了这两个世纪的思想联结。从这个角度看，以文化哲学的研究范式反思 20 世纪马克思主义哲学、研究 20 世纪马克思主义哲学理论，绝不只是一种哲学史的研究，它同时也是对 21 世纪人类文明发展的一种哲学思考。

当代中国马克思主义哲学的研究范式

汪信砚

当代中国马克思主义哲学研究已走过半个多世纪的曲折发展历程，既取得了令人瞩目的重要成就，也留下了很多发人深省的经验教训，其中，最重要的经验教训之一，就是中国马克思主义哲学研究必须透彻地进行自我反思，以便在方法论上达致应有的自觉。事实上，当代中国马克思主义哲学研究一直受到方法论上的严重困扰，其突出表现就是始终未能对马克思主义哲学中国化这一应有的研究范式形成真正普遍的共识。要推进当代中国马克思主义哲学研究的深入发展，首先必须摆脱这一方法论上的困扰，牢固确立马克思主义哲学中国化的研究范式。

一

所谓范式，就是学术共同体中的研究者们自觉认同和共同持有的一套信念、原则和标准。科学哲学家库恩认为，范式是共同体成员们借以指导其研究活动的“一种公认的模型或模式”，它“决定了什么样的问题有待解决”，“规定了一个研究领域的合理问题和方法”①，并由此必然形成一种连贯的学术传统。这样一种对学术探索活动起重要规范作用的范式，无论是在科学研究还是在哲学研究中都是普遍存在的。从哲学史上看，不同的哲学流派都各有其独特的研究范式，而哲学流派的兴衰更迭则意味着哲学研究范式的转换。不过，我

① 托马斯·库恩：《科学革命的结构》，北京大学出版社 2003 年版，第 21、24—25、9 页。

们并不同意库恩关于不同范式无法通约、不可比较的看法。至少在哲学研究中，范式是有优劣之分、实有与应有之别的。

当代中国马克思主义哲学研究要坚持和发展马克思主义哲学，要完成它所肩负的理论使命，就必须自觉以马克思主义哲学中国化为研究范式。毛泽东曾说："共产党员是国际主义的马克思主义者，但是马克思主义必须和我国的具体特点相结合并通过一定的民族形式才能实现。马克思列宁主义的伟大力量，就在于它是和各个国家具体的革命实践相联系的。对于中国共产党来说，就是要学会把马克思列宁主义的理论应用于中国的具体的环境。成为伟大中华民族的一部分而和这个民族血肉相联的共产党员，离开中国特点来谈马克思主义，只是抽象的空洞的马克思主义。因此，使马克思主义在中国具体化，使之在其每一表现中带着必须有的中国的特性，即是说，按照中国的特点去应用它，成为全党亟待了解并亟待解决的问题。"① 根据毛泽东的这一论述，马克思主义哲学中国化，就是把马克思主义哲学与中国的具体实际相结合，就是立足于中国的具体实际来开展中国马克思主义哲学研究。

"中国的具体实际"是一个内涵丰富的概念，它是包含在特定时代中的中国的历史、现实和未来发展趋势的总和，是对特定时代中国社会的政治、经济、文化等等的发展状况及其影响因素的总概括。从总体上看，中国的具体实际主要有两重内容：一是中国的文化传统。在任何时代，中国的文化传统都是中国的具体实际的一个有机组成部分，因为传统"是现存的过去，但它又与任何新事物一样，是现在的一部分"②。也正因如此，毛泽东在谈到中国的具体实际时曾说："我们这个民族有数千年的历史，有它的特点，有它的许多珍贵品。……今天的中国是历史的中国的一个发展；我们是马克思主义的历史主义者，我们不应当割断历史。从孔夫子到孙中山，我们应当给以总结，承继这一

① 《毛泽东选集》第二卷，人民出版社 1991 年版，第 534 页。

② E. 希尔斯：《论传统》，上海人民出版社 1991 年版，第 16 页。

份珍贵的遗产。”① 二是中国的当前现实。不论是在哪个时代，中国的当前现实都是中国的具体实际的更为重要的方面，它有着时间和空间两方面的规定性。作为一种时间性的存在，中国的当前现实不仅延传和积淀着中国的历史文化传统，而且也包孕着中国社会未来发展的种种可能和趋势；而作为一种空间性的存在，中国的当前现实与当前世界处于一种复杂的关系之中，它既以当前世界作为自己存在和发展的外部环境，又是当前世界的一个不可分割的组成部分，因此，它既包括从当前中国来看的和当前中国必然受其影响的当前世界，也包括从当前世界来看的并必然与当前世界互动的当前中国。

与“中国的具体实际”的丰富内涵相适应，马克思主义哲学中国化也包括两大方面的内容：第一，把马克思主义哲学与中国的传统文化相结合。把马克思主义哲学与中国的传统文化相结合，就是既要运用马克思主义哲学来审视、反思和改铸中国的传统文化，推动和促进中国先进文化的形成和发展，又要吸取中国传统文化、特别是中国传统哲学的精粹，用以丰富马克思主义哲学的内容和强化中国马克思主义哲学的民族特色，使马克思哲学具有“为中国老百姓所喜闻乐见的中国作风和中国气派”②。把马克思主义哲学与中国的传统文化相结合，尤其要重视运用马克思主义哲学来批判、扬弃和提升中国传统哲学，并用经过创造性转换的中国传统哲学来阐释马克思主义哲学。从这个角度来看，中国传统哲学的现代化与马克思主义哲学的中国化乃是一个统一的过程。需要说明的是，把马克思主义哲学与中国的传统文化相结合，不是为了使马克思主义哲学适应或同化于中国的传统文化，而是要把中国传统文化、特别是中国传统哲学中的精华吸纳到马克思主义哲学中来。那种把马克思主义哲学的中国化视为“儒化”、视为马克思主义哲学的变形过程和向中国传统哲学的复归、甚至视为马克思主义哲学的封建化的观点，是对马克思主义哲学中国化的严重歪曲。第二，把马克思主义哲学与中国的当前现实相结合。把马克思主义哲学与

---

① 《毛泽东选集》第二卷，人民出版社 1991 年版，第 533—534 页。

② 《毛泽东选集》第二卷，人民出版社 1991 年版，第 534 页。

中国的当前现实相结合，就是要运用马克思主义哲学考察和分析中国的当前现实，从中提升出具有时代性和普遍性的哲学问题，并通过对这些问题的创造性的回答，指导中国的当前实践，推进马克思主义哲学的发展。把马克思主义哲学中国化，关键在于要在研究中国的现实社会问题的过程中坚持、运用和发展马克思主义哲学。对此，艾思奇早在20世纪40年代就曾说过："在中国应用马克思主义，或使马克思主义中国化，就是要坚定地站在马克思主义的观点上，在马克思主义基本原则和基本精神上，用马克思、恩格斯所奠定了的、辩证唯物论的和政治经济学的科学方法，来具体地客观地研究中国社会经济关系，来决定中国无产阶级在中国民族革命斗争中的具体任务及战略策略。""中国化决不是丢开马克思主义的立场的意思，相反地，愈要更能够中国化，就是指愈更能够正确坚决地实践马克思主义的立场的意思，愈更能创造，就是指愈更能够开展真正的马克思主义的意思。"① 整个马克思主义中国化是这样，马克思主义哲学中国化亦复如此。值得指出的是，由于中国的具体实际是不断变化发展着的，它在不同的时代往往具有不同的内容和特点，因此，马克思主义哲学中国化即把马克思主义哲学与中国的具体实际相结合，也内在地包含着把马克思主义哲学与时代特征相结合、在马克思主义哲学研究中及时地总结与概括人类实践和科学发展的最新成果。具有如是规定的马克思主义哲学中国化，就是当代中国马克思主义哲学研究的应有范式。

所谓马克思主义哲学中国化是当代中国马克思主义哲学研究的应有范式，是指当代中国马克思主义哲学研究应该紧紧围绕着马克思主义哲学中国化这个中心任务来展开，它的理论目标就是要在当代条件下推进马克思主义哲学中国化；是否有利于推进马克思主义哲学中国化，应该成为衡量当代中国马克思主义哲学研究的问题和成果的意义的标准。这是由马克思主义哲学自身的本质特点、当代中国社会发展的客观需要及当代中国马克思主义哲学研究的特殊性质

① 《艾思奇文集》第1卷，人民出版社1981年版，第481、480页。

决定的。

首先，以马克思主义哲学中国化为范式开展当代中国马克思主义哲学研究，是马克思主义哲学自身的本质要求。实践性是马克思主义哲学的本质特点，也是马克思主义哲学与时俱进、始终成为时代精神精华的根本基础。在马克思主义哲学看来，实践是作为哲学研究对象的全部人与世界关系的根本基础，从而也是哲学思维应有的出发点和落脚点。也正因如此，实践的观点成为马克思主义哲学的首要的、基本的观点。然而，实践并不是一种抽象的、一成不变的东西，它的最大特点就是直接现实性。一方面，实践总是具体的，它总是在特定的历史背景和特定的现实条件下进行的；另一方面，实践又是历史的和不断发展着的，它在不同的时代有着很不相同的规定性。因此，坚持马克思主义哲学的实践观点，就必须注重把马克思主义哲学与各国的具体实际相结合、立足于各国的具体实际来开展马克思主义哲学研究。马克思、恩格斯在谈到他们所创立的马克思主义哲学时，曾反复强调人们应该“把这一理论应用于本国的经济条件和政治条件”①，强调“这些原理的实际运用”“随时随地要以当时的历史条件为转移”②。列宁把马克思主义哲学的这一本质要求概括为“具体地分析具体的情况”的原则，并根据这一原则明确地提出了马克思主义（包括马克思主义哲学）民族化的思想。他说：“对于俄国社会党人来说，尤其需要独立地探讨马克思的理论。因为它所提供的只是总的指导原理，而这些原理的应用具体地说，在英国不同于法国，在法国不同于德国，在德国又不同于俄国。”③ 马克思主义哲学中国化就是马克思主义哲学民族化的重要表现形式之一。当代中国马克思主义哲学研究只有坚持马克思主义哲学中国化这一研究范式，才能真正体现马克思主义哲学的本质要求。

其次，以马克思主义哲学中国化为范式开展当代中国马克思主义哲学研

---

① 《马克思恩格斯选集》第 4 卷，人民出版社 1995 年版，第 669 页。

② 《马克思恩格斯选集》第 1 卷，人民出版社 1995 年版，第 348 页。

③ 《列宁全集》第 4 卷，人民出版社 1984 年版，第 161 页。

究，是当代中国社会发展的客观需要。马克思主义哲学中国化是整个马克思主义中国化的一个重要组成部分，而马克思主义中国化历来都包含着两个重要层面：一是理论层面，即把马克思主义与中国具体实际相结合的理论探索，其已经产生的标志性成果就是毛泽东思想、邓小平理论、“三个代表”重要思想和科学发展观；二是实践层面，即把马克思主义与中国具体实际相结合的实践探索，其已经取得的重大成就就是找到了一条中国特色的新民主主义革命道路、中国特色的社会主义改造道路和中国特色的社会主义现代化建设道路。马克思主义中国化的这两个层面是紧密联系着的，其中，马克思主义中国化的实践直接就是马克思主义中国化的理论的现实化；没有马克思主义中国化的理论探索及其标志性成果，就不可能有马克思主义中国化的实践和上述三条道路的确立。当代中国正在进行中国特色社会主义现代化建设的伟大实践，它一刻也离不开中国化的马克思主义的指导；只有坚持把马克思主义与当代中国具体实际相结合，着力进行当代条件下马克思主义中国化、包括马克思主义哲学中国化的理论探索，才能把中国特色社会主义现代化建设实践不断推向前进。毫无疑问，当代条件下马克思主义哲学中国化的理论探索的任务应该由当代中国马克思主义哲学研究来承担；只有自觉坚持马克思主义哲学中国化的研究范式，当代中国马克思主义哲学研究才能完成这一任务、适应当代中国社会发展的客观需要。

再次，以马克思主义哲学中国化为范式开展当代中国马克思主义哲学研究，也是当代中国马克思主义哲学研究健康发展的重要保证。当代中国马克思主义哲学研究有着两方面的规定性：其一，它是“当代中国的”，必须具有当代中国特色；其二，它又是“马克思主义哲学”的，必须服务于马克思主义哲学的当代发展。因此，要推进当代中国马克思主义哲学的健康发展，至少必须做到以下三点：第一，必须坚持实事求是的科学态度。毛泽东指出：“在这种态度下，就是不要割断历史，不单是懂得希腊就行了，还要懂得中国；不但要懂得外国革命史，还要懂得中国革命史；不但要懂得中国的今天，还要懂得中国的昨天和前天。在这种态度下，就是要有目的地去研究马克思列宁主义的理论，要使马克思列宁主义的理论和中国革命的实际运动结合起来，是为着解决中国革命的理论问题和策略问题而去从它找立场，找观点，找方法的。这种态度，就是有的放矢的态度。'的'就是中国革命，'矢'就是马克思列宁主义。"① 正是由于坚持了实事求是的科学态度，坚持把马克思主义哲学与中国革命的具体实际相结合，毛泽东才创造了具有鲜明中国特色的毛泽东哲学思想。在当代，中国的具体实际发生了重大变化，特别是近三十年来，中国进入了全方位改革开放的新时期。正如党的十七大报告所指出，"新时期最鲜明的特点是改革开放"；"事实雄辩地证明，改革开放是决定当代中国命运的关键抉择，是发展中国特色社会主义、实现中华民族伟大复兴的必由之路；只有社会主义才能救中国，只有改革开放才能发展中国、发展社会主义、发展马克思主义。"② 可以说，改革开放是当代中国实践最鲜明的主题和当代中国最大的具体实际。因此，只有坚持实事求是的科学态度，坚持把马克思主义哲学与当代中国的具体实际、特别是与当代中国的改革开放实践相结合，当代中国的马克思主义哲学研究才能成为名副其实的"当代中国的"马克思主义哲学研究。第二，必须建构中国马克思主义哲学研究的学术话语体系。当代中国马克思主义哲学研究是当代世界哲学研究、特别是当代世界马克思主义哲学研究的一个重要组成部分，它不可避免地置身于与当代世界上的其他各种马克思主义的和非马克思主义的哲学研究的某种关系之中。当代中国马克思主义哲学研究要走向世界，要与当代世界上的其他各种哲学研究展开积极的对话，特别是要对当代世界马克思主义哲学研究作出自己的贡献，就必须建构自己的学术话语体系，使自己的对象与问题、观点与方法、概念框架、表达方式等等都具有鲜明的实践特色、民族特色和时代特色，亦即具有鲜明的中国作风和中国气派。显然，对于当代

---

① 《毛泽东选集》第三卷，人民出版社 1991 年版，第 801 页。

② 胡锦涛：《高举中国特色社会主义伟大旗帜　为夺取全面建设小康社会新胜利而奋斗——在中国共产党第十七次全国代表大会上的报告》，人民出版社 2007 年版。

中国马克思主义哲学研究而言，这样的学术话语体系只能在马克思主义哲学中国化的基础上才能形成。第三，必须不断推进马克思主义哲学的理论创新。马克思说过：“一切划时代的体系的真正的内容都是由于产生这些体系的那个时期的需要而形成起来的。所有这些体系都是以本国过去的整个发展为基础的，是以阶级关系的历史形式及其政治的、道德的、哲学的以及其他的后果为基础的。”① 这就是说，真正的理论创新总是源自一定时代社会实践的需要，也总是以本民族的历史文化传统为基础。我们民族当前正在进行有中国特色社会主义现代化建设的伟大实践，伟大的实践需要创新性的理论；我们民族也有着悠久的历史文化传统，它为我们的理论创新提供了厚实的基础。当代中国马克思主义哲学研究只有把马克思主义哲学与当代中国的具体实际相结合，自觉立足于当代中国改革开放实践的需要，积极开掘中国传统文化的思想资源，才能真正实现马克思主义哲学的理论创新，也才能促进马克思主义哲学的当代发展。总之，无论从哪方面看，只有自觉坚持以马克思主义哲学中国化为研究范式，才能推进当代中国马克思主义哲学研究的健康发展。

二

我们说马克思主义哲学中国化是当代中国马克思主义哲学研究的应有范式，并不意味着它已然成为当代中国马克思主义哲学研究的范式。事实上，回顾新中国成立多年来的中国马克思主义哲学研究所走过的历程，我们看到，当代中国马克思主义哲学研究至今也没有确立起马克思主义哲学中国化的研究范式，而是在不同的时期都表现出对于这一应有研究范式的这样那样的偏离。

近年来，孙正聿教授在一些论著中把当代中国马克思主义哲学研究所走过的历程划分为三个阶段，即20世纪80年代以前（即新中国成立以后的前30年）

---

① 《马克思恩格斯全集》第3卷，人民出版社1960年版，第544页。

的教科书哲学、20 世纪 80 年代的教科书改革哲学和 20 世纪 90 年代以来的后教科书哲学。① 他认为，与这三个阶段相适应，当代中国马克思主义哲学研究历经了三种不同的范式，即教科书范式、教科书改革范式和后教科书范式。② 孙正聿教授的这一划分“是以教科书为标准的”,③ 因而并非完全没有可争议之处，但它至少为我们考察当代中国马克思主义哲学研究范式提供了一个有启发意义的分析框架。

新中国成立以后的前 30 年间，当代中国马克思主义哲学研究所遵循的的确是一种“教科书范式”。正如孙正聿教授所说，那时，人们“把全国通行的哲学原理教科书作为标准的马克思主义哲学概念框架，以这个教科书模式去宣传、讲授、解释和研究马克思主义哲学，并以这个教科书模式为标准区分马克思主义哲学与非马克思主义哲学”，同时，也“以这个教科书模式作为最基本的哲学理论框架和解释原则，去建构包括中外哲学史、伦理学、宗教学、逻辑学和美学等在内的全部哲学学科，并用它去研究、评述和批判古今中外的各种哲学理论、哲学派别和哲学思潮”④。那个年代的中国马克思主义哲学研究，就是为了服务于宣传和普及哲学的需要、服务于全民学哲学的需要而阐释和完善哲学原理教科书，人们所探讨和论争的问题，如生产力、生产关系、经济基础、上层建筑、矛盾（“一分为二”或“一分为多”）、同一性、斗争性、客观规律性、主动能动性等，一般都没有超出哲学原理教科书内容的范围。实际上，这种马克思主义哲学研究的目的或目标就是为了阐释和完善哲学原理教科书，因而它总是从通行的哲学原理教科书中寻找和提出问题，

① 参见孙正聿：《思想中的时代——当代哲学的理论自觉》，北京师范大学出版社 2004 年版，第 314—322 页；孙正聿：《当代中国的马克思主义哲学研究》，《河南大学学报》（社会科学版）2005 年第 4 期。

② 参见孙正聿：《我国人文社会科学研究的范式转换及其他——关于文科研究的几点体会》，《学术界》2005 年第 2 期。

③ 孙正聿：《当代中国的马克思主义哲学研究》，《河南大学学报》(社会科学版)2005 年第 4 期。

④ 孙正聿：《思想中的时代——当代哲学的理论自觉》，北京师范大学出版社 2004 年版，第 315 页。

所论问题的意义取决于其在教科书体系中的地位，研究成果的价值也取决于它对于阐释和完善哲学原理教科书的贡献。可见，这种教科书范式的马克思主义哲学研究的总的特点，就是以阐释和完善哲学原理教科书为目标、以通行的哲学原理教科书作为基本的解释原则、概念框架和评价标准。显然，这种教科书范式及其所规范的马克思主义哲学研究是严重偏离马克思主义哲学中国化的研究范式的。

20 世纪 80 年代的中国马克思主义哲学研究是在中国社会走向全方位的改革开放这个大背景下展开的，其所遵循的也完全可以称为“教科书改革范式”。在这一范式的规范下，80 年代的中国马克思主义哲学研究紧紧围绕着哲学原理教科书体系改革这个中心任务，对以往长期通行的哲学原理教科书体系在理论框架、基本结构、主要内容等方面存在的问题及其历史成因和克服途径进行了多方面的反思，并试图在重新理解马克思主义哲学的基础上重构教科书体系。从实际的展开过程看，这一关于哲学原理教科书体系改革的研究和讨论，以深化关于实践标准的讨论为开端和突破口，以关于主体性、特别是关于实践的主体性的讨论为中间环节，最后汇集成了关于实践唯物主义的热烈争鸣。这一系列的研究和讨论，较充分地暴露了以往通行的哲学原理教科书体系的弊端，通过实践唯物主义的讨论也确实深化了对马克思主义哲学的理解，但它并没有达到重构教科书体系的目的。究其原因，乃在于规范这一研究和讨论的教科书改革范式仍然是有问题的，它本身只具有“破”的意义，并且即使在“破”的方面也是不彻底的。应该说，这种教科书改革范式及其所规范的马克思主义哲学研究是存在着走向马克思主义哲学中国化的研究范式的可能性的，因为要确立马克思主义哲学中国化的研究范式，就必须首先反思、批判和突破教科书范式，也必须首先正确地理解马克思主义哲学本身。但是，教科书改革范式规范下的马克思主义哲学研究仍然只是从哲学原理教科书中寻找和提出问题，因而它在致思方式上与教科书范式规范下的马克思主义哲学研究如出一辙，只不过一个是要完善原有的教科书体系，而另一个则是要突破原有的教科书体系。

因此，教科书改革范式不可能真正发展为马克思主义哲学中国化的研究范式，它甚至也没有完全摆脱教科书范式的影响。在教科书改革范式的规范下，即使人们真的重构了一个教科书体系，它也必定与原有的教科书体系有着惊人的相似。可见，在当代中国马克思主义哲学发展过程中，教科书改革范式充其量也只是一种过渡性的研究范式，这种范式及其所规范的马克思主义哲学研究仍然偏离了马克思主义哲学中国化这一应有的研究范式。

20 世纪 90 年代以来，中国马克思主义哲学研究进入了一个新的阶段。孙正聿教授认为，与这一阶段相适应的是“后教科书范式”，它的基本特征是由“体系意识”转向“问题意识”。在我看来，所谓“后教科书范式”，实际上就是没有范式或没有形成新的统一的研究范式。这主要体现在以下四个方面：

第一，90 年代以来的中国马克思主义哲学研究不再有人们共同关注和研究的“热点”和“焦点”问题。在学术研究中，研究范式总是决定着人们所探讨的问题的意义；问题相对于研究范式的意义和重要性越大，人们对它的关注和重视程度必定越高。因此，在存在着统一的研究范式的情况下，学术研究中必然会涌现出一些“热点”和“焦点”问题。在新中国成立后前 30 年教科书范式规范下的中国马克思主义哲学研究中，是存在着这样的“热点”和“焦点”问题的，如那时人们就生产力与生产关系、经济基础与上层建筑、矛盾的同一性与斗争性、客观规律性与主观能动性的关系问题展开了激烈的论争。在 80 年代教科书改革范式规范下的中国马克思主义哲学研究中，也是存在着这样的“热点”和“焦点”问题的，如 80 年代人们曾“一窝蜂地”讨论实践标准、主体性、实践唯物主义等问题。然而，在 90 年代以来的中国马克思主义哲学研究中，人们的理论兴趣日渐泛化，基本上没有什么问题能够引起人们共同而持续的关注，因而我们再也看不到以往那样的“热点”和“焦点”问题。在我看来，这就是 90 年代以来中国马克思主义哲学研究缺少统一研究范式的明显表征。

第二，90 年代以来的中国马克思主义哲学研究缺乏共同的“问题意识”。应该说，强烈的体系意识是教科书范式和教科书改革范式所规范的马克思主义哲学研究的共同特征。进入 90 年代以后，由于重构教科书体系的各种努力并没有取得预期的结果，中国马克思主义哲学研究的体系意识日渐淡薄，人们转而开始关注和研究各个领域中的具体理论问题。从这个角度看，进入 90 年代以后，中国马克思主义哲学研究确实表现出了从“体系意识”到“问题意识”的转向。问题在于，在 90 年代以来的中国马克思主义哲学研究中，人们虽然关注和研究了大量的具体理论问题，但并没有形成共同的问题意识，即人们在应该提出什么样的问题、怎样提出问题、什么样的问题才是有意义的、怎样去解决问题等方面并没有形成共识。在实际的马克思主义哲学研究中，有人关注时代和实践的发展，注重从现实生活中提出问题；有人专注文本，着力于在马克思主义哲学经典著作中发现甚至“制造”问题；有人强调与当代世界哲学的“对话”和“接轨”，致力于从当代西方哲学的发展中寻找和发现问题；有人至今也摆脱不了“教科书批判情结”，仍然拘泥于从过去的教科书中找寻问题。与此同时，人们面对问题的致思方法也各异其趣，如有人坚持理论联系实际，注重结合现实实践来探寻问题的答案；有人力图规避现实，把对问题的探讨转变成了纯概念的逻辑推演和自娱性的智力游戏；有人虚化问题，醉心于制造各种新词新说；有人热衷于以西解马，力主以现代西方哲学家为中介重新读解马克思主义哲学研究中的问题，等等。所有这些，都是 90 年代以来中国马克思主义哲学研究缺乏共同的问题意识的表现。正如前述，学术研究的范式“决定了什么样的问题有待解决”，“规定了一个研究领域的合理问题和方法”。因此，在形成了统一的研究范式的情况下，研究者们必定会形成共同的问题意识。而 90 年代以来的中国马克思主义哲学研究之所以没有形成共同的问题意识，其根源正在于它没有形成统一的研究范式。

第三，90 年代以来的中国马克思主义哲学研究也缺乏共同的目标、信念和评价标准。有人说，90 年代以来的十多年间是当代中国马克思主义哲学研究最繁荣的时期。我不想否认这一时期中国马克思主义哲学研究的成就，如孙正聿教授所概括的“开拓性哲学”、“准原理哲学”和“专门化哲学”的兴起和发展，这些成就基本上都是通过对一些具体问题或具体领域的研究取得的。但是，我认为，这种“繁荣”显得多少有些虚假，其间夹杂了太多的泡沫。在这一时期，人们确实研究了很多问题和领域，但人们往往并不真的知道为什么要进行这些研究或这些研究的意义何在，至少人们在这些问题上并没有形成普遍的共识；人们提出了许多新的概念、口号和学说，它们可以说是张三的哲学创新或李四的哲学创新，却断难被公认为马克思主义哲学的创新。既然90年代以来中国马克思主义哲学研究缺乏共同的目标、信念和评价标准，那么，还能说它有什么统一的研究范式吗？

第四，90年代以来的中国马克思主义哲学研究在整体思路上已出现了严重分化。近十多年来，中国马克思主义哲学研究逐渐形成和表现出了几种很不相同的基本思路：一是“回到文本”的研究思路。在这种研究思路看来，马克思主义哲学的经典文本是我们讨论马克思主义哲学的唯一合法的依据，我们过去对马克思主义哲学的诸多误解均源于对马克思主义哲学文本的误读；要重新准确地理解马克思主义哲学就必须回到文本，要推进和深化马克思主义哲学研究也必须首先返回到文本，即只有返本才能开新。二是关注现实的研究思路。在这种研究思路看来，实践是马克思主义哲学最重要的对象性基础，实践性是马克思主义哲学的根本特点；马克思主义哲学要保持其作为时代精神的精华的地位，就必须始终关注现实实践的发展，注重从当代世界和当代中国的现实中提出具有普遍性的哲学问题并对之作出创造性的回答。三是立足于基本理论创新的研究思路。在这种研究思路看来，作为人类把握世界的一种基本方式，哲学首先是对人类把握世界的各种基本方式如常识、宗教、艺术、科学、特别是哲学本身的前提批判，正是在这种前提批判中，才有了哲学的本体论、辩证法、认识论、价值论等不同的领域和内容；在今天的马克思主义哲学研究中，只有深入进行对现时代人类把握世界的各种基本方式的前提批判，推动马克思主义哲学各个领域的基本理论创新，我们才能在当代条件下推进马克思主义哲学的发展。四是以问题为中心的研究思路。

根据这种研究思路，哲学是思想中所把握的时代，而问题就是时代的声音；马克思主义哲学研究应该不断地发现和探索当代实践、科学和哲学发展中涌现出来的各种问题，并由此实现马克思主义哲学的与时俱进。前文已经指出，在学术研究中，统一的研究范式必然形成一种连贯的学术传统。90 年代以来中国马克思主义哲学研究在整体思路上的分化已使得那种统一而连贯的学术传统化为乌有，它是 90 年代以来中国马克思主义哲学研究缺少统一研究范式的最突出的表现。

90 年代以来中国马克思主义哲学研究缺少统一研究范式的诸种表现，正是库恩所说的科学发展过程中新旧范式交替时期即科学危机时期的典型征兆。当代中国马克思主义哲学研究正处于这样一个旧的范式既已失去约束力、新的范式又尚未形成的“危机时期”。可以说，在当代中国马克思主义哲学研究的发展过程中，人们从来没有像这一时期、特别是像今天这样对于到底应该如何从事马克思主义哲学研究的问题众说纷纭和感到迷茫与困惑。这样说并非危言耸听，这一事实也不值得大惊小怪，因为它并不意味着当代中国马克思主义哲学研究已经走到了尽头。实际上，处于“危机时期”的当代中国马克思主义哲学研究面临着两种可能的前途和命运：一是任由目前这种无范式的危机状况持续下去，最后使当代中国马克思主义哲学研究消融于对各种具体问题的无原则的议论之中，甚至消融于与其他各种哲学的“对话”和“互动”之中；二是按照马克思主义哲学的本质要求和当代中国社会发展的客观需要，自觉认同马克思主义哲学中国化这一应有的研究范式，并由此结束目前无范式的危机状态和整合已经取得的研究成果，从而保证自身的健康发展。因此，虽然 90 年代以来的中国马克思主义哲学研究从整体上看也是偏离马克思主义哲学中国化这一应有研究范式的，但这一状况已不可能长期持续下去。在未来，要使当代中国马克思主义哲学研究得到进一步的发展，就必须自觉认同马克思主义哲学中国化的研究范式。

三

既然马克思主义哲学中国化是当代中国马克思主义哲学研究的应有范式，而既往的当代中国马克思主义哲学研究实际上这样那样地偏离了马克思主义哲学中国化的研究范式，那么，很明显，我们所面临的一个重要任务就是要将当代中国马克思主义哲学研究纳入马克思主义哲学中国化这一范式，即真正以马克思主义哲学中国化为范式来开展当代中国马克思主义哲学研究。

库恩认为，一切危机都会随着新范式的出现及其被接受而宣告结束。虽然马克思主义哲学中国化这一范式的确立必将能够结束当前中国马克思主义哲学研究的危机状态，但相对于整个中国马克思主义哲学研究而言，马克思主义哲学中国化也并非全新的研究范式。实际上，在马克思主义哲学传入中国以后，至少在自 1938 年毛泽东写作《论新阶段》起的相当一段时期内，马克思主义哲学中国化曾经成为中国马克思主义哲学研究自觉认同的范式。那时，马克思主义哲学在中国思想界尚属“异端”，马克思主义哲学研究面临着重重困难和阻挠，但中国的马克思主义者不惧白色恐怖、甚至冒着生命危险研究马克思主义哲学，自觉把马克思主义哲学与中国的具体实际相结合，并由此创造了一种全新的马克思主义哲学的民族化形式。正是由于有了马克思主义哲学中国化的研究范式，才有了真正意义上的即具有鲜明中国特色的中国马克思主义哲学，才有了《实践论》《矛盾论》等中国马克思主义哲学的经典之作。遗憾的是，新中国成立以后，马克思主义哲学中国化这一研究范式逐渐被前述教科书范式所取代。因此，从整个中国马克思主义哲学研究的发展过程来看，我们说应以马克思在当代中国化为范式开展当代中国马克思主义哲学研究，实际上是要在当代中国马克思主义哲学研究中恢复或重新确立马克思主义哲学中国化的研究范式。

在当代中国马克思主义哲学研究中恢复或重新确立马克思主义哲学中国化

的研究范式，决不可能是一蹴而就的事情。要使人们自觉地认同和遵循这一研究范式，尚有许多工作要做。其中，最为迫切和紧要的有以下几个方面：

第一，必须坚决反对各种形式的教条主义。以马克思主义哲学中国化为范式开展当代中国马克思主义哲学研究，要求我们从中国的具体实际出发、用马克思主义哲学的立场、观点和方法研究中国的具体问题，而教条主义总是从书本、概念或命题出发，把既有的理论、概念、命题当作万古不变的教条，用理论剪裁现实，用抽象的一般抹杀生动的个性，从而人为地阻隔了马克思主义哲学与中国具体实际相结合的通道。因此，教条主义历来都是以马克思主义哲学中国化为范式开展中国马克思主义哲学研究的大敌。在马克思主义哲学发展史上，教条主义曾受到马克思主义哲学经典作家的尖锐批判。例如，针对把马克思主义哲学教条化的错误，恩格斯明确指出："我们的理论是发展着的理论，而不是必须背得烂熟并机械地加以重复的教条。"① 恩格斯还曾辛辣地讽刺德国社会民主党内的教条主义者"青年派"说："所有这些先生们都在搞马克思主义，……关于这种马克思主义者，马克思曾经说过：'我只知道我自己不是马克思主义者。'马克思大概会把海涅对自己的模仿者说的话送给这些先生们：'我播下的是龙种，而收获的却是跳蚤。'"② 在中国马克思主义哲学发展的早期阶段，王明也是这种形式的教条主义的典型代表，他把马克思主义哲学的概念和命题当作包医百病的灵丹妙药，似乎只要重复一下马克思主义经典作家的现成词句就能解决一切问题。为了反对这种形式的教条主义，毛泽东在20世纪三四十年代先后写作了《反对本本主义》《改造我们的学习》等一系列重要文章，并发动和领导了延安整风运动。也正是在反对王明式的教条主义的过程中，毛泽东提出和确立了马克思主义哲学中国化的研究范式，并由此实现了中国马克思主义哲学的伟大理论创造，形成了毛泽东哲学思想。然而，在20世纪90年代以来的中国马克思主义哲学研究中，教条主义又一次卷土重来，甚至成为一

① 《马克思恩格斯选集》第4卷，人民出版社1995年版，第681页。

② 《马克思恩格斯选集》第4卷，人民出版社1995年版，第695页。

种时尚，并主要采取了以下两种形式：一是“文本崇拜”。众所周知，致力于马克思主义哲学的研究，必须以准确、全面地理解马克思主义哲学经典文本为基础。但是，在近年来的中国马克思主义哲学研究中，一些人并非一般地强调对文本的研究，而是把文本研究视为马克思主义哲学研究的基本思路，即主张马克思主义哲学研究就是对马克思主义哲学经典文本的研究，从而陷入了一种以“文本崇拜”的形式表现出来的教条主义。这种“文本崇拜”形式的教条主义，不过是老式的教条主义即王明式的教条主义的最新版本。二是洋教条迷信。在近年来的中国马克思主义哲学研究中，不仅那种老式的教条主义仍在禁锢着一些人的头脑，而且一种新式的教条主义即对洋教条的迷信也极为盛行。所谓对洋教条的迷信，就是一些中国马克思主义哲学研究者居然把某些现代西方哲学家的理论和观点奉为教条，其最突出的表现就是“以西解马”，如以海德格尔的观点来解读马克思主义哲学。这种洋教条迷信，有人美其名曰为马克思主义哲学研究的“中介式方法”，它无非是说，我们以往对马克思主义哲学的理解是成问题的，现在我们应该通过现代西方哲学家这个中介来理解和研究马克思主义哲学。尽管这两种形式的教条主义之间有很大的差异，但它们却有一个共同点，即都从根本上丢弃了中国的具体实际这个中国马克思主义哲学研究的应有立足点。不从根本上破除这两种形式的教条主义，就不可能真正以马克思主义哲学中国化为范式开展中国马克思主义哲学研究。

第二，必须纠正对于马克思主义哲学中国化的性质的误读。关于马克思主义哲学中国化的性质问题，历来都有诸多的误解或歪曲。例如，海外中国学研究中很早就有人把马克思主义哲学中国化归结为儒家化甚至封建化，认为它实际上是把马克思主义哲学化为乌有，其结果充其量也只是变形走样的马克思主义哲学。近年来，有些人又对马克思主义哲学中国化的性质作了另类误读，即把马克思主义哲学中国化归结为 20 世纪西学东渐史的一个组成部分，这也是对马克思主义哲学中国化的严重曲解。首先，这种观点把马克思主义哲学在中国的广泛传播视为 19 世纪中叶以后随着西方列强的入侵而潮水般地涌入中国的西方文化的一部分，歪曲了马克思主义哲学中国化的历史。实际上，虽然西方列强的入侵在客观上强化了马克思主义哲学在中国传播的必要性和可能性，但马克思主义哲学在中国的传播决不是西方列强入侵的伴生物，马克思主义哲学也不是自动“涌入”中国的。20 世纪初马克思主义哲学在中国的广泛传播，是当时先进的中国人苦苦寻找救国救民真理的结果。关于这一点，毛泽东说得再清楚不过了：“自一八四〇年鸦片战争失败起，先进的中国人，经过千辛万苦，向西方国家寻找真理。”“中国人向西方学得很不少，但是行不通，理想总是不能实现。多次奋斗，包括辛亥革命那样全国规模的运动，都失败了。国家的情况一天一天坏，环境迫使人们活不下去。怀疑产生了，增长了，发展了。”最后，“十月革命一声炮响，给我们送来了马克思列宁主义。十月革命帮助了全世界的也帮助了中国的先进分子，用无产阶级的宇宙观作为观察国家命运的工具，重新考虑自己的问题。”① 这里所说的“无产阶级的宇宙观”也就是马克思主义哲学。其次，这种观点用“马克思主义哲学在中国”的命题来替代“马克思主义哲学中国化”命题，曲解了马克思主义哲学中国化的基本内涵，实质上从根本上否认了马克思主义哲学中国化的事实。在这里，“马克思主义哲学在中国”这一命题所强调的是作为一种西方文化的马克思主义哲学在中国的际遇，就像一个人客居他乡的所作所为。按照一些人的描述，产生于西方的马克思主义哲学约一百年前传播到了中国，然后就指导了中国革命的胜利并成为指导思想，使中国社会历史发生了深刻的变化，其自身也经历了相当曲折的进程。在这幅题为“马克思主义哲学在中国”的漫画式图景中，马克思主义哲学中国化即把马克思主义哲学与中国具体实际相结合已变成子虚乌有的事情。再次，这种观点还将“马克思主义哲学在中国”与“进化主义在中国”、“唯意志论哲学在中国”、“实用主义在中国”等相提并论，混淆了马克思主义哲学与其他西方近现代思潮之间的原则界限，实际上完全否定了马克思主义哲学中国化

---

① 《毛泽东选集》第四卷，人民出版社 1991 年版，第 1469—1471 页。

的意义。按照这种观点，既然马克思主义哲学与其他西方近现代思潮一样都是伴随着西方列强的入侵而涌入中国的，那么，即使存在着马克思主义哲学中国化的事实，它也只不过是西方文化入侵或文化殖民的一种表现。如此一来，不要说什么以马克思主义哲学中国化为范式开展当代中国马克思主义哲学研究，就是以往的马克思主义哲学中国化的理论和实践的合法性也必须加以拷问。总之，不纠正上述对于马克思主义哲学中国化的性质的误读，就不可能在当代中国马克思主义哲学研究中恢复或重新确立马克思主义哲学中国化的研究范式。

第三，必须对马克思主义哲学中国化进行正确的学术定位。所谓对马克思主义哲学中国化的学术定位，是指对马克思主义哲学中国化的学理意涵的界定，它涉及如何看待马克思主义哲学中国化的学术性或在学术上如何致力于马克思主义哲学中国化的问题。近年来，一些人主张区分马克思主义哲学中国化的学术层面与政治层面，认为政治层面的马克思主义哲学中国化的着眼点是解决中国革命和建设过程中所遇到的实际问题和理论问题，其重点是把马克思主义哲学与中国的当前现实相结合，它属于革命家、政治家的事情；而学术层面的马克思主义哲学中国化则是指马克思主义哲学这一学科的中国化，其重点是吸取和改造中国传统文化、特别是中国传统哲学思想，其任务是创造具有中国特色的马克思主义哲学。显然，这里所谓的学术层面的马克思主义哲学中国化也就相当于我们所说的以马克思主义哲学中国化为范式的马克思主义哲学研究，与此相应，对马克思主义哲学中国化的学术定位实即对以马克思主义哲学中国化为范式的马克思主义哲学研究的学术定位。在这种观点看来，以往的中国马克思主义哲学研究存在着学术含量严重不足的问题，而其原因正在于它缺乏准确的学术定位，经常越位到政治层面去干本属于革命家、政治家的事情。应该承认，在马克思主义哲学中国化过程中，革命家、政治家与理论家确有不同的职责和任务。但是，如果认为把马克思主义哲学与中国的当前现实相结合主要是革命家、政治家的事情，而把马克思主义哲学与中国传统文化相结合才是致力于中国马克思主义哲学研究的理论家的本务，那就大谬不然了。这种力主对马克思主义哲学中国化的学术层面与政治层面作截然二分、试图通过规避政治和现实来强化中国马克思主义哲学研究的学术性的观点，不过是近年来中国学术界以“政治淡出，学术凸显”的时髦口号为症候的“流行病”在马克思主义哲学研究中的表现。其实，研究中国社会生活中的现实问题与吸取中国传统文化的优秀思想，都是马克思主义哲学中国化即把马克思主义哲学与中国具体实际相结合的题中应有之义，无论是革命家、政治家还是理论家都不应该偏废任何一方面。作为学术事业的马克思主义哲学中国化即中国的马克思主义哲学研究，当然要重视从中国传统文化、特别是中国传统哲学思想中吸取思想养分，但更应该关注中国的当前现实，其研究中国传统文化也是为解决中国当前现实中的问题寻觅思想资源。如果无视时代和中国社会发展的现实需要，对中国社会发展中的现实问题漠不关心，不仅会因缺乏现实立足点和取舍标准而使从中国传统文化中吸取思想养分成为空话，而且还会使马克思主义哲学中国化面临合法性危机，更遑论什么强化它的学术性和创造具有中国特色的马克思主义哲学了。可见，如果缺乏对马克思主义哲学中国化的正确的学术定位，即使我们能够以马克思主义哲学中国化为范式开展当代中国马克思主义哲学研究，也不能保证当代中国马克思主义哲学研究的健康发展。

第四，必须明确以马克思主义哲学中国化为范式的马克思主义哲学研究与对马克思主义哲学中国化这一领域的研究之间的重要区别。我们说当代中国马克思主义哲学研究一直是这样那样地偏离并且至今也没有确立起马克思主义哲学中国化的研究范式，并不是说当代中国就没有或完全不重视对马克思主义哲学中国化的研究。事实上，马克思主义哲学中国化研究始终是当代中国马克思主义哲学研究的一个重要组成部分，并在不同的时期都得到了一定程度的推进。即使是在教科书范式或教科书改革范式占主导地位的时期，人们也并未停止对马克思主义哲学中国化问题的探索。至于在 90 年代以来、特别是新世纪以来的中国马克思主义哲学研究中，马克思主义哲学中国化更是成为一个受到众多学者高度关注的研究领域，甚至可以说已经兴起了一股马克思主义哲学中国化研究的热潮。但是，在近五十多年来的当代中国马克思主义哲学研究中，马克思主义哲学中国化基本上只是作为与马克思主义哲学基础理论、马克思主义哲学史（包括马克思主义哲学经典文本）、现当代国外马克思主义哲学等相并列的一个研究领域、有时甚至只是作为马克思主义哲学史领域中的一个研究方向而受到人们的重视。在这种情况下，马克思主义哲学基础理论、马克思主义哲学史（包括马克思主义哲学经典文本）、现当代国外马克思主义哲学等领域的研究是可以游离于马克思主义哲学中国化之外的，甚至是完全无关于马克思主义哲学中国化的；一个中国学者可能终生都在从事马克思主义哲学研究，但他可以与马克思主义哲学中国化从不发生任何联系。与此不同，以马克思主义哲学中国化为范式开展马克思主义哲学研究，则意味着整个中国马克思主义哲学研究都是为了把马克思主义哲学中国化，意味着包括马克思主义哲学基础理论、马克思主义哲学史（包括马克思主义哲学经典文本）、现当代国外马克思主义哲学等中国马克思主义哲学各个领域的研究都要以马克思主义哲学中国化为理论目标、解释原则和评价标准。显然，以马克思主义哲学中国化为范式的马克思主义哲学研究与对马克思主义哲学中国化这一领域的研究之间是有重要区别的。其中，对马克思主义哲学中国化这一领域的研究，属于一种狭义的马克思主义哲学中国化研究；而以马克思主义哲学中国化为范式的马克思主义哲学研究，则属于一种广义的马克思主义哲学中国化研究。这里尤其要强调的是，从广义上说，马克思主义哲学中国化研究与马克思主义哲学基础理论、马克思主义哲学史（包括马克思主义哲学经典文本）、现当代国外马克思主义哲学等领域的研究决非毫不相干，更不是相互排斥的，而是有着内在的相互依存关系。一方面，只有通过对马克思主义哲学基础理论、马克思主义哲学史（包括马克思主义哲学经典文本）、现当代国外马克思主义哲学等领域的创造性研究，马克思主义哲学中国化研究才能获得它应有的广度和深度，才能得到切实的推进；另一方面，只有以马克思主义哲学中国化为理论目标并自觉融入到马克思主义哲学中国化研究中去，马克思主义哲学基础理论、马克思主义哲学史

（包括马克思主义哲学经典文本）、现当代国外马克思主义哲学等领域的研究才是真正有意义的，也才能真正推进中国马克思主义哲学的发展。在当代中国马克思主义哲学研究中恢复或重新确立马克思主义哲学中国化的研究范式，就必须突破对于马克思主义哲学中国化研究的狭隘理解，使当代中国马克思主义哲学研究成为一种广义的马克思主义哲学中国化研究。

（原载《中国社会科学》2008 年第 2 期）

宗教哲学方法论的理论探索

麻天祥

哲学是爱智之学，宗教哲学是以智慧思虑、认识无限或本体之学。智慧则是如何认识无限的进路，或者说怎样实现终极关怀的合理性过程。就学术研究而言，方法论显然是至关重要的。宗教哲学的研究方法及领域可以概括为疑虑、诠释、比较和体悟四个方面。

一、疑虑

人类的智慧不会囿于有限的感知，对无限的向往与好奇是宗教、哲学，也是科学发生的内驱力或者说策源地。宇宙之大，事物之千变万化，教人不可思议，眼花缭乱，无时无处不引发人的惊讶与发问：怎么会是这样？为什么不是那样？如何才会成为那样？即使对人类自身，既不能知死，也难于知生，只能感叹“逝者如斯”，“生死事大”，“念天地之悠悠，独怆然而涕下”。人云，哲学源于惊讶，力图超越有限，领悟无限，实现人生终极价值的宗教正是基于对有限的怀疑，而思虑、期盼无限的。更何况，感觉经验，理性认识也常常会给人们传递某些错误信息。宗教不是植根于“信”，而是发端于“疑”的合理性过程。宗教哲学尤其对超越有限的“无限”的理性思考，是以对“有限”的怀疑为前提的。没有怀疑就没有思虑，没有思虑就没有认识，没有认识就没有所得，也就没有人类思维与社会历史的发展。笛卡尔所说“怀疑一切”也是这个意思——怀疑不是目的，而是荡涤习焉不察、习以为常的错误认识和错误观念，为思想的发展清扫出一块空旷之地。胡适的“大胆假设”显然是建立在对以往一切现有思想怀疑的基础上，“重新估定一切价值”的。哲学研究就是要“于不疑处有疑”，于疑处才能审思释然。试想，释伽若不虑疑人生之苦，哪里有觉悟的追求？老庄若无对现象世界的怀疑，怎么能产生恍兮惚兮的“道”的猜测？进一步说，没有对纯粹的基督教信仰的怀疑就没有系统的基督教神学的产生和基督教哲学的发展，也就没有西方新教伦理对资本主义的渗透与亲合；没有对印度佛教的审视就没有对它的改造和理论的增益，也就没有中国化的佛教对中国哲学的丰富和对中国人生观念的重铸。可以说，哲学、宗教哲学的发展，都是在疑虑的母腹中孕育并产生的。而且，几乎所有的哲学、宗教哲学命题，都可以提出一个截然相反，同样合理性的命题，予以质疑和挑战。所以，原本寻求终极真理的哲学、宗教哲学，从事物存在的无限性而言，都不可能终极真理。这里也表现了信仰与理性的悖论。

严格分析，疑虑不是哲学、宗教哲学的具体方法，只是通过怀疑，以无限的观念审思制度化宗教理论的合理性，衡量它的价值，发挥它的效用。因此应当说疑虑是哲学、宗教哲学研究的思维的前提或必要条件。

二、诠释

以本体标识的无限，虽然不仅仅是思维中的概念，但在有限的现实生活中，有限语言的阐释中，毕竟还是哲学的概念或范畴。回答本体是什么，自然无法像回答有限事物那样，“拿证据来”，而且有限的语言常常不足以表述本体或无限的真相，所谓“道可道，非常道”、“说似一物即不中”是也，尽管西方哲学，特别是基督教哲学视语言为本体。但是，从不满足有限世界，有限生存方式，力图摆脱有限的人类理性，尤其是哲学思维，还是要讲超越有限的存在，即说“不可说”而有本体的诠释。正因为如此，诠释则如万花筒色彩斑斓，光怪陆离，表现了它的多样性和它的繁难艰涩。统而言之曰肯定性诠释和否定性诠释，佛学谓之表诠和遮诠。

（一）肯定性诠释

首先是推理，用逻辑的方法证明作为无限的本体，如上帝、道、理、心性之类存在的合理性及其性质。由个别推论一般，而有归纳；由普遍推衍特殊，而有演绎。前者尚官感，置个别事象于推理之前，最终有事物普遍性质的结论；后者重心思，以一般性的命题为预设，继而推导出个体事物的特殊性。或以因果论相推导，因而生果，果而有因，如上帝创世，上帝以第一因而得成立；道生一，终至三生万物，物是道之果，道是万物因。或设一物为本体，继以正、反、合反复辩说。此为先验的，佛教学者称之“结论后之研究”，用胡适的话说就是“大胆假设，小心求证”，所谓求证，实在也包含了类似求证的推理。至于儒家性命天道之说，天命而性，率性而道，也属于辩证的逻辑推理。佛教的缘生之理，以因缘相合而结兹果，果为因之果，因为果之因，说明事物互为因果，表现明显的非本体倾向，表面看似因果论，本质上却包含了远比一般因果论多得多的辩证思维。

推理就要靠逻辑，无论是辩证逻辑还是形式逻辑，严密的逻辑既可以避免不全归纳，也可以扬弃无效的演绎，获得不可能通过有限感觉，以有限事实证明的无限本体。辩证逻辑若理学的“理一分殊”，佛教的名相分析等不一而足。名家的辩证思维在中国宗教哲学中也有它的一席之地。至于形式逻辑，西方的三段论、墨家的三表法（其实它包含了辩证逻辑），在中国宗教哲学中，也是不可或缺的方法；佛教的因明，以宗、因、喻三支说法，形成并完善为系统的逻辑规范，不仅为佛教哲学，实际上也为中国宗教哲学、中国哲学，乃至世界哲学提供了诠释的手段。类比也是一种推理，但在宗教哲学中，也是寓比较、譬喻于其中的推理。如以人的属性升华，类推神的属性，所谓止于至善者。它包含了更多的或然性，自然宜谨慎运用。

其次是分析。哲学既然是本体之学，当然也是探求事物普遍性质之学，从方法论的角度讲，哲学就是概念分析，是概念的游戏。所以不仅要解析本体，而且要诠释本体以及与本体相关的名相，即指称本体和事物的概念。章太炎说法相之学“以分析名相始，以排遣名相终”，名自然是概念，相虽不同于名，但并非事物相状的本身，也是指称相状的概念。由此可见，概念分析是哲学和宗教哲学的主要方法。固然，无限或本体不可以“名”言，是不可道的，语言无法反映超现实的本体的真相，但是，人类毕竟生活在不同程度的语境之中，凭借语言符号传递信息，而且，语言在特定的条件下，也能够超越它的本身，从根本上改变指称对象的性质，将特殊性消融在普遍的规定性之中。本体、无限以及空、无、理、道、心、性等概念，正是借语言表述的超越有限，“意在言外”的存在。中国玄学的言意之辨，佛门的“妙万物以为言”，“语言者，心之缘，道之标帜”，都在于实践或说明，本体的无限性虽“不可以语言传，而可以语言见”，突出概念分析的必要性和可能性。佛教超二元对立的“中”的观念就是建立在对现象世界的“空”、“假”分析的基础上的必然结论；借重分析 logos、calling、original sin、道成肉身、三位一体、属性交流、因信称义诸多概念。中国传统的义理之学，无论儒、道、释，“引传文以解经，转相发明”，也都是对概念的条分缕析；尤其是西方本体诠释学（Onto-Hermeneutics）在中国哲学中的应用，才促进了当代新儒家的崛起。显而易见，概念分析也是中国宗教哲学的常用方法。诠释本体性质，分析体用关系，分析事物的相状，首要的任务是对各种同类的、不同类的，相似的、相异的概念作精密的分析，如体用、道器、谶纬、知行、天人、名相、心性、理欲、有无、动静、因果、性命、诚正、仁礼、元一、言意、净染、善恶、真幻、内丹外丹、无极太极等等，在此基础上，进而在条分缕析事物个别性的同时，抽象出事物的本质特性。

再次是譬喻。对于不可言诠的天道、性理等本体问题，特别是宗教哲学超二元对立的终极问题，譬喻尤其显得重要。中国传统哲学早已注意到这一方法的运用。如《淮南子·要略》云：“言道不明终始，则不知所仿依”，“不引譬援类，则不知精微”，“不知譬喻，则无以推明事”。作为方法，佛教尤多采纳，而有众多的寓言故事。《金刚经》以梦幻泡影、雷、电比喻有为法，理学以“月印万川”喻理事关系，禅宗思想以镜、台、菩提树喻染心、净心，都是譬喻的运用。类比的方法与此相似，多以至善至美的人性比附、推求神性，从逻辑学上讲是推理，但就比附而言，更应当说是譬喻。如托马斯的基督教神学，以人性推类上帝之性；明儒“心即理”之说，也是以至善之德比附天理。佛教索性将譬喻引入因明，形成自己独具特色的逻辑规则，无论三支还是五支，不仅设同喻，而且设异喻，目的显然在于尽量避免或然性，增强说理的可靠性。因此，宗教哲学研究，既要注意理解寓于比喻中的形而上的意义，也要掌握运用譬喻，实行哲学的解析。

（二）否定性诠释

宗教哲学关注的是超越有限的无限，无论怎么讲，它都是不可言诠的，用严复的话说，也是不可思议的。上帝的神性不可说，道的体性也不可说，宇宙之始不可说，人本性的善恶亦不可说，犹如现代数学中的多值逻辑，也常在“是否”、“有无”、“大小”二元对立之间，而难以言诠。故中国的玄学家以“得意忘言”、“得意忘象”之说，提出了“言意之辨”的命题，佛教禅门明确提出“不落言诠”、“不可说”指称“觉”的境界。然而，作为信仰可以不说，置身哲学领域则非说不可，于是而有说不可说。除上述肯定性诠释外，否定性诠释显然是最稳妥的方法，虽然是不精确的，却是无差错的。佛教主张“理绝名言”，不着两边，以“不生不灭，不一不异，不来不去，不常不断”的八不中道表述事物缘生的本质，可以说是否定性诠释的经典性应用。即使儒家以性善论问鼎天下，但至理学“天理”“人欲”之辨而接受挑战，于是有明儒“无善无恶”的否定性诠释。至于佛教的思维方式，当然不能说是先肯定后否定，也不是同时肯定、同时否定以及否定之否定的绝对肯定（铃木大拙语），应当说是超二元对立的双向否定，即否定性诠释。在宗教哲学中否定性诠释的应用不亚于肯定性诠释，甚至有过之而无不及。

显然，诠释不能离开语言。学习以至研究宗教哲学，作为诠释的工具，无论是肯定还是否定，语言都是非常重要的。原因不仅在于它是传递信息的符号，是不得不采用，也只能用作诠释的工具。同时还应当注意到，作为思维的符号，它与人类无限的观念紧密相联，并可无穷伸展，所以能消除特殊性，而使指称的对象具有普遍的规定性。从这个意义上讲，语言就是无限和本体。正因为如此，我们不仅要熟练运用现代汉语，而且要熟谙文言文，不仅要懂一种或多种外国语，而且要学习如巴利文、梵文、希腊文这样的经典文字。前辈学者为我们树立了很好的榜样。

三、比较

缪勒说，只懂得一门宗教（实指某种宗教组织）的人，其实什么宗教也不懂。这显然是从比较宗教学的意义上谈宗教和宗教哲学研究的。可见比较的方法在宗教哲学中的重要地位。如前所言，在人类社会历史中，制度化的宗教不仅有各自的组织形态，而且创立、形成并发展一套各具特色的，关于无限、终极追求，以及实现终极追求的系统的理性思维。因此，宗教哲学研究，不仅要纠正对宗教的误解，而且要以同情理解的态度，认真求实的精神，对各不相同的制度化的宗教组织作历史的、逻辑的认识，以避免偏见，如此则不可避免地涉及比较。比较宗教学（Comparative religion）则应运而生。西方的某些学者认为，比较宗教学的历史渊源可以上溯到远古的诸神崇拜时期，他们在比较中，逐步摆脱单纯的恐惧和信仰，不断地提高探索的水平，而迎来了神学和哲学的黎明。从这个意义上说，宗教学，或者说宗教哲学就是比较宗教学。它比较那些曾经影响甚至还在影响人类社会的宗教组织和它们的思想的起源、结构以及特殊和一般的意义，比较它们的一致与歧异，比较它们之间的关系与优劣。如此判断正确与否姑且不论，但是足以反映，比较的方法在宗教哲学研究中的重要地位。

事实上，制度化的宗教组织，无论是国外各大宗教，还是中国的儒、道、释，它们对无限的观念都有各自的理解，都有名称不同，也就是概念不同的终极关怀和终极寄托。与此相应，自然又有相互区别的进至无限的手段与途径，换句话说就是实现终极关怀的思维方式也不同。它们无论在理论上，还是在实践中，或者相互吸引、渗透，或者排斥、消融，而且在有限的社会生存发展中，世俗化，特别是政治、经济驾驭的必然趋势，导致了它们的两难选择：或者对无限观念的认同，或者与终极关怀的背离，如是色彩纷呈，尤其表现出各种悖论的思辨——出世入世、超越参与、无限有限、信仰理性等等。和而不同的宗教组织，在根本性质上的一致性，在形式、思辨方式上不同程度的差异，甚至不同的致力方向，在不同的历史阶段所起的不同的社会作用，都需要在比较中透彻认识并予以抉择。比较在宗教哲学中的重要性也就不言而喻了。

事实上，在有限世界内，事物的存在都有一定的相互关系，都是比较的，或者说是相对的。因此，离开比较就无法给予事物作明确的定位，比如多寡、大小、新旧、异同、优劣等。所以，日常生活中，“比较”一法普遍采用而习以为常。可见，比较并非哲学特有的方法，只是由于比较宗教学作为一门科学的兴起而备受关注，而且，比较常常和分析推理（特别是类比推理）、譬喻同时应用。但是在比较宗教学中，着眼点大多放在不同宗教组织间的横向比较，比较它们的异同，比较它们之间的高低优劣。当然这是无可非议的。也正是在这种比较中，越来越深入认识它们之间对于大千世界本原以及价值取向的一致性，展示它们进至无限的道路的差异。另一方面，当然还应当有宗教组织自身发展的纵向比较，惟有如此，方能显示各种宗教组织产生的心理依据和文化背景，以及在不同历史阶段与异质文化冲突交融过程中，概念范畴的更新或变化。简单地说，非横向比较无以观异同，无以观不同宗教组织的渗透与交融；非纵向比较，则无以观不同宗教哲学理论的发展和变化。总之，没有比较就无法实现曾经冲突，甚至正在冲突，或者“鸡犬之声相闻”却视同陌路的各种宗教组织之间对话的思想基础。汤用彤先生的中国佛教史研究，于比较的方法驾轻就熟，既有横向的佛道、佛玄、佛儒，以及佛教各宗哲学的比较，同时也注重佛教传入中国后一千余年，在不同历史时期，思想理念的自我调适，为我们树立了最佳的典范。从这个意义上讲，也可以说是历史和逻辑相结合的方法，是研究宗教哲学史，特别是中国宗教哲学史的至高价值和导引。

四、体悟

宗教是对无限的终极关怀，宗教哲学是对超越有限的阐释，而无限又是不可思议，不可言诠的，虽然不得不议，不得不说，但是，还得要求超越语言逻辑的方法，才能心领神会而不致舛错。这就是体悟的方法。平心而论，哲学研究，语言逻辑的方法是必要的方法，也是可行的方法。缺乏逻辑训练的人难以承担哲学研究的任务。然而，无限的问题是超越感觉世界，超越有限知识，也就是超理性、超逻辑、超科学的，任何语言、理性、逻辑都有其局限性，而难以准确把握。依靠逻辑思维，语言诠释，实难获得对无限的认知。臻至最高的境界不是循逻辑理性，而是靠直觉体悟。所以，很多的哲学家认为，分析的方法不能解决哲学问题，分析哲学走到哪里，哪里的哲学就死了。正如中国宗教哲学反复强调的“道可道，非常道”、“明道若昧”、“得意忘言”、“不落言诠”、“说似一物即不中”，突出的就是“悟”。即使是处处讲“拿证据来”的实证主义者胡适，论禅的方法，一是强调从教的方面要“不说破”，二是站在学的立场上“贵在自得”，所指也是直觉体悟。儒家发展至理学，在哲学层面思考，认为所求至极，实即无限之理，靠的是日积月累的“用力”，“一旦豁然贯通焉，则众物之表里精粗无不到，而吾心之全体大用无不明”，所谓“向来枉费推移力，今朝水中自在行”是也。所有这些无疑显示体悟的方法对于认知无限，即认知理、道、禅、神、本心，实现天人合一、与本体合一是何等的重要且无可替代的通途。

体悟的特点是靠直觉，而非理性和逻辑；不是对事物表面的直观，而是透过表象对事物深层质的规定性整体把握，是一种创造性的思维活动。道家谓之“玄览”，佛教直呼之“悟”，佛教哲学专以“现量”的概念，与“比量”相对，解析“悟”的本质。有人说它是非理性的也好，也有人说它是理性的最高形式也罢，实际上指的是斩断逻辑程序，超越时空，直达本体的整体思维。所谓“顿悟”不是指时间的短暂，而意味思维逻辑的退隐。禅门的机锋棒喝、指东说西，若“羚羊挂角，无迹可求”，目的仅仅在于抛却寻言逐句的习惯，截断通常的思维模式，于茫然不知所措的状态中，恍然大悟事物的本来面目。所谓随物应机、截断众流、涵盖乾坤，正是宋初云门的“体悟”哲学，也是直觉体悟方法的诗化。

体悟的另一个特点是它的否定性。直觉的方法是超时空的，具有无限性质的本体又是超现象的，道断语言的体悟方式自然倾向于否定，排中律显然是不成立的。既否定有，同时否定无，依照直觉逻辑的公式是：非非 A 中不包含 A，也就是说非 A 不是 A，也不是 B；非 B 不是 B，也不是 A，完全是超二元对立的思维方式和多值逻辑。佛学中的八不中道可以说是佛教“顿悟”的实施或导引，于是有不思善，不思恶，不落两边，不着理路，单刀直入，以否定之否定为显著特色的创造性思维。

应当说明，体悟的方法并非神秘而遥不可及，它既是感觉经验长期积淀的结果，又是以逻辑手段为基础。紧张、细密的逻辑思维之后，直觉体悟才能充分展示它的魅力。在宗教哲学中，任何夸大“体悟”神秘性的思想、行为，都是不足取的。遗憾的是，不少的宗教组织，或多或少地将“悟”蒙上一层神秘的面纱，以此坚定它们对某种有形之物的崇拜，坚定它们绝对不可移易的信仰。如禅宗末流，炫玉贾石，借“悟”的方法花样翻新，把简明直截的方法，沉入神秘主义的信仰，与宗教哲学也就相去千里了。

胡塞尔与黑格尔：政治现象学何以可能 *

郝长墀

在形式上，我们可以说，现象学涉及人的主体经验的方方面面，特别是关于主体的几类主要经验。与之相对应的，现象学的主要分支包括认知现象学、存在论现象学、艺术现象学、伦理现象学、宗教现象学等。而在所有的经验中，政治经验是人类最普遍的人生经验之一。政治现象学应该是现象学的重要部分。那么，什么是政治经验？它包含的主要现象学关系和内容又是什么？对于政治或政治经验，我们不仅经历过，而且，我们似乎都有某种程度的理解。这种经验的本质结构是什么呢？

莱维纳斯（Emmanuel Levinas）在《整体与无限》序言的开篇就强调说，对于我们而言，政治经验中所显现的实在是显而易见的。与政治相比，我们是不是被道德所欺骗？在战争中，道德不仅被搁置起来了，而且，战争使得道德显得可笑。“预见战争并不惜一切赢得战争的艺术—政治—因此被理所当然的视为理性的真正运用。政治与道德的对立，就如哲学与天真的对立。”莱维纳斯认为，战争是政治的最高和最本质的体现，在其中，理性是战争或政治的本质。战争告诉我们的“实在”是“残酷的事实”，是关于“纯存在的纯粹的经验”。“个人被简约为力量的承载者，在不知觉中被它所驱使”①。因此，对于莱维纳斯而言，在战争中，人类充分体会到纯粹的存在，而这种存在的显现在西方哲

* 本篇旨在结合胡塞尔和黑格尔的现象学理论提出政治现象学理论的基本框架和问题。在黑格尔、萨特、阿伦特、福柯的论著中可以发现关于政治现象学的不同论述，而且他们互相之间有本质的联系。作者将会另篇讨论其他三位现象学家的政治现象学思想。

① 以上参见 Emmanuel Levinas，*Totality and Infinity: An Essay on Exteriority*，trans. Alphonso Lingis，Pittsburgh，PA: Duquesne University Press，1969，p.21。

学中占主导地位，用以表达它的概念就是“整体性”。依据莱维纳斯的观点来看，整个西方哲学都是政治哲学，即关于赤裸裸的存在的哲学（本体论）。与之形成鲜明对比的是道德经验：道德的力量如此软弱，似乎是虚幻的。哲学就是政治，就是理性，就是整体，而道德就是幼稚和非理性的。当然，莱维纳斯在《整体与无限》中所要做的就是对于这种无论在理论上还是实际生活中关于政治和道德的观点进行挑战。

我们所关心的是，这里，莱维纳斯给我们提出了一个问题：我们在日常经验中，特别是在战争中，所体会到的实在的真理，究竟是什么样的真理？难道真的如莱维纳斯所说的，暴力或战争使得人们扮演连自己都不认识的角色，被动地出卖自己，从而失去自己吗？①在政治中，我们为何一方面体会到的是冷冰冰的现实，面对的是无能为力的实在，另外一方面在其中又找不到自我呢？政治经验究竟是一种什么样的经验？在政治中，我们真的是被无名的力量或暴力所驱使吗？

在本文中，我首先分析在现象学中如何界定政治经验和政治现象概念并提出政治现象学的三个基本问题；其次，论述了为何在胡塞尔现象学文献中无法发展出政治现象学理论；然后，依据对于黑格尔《精神现象学》中的主奴关系的解读，认为在黑格尔中，“认可”概念是其政治现象学核心概念，政治空间是关于自我意识如何实现的问题。

一、政治经验与政治现象

政治现象学的核心问题是，在政治经验中，我们体验到的“对象”是什么以及它是如何在我们的体验中显现出来？为了回答这个问题，我们不是把现象学的方法运用到政治经验中进行分析和描述，而是通过对于政治现象本身的分

① Emmanuel Levinas, *Totality and Infinity: An Essay on Exteriority*, trans. Alphonso Lingis, Pittsburgh, PA: Duquesne University Press, 1969, p.21.

析和描述来展示政治现象学可能的形态。这里，我们首先需要对于“政治现象”做一个简要理论上的澄清。

人的存在包含多个维度，每一个维度都体现了人的独特的方面。对于现象学主体而言，每一种对象都有其独特的显现的方式或者或被给予的方式，现象学研究的就是事物如何被给予的。现象学是关于“如何”的问题。在《逻辑研究》(1900）中，胡塞尔关心的问题是，在概念和法则中的普遍的理念是如何在时间之中的意识之流中呈现出来的？简而言之，在知识中，对象性的内在存在如何被把握或呈现出来？针对这样的问题，在《现象学观念》(1906）中胡塞尔明确指出，显现与显现者，或知识与被认知的对象性，构成了现象概念不可分割的两个方面。也就是说，对于胡塞尔而言，对象如何在认知活动中构成自身，这是现象学的核心问题，更准确地说，这是认知现象学的核心问题。后来的现象学家对于胡塞尔的批评，不是否定他对于现象概念的定义，而是拓宽现象两个构成部分的内涵以及揭示两者之间的内在的关系。比如，对于莱维纳斯来说，在伦理关系中，我与他者的关系，他者如何在我之中显现的问题显然不能够用胡塞尔的认知关系来分析和描述：在他者面前，我是被言说的被动者，他者对于我的道德命令，构成了我的伦理主体的本质：主体性（subjectivity）不再是中心和主动的，而是被动地屈服于他者的道德命令。因此，认知现象学中揭示我作为认知者与物的关系所呈现出来的结构和概念是不适合用于分析和描述我与他者的伦理关系的。这是符合胡塞尔在《观念一》(1913）中所强调的不同的对象有不同的被给予的方式的原则的。

由此看来，政治现象指的是人与人的某种关系，这种关系发生在公共空间。在公共空间中，我与他人之间的关系构成了我的政治经验的内容。政治现象就是指的这种公共空间中的政治经验。在这种政治现象中，他人是如何呈现在我面前的呢？对于这个问题，需要从几个方面来思考。第一，在公共空间中，我与他人的不可分割的政治关系的基础是什么？即我为何离不开他人，他人也离不开我？这种基础说明我是无法逃避政治经验或政治领域的。第二，在政治现象中，他者是以什么样的方式呈现出来的，即他者对于我而言是什么样的，在我的视域或生活中是如何被构成的？第三，因为他者的出现，我又是如何在这种政治经验中被构成的？在现象学中，有一点需要特别指出，现象的两个方面或两端，不仅仅是一方在另外一方中被构成，比如对象在认知主体的视域中被构成，更重要的是，这种构成关系是相互的和动态的。一方面，对象随着主体的视域的变化而呈现不同的内容，另一方面，主体也会随着对象内容的拓宽而拓宽自己的视域。

为了让“事物”自身呈现出来，我们需要对于我们的先见或偏见给予悬置，但是现象学悬置有主动和被动的。我们之所以能够进行现象学悬置，那是因为我们对某个对象已经有某种理解，并明确区分开对于对象的误解和歪曲。在这种理解的基础上，再进行分析和描述，从而能够进一步拓宽视域，消除偏见，让事物自身领引我们。对于政治现象，我们首先可以确定的是，政治不是人与物的关系，而是人与人之间在公共空间发生的关系，我们要避免用人与物的关系（认知的或工具性的或审美的等）来研究政治经验或政治现象，特别是要避免用本体论或形而上学范畴来思考人的政治经验。

我们如何来理解政治经验，特别是在人与人之间的关系中辨别出非政治或反政治的因素，让政治现象自身显现自身？我们上面提到的莱维纳斯关于政治的看法，即政治是与战争、暴力、对抗等相关的，可以作为一个出发点。黑格尔在《精神现象学》中对于主奴关系的分析可以帮助我们理解政治现象。

二、黑格尔的“认可”概念与主奴关系

我们为何从黑格尔开始呢？萨特在《存在与虚无》中第三部分第三节明确指出，从问题的角度出发，黑格尔的现象学已经超越了胡塞尔的现象学。他说的是什么意思呢？这里，我先简单说一下胡塞尔现象学中关于他者如何出现的难题。

在胡塞尔的现象学[①]中，特别是《笛卡尔式的沉思》的第五沉思，胡塞尔讨论的问题是另外一个先验自我如何向作为先验自我的我显现出来？我如何知道另外一个人和我一样是人呢？在我的直观中，另一个先验自我永远无法直接以亲在的方式站在我的面前，我只能通过配对、类比、移情来确定他者和我一样是一个先验自我。再者，我永远无法知道这个世界或世界上的任何一个对象是如何向他者显现出来的，尽管我可以通过与他者互换空间位置，通过我与世界的关系来推知他者与世界的关系。在第五沉思中，胡塞尔是从认知的维度来思考我与他者的关系：我与他者都首要的是先验的认知主体，都是“单子”，我们构成了“多重单子”，而且，“只能存在一个单一的单子共同体，所有共—存单子的共同体，”与之相对应的是“只有一个对象性世界”[②]。单子的相似性在某种程度上（实际是偶然的）保证了对象世界的普遍性。胡塞尔认为，如果一个单子能够以亲知的方式来体验另外一个单子的认知关系，这两个单子就是重合的，不再是分开的。如果是这样，我们可以说，单子之间的多样性仅仅是因为它们之间在观念上的空间性造成的；它们之间被这种特殊空间所分开。这种单子之间的关系在本质上还不是具体的人与人之间的关系；单子还不是人。从认知对象的角度看，任何一个对象或普遍本质在任何一个单子中呈现出来都是一致的，单子之间没有本质的区分。单子与单子之间的关系，从认知的角度，实际上是偶然的，可以忽略的，因为任何一个本质在一个单子中呈现出来就是普遍性的，它不需要多个单子来保障。

因此，在胡塞尔的单子多样性的共同体或空间中，单子之间没有内在必要的关系，不可能存在政治关系。政治空间和政治关系不可能发生在胡塞尔的单子共同体之中。而在黑格尔的《精神现象学》中，我们可以发现关于政治现象

① 在胡塞尔现象学文献中，一定要区分开胡塞尔本人努力发展的认知现象学体系和他的论著中蕴含的一般性现象学理念。对于胡塞尔现象学的局限性的批评主要是指他的认知现象学而不是现象学的一般理念。凡是违背了现象学的一般理念的理论就不能被称为现象学。

② Edmund Husserl, *Cartesian Meditations: An Introduction to Phenomenology*, trans. Dorion Cairns, The Hague: Martinus Nijhoff, 1973, pp.139–140.

学的核心问题和内容，特别是关于政治经验的两种形式：现实政治关系和理想政治状态。这里，我们主要围绕黑格尔关于主奴关系来阐述《精神现象学》中的政治现象学思想。黑格尔的政治现象学核心概念是“认可”，认可的发生可以是单方面（单向的）的或互相的，它是两种自我意识之间的关系。与生命和劳动两个活动相比，“认可”更体现了人之为人的根本特征。所谓“认可”就是一个自我意识对于另外一个自我意识的认同、尊重，感到对方有价值。黑格尔的政治现象学是关于人如何成为人的根本问题，在这一点上，阿伦特不仅在核心问题上（政治是关于人作为人的根本特征），而且在思维框架上（生命或劳动、工作、活动）都继承了黑格尔。①

与胡塞尔不同，黑格尔认为，自我意识是依赖于另外一个独立的自我意识而存在的，是在与另外一个自我意识的统一性中获得自身的确定性的。黑格尔说，“自我意识只有在另外一个自我意识中获得满足”②。也就是说，“自我意识的自在和自为存在的条件是，当且仅当存在这么一个事实，它是为另外一个自我意识的存在；即它仅仅在被认可的时候才存在”③。与胡塞尔《笛卡尔式的沉思》不同，不是先获得我的先验自我之后，再思考另外一个人如何在我的先验自我中被经验为另外一个先验自我，对于黑格尔来说，自我意识的前提是自我意识的多样性存在群体，是自我意识的社会群体。其次，自我意识不是单个个体的行为，而是一个自我意识与另外一个自我意识之间的关系中完成的。单独的一个先验自我不可能有真正的自我意识。第三，自我意识的本质是认可：真正的自我意识（在理想的状态下）是自我意识之间的互相平等的认可。单方面的认可不可能获得真正的自我意识或自由。

---

① 参看 Hannah Arendt, *The Human Condition*, second edition, University Press of Chicago Press, 1998。

② G.W.F. Hegel, *Phenomenology of Spirit*, trans. A.V. Miller, Oxford University Press, 1977, 第177段。

③ G.W.F. Hegel, *Phenomenology of Spirit*, trans. A.V. Miller, Oxford University Press, 1977, 第178段。

关于第三点，黑格尔的现象学还原的方法是这样的。两个自我意识在生死斗争过程中，"只有在冒着生命危险的情况下才能赢得自由；只有这样才能证明，对于自我意识而言，它的本质存在不是仅仅的存在，不是在其中显现的直接的形式，不是淹没在生命的洪流之中"①。自我意识是超越了单纯或光秃秃的存在或（生物学）生命。当奴隶面临着死亡的时候，它的整个存在都被恐惧所占据，它不是畏惧这个或那个存在物，而是在它的存在的每一个纤维中，从根基上动摇了所有的坚实和稳定的东西；这种面对死亡而产生的所有东西的绝对的消失，就是自我意识的简单的本质特征②。自我意识是超越存在或生物学生命形式的，是人的独特的本质特征。自由不是人的存在的自然属性，而是在自我意识之间的斗争中实现的。自由不是一个纯粹的本体论特征。那么，作为人的本质特征的认可或自由是如何实现或获得的呢？

自我意识包含了两种关系：意识与它者的关系，以及意识与自身的关系③。自我意识的程度是与它的对象的独立性成正比的。感性确定性或者理论性综合表面上看起来是意识完全被对象的实在性所占据，而实际上，感性确定性的对象，其本质是虚无的。一匹马，面对着面前的一片草地，不会停留在观察草的颜色或形状以及气味等感性特征，而是毫不犹豫地把它们吃掉。感性对象或理论对象的虚无性说明与之相对应的自我意识内容非常贫乏。胡塞尔关于先验自我的思想历程，从忽视或怀疑先验自我的存在，到把先验自我看作是纯粹的形式，到作为单子的先验自我，也证实了黑格尔关于意识阶段的自我意识理论的正确性。欲望作为人的实践的核心内容，是对于对象的它在性的经验。在欲望之中，对象是作为非实体而存在的，是被消灭的。欲望一方面体验到对象的独

---

① G. W. F. Hegel，*Phenomenology of Spirit*，trans. A. V. Miller，Oxford University Press，1977，第 187 段。

② G. W. F. Hegel，*Phenomenology of Spirit*，trans. A. V. Miller，Oxford University Press，1977，第 194 段。

③ Merold Westphal，*History and Truth in Hegel's Phenomenology*，3rd edition，Indiana University Press，1998，p.125.

立性或它在性，一方面又把对象看作是满足自己的手段。在消灭对象的独立性的过程中，自我意识获得了自身的确定性，① 即肯定了自身。黑格尔说，在消灭独立对象的时候，自身获得对于自己的肯定性是真正的肯定性。② 韦斯特法尔（Merold Westphal）认为，欲望的自我的肯定是建立在主宰他者的基础上的。③

但是，这种满足仅仅是短暂的，随着对象的消失，自身的肯定性也不再存在。虽然相对于理论对象而言，欲望的对象具有一定的独立性，但是，还不是完全的独立。对象独立的程度越高，自我意识的程度就越高。黑格尔说，“因此，由于对象的独立性，只有当对象自身在自身之中进行否定，它（欲望）才能够获得满足”。这种在自身之中进行自我否定又保持自己的独立性的对象只能是另外一个自我意识④。换言之，其他的自我意识是我实现我的自我意识的前提条件。这就意味着，一方面，自我意识首先失去自己，在另外一个它者中发现自己，另外一方面，它又不把他者作为本质存在，在它者中看到的是自己⑤。自我意识是通过另外一个自我意识来看到自身的，另外一个自我意识仅仅是自我意识的中介或手段。由于另外一个自我意识仅仅是映射自我意识，是非本质的存在，两个自我意识的活动就是同一个自我意识活动，我意识到自身既是我自己的活动也同时是另外一个自我意识的活动。要想实现这一点，另外一个自我意识必须自愿地响应自我意识的活动⑥，比如士兵服从指挥官的命令。

---

① Merold Westphal, *History and Truth in Hegel's Phenomenology*, 3rd edition, Indiana University Press, 1998, pp.123–126.

② G.W.F. Hegel, *Phenomenology of Spirit*, trans. A.V. Miller, Oxford University Press, 1977, 第 173 段。

③ Merold Westphal, *History and Truth in Hegel's Phenomenology*, 3rd edition, Indiana University Press, 1998, pp.126–127.

④ G.W.F. Hegel, *Phenomenology of Spirit*, trans. A.V. Miller, Oxford University Press, 1977, 第 175 段。

⑤ G.W.F. Hegel, *Phenomenology of Spirit*, trans. A.V. Miller, Oxford University Press, 1977, 第 179 段。

⑥ G.W.F. Hegel, *Phenomenology of Spirit*, trans. A.V. Miller, Oxford University Press, 1977, 第 182 段。

黑格尔说，“每一个自我意识对于另外一个自我意识都是中介，通过它每一个‘自我意识’与自身发生中介关系并与自身统一起来”。每个自我意识都是自为的，又是为他的[①]。自我意识的自为是通过他者作为中介而实现自身。这种关系是相互的。“每一个‘自我意识’看到他者所做的与自己是一样的；每一个‘自我意识’自己所做的就如要求他者做的一样，而且，只有在做同样的事情的时候才做它所做的。单方面的行动是无用的，因为将要发生的只能双方同时采取行动”[②]。自我意识之间必须采取一直的行为，必须步调一致。这是什么意思呢？黑格尔说，“它们以互相认可的方式认可自身”[③]。互相的认可就是平等关系。黑格尔曾经把这种认可关系描述为爱的关系：在爱中，我们与对象成为一体，不存在主宰或被主宰的关系。爱人的人给予对方的越多，不是越贫乏，而是越富有，而接收爱的人并不会因为接收而变得比对方更加富有[④]。爱使得双方都变得富有。互为认可的关系就如知识的传播者与接收者之间的关系，知识传播者不会因为传播知识而贫乏，接收者也不会比传播者更富有。认可不是通过暴力或权力可以达到的，因为其前提是另外一个自我意识完全出于自愿与自我意识采取同样的行动。举例而言，篮球队员之间的关系，他们在比赛中所体现的合作关系和团队精神，就是自我意识之间的关系。我在他者身上看到了我自己，他者也在我身上看到了他自己。我们同时又是同一个团体，但是互相独立个体组成的团体。用黑格尔的话说，我就是我们，我们就是我。自我意识之间的统一体就是人民，而人民是体现在他们的习俗和法律之中的。韦斯特法尔说，“对于认可的斗争是在社会语境中发生的。它不仅仅是一个个人

---

① G.W.F. Hegel，*Phenomenology of Spirit*，trans. A.V. Miller，Oxford University Press，1977，第 184 段。

② G.W.F. Hegel，*Phenomenology of Spirit*，trans. A.V. Miller，Oxford University Press，1977，第 182 段。

③ G.W.F. Hegel，*Phenomenology of Spirit*，trans. A.V. Miller，Oxford University Press，1977，第 184 段。

④ Merold Westphal，*History and Truth in Hegel's Phenomenology*，3rd edition，Indiana University Press，1998，p.131 页 .

与另外一个个人的关系，更为根本的是，他们与社会的关系，因为，他们之间的所有关系都是在习俗与法律的环境中发生的”①。个体的自我意识在社会整体之中才认识到他自己是什么。因此，对于黑格尔来说，国家和法律制度体现应该是人们之间的互为认可的关系，是自我意识的真理，即个体在国家和法律制度中体会到了自己的存在②。这是指的自我意识的理想性(应该是的）的状态，不一定是现实生活中的实际状态。

互为认可的关系是自我意识的最高阶段。这里需要特别强调的是，真正的认可是以对象的完全独立为前提的，也就是说，对方可以认可你也可以不认可，是独立自愿的行为。一旦失去了这种自愿性和相互性，认可关系就成了单方面的，就与认可这个概念本身的内容不符合。黑格尔关于主奴关系的论述，一方面更能突出认可究竟指什么，另外一方面，阐述的现实政治的实际情况。

所谓认可就是一个自我意识得到另外一个自我意识的赞同、嘉许、肯定，自我意识是在另外一个自我意识对于自己的肯定中获得自己对于自己的肯定的。这个认可过程实际上就是自我意识的复制，使得两个自我意识成为一个自我意识。自我意识作为自为的存在是通过从其自身排除所有其他的东西回到自身的。它者对于自我意识而言就是非本质性的，具有否定性的特征。认可之所以可能就是因为每一个自我意识在其自身中，通过自身的行为，进而通过他者的行为，获得自为的存在③，即另外一个自我意识的活动与我的自我意识活动

---

① Merold Westphal，*History and Truth in Hegel's Phenomenology*，3rd edition，Indiana University Press，1998，p.142.

② 关于这一点参考 Merold Westphal，“Hegel’s Radical Idealism: Family and State as Ethical Communities” in *Hegel*，*Freedom*，*and Modernity*，State University of New York Press，1992. 黑格尔在 *Philosophy of Right* 第 258 段说，” Since the state is spirit objectified，it is only as one of its members that the individual himself has objectivity，genuine individuality，and an ethical life”。国家与个人在 identity 上是一致的关系，作为个体的我只有在国家中才能发现自己的客观的自我认同（参看 Westphal 的这篇文章，特别是第 50—51 页）。

③ G.W.F. Hegel，*Phenomenology of Spirit*，trans. A.V. Miller，Oxford University Press，1977，第 186 段。

合二为一。这种认可过程在主奴关系中，在两个不平等的自我意识之间，是一种什么样的情况呢?

在主奴关系中，一个是独立的自我意识，是自为的存在，另外一个是依赖性的意识，它的本质特征就是“仅仅活着或为它的存在”。前者就是奴隶主，后者就是被奴役者或奴隶①。“一个仅仅被认可的存在，另外一个仅仅是认可‘对方’的存在”②。在这种关系中，奴隶主是通过独立的物质存在的中介与被奴役者建立联系的，即被奴役者直接与自然物打交道，为奴隶主提供物质财富。奴隶主拥有物质财富和被奴役者。奴隶主不直接与自然物接触，是通过被奴役者间接地与物质财富发生关系。由于奴隶主在他与物之间依靠奴隶作为中介，他不直接与物打交道，物对于奴隶主而言就是“完全的否定”“或者说，对于它的享受”③。奴隶主享受的是物的依赖性，把物的独立性交给奴隶去对付，奴隶通过劳动对于自然进行加工处理使之成为可以满足人的欲望的对象。

在这种关系中，奴隶主通过另外一个意识来获得他的被认可。而奴隶作为特殊的存在是非本质性的，是服务于奴隶主的欲望的。奴隶的意识“把自身的自为存在搁置在一边，在这么做的时候，它按照第一个‘自我意识，奴隶主的自我意识’要求去行动”。奴隶的自己的行为就是奴隶主的行为，“因为努力所做的实际上就是奴隶主的行为”。奴隶主的本质特征就是仅仅自为的存在，“他是完全的否定权力，相对于此，物就是虚无”。“因此，在这种关系中，他是纯粹的本质性行为，而奴隶的行为是不纯粹的和非本质性的”④。奴隶对于奴隶主是完全的服从和服务，完全的认可。但是，这种认可是单方面和不平等的，是

① G.W.F. Hegel, *Phenomenology of Spirit*, trans. A.V. Miller, Oxford University Press, 1977, 第 189 段。

② G.W.F. Hegel, *Phenomenology of Spirit*, trans. A.V. Miller, Oxford University Press, 1977, 第 185 段。

③ G.W.F. Hegel, *Phenomenology of Spirit*, trans. A.V. Miller, Oxford University Press, 1977, 第 190 段。

④ G.W.F. Hegel, *Phenomenology of Spirit*, trans. A.V. Miller, Oxford University Press, 1977, 第 191 段。

不符合认可概念本身所蕴含的意义的。

第一，奴隶主在奴隶身上看到的不是一个独立的自我意识，而是一个依赖性意识，“一种非本质的意识和非本质的行为”①。奴隶主的独立意识的真理性相应地就是“奴隶的服务意识”②。奴隶主的这种自我确定性或自我肯定不是来自于一个完全独立的意识。举例而言，在一群羊面前和在一群人面前所获得的自豪感肯定是不一样的；在羊群面前的自我肯定实际上是自我贬低，是与认可这个概念不匹配的。另外，奴隶主对于奴隶的主宰是依赖权力和暴力实现的；奴隶屈服于奴隶主不是出于一种内心的认可，而是外在的力量的较量。就如爱一样，武力在爱的面前是无能为力的，武力不可能获得真正的认可。

这里需要特别指出的是，奴隶主的自我意识完全是建立在相对于另外一个意识的关系上，自然物在其面前仅仅是享受的对象，是完全的虚无。在这个意义上，我们可以说，政治关系中在考量物质财富的时候，完全是被自我意识之间的关系所决定的；纯粹的政治关系是可以脱离物质财富的维度的。这一点也是阿伦特政治现象学中的要突出的观点之一。

第二，奴隶是为奴隶主而存在的，但是，在这种奴役状态中，奴隶也有自为意识，不过是隐含在奴隶的意识之中的。首先，就如我们前面提到的，在生死搏斗的时候，在死亡的面前，在奴隶的眼中，世界上的任何东西都变得无足轻重，奴隶彻底体验到了自我意识的内在性。在奴隶面前，所有的物质的东西都分解了，都“绝对消融了”③。这种分解和消融不仅仅是面临死亡的时候的一种体验，更是体现在奴隶的服务过程之中：在对物质的加工和改造过程中，在

① G.W.F. Hegel，*Phenomenology of Spirit*，trans. A.V. Miller，Oxford University Press，1977，第 192 段。

② G.W.F. Hegel，*Phenomenology of Spirit*，trans. A.V. Miller，Oxford University Press，1977，第 193 段。

③ G.W.F. Hegel，*Phenomenology of Spirit*，trans. A.V. Miller，Oxford University Press，1977，第 194 段。

每一个细节上，他都彻底地与任何自然存在进行分离[①]。"通过劳动，奴隶意识到自己真正是什么"。对于物质财富的享受往往是瞬间即逝的。但是，劳动延缓了欲望的满足，对于对象进行加工和改造，这种塑造的活动是个体性的，是意识的纯粹的自为的存在。作为劳动者的意识在被生产出的产品中看到了持久性和独立性，而产品反映的恰恰是劳动者的独立性[②]。因此，奴隶在两个方面获得了自我意识的独立性，面临死亡的恐惧和面对自然物的改造性劳动。通过否定性的恐惧和肯定性的劳动，奴隶意识到自为的存在是属于他的。在劳动的对象身上，劳动者看到了自己的纯粹的自为的存在。如果说，在与奴隶主的关系中，奴隶失去了自己，在与自然物的关系中，奴隶又发现了自己。由于物质财富是属于奴隶主的，奴隶的劳动产品是异化的。奴隶的劳动或改造活动在本质上是服务（奴役）于奴隶主的。但是，在这种异化的关系中，我们可以看到，奴隶正是通过（面临死亡的）恐惧和服务（奴役）来确定自身的存在的。黑格尔认为，如果没有服从和服务（奴役）的话，对于死亡的恐惧仅仅是形式的或观念性的。如果没有改造性活动（服务），对于死亡的空间仅仅是内在的和无声的[③]。如果没有生死搏斗，没有面临死亡的绝对恐惧，奴隶就不可能在生存论的意义上有自我意识。在形式上，奴隶缺乏独立意识和自我意识，在实质上，正是因为面对一个强大的自我意识，奴隶在恐惧和劳动中获得了自我的确定性。黑格尔甚至认为，除此之外，奴隶不可能获得真正的自我意识。

相对于奴隶主而言，奴隶是依赖性意识，而相对于物而言，奴隶是独立意识。因此，奴隶同时具有依赖性意识和独立意识。他的独立意识在本质上是工

---

① G. W. F. Hegel, *Phenomenology of Spirit*, trans. A. V. Miller, Oxford University Press, 1977, 第 194 段。

② G. W. F. Hegel, *Phenomenology of Spirit*, trans. A. V. Miller, Oxford University Press, 1977, 第 195 段。

③ G. W. F. Hegel, *Phenomenology of Spirit*, trans. A. V. Miller, Oxford University Press, 1977, 第 196 段。

具性的，是服务于依赖性意识的。究其根本而言，奴隶的自我意识是与认可的概念不符合的。

在奴隶的意识中，我们看到，人与物的关系不是政治空间的决定性关系，是依赖于自我意识之间的关系的。在现实的政治空间中，奴隶的自我意识是建立在对于死亡的恐惧之上的。这种恐惧是政治权力行使的前提条件。武力或权力的本质是一种死亡游戏，在其中不可能获得真正的相互的认可。权力或暴力关系中的服从是异化了的认可关系，充分暴露了面对认可权力的无能性。相互的尊重和认可不是建立在死亡的恐惧基础之上的。

因此，对于黑格尔来说，政治领域或空间不是为了保护个人私有财产或分配正义的问题，而是在一个共同体中，平等人追求认可的活动，是关系到人的自我意识实现的问题。

针对我们上面提出的三个政治现象学问题，黑格尔的回答是，在理想和具体的情境中（主奴关系实际上是抽象的政治存在），政治空间是由相互独立而又内在联系的多样个体的自我意识构成的。在这种政治空间中，他者首先是作为一个平等的自我意识出现的，我对于我自己的肯定是否定他者，即我的自我意识与他者的自我意识之间的两个行为是同一个。我的自我意识在另外一个自我意识中获得肯定。第三，自我意识的最高阶段是自我意识之间的相互平等的认可，在这种平等认可中获得对于自身的认识，具体体现在习俗和法律为内容的伦理生活之中。而以主奴关系为特征的现实（抽象）的政治空间，自我意识是不可能达到自由的最高阶段，因为自我意识之间的认可关系是单方面和片面的。这里的问题是，当双方都试图主宰对方，在主奴关系中是不可能实现真正的认可的。

黑格尔在论述意识的自我确定性时，已经暴露出他把自我意识的真理性等同于认识论上的确定性。自我意识是认知性的。同时，我们也看到，在论述奴隶面对死亡的时候，对于死亡的恐惧渗透到奴隶生命中的每个细胞，把整个世界都悬置起来了。黑格尔的精彩的语言已经是生存论意义上的描述。在萨特的

《存在与虚无》中，我们会发现，黑格尔单向的主奴关系如何在生存论意义上成了人与人之间的互相的主奴关系①。

三、非结语的结语

黑格尔对于我们开篇引用的莱维纳斯的问题的回答将会是这样的：以战争为极端例子的人类体验是一种抽象的政治经验，与主奴关系是一样的结构；人们在其中所经验到的认可是与认可的理念不符合的。不过，我们可以从其中直观到认可概念的本质。具体的人类政治经验应该是认可的概念的实现，是神圣天国在地上的实现。黑格尔的这种激进的唯心论对于现实生活中的“我们”而言可以说是理想主义，是有待于实现的真正的可能性。现象学的本质直观或本质还原就是从个别事例或事态直接洞察到事物的本质。几何学家在黑板上画的几何学图形无论如何不完美，都可以帮助几何学家直接洞察到几何学原理。在黑格尔发现的两种政治经验符合胡塞尔在《观念一》中开端所做的“事实与本质”的区分②。我们可以说，黑格尔为我们提供了一种政治现象学思路。

---

① 萨特不仅没有黑格尔那么乐观，认为自我意识之间在根源上不可能完全达到共识，而且他认为，黑格尔在自我意识之间的关系上试图从确定性或认知的层面来给予说明，没有触及到一个自我意识如何与另外一个自我意识具有根本性的关系。对于黑格尔来说，一个自我意识是以另外一个自我意识为中介来认识自己的，但是，这些自我意识都是首先是生活在一个社会共同体，是以社会为前提来确认自己。在这个共同体层面，自我意识达到了相互的认可。但是，黑格尔无法说明，我为何与在路上碰得到的张三或李四具有不可分割的关系。对于萨特而言，一个自我意识与另外一个自我意识之间的关系完全没有必要用主奴生死搏斗的极端例子来说明，不必用面对死亡的恐惧来使得奴隶具有自我意识。萨特认为，每一个自我意识的自为的存在都是为他的存在，是在为他的关系中的自为的存在。

② “Experiencing，or *intuition of something individual* can become transmuted into *eidetic seeing*（ideation）—a possibility which is itself to be understood not as empirical，but as eidetic”（Edmund Husserl，*Ideas Pertaining to a Pure Phenomenology and to a Phenomenological Philosophy*，*first book*，trans. F. Kersten，Martinus Nijhoff Publishers，1982，p.8.

后来的现象学家提出了不同的政治现象学思想。对于萨特而言，我们对于日常生活经验的直观，比如羞耻感（而不是用主奴生死搏斗的极端例子），就可以洞察到我们现实生活的政治经验结构，而且，在萨特的具体细微的描述中，黑格尔的“认可”概念作为一种可能性是根本不可能的。人的存在论状态决定了人在政治存在上是徒劳的努力，是互为空虚的存在。阿伦特认为，在政治空间中，人才真正作为人而显现出来，但是，这种显现不是黑格尔所说的普遍性，而是个体性。福柯的局部批判理论讨论了人在不同的权力关系中如何被构成以及人如何超越现有的权力关系。萨特、阿伦特、福柯等人的现象学中可以发现对于人类的政治经验的不同的描述。

如何写作马克思主义哲学专业的博士学位论文

——以马克思的博士论文为范文[①]

何 萍

如何写作博士学位论文？这是我的研究生们经常向我提出来的问题，也是马克思主义哲学专业的博士研究生培养中带有普遍性的问题。在这里，我想以马克思的博士论文为范文，谈谈马克思主义哲学专业的博士学位论文写作中的几个问题。

一、为什么要选择马克思的博士论文为范文

马克思的博士论文是马克思早期从事哲学研究的最重要成果。对于这一成果，我国学术界主要从学术思想的角度加以研究。在这里，我想转换一个角度，把它作为写作博士学位论文的范文，针对目前马克思主义哲学专业的研究生写作学位论文中存在的问题，谈谈学位论文的写作步骤、写作方法和写作规范等问题。

我之所以选择马克思的博士论文作为范文，是因为马克思的博士论文本身就是按照博士学位论文的格式写的。诚如他自己所说的："这篇论文如果当初不是预定作为博士论文，那么它一方面可能会具有更加严格的科学形式，另一方面在某些叙述上也许会少一点学究气。但是由于一些外在的原因，我

---

① 此文原是为马克思主义哲学专业博士研究生和硕士研究生开设的学位论文写作课的讲稿，超星电子已将此课制作成视频。很多研究生希望能读到原稿，故将讲稿修改成文，在此发表。

只能让它以这种形式付印。此外，我认为在这篇论文里我已经解决了一个在希腊哲学史上至今尚未解决的问题。”① 仔细地分析，在这段话中，马克思陈述了三层意思：第一，这篇论文首先是一篇有学术价值的论文，它是为了解决希腊哲学史上的一个哲学问题，同时也是为了解决青年黑格尔派提出的自我意识批判的哲学问题而写的。正是这篇论文的学术价值，决定了这篇论文的优秀性，也使我们既能从马克思哲学思想发展史的角度来研究它，也可以从哲学学位论文的范文的角度来阅读它。第二，博士学位论文是有相当严格的学术规范的。由于这种规范，写作博士论文与写作一般的学术著作在形式上是有差别的。有些学术著作，是很有学术价值，但由于不符合博士学位论文的规范，在现存的形式上，是不能作为博士学位论文的。当然，也有些著作，比如，一些介绍哲学家思想的著作，不论在内容上，还是在形式上，都是不能成为博士学位论文的。可见，我们要写作博士学位论文，首先要了解博士学位论文写作的规范。第三，马克思的这篇论文是完全遵照博士学位论文的规范而写的，所以，它不仅在内容上，而且在形式上都符合博士学位论文的规范。这三层意思构成了我们以马克思的博士论文作为哲学学位论文写作的范文的根据。当然，从写作学位论文的规范方面看，它也适用于硕士研究生和本科生写作学位论文。

一般地说，学位论文的写作主要包括三个大的部分：第一部分是论文的选题；第二部分是搜集资料，这部分的工作是以读书笔记、参考书目、学术综述等形式体现出来的；第三部分是正文的写作，包括论文的结构和叙述方式。马克思的博士学位论文也大致包括这三个部分。下面，我们就按这三个部分，解读马克思的博士论文。

---

① 《马克思恩格斯全集》第 40 卷，人民出版社 1982 年版，第 188 页。

二、论文的选题

论文的选题是写作学位论文的第一要义。一篇论文写得好不好，能不能成为合格的学位论文，首先要看它的论文选题有没有意义。那么，什么叫论文的选题有意义呢？如何判断一篇选题是否有意义以及意义的大小呢？这是最值得我们思考的问题。

我们通常在论证论文选题的合理性时，都是把选题的意义分为两个方面：一是理论意义，二是实践意义。这种论证要求似乎是非常清楚，其实是相当模糊的。因为现在很多马克思主义哲学专业的研究生在作学位论文的选题意义的论证时，忘记了哲学论文选题的一个最根本的东西，这就是哲学的学术价值，就是说，哲学的学位论文必须是研究哲学问题、解决哲学问题的，而不是随意地选一个有理论意义和实践意义的题目来做。在现实生活中，有很多值得研究的问题，也有很多问题具有理论研究的价值，但这些有实践意义和理论研究价值的问题不一定是哲学的问题，它们有些是经济学研究的问题，如市场管理、信用体系等；有些是法学研究的问题，如解决国际、国内经济纠纷，规范人们的行为方式等；有些是社会学的问题，比如对人口状况的调查等。也就是说，这些问题能够成为经济学的、法学的、社会学的、政治学的研究课题，但它不能成为哲学的研究课题，尤其不能成为哲学学位论文的题目。哲学研究的课题必须是哲学问题，具有哲学的学术价值。这就是说，我们在确定学位论文的选题时，首先要进行筛选，要认定它是一个哲学的问题，而且是一个值得研究的、有现实意义的哲学问题。

那么，我们怎样确定和保证论文的选题是哲学的问题而且是一个十分重要的、必须解决的哲学问题呢？在这个问题上，马克思对他的博士论文的意义的论证是非常具有典范性的。

在前面，我们已经谈到，马克思在论及他的博士论文的意义时强调：“我认为在这篇论文里我已经解决了一个在希腊哲学史上至今尚未解决的问题。”[①]马克思所说的解决希腊哲学史上至今尚未解决的问题是指对希腊化时期的伊壁鸠鲁、斯多葛派和怀疑派的哲学评价的问题，尤其是对伊壁鸠鲁哲学的评价问题。马克思认为，先前哲学没有解决这个问题，是因为哲学家们通常把亚里士多德的哲学看作是希腊哲学的终结，而否认希腊化时期的哲学对于希腊哲学的贡献，尤其是伊壁鸠鲁派、斯多葛派和怀疑派对于希腊哲学的贡献，而在马克思看来，“这些体系是理解希腊哲学的真正历史的钥匙。”[②]为了说明这个问题，马克思在博士论文第一部分专辟“研究的对象”一节加以论述。他指出：“在我看来，如果那些较早的体系在希腊哲学的内容方面是较有意义、较有兴趣的话，那么亚里士多德以后的体系，主要是伊壁鸠鲁派、斯多葛派和怀疑派这一系列学派则在其主观形式，在其性质方面较有意义、较有兴趣。然而正是这个主观形式，即这些哲学体系的精神承担者，由于它们的形而上学的特点，直到现在几乎完全被遗忘了。”[③]在这里，马克思所说的希腊哲学的主观形式就是自我意识、哲学精神的问题。马克思是以哲学史上的质料和形式的概念把希腊时期和希腊化时期的哲学贡献区别开来，强调希腊时期的哲学家重视的是哲学的内容，即对物质存在的研究，而希腊化时期的哲学家重视的是哲学的形式，即对哲学的自由问题的研究。这样，马克思就把他的博士论文的主题定在研究自我意识的问题上。马克思进一步强调，他要“通过一个例子，并且也只从一个方面，即从它们与较早的哲学思想的联系方面”[④]来阐述希腊化时期的哲学对自我意识的研究。这个例子就是“伊壁鸠鲁的自然哲学与德谟克利特的自然哲学的关系”[⑤]。可见，马克思把博士论文的选题定为《德谟克利特的自然哲学和伊壁鸠鲁的自然哲学的差别》实际上是研究伊壁鸠鲁的哲学，并通过伊壁鸠鲁

---

① 《马克思恩格斯全集》第 40 卷，人民出版社 1982 年版，第 188 页。
② 《马克思恩格斯全集》第 40 卷，人民出版社 1982 年版，第 189 页。
③ 《马克思恩格斯全集》第 40 卷，人民出版社 1982 年版，第 195 页。
④ 《马克思恩格斯全集》第 40 卷，人民出版社 1982 年版，第 195 页。
⑤ 《马克思恩格斯全集》第 40 卷，人民出版社 1982 年版，第 195 页。

的哲学来解决自我意识的问题。从论文选题的角度看，马克思是从哲学思想的发展和哲学史研究中尚存在的问题来论证他的博士论文选题的学术价值。这还是他论证论文选题的第一步，也就是对论文选题的理论意义的论证。

第二步，马克思论证了他的博士论文选题的实践意义。在《新序言草稿》中，他说："只是现在，伊壁鸠鲁派、斯多葛派和怀疑派体系为人理解的时代才算到来了。他们是自我意识哲学家。这篇短序将表明，迄今为止的这项任务解决得多么不够。"① 在这里，马克思强调"伊壁鸠鲁派、斯多葛派和怀疑派体系为人理解的时代才算到来了"，是指自我意识的研究在德国是一个具有实践意义的课题。这是和他所处的时代、所属的学术共同体相关的。马克思的哲学创造与"博士俱乐部"紧密相关。"博士俱乐部"由青年黑格尔派组成，其中的主要代表人物鲍威尔就是研究自我意识的。鲍威尔研究自我意识，是为了从黑格尔的哲学体系中脱离出来，把哲学变成批判，并以哲学的批判实现当时德国对宗教的批判和政治的批判。我们说，当时青年黑格尔派把哲学的批判与宗教的批判、政治的批判结合一起，实际上是以哲学的变革来实现宗教批判和政治批判的任务。这就是青年黑格尔派研究自我意识的现实的、实践的意义。马克思作为青年黑格尔派的一个成员，也把自我意识的批判作为宗教批判和政治批判的武器，但是，哲学要完成对宗教和政治的批判，它自身的批判必须是彻底的。在马克思看来，鲍威尔的自我意识批判的哲学是不彻底的，而他就是要解决自我意识批判的彻底性问题。这样，马克思就论证了研究自我意识的哲学的实践意义和他的研究从何讲起的问题。

以马克思对他的博士论文的理论意义和实践意义的论证为范例，我们可以把哲学学位论文选题意义的要素概括为三个方面：

第一，哲学学位论文选题的意义必须以哲学的学术价值为尺度，选题的理论意义和实践意义应该先论证你所选的题目是否具有学术价值，论证它是一个

① 《马克思恩格斯全集》第 40 卷，人民出版社 1982 年版，第 286 页。

哲学问题，并且对于解决哲学史上的问题具有意义，然后，再围绕着这一题目的学术价值论证你所选题目的理论意义和实践意义。这就避免了在论文选题意义论证上的主观性和随意性，也能够避免论文选题意义论证的平面化。应该说，论文选题的哲学的学术价值是论文选题的第一要义。没有哲学的学术价值的论文不能称之为哲学的学位论文，当然也谈不上是合格的学位论文。

第二，哲学学位论文选题要有学术共同体的观念。每一时代、每一民族的哲学论题总是多样化的，这种多样化来自不同的学术共同体，而学术共同体就规范了论文选题所要讨论的问题、它的研究方向和研究起点。由此决定，任何一篇有价值的哲学的学位论文都是对它所属的学术共同体中提出的问题的解决，论文选题的前沿性是相对于这个共同体讨论的问题而言的，如果没有学术共同体的规范，论文选题的前沿性就是随意设定的，是一种虚假的前沿性。这一点就向我们的研究生写作学位论文提出了这样一个要求：博士论文应该是在研究生期间进行科学研究的成果，而不是为写论文而写论文，明确地说，不是为了拿一张硕士学位或博士学位的文凭而写学位论文，而研究生在校攻读学位期间也就是选择学术共同体、学习学术共同体的规范、了解学术共同体的问题的过程，这个过程也就是从事学术研究的过程，学位论文就是一个研究生在几年期间从事科学研究的成果。这是学位论文质量的基本保证。

第三，哲学学位论文的选题要小，不要大。论文选题小，才能分析得细致，才会有深度，选题过太，不能集中问题，只能是泛泛而谈。马克思的博士论文选题就是一个很好的范例。马克思以自我意识为研究对象，但是，他的博士论文不是泛谈自我意识的问题，而是选择伊壁鸠鲁的自然哲学与德谟克利特的自然哲学的关系，而且选择两者之间的有差别的方面来谈自我意识的问题，而这个问题又是青年黑格尔派所没有解决的问题。这就使论文写得有深度、有针对性。事实上，定小题目本身就是研究生几年学习成就的一种检验，凡是没有进行深入的研究工作、没有进入一个研究共同体的人，是选择不了小题目的。所以，老师们往往从选题上就可以看出这个研究生在校期间的学习状况和写作学位论文的态度。

三、写作论文的资料搜集工作

资料搜集是写作学位论文的准备阶段。这个阶段与选题是交叉进行的，选题要以先前的研究工作为基础，但是，一旦选题确定，研究工作就要围绕选题进一步集中和深化。在这个意义上，我们说，资料搜集并不发生在选题确定之后，而是贯穿于整个论文的写作过程中，是一项重要的学术研究工作，论文的完成也只是这一工作的一个结果。马克思写作博士论文所开展的研究工作主要体现在《关于伊壁鸠鲁哲学的笔记》和两个附录中。

《关于伊壁鸠鲁哲学的笔记》有七本：

第一本是根据伽桑狄主编的《评第欧根尼·拉尔修》（第 10 卷）的版本所作的摘录。第欧根尼·拉尔修是罗马帝国时代的作家，它的最重要著作是 10 卷本的《哲学名人的生平和学说》。在这部著作中，他记录了公元前 6 世纪到 3 世纪古希腊哲学家的生平、著作，其中伊壁鸠鲁哲学的篇幅最大。这部著作是研究希腊哲学的最重要的史料。伽桑狄是 17 世纪法国唯物主义哲学家，他的主要哲学活动是研究和宣传伊壁鸠鲁的原子论学说和伦理学。马克思在这本笔记中，不仅研究伊壁鸠鲁的思想，也研究伽桑狄对伊壁鸠鲁的评价。后者构成了马克思评价哲学史上各派哲学家研究伊壁鸠鲁哲学的成就和不足的依据。

第二本笔记到第七本笔记是马克思研究古希腊哲学中与伊壁鸠鲁哲学有关的哲学家的思想，其中所涉及的希腊时期的最重要的哲学家有：恩披里柯、普卢塔克、卢克莱修、西塞罗等。恩披里柯是公元 2 世纪新怀疑主义的代表人物，普卢塔克是罗马帝国时期的传记作家、伦理学家，卢克莱修是古罗马最杰出的唯物主义代表，也是伊壁鸠鲁原子论的继承人，西塞罗是卢克莱修同时代的哲学家，他虽然反对唯物主义学说，并且是伊壁鸠鲁学说的反对者，但他的研究领域还是主要在伦理学领域。马克思在研究他们的著作时，不仅研究他们的学说与伊壁鸠鲁哲学之间的关系，而且还比较了他们的学说与智者派、柏拉图学说的关系。这些研究表明，马克思是把伊壁鸠鲁放到古希腊哲学中以探讨人性、个体自由为主体的人文主义哲学传统中，研究他的思想起源和在哲学史上的地位。这些研究为马克思从哲学传统上理清伊壁鸠鲁的自然哲学与德谟克利特的自然哲学的差别奠定了基础，也表明，马克思的哲学是自古希腊以来的西方人文主义哲学传统的批判继承。在第五本笔记中，马克思还做了黑格尔自然哲学的札记，说明马克思在研究伊壁鸠鲁的哲学时，十分重视黑格尔的哲学。

马克思博士论文的附录部分不全，但从留下的残篇看，是由两个部分组成的：一个部分是对哲学史上伊壁鸠鲁哲学研究的评价和对自己有关自我意识观点的叙述；一个部分是正文引文的注释。这两个部分在文献上与七本笔记是一致的，但对先前哲学家思想的评价，尤其是对德国古典哲学有关哲学和宗教思想的评述则多于七本笔记，不仅如此，在对先前哲学家和德国古典哲学思想的评述中，马克思还写有批判宗教和有关自我意识研究的论断。从这些论断看，马克思博士论文中主要观点是在他的研究工作中确立起来的。比如，附注第一部分的第四节①：德谟克利特的自然哲学和伊壁鸠鲁自然哲学的一般差别，这部分的正文部分已经散失了，但是，在附注中，马克思写下了他对自我意识批判的理解，他提出的哲学自我意识的双重性，并以哲学自我意识的双重性批判自由派哲学和实证哲学，从而把自己的哲学与包括黑格尔、青年黑格尔派在内的以往的哲学区别开来。这些思想构成了他的博士论文的基调。我们还可以读一下附录《批判普卢塔克对伊壁鸠鲁神学的论战》。在这篇附录中，马克思批判了黑格尔、谢林、康德的本体论的神学性质，提出“对神的存在的证明不外是对人的本质的自我意识存在的证明，对自我意识存在的逻辑说明”②。这些论

---

① 见《马克思恩格斯全集》第 40 卷，人民出版社 1982 年版，第 256 页。

② 见《马克思恩格斯全集》第 40 卷，人民出版社 1982 年版，第 285 页。

述既体现了马克思对德国古典哲学的批判态度，也体现了马克思的本体论传统。由此可见，在马克思那里，搜集资料不是一个简单的资料归纳的过程，而是哲学研究的过程。这个过程也是学位论文写作的最重要、费时最长的过程，通常它会在学位论文写作的工作量上占到 80%，甚至还要高。

从马克思的《关于伊壁鸠鲁哲学的笔记》和两个附录中，我们可以看到从事哲学科学研究工作的几个具有规范性的特点：

第一，哲学的研究工作必须有明确的主题。这个主题就是研究者所研究的问题，应该贯穿于搜集资料的过程始终。这也就是说，搜集资料不是盲目的，不是单纯的文献学的分类过程，更不是我们很多研究生所做的上网搜索相关条目的工作，而是围绕着自己的研究主题所进行的艰苦的研究工作，它要随着研究工作的需要，不断地扩大和缩小搜集资料的范围以及对有用资料的筛选、评价，从中形成自己的观点。

第二，资料的搜集、筛选不是杂乱无章的，而应该是有序的、有层次的。第一个层次，是所要研究的对象的原始资料，也就是你所要研究的哲学家的原著。在马克思的《笔记》中，这个部分的比重是最大的。第二个层次，是与研究对象同时代和发生时间上联系的资料，也就是研究你所要研究的哲学家与他同时代的哲学家之间的关系，追溯他的思想起源和后继者对他的思想的发展，厘清他的思想的来龙去脉。这就需要读你所研究的对象的研究者的原著。在这个层次上，马克思对智者派、柏拉图、亚里士多德、怀疑论派、卢克莱修、西塞罗、普卢塔克、伽桑狄等人的有关伊壁鸠鲁哲学研究的原著作了许多摘录和评价。第三个层次，是哲学史的资料，包括史料的记载、哲学史家对所研究的对象在哲学史中地位的评价。马克思《笔记》中的这一层次的内容体现在他对第欧根尼·拉尔修的文献的重视和对黑格尔的有关伊壁鸠鲁思想评价的研究上。第四个层次，是你所在的学术共同体的思想，包括对其中不同成员的思想评价。这一层次的研究是为了确定论文写作的逻辑起点。马克思对德国古典哲学家、对青年黑格尔派、对实证主义哲学的研究都是这一层次研究的体现。

第三，哲学的研究不仅要重视哲学史，而且要重视哲学传统。因为哲学史不是不同哲学派别的论战史，而是不同的哲学传统形成和演变的历史；不同哲学派别的论战总是在某一哲学传统的范式中展开的。所以，研究一个哲学家的思想，必须放到他所属的哲学传统中去，才能看清他的思想的本质及来龙去脉，同样地，研究哲学问题，也应放到一定的哲学传统中去理解。马克思的博士论文是以伊壁鸠鲁的哲学为一个方面来研究自我意识的问题。在马克思看来，伊壁鸠鲁之不同于德谟克利特，就在于他们的哲学分属于两种不同的哲学传统：德谟克利特的哲学属于以因果性的思维方式建构起来的实证哲学的传统，而伊壁鸠鲁哲学则属于以目的论的思维方式建构起来的思辨哲学的传统。他选择伊壁鸠鲁的自我意识哲学为突破点，就是选择哲学史上的目的论的思辨哲学传统，从而把自我意识的研究归于以人的个性自由为研究主题的目的论的哲学传统之中，而反对以物质世界为主体的因果性的思维方式，即以实证科学的哲学传统，来说明自我意识的问题。马克思也是沿着这一思路来研究和评价伊壁鸠鲁的哲学的。正是通过这种研究，马克思突破了近代理性主义哲学的范式，而走向了现代哲学。这说明，重视哲学传统，不仅是研究范式的选择，也是真正的哲学创新和突破；哲学的论文若离开了哲学传统，仅仅从概念到概念的分析，就会失去学术的根基，变得空洞无物。

四、正文的写作

正文的写作是以叙述的方法把先前的研究成果表述出来。所谓叙述的方法，就是用逻辑的形式把自己的思想叙述出来。马克思在谈到《资本论》的研究方法时，明确地把叙述方法与研究方法区分开来。他说："在形式上，叙述方法必须与研究方法不同。研究必须充分地占有材料，分析它的各种发展形式，探寻这些形式的内在联系。只有这项工作完成以后，现实的运动才能适当地叙述出来。这点一旦做到，材料的生命一旦观念地反映出来，呈现在我们面前的就好象是一个先验的结构了。”① 在这里，马克思论述了研究方法和叙述方法的联系和区分。两者的联系是从过程的联结上来说的，这就是，思想叙述是以研究工作为基础的，所以，叙述方法只能在研究方法之后开展；两者的区分是两者运用的逻辑行程不同，研究方法是从现实的具体上升到抽象的过程，叙述方法是从抽象上升到逻辑的具体的过程。叙述方法既然与研究方法有着不同的逻辑行程，那么，叙述方法的确立本身就是一个过程，有其相对的独立性。由此决定，论文的写作既要以先前的研究工作为基础，又不能停留在资料搜集工作的水平上，还必须经过逻辑的抽象，通过细致的分析，充分消化研究的成果，进行思想的提升，才能写出论文来。这一过程表明，论文的写作，或者说，叙述工作，不是简单地罗列研究的成果，而是对先前研究成果的一个提升，是科学研究中的一个十分艰苦的过程。当然，叙述方法并没有统一的格式上的规定，一篇论文、一本著作，采取什么样的叙述方法是由作者表达思想的需要决定的。但是，博士学位论文的叙述方法还是有相对的规范性。在这里，我们可以通过分析马克思博士论文的结构和叙述方式来讲博士学位论文的叙述方式。

首先，我们从目录讲起。目录是全文的结构，体现了作者叙述自己思想的基本思路和问题。一般地说，从目录上，就可把握论文 70% 的内容。我们可以读一下马克思博士论文的目录。这个目录列出了论文结构的三个大的部分：序言、正文和附录。

序言主要讲论文写作的意义、主要内容和各个部分的基本观点，其中，马克思特别强调，他是通过对伊壁鸠鲁哲学的研究来解决希腊哲学史上至今没有解决的问题，而这个问题的解决又是为了完成德国哲学对宗教和哲学的批判。

正文分为两个部分：第一部分：德谟克利特的自然哲学和伊壁鸠鲁的自然

① 《马克思恩格斯选集》第 2 卷，人民出版社 1995 年版，第 111 页。

哲学的一般差别；第二部分：德谟克利特的自然哲学和伊壁鸠鲁的自然哲学在细节上的差别。这个结构表明，马克思是把第一部分作为提出问题和陈述自己的基本观点的部分，而把第二部分作为较为系统地展开自己观点的部分。下面，我们具体地分析这二个部分中的细节安排，看马克思是怎样提出问题和陈述问题的：

第一部分分为五节：第一，研究对象。主要论述如何看待和论述伊壁鸠鲁的哲学，这种论述和前此的观点有什么差别。马克思特别强调，伊壁鸠鲁派、斯多葛派和怀疑派的哲学是自我意识的哲学，他选择伊壁鸠鲁的自然哲学对德谟克利特的自然哲学的关系为一个例子，就是要研究自我意识问题。这样，马克思就在论文的开篇明确了自己的研究主题和基本观点，以及要论述的问题。第二，对德谟克利特的物理学和伊壁鸠鲁的物理学的关系的判断。主要叙述哲学史上不同思想家对伊壁鸠鲁的物理学与德谟克利特的物理学关系的判断，最后得出的结论是："大家一致认为，伊壁鸠鲁的物理学是从德谟克利特那儿剽窃来的。"① 这个结论构成了马克思研究伊壁鸠鲁哲学的起点，也是连结下一节论述的逻辑环节。第三，把德谟克利特的自然哲学和伊壁鸠鲁的自然哲学等同起来所产生的困难。马克思通过比较伊壁鸠鲁与德谟克利特在有关人类知识的真理性和可靠性、追求真理性的方法和反思形式上的差别，驳斥了先前的思想家把伊壁鸠鲁的物理学看作是德谟克利特的物理学的剽窃的观点，以理论的分析为自己的观点立论。第四，德谟克利特的自然哲学和伊壁鸠鲁的自然哲学的一般差别、第五，结论。这两个部分残缺，但从他的附录中相关部分的论述中，可以看出，马克思在第四部分是从哲学传统上区分了伊壁鸠鲁的物理学与德谟克利特的物理学的差别，并论述了自我意识与批判哲学的关系。以上四节的结构及其内容展示了马克思分析问题的思路：首先提出问题，阐明自己的观点，然后再逐一分析哲学史上的观点，以自己研究的成果来驳斥以前的观点，

① 《马克思恩格斯全集》第 40 卷，人民出版社 1982 年版，第 198 页。

在此基础上，较系统地阐发自己的观点。

第二部分，我们已经说了，是具体深入到伊壁鸠鲁的自然哲学和德谟克利特的自然哲学中的具体观点，通过比较分析两者的差别，论证他在第一部分提出的有关伊壁鸠鲁物理学和德谟克利特物理学的一般差别。这一部分分为五章：第一章：原子脱离直线而偏斜；第二章：原子的质；第三章：不可分的本原和不可分的元素；第四章：时间；第五章：天体现象。这五章所列的都是伊壁鸠鲁和德谟克利特的物理学中使用的基本概念，也是原子论哲学用以建构自然哲学的一些基本观念。马克思力图通过对这些基本观念的比较分析，揭示伊壁鸠鲁的自然哲学的非自然主义的传统。从论述上看，马克思列出这五个基本观念不是并列的关系，而是递进的关系，其中每一个观念之间都有着内在的逻辑联系。第一章讲原子脱离直线而偏斜，是从原子在运动中，即从总体上，论述原子具有一般性和个体性。进而从静态上，即从单个的原子结构上，分析原子的内在结构和内在矛盾。这是第二、三章的内容。在第二章中，马克思分析了伊壁鸠鲁原子的内在结构，即原子的形式和质料之间的关系，强调原子的形式，也就是个体性，是原子的质的规定性，而原子的质料是原子的现象，原子的形式的实现只有通过原子的现象才是可能的。第三章，马克思从一和多的关系上分析了原子的形式和质料之间的内在矛盾，揭示了原子实现的内在动力。通过这两章的分析，马克思论证了伊壁鸠鲁的原子论的本质就是坚持自我意识的自由，原子的质、它的个体性，讲的就是自我意识及其自由的问题。但这还是静态的、从逻辑上的分析。第四章和第五章，马克思动态地分析伊壁鸠鲁的原子概念，说明自我意识的自由是如何可能的。通过分析“时间”概念，马克思论证了伊壁鸠鲁的原子，即自我意识获得它的感性形式是如何可能的；通过分析“天体现象”，马克思论证了伊壁鸠鲁的原子作为自我意识的绝对性和自由的客观化过程。从这些分析中，我们可以看到，马克思的这五章是环环相扣，步步深入。正是通过这些分析，马克思在第一部分得出的结论在这里得到了升华，形成了他有关自我意识的完整的观点。如果我们把他的观点作一概括性的说明的话，那就是，研究自我意识，就是要说明感性个体的自由是如何可能的问题。在这里，我们可以清楚地看到马克思的自我意识观点与鲍威尔的自我意识观点的根本区别：首先在自我意识的规定上，鲍威尔的自我意识是脱离了感性的抽象精神，而马克思的自我意识却扎根于感性世界之中，强调感性世界中的个体的自由精神。这就把自我意识的研究诉诸感性世界；其次在思维的结构上，鲍威尔的自我意识是在无矛盾的单向批判中展开的，这就是他所说的“世界的哲学化”，而马克思的自我意识是在与整体、感性的矛盾中获得自己的存在，并在对世界和对自身的双向批判中实现自我，这也就是马克思所说的“世界的哲学化同时也就是哲学的世界化”①。马克思的实践哲学就是从他与鲍威尔的这种哲学区分中发展起来的。这就是马克思博士论文的基调。这一基调表明，马克思的博士论文不是单纯的研究和叙述伊壁鸠鲁的哲学思想，而是在创造自己的哲学。这就是这篇论文的学术价值所在。

附录的附注部分不是单纯的引文出处的注释，而是包含了引证和评论，体现了马克思对文献的把握，这对于支撑正文中的观点是相当有意义的。

从马克思的博士论文的三个部分及其相互之间的关联看，马克思的整个叙述都是围绕他的主题和基本观点展开的。他在开篇明确提出了研究的主题和他的基本观点，然后，把他的基本观点贯穿于全文的各个部分，一一展开论述，既突出了主线，又有层次感，体现了马克思分析问题、论证观点的严密性。马克思的这一叙述方法也体现在各章节的具体论述中。在这里，我们举两个例子来讲马克思的叙述方法。

第一个例子是第一部分的第一节：研究的对象。这是学位论文立题的论证，是每篇学位论文开篇就必须写的。我们来看看马克思是怎么写论文的开篇的。马克思的博士论文的开篇不长，一共只有十二个自然段。但是，在这不长

① 《马克思恩格斯全集》第 40 卷，人民出版社 1982 年版，第 258 页。

的开篇中，马克思采取了开门见山的方法，非常清楚地陈述了选题的理由、研究的方法和研究对象的性质和意义，引人入胜。在第一自然段和第二自然段中，马克思指出了伊壁鸠鲁在哲学史上无地位的事实，并指出，伊壁鸠鲁哲学的这一命运是由于人们不理解希腊化时期的哲学，通常把希腊化时期的伊壁鸠鲁、斯多葛派、怀疑派哲学看作是以前哲学的混合造成的。这就从哲学史的角度提出了问题；在第三自然段和第四自然段中，马克思从思维方式上批判了那种否定伊壁鸠鲁、斯多葛派、怀疑派哲学意义的观点，而主张用否定之否定的观点来评价伊壁鸠鲁派、斯多葛派、怀疑派哲学的意义，指出“英雄之死与太阳落山相似，而和青蛙因胀破了肚皮致死不同”①，强调这三派哲学是希腊精神的真正体现，也是希腊哲学最辉煌、壮丽的结局。这就提出了重新评价和研究希腊化时期哲学的任务，也体现了他对哲学史的新理解。从第五到第九自然段，马克思提出了研究伊壁鸠鲁、斯多葛派和怀疑派哲学的方向问题，明确地把自我意识作为研究这三派哲学的主题，以此明确了全文的研究主题。从第十到第十二自然段，马克思说明了为什么以伊壁鸠鲁的自然哲学和德谟克利特的自然哲学的差别为例来研究自我意识的问题。

第二个例子是第一部分的第三节：把德谟克利特的自然哲学和伊壁鸠鲁的自然哲学等同起来所产生的困难。这个部分明显地是对哲学史上人物思想的分析，尤其是对德谟克利特和伊壁鸠鲁思想的分析。马克思在作这种分析时，并不是一一罗列哲学史上哲学家的不同观点，而是从哲学的理论问题入手，分析德谟克利特和伊壁鸠鲁在哲学的基本问题上的不同解答，揭示两种哲学传统之间的差别。在这一节中，马克思为了驳斥把德谟克利特和伊壁鸠鲁的物理等同起来的观点，阐明两者的差别，而把哲学的基本问题概括为三点：第一点，关于人类知识的真理性和可靠性的判断。这是有关哲学的理性和感性的关系问题，也是对哲学的本体论和认识论的基本问题的解答。在哲学史上，把哲学的

① 《马克思恩格斯全集》第40卷，人民出版社1982年版，第194页。

理性等同于理智，作为哲学的本质，否定现象、感性的真实性，是科学主义哲学传统的路向，而把理性与现象、与感性联系起来，力图从现象、感性中发现哲学的本质，是人文主义哲学传统的路向。在这个问题上，马克思首先分析德谟克利特哲学的内在矛盾，指出，在解答理性和现象的关系上，德谟克利特在认识论上肯定现象的真实性，而在本体论上却否定现象的真实性，这一矛盾注定德谟克利特不能说明现象，不能进入感性，进而分析伊壁鸠鲁是怎样解决德谟克利特哲学的内在矛盾的。他指出，伊壁鸠鲁是通过转变哲学的研究对象，即使哲学由面对物理世界转变为面对人自身的世界，把主观作为自己的研究对象，由于这种转变，感性不仅在认识论上是真实的，而且在本体论上具有本质的意义，因而也是真实的。这样，马克思就从德谟克利特哲学的内在矛盾及其解决中揭示了伊壁鸠鲁与德谟克利特哲学在本体论和认识论上的差别。第二点，关于研究方法上的差别。马克思比较了德谟克利特和伊壁鸠鲁追求现象世界证明的方法，指出，德谟克利特是用经验观察的方法寻求哲学的真理，为了获得哲学的真理，他走遍了半个世界，也没有获得真理，相反，伊壁鸠鲁从哲学本身去寻求哲学的真理，所以，尽管他“只有二、三次离开他的雅典的花园到伊奥尼亚去，目的不是为了研究，而是为了访友”①，但是，他却获得了他所要的东西，即哲学和人的自由。第三点，反思形式上的差别。马克思指出，“德谟克利特把必然性看作现实性的反思形式”②，而伊壁鸠鲁则崇尚偶然性的反思形式。由于这两种反思形式不同，德谟克利特和伊壁鸠鲁对待物理现象的态度也不同：德谟克利特遵循决定论，要求从实在的可能性中找出现象的原因，从而走向了客体；而伊壁鸠鲁则处处打破实在可能性的限制，强调抽象的可能性，从而走向了主体。这两种反思形式的差别本质上是因果性和目的论的思维方式的差别，也是科学的思维方式和哲学的思维方式之间的差别。这样，马克思就通过分析德谟克利特和伊壁鸠鲁在上述三个问题上的不同解答而揭示

① 《马克思恩格斯全集》第 40 卷，人民出版社 1982 年版，第 203 页。

② 《马克思恩格斯全集》第 40 卷，人民出版社 1982 年版，第 203 页。

出两者在哲学传统上的差别，证明要把两者等同起来是十分困难的。

从以上两段的分析中，我们可以看到，尽管马克思论述的问题不同，但有一个共同点：整个论述都是围绕论文的主题展开的，并且是一种哲学理论的叙述，哲学史上的史料只是马克思用以论证自己观点的论据。这与他在笔记中对史料的评论似的叙述是完全不同的，甚至是反向的。从中，我们可以概括出学位论文的写作有以下基本要点：

第一，学位论文的写作应该是作者自己的理论观点的陈述，即使是研究哲学史上的某一人物的思想，也要确立自己的观点，把该哲学家的思想当作叙述自己的哲学思想的一个例子。这是学位论文写作的基本要求，而要达到这个要求就要处理好观点和材料的关系。现在，我们许多研究生写作学位论文时，跟着材料跑，从头到尾都是材料的叙述，读完了也不知道作者自己的观点是什么。这在写作上，是没有区分研究方法和叙述方法，在研究上，是缺乏深入的研究，没有确立自己的观点。我经常听到这样的评论："该论文只叙不评"。这就等于说，该论文根本不是一篇合格的学位论文，因为他没有作者的思想，或者说，作者根本不知道怎样表述自己的思想，不知道论文写作的规范。这个问题在写作论文之初，尤其是在写作论文的提纲、拟定论文目录时，就应该解决的。作为老师，也不能把学位论文的要求定在先叙后评上，因为这是研究阶段使用的方法，根本不适合论文的写作，而且按照这种方法也是写不出好的论文来的。

第二，学位论文的写作应该在导言或前言部分就明确地提出自己的观点，不能把综述堆在导言或前言部分。作者在写导言或前言部分时离不开史料的运用，包括对哲学史上有关本课题研究的评论，但这只能是有选择的，并且要服务于观点的叙述，而不能喧宾夺主，只有史料而无观点，其结果，把导言部分变成了综述，而始终无法进入正题。

第三，哲学的学位论文一定要重视哲学史的传统，要把研究的对象和问题放在一定的哲学传统中去讲，只有这样，才能具有理论性，也使史料的分析和处理得当，分析有序，克服论文写作的随意性。

总起来看，以上三个部分是学位论文写作的不同环节，一个研究生如果把这三个环节都把握好了，就能把研究工作和论文的写作有机地结合起来，就能写出好的学位论文来。

批判性融会与创造性建构

——刘纲纪先生学术方法论略

石长平

一、以马克思主义思想为指导的治学原则

马克思主义实践哲学的历史唯物主义和辩证法是所有实践美学思想的哲学基础和方法论，刘纲纪的实践美学思想当然也是以马克思主义实践唯物主义和实践观为基础的美学思想。在哲学和美学探讨上，刘纲纪始终坚守在马克思主义的旗帜之下，刘纲纪的实践本体论美学的总体特征之一就是它的理论形态属于马克思主义实践观的哲学美学，整体实践观是它的理论基础和逻辑出发点。他说，在从事理论研究的三十多年里，“我写的每一本书、每一篇文章，都离不开马克思主义的指导，离开了马克思主义的哲学基础，我在大量的错综复杂的感性材料面前，就会感到束手无策，就没有办法将它提升到一定的哲学高度加以认识。”① 这些话再清楚不过地表明了马克思主义作为思想根基对刘纲纪的深刻影响，从世界观到方法论，从鸿篇巨制到短文随笔，根本观点的确立、理论框架的搭设、思想系统的构建等等都是在马克思主义思想的指导下进行的，字里行间都深深地打上了马克思主义的烙印，渗透着马克思主义的精神实质，跃动着马克思主义的思想灵魂。

① 陈炎：《马克思主义与现代美学的研究——访刘纲纪教授》，《文史哲》1987 年第 4 期。

刘纲纪实践本体论的提出，是建立在刘纲纪对马克思主义哲学精神或哲学特征的重新认识的基础上的。在“回到马克思，发展马克思”这一思想指导下，刘纲纪对马克思主义哲学中唯物主义问题进行了重新考察，他批判了斯大林主义的“正统”马克思主义，反思了列宁对物质概念的笼统规定，也指出了恩格斯对“实践”的忽视倾向，认为马克思主义的基本特征是人本主义、实践的唯物主义和彻底的自然主义，因之它可以称之为以物质的自然界为基础的实践的人本主义。① 正是在对实践的唯物主义和彻底的自然主义哲学精神的引导下，刘纲纪才创造性地在不同层次和范围中区分出自然本体和实践本体，使对包括美在内的人类的一切社会活动的解释建立在科学的实践本体基础之上；正是在对马克思主义的人本主义思想的理解上，刘纲纪才纠正了实践论美学前期忽视个体、重视理性的理论偏弊，恢复了实践论美学既注重群体、理性也关注个体的感性生存的真实面貌，把实践本体美学的理论指归明确地建立在马克思主义关于人的全面自由发展的经典论述上，赋予了它关爱人生，体念社会的应有的理论品格。

实践、自由、（审美）反映是刘纲纪美学思想的三大理论基石，而这三大核心范畴无一不是从他在对马克思主义理论的忠实阐发中提炼出来的。

实践是马克思主义实践哲学的本体，也是实践美学的逻辑起点，审美活动作为人对世界的对象性活动，是在人类的实践中逐渐发展起来的。马克思没有明确界定过实践概念，在《1844年经济学哲学手稿》中，马克思说：“通过实践创造对象世界，改造无机界，人证明自己是有意识的类存在物。”②“正因为人是类存在物，他才是有意识的存在物，就是说，他自己的生活对他来说是对象。”③“理论的对立本身的解决，只有通过实践方式，只有借助于人的实践的

① 参见刘纲纪：《传统文化、哲学与美学》，武汉大学出版社2006年版，第151、170页。

② 《马克思恩格斯文集》第1卷，人民出版社2009年版，第162页。

③ 《马克思恩格斯文集》第1卷，人民出版社2009年版，第192页。

力量，才是可能的。”① 马克思在《关于费尔巴哈的论纲》中提出的实践观点是哲学上的一次革命。刘纲纪对实践的本体意义的指认，不仅符合《手稿》，而且也是对《提纲》的精确解读，在两者之间，刘纲纪更重视《提纲》中所包含的本体论意义。在《提纲》里，马克思明确地提出，以往的全部哲学——包括唯物主义哲学和唯心主义哲学——的根本问题，就在于不是从人的“实践”的“感性活动”去理解人对世界的关系，因而不能真实地理解人与世界的真实关系。在这里，马克思已经把“人何以存在”的根据，从《手稿》中关于人的“自由自觉活动”的“类特性”，确认为人的“实践”活动，这在马克思哲学思想演进的过程中具有重大意义。在提纲第三条中，马克思又针对近代唯物主义哲学关于“人”与“环境”相互关系的争论，明确地把人的存在的根据归结为“革命的实践”。在提纲的第八条中，马克思把上述思想凝结为一个根本性的论断：“社会生活在本质上是实践的。凡是把理论导致神秘主义方面的神秘东西，都能在人的实践中以及对这个实践的理解中得到合理的解决。”② 这样，马克思就在确认社会生活的“本质”与解决理论的神秘主义相统一的意义上，确认了“实践”的本体地位。刘纲纪正是在对马克思的经典论述作出如此精深理解的基础上，才提出了他的实践本体论这一重大理论创见的。

自由是刘纲纪美学理论由实践通往美的中介，对自由的论述是对马克思关于人的本质、必然王国与自由王国、“人也按照美的规律来创造的”等有关重要论断的合理阐释和发挥。刘纲纪认为，人的本质力量是人之为人的特性，是人从动物状态脱离出来的根本，是人的自由自觉的实践过程和结果。他第一次明确地提出了审美自由不同于一般自由的三个特点，这三个重要特征的提出，都以马克思主义的思想作为立论证据。第一特征是超功利性，第二特征是合规律性，这是刘纲纪结合上述马克思主义的有关命题，从马克思主义哲学关于“自由是人对客观世界必然性的认识和实际支配”作为根本指导思想出发来深

---

① 《马克思恩格斯文集》第 1 卷，人民出版社 2009 年版，第 192 页。

② 《马克思恩格斯选集》第 1 卷，人民出版社 1995 年版，第 60 页。

入分析自由的本质的结果。最后一个特征是个人与社会的高度统一，这是刘纲纪认为最为重要的特征。

在《艺术哲学》的“新版序”中他说：我下决心要写出一本专著，以马克思主义为指导来对艺术哲学中的各种问题作一次系统的考察。事实也正是这样，整本著作都是以此为指导来展开论述的。为了论证审美的自由是个人与社会性的统一，在《艺术哲学》中刘纲纪用了十多页的篇幅，其中引用马克思、恩格斯著作中的话达 17 次之多，涉及《手稿》《关于费尔巴哈的论纲》《资本论》《经济学手稿》《德意志意识形态》《自然辩证法》《反杜林论》等多部著作。在他的《中国美学史》中，在谈到中国美学史研究的基本原则时，他说：根据马克思主义哲学，社会实践是美的根源，美是具有实践能动性的人类改造了客观世界的产物。……本书主张以马克思主义的美学为指导，把历史的分析与逻辑的分析统一起来。① 不仅上述这些，他的所有论著也都是如此。

刘纲纪的审美反映论是建立在对列宁反映论的理解和批判基础之上的，从对马克思、恩格斯著作中找到了关于反映是人脑对外界客观事物的意识的经典论述，不仅找到了反映是感觉和思维，也找到了情感和意志也是反映的有关阐释。② 从而突破了过去只把马克思主义的反映看作认识论意义上的反映的片面性理解，使反映获得了更大也更准确的蕴含，为合理揭示艺术的本质与规律敞亮了一条真理之路。

总之，刘纲纪所有关于对美和艺术本质和规律等问题的解决，都是在马克思主义实践本体论、实践认识论、实践辩证法、实践价值论的根本原则的指导下，对马克思主义的诸如“人的本质力量的对象化”、“人也是按照美的规律来创造的”、“劳动创造了美”、“自然的人化”等经典命题的忠实的、有深度的具有原创意义和启发意义的阐发。

---

① 参见李泽厚、刘纲纪：《中国美学史（先秦两汉编）》，安徽文艺出版社 1999 年版，第 13—15 页。

② 参见刘纲纪：《艺术哲学》，武汉大学出版社 2006 年版，第 13 － 18 页。

二、错综中外——打通“中、西、马”的比较研究方法

刘纲纪美学研究的一以贯之的方法首先是错综中外——打通“中、西、马”，这使得他的理论既有宏阔厚重的历史感，又有动态开放、与时俱化的强烈现实性。其次是弥纶群言——融摄和整合马克思主义实践论美学。中国实践美学的产生在20世纪30年代，中国的马克思主义美学在1942年以毛泽东的《在延安文艺座谈会上的讲话》为标志而确立，而“实践派”的提出则是在20世纪五六十年代，是在毛泽东实践观美学思想上的发展。刘纲纪在兼容并蓄前哲和时贤的基础上，在比较研究中融摄超越，创造性地提出了他的“实践本体论”美学思想。

何谓打通“中、西、马”呢？刘纲纪有个简要的说法：“说简单一点，如何接受、消化西方美学资源使之本土化，和如何发掘、阐释中国传统美学资源，并使之世界化，这是一个完整命题的两个方面，我的立场就是以马克思主义的实践美学对此加以研究。”① 他又说：“打通中（学）、西（学）、马（学），在马（学）的基础上整合中（学）与西（学）。而在西（学）必须与中国的国情相适应这个意义上说，中（学）又应占主要的地位。”他认为，说“学贯中西”还不够全面，要把马（学）加进去，成为“学贯中西马”，在“体”“用”问题上，应当是“以马克思主义为基础的，以中国为本位的中西互为体用”②。

“欲求超胜，必先会通。”“学贯中西”即中西美学比较研究是打通“中、西、马”重要组成部分。对于西方自古希腊以来的丰富的哲学和美学思想资源，刘纲纪一向极为重视，他的哲学和美学研究几乎都是在马克思主义实践观的指导下在整个西方哲学和美学史的学术背景下展开的。《中西美学比较方法论的几

---

① 聂运伟：《路漫漫其修远兮，吾将上下而求索——刘纲纪先生访谈录》，《文艺研究》2004年第6期。

② 刘纲纪：《传统文化、哲学与美学》，武汉大学出版社2006年版，第91－92页。

个问题》可以看作是刘纲纪对这一问题的总结。

他指出，要遵循历史的方法、辩证的方法和逻辑的方法，要从三个方面进行充分的理论准备：一要对马克思主义的哲学和美学有系统深入地了解；二要借鉴西方近现代美学研究的成果，这是对中国古代美学作出现代的科学分析的必要条件；三是深入研究中国古代哲学，非此不可能真正理解中国古代美学。在刘纲纪的《艺术哲学》《中国美学史》等重要著作中，与西方哲学美学的比较处处可见。孔子美学、墨子的美与功利的关系思想、庄子的大美和自由、宗炳的“踪迹”等等都在同古希腊以降的重要美学思想的比较中得以合理阐释，毕达哥拉斯派、赫拉克里特、柏拉图、亚里士多德、朗吉弩斯、博克、康德、席勒、黑格尔、柏格森、苏珊·朗格、弗洛伊德等美学家的身影也不断闪现。同这些美学家的比较研究还充分表现在《周易美学》中，《周易美学》甚至可以说是一本中西美学思想比较研究的经典范本。交感论与模仿说、卦象与卡西尔符号哲学、“辉光”的美学精神与普罗丁和托马斯·阿奎那等神学家对“光”的释解等，构成了《周易美学》深沉厚重的历史感和闳阔辽远的世界视野。

对于马克思主义实践观的美学与中国本土美学学术资源的关系问题，刘纲纪认为它们是完全能够融会贯通的。马克思主义传入中国后，“五四”前后几年间很快就为中国不少进步的知识分子所接受，成为中国最进步的、占主导地位的思想，这说明它一方面符合中国革命的需要，一方面与中国传统的思想文化存在着能够融合会通的地方。在刘纲纪看来，从历史和社会的背景讲，中国的原始氏族社会存在的时间很长，发展到了很成熟的程度。因此，在进入文明社会（阶级社会）之后，原始氏族社会的思想与风习被大量地保存了下来，其中许多思想都可与马克思主义相通，如儒家的仁爱、民本、大同的思想，道家对“耕而食，织而衣，人人无有相害之心”的社会的歌颂，对阶级社会中统治阶级所讲的仁义道德的虚伪性的无情揭露与批判，都有与马克思主义的相通之处。从哲学的层面看，充分肯定人与自然、个体与群体、主体与客体、有限与无限、感性与理性是必须统一、应当统一和能够统一的，两者之间不存在什么无法跨越的鸿沟，这是中国哲学的精华所在。此外，如大量丰富深刻的朴素辩证法思想，相信一切危难最终都是可以克服的思想，高度重视人自身的作为与努力的思想，认为“行”高于“知”、重事功而反空谈的思想，也都是十分宝贵的。上述这些古代哲学特有的精华与宝贵的思想，显然又都可以和马克思主义的哲学相通。从美学的层面说，既然整个中国传统思想文化包含着许多能通向马克思主义的东西，中国传统的美学又是传统思想文化的一个重要组成部分，那么它当然也是能通向马克思主义美学的。也就是说，马克思主义美学能够通过批判地继承中国传统美学而实现中国化，打通中（学）、马（学），在马克思主义美学思想的基础上，继承中国古代美学从人与自然、个体与群体、主观与客观、有限与无限、感性与理性的统一中去寻找美的优秀传统，将中国古代美学的一系列概念、范畴、定义、命题加以改造，以应用于对马克思主义实践观美学的阐述问题。这在刘纲纪的中国美学史和中国书画论等理论实践中都有显在的体现。

为了更好地实践打通中（学）、西（学）、马（学）这一研究理念，刘纲纪还在世界范围内对马克思主义美学的研究进行了深入的清理和分析，对马克思主义美学基本形态进行了比较研究。他认为从19世纪末到20世纪马克思主义美学形成了三种基本形态：苏联马克思主义美学、西方马克思主义美学、中国马克思主义美学。在他看来，苏联马克思主义美学可以称之为本质主义的反映论、认识论美学。西方马克思主义是第一次大战后欧洲先进资本主义国家的无产阶级革命遭到普遍失败，并无法再次形成热潮这一历史条件下的产物，这种马克思主义实际是马克思主义和西方现代唯心主义的混合物。在这种美学中，符合或基本符合马克思主义的正确思想和违背马克思主义的错误思想经常杂然并陈、相互交织在一起的。

中国的马克思主义美学是马克思主义的普遍真理（含马克思主义的美学思想）与中国革命文艺发展的具体实践相结合的产物。从中国的马克思主义观点看，西方马克思主义对马克思主义基本原理的质疑、批评、否定是轻率、主观、任意、没有根据的，而苏联对马克思主义的理解则在许多情况下带有僵硬、武断、教条的特征。这两者都是中国马克思主义所不取的。中国从20世纪30年代始，在鲁迅、瞿秋白等人的努力下，从俄苏系统地输入马克思主义美学，并取得了重要的成绩。但中国是一个有着自己悠久的思想文化传统（包含美学、艺术传统）的大国，在国情上又与西欧、俄苏有很大的差异。因此，从苏联传入的马克思主义美学，没有任何一种思想被中国人简单地认同和接受。1942年，毛泽东的《在延安文艺座谈会上的讲话》的发表标志着中国的马克思主义美学的诞生与建立。刘纲纪指出："在20世纪的马克思主义美学中，以毛泽东为代表的中国的马克思主义美学，是足以同苏联和西方的马克思主义美学并列而无愧的，并且在一些重大问题上作出了超越前两者的贡献。"①

刘纲纪把中国马克思主义美学提到与苏联马克思主义美学、西方马克思主义美学并肩而立的地位，这是一个客观而富有创见的提法。他对三种马克思主义美学形态的合理划分，对于全面地了解马克思主义美学在世界范围内的形成、发展、转化和嬗变提供了一个科学的坐标系。这既是他为中国美学今后在打通"中、西、马"的研究上提供的一种学术路向，也是他这一思想在其理论中的具体实践，因为，对三种马克思主义美学形态的划分本身就是一种打通中、西、马研究的成功范例。

三、弥纶群言——批判性融摄和创造性整合的研究方法

现代以来中国美学对刘纲纪美学思想的影响，主要表现在毛泽东、鲁迅、周扬、王朝闻、朱光潜、宗白华、马采、邓以蛰、李泽厚等人的哲学和美学思想。在这些人中，鲁迅是马克思主义美学的最早输入者之一，周扬是最早使用马克思的实践观点论述美学和文学艺术问题的前期马克思主义实践论美学家，

① 刘纲纪：《略论19世纪末至20世纪马克思主义美学》，《文艺研究》1999年第3期。

毛泽东是中国马克思主义实践论美学的确立者，王朝闻、后期朱光潜与前期李泽厚是马克思主义实践论美学在新中国成立后的主要倡扬者和阐发者，宗白华、马采、邓以蛰尽管不能算作马克思主义实践论美学家，但他们在新中国成立后的美学研究中都自觉地接受马克思主义实践唯物主义的理论指导，对中国古代传统美学和艺术做出了精辟独到的开创性研究。因而，所有这些人无论在其理论思想上，还是在其人格精神上或直接或间接、或显著或潜隐地给了刘纲纪以影响。刘纲纪正是在他们的人格魅力和理论阐发上获得了感染与启发，在中国传统文化和西方哲学美学的富饶土壤中，培植了他的实践本体论美学的智慧之树。

刘纲纪说："我最初学习研究美学，深受毛泽东的《在延安文艺座谈会上的讲话》，周扬译的车尔尼雪夫斯基的《生活与美学》、王朝闻的《新艺术创作论》的影响。"①

毛泽东的实践观美学对他的影响是第一位的。20 世纪 70 年代末至 80 年代初，刘纲纪曾致力于毛泽东哲学的研究，进入 21 世纪，刘纲纪在新的历史条件下又重新阐释毛泽东的《讲话》，以深远的历史眼光和宏阔的全球视阈写出了近十万字的《讲话解读》，依据《在延安文艺座谈会上的讲话》精神实质阐发中国马克思主义实践美学，回答现代以及后现代所提出的包括审美在内的种种文化问题。他认为，毛泽东以《实践论》为他的整个哲学的根本，更符合马克思哲学的精神，"可以说是中国学者对美学研究的一大贡献。"② 刘纲纪认为，以毛泽东的《在延安文艺座谈会上的讲话》为代表的中国马克思主义美学的产生，是马克思主义的普遍真理与五四以来中国文艺发展的具体实践相结合的产物。它不同于苏联和西方的马克思主义美学的特征，集中到一点，就是

① 聂运伟：《路漫漫其修远兮，吾将上下而求索——刘纲纪先生访谈录》，《文艺研究》2004 年第 6 期。

② 聂运伟：《路漫漫其修远兮，吾将上下而求索——刘纲纪先生访谈录》，《文艺研究》2004 年第 6 期。

鲜明地确立和深刻地论述了“以人民大众为本位的马克思主义实践观的美学”，在毛泽东的思想中，实践观点和文艺为人民大众服务的观点是不可分地统一在一起的，这种美学也可表述为以马克思主义实践观为基础的人民大众的美学。

对刘纲纪而言，毛泽东的美学思想首先影响到的是他的自觉为社会为人民服务的人格精神，其次才影响到他的学术思想，或者说是对他作为马克思主义者的思想与作为马克思主义美学家的思想的双重影响。实践本体论的理论指归正在对毛泽东“以人民大众为本位的马克思主义实践观的美学”的忠实继承与创造性发展，“大众文艺”、“能动的革命的反映论”的艺术反映论等也都深刻地体现了与毛泽东实践观美学的渊源关系，而刘纲纪关于“艺术美高于现实美”的观点，除了有黑格尔的影子外，更多的是对毛泽东的《在延安文艺座谈会上的讲话》精神的直接继承。从这个意义上讲，刘纲纪的实践本体论美学一开始就不同于李泽厚的“实践美学”。

中国马克思主义美学的建立既是以马克思主义为指导的，同时又明显受到马克思曾给以高度评价的俄国革命民主主义者车尔尼雪夫斯基的影响，而这要归功于周扬。周扬对中国马克思主义美学的产生起了重要的作用，他在美学和文艺理论上作出了很大的贡献，他的思想对于中国当代的美学和文艺工作者都产生了不容忽视的影响。车尔尼雪夫斯基的美学在30年代“左联”时期已被介绍到中国，到了延安时期，周扬又以毛泽东的《实践论》为指导深人地研究、介绍、评论了车尔尼雪夫斯基的美学，并翻译了他的《艺术与现实的美学关系》(《生活与美学》）一书。周扬在马克思主义实践观点的基础上吸取了车尔尼雪夫斯基“美是生活”，艺术是生活的再现，生活的美比艺术的美更丰富、更生动的思想，同时又消除了它脱离实践的直观唯物主义缺陷。在同笔者的一次谈话里，刘纲纪曾回忆了20世纪60年代初在参与编写由王朝闻主持的《美学概论》时与周扬的交往，和周扬对他在美学研究上的肯定与鼓励，他说：这对我以后深入研究马克思主义哲学和美学是一个很大的鼓励。我始终很敬重他，他不仅是党内意识形态方面的领导人，也是一个学者，一个卓越的马克思主义理论家。

对于老一辈研究美学的学者，有的在思想上直接影响他的马克思主义美学观，如王朝闻等，有的在研究方法、艺术涵养等方面陶冶了他的学养和理论兴趣。他说："中国老一辈研究美学的学者，其实都精通某些艺术门类，有很高的艺术品位，像邓以蛰、宗白华、马采、王朝闻等先生，都可谓艺术鉴赏大家。从他们的言传身教中，我受益匪浅，也正是因为书画，我得以更多地接触了这些著名学者。"① 刘纲纪这样回忆道：

> 我主要谈谈和宗白华、朱光潜、王朝闻三位先生的交往。我在北大念书的时候，宗先生住在未名湖畔健斋的二楼，那是我常去的地方，有时晚上九、十点钟，兴头来了，也跑去拜访。他收藏有许多珍贵的书画，对我有极大的吸引力。……我觉得，在对中国美学特征的体悟上，他比朱光潜先生要深入一些。
>
> 1962 年，我到北京参加王朝闻主编的《美学概论》，王先生请朱先生为编写组的同志专门讲美感问题，这是我第一次见到朱先生。我感到他的论述十分精到，且是一位可亲可敬的老师。随后，我去燕东园拜访他。我记得朱先生很热情，很关心我，和我谈了不少事情，还希望我努力学习外语，现在我还保留着他给我的几封信。……20 世纪 50 年代，朱先生的美学思想转向马克思主义的实践观，这是一个了不起的自我超越。……我与王朝闻先生认识得较早，读书期间，我开始发表一些美术理论的文章，引起了他的注意。他常常让我参加一些学术活动，从编美学教材看，他是主编，是我的上级，从年龄上讲，他是我的前辈，但我们又是"忘年交"，直到现在还经常联系。②

---

① 聂运伟：《路漫漫其修远兮，吾将上下而求索——刘纲纪先生访谈录》，《文艺研究》2004 年第 6 期。

② 聂运伟：《路漫漫其修远兮，吾将上下而求索——刘纲纪先生访谈录》，《文艺研究》2004 年第 6 期。

在刘纲纪的理论研究中，对上述这些学者们思想的总结性论述也构成了他全部理论的有机组成部分。《论鲁迅美学思想的发展》《中国马克思主义美学的建设者与开拓者——王朝闻美学研究的当代意义》《读王朝闻文艺论集》《中国现代美学家和美术史家邓以蛰的生平及其贡献》《马采〈哲学与美学文集〉序》《宗白华对道家美学的阐发》以及主编的《邓以蛰美术文集》等编著中，刘纲纪对他们的思想贡献和理论局限都给予了深入详细的评述和分析。这都清楚地表明了刘纲纪正是在前贤的理论基础上博采众长，海纳百川地弥纶群言，而后融会超越，卓然自成一家、独标一帜的。

在缅怀王朝闻的一篇文章中，刘纲纪写道："王朝闻同志是我多年来所尊敬与眷恋的前辈、师长与友人，我中青年时代的生活和工作的相当大的一部分是和他联系在一起的。……王朝闻在中国马克思主义美学的传播和发展中占有不能忽视的重要地位，他是中国马克思主义美学研究的建设者、开拓者之一，并为此作出了独特的贡献，他的美学思想在今天看来也仍然具有重要的现实意义。"① 实际上，在刘纲纪探索马克思主义中国化的学术理路中，可以找到王朝闻作为"艺术家的美学"的影响，在他对美和美感的理解里，王朝闻主编的《美学概论》的启思也是能够明显地指认出来的。

毫无疑问，朱光潜是在20世纪中国产生了最大影响的美学家。章启群在《百年中国美学史略》中说："在朱光潜之后的几乎每一个中国美学的研究者都是从读朱光潜的书而迈进美学之门的。"② 这并非虚妄之谈。刘纲纪也是读着朱光潜的书进入美学殿堂的。他回忆说："我读初二的时候，班主任很赏识我的读书兴趣，常常借书给我看，并在贵阳买了本朱光潜先生的《谈美》送给我，这本书是我接触美学的启蒙读物。"③ 在北大求学和编写《美学概论》期间与朱

① 刘纲纪：《美学与哲学》，武汉大学出版社2006年版，第536页。

② 章启群：《百年中国美学史略》，北京大学出版社2005年版，《序》第10页。

③ 聂运伟：《路漫漫其修远兮，吾将上下而求索——刘纲纪先生访谈录》，《文艺研究》2004年第6期。

光潜的书信往来和当面畅谈，都使刘纲纪在学术探索上受到了极大的鼓舞，而朱光潜在转向马克思主义美学研究之后，在美学大讨论中对马克思主义实践观美学的阐发也在一定程度上启发了刘纲纪的思想灵感，成为他以后构建实践本体论美学体系的必要的理论语境。

李泽厚作为“实践美学”的前期代表人物，对所有中国后来的实践美学派别的美学家们来说，都是一个永远绕不过去的话题，即使所谓的“后实践美学”，也基本是在后期李泽厚哲学和美学思想的先导下发展而来的。刘纲纪对李泽厚有较高的评价：“他的研究重视宏观的、根本性问题的探讨，很具原创性与启发性，表现出思想家的气度。”① 作为北大时期的学长和后来的老朋友，李泽厚和刘纲纪之间有着比较密切的关系，早在 1956 年的时候，清华大学建筑系开设由蔡仪主讲的美学课，李泽厚和刘纲纪每次都一起去旁听。但不少研究者对两人的关系存在一定的误解，主要表现在对《中国美学史》的写作和两人在美学理论的相互影响上。对于《中国美学史》，李泽厚只是主编，刘纲纪才是真正的撰写者。李泽厚曾明确说过：“和刘纪纲合作写的《中国美学史》，是他执笔写的，所以我始终不把这部书列入我的著作中，尽管我提供了某些基本观点。”② 刘纪纲也曾提到过这一事实：此书之所以能较快地写成，和他对我的热情地鼓励和不断地催促分不开。我写完一章就寄一章给他，当时他自己正在写收入《中国古代思想史论》中的文章，后来我感到在某些文章中他参考吸收了我写的稿子中的一些看法和材料。③ 搞清楚了这一段历史，就可以使我们明晰地了解到他们之间在学术思想上相互碰撞、相互影响的关系。

在美学理论上，有的研究者认为刘纲纪的美学思想是在李泽厚的基础上的进一步阐发。实际上，如上所讲，刘纲纪的实践本体论美学思想一开始就与李

---

① 刘纲纪：《传统文化、哲学与美学》，武汉大学出版社 2006 年版，第 604 页。

② 戴阿宝：《美的历程——李泽厚访谈录》，《文艺争鸣》2003 年第 1 期。

③ 聂运伟：《路漫漫其修远兮，吾将上下而求索——刘纲纪先生访谈录》，《文艺研究》2004 年第 6 期。

泽厚的不同，在对核心概念如实践、自由等的理解上，对美的本质的规定上以至在整个研究理路上，两人都显出迥然相异的旨趣。他们基本相同的，是作为理论基础的马克思主义的某些重要命题或范畴，如“人类社会生活的本质是实践的”等根本观点。一些研究中国实践美学的学者常常以为李泽厚代表了整个实践美学派别，这实在是一个不该有的大误解。但申明这些并不是要否认李泽厚对于刘纲纪的影响，在这里所想要指出的是，李泽厚对刘纲纪美学思想的影响不是如有的研究者所认为是直接的、正面的，而恰恰相反，主要是间接的、逆向的。也就是说，刘纲纪在构建他的实践本体论美学的过程中，不是沿着李泽厚所指向的路径，而是一开始就意识到李泽厚所开辟的美学之途可能是一条充满争议的路径。正是在对李泽厚的深刻反思和理性批判中，他走出了另外一条更切近真理的道路。

在《美学与哲学》的“新版序”中，刘纲纪以更多的篇幅再次谈到了他与李泽厚对美学研究的不同思路和对美的不同认识。这既是刘纲纪对区别于李泽厚美学思想的申明，又是他本人探索马克思主义实践美学心路历程的真实描述。20 世纪 80 年代，刘纲纪明确提出了“实践本体论”，他坦言，直接的动因是他难以同意李泽厚的“人类学本体论”。作为中国马克思主义实践观美学的倡扬者和坚定捍卫者，刘纲纪难以容忍马克思主义实践论美学被随意装饰打扮，“在学术上，从青年时代开始，我的最高目标就是做马克思主义的一个忠实的阐释者，我努力要做的阐释是一种我认为有深度的、有独到之见的阐释。”① 面对李泽厚以康德观点改造马克思主义，对实践美学作出不符合马克思主义原意的阐释，从而使实践美学这一原本科学的理论不能正确解释审美问题和艺术实际的时候，刘纲纪总是以美学家的责任心和马克思主义者的使命感，义不容辞地予以回应和批评，重新作出有深度的合理阐释。刘纲纪的美学思想的一些重大突破，不少都是在对李泽厚学说作正本清源的批判基础上进行的，

---

① 聂运伟：《路漫漫其修远兮，吾将上下而求索——刘纲纪先生访谈录》，《文艺研究》2004 年第 6 期。

很大程度上，李泽厚对刘纲纪的影响基本是在这种意义上表现出来的。

综合以上论述，正是在吸收现当代中国思想家和美学各家所长的基础上，刘纲纪发展了当代中国实践美学思想，形成了他的实践本体论美学思想体系。从实践这个本体和逻辑起点出发，刘纲纪形成了他关于“美是自由的感性显现”、“美感是由于人见到自由获得实现而引起的精神的愉快”、“艺术是对现实生活的审美反映”等关于美、美感和艺术等美学问题的论述，在对以毛泽东、周扬、王朝闻、朱光潜、宗白华、马采、邓以蛰、李泽厚等人的实践美学思想进行总结的基础上，独抒机枢，匠心运营，创造性地发展了当代实践美学思想，建构起来具有中国特色和世界性意义的实践本体论美学思想体系。这一体系的建立，是他综采众长，兼收并蓄，融会贯通的结果，是对当代中国实践美学的总结和发展，具有重大的历史意义和现实意义。

四、科学的治学方法创获卓异的理论品格

概括而论，由于以上所述的思想指导原则和科学的治学方法，使得刘纲纪实践本体论美学总体上获得了如下这些理论品格：

第一，严整精审的体系性显示出巨大的逻辑感。逻辑力量是哲学美学不同于科学美学所特有的品格，这种力量首先表现为撞击人的理论思维的力量，它力图在最深刻的层次上把握世界的统一性，以此去解释纷繁复杂的审美现象；其次，逻辑力量又表现为理性反思和理论批判的力量，在反思和批判中自我构建、自我运动与自我发展，从而思维规定不断丰富，内容不断充实，思想力度不断强化，逻辑层次不断跃迁。刘纲纪以实践本体论为哲学基础，以创造自由论为理论核心，以审美反映论为艺术本质，三者环环相扣构成一个完整的美学问题域，形成了一个层层推衍又互为支撑的立体网络体系结构；再次，逻辑力量又取决于它的彻底性程度。刘纲纪抓着了“实践”这一本原、本体，也就抓住了包括审美现象在内的所有人类社会存在的根本，在揭示与解释美与艺术的

根源、本质、规律、现象等重要问题时，以“实践”统摄全局，从实践到自由再到反映，把实践本体观点一致贯彻到底，产生了巨大的理论力量。

第二，与时俱进的开放性显示出强烈的现实感。刘纲纪立足现实去“改造世界”，指向现实、关注社会的博大的人文关怀的这一维度显示了其与时俱化的现实感，他思想中的现实不是纯粹思辨的产物，而是具有丰厚的时代内容，他以思想理论方式所把握到的现实，又非现实的表象，而是在对时代的整体性把握和批判性反思中得出的实质性结论。由此得出的这种现实感还表现为一种理想性的理论引导，刘纲纪的实践本体论美学理论不仅构成了对现实的反思与批判，更是在其美学所具有的理想性的指导下所展示的新的世界图景——新理想主义和新英雄主义的社会主义新文化建设。

第三，溯根讨源的兼容性显示出厚重的历史感。哲学发展的最基本逻辑就在于它是一种历史性的思想。当我们说“实践本体论”美学是中国马克思主义哲学美学以至世界美学史上的一个阶段或一种形态时，这也许并不算是溢美之言或夸大之辞，因为把实践作为建立在自然物质本体基础上的社会本体，并以此建构一个严整的哲学美学体系，这是美学史上的独特的一章。而这一理论的生发和建构是以巨大的历史尺度去批判地考察和汲取全部美学史的积极成果为前提的，史与论结合，逻辑与历史统一，用史实印证和支撑理论，这无论是在刘纲纪对美和美感的理解，还是对艺术的阐释，都是显而易见的特点。

第四，弥纶群言的容涵性显示出广博的境界感。这种境界感源于向上兼容的历史感和切近时代的现实感，这使得刘纲纪的美学体系本身具有了海纳百川的包容性和与时代同步的开放性，打通“中、西、马”，这正是他的理论所具备的博大境界。同时，非常显明，刘纲纪美学思想的这种境界感还表现在对人类生存关怀的温暖人心的理论构想，表现在最激动人心的审美的理想社会必定实现的人类美好前景。

责任编辑：方国根　夏　青

图书在版编目（CIP）数据

哲学前沿问题与方法论 / 吴根友，黄超 主编 . — 北京：人民出版社，2020.10
ISBN 978 – 7 – 01 – 022070 – 3

I. ①哲…　II. ①吴…②黄…　III. ①哲学 – 研究　IV. ① B

中国版本图书馆 CIP 数据核字（2020）第 068278 号

哲学前沿问题与方法论

ZHEXUE QIANYAN WENTI YU FANGFALUN

吴根友　黄 超　主编

人民出版社 出版发行
（100706　北京市东城区隆福寺街 99 号）

环球东方（北京）印务有限公司印刷　新华书店经销

2020 年 10 月第 1 版　2020 年 10 月北京第 1 次印刷
开本：710 毫米 ×1000 毫米 1/16　印张：30.5
字数：450 千字

ISBN 978 – 7 – 01 – 022070 – 3　定价：88.00 元

邮购地址 100706　北京市东城区隆福寺街 99 号
人民东方图书销售中心　电话（010）65250042　65289539

图书在版编目(CIP)数据